FLAG ON THE MOUNTAIN

Ivo Žanić

FLAG ON THE MOUNTAIN

A Political Anthropology of the War
in Croatia and Bosnia-Herzegovina
1990–1995

Translated from the Croatian by
Graham McMaster
with Celia Hawkesworth

SAQI

in association with
The Bosnian Institute

ISBN 10: 0-86356-815-7
ISBN 13: 978-0-86356-815-2

Originally published as *Prevarena povijest*,
Durieux (Zagreb), 1998

This edition published 2007

© Ivo Žanić, 2007

translated for this edition by
Graham McMaster with Celia Hawkeworth
translation © 2007 The Bosnian Institute (London)

A full CIP record for this book is available from the British Library.
A full CIP record for this book is available from the Library of Congress.

Manufactured in Lebanon

SAQI
26 Westbourne Grove, London W2 5RH
825 Page Street, Suite 203, Berkeley, California 94710
Tabet Building, Mneimneh Street, Hamra, Beirut
www.saqibooks.com

in association with
The Bosnian Institute
14/16 St Mark's Road, London W11 1RQ
www.bosnia.org.uk

For Andrija and Mirjana

Contents

List of Illustrations

Colour-plate section (between pages 256 and 257)

14. The Mijat Tomić *Haiduk* Troop – 'a historic formation of the Croat people in B-H' – poses in 2001 at Doljani, beside the restored tombstone of the *hajduk* after whom it was named.
15. The Mijat Tomić *Haiduk* Troop photographed on the occasion of its foundation in September 1999, in front of the memorial basilica of King Tomislav at Duvna/Tomislavgrad.
16. Front row centre: a Bosniak in the garb of an Ottoman warrior and brandishing a scimitar, as a symbolic member of the Mujo Hrnjica *bölükbaşı* detachment, at the founding conference of the SDA in Velika Kladuša.
17. Idealized mediaeval Bosnian knight as exemplary precursor of the modern Army of B-H – cover illustration of the book *Historija bosanske vojske* [History of the Bosnian Army] by Enver Imamović.
18. Iconography of the Army of B-H when it defined itself as exclusively an army of Bosniaks, and reduced the tradition of Bosnia to its Islamic component: Alija Izetbegović and generals Rasim Delić and Sakib Mahmuljin in a position of prayer, behind them the official poster with a mosque and Moslem tombstones.

ONE

Introduction

By feigning to be a Catholic, I ended the war in the Vendée; by making myself out to be a Muslim, I strengthened my position in Egypt; and by pretending to be an ultramontane, I won over the Italian clergy.

The media, propaganda and tradition

These words of Napoleon's led the French social psychologist Gustave le Bon, at the end of the nineteenth century, to conclude that it was the French emperor who, after Caesar and Alexander, had been the politician with the greatest ability to make an impression upon the imagination of the masses (le Bon 1982). What is meant here is that the statements of any political leader contain, in addition to their manifest or explicit meanings, implicit ones that are at least as important. For to turn oneself into a communicatively effective Catholic, Muslim or ultramontane – or *haiduk*, to introduce at once a concept that will figure many times in this book – does not mean simply to declare oneself as such, to announce *I am this or that*, but to employ a number of associative expressions located in the social, cultural or historical experience of the target audience, which enable it, without explicit instructions, to draw its own conclusions about who and what kind of person the speaker is. If the expressions that are taken from such reservoirs of expressive devices occur often enough, they give a certain consistency to the narrative and make it identifiable. Then a *special world* is evoked before the listener, a world to which the speaker has recourse when he wishes to win others over to his cause.

Of course, there is also a parallel level of speech that is not marked with such particular features, but transmits affectively neutral information. Compared to this, the level first mentioned comes over as a kind of decoration or *embellishment*, which sometimes remains a one-off inspiration, but more often develops into a deliberate and sustained project of persuasion. This level transmits additional, even surplus, information, almost always imaginatively resonant, sometimes with an aesthetic dimension. The images of the spoken statement are then seen as a *system* of structural and semantic resources with an evident function: through vivid, figurative speech, to produce expressiveness, as an essential quality of communication.

The writings of professional journalists and letters to the editor, party proclamations, statements for papers and speeches at public meetings, fliers and posters, the slogans that are shouted out or written on banners, all these are *linguistic works* and hence primarily material for linguistic interpretation, starting with linguistic analysis identifying the lexemes that are specially marked. But a work of language has a social function too, and always relies on the social and historical context of the communication, as a framework in which evocations stemming from the expressive, imaginatively resonant elements of the statement are formed and understood.

The mass media, here primarily the press, are an indispensable source for an analysis of the methods of shaping public opinion and manifesting the idea of history in the consciousness of those who produce the papers, read them, comment on what has been read, and retail them. The mass media, hence, have an enormous importance in the process of socialisation, for they ensure that the knowledge that is necessary for orientation in the world of the everyday is internalised. In their way, they work as translators of professional expertise into the lay formulae necessary for the cognitive mastery of everyday life, and they strengthen the imaginative base of the community through the production of metaphors for popular consumption. To this extent they are comparable with myth, because, like it, they define and reinforce essential categories for the society that generates and absorbs them: the moral, aesthetic and cognitive structures that acquire their legitimacy simply by being repeated in text after text, in programme after programme (cf. Silverstone 1988: 37).

The topics that appeared in political communication in Bosnia-Herzegovina, Croatia, Montenegro and Serbia from the mid-1980s to November 1995, when the Dayton Agreement put an end to the war, together with the manner in which they were stated, the expressive repertoire used by participants in this communicative process, are understood here then as facts of the prevailing culture. These texts interest us because in the given system of semantic expressiveness they manifest certain additional meanings above and beyond the explicit information. In our case, such features imply diverse evocations of traditional culture and targeted allusions to it that go beyond the level of direct, inexpressive and unevocative information with a political function.

Language with the figurative power to direct the imagination towards deeper cultural matters is essential for any political mobilisation that wishes to engage the target audience as widely, deeply and enduringly as possible. Messages, including political ones, do not have just a single meaning, especially not just the most obvious, the most manifest. They also signify aspects of the phenomena that are not noticed on the surface of the text, but are indicated in the form of transferred meanings. They need decoding, translating, which can be done only after establishing the links between the message and the experiential milieu, the social context in which it came into being. This symbolic meaning of the message is examined by content analysis (cf. Krippendorff 1981).

Unlike its symbolic level, manifest meaning is relatively easy to control and direct in line with the changing relationships of political power and the current needs of those taking part in the communication. Designations that are ideologically charged and burdened with the games of day-to-day politics such as *Mujaheddin, Ustashas* and *Chetniks* often stay on the surface, evoke an immediate response, and imply specific ideological, political and historical knowledge, with all the relativisation and complex dynamics that are instinctive in complex social processes in the modern meaning of the word. Meanwhile the deeper-level identifying characteristics are based on a long social memory and on stable cultural experience, as consequences of a process of value filtration, categorical classification and unambiguous semantic systematisation that has already taken place. Here it is impossible not to mention Mark Thompson's study of the *forging of war,* which, as soon as it appeared in May 1994, became for many a point of reference for a judgment about the role of the media in the preparations for and execution of the war. His research has all the virtues, but also the shortcomings, of the analysis of the *manifest* content of media messages, a procedure that is in some sense the opposite of content analysis. Although it does not necessarily entail overemphasis on the formal features of the discourse of the media or over-reliance on quantification, this kind of analysis does not come to terms with the social framework and conditions in which the messages come into being and circulate, or it does so only peripherally. (Thompson 1994)

Not denying the value of this study, two Croatian authors drew attention to the shortcomings inevitably involved in this kind of methodological approach. Both of them noticed that as a result Thompson was unable to see, or at least to judge, the full importance of the delay in political mobilisation among the Croats, and particularly among the Bosniaks, as compared to the analogous process in Serbia, Montenegro and among the Serbs living west of the Drina River. And yet this Serbian preparatory phase, in which there was as yet no armed violence, began very soon after Tito's death, lasting, that is, almost ten years before similar processes began – and then as a defence mechanism – in Croatia and Bosnia-Herzegovina.

Accordingly, the sociologist Josip Županov warned that the media theory, being formal and 'restricting itself to the performance of the media in the active phase of the conflict and ignoring all else', is incapable of recognising either attacker or attacked but, falling into moral nihilism, perhaps even unconsciously, sees only the decontextualised 'belligerent parties'. When the first year of the war is discussed, for example, one has to bear in mind the general context in which the Croatian media transmitted the testimonies of displaced persons about the way their erstwhile Serb neighbours had brutally attacked them. There is no question that this had

> the effect of a forest fire: the refugee stories disseminated by the media, like red hot fir cones, set on fire and destroyed almost the entire primary social network of inter-ethnic relations ... Without the media, the blaze would not have spread with such speed or taken on such proportions.
>
> Today it is easy to condemn such journalists – some people would even put them on trial in The Hague. But one can ask the question: were they supposed, even from the standpoint of the code of ethics of their profession, to ignore these refugee stories? To limit themselves to standing up against ethnic cleansing only on principle?[1]

Another critic, a journalist, writer and media analyst himself, also feels that Thompson overplays the role of the media in the preparation for the war, that he is probably unconsciously subject to the 'typical Western aggrandisement of the power of brain-washing, arising from lack of experience of life in a totalitarian society', and highlights this with the rhetorical question:

> If the media managed so rapidly to inflame the Yugoslav nations to hatred, how was it that they had not managed, over decades, with far more systematic and monopolised information and far more powerful repression, to convince the masses that communism was a Good Thing?[2]

---

1. Josip Županov, ['Intolerance and media propaganda did not start the war'], *Nacional*, 3, 8 December 1995.
2. Jurica Pavičić, ['The most to blame of all'], *Vijenac*, 50, 30 November 1995.

On the basis of Thompson's book it is impossible to give any cogent answer without challenging the method itself.

The symbolic system of news and the folklore matrix

At the level of content analysis, however, the answer is relatively easy to give if one bears in mind that cultural values are regularly involved, in one way or another, in a text reaching us through the media, and that such a text is thus, among other things, a cultural construct. A cultural anthropological approach, which places the narrative features of the news item in the centre of attention, does not deny that it conveys information. Nor does it suggest that the information and the story are mutually exclusive. But it warns that the rhetorical and structural means cannot be treated simply as methods by which some item of information is communicated properly and precisely. Journalists also invent things, not always with the deliberate intention of deceiving their audience, but by using culturally defined definitions, which they narrate in the culturally prescribed manner, as sharers in the culture and 'cultural grammar' that sets forth the rules of narrative construction. Nor is the position of the recipients different: readers often ignore some parts of a newspaper because they are not interested in the topic, but they may also do so because the narrative form is off-putting (Bird and Dardenne 1988: 76). To this extent most of what the listener or reader finds out from media news

> may have little to do with the 'facts', 'names' and 'figures' that journalists try to present so accurately. These details – both significant and insignificant – all contribute to the larger symbolic system of news. The facts, names, and details change almost daily, but the framework into which they fit – the symbolic system – is more enduring. And it could be argued that the totality of news as an enduring symbolic system 'teaches' audiences more than any of its component parts, no matter whether these parts are intended to inform, irritate, or entertain (Bird and Dardenne 1988: 69).

Since journalists will always, willy-nilly, locate new topics within a stable cultural pattern and the interpretive model it mediates, they come very close to oral story-tellers: since both carry out 'the routinization of the unexpected', that is, since 'news does a great deal of chronicling, recording newsworthy events in a routine fashion' (Bird and Dardenne 1988: 75) reporting facts and telling stories are not incompatible activities. And then, since the meaning of the message is related to this kind of encoding process, control of its transmission also entails control and presentation of the dominant 'world of meaning' or the world of values of a society or a social group. It is this connotative level that is important for the ultimate understanding of a message, because it will determine the way some idea or other is understood. The relevant deep level of the basic meaning of the message is directed or determined by the cultural experience, but also by ideology. That is, it

> always carries out some sifting and sets up a value system, and with it a scale of values the purpose of which is primarily to separate out 'that which has meaning' from 'that which does not', the important from the unimportant, the desired from the undesired, the valuable from the worthless, and in connection with morality and justice, the permissible from the impermissible, and then to have an immediate impact on the shaping, directing, reforming and renovation of a more or less coherent *Weltanschauung* (a systematised 'world of meanings') and then, via this, to have an indirect effect on the forms, dynamics and character of social relations. [The ideological structure of a society must have] this dominant axis of projection around which all the relevant components of the *Weltanschauung* can gather and be distinguished from the irrelevant (Dragojević 1989: 48).

Thus, every information or communication process implicitly contains certain elements of direction, and it is not easy to draw a line between the end of everyday communication and the beginning of propaganda, that is, deliberate, planned work for the sake of changing and controlling attitudes so as to create a predisposition for certain behaviour, to create a *systematised world of meanings* (Šiber 1992: 6). With respect to the openness of the objectives and the directness of the action, propaganda can be

1. *open and direct,* when the aims are known from the outset;
2. *deferred,* when, even before the declaration of a clear political aim, a certain process of psychological preparation is carried out, that is, an appropriate atmosphere and emotional saturation are created;
3. *indirect and deferred,* when because of a certain resistance to the substance of the propaganda, the psychological conditions which facilitate reception of the message are first created; there being, however, in the first phase no explicit link between this activity and the later overt statement of its aims (cf. Šiber 1992: 21–22).

In other words, only the first form can credibly be covered by analysis at the manifest level. However, it is impotent when this level is abandoned or when it is dressed up in transferred meanings, when images are projected that at first sight have no connection with some current political or social fact, seeming rather to be neutral in value terms and ideologically irrelevant, but in fact, in the long term, they prepare, psychologically and cognitively, for real political action.

Evocations that began to be built into a system in Serbian propaganda from the mid-eighties on belong precisely to this kind of procedure. They promoted not a transparent and explicit message, but a diffuse and implicit, indirect and deferred one. They did not declare their aim clearly; rather, bypassing discursive statements, and in parallel with them, they were fitted into a system of expressive terms and figurative images, the linguistic form of which 'does not mean what it says'. This system, laid out in the scheme of *(Serbian) haiduks versus Latin*[1] *urban upper-classes and Turkish beys*, was nothing but the groundwork for a desirable reaction in an anticipated future situation when the political elite would be able to articulate its objectives clearly. Then this general relationship would be semantically understood in the current social, political and religious situation as a scheme: *the oppressed Orthodox Serbs versus their Catholic (Slovene and Croat) and Muslim (Bosniak and Albanian) oppressors.* They would not then be peoples in themselves, with an autonomous historical identity and political will, but just derivations or the anachronistic remains of empires of which – like the Serbs – they were a part, but with which – unlike the 'never subjugated' Serbs – they merged through sharing the same religious affiliation and cultural orientation (Slovenes and Croats with Austro-Hungary, some Croats with Venice as well; Bosniaks and Albanians with the Ottoman Empire). Since they were so closely connected with imperial rule and accepted it as their own – perhaps not in the political and administrative but certainly in the cultural and ideological sense – they inherited historically and perhaps genetically too its repressive nature and its

---

1. *Latin* – in ethnically mixed areas, the colloquial and in the past even sometimes the official name for members of the Catholic Church, independent of their ethnic affiliation. It was also the semi-official term in the Serbian Orthodox Church (SOC) and regularly among the ordinary people right up to the beginning of the twentieth century for all members of the Catholic Church, and among the Orthodox population in the Dalmatian uplands the term for the inhabitants of the coastal cities, who were Catholics, whether they were Croat or Venetian, or of some other origin, and even for Orthodox who, instead of the traditional garb, would wear urban, 'Italian' clothing. In the last two cases the word had a derogatory meaning, because – from the viewpoint of the value system of patriarchal rural culture – it was associated with moral decadence, the feminisation of men, looseness in women, lack of character and loss of original ethnic virtues as a result of mixing, in society and in marriage, with external communities.

hatred for the indomitable and independent Serbs (and Montenegrins), even after these structures of government had vanished.

These terms and images were a powerful *argument* in the whole of the discourse, for through them, with the help of the representative situations from social memory that they evoked, 'something was concluded through the agency of something else, and something dubious and uncertain became stronger with the help of something undoubted and certain' (Pupovac 1987: 69). With their 'innocent' transferred meanings they undermined any psychological resistance and prepared the ground for the later internalisation of the manifest message.

The pages that follow will abound in telling examples, but it would be useful at the outset to analyse one in which this attitude is shown very precisely, as if in a laboratory. A newspaper commentator describes conditions in Montenegro in 1989, when a government that, although communist in name, had resisted the Milošević project and defended the status of Montenegro as one of the formally equal members of the Yugoslav federation was brought down by demonstrations and street violence organised from Belgrade. In its place came the government of Momir Bulatović and other toadies of Milošević, who openly involved the republic in the political and soon-to-be-military agenda for the creation of Greater Serbia. As the Montenegrin reporter informed viewers of the main news on Croatian TV, after the change in government, there was an 'inconceivably violent and energetic' outbreak of revanchism aimed at all that had anything to do with the communist past, and thus involved hatred for 'several generations of communist leadership in Montenegro'. These politicians 'are now called not only autocrats but *beylerbeys* and other derogatory and insulting names'.[1]

When someone is called an autocrat or tyrant, it may be accurate or inaccurate, but the term stays within the framework of rational discourse, and the debate about his rule remains within the terminology of modern political thinking, in categories of the rational analysis of power relations in a modern society. But when someone is called a *beylerbey*, Bey of Beys, which was the name for the supreme military or civil commander of a larger district or province in the Ottoman Empire, then he is being identified with a particular kind of autocrat, who has not only no political but also no cultural legitimacy, for he is an alien (by origin or faith) or a traitor, i.e., a local man who has converted to Islam and entered the service of the foreigner. And this then activates a completely different level of perception, different social

---

1. Rajko Cerović, 'Vrijeme revanšizma [Time of Revanchism]', *Vjesnik/Panorama subotom*, 31 March 1990, p. 3.

and political attitudes, and requires different categories for situating such a government within the value system of the community. The journalist himself had a good feeling for the difference between the first notion, which belongs to the political sphere, and the second, which transgresses the boundaries and powerfully awakens the socio-cultural imagination: while he simply neutrally stated the use of the term autocrat, he qualified the second as derogatory and insulting.

Put another way, *autocrat* conveys a manifest meaning and *beylerbey* a transferred or symbolic one. The first concept belongs to direct, the second to indirect propaganda. It is a new signifier that means a modification of the first, adding affective content to it, content that it does not itself possess, and that radically changes the meaning of the whole sentence. Speaking from the perspective of stylistic analysis, this is a textbook example of how the same utterance may contain in parallel both the conceptual and logical, and the affective or imaginative side, or function, of language.

The deliberate evocations of the folklore matrix, produced in a range from suggestion through reminiscence to explication were enchained in sets of quotations. They created developed hierarchical structures, and thus became the means of establishing the Big Propaganda Text: the construction of the strategic paradigm that would ensure and motivate the associative capacities of both speakers and listeners, senders and receivers of messages. No statement can be ascribed evocativeness if it does not have built into its structure a special kind of matrix that is based on 'common conventions for the productive and receptive consciousness' (Moranjak-Bamburać 1991: 34). It was tradition that served as such a matrix – it was the paradigm on the basis of which it was possible for individual texts to be enchained; it had the importance of exemplary history that was at the same time a manner of consecrating history and a system of signs that guaranteed mutual understanding within the framework of the group.

Unreliable and ahistorical in its facts, oral traditional history is indispensable as material for getting to know the normative value system at a given time and the ways in which certain events are experienced, judged and interpreted.

For the philosopher, tradition is *an intergenerational event*. Every generation is for this reason historical and historical to the extent that it genuinely accepts what has been, reshapes and renews it, putting its own stamp upon it. Tradition makes possible the continuity of experience with the world, prepares conditions for the new and puts it in the right place in the totality of historical events. The content of the tradition as of *the old that is never entirely old and never becomes outdated* consists less of knowledge of facts and technical skill, and more of a certain manner of relations towards a comprehensive mindset. It is primarily manifested in recalling a time of myth, the heroic period of a nation, in the particularity of its religious, moral and legal customs, in the authority of inherited institutions and the renown of great individuals. These are *the forms of life in common* that provide their own obligations, an authority that is accepted directly and admitted without consideration, and they are also a set of common prejudices (Pejović 1968).

For the social anthropologist, too, tradition is not complete and unchangeable but rather an enduring process of interpreting the past, which consists equally of continuity and discontinuity. It is constituted symbolically, it usually has an ideological content, and attitudes to the past can be changed by conscious interpretation, though this in no way implies that current actions and ideas have no link with the past. Traditions

> are neither genuine nor spurious, for if genuine tradition refers to the pristine and immutable heritage of the past, then all genuine traditions are spurious. But if, as we have argued, tradition is always defined in the present, then all spurious traditions are genuine. Genuine and spurious – terms that have been used to distinguish objective reality from hocus-pocus – are inappropriate when applied to social phenomena, which never exist apart from our interpretation of them (Handler and Linnekin 1984: 288).

However it is acquired, then, tradition is always a matter of the shared knowledge of interlocutors that has to attain a certain scope or volume for them to be able to understand each other. It has to be known to its recipients through characteristics that are relevant for understanding a text. Knowing the tradition is one of the conditions that a recipient has to satisfy in order to decipher the mechanism of the consistency of a (propaganda) text. These mechanisms are more or less concealed and can demand more or less active input from the recipient, varying amounts of knowledge and different degrees of resistance, in order for him to fill in the semantic gaps and discover the mechanisms of consistency: to explain the meaning of a word, recover in his own mind the parts that are missing, to connect images separated by the composition, identify the links between narratives and so on (cf. Mayenowa 1969, 1974).

A citation from the tradition, from the folklore matrix, is a symbol through which one historical time is included in another, making parallel events possible. Faced with a text shaped according to the indirect propaganda principle, a sensitive receptive awareness will recognise evocation as an *initiatory stimulus*, as an *image of opening up* to new territory where the recipient will gain different knowledge about life, and understand events in a different way. The example quoted above of the use of the term *beylerbey* for contemporary Montenegrin politicians is precisely this – an initiatory stimulus, a passage into a different time.

For this purpose the discourse has to have some connection, informed with meaning, with one or more older works. This relationship is crucial for its meaning, because a whole series of associations and semantic links is set up. Thus two texts – the current discourse and the matrix, i.e. the narration transmitted by the tradition and the narration currently formulated – set up a relationship of intertextuality, because other people's texts, precursor texts, become the subject or material of one's own, which can then be understood only in its relationship with them, in a dynamic process in which the new formulations semantically confirm their precursors, and vice-versa.[1] Tradition, here above all else the *haiduk* epic as precursor text, gives an outline identification of the world, saying that the events happening now have happened since time out of mind. Everything can be repeated – persons, events and circumstances – because they bear the structure of myth and explain every causality with this generally internalised truth.

The following are included in the folklore matrix as precursor texts in the process of shaping an indirect propaganda text: 1) works of oral literature and 2) works in the genre of popular vernacular creation, works of literature by self-taught vernacular writers and texts that have been written for the populace by educated individuals. The matrix also includes those works of literature by major authors that in their spirit and poetics are the inheritors of the oral tradition, above all *The Mountain Wreath (Gorski vijenac)* by Petar II Petrović Njegoš (1847), *Smrt Smail-age Čengića (The Death of Smail-aga Čengić)* by Ivan Mažuranić and *Razgovor ugodni naroda slovinskoga (A Pleasant Conversation of the Slav People)* by Andrija Kačić Miošić (1756). Kačić's *Conversation* became immediately popular, and 'some of the songs entered into the oral tradition whence they had not come' (Lord 1960: 136). All three works deal with events and figures from the times of the Ottoman wars and Ottoman government in the South Slav lands (in fact, the *Conversation* is a chronicle of the South Slavs from the beginnings to Kačić's own day, partly in verse, partly in prose). They celebrate the same heroes that appear in the popular epics, convey more or less the same value system, above all the heroic ethos of resistance, and then add to them creatively. For Njegoš and Mažuranić it is thus important to point out that 'these authors are not

---

1. See Oraić Tolić 1990; Moranjak-Bamburać 1991.

imitating oral epic, not writing "in its style". They have developed a native literary tradition of epic', they used the native ten-syllable line 'for what is clearly written for literary purposes' (Lord 1960: 133–134). Particularly important roles in the national integration ideologies of the second half of the nineteenth century were played by the two classic works of nationalist Romanticism: the dramatic poem by Njegoš, the Montenegrin Orthodox prince-bishop, dealing with the issue of the massacre of Montenegrin converts to Islam in the eighteenth century; and the poem by Ivan Mažuranić, a Croatian politician, based on an event in the eighteenth century, when Aga Čengić, lord of Eastern Herzegovina, was ambushed and killed.

What is more, as witnessed by the poet Miroslav Krleža, the rebellious Croatian peasants defended themselves in courts in Varaždin, Bjelovar and Zagreb in 1937–8 with quotations from his collection of *Balade Petrice Kerempuha (Ballads of Petrica Kerempuh)*, published only a little earlier, in 1936 (Matvejević 1987: 133). Although Krleža is not precise about what they quoted, it is not hard to discern the framework in which this was possible. The *Ballads* were shot through with motifs of the Peasants' Revolt of 1573 in northwestern Croatia, which from the end of the nineteenth century had a very active life in the Croatian political imagination both as lesson and as inspiration, and for Krleža was a symbol of the ongoing revolt of the oppressed, an example at the social level of the indestructible aspiration for the establishment of a more just society, and at the political as a call to resistance against foreign and in general every ruthless government, which in the new conditions meant the royal dictatorship in Yugoslavia. Although his work is not, like Kačić's, a poem in the popular style, it is an artistic endorsement of the vernacular view of life and history as the eternal Way of the Cross suffered by the disenfranchised masses. For this reason the 'distance of the modern urban writer' (Bošković-Stulli 1984: 7) in his approach to popular themes could not be any threat to the perception of the *Ballads* that resulted in their being evoked in court, in a functionally identical way to that in which the 'pure' folklore matrix is evoked.

The basic fund of knowledge

The key moment in shaping the deferred propaganda message comes when it is necessary to choose which segment of the folklore matrix, which precursor text, to take as the source of the evocations. In its stock of symbolic props, traditional narratives and motifs, nearly every community has 'a particular group which is thought of as more serious, more authoritative, more educational and closer to fact and truth than the rest' (Frye 1971: 54). But what is held to be so in a given historical or political situation, or from the angle of a particular political force, is not necessarily experienced in the same way in a different situation, or in the imagination of a different and competing power.

The choice of matrix is thus always also the selection of point of view, a decision that is made after considering needs and challenges that have been identified. The choice may be made spontaneously by participants in a political communication, when they recognise something that arouses an active and positive response. But it may also be made by an individual political authority. His choice is then reproduced and elaborated, either spontaneously or on command. Such an individual can do this without being aware of all the consequences of his act, but also consciously, and this then gives rise to 'intentionally consistent texts' (Mayenowa 1969: 164). A decision may also be made outside the sphere of political communication, and be suggested to the social group that is politically active. But it always involves the recommendation of a social, religious or political authority about how to build a productive discourse, which topics, motifs and metaphors to privilege, how, within the dominant set of requisites, to systematise a given type of image and develop directed analogies in terms of motif and expression.

On one occasion, the source of a decision can be precisely identified from extant documents, as in the case of the instructions of the Staff of the Communist-led resistance movement detachments in the Kordun region of Croatia in March 1943 to the political commissars. They were told that on entering Croatian villages, where the peasants were suspicious of the communists, they should sing songs about Matija Gubec, the legendary leader of the Peasant Revolt in NW Croatia, as a psychological and symbolic preparation for political action (Jelić 1973: 336). On another occasion, the source may be revealed by the participants themselves when they subsequently describe the process of making the appropriate decision. In the following pages several such statements are quoted from persons who, as the political scientist Ivan Šiber would say, decided at what box-office 'a ticket into the group' could be bought (1992: 59). The choice of the matrix is neither a rapid nor an unambiguous procedure, but part of a complex interweaving of conscious decisions and spontaneously formed expressive repertoires, a point at which diverse incentives and influences come together. It always involves the creative competition of two factors: tradition, or the habits of a given community, and the decision of the individual, who is more or less caught up in those habits.

The basic fund of cultural knowledge, a prerequisite for any political force to be able to make a coherent choice of evocative repertoire, is acquired in two places.

One is the school, which is always seen as a cultural thesaurus. And if certain texts or authors do not appear there, then they will not exist in the consciousness of the new generations. The creators and owners of the school system are always the creators or the proprietors of the cultural canon, and to destroy a certain type of school means to destroy its manner of quotation and its type of cultural canon (Oraić Tolić 1990: 61). The school, as organised selector or promoter of knowledge, made it possible in both versions of the Yugoslav state – monarchist and communist – for a large number of people to master at least general knowledge about the *haiduk* phenomenon. Without this those taking part in political communication would not have been capable of revealing the mechanisms of textual consistency. This was not broken down even during the hiatus of 1941–1945, because the communists preserved most of the pre-war system of symbols and exemplary moral models from the Yugoslav *haiduk* tradition.

The second place is the scene of primary socialisation, above all the family, central site of the intergenerational transmission of basic values and attitudes. It is not uninteresting therefore to consider how the leaders of the main military and political forces on the territory of Yugoslavia during World War II might have become acquainted with the heroic epic and the motif of the *haiduk* during this primary socialisation process. This does not in itself define the way a future leader would actively call on knowledge obtained in this way (or whether he would at all), but it does mean incontrovertibly that he had acquired the basic ability to do so and to decode other people's evocations whenever he encountered them in the communication process.

Politicians, ideologues and the heroic epic

As a boy, the Ustasha leader and supremo, *poglavnik*, of the NDH [Independent State of Croatia] Ante Pavelić (born in 1889 in Bradina near Konjic, Herzegovina, but into a Lika family), by profession a lawyer, read 'incessantly', as he put it, from Kačić Miošić's book of epic songs and from 'a thick collection of popular poetry', 'out loud, of course, and chanting, as the traditional national songs are read or recited' (Pavelić 1968: 95). The Chetnik leader and commanding officer of the *Yugoslav Army in the Fatherland*, as these mainly Serbian royalists and Nazi-collaborators were called, Dragoljub Draža Mihailović (born in Ivanjica near Čačak, central Serbia, in 1893), a professional soldier by training, left no autobiographical records, but the memoirs of his close colleague, commander of the First Ravna Gora Corps (Vučković 1980, 1984), and of a politician who spent 1944 in his HQ (Topalović 1967, 1968), leave no doubt: the general knew the Serbian *haiduk* epic tradition very well and used it systematically – although not very inventively it seems – in his communications with the army and the people. From the very first day when the capitulation of Yugoslavia in April 1941 found them in northern Bosnia, Mihailović and those officers who had stayed with him saw themselves as inheritors of the *haiduk* tradition. As witnessed by one member of the group, who later went over to the Partisans and ended the war as a general of the JNA [the Yugoslav People's Army], they very soon decided that they were 'more a *haiduk* army than a Yugoslav one' and that they 'had no alternative but to "*haiduk*" it', 'to find people to harbour them (*yataks*), and seize booty from the Germans'. And so they headed into Serbia, believing in the *haiduk* tradition of the area. In the mountains on St George's Day they even had a rather better than usual dinner to celebrate this day on which the *haiduk* bands would traditionally get together after the winter (Martinović 1979: 87–94).

The Partisan leader, top man of the CPY/LCY and lifetime president of Yugoslavia Josip Broz Tito (born in Kumrovec, Croatia, in 1892), a metalworker by occupation, was well behind from this point of view. Unlike Mihailović's Šumadija or Pavelić's Lika and Bosnia-Herzegovina, Tito's Zagorje in northwest Croatia knew nothing of Ottoman rule, and hence nothing of the *haiduk* way of life. Nor could he have learned anything of the tradition during his apprenticeship and employment – in Sisak and Zagreb, two relatively developed industrial cities in regions that the Ottomans had never occupied, or in Slovenia, the Czech lands, Germany and Austria. Only the very occasional example shows that as a returnee from revolutionary Russia to the newly created Kingdom of the Serbs, Croats and Slovenes he successfully internalised the evocation of the Ottoman period as a kind of political *lingua franca* for the presentation of repressive social relations.

This coded language was very familiar to every inhabitant of those parts of the new state that had until a short time before been under Ottoman rule. Then, through the centralised educational system and the discourse of the nationalistic (Greater) Serbian parties, it became increasingly familiar to those in areas where this kind of memory had not existed (Slovenia) or had faded away, and political discourse resorted to different metaphors (Croatia, Vojvodina). According to an article Tito published in 1927, the following conditions prevailed in the country: the government had divided it into '*pashaliks* and *bölüks* [territorially organised military units]', 'and every pasha in his *pashalik* "pashaed" it according to his whim' and the '*bölük-başis* [company leaders, often commanders of mercenary units] were still worse.' (Broz 1977: I, 42–43) Although the article does not mention the *haiduks*, it contains all the other imaginatively resonant terms that evoke a recognisable exemplary historical situation: the names of the organisational units in the Ottoman Empire, and the names of civil servants and military commanders who were bywords for arbitrary behaviour, corruption and cruelty. Thus anyone possessed of this basic stock of knowledge could easily, by imaginative intuition, decode the term for anyone who, in this general framework, appeared as the adversary of pashas and *bölük-başi*. Once these were the *haiduks*, and in more recent times, this same role of fighter for freedom was played by the communists.

At the same time, Tito's shortcomings were abundantly compensated for by many from his immediate entourage, the Partisan leaders and the organisers of the uprising, later the highest Partisan officers or state officials, socialised in areas in which the *haiduk* way of life was vividly remembered or may even have existed in their childhood, as the *haiduk* epic was valued and cultivated. One such man was Milovan Đilas, who during a lull in the Partisan campaigns would sometimes sing heroic popular songs to the *gusle* by the campfire (Stilinović 1986: 167). General Đoko Jovanić, from the province of Lika, had a father who was a 'well-known *gusle*-player of Yugoslav rank', who would perform songs about *haiduks* and *Uskoks* at home (Jovanić 1998). Rodoljub Čolaković (born in Bijeljina, northeast Bosnia, 1900), key man of the CPY in eastern Bosnia in 1941/42, would often evoke epic images in his speeches and articles as a young agitator on the left. In the twenties he explained to the Bosnian Serb peasants that agrarian reform would not be just until the peasants acted in line with the verse 'everyone kills his own *subaşi*' from the epic poem 'The beginning of the revolt against the *dayis*' (Čolaković 1985/6: 70).[1] As a small child, his mother had read him

1. *Subaşi (subaša);* estate steward or bailiff, collecting the revenues on the feudal estates from the peasants from the aga and the bey; also a military commander with a police function. *Dayi (dahija):* originally a war hero or Janissary commandant, in time began to mean a local tyrant who rebelled against the law and the central government, and was at the same time an oppressor of the people, for in Serbia at the beginning of the nineteenth century these Janissary commanders began to draw all the power into their own hands. Both concepts are alive in the Serbian language today as metaphors for government that is incorrigible and has to be overthrown without consideration, by any means whatsoever. In order to see the vitality, semantic stability and wide diffusion of such metaphorical terminology, it is useful to mention here that, for example, in the communist proclamation to the Serbs in Central Bosnia in September 1941, the Ustasha leader Pavelić was called the '*subaşi* of Hitler's fascism' (Zbornik NOR 1951, IV/1: 332.

heroic songs at bedtime, and at home his grandfather's servant often played the *gusle* and sang:

> We all listened to him with well nigh religious attention ... That brilliance of weapons and clothing, those shining swords and golden buttons, and above all these fearless men who shared battles, received terrible wounds, tended them with herbs and once again mounted their warhorses and set off to new battles all carried the boyish soul away ... I was a firm believer in the reality of that world. (32–3)

From the beginning of the upsurge of contemporary Serbian populism it was noted as significant that the two Serbian parties west of the Drina River were headed by psychiatrists – Jovan Rašković in Croatia and Radovan Karadžić in Bosnia-Herzegovina. Rašković stated explicitly that for him political activity was a 'new attempt at therapy' and that he was 'obsessed with the rhetorical metaphors that were the foundation of politics and political influence' (Rašković 1990: 296). One Belgrade journalist wrote that, unlike 'the other new-style Serbian leaders who manipulated the people like laymen', Karadžić did so 'on a scientific basis'. The tinge of irony did not overshadow the fact that he himself had defined to her his 'technology of encounters with the people' as the tripartite procedure of a professional 'group analyst in training' who could 'train a considerable number of patients in a short time' in the Psychiatric Clinic in Sarajevo (Vujasinović, 1995: 138).[1]

Nevertheless, it is at least equally important that in the Serbian leadership, in addition to the two people mentioned, there were others well versed in the popular culture and its epic tradition. Some of them were even connected professionally to it: Novak Kilibarda, president of the Narodna Stranka [National Party], who appeared with Rašković and Karadžić in 1990 at mass rallies in Montenegro, eastern Herzegovina and the Bosnian Drina region, is a professor of traditional popular culture at the Teachers' Training College in Nikšić. Ljubomir Zuković, minister of culture in the self-proclaimed Serbian government in Bosnia-Herzegovina and a writer of programmatic articles in its weekly, *Javnost*, taught in the same school and was until the war a professor of traditional popular culture at Sarajevo University. Both of

---

1. For Rašković's metaphors see Žanić 1993a: 39–44. Karadžić's colleague, a Muslim doctor, was to say after the war that the future leader of the self-proclaimed Serbian State of Bosnia-Herzegovina 'handled words and emotions with facility. He was good with psychotherapeutic tools, left the impression that he understood and sympathised with people, was a master of the skill of reinterpretation, seemed convincing and manipulative'. Armin Bešlija: [Doctor or Patient], *Dani*, 64, December 1997.

them have published numerous articles and books on oral literature.

The *gusle*-player and vernacular poet Božidar Vučurević from Zubci near Trebinje, a trucker before the war, who dealt in manure and firewood in the Dubrovnik region, became the chairman of the Herzegovina regional committee of the SDS [Serbian Democratic Party] of Bosnia-Herzegovina. After the elections at the end of the year he became president of the Trebinje municipality, later the self-styled Serbian Autonomous Region of Herzegovina, and in fact, the unchallenged Serbian leader in eastern Herzegovina. His songs offer a worldview in which the town is a place of moral infection and education that introduces foreign customs and destroys traditional values – above all male authority in the family – while the countryside is the only place in which a man can develop his real abilities. In an extensive autobiographical account to a journalist of Radio Belgrade he presented himself in this way: on the wall in his house he had set up a kind of shrine, where side by side there were a *gusle* and the icon of his patron saint, and above them the novel *Time of Death (Vreme smrti)* by Dobrica Ćosić. He lived alone, but was not lonely, because 'my solitude was full of the epic poems that I love, that I read and that I write'; 'they are my great love, and I could never give them up'; what is more 'if he did not write epic poems' he would find political operations hard to put up with, for they were a chore, that – unlike making war – he did not value (Mihović 1993: 46, 74, 81).

Notwithstanding the power he had acquired in politics, Vučurević went on appearing as a *gusle*-player, on his own or at festivals and tours in Republika Srpska [the Serbian entity of Bosnia-Herzegovina], and his works were allegedly read by Milošević himself. Having published his 'Greetings from Serbian Herzegovina', a poem in which he accuses official Serbia of giving only weak support to the Herzegovinan Serbs, Vučurević telephoned Milošević 'at home' and heard the following comments from him: 'Božo, I read your poem in bed last night. It's good. Criticism from a true brother and comrade. But I am going to make you write another one soon.' (*Vreme*, 129, 12 April 1993).

The poet and ideologue Rajko Petrov Nogo, born in Borije near Kalinovik, an area connected with the epic character Ljutica Bogdan ('to this very day people point out where his tower used to be'), says that his 'first and last reading was the epic decasyllable', and he was even lulled to sleep in his cradle by his father's *gusle*-playing (*Javnost*, 218/219, 3 June 1995). The writer Vuk Drašković, the exalted populist who in the second half of the 1980s made the most systematic use of evocations of the epic, and supplied Milošević with a fully worked-out political imaginative vision for the war, grew up in Slivlje near Gacko, eastern Herzegovina, also an area with a living epic tradition, alongside the *gusle*-players who appeared at evening gatherings and weddings (Drašković 1989: 93–101). The journalist who asked the Montenegrin president Momir Bulatović whether 'he could sing to the *gusle*' did, it is true, receive a negative answer, but with the information that the politician's father, a colonel of the JNA [Yugoslav National Army], kept a *gusle* in his house in the Kuči region, 'as happened in every other house in Montenegro' (Nebojša Jevrić; *Duga*, 442, 2 February 1991).

Like Tito, the leader of the HDZ [Croatian Democratic Union] and President of the Republic of Croatia Franjo Tuđman underwent his youthful political socialisation within the framework of communist ideology, and in a score of years after the war climbed relatively high in the Yugoslav military and Communist Party hierarchy. But at the end of the eighties, his discourse did not perpetuate the militant phraseology of this ideology, particularly not the cult of heroism, but was powerfully suffused with historicism and Croatian political mythologemes that either referred to the 'state rights' tradition or played with the motif of the 'bulwark of Christianity', *antemurale christianitatis*. This was the notion that Croatia, in defending Western Europe and its faith and culture against the Ottoman invasion, at great cost to itself, had acquired a reputation that gave it the right to expect respect, help and gratitude (cf. Tuđman 1995). There was not a trace of *haiduk* motivation in him, very likely because of the same local background handicap that we observed in the case of Tito. Nevertheless, the lengthy book *Rat protiv rata* [*War against War*] (1970), written with great ambitions in the way of military theory, shows that the author had in the meantime got to know most of the *haiduk* epics and the literature about the phenomenon, although mostly from the pens of nineteenth-century Romantic writers or else from twentieth-century school anthologists, in an idealised Marxist interpretation that presented the *haiduks* as politically aware protagonists of ethnic and social struggle.

But these shortcomings were abundantly compensated for in the nineties by the writer Ivan Aralica, Tuđman's adviser, a man who was to the greatest possible extent in his personal confidence, a member of the HDZ leadership, and writer of a number of political essays setting forth its agenda. As he himself said several times, Tuđman had his novels, the subject of which was the period of the Ottoman wars in the seventeenth and eighteenth centuries, constantly to hand. He also discussed the past of Bosnia with the writer. In the mid-nineties Tuđman appointed him chairman of the obscure National Council for Strategic Development. Aralica himself, a long-time teacher of literature in the hills of inland Dalmatia, described, in a long autobiographical interview the day after Tuđman died, the ambience in which he had grown up. 'We had a *gusle* in the family, but we didn't know how to play in it, except as a joke', but to make up for this he read Kačić's song-book, and everything like it, frequently. He would read the epic songs 'aloud, sometimes chanting, and sometimes the way one usually reads'. His uncle 'knew a lot of the songs by heart' while another uncle, after World War II, brought his nephew home a book of poems by a vernacular writer who had written of Tito and events from the Partisan struggle in the manner of the old epics. Young Ivan learned it by heart (*Globus*, 590, 29 March 2002).

Equally interesting is Mate Boban, an economist who was employed in several minor firms in Herzegovina and Dalmatia, and was from the beginning of 1992 leader of the HDZ in Bosnia-Herzegovina and the self-proclaimed Croatian Republic of Herceg-Bosna. Born and brought up in Herzegovina's Grude, an area with a living epic tradition, he was friendly with the *gusle*-player Željko Šimić from Alagovac near Grude, and with the naturalised citizen Osijek Mile Krajina, from the Dalmatian hinterland region along the Herzegovina border, one of the most productive authors of new epics among the Croats. The two of them, says Šimić, were 'old pals' and it was the young Boban in 1967 who took him to Zagvozd to perform his song about the nineteenth century *haiduk* Andrijica Šimić, also from Alagovac, at a party for Partisan veterans, which was a 'launch' for this *gusle*-player (*Panorama*, 126, 25 September 1996).[1] A journalist who visited Boban immediately after he had been forced to retire from open politics found him reading Kačić Miošić's song-book. The host's comment at the time that 'after all history is the best teacher of life' (*Nedjeljna Dalmacija*, 1200, 27 April 1994) indicates not only his enduring fondness for the heroic epic, but also that he thought of the two-and-a-half-century-old epic transposition of reality by Kačić Miošić a reliable document, actually a work of history.

Among Bosniak politicians, it was Fikret Abdić, also an economist, who grew up in the village of Donja Vidovska near Velika Kladuša, who made by far the most elaborate use of an epic character, that of Mujo Hrnjica. During winter evening gatherings, Abdić's elder brother Muhamed, the only high school pupil in the village, would read out or sing the Muslim heroic epic

---

1. Šimić returned this friendship three decades later when, dissatisfied that the Federation of Bosnia-Herzegovina had been created instead of Herzegovina being annexed to Croatia, he sang the verses: 'If Boban had an officer stayed / Vitina would not its eyes on Turks have laid' (Šimić 1996). The village of Vitina is symbolic here, because it is among the few western Herzegovina settlements with a Bosniak population and is the closest to Croatia, on the very border.

in which it was the brothers Mujo and Halil Hrnjica who stood out for 'their bravery, sense of justice and heroism'. Listening to the songs, the 'older people' would 'cry for joy, admiring their heroism' (Abdić 1992: 37). And the experience of Muhamed's younger brother cannot have been essentially different from that described in his memoirs by Rodoljub Čolaković, with the difference, of course, that in the case of Čolaković it was a Christian or Serbian milieu, and its corresponding epic.

Slobodan Milošević and astuteness of discourse

According to the writer Mirko Kovač, Slobodan Milošević too 'is most fond of reading epic literature and prose about *haiduks*'.[1] There is no reason to doubt this a priori, but those who have studied his discourse, particularly the collection of speeches *Godine raspleta* [*The Years of Denouement*], did not find any phrases or allusions inspired by or quoted from heroic epics, but only features of the so-called 'conference', bureaucratic speech, above all a great frequency of formulas and terms of communist ideology along the lines of the *Little Red Book* of Mao Zedong or Stalin's *Short Course*. Only the Slovene sociologist Rastko Močnik noted in this discourse a procedure that has its equivalent in the poetics of South Slav traditional poetry. In Milošević, he states, 'negative constructions play a great role', this being a figure 'provided him by traditional poetry' the most commonly quoted model being the beginning of 'Hasanaginica': 'What is that? Is it this or that? It is neither this nor that, but something else',

> or a double construction

> 'not only ... but also', thus fulfilling the demand for a negative beginning... and giving itself the possibility of an antithetical linkage, for repetition, amplification ...'[2]

More detailed analysis along these lines can provide interesting perceptions, but may also result in misunderstandings.

The Slav or negative antithesis is expounded according to the logical formula: $A - not\ A - A$, but the basic form of the total antithesis would be: $A\ is\ m;\ A\ is\ not\ m$ but $B\ is\ m$ (Zima 1988: 85–86). One can use this pattern

---

1. Kovač's article was originally published in the French daily *Liberation*, 28 February 1992; here it is quoted according to a translation headlined 'The greatest Serbian writer is a traitor to things Serbian!', *Slobodni tjednik*, Zagreb, 106, 1 April 1992.
2. Rastko Močnik, 'The strategy of negative rhetoric', *Start*, Zagreb, 528, 15 April 1989, pp. 36–37.

to analyse Milošević's speech at the Extraordinary Conference of the LC [League of Communists] of Vojvodina in Novi Sad in January 1989:

> The changes in the Constitution that are under way, which have, as is known, as their only aim the establishment of the unity of Serbia as a republic,
>
> *A_1 is m_1:*
>
> were supposed, according to interpreters from the ranks of the Vojvodina bureaucracy, to have called into question the economic existence and prospects of Vojvodina.
>
> (*figure of surprise*):
>
> As if Serbia could possible exploit part of the territory of its own republic and a section of its own people whose unity it so much favours. In addition,
>
> *A_2 is m_2:*
>
> according to them the many ethnic groups in Vojvodina ought to do very badly with the changes in the political system, above all the Hungarians.
>
> (*figure of surprise*):
>
> As if in any part of our country today, and particularly in multi-ethnic Vojvodina, any policy of ethnic discrimination could pass, while at the same time counting on the support of its own people. And indeed,
>
> *A_1 is not m_2:*
>
> nor will Vojvodina lose out economically with the changes in the Constitution,
>
> *A_2 is not m_2:*
>
> or politically. On the contrary,
>
> *rather B_1 is m_1:*
>
> the stagnation in the economic development of Vojvodina... will be obviated with the social and economic reform, which is starting to be implemented ... At the same time,
>
> *but, also, B_2 is m_2:*
>
> the point of the changes in the political system, above all the changes of the Constitution, is to ensure an equal legal, material, political and cultural position for all citizens of Serbia, irrespective of their ethnicity (Milošević 1989: 322).

But this kind of coincidence, however fascinating, does not in itself mean much in the sense that we are interested in here. What is involved is a compositional element of formal rhetorical analysis, rather than words, phrases or images in a particular semantic relationship. This is a purely neutral structure without any affective content, symbols or recognisable cultural pattern.

The statement of the President of the Presidency of Bosnia-Herzegovina Alija Izetbegović provoked by announcements that the JNA was going to interfere directly in the political life of the country may be set out according to the same pattern. In order for this to be more clearly displayed, in parallel with Izetbegović's words (*Oslobođenje*, 16 March 1991), the relevant lines from 'Hasanaginica' are quoted in brackets:[1]

We cannot see what is currently endangered in Yugoslavia for there to be a need to involve the army in the solution of the problem
(What whitens in the mountain green?)
A_1:
Is there any attack upon the external frontiers?
(Is it the snows?)
not A_1:
No there are not.
(It is not the snows.)
A_2:
Are there inter-ethnic conflicts?
(Is it the swans?)
not A_2:
There are not, they are only invented.
(It is not the swans,)
B:
But what is then endangered, for something is indeed endangered?
What is endangered is the remains of the old totalitarian system,
what is endangered is totalitarianism in the land.
(but the tent of Aga Hasan-aga).

---

1. 'Hasanaginica' is a Croatian and Bosniak popular ballad, written down in the mid-eighteenth century in the Herzegovina-Dalmatia borderlands. It is one of the most intellectual and beautiful of all the South Slav ballads. Here we are concerned with the introductory lines, translated from the Croatian/Bosnian by the author of the whole of this translation. But thanks to the Italian translation of the book of Albert Fortis, *Viaggio in Dalmazia* (1774), it was at once translated into many languages, including three English versions: the translation of Walter Scott was long unpublished; John Boyd Greenshields printed his in *Selim and Zaida, an Oriental Poem with other Pieces* (1800), and William Edmondstoune Ayton his own entitled 'The Doleful Lay of the Noble Wife of Asan Aga', in the collection *Poems and Ballads of Goethe* (1859). But none of them, based on Goethe's German translation, sometimes combined with a French version, produced in turn from the Italian, succeeds in catching the rhythm or spirit of the original.

Both speakers here separate the first member of the antithesis and use syntactic parallelism that follows the two topics that they are treating: the economic situation and ethnic relations in the first case and the possibility of external attack on the country and ethnic relations again in the second. Both, also, fail to rise above the structural level. For this reason, such examples, though quite intriguing, are really only pseudo-evocations.

To this extent it is quite accurate to say that Milošević (to let Izetbegović be for the moment) makes uninventive use of the totalitarian language as he found it. What is more, in his discourse, right up to the speech on Kosovo Polje in April 1987, the ethnic issue is mentioned exclusively with negative connotations, and every foregrounding of Serbian ethnic content is considered a danger that has to be repressed, even 'a very snake in the bosom of the Serbian people' (Milošević 1989: 171), as he said at the notorious eighth Session of the Central Committee of the League of Communists of Serbia in September 1987. It is a fact, however, that in a Milošević speech of 1984, the pronoun 'we' means 'the communists', while the 'Serbian people' in the printed version of 1989 (Popov 1993: 20) both is and is not a change: it is at the manifest rather than the content level, and not only because in each case it is a question of a populist appeal to the incontestable authority of the collective. The pith and marrow of things is broached when the question is asked as to what the fundamental *virtue* or *feature* of a given collective is, what its members perceive as their own central qualitative characteristic as against those of competitive collectives. And in both cases, this characteristic is heroism and indomitability, or the *virtue of heroism* – *we communists* and *we Serbs* are nothing if not heroes. This book seeks to show what, in concrete historical and social circumstances, the phrase 'we *haiduks*' can and does mean.

For this reason Milošević's discourse belongs authentically to the folklore matrix, not because it abounds in the appropriate terminological and phraseological evocations, rather because it is reducible to its fundamental binary opposition of *them* and *us*, to an agonistic approach of the kind that the heroic epic is also based on when it deals with the theme of the conflict between two clearly demarcated sides. To this extent, then, Milošević perpetuates its spirit, for the binary opposition of *us/good* – *them/evil* provides a suggestive horizon for discrimination, identifying the world as clearly divided in two, and thus promotes a frame of reference for the further identification or specification of this world. His disciples will undertake this independently, selecting from their reserves of knowledge certain concrete categories, including the *haiduk* way of life.

What is more, with this type of discourse, limited to the perpetuation of a non-specific binary structure, Milošević sets up an ideal situation, above and beyond every concrete ideology or political programme, and hence beyond the responsibility that can be derived from the facts of the discourse. With his cognitive perspective divorced from any realistic social and historical context, he restricts himself only to the task of identifying the world in this way or that, of activating a general impression about it, which in itself has no effective mobilising energy, because it is overgeneralised. But the moment this interpretative model really starts to be put into practice in all its individual implications and concrete culturological evocations – Milošević is no longer an active participant. Hence the remark that his discourse is expressively feeble and lexically impoverished turns out to be relative. It is just what it needs to be and contains everything it needs. Others can carry out the filling-in at the lower levels, the insertion of expressive terms and figurative images into the firm and solid supporting structure.

Many noticed the dangerous and aggressive nature of Milošević's politics only when, on St Vitus' Day [Vidovdan] 1989 at Gazimestan, he said of the sixth centenary of the Battle of Kosovo: 'Six centuries later, today, we are again engaged in a battle, facing more battles. They are not armed, although armed battles are not yet to be excluded' (*Politika*, 29 June 1989).

But *battles* were from the very beginning contained in his discourse as the most suggestive image in the semantic sets that they built. These sets – like 'the battle for self-management' that 'is fought on the ground of the economy' (Milošević 1989: 108) – unavoidably stir imaginative resonance in the collaborators in the vernacular, popular worldview, especially given the prototype of the patriarchal cult of heroism. The order in which a political rally at Valjevo, western Serbia, in 1986 he stood for the virtues necessary for the solution of the Yugoslav crisis – 'for that courage and determination, for that intelligence, for that knowledge, and for that capability' (Milošević 1989: 100) – is an exemplary specimen of heroic communist discourse, but it is equally an exemplary evocation of the ethos of the epic and the hierarchy of its values. In both of these aspects it is equally distant from modern, civil political thinking, which would, for pragmatic reasons at least, put 'knowledge' in the first place, knowing that it would thus satisfy its audience's horizon of expectations.

However, Milošević was also capable of addressing a different kind of audience. Privileging the virtues of courage and determination, he was at the same time appealing equally to two audiences: the ideologically communist and the supra-ideologically patriarchal. The first, who are so fond of calling themselves *a special brand of men*, need these heroic virtues to be able to 'break through the front of capital', 'hold command positions in the national economy', 'organise a political army', 'carry out an offensive on the class struggle front', making of their country 'the shock brigade of the proletarians of all countries', because 'there are no fortresses that the Bolsheviks cannot take', etc. The second audience, on the other hand, knows them quite simply as the virtues of the epic hero, *sans peur et sans tache*, above all that of the *haiduks,* from whom fearlessness and toughness, resilience and speed are sought, who 'care not for their heroic heads' and who if a bolt shot down from the sky 'would greet it with their bare hands'. At the moment of its repetition in the communication process, every statement (or image) corresponds to certain expectations and arouses in the recipients a certain horizon of expectations, and it is only there that an image that is formally identical may be recognised in this or that context. A statement always contains several potential meanings, several aspects, and the recipient will accept it sincerely only if he manages to place it in an apposite reference system of his own expectations (Jauss 1978). Accordingly, the communist recipient will understand the heralding of the battle within his own experiential horizon, and the recipient who shares in the epic culture in his own, but both will see the image as containing a very similar meaning.

In his victory speech at the Belgrade conference of the League of Communists of Serbia in 1988, a month after the Vojvodina *autonomists* had been overthrown at mass rallies, but also after a simultaneous attempt to bring down the government in Montenegro had come to nothing, Milošević said that 'the mature democratic forces of society had halted and broken the siege by the bureaucrats and magnates' (1989: 303). This seeming meld of terms from two different historical periods, the bourgeois bureaucrats and the feudal magnates, is actually deeply natural and shows in an ideal way how the expansion of a single sign system can unfold simultaneously in two directions, to two different audiences – urban and rural. The images of combat and heroism were compact, single-termed, and were directed, as a whole, simultaneously to both audiences. The image just quoted of the siege is two-termed, composed of elements from two kinds of imaginary, and at the moment of its transmission it is divided in two, and each half of it fits within the horizon of expectations of the pertinent audience. In other words, it perfectly sums up the two components of the core content of the contemporary movement, which was even then officially named the *antibureaucratic revolution*, and of its traditional inspiration, or interpretive model, which could be called the antifeudal revolt, evoked even then at the rallies with banners proclaiming lines from Njegoš:

> *The magnates damn their souls!*
> *ground the Empire into pieces*
> ...
> *Sowed the bitter seed of schism*
> *the Serbian tribe to poison.*[1]

These words are spoken by the chorus, the *Kolo,* that is the people itself, by way of warning to the chiefs that they must live up to their historical responsibility. It would seem that in his concept of history, Njegoš was thinking of the feudal magnates who had become too independent after the death of Emperor Dušan's son Uroš, the result being that the Ottoman thrust caught Serbia with no powerful central government. However, the sense of the message surpasses any particular historical circumstance. It is universal, and the curse is addressed to all those who for the sake of their personal ambitions neglect their duty and obligations to the state. The rulers, having the greater responsibility, have a greater guilt when they transfer their disharmony to the people, when they 'sow the seed' of dissension among them.[2]

Milošević's phrase is semantically realised precisely in this horizon of expectations, with an audience that must have been able to understand the negative connotations of the idea of bureaucrats, while the concept of magnates would simply evoke an emotional response and explain the higher point of the events in which it was participating. Thus, through an overtly

---

1. Njegoš, 1987, 207–208, 211–212. The lines – whether the first alone, or the first and the second, the first and the third – were carried in Podgorica [then Titograd] during the first attempt to overthrow the Montenegrin authorities (*Politika,* 9 October 1988), at the associated rallies in Kolašin and Andrijevica (*Politika,* 11 October 1988), at the election meetings of Kilibarda's NS and Rašković's SDS in Zeta (*Svet,* 220, 19 September 1990), and so on.

2. There is more detail in Žanić (1996a) about the contemporary damning of politicians. The irony of political relations would lead to Milošević himself being identified as a decadent magnate when a few years later he agreed to negotiate with the international community. Standing by the side of Radovan Karadžić, the Synod of the Serbian Orthodox Church was to accuse Milošević of leading the way to national schism 'at a decisive moment', when general harmony was necessary, and of making it possible that 'in this Serbian generation too the terrible national curse should come true', and four of Njegoš's lines were quoted (Communiqué of the Bishops of the Serbian Orthodox Church, *NIN,* 2276, 12 August 1994). A year later, after the collapse of Republika Srpska Krajina and the beginning of disintegration among the Serbs in Bosnia-Herzegovina, the same ecclesiastical body called upon their leaders not to let the 'historical national curse fall upon them: *The magnates damn their souls/ ground the empire into pieces.*' (*NIN,* 2328, 11 August 1995 – original italics).

unusual phrase, the speaker presented himself very clearly as the embodiment of the oppressed and humiliated people, as the authentic executor of its aspirations for a renewal of the golden age of harmony.

Furthermore, these same selfish and fractious magnates, the causal agents of the national disaster, are directly linked to another important topos in the Milošević discourse – round tables. As he stated back in May 1986 'in no version whatsoever was it possible' that the political actions of the communists should be determined by round tables (Milošević 1989: 93). They gave an a priori negative image, metaphor and symbol of fruitless talk, but also in the vernacular worldview and presentiments secretive, behind-the-scenes conspiracies the point of which was impossible to fathom and which were carried out in some unintelligible language of faceless bureaucrats and decadent magnates.

Finally, is there any point in wondering how much the average consciousness, with its forty-five years of habituation to militant communist rhetoric and made insensitive to the meaning of words stated with empty pathos by countless state officials, would be capable of noticing that there was after all a difference between the symbolic 'declaration of war on opportunism and bureaucracy' (Milošević 1989: 202) and the real declaration of war against the Croats and the Bosniaks? And would they not react equally to each call to war – whether with an indifferent wave of the hand and the apathetic hope that yet another bit of bother thought up by the government that did not touch the ordinary man would blow over, or with wholehearted involvement in the hunt for the archetypal enemy, with a fierce desire to return with as much loot as possible, to prove their own real value to themselves, and their orthodoxy to their master?

TWO

———

The Kosovo Crisis

The gusle, tambouritza and saz are good instruments. Though primitive, they can provide a lot of musically and in particular 'ethically' worthwhile results, but only individually. Not even Mokranjac [Serbian composer, 1856–1914] could possibly write a score to combine all three of them as an ensemble, without the playing being dissonant and cacophonous... And that is how it will be as long as this unnatural and cacophonous orchestra exists or, perhaps, until a drum is introduced into the playing.
(Mensur Čamo, 'The *saz, gusle* and *tambouritza*', *Nedjelja* 92, 24 November 1991)

Oral political journalism

It was with this metaphor that a journalist of a Sarajevo political weekly, and the editor who drew attention to it by including it in the headline, presented conditions in Bosnia-Herzegovina on the first anniversary of free, multiparty elections. A year after the election victories of the *gusle* players of the Bosnian Serb SDS, the *tambouritza* players of the Bosnia-Herzegovina Croat HDZ and the *saz* players of the Bosniak [Muslim] SDA, the country was on the edge of an abyss. The JNA had armed the Serbian villages, the SDS was declaring Serbian autonomy all over the country and obstructing the parliament, and what collaboration there was between the HDZ and the SDA, fraught with calculation and suspicion on both sides, was more of a spontaneous defence mechanism than the result of a carefully thought-out political platform.

However, while the symbolism of the three instruments, representing the three major Bosnian ethnic communities and their political relationships, is fairly clear, one may still speculate as to who the enigmatic drummer might be. Historically, it could be one of those complicated political orchestrations – Ottoman, Austro-Hungarian or Yugoslav – within which the dissonances of the three stringed instruments were really or least ostensibly smoothed over, most frequently by one of the players getting a score from Istanbul, Vienna (sometimes directly, sometimes via Zagreb) or Belgrade, sometimes bringing over a drummer as well. But at the time when the article was written, things were not all that clear. Some people naively believed in the JNA, some in almighty NATO, some in the European Community and the United Nations, some just in themselves, some in nobody. Since the Dayton Agreement was signed on the fourth anniversary of the publication of this article, one might say that the authoritative drummer came from the other side of the Atlantic, except that not even then had it become finally clear whether auditions for the quartet were over.

But if one pushes aside all the ruins and graves that had covered the country in the meantime, it may be seen that, from the outset, the stage had been crowded with instruments, especially one of them. A character in a late nineteenth-century romantic fable dreams about this in a clearing in a forest, surrounded by members of his own *haiduk* band:

> How easily his fingers flitted over the strings. And the sound rose and flickered over their heads. But however melancholy it was, it did not confound the soul ... Marvellous are the sounds of the *gusle*! They are like a wounded man on his deathbed, who with his last breath implores you to avenge him (Veselinović 1987 [1896]: 86).

Five years before the quotation with which we opened this chapter, the front page of *Oslobođenje*, the main daily newspaper in Bosnia-Herzegovina, had carried a comment about the *Master Gusle Players* tour that had covered twenty-five Bosnian cities at the end of 1986. During the tour, the epic poem by the Montenegrin bard Božidar Đukić, 'The Tragical Fate of Branka Đukić', had particularly 'raised the temperature and awoken passions'.[1] Its author was from the Vasojević clan, Northern Montenegro, and he recorded his epic on an audio cassette. The song concerns the attempted rape and the murder of a nineteen-year-old Montenegrin girl on 3 September 1975 on Mt Čakor, on the border between Montenegro and Kosovo, and later events related to this incident (Đukić 1985).

Given the political power relations of the time, this newspaper commentary could not have been published without some political patronage,

---

1. Emir Habul, ['Nationalism on the stage'], *Oslobođenje*, 10 January 1987.

even without direct encouragement from the political establishment of the republic. But within the context of the standard ideological criticism of nationalism and along the lines of the regular stereotypes and ideologemes of Yugoslav political discourse, it also developed certain assumptions that were to some extent unexpected:

> Unfortunately, as confirmed by the most competent political bodies, nationalism is on the rise ... At the moment there are increasingly widespread attempts to stir up nationalistic and other primitive passions through the *gusle*, which in these regions has always been a symbol of the preservation of aspirations to freedom, the safeguarding of national identity and freedom.

At concerts, the announcers always insisted that the murderers of Branka Đukić had been Albanians, and some of the participants from Belgrade stated that 'the *gusle* players should leave a special impression on every Serb, so that after the concert they should start thinking about the Serbian cause more profoundly and studiously.' Such a mood at a quite ordinary folk music concert gave grounds for thinking that there was something really serious involved:

> If a compère insists that 'Kosovo has been black and bloody since that fatal year of 1389 and it will stay that way', if he recites the lines: 'Don't be amazed, my heroes, if there are bloodstained Christmas Eves',[1] or, if before a concert at Kalinovik he asks if there are any Muslims in the room so that the repertoire can be adjusted, then it is clear what kind of motivation is at issue.
>
> It is obviously intended to inflame the audience in an 'ethnically pure' hall. The revolutionary *gusle* songs played a subordinate role in these concerts, while the mythical ones produced effects in the style of 'That's the real stuff, voevod'[2] or 'Lay on, brothers, there

---

1. An allusion to the central motif of Njegoš's *The Mountain Wreath* in which the massacre of Montenegrin converts to Islam took place on Christmas Eve, as in the Christian heroic epic altogether this day is symbolic and consecrated for an attack on Muslims. In fact, in the context of the concerts described, when the audience, mainly Serbs, was systematically sensitised in this way, it was not really an allusion, more of a direct call to violence.

2. Voevod (*voyvoda, vojvoda*) – a word that was diffused for centuries over the whole of the South Slav area in the sense of senior military commander, in very varied contexts. It was value-neutral, except that at the end of the nineteenth century its official use was narrowed to Serbia, and so after the creation of the Kingdom of Yugoslavia it started to be perceived as only Serbian in other parts of the country. In WWII it was the official title for Chetnik commanders, and after that experience, it remained associated in the minds of the populace only with them, sometimes with extremely

are more of us yet'.

The problem, says the commentator, is not that the crime is condemned in the epic but that it is 'imbued with a cry for vengeance' and that it 'indirectly casts doubt upon the likelihood that the court will justly condemn the murderers'. At the trial of the two alleged criminals in the District Court in Bijelo Polje on 4 December 1975, the girl's father, Rade, took a pistol into the courtroom and killed one of the defendants, because he 'suspected the court would not send them to the gallows'. When he tried to shoot the second one, his pistol did not work. His action was greeted with delight by those in the court: 'The crowd all cried as one: / Rade from under Kom [a mountain in the Vasojević area], well done / For you've done your sacred duty' (Đukić 1985). Then the epic shifts to the scene in which Rade Đukić is being tried in the very same chamber, when he justifies himself by referring to Prince-Bishop Petar Petrović Njegoš, or rather to the quotation of an idea from his play *The False King Šćepan the Small (Lažni car Šćepan Mali,* 1851):

> *to do ill, defending himself from ill*
> *here there is no crime.*
> (Njegoš 1851: V, 178–182).

Since this kind of revenge was allowed by traditional law, given that the criminals had 'attacked human decency / and the public voice condemned them', the father was entitled to take the law into his own hands, without this being an act of self-will, rather the fulfilment of an obligation that went beyond both him as an individual and the formal laws of the state, whose existence he was aware of but he considered them to belong to an inferior category. Furthermore, he did not make his decision about it as a matter of individual choice, rather he simply responded to the challenge of his enemy:

> *and I on behalf of the people*
> *stood in defence of my home*
> *and responded to the slayer*
> *perforce to break the law*
> *to commit a deed like this.*

Under its ideological and political garb, whether the author was aware of it or not, the article in *Oslobođenje* contained a series of important

---

negative, although in other circumstances, as may be seen from this example, highly positive connotations.

references to the life of epic songs in contemporary social conditions, to their functionality as communication in times of social tension and to the value system they reproduce, which affects the social conduct of their consumers. The article also raised other, no less important, questions about the range and scope of this kind of propaganda, this kind of oral journalism, about the ways in which current political messages are involved in the channels of traditional communication and built into the poetics of its genres. In what way do they assume its authority, which then functions, all by itself, as an unquestioned source of legitimacy for this particular kind of politics?

This very particular subculture, the *gusle* player-singer pop scene, and derivations from it, the *gusle*, then, as medium of public communication, one no less important than TV, radio or the press, conceals an enormous amount of material for studying both the ideological and political background as well as the sociocultural context of the war of 1990–1995. The pages that follow are thus a parallel study of two media systems, two kinds of journalism. They will show that, in certain conditions and environments, the two systems were very largely characterised by identical terminology and phraseology, themes, metaphors and symbols, the natural consequence of reaching for the same evocative box of tricks. These two kinds of journalism were coexistent, in a dynamic interaction, imbuing each other at several levels of expression, creating cognate or complementary messages and parallelisms of content and typology.

New epics and their authors

Such the was the esteem in which the heroic epic was held among the people for centuries that even those who endeavoured to eliminate its negative effects, including Franciscan educators such as Tomo Babić, were forced to clothe their messages in decasyllabics, the typical style of the South Slav epic, if they wanted to reach the public. The old songs were joined at the end of the nineteenth century by new creations that sang of the battles of the Herzegovinians, Montenegrins and Serbs in 1875–1878 and events from the Greek and Turkish, Russian and Japanese, Italian and Turkish, Balkan and First World wars. In Serbia, Bosnia and the Dalmatian Highlands decasyllabics were the vehicle for election addresses, proclamations and the celebration of political leaders. After the assassination in 1928 of Stjepan Radić, the leader of the Croatian Peasants' Party, the strongest opposition force in the Kingdom of Yugoslavia, there were so many songs about him among the Herzegovinian Croats that one may call them a cycle. Some of these were performed in secret, hidden even from the Franciscans, because the Yugoslav gendarmes had orders to arrest the *gusle* players. Under Austro-Hungarian rule, the Land Government in Sarajevo received complaints and appeals composed in the traditional decasyllabic line. The decasyllabic spread the platform of the Popular Party (*Pučka stranka*) in Dalmatia immediately after World War I. The peasants were catechised in it in Serbia, and it was used to popularise the *Sokol* movement in Herzegovina (Murko 1951).

In the first Yugoslavia, fierce polemics were carried on in anonymous songs printed as leaflets and handed out in trains, schools and government offices, such as the one for and against the president of the Yugoslav Muslim Organization (JMO) Džafer Kulenović (Kulenović 1978: 10). The NDH performed and printed songs about the exploits of the Ustasha and the glory of Ante Pavelić. In Chetnik areas they glorified Draža Mihailović, in Belgrade General Milan Nedić, the occupation governor of Serbia. Even after World War II government and Communist Party bodies received reports from the field in decasyllabic verse, and the example of the woman who at the meeting of the Anti-Fascist Women's Association (AFŽ) would in the blink of an eye recast in decasyllabics a whole copy of the magazine *Woman in Combat* (*Žena u borbi*) led to the use of the line in literacy campaigns (Visković 1947: 7): people deeply familiar with that verse form would take in messages in it more easily than in a standard teaching format.

Whether or not they were created spontaneously, or for political propaganda purposes, whether they have artistic value or remain at the level of uninventive versified chronicle, all of these songs show that epic verse was still very much alive among considerable sections of the Yugoslav population, where it had a vital and unique social and aesthetic function. The epic, 'the art of narration', wrote an American Slavic studies expert in 1960, flourishes, 'provided that the culture is in other respects of a sort to foster the singing of the tales. If the way of life of a people furnishes subjects for story and affords occasion for the telling, this art will be fostered' (Lord 1960: 20). Although the area for it is narrowing historically, wars are undoubtedly the kind of situation when it can expand for a shorter or longer period. For example, Father Stjepan Džalto described the seizure of Bugojno, Central Bosnia, by the AB-H [Army of Bosnia-Herzegovina] in 1993, the expulsion of the Croats from the town and the slaughter of Croatian civilians in the nearby village of Uzdol, where he was priest, in decasyllabics. Similar works would continue to be created, he said, because 'war gives rise to heroic songs' (*Glas Koncila*, 14, 3 April 1994).

According to Lord, the epic songs have died out in the cities 'not because life in a large community is an unfitting environment for them' but because it was there that, thanks to regular education, literacy first took root, and what this public had previously sought, and found, in live performances, it now started to get from books (Lord 1960: 20). But the problem cannot be reduced to a question of literacy alone. Its real context is the spread of the means of mass communication as a new and increasingly accessible source of information. This would tend to be borne out by the experience of the popular poet Ante Škrapić, a worker in the Šibenik light metals factory TLM, who wrote of many events of the war in Croatia. 'Once upon a time,' he said, 'before there was radio or television, he read his poems to the workers, who liked them, but now there were practically no such performances.' (*Slobodna Dalmacija,* 2 February 1992).

There is a great deal of evidence that the decasyllabic epic song, whether it is promoted in live performances by *gusle* players, sold in printed form, most often at village or country fairs, or recorded on LPs or audio-cassettes, is even today for a large part of the population not only a source of aesthetic pleasure but also an important, sometimes the main, medium through which information about current events is conveyed, on which they build their value system, form political judgments and model their general social conduct. In such environments, the epic is socially sanctioned as a medium that is suitable for the exchange of relevant collective experience and ways of settling certain problems. Investigating the influence of the global social and cultural system on the specific culture of the firm, Dunja Rihtman-Auguštin noticed the broader significance of the worker who described conditions in his firm in decasyllabics ('Empty hands and empty machinery, / no raw materials and no money') and found himself charged in court with 'inciting the people and spreading false news'. This shows that

> in this country a given situation, the difficulties, problems and conflicts in an area may be successfully expressed both in a political or an academic vocabulary using the terminology of organisation theory, and also in decasyllabics. Clearly, this genre expresses very well a certain value orientation [that has] come into conflict with the existing institutional system (Rihtman-Auguštin 1972: 149).

Such new epics, new *gusle* players' songs, as contemporary offshoots of the folklore tradition or its counterparts, cover an extraordinarily wide range of themes: natural disasters (the earthquakes in Skopje and Banjaluka of 1963 and 1969, the Zagreb floods of 1964); crimes such as that sung of by Božidar Đukić; and traffic accidents that capture attention either by the number of victims or by the death of some outstanding individual in them.

World events were also sung of: for example the murder of John F. Kennedy in 1963 and the Yugoslav ambassador to Sweden, Vladimir Rolović, in 1971. An inexhaustible theme during the whole forty-five years of the second Yugoslavia was provided by the events of World War II, seen, of course, from the Partisan perspective and in terms of official ideological paradigms. Also handled were the lives of members of the *nomenklatura*, and, in version after version, the life, travels and funeral of Josip Broz Tito. One vernacular poet from the Kozara area, Western Bosnia, even put into verse a rather long speech he made in Prijedor on 10 September 1972 (Rodić 1982). Another *gusle* player and poet from Montenegro readjusted priorities among the figures he sang of: he wrote the epic 'Blažo Jovanović in India', in which he compares this very powerful Montenegrin politician with the Kosovo heroes, the knights. He emphasised in all kinds of ways how important he was on the journey and in the politics of the non-aligned movement, without once mentioning Tito, although Jovanović had gone to India only as a member of Tito's entourage. The poem was banned for this oversight (Dedijer 1981b: 111). Although the new epics were not the same as those contained in the classic collections, they were still, in their manner of existence and their function in their own community, part of the epic traditional or oral poetry, with a vital function and value within it (Bošković-Stulli 1983: 184–185).

Even in the 1920s many of the contemporary songs had literary origins, that is, their authors found stimulus, themes and information in books and the press, which is largely what they do today. The *gusle* player Mile Krajina describes his creative process as follows: 'I sing when some event arouses me so much that I cannot restrain myself from singing of it ... Writing the songs, I get deeper into the historical background, and study the same event from several sources, because that is the only way to find out the truth about history. When I read, I read what it says, and also between the lines. I learn most about the events of today from the papers' (*Globus*, 164, 28 January 1994). In more recent times, the television is also a source of information. Thus the *gusle* player Željko Šimić explained one of the motifs in his poem against the establishment of the Federation of Bosnia-Herzegovina (FBH): 'Perhaps a lot of people won't know what book of Turkish grammar and usage is mentioned in the song. Where does it come from? I saw a Croatian TV report about the printing of a Turkish grammar in Croatia! Are we going to have this grammar here in the Federation?' (*Panorama*, 126, 25 September 1996). The explanation relates to the following lines:

> *Croatia glories in a grammar*
> *written in the Turkish language*

the Muslim brothers have published it
and the city of Zagreb made it public.
We have still not learned Croatian
I'll not learn the Turkish script.
Oh, Minister Vokić,[1] do you care at all
which books teach Herzegovina Croats?
(Šimić 1996)

At issue is the *Grammar of Contemporary Turkish* by Dr Ekrem Čaušević, founder of the Chair of Turkish Studies at the Faculty of Philosophy in Zagreb, which was published there in 1996. A lot of attention was devoted to it in the news programmes of HTV [Croatian Television], and that is evidently where he got the information from, while completely missing the point.[2]

The author of a popular song about an air crash sought data about the dead – and got them – directly from their families, and described all the casualties in detail in his epic, giving their names, surnames, occupations, all their virtues and making the inevitable final point about the curse of destiny (*Nedjeljna Dalmacija*, 13 May 1984). When on 7 May 1991, in Polog, the population of western Herzegovina prevented the passage of the JNA tanks, quite reasonably not believing the official explanation of a routine exercise, the *gusle* player Šimun Vukoja from Ljubotići worked day after day, at the scene of the event, as both witness and participant, on his epic 'The Landing on Široki Brijeg' ('Desant na Široki Brijeg'). When a journalist met him, he already had 'five closely typed pages of lines', including an episode about the arrival of the President of the Presidency of Bosnia-Herzegovina, Alija Izetbegović, among the agitated people, putting his speech into verse:

The day went past, Hail to Maria
and now has come President Alija,
he at once to the people spoke,
and back came the plaudits of the folk:
Good people of Lištica commune,
let us let pass this army unit,
you are folk with sensible heads,
listen to me and to President Tuđman,

---

1. Minister of Education of the Republic of Croatia.
2. Šimić must have been even more surprised in September 1997 when in the space of two days he could have seen an interview with President Tuđman, according to which Islam and Christianity were said to be in a state of irreconcilable conflict, and then the ceremonial arrival in Zagreb of the Turkish President Süleyman Demirel and that same Tuđman and the Croatian Presidential Guard greeting him while the Turkish – Šimić would probably say Ottoman – crescent flag was freely waving.

> *allow this column of tanks to pass,*
> *their caterpillars scaring our kids.*
> *You've held them two and sixty hours*
> *so now you can open up the doors.*
> *Move aside these barricades,*
> *and let them have free passage.*
> *Even if it's against your will,*
> *let them go to the Kupres field.*[1]

Some authors sent their songs and poems to the newspapers themselves. In April 1953, after the death of a federal government member, Boris Kidrič, one paper in the Serbian heartland received so many that it had to make excuses for 'not being in a position to publish more than one' (*NIN*, 2 August 1981).

I myself saw, at the end of March 1989, an author bringing into the office of the Zagreb evening paper *Večernji list*, an epic about the current president of the parliament of Croatia, Anđelko Runjić. As far as I could gather in a short reading, the poem celebrated Runjić as champion of the construction of the Zagreb-Split motorway and laid stress on the importance of maritime affairs in the Croatian economy. In my private documentation I have a similar work about the president of the Croatian unions Bernardo Jurlina, offered the following year to the daily *Vjesnik*. The 'marvellous falcon' Jurlina is sung of as a hero, defender of Croatia, for only he of all the Croatian communist *nomenklatura* stood out openly against Serbian repression of the Kosovars. Since in the nature of his work he often travelled to Belgrade, the poet warned him: 'Beware the fate of Stjepan Radić / Now too there is a Puniša Račić.'

The reference to the assassination of Stjepan Radić, who was shot by the extreme Serbian nationalist Račić in the Belgrade Assembly in 1928, is a standard motif in modern songs about Croatian politicians. In an epic about the last congress of the League of Communists of Yugoslavia in January 1990, prepared in a mood of violence and open threats from Milošević, a *gusle* player warned the LCC delegation, on the eve of their departure for Belgrade:

> *Watch out, our brothers and comrades,*
> *that twenty eight be not repeated!*
> *Do you know, Ivo [Račan], that Stipe Radić*
> *was wounded for his principles there ...*
> *Careful, Ivo, lest in the Sava Centre*

---

1. Miljenko Karačić, 'Tanks sent Lištica into the world', *Bosanski pogledi*, 12, 13 May 1991.

some Croat has his head blown off.
(Šimić 1990a)

It was no different at the beginning of 1991 when it seemed that there would be a massive JNA coup in Croatia to install a pro-Belgrade government in just a matter of days. The departure of Tuđman and the Croatian leadership to Belgrade for talks on the dramatic night of 25 January led a vernacular poet to 'recall Stjepan Radić' and describe the feeling of the time in verse: 'Croatia was again all in terror / that history would be repeated' (Krajina 1994: 22).

It was the same among the expatriates. Some authors published poems at their own expense. Many Chetnik and Ustasha-oriented papers regularly published such epics, while the targets of the vernacular poets were often also modern publications edited along pluralist lines. The former Ustasha ensign Ante Vukić sent his decasyllabic comments on political events tirelessly to the *Poruka slobodne Hrvatske* [Message of Free Croatia] issued in the seventies in Switzerland by a group of Radić's followers, not remotely troubled by its failure to oblige with publication.[1]

From the wide range of issues concerning the overall position of vernacular, traditional, folk culture in a society that was becoming urbanised, socially transformed and administratively organised on modern principles, we can pick out three that follow on directly from that leader in *Oslobođenje*. They are:

1. the adaptation of the epic repertoire to the religious and ethnic composition of the audience, which happened in the eastern Bosnian town of Kalinovik, but was probably no different anywhere else;
2. the cult of the *gusle,* 'the symbol of freedom and ethnic identity', as the commentator put it, indicating that he considered the very form of the composition a political message with a particular profile;
3. the social context and the functionality of the *gusle* player's performance as communication, part of a more broadly based propaganda project.

Fitting the gusle *player to the public*

In itself, both in the Balkans and in the Middle East, this procedure is not unusual. The Slovene Slavonic studies expert M. Murko, who carried out

---

1. I am grateful for this information to Dr Tihomil Rađa, the paper's editor.

Ensemble of Serbs and Moslems from Sandžak in the early 1930s, among them three eminent local *gusle* players: the Moslem Rešo Alihadžić (second from left in the front row), and the Orthodox Simo Džagarija (beside him) and Dušan Jerinić (first from right in back row). (Murko 1951)

detailed field-research between the two wars, left a mass of evidence about how in their choice of material the singers took the feelings of the audience into account and could modify the outcome of the song, or the tone in which it was sung, according to whether they had a Muslim or a Christian audience. In eastern Bosnia he saw the way that the Orthodox and the Muslims listened to each other's *gusle* players' performances, and laughed good-naturedly when the singer of one side killed a mass of members of the other. In Trnovo the Serbs told him how their *gusle* players 'cut up the Turks, and theirs the Serbs, and we always laugh, but when we are together we don't want to give offence, and we choose songs we have in common'. Elsewhere, he was surprised when he saw a Catholic singing to Muslims about Ramadan, but it was explained to him that they 'honoured every kind of heroism' (Murko 1951).[1] Filip

---

1. In the tavern of a mixed-religion village between Goražde and Foča they kept two *gusles*, one for Orthodox singers, the other for Muslims, which would at first sight seem to be a sign of intolerance or distrust. In conversation with the locals, however, Murko realised that quite the opposite was true. It was actually a way of cooling tensions and avoiding unnecessary problems, for Christians tended to inscribe a cross on the bottom of their *gusle*, which meant it could not be used by the Muslims. And

The *gusle* player Marko Bandur from Ljubuški, photographed in the early 1930s: there is nothing unusual about his being dressed as a 'Turk', since this was then the normal apparel of Catholic Croats in Herzegovinian villages. (Murko 1951)

Višnjić, the greatest of the nineteenth-century Serbian *gusle* players and singers, was able to switch the scene of events in order to meet the taste of his Bosnian Muslim audience, and cast aside his Muslim repertoire only when he was completely taken up with the theme of the First Serbian Insurrection. This adaptability helped the professionals to make a living. In the inter-war years, a certain Catholic from Bihać would sing Muslim songs to Muslims, 'or his own songs in such a way that the Moslems won the battles', and Serbian songs when he was with Serbs, quite aware that he had to please his audience or otherwise he would not be able to count on the fee he depended on to support his family (Lord 1960: 19).

A Muslim in whose presence a Christian slaughtered the Turks would himself seek the *gusle* so that he could 'cut down a few Vlachs in return' or ask the performer to extend a song in which the Muslim hero had landed in jail and free him. Sometimes it would end like this, and sometimes there would be a punch-up, the overture to which was breaking the *gusle* over the

so there were two *gusles*, so that a singer could choose the one that suited his way of seeing things (Murko 1951: 334).

53

gusle player's own head. For this reason, from time to time, heroic songs to the *gusle* were forbidden, as they were in Montenegro, so as not to stir up old rivalries and resentments among the fraternities and clans (Medenica 1938). The Turks had also banned the *gusle*, particularly in Kosovo. In Herzegovina, the Catholic priest of Trebinje who composed and sang to the *gusle* songs about Turkish (bad) deeds was summoned in 1748 before the ecclesiastical court in Dubrovnik, because the citizens of Dubrovnik were afraid that his media exposure might have repercussions in their relations with their powerful Ottoman neighbour.

The knowledge of participants in the vernacular culture of current events is given shape in some general, non-historical categories of justice and injustice, heroism and cowardice, loyalty and treachery, faith and lack of faith, as the manifestation of a single, unified cognitive and value system that was untouched by history. The attention of the contemporary creator or consumer of the epic was focused, above all, on the hero, the person who was the mover of, or an important participant in, dramatic events, who overcame trials and lived through perilous situations. The concept of heroism as an enduring norm in the life of the traditional community, as a tried and unquestioned manner of organising reality, was in fact a common denominator that in the deep structure reconciled features that on the surface would seem irreconcilably opposed. Everything that happened in the life of the community would be measured against these universally applicable values, and the vernacular author did not appear as the bearer or representative of his own individuality, his own views on life, rather as a representative of a collective understanding of basic human values. In fact he

> did not sing of heroes or some individual figure of a hero, rather of *heroism*, the heroes figuring as bearers of the quality of heroism ... By foregrounding the quality, the abstract historical and contemporary heroes, the protagonists of the heroism, were abstracted (Zečević 1978: 378).

On the face of it, it would be hard to find two more incompatible personalities than the Slovene politician Boris Kraigher, war veteran, vice-president of the Yugoslav Federal executive government [SIV] and one of the creators of the Yugoslav economic reforms of the 1960s, and Dragan Mance, a 22-year-old football player from Belgrade's Partizan football club and a member of the Yugoslav national team. Only a rather strained formal coincidence would seem to link the two: both were killed in traffic accidents, Kraigher in 1967, Mance in 1985. But when the epics arising as a result of these events are compared – 'The Tragic Death of Dragan Mance' ('Tragična smrt Dragana Mancea') and 'The Sudden Death of Boris Kraigher' ('Nenadna smrt Borisa Kraighera'), the first recorded on cassette by a *gusle* player, the second printed by the author himself – one may discern a fundamental kinship between them, from the point of view of the participant in the epic tradition. Both deaths are described in the way that the deaths of the one-time epic heroes were described, in the style, sensibility and metre of the traditional epic, but with the technical concessions required by the new reality. Kraigher, that is, set off to 'to the battle' of new social and economic relations not on horseback but 'in his car / on the broad asphalted road', just like Mance, who had set off in his car on a city boulevard for a training session.[1]

Just as, in the creative process described above, the creations of the vernacular authors seem monotonous only to those who approach them from outside, so it is a mistake to see the celebration of ideologically different and even opposed personalities by the same author as political fickleness or morally dubious opportunism. At the end of 1989 the already mentioned Šimić called upon the Madonna of Međugorje 'to help Marković Ante / to gain glory with his reforms', greeting the then Yugoslav prime minister – ideologically a communist, though a liberal one – as 'my own Herzegovinan fellow-countryman' (Šimić 1990a). For Marković was born in the town of Konjic in Herzegovina, although his family had moved to Zagreb very soon afterwards, and he himself had no connection whatever with his native area, nor was this at all relevant to the public. On the basis of this fact, however, Šimić built up a relation of territorial solidarity, typical of the traditional patriarchal culture, in which origin was always an essential criterion of identity, irrespective of one's subsequent life's journey. Only a month or so later he celebrated the departure of the communists from power, calling Croatian President Franjo Tuđman, just elected on an anti-communist platform, 'the pride of the region' and calling upon him to bring to Međugorje 'the whole new Parliament / for the Mother of God to bless' (Šimić 1990b). In Herzegovina, he said, they hold it against him that in the time of Yugoslavia he performed an epic about the Battle of the Neretva in 1943, celebrating, of course, a Partisan victory over the 'cursed' Ustashas. But, he said, he had only performed the work, it had been written by a colonel in the JNA. 'All in all, I can say that it is impossible to play the *gusle* for so many years and not offend anyone. So I sing, no matter

1. For these epics, see Jovan Mihajlović, ['On the figure of the contemporary national epic Boris Krajger' in *Proceedings of the 1ˢᵗ Congress of Yugoslav Ethnologists and Folklore Studies Experts (Rogaška Slatina, 5–9 October 1983)*, Ljubljana, 1983: 699–705. Miroslav Kos 'Grave-diggers of the Spirit', *Duga*, 337, 24 October 1987.

who does or doesn't like it' (*Panorama*, 126, 25 March 1996).[1]

The contemporary epic singers are simply bards, who sing of the exemplary deeds of exemplary people and satisfy the expectations of their consumers. Today this hero and fighter for justice will be a *revolutionary*, tomorrow a *counter-revolutionary*. Once again, both the singers and their audience manifest 'the power of a tradition that works in spite of all intellectual changes, precisely at the level of style and poetics.' (Bošković-Stulli 1983: 181).

Also important is the note in the *Oslobođenje* article that at the contentious *gusle* players' tournament at the end of 1986, in parallel with dangerous nationalistic songs, which the author labelled 'mythic', they also performed desirable revolutionary songs, which could only have been about the Partisan victories, 'the revolutionary transformation of society', 'brotherhood and unity', Josip Broz 'Tito' and other members of the Yugoslav *nomenklatura*. This shows at least two things. On the one hand, it had seized a moment when, from a formal perspective, two political conceptions were in some kind of equilibrium, still capable of coexisting in the same context and genre, with the proviso that one was rising and the other declining. On the other hand, they were actually able to do this because at some deep level they did not differ at all, and the defeated concept would have to withdraw only when the emotional saturation of the audience reached a level at which it would no longer be able to tolerate the *names* of its heroes or their characteristics. The very same virtues, the same type of situations, would then be transferred to new names – and everything would continue as if nothing had happened, since both sets of heroes did not, in any case, exist just by themselves, but as current embodiments of their mythic forbears and continuers of their exemplary exploits.

The murder in Paraćin and 'political rapes'

When the Kosovo crisis flared up, the authors of the new epics looked to it with increasing frequency for topics, interpreting them according to the historical and political key suggested to them by the official media and also by their own traditionally sanctioned understanding of reality, whether or not such events really did have a political background. One of them sang how on 13 May 1981 five Serb policemen were killed in a clash with two Albanians who had holed up in their house in the village of Prekaze (Jeknić

---

1. In the same interview he spoke about other problems, for example, that some local political leaders had made trouble for him when in the 1993 epic 'Who is stealing Herceg-Bosna's marks' ('Tko ukrade Herceg-Bosne marke') he had accused them by name of money-laundering and embezzlement.

1987). The *gusle* players reacted with speed to the crime in the JNA Paraćin Barracks, where on 3 September 1987 an Albanian soldier had killed four soldiers while they slept and wounded several more (Rosić 1988, Miljanić 1988). There are plenty of indicators that the first event was a shoot-out with common criminals, the second the crime of a deranged individual. But officially, they were put in the context of organised anti-Serb activities and interpreted as episodes in a coordinated Greater Albanian conspiracy against Yugoslavia or rather Serbia.

The fact that the authors of the epics did not mention the names of the criminals, although they were well known to the public throughout the then Yugoslavia, and hence to the writers and their intended audience, contributed to the mysterious mood of conspiracy and murky danger that loomed over the community. The perpetrators were referred to metaphorically, in a depersonalised way, as 'the Kosovan plague', 'the beast of Kosovo' and the 'Kosovo spectre', while their victims were described as heroes who had fallen for freedom, irrespective of how they had died or whether there had been any political dimension to their previous lives. The *gusle* player Rosić, for example, put the Paraćin murders in the context of the well-thought-out activities of those Greater Albanians who 'murder and rape our sisters / round Čakor and Kosovo polje'. The mention of the Čakor rape, evidently the same as had been sung of by Božidar Đukić, suggests at least two things. First, since they were following the same generic rules and promoting the same value system, the popular singers, independently of each other, noted the same events as being particularly symbolic and dramatic, and fitted them into new plots, or cited them later as being paradigmatic. Secondly, in such a procedure, the *gusle* players were no different from the journalists, because in both the controlled media and in the new epics sexual violence, in which there were cross-connections of violence, sex and ethnicity, was placed quite unambiguously in a political context, treated paradigmatically, and interpreted as organised anti-Serbian activity. Of course, sometimes the two processes took place to some extent independently of each other, sometimes there are clear mutual borrowings and influences. And it would certainly be possible to investigate the extent to which the official interpretation of events in Kosovo influenced subsequent *gusle* players' interpretations of the Čakor crime. For the moment, it is enough to note that the vernacular singers also manipulated the rape for political purposes, and promoted the idea of the Albanian as a congenital sexual maniac.[1]

---

1. For the political use of rape, where the anti-Albanian campaign in Kosovo is seen as an overture for the real – systematic – rapes of Bosniak women that the Serbian paramilitary forces carried out in Bosnia-Herzegovina, see Bracewell (2000) and

What is more, the authors of the new epics put contemporary events in the context of the Battle of Kosovo, seeing them as a continuation of this event. Nevertheless, in this period the idea still prevailed that this was a crime it was hard to imagine being thought up 'at the time of Brotherhood and Unity' (Đukić 1985), as an attack on Yugoslavia and the work of Tito, on the 'brotherly ring-dance (*kolo*) of Branko Radičević' (Miljanić 1988) or 'the brotherly ring-dance that winds / from Triglav to Đevđelija' (Jeknić 1987).[1] We should therefore deal in more detail with Đukić's epic about the crime in Čakor.

At the time it happened, at the end of 1975, this event aroused considerable interest in Montenegro and Serbia. But it was not so much the actual murder of the girl that captured public attention, and particularly not the ethnicity of victim and murderers, rather the fate of the girl's father, and his trial on a charge of murder motivated by ruthless vengeance (he was sentenced to eight years, later commuted to four). Sympathising with him, the public thought more or less as he did when he justified himself by reference to those lines by Njegoš. This central drama, the conflict between legality and legitimacy, the rule of law and cultural norms (Giordano 1996), was in essence preserved in Đukić's epic, although it was recorded as long as ten years after the events and in radically different social circumstances, when the most ordinary street brawls would be interpreted in a political light, if there were Albanians and Serbs involved in them. In the foreground was the tragedy of parents who had with enormous sacrifice brought up five children, and then in a single year lost their only son, in a traffic accident, and their daughter, Branka, an 'A' student.

While the Đukićs, a 'clan of three hundred years' standing', were discussed at length and by name, the attackers were neither named nor identified ethnically. They were simply nameless scum and evil-doers, robbers, 'trash / from near the wretched town of Peć [Alb. Peja]'. The *gusle* player explicitly discounted the political, ethnic and confessional background of the crime, determining it classically as a deed of violence out of lust: they attacked 'the

---

Mežnarić (1993). The *ideological* treatment of such events is shown in the fact that Božidar Đukić's epic was printed in the Christmas number of the Šabac *Glas Crkve* [Voice of the Church] 1 1987: 61–64, at the height of the 'political rapes' campaign.

1. The first case is a direct reference to a poem by the Serbian Romantic poet B. Radičević (1824–1853) in which representatives of all the South Slav areas together harmoniously dance a *kolo*, a traditional ring-dance. The poem had to be learned by heart in the schools of both Yugoslavias, and was interpreted as a poetic prophecy and powerful political symbol. The second case was a universally known metaphor that was used daily in the press, meaning something like 'from Land's End to John o'Groats'.

frightened female'

> *neither for money nor faith-strong love*
> *nor from need or out of trouble*
> *rather to feed their awful lusts.*

And when he described the decision of the victim's father to take the law into his own hands, Božidar Đukić stressed that he did this

> *against neither nation nor faith*
> *rather to cleanse the human face,*

the 'clean face (*obraz*)' being a synonym for honour, that is, exclusively from the perspective of the patriarchal moral code in which fornication was the gravest of crimes, and paternal and fraternal vendetta was not only permitted but actually prescribed. The father was defending the honour of the family, doing something that, by force of circumstances, was not legal but was incontrovertibly legitimate.

From this kind of basic attitude it could be concluded that during this phase of the Kosovo or Yugoslav crisis at least some of the vernacular poets were not ready to join in open haranguing, but described events within the value system of the original epic ethics and official Yugoslav ideology. It was the compères at their public performances who took on the role of explicitly explaining to the audiences the historical and political dimension of the events described, just as the commentator in the Sarajevo paper stated that it was the announcer who stressed the fact that the criminals were Albanians, because this is not mentioned in Đukić's epic.

If it had not been for such interpolations from the announcers, it is very likely that Đukić would have been able to perform his epic freely not only to a Bosnian Muslim but also an Albanian audience, if they were genuine participants in the epic culture: they would have understood it in its original categories, which were metapolitical and ahistorical. Informants often told the folk-song collector Murko that a singer could sing any song if it met the basic condition: if it contained 'a good hero, of whatever religion, it was listened to without distinction' (Murko 1951: 241). In 1944 in Belgrade a certain Partisan major from Lika, clearly of Serbian Orthodox peasant origin, expressed his admiration for Tito to a Croatian journalist with the cry: 'He is indeed a great man although he is a Catholic!' (Radica 1992: 57). At the beginning of the century, the future Ustasha leader, then a schoolboy, met a Muslim audience that listened with as much excitement to their *gusle* player when he sang about the battles of the golden age of the Ottoman Empire, with which they identified, as they did when at their request he read from Kačić Miošić about Christian victories. They knew all the main heroes of the Balkan nations and put 'each of them in his place and judged them by their heroic deeds,' admiring every act of courage and wisdom and despising every act of treason (Pavelić 1968: 114–116). Then not even the Čakor criminals would be perceived as Muslim Albanians, rather as despicable universal villains, while the girl's father was not the archetypal national avenger of the defeat of Kosovo some six centuries earlier, rather the perpetrator of individual justice, simply a great man, a giant among men, possibly with the benign addition 'although he was Orthodox'.

But a comparison of this Đukić epic with another of his songs recorded just a bit more than a year later, in the spring of 1987, entitled 'Extinguished Kosovo Hearths' ('Ugašena kosovska ognjišta'), shows how much had changed in a short time.[1] In the meantime the so-called Memorandum of the Serbian Academy of Science and Arts had reached the public, and Milošević had been transformed from anonymous apparatchik into charismatic national leader. In April, on the Field of Kosovo, he had without any reserve stood by the side of the local Serbian leaders, and in September, at the eighth session of the Central Committee of the League of Communists of Serbia he

1. Božidar Đukić, 'Extinguished Kosovo Hearths', *Glas Crkve*, year 15/III, no. 3 (St Vitus Day number), 1987, pp. 68–70. This is a quarterly issued by the (Orthodox) Eparchy of Šabac and Valjevo, Western Serbia. The editorial board recommended to their readers a cassette on which the song was recorded, as well as the one containing 'The Tragic Fate of Branka Đukić', both of them because of their 'topicality', which is a very strong pointer to the context in which they should be read. There are two interesting facts about the later fate of this epic and its author. At the end of 2001, the Serbs and Montenegrins in the northeast of Montenegro explained their lack of trust in the Albanians by the lesson that had come out of the tragedy at Čakor, and invoked the Đukić epic as a truthful depiction of events. cf. Božo Nikolić: 'Dolina sjenki i nade [Valley of shadows and hope]', *Monitor*, 577, 9 November 2001.

   Half a year later the Vuk Karadžić *Gusle* Association of Belgrade put on a *gusle* evening with fourteen participants. There were pictures of Milošević, even then in The Hague, Karadžić and Mladić in the lobby, for a large number of epics were actually devoted to them, while the audience was partially composed of officers of the Army of Yugoslavia and policemen in uniform. They performed the classic songs about *haiduks* and Kosovo, some from the early twentieth century, about the Russo-Japanese war, for example, and new ones about the NATO bombing of Serbia, against the government of Đinđić that had overthrown Milošević, and about Karadžić. Among the performers was Božidar Đukić, whom the audience 'applauded wildly, more so than the others'. He performed a song about a duel between a Christian and a Muslim over a woman, at which the audience jumped to their feet in delight when the dying woman begged her son: 'Oh, don't let your wife be kissed by a Turk'. cf. Ljubomir Živkov, 'Hoćemo li, moj đetiću, zapjevati Karadžiću [Let's sing, lad, of Karadžić]', *Vreme*, 589, 18 April 2002.

had taken over complete control in an internal coup.

Created in such circumstances, the new Đukić epic contained the lines

> *the bright Sun shines from Kosovo*
> *we shall not surrender you, land of Dušan,*

which had already been sung or written on banners during the assemblies and mass rallies of the Kosovo Serbs. And on 9 September the whole country was to get to know them when it watched on television the peak of the previous *happening of the people* – the Novi Sad rally in solidarity with the Kosovo Serbs. While in his previous epic Đukić had nothing but contempt for the rapists, now he was decidedly threatening all who

> *raped the children and the feeble*
> *and anyone weaker than them*

which, in context, was understood as a threat to Albanians in general. The whole motif was developed along national propaganda lines. The concrete event was just an opportunity to highlight Serbian casualties throughout history. The alleged current rapes in Kosovo were naturally connected with a series of 'foes' who 'slaughtered us over the ages' – from the Turks to the Ustashas. While a year earlier he had explicitly denied any political or ethnic connotations in the matter of the Čakor rape, and concentrated on the human drama of the protagonists, this time he depicted sexual violence as something carried out systematically, with no end in sight:

> *They are raping our maidens and our matrons*
> *Every day the same thing goes on.*

Nevertheless, only two cases were mentioned to back up this claim. One was the already twelve-year-old case of Branka Đukić, which now turned out to be paradigmatic, and the father's conduct still more laudable ('He avenged her, his clan sang out to him'), and a new case of the murder of a Serbian schoolgirl in a Prizren street. However, the description mentions only curses against her 'Serbian faith' and in no way suggests that the murder was preceded by attempted rape. There is something else that suggests a fundamental change of angle and accent. In 'The Tragic Fate of Branka Đukić', the murderers were nameless, while the victim was introduced by name, surname and broader family origin. However, in 'Extinguished Kosovo Hearths', the victim was anonymous, while it was the murderer who had name, surname and ethnicity: 'Mehmet Afa, Albanian from Kosovo'. This change faithfully follows the change in the dominant political objective and the shift from the category of the individual and the human to the category of the collective and the national, within the dominant value system of society. In the first instance, it was the tragedy of the particular family and the personal drama of the victim's father that was focal point. In the second, the individual misfortune was just a part of the collective misfortune and it was only as such that it could be finally understood, explained and, in the end, redeemed.

The cult of the gusle *in the nineteenth and twentieth centuries*

When the commentator in the Sarajevo daily stated that the *gusle* was the symbol of freedom, he was simply transmitting one of the standard official ideologemes of the Yugoslav communists, behind which there was, however, a very complicated story. The *gusle* was one of those instruments that in many nations, in the context of the ideology of national integration, had made the journey from being thought of as a folk instrument to a national one, and sometimes back again. Through the broader social attitude towards such instruments one may identify a series of practices – musical, social and verbal – the aim of which is 'to mediate between various dichotomies: traditional / modern, rural / urban, Balkan / civilised, lower / upper class, insider / outsider' (Bonifačić 1995: 75). This happened with the bagpipes in Scotland, the Celtic harp in Ireland, the banjo in the USA, the balalaika in Russia, and with the *gusle*, *tambouritza* and *saz* among the Serbs and Montenegrins, Croats and Bosniaks respectively.

A particularly romantic attitude towards certain instruments was created in the nineteenth century under the influence of Herder's ideas that folklore, as preserved among the simple people, was the embodiment of the national spirit, *Volksgeist*, of some unadulterated national culture upon which the modern national culture should be founded. It was along these lines that the idea was developed among the Croats, Serbs and Montenegrins of the blind *gusle* player, the *guslar*, as poet born, given his instrument by nymphs in order to sing about the glorious national past. What ideologues and politicians said in their discourse was put into verse by the Croat Silvije Strahimir Kranjčević (1865–1908): 'that all the history of my race / from the *gusle*'s strings was heard', while the Serbian poet Jovan Jovanović Zmaj (1833-1904) wrote that '*gusles* – Serbian *gusles* / know not how to lie'. The Montenegrin poet Njegoš wrote that during times of foreign rule 'our tears were wiped away / by the skilful sounds of wonderful *gusles*'.

The patriotic lyric of the Bosnian Muslims also used the same national and patriotic ideas, romantic motifs and schemes. The orientalist, politician and prominent writer Safvet-beg Bašagić (1870–1934) wrote that he was strongest when his 'buoyant thoughts / the sycamore *gusle* matched'. For Hamid Šahinović, the *gusle* was a device for celebrating the forbears and preserving their memory (cf. Rizvić 1990). But because the nineteenth-century ideologies of national integration among the Balkan Christian peoples had particularly stressed historical recollections of war with the Ottoman conqueror, during which the Bosnian Muslims would sometimes be denied any Slav attributes, the *gusle* had become a symbol of Christianity, or of perseverance in that faith. In 1897, provoked by the statement of a Serbian writer that to convert to Islam meant *to lose the gusle*, that is, it implied a substantial change of identity, the Bosniak writer Edhem Mulabdić answered in Kranjčević-style rhetoric. It was not true that the Bosnians who had 'replaced the cross with the crescent' had thereby automatically replaced the *gusle* with the oriental *šarkija* instrument. It was true that the *šarkija* was a kind of 'dowry' from the Turkish *saz*, but it was also true that their *gusle* players' epic was still alive and that the Muslim nation 'read its own history from nought else but from the *gusle*' (Rizvić 1990: 100).[1]

But among the Croats, in certain circumstances, alongside the *gusle* another symbolically significant instrument appeared. While the *gusle* was the symbol of virility and heroism, the other half of reality – peace and social harmony, love itself – was represented by the *tambouritza*, and it was only with both poles that the land achieved fullness. In the 'Ages of Illyria' ('Vjekovi Ilirije'), Ivan Mažuranić (1814–1890) interpreted the point of historical events through the alternation of the two instruments. In the original 'blessed age' of peace and harmony the Illyrian 'merrily plucked / at the pastoral *tambouritza* strings'. With the incursions of the alien aggressor the 'peace-loving *tambouritza* strings perished' and a time of heroic resistance ensued. At the end of this, the 'joyful' sounds of the sycamore-*gusle* marked freedom restored, and self-awareness enhanced through battle (Mažuranić 1979: II, 63–67).

But still, South Slav political musicology would be too simple a discipline if it did not contain at least a crumb of historical irony. And this irony lies in the fact that all these dissonant instruments, the *gusle, saz* and *tambouritza,*

---

1. *Saz* – in Bosnia and Herzegovina, Macedonia and Kosovo, a kind of tambouritza, the player either accompanies a vocalist or performs solo. It has a long neck, a variable number of strings (eight or ten are the most common), all tuned to the same key, and all struck at once, to obtain greater sonority. In many Bosnian villages the *saz* player had considerable social status. *Šargija* or *šarkija* (Tur. *şarki*) is a variant of the *saz*, and is often used as a synonym.

are linked by a common origin.

The original home of today's *gusle* is western and central Asia, from where through the influence of Islamic culture, between the eighth and the tenth centuries, via Byzantium, it was adopted by the South Slavs. The area of the *gusle* once extended to the west as far as the Kupa River, the central part of the Slovenia-Croatia border, excluding the coastal towns of Dalmatia. But from the beginning of the twentieth century it narrowed abruptly. The urban Muslims, especially the agas and beys, themselves hardly played the *gusle*, considering it a rural instrument. Nevertheless, they were happy to bring *gusle* players from the countryside, and most Muslim cafés would hire a *gusle* player to entertain guests during the fast of Ramadan (Murko 1951, Balić 1973, Lord 1960). It is then too little to say that it is a paradox that in both the Croatian and particularly the Serbian national imaginative repertoire, as in that of unitarist Yugoslavism, the *gusle* should have become a symbol of resistance to the Turks and to Islam. In no nation, wrote an ideologue with philosophical ambitions on the eve of World War I, had any instrument had 'such a strong and fertile effect on the development of cultural, social and political events as the *gusle* among the South Slavs'. The *gusle* players were 'the strongest movers of the masses at moments of destiny, they were worthy teachers, conscientious judges and honourable journalists of the nation', 'the strongest awakeners of heroic virtues and the sweetest consolers of the afflicted.'[1] Twelve years later the Bosnian Serb writer Čedomil Mitrinović argued that the Muslims in Bosnia-Herzegovina should be 'socially de-Islamised'. Otherwise, should the process of their 'nationalization' fail, 'there remains only one solution: short, clear, and inexorable. The singer of folk songs has foretold it and sung about it, he still sings about it today. We shall not repeat it here, because we all know it'.[2]

This kind of symbolisation reached its peak in the wars of 1990–5, when the hypertrophied Serbian cult of the *gusle* reached a paroxysm. And therefore the reaction could not be any less emotional. After the slaughter in Srebrenica, in powerless rage, the Bosniak writer Rasim Muminović called *gusle* playing 'screeching to the hair of the horse's tail', or 'the opium that reeks of the hair of the horse's tail' (*Bošnjak*, 22, 22 August 1995) (referring to the fact that the

---

1. Miloš Gjurić, [The St Vitus Day Ethic (Prelude to *Gusle* players' Philosophy)], *Vihor*, I, 2, Zagreb, 1 April 1914, p. 68.
2. Čedomil Mitrinović, *Naši muslimani. Studija za orijentaciju pitanja bosansko-hercegovačkih muslimana*, Belgrade 1926 (translation by I. Banac, quoted from Banac 1984: 372). It is worth mentioning that the expressions 'the singer of folk songs' and 'sings', which are a bit generalised, are in the original more precise: *the* gusle *player*, or *sings to* gusle *accompaniment*. And the 'solution' referred to 'was genocide' (Banac 1984: 372).

instrument's single string is made of horse hair). This was a drastic but logical settling of accounts with an instrument that Serbian ideology had made perhaps the most radical material symbol of its plan for national expansion. And, at the same time, it was a radical rejection of any Muslim link with an instrument that because of the aggressive ideological identification it had undergone would necessarily at one time or another be perceived among the victims if not as a sign of almost demonic evil then certainly as the embodiment of barbarism and lack of culture. Muminović's statement seems from this point of view a logical counterpoint to the century-and-a-half-old metaphor of the Serbian Romantic writer and national ideologue Jakov Ignjatović, who had seen, in the same string, 'genuine hair from the spirit world, dewed with the blood and tears of the Serbs' (Ignjatović 1951: 18).

A hundred years after Mulabdić's fervent defence of the Bosniaks' right to the *gusle*, the wheel had come full circle: the instrument had become for him a crucial piece of evidence that the Bosnian Muslims were no Asian newcomers but an indigenous part of the Slav world. The extent to which it was disseminated was supposed to show that it was precisely through this instrument that the fundamental layer of vernacular culture and Herder's *spirit of the people* overcame the religious differences among the South Slavs, but now it was contemptuously mocked, among other things, as a symbol of Orthodoxy, of religious differences that proved unbridgeable. The Greater Serbian ideologues were given what they had long demanded – exclusive rights to the *gusle*.

Nor is the tale of the *tambouritza* without its unexpected turns. From the beginning it was intertwined with the story of the *gusle* in the spread of Croatian romantic national ideology, and within the para-history of Croatian-Serbian relations. Some identical or cognate ideologemes that metamorphosed within the two ideologies of national integration in the nineteenth century with the aid of the *gusle* could not eliminate the cultural, political and ideological differences, which were expressed through the Croatian attitude to the *tambouritza*. In other words, from the outset, while it worked together with the *gusle* in some respects, the *tambouritza* was also in conflict with it.

This instrument too was originally used among the Muslims in Bosnia, Macedonia and in Kosovo. It gradually spread to all the South Slav regions, and at the turn of the eighteenth and nineteenth centuries was particularly loved in Slavonia and Vojvodina. In the ideology and work of the Illyrian Movement, the *tambouritza* was made a symbol: the Croatian national instrument. What is more, since it was also accepted by the Czechs, although it was not a part of their vernacular tradition, and in particular by the Serbs north of the Sava and the Danube, it grew into a symbol of the broader anti-assimilative ideology of the Slav peoples in the Austro-Hungarian monarchy, their common sign of resistance to the tendencies of Germanisation and Magyarisation (Bonifačić 1995). After 1918, as a sublimation of the vernacular tradition in the political imaginative repertoire of the Croatian Peasants' Party [HSS], the *tambouritza* sent out messages in two directions: it remained a means of resistance to foreign domination, now Serbian domination within Yugoslavia, but it was also the incarnation of 'pure' Croatian peasant culture in opposition to undesirable urban culture, subject to foreign influences. Since *tambouritza* players in national costume were such an essential part of the iconography of the party and the mass political meetings it called throughout the country, the HSS leader Stjepan Radić himself being happy to play it, political opponents of the HSS sneeringly called them '*tambouritza* players'. In the essay 'Stjepan Radić in Belgrade' ('Stjepan Radić u Beogradu', 1926), the most influential Croatian Marxist writer Miroslav Krleža saw Radić as a 'naïve *tambouritza* player' who could not see how base the Belgrade politicians were but was happier to flirt with them than once again in 'his Lepoglava solitary confinement to kill fleas and play the *tambouritza*' (Krleža 1971: 242, 255). But two years later, when he expressed respect for him in his essay 'Stjepan Radić on the bier ('Stjepan Radić na odru')', he was to see the *tambouritza* as a symbol of Radić's personal and political decency, his 'Tolstoyan love of peace' (ibid. 281).

However, the murder of Radić, who had urged a parliamentary solution to the problem, as well as democratic negotiations between Croats and Serbs over decentralisation of the country, and the dictatorship proclaimed on 6 January 1929 by King Alexander, led the former member of parliament Ante Pavelić to the conclusion that violence was the only option left for Croatian political objectives. In one of his own proclamations, of 20 April 1929, only three and a half months after he had become an émigré, he started systematically building up not only an ideology but also a symbolism that was quite opposite to that of Radić. First of all came trees, birds and garments:

> Friends and brothers – we have as our symbol the linden, the only gentle tree, and the dove, the only gentle, tame bird, but when we need, we shall take the hawk, the eagle and the oak as our symbols ...
> When we go to a party, we put on tails, but when we go to fight, we'll put on different clothing.[1]

1. cf. Tomislav Jonjić, 'Povijesno-politički okvir postanka ustaškog pokreta [Historical

Ivan Tišov, 'Stjepan Radić among the peasants' (1928, oil on canvas): typical portrayal of the Croats as a peace-loving people listening to the music of the *tamburitza* in the shade of 'the sacred Slav tree' or lime.

The universal symbolism of dove as opposed to hawk and eagle is clear. The linden, sacred tree of pre-Christian Slav myths, which in the romantic nineteenth century among almost all the Slav nations, including the Croats, was turned into a symbol of their pacific nature, and their liking for a quiet and orderly rural life as opposed to the politically expansive and rapidly urbanising western nations, was replaced by the oak as symbol of toughness, virility and strength. Soon after that the transformation of musical symbolism made the framework complete. In February 1932, the Ustasha leader Pavelić contrasted, in his editorial for the paper *Ustasha*, the *tambouritza* with another tune, another instrument and other methods:

THE KNIFE, REVOLVER, BOMB AND THE EXPLOSIVE DEVICE ... These are the *gusles* on which the Croatian people must play out the death march of foreign government (Požar 1995: 55).

As he boasted as soon as he came to power in a speech in St Mark's Square,

and political framework of the origins of the Ustasha movement] (4)', *Hrvatska obzorja*, X, 1/ 2002, p. 43.

Zagreb, on 21 May 1941, Pavelić knew from the beginning that 'no nation in the course of history had ever freed itself with songs and *tambouritzas*' (Požar 1995: 185), and the Ustasha police chief Eugen Dido Kvaternik explained to his old schoolmate, Branko Pešelj, an HSS leader, that he had to let the Ustashas settle 'the Serbian problem' because the Radić '*tambouritza* players' did not know 'how it was to be done' (Pešelj 1989: 12).[1]

Chronologically, Pavelić's glorification of the *gusle* as the instrument of bold and resolute men was a reaction to the Greater Serbian ideologemes of racial superiority and the cult of Serbian heroism that deeply imbued the state that was created in 1918. For just as Č. Mitrinović summed up the attitude of this ideology to the Bosniak *saz* players in his invitation to listen to the ancient message of the *gusle*, so Jovan Dučić, poet and royal diplomat, in a 1942 article called 'Yugoslav ideology' in the *Amerikanski Srbobran* made a metaphor of the equally non-virile Croatian *tambouritza* players: 'The Serbs are a *gusle*-playing nation, and the Croats a *tambouritza* nation; and while the Serbs were building their glorious epics, the Croats were building jigs' (according to Radica 1984: 183).

But in the wartime nightmare of Yugoslavia, things developed differently. The *tambouritza* players, partly through their own fault, were outwitted and driven off the stage. However the two exclusivist *gusle* ensembles fared badly in the face of the victorious strumming of the Partisans. In communist Yugoslavia the *tambouritza* had its ups and downs: sometimes it was out of favour because it recalled the old way of life; while at others it occupied an important place within the general promotion of the ideology of *brotherhood and unity* through culture and art (Bonifačić 1995). The *gusle* fitted better into the new circumstances, primarily because these conditions were not all that new. Although it did not keep the status of de facto state-sponsored musical instrument of the first Yugoslavia, it did not do badly in the second. The new political musicologists proclaimed all instruments formally equal, but one of them was, willy-nilly, more equal than the others. The score that grew out of such a solution gave birth directly to the deafening *gusle* players' fortissimo four and a half decades later. 'My heart, comrades, flutters only when I hear the [Yugoslav] anthem, the *Internationale* and the *gusle*', said one of Milošević's supporters during a session of the City Committee of the League of Communists of Belgrade in June 1988 (Bogdanović 1988: 306).

---

1. Serbian jargon expressed the wimps / heroes opposition through the pair *frula* (shepherd's flute) –*gusle*; the shepherd's flute players (*frulaši*) were Milošević and all who wanted to negotiate with the international community, and the *gusle* players were the 'brave' Serb leaders in Bosnia-Herzegovina and all who were for fighting until victory.

Gusle *players in election campaigns*

From the outset, Serbian political parties made the symbolic act of publicly donating a *gusle* into a kind of ritual of political initiation. For example, a member of the leadership of the League of Communists of Montenegro who, despite the official party line, supported an alliance with the pro-Serbian NS [People's Party], was given a *gusle* by its leaders at a large meeting in Pavino Polje in 1990. The Greek Prime Minister Konstantin Mitsotakis was given one by Radovan Karadžić on 6 May, when he attended a session of the National Assembly of Republika Srpska at Pale. At Pale, *gusle*s were regularly given to members of UNPROFOR, UNHCR and other international organisations. They would hang these souvenirs on the walls of their Sarajevo offices, without any inkling of the irritation this caused to the inhabitants of the besieged city.

Gusle players appeared at many of the meetings of the SDS of Bosnia-Herzegovina, particularly as these were often held on church holidays, when the *gusle* was in any case a regular feature. That is how it was, for example, in the central square of Bijeljina at the founding meeting of SDS Bosnia-Herzegovina for northern Bosnia on 9 August 1990, on St Panteleimon's Day, when the town traditionally held a big fair. A branch of the same party was founded in Foča on 28 August, feast of the Assumption, when fairs and national meetings were also traditionally held. On 29 August a branch of the SPO [Serbian Renewal Movement] was founded in Avtovac near Gacko, eastern Herzegovina, in the native area of its leader Vuk Drašković, on the feast of the Transfiguration, also a day traditionally given over to fairs and popular merrymaking. *Gusle* players would also appear even when a meeting was held indoors, as was the case with the founding assembly of the pro-Milošević NS in Podgorica the same year. Sometimes the players were very young, as Murko had testified in the 1930s. As part of the NS meeting in Zeta, a six-year-old *gusle*-player played and sang in honour of Jovan Rašković 'who shields our brothers from the Croats', and Radovan Karadžić 'on the side of Kosovo's prince' (*Nedjelja*, 29, 2 September 1990). The phrase 'Kosovo's prince' did not mean just the medieval Prince Lazar, leader of the Serbian army in the lost battle of 1389, but also, and much more, his current reincarnation, Milošević, as leader of the new army that would avenge the ancient defeat and restore national history to its 'natural course'.

By the end of the 1980s, in Serbia and the Serbian settlements west of the Drina, the cult of the *gusle* was established as a rounded and politically clearly defined system, and the *gusle* player in the role of oral political journalist, even of political party spokesman, had become a regular and legal participant in public meetings. In Croatia, by contrast, as late as September 1989, the police prevented 'a well-known follower of the Zadar *mass movement*'[1] from appearing in front of the Church of St Chrysogonus, on the occasion of the celebration of *Branimir's year*, and bringing an unnamed *gusle* player who 'was, it is assumed, to have sung nationalistic songs' in that main city square (Marinko Čulić; *Danas*, 395, 12 September 1989). It was not until the eve of the first multiparty elections that Croatian *gusle* players started entering into political life without hindrance, most often as part of the campaign of the party that was to win – Tuđman's Croatian Democratic Union (HDZ). At the popular celebration in Cista Provo not far from Imotski, organised by the HDZ after the first round of elections, Šimun Vrančić, a *gusle* player from Tijarica near Sinj, performed an epic that warned of Greater Serbian pretensions, called upon expatriates to return, celebrated Tuđman as prince and knight and appealed to the medieval Croatian kings to assist current political aspirations with their spirit (*Nedjeljna Dalmacija*, 20 May 1990). The *gusle* player Marko Kunac of Potravlje appeared at an election meeting of the HDZ in the central square in Sinj. According to a newspaper report, to the 'general delight of those present', who included the president of the party, he sang of him as 'tireless traveller and great son of Croatia' and 'won thunderous applause and hurrahs' (*Vjesnik*, 25 March 1990):

> *It's Easter, people, stir yourselves,*
> *Here is Tuđman, a new dawn gleams.*
> *After a full twenty years*
> *We have seen a son of Croatia ...*
> *Around him, all Croats brothers;*
> *He holds us, and our sense returns.*[2]

In terms of activity and media presence, as well as political status, Mile

---

1. In Yugoslav communist ideology, *maspok*, or 'mass movement', was a derogatory expression for the endeavours of the younger, liberal generation of Croatian communists in 1967–1971 to modernise the country economically and politically and open it up to the West. The reforms were crushed violently by Tito and a group of Serbian generals around him, who proclaimed the reformists 'extremely nationalistic'.
2. This is a quote from a fragment (twenty-one lines) that Kunac sent me when I wrote to him asking for it, in response to the article in *Vjesnik*. In the accompanying letter he stated that he was preparing epics about Milošević, Stipe Šuvar, a rigid and unattractive Croatian communist, who, at that time had acquired a certain amount of popularity for having stood up to Milošević, and Bogdan Kecman, leader of the Kosovo Serbs who had attracted the attention of the public because of his intention to organise a Serbian rally in Ljubljana on 1 December 1989.

Krajina, from Osijek, whose family came from Sinj, was without peer among the Croatian *gusle* players. He appeared at many HDZ meetings and on the day of the constitution of the first multiparty parliament, 30 May 1990, on Jelačić Square, dressed in the uniform of an *Alkar* squire, he had the honour of carrying the Ban's flag, borrowed from a museum for the occasion. The occasions at which he appeared range from the Rural Sports Olympics in the Dalmatian highlands to the programme organised after the parade at Zagreb's Jarun Park on Statehood Day (*Dan državnosti*) 1995.

The reasons for including *gusle* players were diverse, but it was always a procedure through which more truth and a greater sense of occasion were instilled into any given situation. This situation might be the founding of the local branch of a party or it might be a political meeting stimulated by electoral rivalry. These could not always be distinguished since the first free multi-party elections were held in spring 1990, and many meetings were both one and the other. The Bosnian *Master Gusle Players* tour of December 1986 shows that an organised *gusle* player's appearance could be a very effective means of promoting a political message to an audience that did not follow other media. Or, if they did, they did not accord them the same degree of credibility that they did to the epic presentation of the same event. Nor did they ascribe the same moral dignity and social authority to the modern journalist as they did to the *gusle* player.

A *gusle* player's appearance, including one at a political rally, has a 'pronounced social function' that does not depend on poetic expressiveness, nor is it crucially determined by it (Bošković-Stulli 1983: 184–185). Its purpose is above all to develop social solidarity and encourage national identification, that is, to renew the common value system into which contemporary relations, events and personalities will then automatically fit. It may be said that the appearance of a *gusle* player, then, as a preliminary event, before the actual speakers, opens the meeting up to explicit political meanings and symbolically guarantees that the anticipated discursive expression will correspond intellectually to the traditional worldview. The same kind of performance at the end, after the speakers, closes off the meeting, returns it to the initial mood of the popular fete. The *gusle* player demarcates the central episode, the appearance of the charismatic speaker, and thus serves as a kind of structural device, a metaphorical stage direction in the dramaturgy of the public assembly. From a contextual point of view, as already stated, appearances at mass party rallies are interwoven into situations where singing was already common – public holidays and ceremonies, carnival festivities, particularly during fetes around churches and monasteries on the day of some patron saint or when the people gathered at fairs, or public celebrations such as those for St Sava and St Vitus. In the first Yugoslavia *gusle* players also appeared at *Sokol* [a state-sponsored organisation promoting sports and gymnastics] celebrations, and in some cities there was singing to the *gusle* in hotels and cafés during annual or weekly fairs.

The presence of a *gusle* player at a political meeting is not, then, mere decoration, but a part of the process and a pattern through which communicative events unfold. It is a part of the totality of the interpersonal relationships of a communicative form and function. It is a deed that is not simply a functional but also an organic part of the context, an essential component of the *contextual coherence of the message*. If the political speaker promotes recognisable evocations of traditional matters, the introductory or concluding performance of the *gusle* player, who often remains on the platform with the speakers, reinforces the semantic field of the message and is a joint shaper of the evocation, uniting with it as an equal component of the event.

But even if the (political) speaker did not aim for explicit evocations, the *gusle* in itself would suggest one possible interpretation, a non-verbal message so that the verbal message could, and should be understood (also) within the value system of traditional culture. As a prop, the *gusle* would serve to define the type of stage from which the speaker was addressing his audience, because the instrument was per se evocative of the heroic tradition. The result would be to establish a unity of content and worldview between the elite culture, represented by the central speaker, generally from *the big city*, almost always dressed in a city suit and tie, and the popular, vernacular culture, embodied by the *gusle* player, usually dressed in folk costume with some ancient weapon at his belt, as authorised mediator of the authentic national spirit. Awareness of this functional demarcation of the two worlds was later expressed by the *gusle* player Petar Maroš in Trilj near Sinj, at a celebration of the eleventh anniversary of the founding of the local HDZ. Since he was also the chairman of the local party organisation, he began, dressed in a city suit, by making a standard political speech in line with the official views of his party, using its regular terminology and discourse. He called the new government elected after the death of Tuđman 'communist', claiming it was ruining the country and said that the 'nation would judge it harshly'. Then he changed into the folk dress of the area (though retaining his ordinary trousers and shoes for speed's sake), took up the *gusle*, and repeated more or less the same views in epic discourse, translating the speech into different categories: 'Oh, Tuđman, were you now to rise / and see Croatia where it lies' (*Novi list*, 27 February 2001).

As a person of repute in his own milieu, whose songs keep alive the possibility of identification with epic heroes, and may at decisive moments increase self-confidence, the *gusle* player could affect other members of the community, through his choice of party. The impression, of course, was the stronger if a whole *gusle* players' association were to join a party, which is what happened in the case of Kilibarda's NS in Montenegro.

This kind of association between *gusle* player and political party and programme was no new phenomenon, particularly not in Serbia. In the first Yugoslavia there were many *gusle* players who were on the payrolls of various political parties, even the government in Belgrade itself. They were sent to areas where the majority population was suspect, i.e., non-Serbian, in order to promote the 'national spirit' and the 'idea of national and state unity' in line with the ideology of Yugoslav integration, by performing in the open air, in schools and barracks. As well as the occasional song from the classical repertoire, they would also perform new epics, in which they glorified the Karađorđević royal family and sang of Serbian victories in the Balkan and First World wars (Murko 1951).

During the 1991–1995 war, the *gusle* in Croatia became a symbol of Serbian 'primitivism and lack of culture', as it did among the Bosniaks. Although official cultural policy restored the *tambouritza* to the status of national instrument and made it a symbol of the Central European cultural mainstream, by way of counterpoint to Balkan culture (Bonifačić 1995: 75), it neither wanted, nor was it able to reject, the symbolic value of the *gusle*, despite all the negative emotions that had accrued around it. Had it attempted to do so, it would have faced the resistance of the population in areas where the epic tradition was still alive, primarily in Herzegovina and the Dalmatian highlands. Here, the *gusle* cult was in many respects founded on the same set of meanings as it was among the Serbs. It not only survived the 1990–1995 war intact, but when it was over, set off on a determined *reconquista* at the national level.

An interesting attempt to make practical use of the ideological cult of the *tambouritza* occurred in Zagreb's Municipal Court. On trial for taking illegal loans, the director of the firm Muzička Naklada defended himself by saying that he had acted in order to save a firm 'that was the only Croatian producer of instruments, including the *tambouritza*, the national instrument' (*Večernji list,* 14/15 August 1997). It was also impossible for the war not to add certain new semantic associations to the *tambouritza* and thus partially to distort the stable border between this instrument, as symbol of peace and belonging to Europe, and the *gusle,* as symbol of belligerence and the Balkans.

For the final military victory was after all not won by the docile sounds of the *tambouritza* orchestra but the only way it could be – by arms, courage and military skill. This fact was in line with the connotations of the *gusle*, but inevitably also influenced the message of the *tambouritza*. Otherwise, the implication would have been that the *tambouritza*-playing section of the Croatian people had not taken part in the liberation of the country, and, furthermore, that it was not even capable of such a thing. Rather, it was condemned to wait while the *gusle*-playing section carried out the hard and dangerous task. Thus the *tambouritza* had to be granted its share of military dignity: 'The *tambouritza* is really a symbol of being Croatian ... We all went to war with the *tambouritza*,' said music teacher and composer Zdravko Šljivac (*Nedjeljna Dalmacija*, 1410, 1 May 1998).

However, in this duel between *gusle* and *tambouritza* for the place of authentic representative of the Croatian national spirit, it was not the formal outcome that was important, but something else. Although opposed on the surface, both *gusle* players and *tambouritza* players came together in essential matters. There was no difference between statements that Croatia had not been built with top hat and tails but by the plough and the 'horny peasant hand', that the source of Croatian culture was not the 'piano, harp or fashionable electronic rubbish, but the *tambouritza*, the tenor *tambouritza* (*bisernica*) and the alto *tambouritza* (*brač*)' (Predrag Haramija; *Državnost*, 40, 1 March 1996) and the claim that it was to the *gusle* and in the epic decasyllabic that the Croats had 'honed their national awareness and preserved many a Croatian hero from oblivion'. And only those 'who considered *brotherhood and unity* their greatest inheritance' or who had grown up in ethnically mixed surroundings could fail to understand this.[1]

---

1. Letter from the Students' Association of Imotski in Zagreb to *Slobodna Dalmacija*, 17 June 1996. This is a reaction to an article by Miljenko Jergović, '*Gusle* player of the Square', *Slobodna Dalmacija*, 10 June 1996, in which the author complained that a *gusle* player had been performing in the central square of Zagreb, in a place where jazz and chansons were usually performed. Jergović was not considered competent to judge about *gusles* because although a Croat he was born and brought up in 'impure' Sarajevo.

On the other hand, the commentator of the Bosnian Serb paper *Javnost*, Dragoljub Jeknić, complained of the 'spiritual devastation' of Serbian city youths who had no feeling for the heroic epic. According to him this negative 'attitude to the epic sound of the *gusle* player, was actually just typical of Catholics.' 'The shame they felt that even they should come from a *gusle*-playing tribe' was the fault of Vatican plots and home-bred degenerates (according to *Vreme International*, 191, 20 June 1994). That is, once again, it was some kind of brotherhood and unity that had introduced external cultural influences, in this case to the detriment of authentic Orthodox culture. And if they were to agree on this with the Serb Jeknić, the patriotic Imotski Croats, all of them Catholics, would be genuinely surprised to hear that he held alienation from

In each case the instrument was the symbol of a romantically understood indigenous culture as opposed to the degenerate culture of modern civilisation. Because independently of the kind of practical political procedure it employs, every nationalist ideology starts from the perspective that the enlightened countryside is the mover and creator of history, and the peasantry, with its sense of justice intact, is the most aware part of the nation, providentially called upon to fight for its emancipation.

The countryside and the city, the countryside in the city

Like other countries that came within the Soviet orbit in 1945, Yugoslavia imitated the Stalin model of development, according to which only heavy industry guaranteed economic independence and was effective in transforming the 'socialist base' in a country with a mainly agrarian population. The regime embarked on an enormous undertaking that completely changed the lives of many families within a single generation. In Yugoslavia, the percentage of the population that lived from agriculture was reduced from 68 percent in 1953, to 47 percent in 1971. In the 1948–1981 period, an amazing six and a half million migrants moved from countryside to city.

However, many of the peasants who had thus become members of the working class would often go back to their village, some even living there and commuting into the cities. They became a special class of (industrial) worker-peasants who obtained benefits in both economic and social settings. But in cultural terms they were examples of *homo duplex*, with their loyalties divided between the vernacular culture and the new urban subculture. This world was frozen in the gap between countryside – from where it had been torn by forced industrialisation and the 'five-year plans' through which the ruling ideology created a working class *post festum* – and the city, with which it had never fully come to terms, and in which it was forced to play social roles it was not prepared for. And because of its patriarchal culture this world was predisposed to embrace the anti-intellectualism of communist propagandists and ideologues. This meant supporting their enduring suspicion of the humanist intelligentsia and other 'rotten bourgeois upperclasses', implicitly agreeing with the idea that power was one of the spoils of war, gained once and forever, and that, from a functional point of view, society was the same as the patriarchal family with an unerring and authoritative, strict but just and ultimately benign, householder, or *pater familias*, at its head.

Despite the changes in the ideological wrapping and quantitative indicators

---

the epic a bad, Catholic characteristic.

of the modernisation of society, there remained a deep-seated, largely intact cultural pattern the characteristics of which were military organisation and aptitude for military actions, a bellicose spirit, an indisposition for productive work and a lack of concern for the market. On the whole, neither the political nor the academic elite that discussed the relationship between countryside and town and endeavoured to define it saw that this was 'in fact the phenomenon of the countryside in the city' (Rihtman-Auguštin 1970: 34). The year 1945 brought the victory of one army, one ideology and one political project over its two strongest rivals, but underneath that little had changed. A cynic might even say that the Chetniks and the Ustashas did not even know they had lost the war, just as many sincerely pluralistically inclined Partisans and anti-fascists did not notice that at the deep or cultural level they had not won it.

> By force of circumstance, the manner of Partisan life (and this is also culture) often coincided with the peasant way of life. For this reason there was no break with tradition. On the contrary, some of the traditional ways of understanding were confirmed and enhanced. A very particular folklore developed, entirely within the framework of the traditional (Rihtman-Auguštin 1970: 41–42).

When they came to power, the communists did not even need to win a large number of people over to their project for the transformation of society. It was enough for them to inherit certain important elements of the popular, patriarchal worldview, which were neutral from the point of view of the formally or manifestly understood communist ideology, and which many deeply believed in and were at home with. In the government-controlled media these elements were, it is true, subjected to a narrative transformation, but not so great that they lost their links with the living, original oral culture. As late as the early 1980s, in the value system of Yugoslav society, there still persisted traditional values such as radical egalitarianism, the heroic code and authoritarianism, as their essential components (cf. Županov 1983).

When Tito was accused, at his trial in 1927, as a member of the illegal Communist Party, of fomenting terrorism, he stated that he 'acknowledged only the authority of his party'. Neither the culturally stable inhabitants of the real countryside or the culturally disorientated inhabitants of 'the countryside in the city' could have been aware that the official interpretation of this statement and the cult significance attached to it in the value system of Yugoslav communism in fact meant the destruction of general legal security and acted as a psychological brake on the modernisation of society. On the contrary, from their traditional perspective, they intuitively recognised in Tito's words the affirmation of the epic concept of *heroic freedom (junačka sloboda)* with which many of them had grown up. This was a concept that embodied permanent resistance by the heroic patriarchy to every organised law and formal government. The political elite's often repeated slogan: 'we would all rather eat roots – or grass – than be subject to the dictates of the imperialist forces' was a not very distant echo of the concept of *heroic poverty (junačka siromaština)*. In archaic society this grew out of the heroic belief system and the whole hierarchy of ethical and social values according to which it was not important to partake in the goods of this world (Gesemann 1968).

The hypertrophied cult of heroism might occasionally have seemed ridiculous to these people, especially when the medals of *Heroes of Labour* were awarded to tongue-tied rank-and-file party members, but the cult itself was not in doubt, because it derived naturally from far older ideas about social relationships, sanctioned by tradition and experience.

The media painted a picture of a society under permanent threat from outside, and engaged in a lasting internal war, polarised between friends and enemies. This picture was enhanced by the militant or military terminology that suffused all political discourse. The motif of the heroic warlike nation was a lasting identity myth of the Yugoslav elite: throughout the forty-five years of communist rule, the official discourse was extremely militarised, with belligerent metaphors providing its key characteristics. The party was an army, its leaders the leading echelon, every activity was a battle, a siege, a front, a first line, trench warfare, breaking through a corridor, and the state itself was defined as bastion or fortress of self-managing socialism, brotherhood and unity. In short, warfare was a universal sign system. (cf. Žanić 1987). The extent to which the hierarchy of values in the country was militarised can be seen from a debate in the Croatian parliament in 1988 on the passage of a new law concerning admission to the civil service, just before Milošević's rise to power. A female member complained that 'professional qualification' came only eighth in the list of desirable qualities for employees, while the first seven places were occupied by 'fighting spirit', 'revolutionary determination', 'bravery in the face of the enemies of socialism', 'ideological tenacity' and so on.

Given this universal, ahistorical model, it was not only possible, but indeed to an extent natural, that Slobodan Milošević should have been transformed overnight from a standard communist apparatchik, operating with a score or so of bland phrases from party conferences, into the idol of the million-strong masses of the inhabitants of 'the countryside in the city', who demanded the redress of injustices several hundred years old, and the leader of an army eager to settle scores with 'Latins' and 'Turks' that only it could see.

In such a social and psychological context, it may be said that it was not the *gusle* players who, after 1945 or at the end of the eighties, changed the setting of their performances and appearances and overtly offered themselves to this or that person as transmitters of his views. It was rather that such a current political leader, or pretender to that status, came to them, or through his actions and value system caused himself to be recognised, within their socially variegated but psychologically homogeneous audience, as a hero worthy of support and *being sung of to the gusle*.

The *gusle* player Milomir Miljanić is a good example of how little contemporary political and ideological categories meant in the epic subculture. Up to the end of the 1980s his repertoire contained songs that were in harmony, in theme and ideology, with the official Yugoslav paradigms. In fact, it could not have been otherwise if he wished to perform legally, whether or not he was a member of the only legally allowed political organisation, the League of Communists. However, after the breakdown of communism he could freely choose both: party and topic. He chose the same themes as the other Serbian and Montenegrin players: he condemned the communists for having deliberately laid waste to Serbia and stood up for the Serb paramilitaries in Croatia and Bosnia. And in 1995–6, with the declared Chetnik Vučurević, he recorded a cassette, *God damn you, pagan traitors (Bog vas kleo, pogani izrodi),* and took part in a tour round the Serbian lands, which is to say Greater Serbia. He had particular success with an epic glorifying Karadžić. In terms of parties, he did not choose a single one of the many that had similar agendas and attracted other *gusle* players. He enrolled in the marginal and Stalinist New Communist Party of Yugoslavia, founded on 30 June 1990 in Belgrade, which did not acknowledge the collapse of Tito's Yugoslavia. During the nineties, its premises were decorated with the flags of SFRY and the USSR.[1]

The gusle *playing scene, festivals, the market*

The processes that marked the rebirth of the methods and activities of the pre-war *gusle*-playing scene, irrespective of their different ideological packaging, emerged in the second Yugoslavia precisely within the particular class under discussion: the (industrial) worker-peasantry. In Belgrade, in union branches, *gusle*-playing sections were set up, with members making

---

1. Statement of the party chairman Branko Kitanović in the weekly *Nacional*, 165, 13 January 1999.

appearances in schools and factories. Fifteen years after the war, Serbian and Montenegrin *gusle* players started to get together with greater ambitions. This led to a curious phenomenon, which, in the second half of the 1980s, came to be seen as a useful organisational infrastructure in the cognitive and psychological preparation of the Serbian population for a war of conquest of Croatian and Bosnian land and for genocide.

The Filip Višnjić *Gusle* Association, founded in 1961 in the Sarajevo suburb of Vrace, was the first in the second Yugoslavia to function continuously and to have the status of a legal entity. It thus became a model for the foundation of other associations. Very soon it had 200 members, and it was pioneering in that it introduced a new element, one that had been unnecessary to the original consumers of the genre. Before every performance, a compère, usually the chairman of the association, would tell the audience about the event described in the song, who its characters were, and what political and historical importance it had. *Gusle* players regularly appeared on the local radio programmes Radio Romanija and Radio Ilijaš, and in the suburbs of Sarajevo. They went on tour, and their outstanding success in their first appearance in Belgrade directly stimulated the formation of two associations or clubs in the city – Vuk Karadžić (180 members) and Yugoslavia in New Belgrade. Clubs were then founded in Kragujevac, Smederevo, Nikšić, Prijepolje, Podgorica and Kula (Radovanović and Lovrenski 1985).[1]

The members of these clubs were of various professions – from factory workers and teachers, shop assistants and machine technicians, to lawyers, economists, engineers and company directors. However, their biographies show that in most cases they are the typical socialist semi-worker/semi-peasant, regardless of the formal education or status they have acquired. To some extent an extreme case, but not an untypical example from this point of view is Momčilo Lutovac, with a PhD in geography, a Belgrade university

---

1. Although the authors consistently present the *gusle*-playing scene as Yugoslav, and although the actual *gusle* players put their work in this context, according to their biographies it is clear that they are all Serbs and Montenegrins, and that the clubs are too, however they present themselves. This conclusion is confirmed implicitly by their concluding remarks that in Yugoslavia, apart from those mentioned so far, there are some other good *gusle* players at work: two Muslim *gusle* players, one from Nevesinje and another from Konjic, one Albanian from Montenegrin Malesija, and one Croat, i.e., the already mentioned Ž. Šimić. Since previously there was no mention of ethnicity, it is clear that the authors understood the Serbian and Montenegrin epic tradition to be pan-Yugoslav. This identification of Serbia with Yugoslavia, not in modern ideological but in traditional epic categories, goes some way to explaining how it was possible for Miljanić, discussed above, to celebrate the creation of Greater Serbia and at the same time to be a member of a neo-Bolshevik and pro-Yugoslav party.

professor. For a long time he was an active *gusle* player, and when his age prevented him from appearing any more, he dedicated himself to writing epics for other *gusle* players. He specialised in songs in which he 'unmasked' the champions of Montenegrin independence and statehood (see Đukić 1988). All of them played the *gusle* in their spare time. When they went on tour and to competitions, they would take paid or unpaid leave, and in this way the otherwise considerable differences in status, education and wealth were evened out.

There is another striking factor: the disproportionately high share of professional soldiers or civil servants connected with the JNA engaged in the sudden revival and expansion of the *gusle* playing scene. One of the most active and renowned *gusle* players worked as a people's defence officer in the *Prva Iskra* factory in Belgrade. The chairman of 'Vuk Karadžić', who was, as we have seen, usually the compère at public performances, was an army captain. One of the 'two enthusiasts' who contributed most to the union *gusle*-playing sections becoming independent organisations and turning into clubs or associations was a JNA colonel (the other was a ticket inspector on the Belgrade tram system). Two of the four founders of Filip Višnjić were ensigns (the other two were a working man and a shop assistant), while it was a JNA lieutenant colonel, a Belgrader who had served in Sarajevo from 1959 to 1973, who was elected the first president (cf. Radovanović and Lovrenski 1985). These facts are additionally intriguing considering the war experience of 1990–5, as well as the general social exclusiveness of the army and the degree to which its members kept themselves professionally apart in the second Yugoslavia.

The *gusle*-playing scene spread and strengthened particularly in the eighties, with the deepening crisis in Kosovo and the rise of Milošević's populism. This was facilitated by the already existing organisational network, the well-established market and an audience accustomed and eager to consume such works. According to a publication that gives a survey of the scene at precisely this watershed moment 'the Renaissance of *gusle* playing started some ten years ago and now there is a great demand for such performances'. Some of the *gusle* players 'had become real stars' and their records were being sold in 'tens of thousands of copies' (Radovanović and Lovrenski 1985: 11). It was no exception to get a *gold disc*, i.e. to sell 50,000 copies of a disc or cassette. In 1980, one record by four *gusle* players, originally produced in 1,500 copies, was reissued so fast that in a very short time sales leaped to 100,000 copies. By that year a *gusle* player from the Montenegrin region of Drobnjaci Boško Vujačić, an engineer in the Podgorica Aluminium Firm, had sold a total of half a million records and cassettes.

A new club, the Petar I. Petrović Njegoš Club, founded in the summer of 1988 in Podgorica, had by the end of the year attracted 180 members, who performed 'the classical ethnic/national repertoire' and songs about the WWII Resistance movement, but who also wrote new songs about murders or tragic car accidents. According to the chairman of the club, M. Filipović, his cassette *Serdar Jole and Vojvoda Peko*, about two Montenegrin captains of border units in the mid-nineteenth century, sold 65,000 copies in eight years of continuous production, while a cassette by a club member, Milomir Miljanić, *Vjetrovi Kosova (The Winds of Kosovo)*, sold 300 copies a day (*Pobjeda*, 22 January 1989). The Croatian *gusle* player Željko Šimić considered a far smaller run outstanding, at least with hindsight. During the time of Yugoslavia, he says, he had earned well, selling 'six thousand copies of cassettes' in Montenegro, Bosnia and Croatia and 'even' Serbia, but today 'the market has got smaller, and now we Herzegovinians play our *gusles* just for Herzegovina' (*Panorama*, 126, 25 September 1996). By the reduction of the market he is not of course thinking of a decline of interest in the *gusle*, but of the new state, and therefore ethnic, borders.

In the parts of Bosnia-Herzegovina under Serbian rule *gusle* playing was systematically promoted from the outset as a kind of official art, and the *gusle* was elevated to the rank of state instrument. There was even a proposal that a *gusle* course be started at the Music Academy of Banja Luka University. The number of *gusle* playing clubs under the umbrella of the Gusle Players' Association of Republika Srpska kept on growing, a particular incentive being the Festival of Serbian Poetry and *Gusle* players of Republika Srpska, organised as a competition. This 'important event in our spiritual culture', as it was called by the Banja Luka daily (*Glas srpski*, 19 June 1995) is part of the observance of St Vitus' Day as an official public holiday in Republika Srpska, the Day of the Army of Republika Srpska, and is thus connected with one more tradition – the connection between the army and the *gusle* players.

At the first festival in Trebinje in 1994, fifty-five *gusle* players appeared, from eight clubs. At the next in Milići the following year, there were sixty players from ten clubs. The most numerous of them, the Stojan Janković Club from Banja Luka, was ceremonially founded on 6 June 1994 in Banski dvor, and at once gave two concerts in the Army Hall. It had eighty members, ranging in profession from soldier to professor, and fifteen juvenile members, who were elementary school pupils (*Glas srpski*, 14 July 1994). The Republika Srpska Gusle Players Association chairman Kosta Plakalović explained, during a tour of Serb expatriate communities in the USA and Canada at the end of 2002, that *gusle* activities went on developing even after the war. He said that there were fifteen clubs in Republika Srpska, with about 300 active *gusle* players, some 150 of them regularly taking part in competitions in that part of Bosnia-Herzegovina, or in Serbia and Montenegro (as it is now), where there are another 300 players. 'What is essential for all of us,' he said, 'are the young players, boys of nine to ten who are already playing and going on tour.' Plenty of young people came to listen, he said, and 'I'm doing my best to make sure that the young people play the *gusle* as much as possible, for that's the only way for it to survive as an instrument.'[1]

Gusle-playing competitions had been held in the Kingdom of Yugoslavia as well. They were started in 1927 by the Minister of Culture, V. Vukićević, whose 'ideal was to base national culture and upbringing on the traditional songs' (Murko 1951: 377). In the first post-war years the communist authorities did put on *gusle*-playing evenings in regions with an epic tradition, but they were not competitive, rather 'a response to the people's interest in the singing of epic songs' (Mimica 1988: 37). As in many other things connected with the *gusle*-playing scene in the second Yugoslavia, Sarajevo's Filip Višnjić had a pioneering role in the revival of competitive festivals, during which the title of best Yugoslav *gusle* player was awarded. At the first, held in Sarajevo in 1971, 180 *gusle* players registered, which 'even today is considered the largest gathering in the history of *gusle* playing' (Radovanović and Lovrenski 1985: 35). The second and third festivals were held in Kosovo Polje near Priština, a Serbian and Montenegrin colonist settlement founded in 1921, which in the eighties was reputed to be the centre of extra-institutional Serbian political action. After that the *gusle* players gathered in Zenica, Nikšić and Podgorica, twice running in Belgrade, then in Sarajevo (Vogošća suburb), and again in Belgrade.

On the other hand, it would seem that in the Croatian part of Herzegovina, despite the living epic tradition and the persistence of a few individuals, even the war failed to give *gusle* playing new life in the long run. It is true that Željko Šimić heralded the foundation of the Herzegovina association in 1996, but he complained of the lack of interest, particularly among potential newcomers – the youngest *gusle* player was 18, which is on the old side for starting to learn. The only talented boy, who had started to learn the trade with Šimić, was talked out of *gusle* playing by his father, and the audience were all over thirty (*Panorama*, 126, 25 September 1996).

Šimić's colleague, Anđelko Češkić, who had issued eleven songs on eight cassettes, makes an important distinction among *gusle* players: 'there

---

1. http://www.novine.ca/vesti/intervju/intervju/intervju28.html

are five or six professionals who have recorded cassettes, but there are more plagiarisers'. Such people sing about anything at all, sex for instance, and one of them had sung about the soap opera *Santa Barbara*, which was 'a disgrace to the instrument'. He did not sing about the 'heroes' of the recent war, because he considered that would be mere currying political favour for profit. Rather, his heroes were from medieval Croatian history, the victims of the Yugoslav secret police, events surrounding the vision of the Madonna of Međugorje and various church feasts and celebrations. It is worth quoting his opinion of Montenegrin and Serbian *gusle* players at greater length:

> I know many of the Montenegrin *gusle* players from those times ... They were really good, that has to be said, better than us. I never heard a single Chetnik song from them, though what they sing these days, I don't know. They mostly sang heroic songs, and one of them on Romanija actually made me a *gusle*. This Montenegrin performed the one about King Tomislav and our hero Mijat Tomić on this *gusle* I have now ... They never sang anything except Mijat Tomić and the old heroic songs in my presence ... There are good and bad people everywhere, all people are the same for me, only they have different customs and religions. It's a sin to generalise about a whole people, and I am above all a Catholic, and then a Croat, and I would be cursed if it were otherwise.

As for the Serbian *gusle* players in eastern Herzegovina, they play nicely, but he does not like their songs because they are mainly of Chetnik orientation:

> But in spite of the songs, I would like to listen to one such *gusle* player because of their voice and touch. I would try to learn something from them, but what they sing would never stick in my head.

It was at a festival in Croatia in 1990 that he last saw those who had come to western Herzegovina before the war, 'but they were never allowed to sing Chetnik songs'. And 'if I were to sing about Maks Luburić, I think they would lynch me'.[1] Predictably, Češkić did not see that the impossibility of him performing to them a song about the Ustasha commander who was responsible for the massacre of many Serbs in WWII was equivalent to their inability to sing songs to the Croats about the Chetnik leaders who had

1. Igor Kolovrat, 'U zapadnoj Hercegovini najnoviji je guslarski hit ... [In western Herzegovina the latest *gusle* hit ...]', *Globus*, 392, 12 June 12 1998.

perpetrated the same kind of crimes against the Croat population.

On the one hand, this kind of censorship fits into the general situation of the *gusle* player's adapting to his audience that we have already discussed. In the original epic culture, the problem was easily solved by simply leaving out of the repertoire songs that referred to opposing historical memories. (This clearly happened before 1990, although they were certainly performed, even then, to an audience that shared the same worldview.) On the other hand, despite Češkić's repeated claims that he was a Christian humanist and a Croatian patriot who condemned all kinds of chauvinism and all crime, it is clear that he held the Ustashas to be above all Croatian freedom fighters, and, as such, incapable of committing crimes. Such crimes as they did commit were of a passing nature, something unavoidable, provoked by the crimes of the opposite side, in short, legitimate self-defence. The problem, however, is that the Serbian *gusle* players have precisely the same views about the Chetniks and their crimes and that, *mutatis mutandis*, the same speech would fit easily into the mouths of Kosta Plakalović or Božidar Vučurević.

After the war, there were two processes in western Herzegovina connected with the *gusle* that have no equivalent in Serbia and Montenegro. Although they caused controversies and did not last long, they show in a particular way that the *gusle* scene, in an area that was not as autarchic as Republika Srpska, inevitably had to deal with the challenges of modernisation, or with a key feature of it that was totally unknown to patriarchal culture – irony and self-deprecation.

Almost on the same day that Šimić complained that the *gusle* was dying out, a pop group called Mobitel, from Mostar, shaped its appearance at a pop festival, where patriotic songs dominated, as a parody of the key features of local mythology and the self-identification of Croatian Herzegovinians and their way of life. This is implied by their very name, for the Herzegovina Croats were the first in the country to take en masse to mobile phone use, which gave rise to many jokes and anecdotes. As well as a modern light show, digital drums and so on, they had a *gusle*, played by two glamorously dressed girls. The band had found them a month earlier through the model agency Glamour Fashion, asking for 'girls who wouldn't be too shy to play the *gusle*'. They already knew something about the *gusle* and showed up, while the other models commented with a sneer – 'look at those rednecks', said one of them, a nineteen-year-old student. The second one, a fifteen-year-old schoolgirl, said that she had learned it from her granddad, to whom she had been very attached. They had never played it at home, but she appreciated it as 'one of the trademarks of my people'. The reaction was diverse. The city Croats, who had grown up in Mostar, where the girls were also from, told jokes at their own expense. Those who had come into the town during the war from the rural areas 'on the whole couldn't see that we were making fun in the songs and they didn't like the Mobitel group.' They laughed at the girls, and constantly quipped at one of them who worked in a café during the summer – 'look folks, a model sweeping, where's her *gusle*?'[1]

Two years later the successful producer of electronic dance music Denis Curman from Zagreb tried to fuse techno and high energy arrangements with traditional Herzegovina polyphonic singing and the *gusle*. A six-member band called the Herceg-Boys cut a disk, but without much commercial success. Two *gusle* players admitted they were 'surprised at this unusual combination' but 'impressed' that the music that they 'had known only in the original and intact form could be transformed.'[2] From the interview it is clear that they saw no contradiction between their belief that the project would succeed not only in Croatia but elsewhere and the fact that their *gusles* were still decorated with a map of the NDH, a portrait of Ante Pavelić, and Ustasha symbols. Their friend Damir Zorić, a member of parliament and Zagreb politician, a Herzegovinian by descent, showed more political savvy when he ordered one for 500 euros from one of them, who made *gusles* as well as playing them – but without the Ustasha symbols.

Although the Croatian Herzegovina *gusle* players often attacked the international administration in Bosnia-Herzegovina as being unjust to the Croats, and were sorry that the project for annexing Herzegovina to Croatia had come to nothing, and promoted negative stereotypes about Bosniaks and celebrated people who had played very dubious roles in the war of 1992–5, they still did not experience what their Serb colleagues did. At the beginning of 1998, after the performance of *gusle* songs had already been banned on Serbian Radio Television, the Office of the High Representative in Sarajevo banned all other *gusle* performances in Republika Srpska, because these new epic songs 'promoted inter-ethnic hatred, stirred up national passions and aggrandised persons whom the ICTY had indicted for war crimes'. To which the *gusle* players replied: 'They can impose sanctions on us, but we won't listen. We're going to go right on playing, in spite of their bans.'[3] And so they did.

1.   Mark Cigoj, 'Zamislite, ni Hercegovci ne uživaju u našem guslanju [Fancy, not even the Herzegovinans enjoy our *gusle* playing]', *Globus*, 30 August 1996.
2.   Darko Hudelist, 'Techno-gange ...', *Globus*, 420, 25 December 1998.
3.   'Izjava guslara iz Republike Srpske [Statement of *gusle* players of the RS]', *Nedeljni telegraf*, 18 March 1998.

Two Serb and two Bosniak singers of epic ballads with their audience at a summer camp of the Yugoslav army at Kalinovik in 1930.

Gusle *players and the army*

Photographs from the time of the aggression against Croatia and Bosnia-Herzegovina show that the *gusle* player retained, or rather renewed, his role as camp follower. During the Balkan Wars, in order to keep up the spirit of heroism, there was a lot of singing to the *gusle* in the Serbian and Montenegrin armies, as well as in the Austro-Hungarian units in which there were soldiers from Bosnia, Herzegovina, the Dalmatian highlands and Lika. There were even *gusle* players in the Turkish army, where Muslim soldiers from Bosnia and Sandžak served. There were *gusle* players who celebrated even rather minor participants in the battles if the subjects were willing to pay for their deed to be mentioned, while the regular Montenegrin army had a separate *gusle*-playing unit with its own captain (Murko 1951). Sometimes the actual participants in the wartime events described their own experiences in song, and if they were *gusle* players, performed them extempore. There were such poets in World War II also, when many *gusle* players, going off to one army or another, Ustasha, Chetnik or Partisan, would take their instrument with them. At a Partisan performance in the summer of 1942 in eastern Bosnia, by a vast bonfire in the shape of a five-pointed star, one of the combatants, a peasant from Romanija, composed and immediately performed a song about the collapse of Yugoslavia 'betrayed by the king and the magnates', about

Gusle player relaxing for a moment in Knez Mihajlov Street (central Belgrade), summer 1992. (photograph by Boža Petrović)

Anonymous Croat legionary, member of the 369th infantry division of the Wehrmacht that was operating in Bosnia in 1943–5, playing an improvised *gusle* on the battlefield. (photograph published under the title 'Meal-time idyll' in the Croatian edition of the German military magazine *Signal*, July 1943)

Hitler, Pavelić, the communists and various combatants from Romanija such as Slaviša Vajner (Čolaković 1977: II, 47). Stanko Škare, a peasant from near Imotski, was not a *gusle* player, but wrote about the events of the war in rhymed decasyllabics along the lines of Kačić-Miošić, and read them out to the peasants, who would 'remember, note down and copy out' his offerings (Nazor 1977: XVII, 217–222). Almost every region, particularly those with a tradition of animal husbandry and the evening get-together with the *gusle*, had its own chronicler who described the battles in the region, in the language and style of the epic tradition. After the war, some of them had a virtual monopoly on treating local wartime topics and exemplary biographies.

According to the testimony of someone who travelled by car from Sarajevo to Sofia towards the end of the summer of 1991, a *gusle*-playing performance was the emotional highlight of a mass political rally in Kraljevo, Central Serbia, when the JNA was sent off to its attack on Croatia, after a fiery speech by the Serbian Radical Party leader Vojislav Šešelj (Mladen Matić; *Vijenac*, 15,

4 August 1994). It is quite reasonable to suppose that there were plenty more such farewells with a garnishing of *gusle* players, particularly in central Serbia.

It was Montenegrin *gusle* players who became most numerously and systematically involved in the military operations. In Doljani, near Podgorica, where the JNA mustered in September 1991 for an attack on Konavle and Dubrovnik, the authorities put on a *gusle*-playing performance for the soldiers. There were songs about old battles against the Turks, as well as about the threats faced by the Serbs and the Orthodox religion throughout history. In addition, new songs were spontaneously composed about 'Tuđman's Ustashas and our wretched brothers across the Drina' who had to be protected (Koprivica 1996: 12). According to a post-war statement by Plakalović, who during communist Yugoslavia had issued LPs that sold well, singing then of course about Tito and *brotherhood and unity*, all the Serb *gusle* players in the country spent the war with the army in the trenches, encouraging the soldiers.[1] Just before the open aggression began, in early March 1992, Col. Hasan Efendić, the Bosnian Civil Defence commander, went round the barracks of the JNA at Lukavica above Sarajevo to see if he could get the Serbian street barricades peacefully removed. He saw that the Serbs were then listening to *gusle* songs (*Dani*, 98, 29 March 1999). A writer who joined the Karadžić forces outside the city tells that, throughout the siege, on Mt Jahorina, where the Bosnian Serb army had taken over a former JNA radar station, the commander of the station, an ensign, regularly played the *gusle*, particularly when he and the soldiers had been drinking.[2]

In the autumn of 1991, it was common to see in the news programmes on national radio and television in Serbia and in Montenegro, as part of their battle zone reports, soldiers, then still in the uniform of the JNA, listening intently to *gusle* players and occasionally cheering them on. In one such bulletin, shown on 10 November, after the JNA and the paramilitaries had taken the Dubrovnik neighbourhood of Mokošica, a major could be seen playing the *gusle* to a group of ten soldiers leaning on an APC. The shot lasted long enough for the following lines to be heard: 'Let Europe come to help / And we'll fire our big guns.' In another story, ten days later, among debris and the traces of fighting on the badly damaged road above

---

1. http://www.novine.ca/VESTI/intervju/intervju28.html (accessed 24 April 2003). Here the most appropriate term would be that introduced by the American forces during the Iraqi Freedom campaign in March and April 2003 when journalists were on the front lines with the soldiers. *Gusle* players were *embedded* with military units in the same way.

2. Neđo Šipovac, 'Čudne kape i crne naočari [Strange caps and black glasses]', *NIN*, 2547, 21 October 1999.

Dubrovnik, with the besieged old part of the city in the background, a soldier was shown with a *gusle* singing: 'From Durmitor cries the nymph / where are you, Serbian Dubrovnik?' This connection continued after the war. The Leopards, a commando group of the Army of Yugoslavia, deployed in Montenegro, and largely composed of veterans of 1991, had on its official emblem the inscription *For the Honoured Cross and Golden Freedom*, a typical formulation from the anti-Ottoman epic, and special *gusle* festivities were put on in its honour, in Herceg Novi, for example, funded by the pro-Serbian Montenegrin parties (*Monitor*, 3 August 2003).

The whole semantic and emotional charge added by the *gusles* to the campaigns of aggression against Croatia and Bosnia-Herzegovina may perhaps be best summed up in a newspaper report by the popular writer of light fiction Momo Kapor. After travelling through the burned-out and looted region of Konavle at New Year 1992, he found himself in the evening, at the Luksor Hotel, Trebinje, together with the poet Matija Bećković. Kapor listened as 'a lad in camouflage uniform' played a *gusle* and sang a song about the battle between the Montenegrin and Turkish armies in Vučji dol, 1876. Although a city man, a Belgrader, it was then, as 'the mighty mountains of Herzegovina were ringing', surrounded by armed men who were 'serious in their mission on the border' of Catholicism and Orthodoxy, that Kapor recalled that he was by origin actually from eastern Herzegovina. The 'forgotten essence' stirred in him, and 'the phoney overlay of intellectualism' dropped from him; forgotten were the 'Joyces and Eliots, the Sheratons and the intercontinental flights, the courtesies and the quotes' because 'this sound was older than us, and older than this war'. The confrontation of the two cultures, the two value systems was final, total, irrevocable, and the border that was being set up or rather restored between them could not be crossed. The transformation that occurred then was absolute, predestined:

> Never has Johann Sebastian Bach managed to give me such goose-pimples or Mozart to bring a tear to these eyes that have seen all the wonders of the world. But this sound, this voice, that cried, that raged, that threatened and moaned, defiantly, and in falsetto when it was excited, was capable of taking me wherever it wanted. No one can withstand [the sound of the *gusle*], and nor could that lad in uniform who picked up his automatic rifle, raised it and scattered a burst into the sky.[1]

---

1. Momo Kapor, '[An area fried in hatred]', *Pogledi*, 100, 17 January 1992. For the analysis of a report in the fortnightly *Duga*, with scenes of JNA soldiers who were doing ritual dances to the sound of the *gusle* among the burned-out buildings in

Konavle (southern Croatia), autumn 1991: a JNA soldier plays the *gusle* in the ruins. (photograph by Željko Sinobad)

Early in the autumn of 1991, JNA soldiers in Konavle, among whom there were some professional *gusle* players, explained to a journalist from the Podgorica daily *Pobjeda* that 'it was easier to make war with the *gusle*'. The journalist agreed, concluding that 'with the *gusle* it was as if all those heroes who told the story of freedom from our hearts and lips were joining the ranks of the unit commanded by Peronić'. In the Konavle combat zone he met three volunteers, members of the Starac Milija Gusle Club in Bijelo Polje. 'Because I am a *gusle* player I sort of feel an obligation to be in the lead in everything,' explained one, another adding:

> Who could believe in our songs if we were not in the front line today ... Battle and liberty are taken for granted when you say '*gusle* player'. For us the war is like a kind of advanced course in the profession. We've earned the right for our soul and throat to put heroes into the song. Whenever there is no firing, then we play the *gusle*. First a volley, then a song.

A third drew his attention to the particular tactical effect that their playing and singing had on the other side – the defenders of Dubrovnik.

> They hear our *gusles*. And they fear our songs. Whenever we start

Konavle, see Čolović 1993: 74.

playing the *gusle*, the snipers start firing.[1]

Eight years later, in the new wartime situation in Serbia when NATO launched its bombing campaign in the spring of 1999, the *gusle* player Milomir Miljanić gave an identical explanation of his activities, in a newspaper issued by the Army of Yugoslavia [VJ]. Just because he was a 'folk *gusle* player' he 'thought it his duty in time of war to be with the people, or with the army, part of the people'. He enlisted voluntarily, and sang heroic songs in units throughout the country, as well as in the Central Army Club in Belgrade, to 'alleviate for a moment the trouble and misfortune that had overcome our people'.

It is worth quoting a longer account he gave of this experience, from which it can be seen how he perceived the ongoing conflict. Unlike the wars in Croatia and Bosnia-Herzegovina, when the Serbian units were manned largely either by local people or men imported from Serbia proper, or from the urban populations that still preserved rural cultural habits and preferences, including listening to the *gusle*, this time he was in the milieu of the regular army, manned through the regular recruiting system. The audience therefore included the regular city youth, from a different social and cultural background, which if it had a free choice would not have elected to go to *gusle* concerts. In addition, this was a generation that was too young to have taken part in the war against Croatia and Bosnia-Herzegovina, and did not have the wartime or the accompanying cultural, that is, epic, experience.

> Even if the aggression had gone on far longer, there would always have been something to sing about to the army, without repeating the same song. For many of the younger combatants in this war it was the first time they had come across a *gusle*, or seen a *gusle* player, but they all listened with special attention to what was being sung to them and paid it great respect. By a trick of circumstance, it happened that they were once again defending Kosovo from a new enemy, while Prince Lazar and his fellow fighters [Kosovo, 1389], of whom we sang, had done the same thing in their own day, only in different circumstances. Such songs sung in time of war enabled the combatants to identify with the former heroes of Kosovo.[2]

---

1. Unsigned, '[Bursts of firing from the *gusle*]', in *The War for Peace*, special number of *Pobjeda*, October 1991, p. 77.
2. Sanja Krajnović, 'Poezija opstanka [Poetry of survival]', *Vojska*, 27 July 1999, p. 24.

It is hard to assess the accuracy of his estimate of the many young combatants who met the *gusle* for the first time and at once fell in love with it, but there is no doubt that he himself did experience the armed conflict of the time as a conceptual and substantial continuity with that of about six centuries earlier. And he was clearly not alone.

In conclusion, it is obvious that the profound crisis of Yugoslav society, the rise of Greater Serbian populism in the 1980s, and the war that accompanied the collapse of the SFRY, saw the restoration of multiple links between the protagonists of the *gusle*-playing scene and the military and political figures who had launched the war. These were links that existed at the beginning of the century, and were never broken. The interest and benefits were mutual: in the *gusle* players, the elite gained an extensive, well-developed network that celebrated heroism and promoted its cult. This gave it legitimacy in that section of the population where the phrases of its regular propaganda, its discursive phraseology of legitimation, would only have penetrated with great difficulty, if at all. Meanwhile, the *gusle* players had the opportunity to reconquer areas and social classes that they seemed to have lost irrevocably in the processes of urbanisation and modernisation of the early twentieth century. The particular development of Yugoslav society after 1945 enabled the *gusle* player to bridge the gap in communication and worldview between the town and the country. Through the united working man-peasant class and the phenomenon of *the countryside in the town, the rural in the urban*, he was able naturally to enter the cities, especially the peripheral slums and new tower block estates such as those in New Belgrade and Vogošća. There he was greeted by an audience that belonged only formally to such agglomerations, but was in fact, in terms of worldview and cultural needs, the same as that he had originally addressed at country fairs, fetes and gatherings.

Two additional processes reinforced this expansion, and brought the Serbian and Montenegrin *gusle* players into surroundings that were completely inaccessible to them for demographic reasons, but which had proved in the eighties to be vital centres of the *gusle*-playing subculture and nuclei of the mass extra-institutional movements exploited by the Milošević project. The first was state-fostered colonisation by Montenegrins and Serbs from Croatia and Bosnia-Herzegovina, either by the creation of new settlements within the compact territory of some other ethnic community, such as the phenomenon of Kosovo Polje in predominantly Albanian Kosovo, or by the colonisation of a settlement from which 'unsuitable' communities had been previously forcibly moved out, primarily Germans and to some extent Hungarians, as in the case of Kula in Vojvodina. The other process consisted of official postings of the

In the lobby of a captured hotel, Serb soldiers around one of their number playing the *gusle*. (*Vreme*, 230, 20 March 1995)

JNA officer corps, during which a large number of them evidently became authoritative promoters of the *gusle*-playing scene and a personal link among its various sections. Their authority in this process was enhanced by widespread respect for the military profession in patriarchal settings and the political status accorded to members of a military corporation sponsored by the party.

Thanks to all this, and backed up by advanced technical opportunities for the distribution of their products (radio, records, cassettes), in time the *gusle*-playing scene became not only a parallel information and communication network, with some hundreds of very mobile journalists, but also a powerful political factor, acquiring a social influence that it had never expected. On the eve of the war, a *gusle*-playing club was an authoritative press centre, with a reliable translation service, that simultaneously interpreted the messages of current politics into ancient epic images and categories, and vice versa.

The twilight of communism and the declaration of war

One of the new epic songs shows particularly well the subtlety with which political messages can sometimes be framed as well as the way what is often unintelligible for the outsider contains easily recognisable and instructive meanings for regular consumers of the genre. This is the epic 'Twilight of the Gods at Žuta greda' ('Sumrak bogova kod Žute grede'), performed by the

Chetniks and a *gusle* player on the front not far from Kupres in May 1993. (recorded from SRT – Banja Luka)

gusle player Vojo Radusinović (1989), written by the vernacular poet Žarko Šobić (from Gornja Bijela near Šavnik in Drobnjaci), an engineer at the Piva hydroelectric generating station in nearby Mratinje.[1] The poem is inspired by an event at Žuta greda, a bend on the Nikšić to Podgorica road, where on 8 October 1988, a group of workmen from the Nikšić steelworks was prevented from joining a Podgorica rally in the course of Milošević's first attempt to overthrow the Montenegrin authorities. In the scuffle on the narrow road, where police loyal to the Montengrin government set up a blockade and used tear gas, several workers were injured. In the next few months the pro-Milošević media assigned the event almost mythic dimensions, turning it into the propaganda core for the preparation of a new, violent attempt to take power in Podgorica, which succeeded in January 1989.

With some exaggeration, perhaps, but not in essence inaccurately, one of the most militant pro-Milošević journalists said that 'in a month' this and cognate epics (Jeknić 1990, Đukić 1988) had a greater effect in undermining the authority of the republican government than the 'entire writing of the press' and well-supported data about abuses of power perpetrated by members of the previous government (Nebojša Jevrić, *Duga*, 424, 26 May 1990). And this kind of propaganda operation, waged in parallel through the interpretative categories of two kinds of journalism, printed and oral, is not unprecedented. A similar campaign was carried out by the Serbian government when, towards the end of World War I, it was necessary to

1. Renowned *gusle* players called Radusinović from Podgorica are mentioned by Murko 1951: 129. Vojo Radusinović lives in Nikšić.

compromise the Montenegrin army and King Nikola as much as possible, in order for Montenegro to be eliminated as an independent legal, military and political factor in the creation of the Kingdom of the Serbs, Croats and Slovenes. What the police action at Žuta greda was in 1988, the Austro-Hungarian capture of Mt Lovćen was in January 1916 – a highly symbolic core around which a comprehensive set of meanings was to be built. Then, together with explicit propaganda accusations and commissioned 'analyses' whose discourse was supposed to show their own audience that this had been an unnecessary withdrawal, even a cowardly flight, by the Montenegrins, depriving its king and government of the moral legitimacy to take part in the creation of the new state, the epic 'Lovćen Anathema' ('Lovćenska anatema') was printed and played, transmitting the same message, through its own discourse and interpretative categories, to its own audience. Knowing, that is, that 'some Montenegrin peasants believed in the truthfulness of the decasyllabic songs', Belgrade adapted its political propaganda to the patriarchal frame of mind of these people, hoping that it would be easier to reach the uneducated populace with the *gusle* (Radojević 1971: 79).

Starting from a conflict between police and workmen, Šobić's 'Twilight of the Gods at Žuta greda' also gives shape to a far more comprehensive and complex vision of social and political relationships in Yugoslavia in the last year of peace. The epic consists of 349 decasyllabic lines, starting with images of a looted and devastated country, 'a homeland gnawed away' that the 'pseudo bigwigs' had sold to the 'fat cats' of the International Monetary Fund. This relates to the fact that the incompetent and disoriented post-Tito nomenklatura solved the spiralling economic problems of the eighties by taking out yet more loans that the country was incapable of servicing. The world was turned upside down: a river was smaller than a brook, a fox hunted a lion, a son did not respect paternal authority, hawks lost their wings, while hens 'flew towards the skies'. This ancient topos, so suggestively worked out in Šobić, was a favourite theme in the vernacular culture of pre-industrial Europe. It functioned particularly in carnival parades, and from the mid-sixteenth century it was nourished by popular broadsheet writers and illustrators, because it was suitable for illustrations presenting a physical revolution as well as a revolution – or reversal – in interpersonal, familial and social relations: fish flying, horses turning into farriers shoeing men, sons beating their fathers, the king walking while the peasant rides, the husband holding the baby and spinning while his wife smokes and holds a gun (cf. Burke 1978: 186–191).

The continuity of the world turned upside down as an image for rebuking and complaining about the present can be followed in literature from the Greek and Roman classics through the Middle Ages to the Renaissance (Curtius 1963: 94–98), and entered into the discourse of the Yugoslav political elite and the media in a big way in 1984, along with cyclical inflation and shortages. The previous, pre-inflationary world was orderly, and everything in it went on in the natural way, while the current world was upside-down. Price rises were not feared by the producer, which would have been normal, for his market would be threatened, rather by the consumer; instead of avoiding borrowing in these uncertain conditions, the people were happy to get into debt under and the old proverb 'Debt is a bad friend' was turned into a new phrase 'Debt is your best friend', as commentators and politicians often said. Inflation led people to get rid of their money, and everyone felt that he had won if he was penniless, wrote the Zagreb daily *Vjesnik*, 14 January 1986. The country was obliged to import wheat from Austria 'which had once been a big importer of Yugoslav grain' wrote *NIN* in Belgrade, in September of the same year (cf. Žanić 1987: 28–30).

The epic images of chaos used by Šobić drew strength easily and naturally from this kind of metaphor, with which the Yugoslav public had been bombarded for years. It was also an ideal point of departure from which to launch a new political agenda.

In the ominous silence, in a Yugoslavia benumbed in expectation of some momentous upheaval, came the first indication of action aimed at restoring the broken order:

> *the Serbian people took out of its sheath*
> *the Scourge of God of Saint Elijah.*

The mention of Elijah had powerful resonance, for he inherited a pre-Christian tradition that made him an ideal symbol for heralding important events. He was the thunderer, the storm god, who determined when there would be thunder and lightning. In many areas, particularly among the Vasojević and other Montenegrin mountain clans, on St Elijah's Day (*Ilindan*) the people would go up into the hills and make merry, shooting their rifles into the air. Henceforth there was a constant contrast of alternating images of the ruined country and of the resistance that was in full swing: 'the folk sharpened their rusty sabres' and 'the folk broke down republics' borders', 'the people's tribunes made their speeches' – heralding the mass demonstrations launched by Milošević and the demands that were heard at them. As the song progresses, images and messages concentrate with increasing suggestiveness around the motif of betrayal, taking two directions.

The Yugoslav or Serbian communists had, on the one hand, betrayed their own project for a social Arcadia, 'they tarnished their honour / cast the hammer and sickle beneath their feet' and 'trampled on the grave of the Comintern,' making the ideas of Marx and Lenin into mere dead museum exhibits. And, on the other hand, they had rejected the genuine traditions of the people, 'trampled down the Serbian great men' and 'sold at the market place/ the customs of the Slav nations' – Christmas Eve, Christmas and the lighting of the Yule log. The deep-level correspondence between these two crimes confirms once again the way the popular mind tended to understand the communist ideological project as a restoration of the original golden age of justice, harmony and equality, as a manner of cancelling out all social development that threatened the values of the patriarchal countryside, at one in its worldview and economically self-sufficient. The accusation of betrayal is exhausted in the condemnation of 'scramble and plunder' and the moral category of 'loss of face', that is, the epic conception that demands that the hero should die rather than besmirch his honour. This is a non-ideological or trans-ideological message, equivalent to Milošević's suggestion that some people had to leave the League of Communists 'because they have stolen from us and because they have disgraced us' (Milošević 1989: 225).

Having indicated the main lines of the historical situation and the value system in which the denouement was to unfold, Šobić builds up the central image – the group of 'Slavonic rulers', the typical epic scene of counsel-taking, the assembly of the chiefs, when the key decisions were made. The remark that the agreement occurred 'on the feast of Kosovo's prince' refers to a concrete instance – the banquet in Kruševac, described in perhaps the best known and most published epic song of the Kosovo cycle, 'The Prince's Dinner' ('Kneževa večera', transcribed by Vuk Stefanović Karadžić, and published in the second volume of *Serbian Popular Poems* (*Srpske narodne pjesme*) in 1841, when Prince Lazar gathered the Serbian heroes on the eve of the fateful battle at Kosovo, where men were to prove their mettle.

> *Serbian Prince Lazar celebrates his patron saint*
> *In Kruševac secluded town,*
> *He placed the gentry at the table.*
> *All the lords and all the barons.*

Then comes a list of heroes and magnates at the meeting, in an image corresponding to the Last Supper, including the motif of Lazar sensing he would be betrayed the next day, which the greatest hero Miloš Obilić also

The *gusle* player Tanasije Vučić (1888–1931)
who followed the Serbian and Montenegrin
army in the Balkan and First World wars.
(Murko 1951)

knew. But he would not say who it was, telling the guests and the prince that
it was one whom none of them would suspect:

> For traitor have I never been,
> Neither have been, nor shall I,
> Treason sits at your right knee,
> Drinks cool wine ' neath your coattails.

In 'The Twilight of the Gods at Žuta greda', as well, the meeting is
attended by several of the figures from the original 'The Prince's Banquet'
– primarily Lazar himself, and Toplica Milan and Miloš Obilić, some of
the characters from the post-Kosovo epic, as well as some non-epic figures
symbolising the new political circumstances and meanings that the original
epic tradition could not encompass. This key scene is preceded by a no less
important introduction:

> Sang the gusle *player Tanasije Vučić*
> Višnjić's 'Revolt Against the dayis'.

This *gusle* player was a real person, and one chosen deliberately for his origin and significance. Born in 1883 and dying in 1931, he was by origin from Drobnjaci, like Vuk Karadžić. In the Balkan Wars and the First World War he had gone with the Serbian and Montenegrin armies, performing heroic songs to the soldiers and officers. After 1918, he toured tirelessly, becoming, for many, the most prominent popular singer in the South Slav lands (Murko 1951). Brought in to open the imaginary counsel, he really does most authentically symbolise not only the social status of the epic but all the *gusle* players who had by then, through their cassettes and tours, in their appearance at party congresses and protest meetings, promoted the renewed ideology of a final 'revenge for Kosovo', as well as all those who were soon to join the Serb paramilitary forces in their military campaigns. Chosen with equal care is the song that Vučić performs, for it conveys, more clearly than anything else, the idea that the insurrection just starting is a replica of the 1804 Serbian Insurrection under Karađorđe, just as it was a replica, or vengeance, of Kosovo. Historical time is abolished and compressed into a single moment, because 'ages pass in a single day'.[1] The blind *gusle* player Filip Višnjić, born in 1765 not far from Zvornik in Bosnia, defected in 1809 to insurrectionary Serbia, and then sang of the most important events of the time. 'The Beginning of the Revolt against the Dayis' ('Početak bune protiv dahija', Karadžić IV) is the peak of his epic vision of the anti-Ottoman insurrection and contains a number of tested historical elements, integrated of course into the vernacular vision of the world and sense of history. As distinct from some other traditional songs, its popularity was not created by 'literary criticism and school anthologies'; they 'came upon it already popular' (Veljković 1928: 376).

This song was a perpetual emitter of messages to be used in new historical circumstances, many of the images and phrases entering at once into the colloquial language. Its vernacular worldview with its sharp division of the world into two irreconcilable poles in a predestined clash enabled the most diverse of ideologues to dehistoricise the present according to this metaphorical pattern and to present themselves as authentic continuers of the archetypal resistance to the outsider and the oppressor. Naturally, in World War II, the communists saw in the poem a paradigm of a non-ethnic class conflict, a showdown between the exploited and the exploiters, while the Chetniks saw it as an archetypal image of the fatal clash between cross and crescent.

---

1. The Russian revolutionary poet Vladimir Mayakovsky would say that historical time is speeded up, and later it will be seen that this allusion to him in a context that has no ostensible connection with Bolshevik propaganda is actually not at all out of place.

'We carried out' the uprising in Serbia in 1941 'in the tradition of the First and Second Serbian Insurrections', 'of the traditional poetry that is a sublimate of it all', recalled the Partisan commissar of the time, Tanasije Mladenović (*Svet*, 219, 5 September 1990). On one occasion, the pre-war unionist Živko Topalović, who was in Mihailović's HQ from January 1944, addressed the formally drawn-up ranks of Chetniks, and in the name of all their forbears who 'had been *haiduks* in our mountains' called upon them to spread the word 'that the summons of the song was being repeated: 'The enemy's here, time to go to war, Let all the horsemen pull on their boots, And all the infantrymen pull on their sandals''. (Topalović 1967: 191).[1] It is no exaggeration to say that in the countryside it was not informed political views that determined whether the men would join one army or the other, rather whose representative was quicker and more convincing in evoking the archetypal motif of revolt against injustice. Thus, when Šobić states that those attending the counsel listened to Višnjić's song by way of introduction, he is in fact imaginatively repeating what the communists had done in Užice in October 1941 by 'realistically staging' the song (Nedeljković 1973: 262) or when they took a song from the first Serbian insurrection as the unofficial anthem of the Užice Republic (as they called the first major piece of territory under their control in western Serbia), except that instead of the original 'Turkish *dayis*' they gave it a more contemporary adversary, and sang 'The Užice people has risen up / against the raging German *dayis*' (Nedeljković 1981: 37).

Thus Šobić's 'young proletarians' who, half a century later, raised another 'proletarian revolt' or his image that during the time 'the Partisan nymphs started to sing again' are not a sign of communist ideology, still less of its conscious promotion. This is particularly reinforced with the phrase '(Partisan) nymphs', *vile* in the original, pretty young women of magical powers that in the South Slav traditional epics correspond to the classical muses. They inspire the hero to acts of bravery, warn him of danger, help and advise him and protect him in difficult situations. The image of them starting to sing again means that the nation has awoken, that it is prepared for resistance, and that no one is left on his own, for up to then, while the nation was chaotic and apathetic, they had been silenced and degraded. So, the point of his epic is not at all to promote this or that ideology, rather to maintain the core of the common *Weltanschauung* lying below the surface of both ideologies and both political imaginative inventories, Partisan and

1. The first line is from 'The Beginning of the Revolt against the Dayis' and the second two from the epic poem 'The Insurrection of Prince Miloš against the Turks' ('Ustanak kneza Miloša na Turke').

Chetnik. This epic was created at a time when the 'class' *anti-bureaucratic revolution (antibirokratska revolucija)* was transformed smoothly – and for the ordinary participants quite imperceptibly – into an ethnic or nationalist revolution, when the demand for social justice, that is for the correction of injustice inflicted on the proletariat, whichever people they belonged to, gave way to the demand for ethnic justice, i.e. for a correction of injustices inflicted on the Serbs, whichever social group they belonged to, and the mass rage against the ethnically non-defined gentry and rotten upperclasses was redirected to the religiously and ethnically determined *Turks* and *Latins*.

Višnjić's line 'the folk sprang up like grass from the ground' on one of the banners at Aranđelovac, one of the first pro-Milošević rallies (*Politika*, 8 October 1988), was an immediately obvious instruction as to how contemporary events ought to be interpreted. This evoked the very same archetypal image of an unstoppable national movement, implanted in 'the collective mind of this people', as Amfilohije, Orthodox Bishop of Banat, when at the beginning of 1990 he defined not only the point of the political protests, but also the mission of the Church itself in the new circumstances. The rallies, he said, were unfolding according to the same predestined logic as the Karađorđe insurrection:

> You recall the traditional song 'The Revolt against the Dayis' – 'The folk sprang up like the grass from the ground' (*usta raja ko iz zemlje trava*). This is something that is going on according to spiritual laws in the spirit of the nation and the Church (Radović 1992: 130–131).

In Višnjić's understanding of history, the insurrection is not just a human act but also the 'will of heaven', and the saints encouraged wavering Serbs to action through heavenly signs – the eclipse of the sun and the moon, the appearance of a comet, thunderstorms, all founded on popular beliefs that major events were heralded by remarkable phenomena on earth and in heaven. For this reason the revolt was actually divine retribution, the execution of divine justice, and there was no power that could save the Turks. That is, before the insurrection the same heavenly omens appeared as five centuries earlier, on the eve of the Battle of Kosovo, when 'the Serbian empire perished', and now they meant that 'someone [would] lose an empire' (Veljković 1928: 380).

The autonomy of Vojvodina and Kosovo was forcibly revoked, and after the conflict at Žuta greda and his failure at that time, Milošević's new coup in Montenegro in January bore fruit. The federal government of Branko

Mikulić resigned on 2 January, on 20 February the Albanian miners in Stari Trg started a hunger strike demanding the restoration of autonomy for Kosovo, the Belgrade mob yelled anti-Albanian slogans and demanded arrests, and on 27 February, under pressure from Milošević, the presidency of the SFRY approved sending JNA tanks onto the streets in Kosovo, while a pro-Milošević rally the very next day in Knin meant the start of the Serbian rebellion in Croatia. The whole of Serbia was in a trance, and Milošević at the height of his power and popularity. It was time then, on the eve of the final impulse, to announce prophetically the higher purpose of the events through an ageless topos. This was done particularly by three writers who from the very beginning had been installing some of the most suggestive images into the imaginative equipment of the *happening of the people (događanje naroda)*.

Vuk Drašković saw once again over Serbia 'heavenly omens' as a reliable announcement of a new insurrection (Drašković 1989: 99). The same 'omens that the saints today are placing in the clear sky over Serbia' were recognised by Matija Bećković (*Nedjelja*, 34, 14 October 1990). And according to Vojislav Lubarda, Yugoslavia was ruled by 'socialist *dayis*', and Bosnia by 'viziers and pashas', and some two years earlier '*new signs* and *new omens* had appeared in the sky over Serbia' because 'the *raya* [disenfranchised Christian Turkish subjects] once again could no longer stand the *zulüm* [violence, reign of terror, exercised by the Ottoman authorities]'. Its leader, the 'new Serbian leader', Milošević, was 'not *black* like his famed predecessor', Black George [Karađorđe], but even so it was clear that events were ineluctably following some deep internal logic of history (Lubarda 1990b: 9–33, original italics, used so as additionally to point out the use of terms of Turkish origin, related to Ottoman rule, thus suggesting an analogy between two historical situations and their protagonists). Supernatural portents also appeared in Njegoš's *The Mountain Wreath (Gorski vijenac)*, just before crucial decisions were made: lightning created a cross in the sky, the mountains shook, and the moon went as red as fire. Authentically inheriting the tradition, Šobić too places his image of stones falling from the sky between the moment of tense expectation, when

> *in the calm before the storm*
> *the folk await the destined hour,*

and the beginning of the counsel, at which the national leaders were to decide about the start of the final reckoning. Then 'stones began to fall from the sky' and 'lightning flashed down the Pješivci clan', which is a precise indication of the event that signalled the new revolt, for the Pješivci means the tribe, clan and also the clan ground, or the region around Nikšić, which was where the demonstrators had come from when the police halted them at Žuta greda.[1]

Although Višnjić clearly stated that the common folk were rising, because they could no longer endure the reign of terror, a parallel interpretation is built into the song according to which the Turkish oppression was only the trigger, and the real objective and nature of the insurrection were different. It went beyond the concrete social and historical framework and simply could not be avoided, because it was directed by a supra-historical purpose:

> *for the blood had welled up from the ground*
> *the time has come, it is right to do battle*
> *to shed blood for the honoured cross*
> *each one to redeem his old ones.*

This picture of a land running with blood was evoked by a speaker at a Podgorica rally, threatening all who had grown used to serving the 'Sultan' – the Albanians and Bosniaks – as well as those who served the 'Kaiser' – the Slovenes and Croats. They 'have to be aware that the time has come and the blood has welled out of the ground, and woe to the country an army marches over' (*Pobjeda*, 1 February 1990). The image is based on the ancient conception of the blood as the centre of vital force in a body, which remains so even when it is separated from the body. The blood of a murdered man is never still, but, when the time comes, seethes, becomes agitated and foams, heralding imminent revenge as the wish of the deceased, or of his soul (Bandić 1974).

The motif of fighting for the faith, for the honoured cross, was common in the discourse of Serbian political leaders that year. At the *Jovandan* [St John's Day] church and folk meeting in Strmica, a month before the rebellion in Knin, the SDS leader Jovan Opačić announced that the 'sons of

---

1. A Croatian *gusle* player used the same ancient topos when he described the course of the 14th Congress of the LCY and political relationships of the time. The Macedonian and Bosnian-Herzegovinan communists cowered silently, and the Slovene, and then the Croatian leaders, in solidarity with the Slovenes, held out against the onslaught of the Serbian and Montenegrin ralliers and attempted to stop Milošević taking control of the LCY. The congress collapsed because the Slovene and Croatian delegates walked out demonstratively, and the two republics decided to call free elections: 'Every day the pressures are stronger / but one morning the clouds came over/ the lightning flashed from Ljubljana town / the bolt struck in the centre of Belgrade./ Then they flashed from white Zagreb / and the whole of Yugoslavia shook' (Šimić 1990a).

the legendary, rebellious Tristate Border', *tromeđa, Triplex Confinum*, that point near Knin where the borders of the Ottoman Empire, Austria and Venice had intersected (i.e. Bosnia, Lika and Dalmatia), would rather 'wage war for the honoured cross and golden freedom (*krst časni i slobodu zlatnu*)' than accept the new Croatian government (*Borba*, 9 July 1990). He repeated this some two weeks later at a rally named the All Serbian Parliament in Srb, Lika, at a place where 'revolts and insurrections had always been raised' and people had 'perished for the honoured cross and golden freedom' (*Borba*, 26 July 1990). At the Podgorica rally in October 1990 the speakers also called for a 'war for the honoured cross' against Slovenia (*Nedjeljna Dalmacija*, 1019, 11 November 1990).

A battle for the honoured cross in Višnjić's mental horizon is on the one hand a battle for freedom and on the other the aspiration, by avenging 'the old ones', the ancestors who fell by the Turkish sword, to carry on their work and receive their heritage. To this extent war was 'a natural periodic event, which came after some rather large blow, and to which Serbia, in this case, was being directed in the most immediate way by higher forces.' (Ćorović 1936: 78). In Višnjić's glossary, the word *pokajati*, commonly meaning *to reedem oneself, to atone for one's sins*, also *to repent*, in the call 'each one [is obliged] to redeem [to repent for] his ancestors (*svako svoje nek pokaje stare*)', actually means *to avenge*, that is, to comit those addressed to a blood feud, and the word in this meaning may be found in almost all his songs (Maticki 1982: 84–92).

In addition, Karađorđe's historically authentic message to the insurgents to kill the representatives of the Ottoman authorities and to send their own families to safety in groups of refugees was turned, in the lines, 'each kill your own *subaşi*/ hide your wives and children in fleeing columns', into a 'classic formula', into a cry full of dramatic strength and internal rhythm (Veljković 1928: 382). The effect to date of the *anti-bureaucratic revolution* was summed up by a participant of many a rally precisely according to this model: 'the pashas have fallen, but in many places the *subaşis* have remained', although they would not last long, because 'no one could any longer stop a people once they have set off like this' (Miodrag Perunović; *Politika ekspres*, 12 August 1989). Another almost simultaneous evocation of the same archetypal situation is worked out in greater detail still: 'all our songs about rebellions begin with lines: May / Let each one kill his *sipahi* [Ottoman soldier rewarded with a fief complete with serfs]', and since the mass rallies in Montenegro had successfully 'pulled down the pashas and *beys*', it remained only to have it out with the '*subaşis*' (Nebojša Jevrić, *Duga*, 403, 5 August

1989). Višnjić's song ends with the scene in which Karađorđe, after he has conquered Serbia and expelled the Turks, turns to the Drina 'border/ twixt Bosnia and Serbia' and solemnly announces that he will soon cross it and 'set out into honest Bosnia'.

As one Serbian historian put it, these 'few lines by a blind Bosnian *gusle* player ... contributed more than the work of a single educated man' to the annexation of Bosnia-Herzegovina becoming one of the priorities of the Serbian foreign policy programme in the last century (Čubrilović 1939: 24). It is not surprising therefore that from the outset contemporary political leaders were called 'leaders of the Third Serbian insurrection' – from the SDS president Jovan Rašković (*Duga,* 431, 1 September 1990) to the leaders of the Kosovo Serbs Miroslav Šolević and Kosta Bulatović (*Duga,* 424, 26 May 1990). In June 1991, ten months before the aggression against Bosnia-Herzegovina, the novelist Vojislav Lubarda wrote that there was nothing else for the Serbs of that area to do 'than what the Serbs in Serbia did in 1904 under Black George. The Serbs always have some Black or Saint George' (Lubarda 1993: 107).

Now, however, it is time to return to the Radusinović-Šobić epic and observe how, after the evocation of the charismatic figure of the *gusle* player Tanasije Vučić and the paradigmatic songs of Filip Višnjić, his meanings focus on the final definition of the contemporary historical situation, on the crucial counsel that gives an impression of the Yugoslavia that existed at that moment in the minds of those taking part in the *happening of the people.*

> *The prince of Serbia puts the cup*
> *on the knee of Matija Gubec,*
> *Goce Delčev drinks the crimson wine,*
> *below the crown of St Elijah,*
> *Montenegrin bishop prince Danilo*
> *places on his lap the sharp sword;*
> *a house full of Slavonic rulers,*
> *each with each in brotherly talk ...*
> *the anthem of heroic Slavs roars out ...*

Within the general outline of the Kosovo myth – and the ideological paradigm according to which Yugoslavia was merely an extension of Serbia, and its peoples worth something to the extent to which they cooperated with the Serbs – each of the participants in the council represented one of the peoples. The Serbs, as at the original Kosovo supper, were represented by Prince Lazar, the host of the gathering; the Macedonians by Goce Delčev, leader of the anti-Ottoman Ilindan Insurrection of 1903. Montenegro is represented by an unambiguously readable figure – Prince Bishop Danilo, in whose time the extirpation of the Montenegrin converts to Islam (*istraga poturica*) was carried out, while the peasant leader Matija Gubec was there to stand for Croatia.

Gubec functioned quite regularly in the political imagination of the second Yugoslavia as a symbol of the Croatian component. Šobić himself had already treated a Gubec understood in this way in his epic 'The Peasants' Revolt of 1573' ('Seljačka buna 1573'): during the fatal battle with the official army at Stubica, the peasant leader called on God not to allow the 'Croatian banners to be broken', and bore his later torture heroically 'for his Croatian homeland' (Šobić 1983a: 15). As against the magnates and the prelates who were either foreign or alienated from their own people, Gubec embodied the original Croatian- Slav- soul, an ideological concept that rejected foreign, above all 'Latin' and Germanic, cultural influences, seeing the future for the Croats only in a community with the South Slav peoples. Realising that the fortunes of war were abandoning the peasant army, he prayed to God to save his martyred people 'for the love of the Old Slavs' (Šobić 1983a: 13), not to let the Slav nature of the Croats be wiped out, for the Croats to persist in their resistance to non-Slav influences and all of those who wanted economic and political links with the morally corrupt Latin and Germanic West, rather than with their *Slav brothers,* in Yugoslavia.

Since, however, at the time of Milošević's campaigns against the legal authorities in Kosovo, Vojvodina and Montenegro the Croatian communist *nomenklatura* largely kept their mouths shut, in confusion or hypocrisy, the message of Šobić's epic is that the Serbs expected from the Croats, or rather from their political elite, if not active alliance, then at least understanding for their important national efforts. What is more, Prince Lazar turns in a familiar manner to Gubec, placing the wine goblet with comradely care upon his knee.

Since it is stressed several times that this is about the Slavs, it is clear why there are no Albanians at the council of war, and it is not hard to guess why the Bosniaks have been left out. For they, in the Greater Serbian ideology and in romantic pan-Slavism, into which the popular mind quite often translated this ideology, were simply Turks, the consequence of religious apostasy and a foreign body in the Slav Balkans. The absence of the Slav Slovenes might be a little strange for a moment, but this is the element that shows the exactitude of Šobić's vernacular copy of Milošević's discursive interpretation of Yugoslav reality. The Catholicism of the Slovenes could not be the reason, because this was the phase when the *anti-bureaucratic revolution* evoked the All Christian alliance against 'the Turks', before, that is, it was transformed into Orthodox resistance to the 'Latins'. This is shown by the presence of the Catholic Gubec at the crucial gathering.

But what seems unintelligible to the outside observer is explained so clearly to the consumer of the genre and connoisseur of the tradition that it could not possibly be clearer. Šobić is explicit: Skender-bey, the representative Albanian, their national symbol and hero, has gone to the representative Slovene, the nineteenth century romantic poet France Prešeren, 'to take part in his wedding feast'. The image of *going to a wedding feast* is clearly adopted from *The Mountain Wreath,* which shows once again not only the persistence of the ancient images and expressive models in the new epic, but also their active communicative value within the social groups that consumed it. Prince Bishop Danilo is afraid that, should there be dissension because of the extirpation of the converts to Islam, if, that is, the Montenegrins took their Islamised relatives under their protection, 'Satan would come to the devil's nuptials / and put out the candle of Serbia' (Njegoš 1987: 536–537). And this is precisely what the Slovenes had done when 'the devil' Prešeren had invited 'the Satan' Skender-bey to the wedding feast.

The Slovenes, then, have betrayed the common cause, linked up with the archetypal non-Slav enemy, because – in a parallel reality – in 1989, at a meeting in the Cankar Hall in Ljubljana, President Milan Kučan and other members of the Slovene elite had expressed their solidarity with the Albanian hunger-strikers and condemned Serbian repression in Kosovo. In other words, Slovenia had shut itself out of the (South/Yugo)Slav alliance, had become de-Slavicised, Albanianised.

The deliberations were rounded off by an element that had been missing and without which the political message could not be completed. One personality is absent, although the participants had very much wanted to confront this person with some tough questions that were from the very beginning the motivation of the *happening of the people* and could at last be asked openly. These were above all, questions about the so-called AVNOJ (i.e. Tito) borders between the Yugoslav republics that Serbian populism never recognised. If, then, the unnamed but recognisable 'leader of the Partisans' were to appear, the Kosovo heroes Miloš Oblić and Milan Toplica would ask him a few short and sharp questions:

> *who has altered the Serbian borders*
> *who brothers dear divided*
> *who has sent the homeland to the devil.*

However, no matter what Tito might have answered, nothing would have changed. The council members had no more time for discussion with him, but only wanted to tell him bluntly where to get off, and then carry on with the job, for the decision had already been taken, regardless of any counter-arguments Tito might have used to justify having organised Yugoslavia as a federation and explain why just such borders were drawn between the federal units. At the beginning of 1989, militant and full of self-confidence, their idol, the new Karađorđe, had only just – from the rostrum of the Central Committee of the League of Communists of Yugoslavia, in his strongest apologia for lawlessness to date, as civil lawyers would say, or rather, for the concept of *heroic freedom*, as the inhabitants of *the countryside in the city* correctly understood him – given them carte blanche to run down anything that might get in their way 'institutionally, or non-institutionally, statutorily or non-statutorily, on the streets and inside, in populist or elitist ways, with good arguments or without them' (Milošević 1989: 333), convinced, together with them, that all the preliminary work had been done well:

> *of nobody is Serbia afraid.*
> *It has some good Slav backing*
> *when it wants to bend the borders.*

THREE

The Attack on Croatia

The haiduk *band, that scarecrow in human form that prevented the public traffic, repelled trade and eliminated all kinds of communication, is being warmed up for the commonalty in today's ominous times.*

(The mayor of Obrovac, northern Dalmatia, in a report to his superiors, 15 July 1878. (Peričić, 1991).)

Gathering of the band

It is hard to say whether the Radusinović-Šobić *prince of Serbia,* when he seated Matija Gubec so gallantly by his side and served him wine, was really thinking that he would be able to agree with him about *bending the borders,* especially at the expense of the *Turks,* or whether he was just buttering him up to lull him into a sense of security and gain time. It is easier to spot that in any event he miscalculated, because very soon nobody in Croatia would be asking Gubec about anything at all. Among the Croatian communists, the party that had for forty-five years respected him as the embodiment of the anational class struggle and Tito's symbolic forbear – for both had fought for the oppressed, and came, what is more, from the same region – it was the reformist trend of Ivica Račan that won the day, and at the end of the year in which Radusinović recorded the Šobić epic it announced multi-party elections, the first since World War II. Both they and the future electoral victor the HDZ, as well as the other newly-founded parties, like almost the whole Croatian public, had realised that Yugoslavia was historically defunct, that Milošević's pro-Yugoslav rhetoric, full of come-on phrases about a 'modern federation', national equality and the fight against all extremists, was just a mask behind which stood a reinvigorated Greater Serbian and Chetnik project, and that Croatia could be defended only by the establishment of democracy and strengthening statehood. For this reason it was impossible for there to be any continuance, even in the relations of the two political imaginaries, of that misalliance of the Croatian serf and the Serbian emperor (called upon for two years already in the cry from so many rallies: *We seek nothing new – only the Empire of Dušan!*).

The multi-party convocation of the Sabor [the Croatian parliament] met on 30 May 1990, and the president of the majority party, the newly elected president of the Presidency of the Socialist Republic of Croatia, Franjo Tuđman, gave a review of Croatian history in the preamble to his inaugural speech. He mentioned the crowning of King Tomislav and of Dmitar Zvonimir, rulers of the medieval Croatian kingdom at the time of its greatest power and territorial extent in the tenth and eleventh centuries, a deed of gift of King Petar Krešimir IV, from which it could be seen that the Croatian state as it was then had established its sovereignty over the eastern part of the Adriatic, after a long struggle with Byzantium and Venice. More particularly, he stated that 'during all these long centuries and during the trials of our history' it was the Sabor that had been 'the guardian of the sovereignty of the Croatian people vis-à-vis other nation states and state communities' (*Vjesnik*, 31 May 1990). This was too over-generalised and rather too historicist, but the fundamental message was accurate and it met the mood of the overwhelming mass of the Croatian public. In the months when Serbian propaganda denounced the Croats and the Slovenes as a Habsburg invention, 'Viennese grooms', and denied them any political or historical identity, it was not inappropriate to recall that Croatia had had its own legislature, and perfectly legitimate equivalents of the Serbian medieval kings, and that in contemporary times Croatia was just as much a state as Serbia was.

Two months later, the Sabor reinstated the Croatian national coat-of-arms on the Croatian flag, replacing the five-pointed red star that had ruled there up to then. Repeating *ad nauseam* the formula that this was the restoration of Ustasha insignia, propaganda coming from the Milošević-controlled Belgrade media, with material support from the JNA and organisational help from the pro-Serb and unitarist sections of the secret police, managed to convince a large section of the Serbian minority in Croatia that a pogrom was being prepared for it. The SDS, which had obstructed political life from the very beginning and systematically encouraged a lack of trust in the new government, finally started the process of *bending the borders*, long prepared from every point of view, including the symbolic and terminological.

At dawn on 17 August armed Serbs blocked the roads around Obrovac, Benkovac and elsewhere in northwest Dalmatia and southern Lika with felled tree trunks, logs, rocks and dumped soil, sometimes maltreating drivers in the vehicles they halted. Arms were hijacked from police depots, and JNA fighter-planes prevented two legal police helicopters from intervening. In Stara Pazova, Vojvodina, the SNO held a great rally in support of these actions and announced that volunteers would be going off to Knin. The Montenegrin NS did the same.

A week later, an extraordinary session of the Sabor was held in Zagreb. This was a moment at which – independently of the concepts used in newspaper reports and everyday talk – it was necessary not only to take up a legal and political position towards the events but also to give them a name stamped with the authority of government. The President of the Republic, Franjo Tuđman, and the Prime Minister, Stjepan Mesić, made introductory speeches at the session. What interests us here is the fact that they were identically structured: first of all an account of previous forms of Serbian obstruction of law and order, then a description of the process that indicated a transition to a qualitatively new type of obstruction, and finally a choice of term for this new quality. Both of them designated the previous phase by a term from a neutral civil service and legal style (or discourse), that is, *civil disobedience* (Tuđman) or *general civil disobedience* (Mesić), which then, when the barricades and the armed guards appeared *culminated* (Tuđman) or *escalated* (Mesić), once again in standard terms of political jargon, in *open rebellion, in what throughout the world and in international law is called terrorism,* as Tuđman put it, or *armed rebellion, sabotage, highway 'haidukery' and violence,* as Mesić phrased it (*Vjesnik*, 25 August 1990).

There were essential differences in the two accounts, however.

The first speaker used the terms *rebellion* and *terrorism*, which, as he said himself, belonged to internationally codified legal terminology, while the other used terms belonging to various areas: *armed rebellion, violence* and *sabotage*, also stylistically neutral, but the phrase *highway 'haidukery' (cestovna hajdučija)* consists of a non-affective attribute and a noun that is affective, stylistically marked, in relation not only to the attribute but also to the other items in the sequence.

The two speeches thus indicated not only the legal and political framework for the interpretation of the Knin events, but also the key terms for their designation. Considering the objective distribution of political power and the functional scheme of social communication, the lexical choice of the two leading speeches was an implicit instruction to delegates, and then to the whole Croatian public, as to the referential terminological code into which these events were to be put. In other words, this is an authoritative, exemplary text of how to organise appropriate linguistic behaviour with respect to a given semantic unit (the theme). Potentially, each of the five terms figures before later speakers as a completely equal *indicative word* for further semantic motivation of their personal discourse, and also for the creation of verbal density in the collective, national discourse, including the news media. Thanks to this density, the discourse became a normative style within which understanding was based on the clarity of a typical linguistic field, or of its components (cf. Suško 1974).

From this point of view, although they are formally equal, the five terms form two groups: on the one hand there are *terrorism, rebellion, sabotage* and *violence*, which are non-affective, and on the other *'haidukery'*, which is affective. For each word is surrounded by a network of mental associations that link it to other words, with which it creates a single associative field or paradigmatic sequence, and then, through his choice of the indicative words, each speaker creates an axis of associations, which seeks to connect with cognate lexical items and exclude disparate ones, thereby creating its own kind of verbal density.

The introductory speakers did this according to their own internal motivation. Those who later joined in the communication did so under the influence of their own choices, and henceforth in Croatian discourse there would be two terminological sequences. The elements of each person's expression were objectively lined up either with the neutral, civil law, or with the evocative, traditional glossary. Most of the members spoke in the debate about *terrorists, extremists, insurgents (odmetnici)* and *rebels (pobunjenici)*, that is, they remained within stylistically unmarked discourse. However, there were some, like Milivoj Franić (HDZ), who referred to *'haiduks* on the roads', or in newspaper commentary their *harami baši* [chief of a *haiduk* band] Milan Babić (Vojko Mirković, *Slobodna Dalmacija*, 25 August 1990), that is, they adopted and continued to promote the traditional terminology.

In the following few months the discourse of the Croatian political elite and the news media stabilised on a neutral stylistic level, for in some important places the barricades had been temporarily lifted, and a significant section of the Serb minority in Croatia was still uncommitted. At that moment it might have seemed that a peaceful outcome to the crisis was not impossible. But at the end of the year the harangues from Belgrade and the activities of the paramilitaries in Croatia showed this to be an illusion. President Tuđman spoke of it at the celebration of the anniversary of the creation of the Croatian anthem in Zelenjak, not far from his own birthplace. The music was composed, in 1846, by an Orthodox border officer, Josip Runjanin. Tuđman accordingly cited him as a patriot and loyal Croatian citizen who should be remembered by

> those who incited the Knin log revolution (*balvan-revolucija*), the Knin '*haidukery*' against the state of Croatia, against the Croatian people, [however] much it had to be admitted that the majority of the Serbian populace in Croatia did not go along with the Knin '*haidukery*' (*Vjesnik*, 30 December 1990).

Marked terminology appeared again systematically at the beginning of March the following year, once again from an authoritative source. The national news agency HINA announced that the arrest of the Kijevo local community chairman[1] was the 'most recent and the most ruthless act of '*haidukery*' to date in the already familiar Knin version of it', and the term '*haidukery*' (*hajdučija*) was deliberately placed in the title by the editor, who clearly recognised the powerful collocation and obvious value judgment in it (*Večernji list*, 5 March 1991). Towards the end of the month, at a press conference in Split, President Tuđman admitted that, for all his personal courage, he would not dare to go to Knin to be 'subjected there to '*haidukery*'' (*Vjesnik*, 29 March 1991). With the clash at Plitvice between the regular Croatian police and Milošević's self-styled SAO Krajina two days later, '*haidukery*' was finally established in Croatian political discourse as an explanatory term for the proceedings of the SDS and the rebellious, illegally armed section of the Serbian minority.

This term was, very largely spontaneously, sanctioned at all relevant points of public communication – in various types of newspaper account and in the statements of members of the political elite, whether given during an interview or as independent declarations or from the rostrum of the parliament, whether mediated as party communication, or with the status of a document such as the president's address to the nation.

This is confirmed above all by the different statements of the officials of state institutions that naturally have direct jurisdiction for such activities in every country – such as those of the Interior Ministry official Josip Boljkovac and Assistant Minister Slavko Degoricija – in *Vjesnik* and *Večernji list* on 1 and 2 April 1991. In a statement on HRTV on 2 May 1991, printed the following morning in all the dailies, President Tuđman spoke of 'rebellion and '*haidukery*'' and therefore also terrorism', while Stjepan Kljuić, President of the HDZ of Bosnia-Herzegovina and member of the Presidency of Bosnia-Herzegovina, called the same proceedings of the SDS of Bosnia-

---

1. A village 8 km from Knin, populated by Croats, surrounded by villages inhabited by Serbs, which was for this reason exposed to extremist violence.

Herzegovina 'the *'haidukery'* reigning in Eastern Herzegovina and the [Bosnian] Krajina' (*Vjesnik*, 16 June 1991). Communiqués from parties and associations in support of the authorities were read out on the television. They included references to 'these *haiduks*', by the Executive Committee of Croatian World War II Veterans, '*haiduk* actions of the Chetnik terrorists of Knin', by the municipal government of Slavonski Brod, Slavonia, 'Greater Serbian *'haidukery'* abetted by the Bolshevik part of the JNA', by the municipal government of Bjelovar, northern Croatia, 'the terrorist actions and *'haidukery'* of Martić's police', by the municipal committee of Benkovac HDZ, north-west Dalmatia, and so on.[1]

Although the non-affective terminology continued to dominate quantitatively, the affective term would be established as qualitatively equal, a parallel system that would keep constantly open the possibility for contemporary events to be understood through the semantic model of former conditions and with a strong imaginative resonance.

Naturally, the Serbian side was also faced with the need to select an indicative word from its own political angle and value judgment in order to describe the same events and to designate the actors. Thus a Belgrade fortnightly published an extensive report from 'the free territory of autonomous Knin', made up of a series of short, free-standing images that gave an anecdotal summary of the reporter's adventures while visiting the Serbian armed night watches. Each one deals with some national stereotype: Serbs speak one dialect, shot through with vernacular phraseology and the occasional curse, while the Croats are constantly inventing some impossible newfangled words that they often cannot get their own tongues round; the Serb *is glad to go to war*, is accustomed to arms and cleans his old rifle in front of his admiring children and grandchildren, while the Croat, terrified, leaps through the window of his house and runs headlong into the night when his Serb neighbour shoots into the air to celebrate the birth of his son.

There is one image that is meant to describe the typical manner in which the Serb joins a contemporary national or ethnic movement, and introduces to the reader the unnamed and hence symbolic soldier / loner who recognises no one's authority, needs no one's formal command. He responds to the call of his own profound internal memory, and sees in the act of going off to war the culmination of his existence to date, the fulfilment even of a kind of mission.

---

1. All in *Večernji list*, 3 April 1991. cf. newspaper commentaries: e.g. 'the *haiduk* attack of the self-styled Knin police' (Aleksandar Milošević, 'Plitvice', *Vjesnik*, 1 April 1991), 'the *'haidukery'* of the self-styled [authorities] of Knin' (Branko Tuđen: '[The noose has to be cut]', *Večernji list*, 1 May 1991); 'a *haiduk* surprise attack' (Vladimir Vuković: ['Hijacked, damned'], *Glasnik HDZ*, March 1991).

114

He kissed his grandchildren on their hair.
He rummaged in the stonework over the door. Took out a gun.
Cleaned off the grease.
'Wife, get the nosebag ready!'
'Oh, where are you going?'
'A-*haiduking*!'
'Have you gone mad?'
'I have waited all my life for it.'
'Are you sick?'
'This will heal me.'
He took his rifle, bread and bacon. He did not go to the HQ, or
to the watch. But alone. Into the mountain.
They only just found him, in Bukovica, and brought him back
home![1]

The political leaders set the imaginations of their audience off in the
same direction: when journalists asked Mirko Jović, president of the SNO
(Serbian People's Defence), whether the volunteers that the party was
organising and sending 'to defend the newly established western borders
of Serbia' were armed, he replied that 'the Serbs are competent *haiduks*,
and they will cope if need be' (*Vjesnik*, 16 April 1991). In a debate in the
Serbian parliament about the position of the Serbs in Croatia, the SPO
delegate Predrag Mijailović stated that 'one has to be proud of our *komitas*
[guerillas] and *haiduks*' who were defending the people there, in the Knin
region (*Politika*, 8 May 1991).

The most influential Serbian weekly had promoted '*haidukery*' as a
model of relations between the local Serbian population and the Croatian
government a few days before the actual blockading of the roads. Its journalist
stated that the Knin people had heard that ethnic Serbs in the Croatian police
force had not wanted to put on the new black uniforms with the Croatian
coat of arms instead of the red star, and had had the following dialogue with
the head of the Šibenik police, a Croat:

If you don't want what is offered you here, you are free to go into
'*haidukery*'.
Perhaps we will become *haiduks*. But not alone. Our whole
people will go with us.'[2]

---

1. Zoran Bogavac and Dragutin Spaić, ['Croatia in my heart'], *Svet*, 222, 17 October
1990.
2. Vasko Ivanović, Dragan Bećirević, (Mysterious guard), *Politika*, 13 August 1990. No
'new black uniforms' existed for the regular police, for this was an invention of Belgrade

These examples show that both the rival national discourses called the events and participants in them by the same name and recognised a recurrence, or continuity, of the same phenomenon – *the haiduk*, *'haidukery'*, setting of course different values upon it: in the Croatian case, consistently negative, in the Serbian positive. The opposition in values is not at all surprising considering the direct political, and already military, confrontation of the two communities and their political elites. However, more detailed analysis will reveal that many far deeper oppositions lie in the background, and that what is involved is not remotely what might be called rhetorical rivalry or terminological hair-splitting.

Haiduks *and their* yataks – *reality and romanticism*

...essi Haiduzzi ladri ed assassini ...

(Standard formulation in the complaints of the authorities of Dubrovnik to the Venetians about the attacks of the *haiduks*, Nazečić 1959)

You hound me, instead of doing the right thing, which would be hounding those who have stolen and flayed.

(From a letter from a *haiduk* on the Herzegovina-Dalmatia border to a representative of the authorities in 1829, Peričić 1991: 201).

The phenomenon of *'haidukery'*, or outlawry, in the Balkans in the Ottoman period cannot be considered apart from cognate phenomena in both a temporal and spatial perspective. On the one hand, it is a very ancient Balkan affair, with a continuity stretching from Illyrian and Thracian times, 'one of the Old Balkan highlander life forms, the traces of which go right on down to our own times, through a Slav layer of more than a thousand years, through all the political and cultural epochs.' (Dvorniković 1991: 362).

On the other hand, its context is also the epoch of 'classical' European brigandage from the fifteenth to the end of the eighteenth century. At that time, it became an institution in all those major land and sea areas in which

---

propaganda, to identify the new Croatian government with the Ustashas and their infamous Black Legion (cf. also an article by Željko Luburović [St Savan agitprop in the service of war] *Vjesnik*, 20 August 1990, where this account is discussed from a Croatian point of view. After having correctly retailed it, quoting *Politika*, Luburović, subjects the key term to irony: 'The devil won't be still, hardly a day had passed, but the Serbs went off to the *haiduks*. And what for? Because they wanted by force to resist the disarming of the police reservists through a parliamentary decision – and this is nothing more than armed rebellion – which every civilised country condemns through the criminal code.'

the Islamic and Christian worlds met and clashed, as well as in the similar situation that was created by the Swedish-Danish War, and among the rural masses all over the continent affected by wars, epidemics, economic crises and migrations. The frequently violent efforts of the authorities to collect military, administrative and fiscal contributions were a hindrance to commerce and encouraged the creation of private and illegal commercial networks, smuggling, in other words, in France of salt and tobacco, in England of tea. Before unification, fragmented Italy and Germany were an ideal space for the activities of armed bands – someone who had committed a crime or a theft in one petty state could in an instant take cover in another, its ruler often understanding his sovereignty as a means of refusing to extradite someone who had taken refuge on his territory (Bertoša 1989: 14–15, Hobsbawm 1978, 2000).

Poorly paid soldiers, impoverished bearers of feudal rights, peasants who watched helplessly as taxes and families grew and holdings and income fell, village notables threatened with decline on the social scale by new circumstances, all these

> saw in the state and its expensive and useless apparatus their main enemy which had distorted the traditional social balance and, above all, was endeavouring to alter the organisation of the space within which they had for centuries had ensured prestige, reliable defence points and a secure life. That is why in certain parts of Europe and in many social groups *banditry* appeared as a form of resistance to change, although this was not its only source. (Bertoša 1989: 16)

As elsewhere, in South Slav *'haidukery'* there was an interweaving of elements of highway robbery and a predatory economy, social resistance and a national political struggle, and it is not always easy to distinguish where one ends and the other begins, the more so since there are great differences with respect to its causes and forms in various areas. *'Haidukery'* was one thing in Serbia before the insurrection, and another after it. It was something else in Montenegro, and something else again in Bosnia, and different again in the broad hinterland from Zadar to Kotor, where the *haiduks* and *Uskoks* merged into a single type of warrior – who was now a highland *haiduk*, outlaw from the law of the Turkish land, now a Venetian *Uskok*, who did military service for his new master. *'Haidukery'* (*hajdukovanje*) was to an extent akin to fighting in the border bands (*četovanje*), with the difference that these bands were formed mainly at the instigation or at least with the

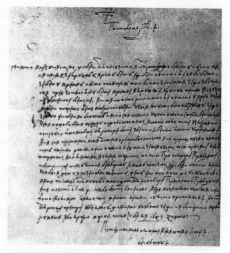

Stanislav Stanko Radović, alias Sočivica, the most famous Hercegovinian-Dalmatian *haiduk* of the eighteenth century, portrayed at the age of seventeen wearing cloth apparel and a fur cap in the Turkish style, pistol and scimitar at his belt, and a long musket (*diljka*) in his right hand. (Lovrić 1776)

Letter written on 29 June 1647 by Petar Kulišić, the most famous *harambaša* between the Cetina and the Neretva, demanding of the Dubrovnik authorities to free captive *haiduks* and return their plunder, since otherwise all *haiduks* would 'prepare honourably for combat and all honourably avenge our brethren'.

knowledge of the political authorities, while the *haiduks* were more or less independent, rebels against any authority at all, even though from time to time they too would work together with either the Venetians or the Turks, just as the soldiers from the border troop would in peaceful times desert and carry out attacks on their own account. The *Uskoks* actually differed from the *haiduks* only in that they lived outside the Turkish confines, and would make their attacks upon the Ottomans by 'jumping' (the name *Uskok* derives from the verb 'to jump in', *uskočiti*) into their regions.[1] Anyway, there too the

---

1. For an excellent historiographical study about the *Uskoks*, based on archival research, and with powerful social-anthropological and cultural/historical information, see Bracewell (1992). For *haiduks* in Bulgaria, see Cvetkova (1982), and for the *klephts* see Kolioupoulos 1987. These discussions also tell of the same dilemmas about the ethical and political evaluation of outlawry that are discussed in this chapter in connection with the Serbs, Croats and Bosniaks. Among works that deal with various types of outlaws, including *haiduks*, the greatest popularity was achieved by Hobsbawm (1979 and 2000). Hobsbawm must be credited with being the first in modern historiography to have drawn attention to this phenomenon; he minutely collected and systematised material from all over the world and from all periods. However, following the Marxist tradition of studying the exploitation of the

border zone 'was an integral part of what might be described as a system of checked and manipulated lawlessness' (Koliopoulos 1987: 319).

In addition, the manner in which the *haiduks* were organised and behaved differed from region to region. 'Classical' *'haidukery'* had a stable annual rhythm and a stable band composition, while in Montenegro, *'haidukery'* implied coming together if and when needed and splitting up when the need had passed, so the composition of the troop consequently changed. Sometimes, for larger operations, troops would combine into *haiduk* armies of 1,000 or 2,000 members, which had no hesitation in attacking large fortified cities. If in a given area there were several troops at work, a hierarchy would come into being among the *harami başis*. The most prominent of them would be gradually transformed into national leaders and carry on a wide correspondence. The richest would start to imitate the Turks, Venetians and the gentry in the coastal towns, building towers, buying estates and surrounding themselves with servants. Their descendants then gentrified themselves fully and added noble titles to their names (Samardžić 1972).

At the time of the decline of Ottoman power in the nineteenth century, 'the whole of Bosnia was swelling with *haiduks* like a loaf with yeast', as the Franciscan chronicler Grga Martić put it, and the authorities, particularly the local officials, often made pacts with them, either because they were powerless to control them, or in order to get some benefit for themselves.

The Ottoman authorities persecuted the *haiduks* with great severity. They would send out punitive expeditions against them, often with regular military formations, they took their families hostage; tortured and publicly executed, as an example, those they captured. But at the same time, they endeavoured to win them over, to include them at least to some extent in the regular structure of society. The interaction of various kinds of outlaws with the state is very important for determining the nature of their activities, motives and behaviour. For, 'although the state was clearly against them, it dealt with them in different ways' and one was 'to bargain over acceptance of government positions' (Barkey 1994: 181).

---

peasantry by the large agrarian state, he gave a very one-sided interpretation, fairly ideologised definitions, and presented one particular form of banditry as the essential form, i.e. social banditry. For a well-argued critique of Hobsbawm from the aspect of the complex and dynamic social and political structure of the Ottoman state from the mid-fifteenth to the end of the seventeenth century, see Barkey (1994: 178– 185), which includes references to other relevant works. Although her research was concentrated on western Anatolia, many of the social situations, the constellation of military and political power, relations between centre and periphery, the causes and results of outlawry, and hence the conclusions, also apply to the activity of the *haiduks* in the South Slav countries ruled by the Ottomans.

Since it was the roads that were the most dangerous, there was a two-fold effort to solve the problem. Sometimes the Turks would burn the forest on both sides to forestall *haiduk* ambushes. In Serbia, they gave the villages along the roads certain privileges, even their own village self-government, and armed them, so that in return they should keep watch against the *haiduks*. The results, however, were fairly ambiguous. In the seventeenth century, the same Orthodox border villages in Herzegovina, set up as an armed buffer zone with Dubrovnik and Venice, that provided pandours also gave rise to *haiduks*. Neither group did anything without clearing it with the other side, and together 'they were in sovereign control of [eastern] Herzegovina' (Sarmardžić 1952: 19). At the time of the Cretan War, 1645–1669, the *haiduks* created their own de facto state and 'forced tributes out of all the Vlach villages between the Ragusan border and Gacko' (Samardžić 1955: 189). In the second half of the nineteenth century the Austrian authorities in Lika faced the same problems: instead of working 'for the general security', the 'columnists' (*kolunaši*, members of the mobile troops that were founded to hunt down the *haiduks*) would make deals with the *haiduks*, who would often operate quite openly even in the vicinity of major settlements' (Peričić 1991: 197).[1]

Even earlier the Venetian government in Dalmatia had attempted to win over the *haiduks*, seeing that the officers from the karst area in its service would not and could not go against them without seriously offending the local people, which they were determined to avoid. Individuals, even whole families, would accept the official Venetian proposals and go over to the side of the authorities against the *haiduks*. At the beginning of the 18th century, the Rašković family obtained a profitable hereditary post at the border crossing at Grab in Strmica above Knin (Grgić 1958: 249). In Serbia, *haiduks* who voluntarily surrendered and obtained pardons would most commonly become pandours, 'for they had grown unused to working in the fields' (Karadžić 1898), and some of the Bosnian-Herzegovinan *haiduks*, after 1878, surrendered to the new Austro-Hungarian government, which

1. For this kind of collaboration, see also Nazečić (1951). Here it is very difficult to resist making connections with the events of 1990. A Zagreb journalist came back from Gračac, an eastern Lika area with a Serbian majority where the road blockades and paramilitaries had appeared at the same time as those in Knin area, fairly relieved because at the police station they had told him that there had 'been no major incidents' in the night of 17–18 August precisely because the 'police patrols had kept watch [on the highways] together with *haiduk* groups' (Darko Pavičić, 'Terrified and worn out from 'haidukery'', *Vjesnik*, 19 August 1990). The actual term *haiduk* here is clearly the journalist's, but this does not cancel out the news that the local police, composed of ethnic Serbs, were working with the irregular armed groups.

amnestied them. Amnesty was proclaimed by Dubrovnik too, for those of its subjects, mainly peasants from Konavle, who had joined the Herzegovinan *haiduks* in operations against the republic. In 1693, before being able to return home freely, such men had to serve a term in the fleet of the King of Spain, as a neutral side (Nazečić 1959: 111). The Ragusans sometimes hired certain *haiduks* to escort their caravans and protect them from the attacks of other *haiduks*, and it would seem that at the end of the eighteenth century they even founded their own band of *haiduks* around Popovo polje.

Some initiatives sprang from the fact that the *haiduks* had a fine reputation among the ordinary people, that, as E. Hobsbawm puts it, there is no banditry without legend, that 'the bandit is not only a man, but a symbol' (Hobsbawm 2000: 139), and that consequently *'haidukery'* could be reduced if the celebration of their exploits could be stopped. In 1729 it was suggested to the Austrian authorities that those who told admiring stories about the *haiduks* should be flogged, and if they persisted even put to death. At one time, the Ottoman government considered having all the *gusle* players killed. The authorities in the Principality of Serbia in the second half of the nineteenth century occasionally forbade *gusle* players from singing at public meetings about the exploits of the *haiduks* (Popović 1930: 112). In the first half of the eighteenth century in Syrmium the Austrian government raided taverns where *haiduks*, peasants and townspeople would all gather round the *gusle* players. It also worked together with the Orthodox Metropolitan of Karlowitz who anathematised the outlaws (Gavrilović 1986: 242), to no avail, as did the Dalmatian Orthodox Prince-Bishop Stefan in 1809, condemning the 'disobedient, the criminals, the bloodthirsty rebels, and the damned monk Stevan Dubajić' who had joined them (Peričić 1991: 190).

In parallel with the desperate position of the Christian common people, the *rayah*, who were driven into *'haidukery'* by poverty, the increasingly heavy taxes and the unrestrained reign of terror, especially of the undisciplined military units and the self-willed local Ottoman authorities, there were also increasing numbers of quite ordinary robbers. Sometimes the choice of victim did not at all depend on his riches or social status. There were Muslim *haiduks* who robbed only Christians, Orthodox who robbed only Catholics, Catholics who stole only from the Orthodox. But there were also examples of very efficient, as Tito would put it, *brotherhood and unity:* in the mid-nineteenth century in the Glamoč-Livno-Kupres triangle there was one trio of *haiduks* at work composed of one Muslim, one Orthodox Christian and one Catholic. (When they were granted amnesty, the first was taken into the government service, and the two Christians became gendarmes.) There

Lazar Škundrić, 'the last Lika *harambaša*', photographed at Gospić just prior to his death in 1901.

was a Catholic, Vid Marinčić, in the band of the Muslim *harami baši* Mujo Jelečković, while there were five Othodox *haiduks* serving under the Catholic Andrijica Šimić. He himself in turn started his '*haidukery*' in the band of the famed *harami baši* Jovo Kadijević, an Orthodox Christian from the Imotski village of Glavina.

There were also '*haidukettes*', not only Christian, but Muslim too, and some of them had songs sung of them as being bold and capable leaders of bands whom the men would respect and follow devotedly. In the first half of the eighteenth century, a certain Rabija led a band in the Bosanska Krajina, under the name Deli Ibrahim, until she was captured and hanged in public in Banja Luka. In more recent times, there was a *haiduk* band in Banija that raided as far as Zagreb and into Bosnia, led by Karolina Novosel, who dressed in man's clothing. She was captured near Velika Gorica in 1866, flogged in Petrinja, condemned to death and publicly hanged.

How complicated a phenomenon '*haidukery*' was may be seen from the group without which it was inconceivable, that is, the harbourers, *yataks*, the people with whom the *haiduks* spent the winter and who supplied them with food, informed them about patrols and looked after their loot. These were most often peasants, some acting out of fear of revenge, others because of family connections, but

> one need not rule out those who became *yataks* because they admired the acts of the brigands, the heroic ethic of the epic songs, and who, in that sorrowful time [Syrmium in the eighteenth century] sought their 'own glory', their 'pride' and revenge among the brigands, equating every rebel and outlaw with the *haiduk*,

avenger, fighter for justice, fighter against the rich, the powerful, fighter against authority (Gavrilović 1986: 242).

In Bosnia there were also *yataks* who were traders and monks, mainly Christians, but it was not unknown for the city 'Turks' to act as harbourers and to share in the loot, even respected Muslim houses such as the beys of Ljubović in Herzegovina (Popović 1930: 154). Just as friendship and blood-brotherhood between Christians and Muslims was not rare, practically every *haiduk* had some Muslim if not as *yatak* then at least as blood brother or trusted friend (Popović 1931: 38). They seized slaves from each other, yet they would also help each other during their sale, as is recorded in one traditional song, in which the Zadar governor reproaches two *harami başis* who were friendly with the Ottoman authorities: 'the whore and the hero met / you sell the Turks to the *giaours* / and the *giaours* around the land of the Turks' (Nazečić 1959: 151). The old habits remained even after the establishment of the new Venetian-Ottoman border on the Dinaric mountains at the beginning of the eighteenth century, which slowed down the introduction of the new system: traders sold *haiduk* booty for about a third of its real value, thus making vast profits (Pandžić 1979: 111).

In Serbia, *haiduks* operated right up until World War II as robbers,[1] but they were also hired as thugs to scare off competition in political struggles, and at every arrest great chains of *yataks* would be come to light, ranging from impoverished peasants to chairmen of municipalities. This situation prompted Vladimir Dvorniković to say that from a social point of view the real focus was not the problem of '*haidukery*' but of harbouring.

> There is something wrong in the mental and social attitude of the *yatak*. His feeling for the law, society and the state is wrong. In his soul he does not acknowledge these laws because they 'are not his' ... Just as in the old days he did not consider the *haiduk* who avenged him and thrashed the Turks a criminal, so too he does not now sense the criminal in the *haiduk*, not even where the worst cut-throat is concerned (Dvorniković 1991: 365).

Consequently, he believed that this kind of psychological, covert *haiduk* was more dangerous to society than the actual outlaw. Sometimes in accordance with the truth of history, sometimes in contrast to it, traditional

---

1. In Greece too some brigands survived until the end of the 1920s, but they were 'never more than hunted outlaws, survivors of an era that had come to an end' (Kolioupoulos 1987: 19).

songs and customs would systematically idealise the *haiduk* as the type of the hero who summoned up the strength to oppose the oppressor, and who was therefore above the ordinary man, and increasingly represented the unattainable, the impossible.

In a memo to the Venetian authorities in 1785, the Zadar lawyer Grgur Stratiko says that the people in the hinterland of the city glorified 'anyone who gave brilliant evidence of his strength, boldness and fearlessness'. If they died in a fight with the regular army, or if the authorities executed them, 'they were considered heroes and the victims of glory, which not even the disgrace of the scaffold could darken' (Grgić 1958). In his *Srpski rječnik (Serbian Dictionary)* of 1818 Vuk Karadžić admits that '*haiduks* did do ill to their own people' but nevertheless it was the greatest shame and mockery to them if they were called thieves or if they were said to attack the weak. An ethnographic questionnaire composed by Baltazar Bogišić in the second half of the nineteenth century shows that the people 'respected the *haiduks* as heroes because the *haiduk* never committed any crime among his own people'. They did not wish to betray him to the authorities, because for them the 'crimes of the *haiduk* and all others who risked their lives were a lesser sin before God and a lesser disgrace before people' than a crime committed randomly or by a betrayal of trust (Bogišić 1974). In Bukovica they did not think very highly of the *Boduls*, the seaboard folk, and yet if one of them killed a gendarme, whatever the reason or occasion, they would admire him. Vladimir Ardalić of Đevrske gives evidence that there, even after the disappearance of the *haiduks*, they still liked wearing the *haiduk* outfit and 'if anyone's dad or grandad was a *haiduk*, he would be proud and glad of it' (Ardalić 1899: 116).

The philosophy of life of the *haiduk*, the way he understood relations between people and attitudes to material goods, was given shape in harsh times of constant fighting and violence, in which a special ethic had developed. One of the essential elements was that money was to be acquired by force and by being exposed to danger. If money or any other good was acquired in this way, possession of it was legitimate and honest. This worldview is contained in the epic songs, in which there are often lines such as 'I won the weapons in the fight / I seized and did not steal them', and can be seen particularly clearly in the complaint of the *haiduk* Stanislav Sočivica, after he had been conned out of his stuff by a friend and relative:

> Is it right for two thieves to have tricked me out of it without any danger at all, everything that I acquired by force and putting myself in danger of my life? If they had attacked me on the road,

I wouldn't have minded ... But to steal like that, in confidence and with no danger, that's the worst kind of filching in the world, because you don't know who to guard yourself against (Lovrić 1948: 209).

However, the idealisation of the *haiduk* and his way of life, and the penetration, or insertion, of this kind of prettified picture into layers of society that were not otherwise in direct contact with the epic tradition is a complex process which can be reconstructed in its essentials through a comparison of songs recorded earlier and later and which came finally to an end in the atmosphere of the romantic worldview and the new nationalist ideologies in the second half of the nineteenth century.

The songs of the oldest collection, the Erlangen MS, from the 1700s, show a greater correlation with the facts in the records about the figures and events they describe, that is with a complex and not at all unambiguous reality: the *haiduks* had their own mutual accounts to settle, betrayal was no rarity, still less was cooperation with the Turks in the trade in Christian slaves. It was not only the caravans and the Turkish money convoys that were attacked, but Christians as well, even wedding groups 'and we all as one lay with the bride / and cut the head off the groom,' as one hero boasted. Battles were 'very often connected with loot, and far less with some heroic or romantic exploit, a duel and the like' (Nazečić 1959: 150). The singers who narrated these songs 'without censorship or social control' to the anonymous transcriber, although 'not all and not equally', also knew of the moral stature of the defeated, of compassion, the relativity and transience of the fortunes of war and they acknowledged 'a kind of closeness and understanding between the historically embattled sides, which resulted from the fate they shared in common, some attacking and others defending the military border' (Krnjević 1980: 243).

In this collection there are no songs about the Battle of Kosovo, and more than half of those in which *haiduks* are the protagonists make no mention of the battles with the Turks and conscious sacrifice 'for the honoured cross and golden freedom'. A century later, in the Vuk Karadžić collection, three quarters of the *haiduk* and *Uskok* songs describe the struggle with the Turks. This 'certainly very obvious difference'

it seems to us, shows very clearly that the song was directed towards the current situation: if the struggle against the Turks was in the foreground of the people's life, then it was also in the foreground of the epic song. And even where, in the older songs, it was not entirely clear against whom the battle was being waged, the new song made it quite clear, identifying the Turks rather than some vague enemies. (Nazečić 1959: 180–181)

And it was precisely Vuk Karadžić's collection, which contained the vernacular singer's new view of the phenomenon of *'haidukery'* and a considerable degree of idealisation created in conditions when anti-Ottoman actions were increasing, that became a kind of canon of and basis for the cult of the *haiduk* in nineteenth century Serbia, and later in both Yugoslavias. This collection was the main source, and where Serbian editors were concerned, often the only source of examples for schoolbooks and popular anthologies. The later way of looking at the heroic epic, according to which it occupied an important place, like all traditional artefacts, in the context of its own national literature, derives from the fact that the same man, Vuk Karadžić, was both the founder of the Serbian standard language and modern national literature and at the same time the classical collector and publisher of the literary treasures of the common people. Thus vernacular poetry became 'the inviolable domain of literary and aesthetic evaluations, which was at quiet war with the approaches of students of folklore and ethnology' (Bošković-Stulli 1975: 148).

In addition to this, and inseparable from it, as collector, Karadžić participated in the shaping of the standards and value system of an ideal national culture and its ethnic borders. Anyone who makes any selection does this, of course, in line with certain criteria. However, Karadžić's criteria were not just literary and aesthetic, rather 'overtly nationalist and political' (Rihtman-Auguštin 1989: 90). In other words, he systematically stylised the material and promoted through it a deliberately planned political programme of national integration in which the romantically understood countryside was to be the ideal of the life of the nation. He did not describe the real situation, but rather furnished exemplary models that only ever existed as a romanticist utopia or fiction.

This kind of concept was powerfully manifested in the noisy celebration *Two Centuries of Vuk*, 1987, on the second centenary of his birth, when the Romantic conception of vernacular culture became the central content and main source of slogans of the *anti-bureaucratic revolution* and the *happening of the people* (nor is it irrelevant that this slogan was forged precisely by the scriptwriter of the TV series about Karadžić's life, the writer Milan Vitezović, at the million-strong rally at Belgrade's Ušće). The populist ideologues made first-rate use of an anniversary that really did have a major significance for Serbian history and cultural history, and through a barrage of ideologised media stories they were able to pass off a whole worldview as a model for the present. Inspired by this concept, the masses drew from it slogans and ideals, and recognised its exemplary characters. One of these, and a not unimportant one, was the archetypal epic *haiduk*, who went into outlawry in the 'green hills,' to take his revenge for injustice, to chastise the degenerate 'gentry' and renew the utopia of social harmony and equality.

It could be said that one important psychological aspect of the war was conditioned by the fact that it was precisely Vuk Karadžić's collections and the popular anthologies based on them that were the long-term foundation of the *haiduk* cult, and that they were also the matrix from which evocations in contemporary Serbian political discourse were derived. That is, the poetic (epic) idea of the hero, his epic character and the intellectual content of a given song are the most reliable way of determining its age, for this is the element that lies at its very core. The *haiduk*'s great self-confidence and his sense of being uncatchable, the high degree of hyperbole in the depictions of his physical strength, the facility with which he vanquishes in combat, the descriptions of the battles in which no resistance from the adversary is either seen or felt, scenes in which the Turk is harmless and comical, caricatured as a dull bully who can be easily cheated and made fun of – all these are features that reliably indicate the more recent origin of a given song (Organdžieva 1986). That is, they suggest that such songs were created precisely at a time when, consciously or not, their authors were starting to be influenced by at least the rudimentary workings of the nationalist ideologies and political agendas, when they were retreating from the complexity of real life and starting to stylise their knowledge in a one-sided way.

By using just these songs as their psychological-propaganda foundation, and convincing their target audience, in any case brought up on them, that every single one of them embodied an invincible *haiduk* such as the one depicted in the song 'Starina Novak and Headman Bogosav' ('Starina Novak i knez Bogosav') – one of the key metaphors in the aggression against Bosnia-Herzegovina – the creators of the Greater Serbian political imaginary at the end of the 1980s actually fatally deceived those whom they thrust into war, as well as themselves. Through such symbolic identification and psychologically suggestive interpretation they told them what an easy job awaited them in their militarily incompetent and stupid adversary, in the contemptible 'Jerry grooms and Turkish lackeys'. By suppressing in them any self-critical rationality they instilled in them a self-confidence of almost mythic proportions, only for this ostensibly impressive psychological structure to burst like a bubble at the first serious counter-strikes from the

Croatian Army [HV] and the AB-H [Army of Bosnia-Herzegovina].

For the traditional vernacular singer the main reasons for resorting to *'haidukery'* were the 'corvée', *kulluk* in its Turkish version, taxes and violence, as well as poverty, poor harvests, a rejected marriage proposal or simply love of such a way of life (Krstić 1984). Also not unimportant was the aspiration for fame, the desire to 'live in the songs', to be 'talked of in later times'. The long *haiduk* tradition in Lika is pithily caught in the phrase 'Nor mountain without wolves, nor Lika without *haiduks*'; in Herzegovina by 'Ivan-planina, *haiduk* legacy'; while in Bosnia the *haiduks* most often gathered around 'Romanija, the *haiduk* bride', from where the road led to Istanbul, as well as around Tarčin, where from as far back as the Middle Ages an important trade route had passed from Vrhbosna / Sarajevo to Dubrovnik.

As well as being the peasant's reaction to the intolerable reign of terror of the authorities or pure and simple brigandry, *'haidukery'* had a quite specific motivation in some periods and areas, which reveals all the diversity of the phenomenon. After the Battle of Mohacs in 1526 when the Bosnian frontier did to some extent stabilise, Sultan Suleiman stripped many peasants of privileges they had formerly had because they were in various forms part of the military machine – as *martolos* (irregular troops planted on the borders to weaken the neighbouring states with incessant looting and marauding), as *akincis* (irregular light cavalry troops that carried out incursions deep into enemy territory, without receiving pay and living off their loot), the *voynuks* (special units charged with foraging for the army on a campaign) and the *derbentcis* (men who guarded the passes and canyons). The *martolos* and the *voynuks* were the two basic branches of the army in Ottoman service in the South Slav lands, and were mainly Orthodox but occasionally also Catholic. On their return to the villages, reduced once again to *rayah*, with all their liabilities and burdens, they tended to run away and become *haiduks,* which was the easier course in that they already had weapons and had become unused to the life of the peasant (Nazečić 1959: 186–187).

There had been highway robbery throughout the Balkans before the Ottoman invasions, particularly along important roads, such as around Prijepolje and Plevlje, where the caravan route linked Niš with Kotor and Dubrovnik, and was later regularly taken by Dubrovnik envoys carrying their tribute to Istanbul. In Banat, Bačka, Srijem and Baranya, *haiduk* bands would attack boats ferrying grain along the Sava and Danube rivers. A particular feature of Ras/ Sandžak was that the highway *haiduks*, largely Vlach nomadic herders, came into contact with the mainly agrarian *haiduks* of the plains of Kosovo, Toplica and Macedonia (Hrabak 1979). In the 120 years since the Turks were driven south of the Sava until the time Prince Miloš Obrenović came to power in Serbia, *'haidukery'* in Srijem [Syrmia] passed through several phases. At first it benefitted from the fact that the military and civil authorities squabbled with each other, and some of the stronger bands ran real protection rackets, imposing taxes not only on traders and richer citizens but also on whole municipalities.[1] Towards the end, because of the proximity of insurrectionary Serbia, the *bećari*,[2] vagrants from all parts of the Balkans, flocked there – refugees and tramps from whom it was easy to form mixed bands ready to plunder on both sides of the Sava (Gavrilović 1986). In Slavonia in the second half of the nineteenth century, the main *haiduk* haunts were the mountain forests of Psunj, Papuk and Krndija, the basic reasons being poor harvests, the rebellion of the landless after the abolition of feudal servitude and the inflow of refugees from Bosnia, mainly herders, who found it hard to fit in to the life of the Slavonian arable farmers (Pavličević 1987).

In the north Dalmatian hinterland, from the mid-nineteenth century *'haidukery'* meant the resistance of the patriarchal social milieu to the processes of modernisation that had then started to penetrate from the coastal towns, as well as an expression of poverty and fear of press-gangs. Even in the 1890s, transport from Zagreb to Zadar through Obrovac was not secure (Obad 1990). In the Knin area, the *haiduk*s operated along the caravan routes that linked Bosnia and the coast through Strmica and Unište, as well as on the Lika border. In the first half of the nineteenth century, the authorities were given particular trouble by the *harami başi* Kojo Rašković, who twice set up strong bands that stole cattle, robbed travellers and took contributions in wine from tavern keepers (Peričić 1991). According to some estimates, in this area in the mid-nineteenth century, ninety-one *haiduk*s were driven out, arrested (often hanged) or killed in clashes with pursuers. *'Haidukery'* waned at the end of the century when, with the development of the roads, the caravan trade, the *haiduk*s' main target, declined, and a dense network of police stations was established (Obad 1985). In Bukovica, at the

---

1. Towards the end of the sixteenth century the Uskoks of Senj too would offer terms to the Orthodox villages in the Ottoman hinterland, 'promising not to raid them in return for tribute' (Bracewell 1992: 190). In the second half of the seventeenth century, in western Anatolia, larger bandit companies, even armies, were formed, and 'many of these bandits extorted money from the cities they stopped at', while 'some city dwellers chose to bargain with rebels and offer them large amounts of money to save their city from ransacking' (Barkey 1994: 199).
2. An unmarried unemployed youth, a kind of irregularly employed labourer, a South Slav expression created out of Turkish *bekâr*, whence *bétyar*, the Hungarian term for this social group on the other side of the border.

beginning of the twentieth century, villagers still had a vivid memory of the two last local *haiduk*s, Jovan Kutlača and Mitar Drača, the first as a violent 'real brigand' and the second as a man 'of a more noble temper' who 'robbed the rich and helped the poor', as the local population described them (Tresić-Pavičić 1906: 45). In addition, the collapse of the military border system unleashed destructive *haiduk* forces in large numbers in Banija and Kordun, as well as in Lika, which most often attacked the roads from Karlovac to the sea. On both sides of the border there were also Muslim *haiduk*s from the Cazin region (Roksandić 1988), where, according to the folk song, the last Banija *haiduk*s Mihajlo Tadić and Jovan Kalanja raided Bosnia where 'they took the sultan's purse / and gave to the poor Vlachs' (Begović 1986: 230).

The traditional songs found in the classical collections and anthologies of the nineteenth century do not generally make the distinction that the researcher, constantly hesitating between the data provided by the sources and the interpretation given by the popular song, wishes to indicate through the use of the attributes *good (dobra)* and *bad (loša)*, or *nice (lijepa)* and *nasty (ružna)* '*haidukery*' (Popović 1930: 1931). Sometimes the people themselves would indicate a hero worth celebrating by the word '*haiduk*', and a contemptible robber by the diminutive '*haidučić*' (Grgić 1958: 248), which in this context has a derogatory connotation. A Serbian historian who researched events on the Bosnian-Dalmatian or the Ottoman-Venetian border, uncritically adopting the idealised epic conception of the *haiduk* and the Uskok, says in the conclusion of one of his studies that during the Cretan War, that is, the mid-seventeenth century, in the hinterland of Boka and in Herzegovina a 'degradation of the *haiduk* struggle (*hajdučka borba*) into mere '*haidukery*' (*hajdučija*)' was noticeable, because the *haiduks* committed acts of violence also against the Christian population (Stanojević 1970: 471). Although it is not explicit, from such a formulation and the overall tone of the work it is clear that the *haiduk struggle* was supposed to indicate a highly ethical national-liberation resistance that even 'cemented the unity of Serb and Croat' (ibid. 470), while '*haidukery*' meant common or garden looting raids. The classical philologist and folklorist proposed an explicit tripartite conceptual classification in his comparative study of Yugoslav *haiduks* and Greek *klephts*. *Hajdukovanje* was supposed to be the *nomen actionis*, the neutral term for all forms of outlaw brigandage, and of the other two 'completely opposite terms', *hajdučija* and *hajduštvo*, the first was meant to indicate mere highway robbery while the second 'implied *haiduks* of high morality, protectors of the common people, worthy of the name of freedom fighter' (Stojanović 1984: 21).

But this is just an ideal theoretical possibility, hardly ever usable, for quite frequently both motives were inextricably intermingled in the same *haiduk* or the same band, there being periods in their activities in which either one feature or the other would dominate.

Outlawry and social marginalisation are too complex phenomena 'and have in both their breadth and depth grown too much into the tissue of society to be able to be moulded into the schematic fetters' of this or that phrase, remarked a researcher into conditions in Istria in the seventeenth and eighteenth centuries (Bertoša 1989: 19), and this applies in principle to other areas as well. And there is one other essential observation that goes beyond its original context: all outlaws in Istria, that is, those whom the Venetian government had condemned to exile 'became a part of the world of the marginal, but not all marginal people were criminals – not according to their nature, and not according to the crime of which they had been condemned' (ibid. 28). The Austrian government's severe and excessive penalties contributed directly to the flare-up of 'haidukery' on the Military Border (*Vojna krajina*) in the eighteenth century, where in more peaceful years the poor borderers attempted to set up a kind of border trade with Ottoman Bosnia. As soon as the peasant crossed the border without the special pass that he had a hard time getting, the authorities would proclaim him a military deserter, confiscate his property and drive out his whole family. And then, as a man without a home, he had no choice but to join the *haiduks* (Pandžić 1979).

The epic vernacular poetry, when read without prejudice or preconceived ideas, preserves traces of this complex reality in quite a few places and bears witness to the duality and heterogeneity of the *haiduk business*. Of course, such distinctions are not made – cannot be made, given their social objectives, varying status and political and ideological motivation – by the protagonists of the political discourse quoted and still to be quoted here. For them the *haiduk* was an immutably positive or negative figure.

From a general point of view, there is one more reason why many of the vernacular heroic songs do not pick out and do not condemn those *haiduks* who turned into common robbers. In its worldview, that is, every individual who went into the 'green hills (*gora zelena*)' was ipso facto opposed to all the institutions of the current social, economic and political system, that is, exceptional and worthy of respect, and all the more recent *haiduk* poems are linked by the idea of the inevitability of the struggle with an unjust system. Even when the outlaw was originally just an ordinary robber, whose victims included Turks, or Muslims to be more precise, this had the effect of procuring him the forgiveness of the people, their forgetfulness of things that were otherwise against their moral views – such as breaking up and robbing wedding parties – so that he was increasingly seen as a fighter against the Ottoman authorities (Organdžieva 1985, 1986; Nazečić 1959). One researcher into this phenomenon, using examples from the traditional songs, gives a survey of the gradations of the popular view about *haiduk* violence: *it is an evil – it is a necessary evil – it is the only solution* (Međeši 1988), although this does not in itself refute the observation that, on the other hand, 'such is the need for heroes and champions, that if there are no real ones, unsuitable candidates are pressed into service' (Hobsbawm 2000: 47). It is enough for them to have the courage required by their role, guile and perspicacity, and, of course, victory, but by the standards of the poor, the oppressed or people who are outraged for some other reason 'the mere capacity of the outlaw to survive against the combined forces of the rich and their jailers and policemen is victory enough' (ibid. 130).

For all the authorities, *'haidukery'* was nothing but robbery, a kind of banditry which was judged summarily, while in the eyes of the oppressed masses, the *haiduks* were in a way executors of public opinion, and to side with them was a matter of vengeance, social justice, resistance to the foreign oppressor and a spur to morality.

'Haidukery' was also steeped in rituals, which is not surprising when one bears in mind that, according to one interpretation, the *haiduks* inherited the position of the mythic hero and the sacred king, and for a very long time society would still continue to project onto them certain mythic characteristics. They had something of the omnipotence of the mythic hero: they were invulnerable, no bullet could kill them, they would turn into birds or wolves, they had certain parts of the bodies of animal-shaped deities, and brought the community various magical gains – a fertile year, health, progress (Matić 1976).

The *haiduks* spent the winter with their harbourers, *yataks*, and gathered together *when the hills went green*. This annual rhythm of *'haidukery'* was defined by the vernacular expression 'St George's – *haiduk* meeting, St Demeter's – *haiduk* parting'. These two feast days – the first on 6 May, the second on 8 November,[1] when people neither went out of doors nor received guests, were said by the people to be the 'heads of the house', vestiges of beliefs from the times when these days marked new phases of the year. Although

---

1. According to the Julian calendar, used by the Serbian and Montenegrin Orthodox Christians. The Catholic Mijat Tomić gave his band instructions according to the Gregorian calendar 'On St George's – which falls on 23 April, once again we shall meet, just as we shall part on the feast of St Demeter, which is celebrated on 26 October' (Horvatić 1982: 29).

modern warfare and in particular the German offensive in Serbia at the end of 1941 did not allow of the idea in the *haiduk* tradition of fighting 'from St George's to St Demeter's', the Partisan political commissars in Serbia had a lot of problems with the suggestions of their fighters, mainly peasant volunteers, that on St Demeter's they should split up into squads and overwinter in the villages until St George's (cf. Dedijer, 1981a). And in any case, during their conquests, the Ottoman sultans had usually stood the army down on the same day, 8 November, which was also in that culture traditionally understood as the start of winter.

Mirko Jović, president of the SNO [Serbian People's Defence], called a great Party Meeting at Oplenac, Central Serbia, on St George's Day 1990, and such rallies could be looked at as 'an extraordinary form of popular ritual' (Burke 1978: 203). The feast was proclaimed the patron saint day (*krsna slava*) of the party, and Jović made particular mention of the fact that the meeting was held 'on St George's, the *haiduk* meeting', which was appropriate, because 'the way things are, the Serbs will once again need Rudniks, Topolas and Ravna goras' (*Borba,* 7 May 1990; *Vjesnik* 7 May 1990).

These three places were connected with important events in recent Serbian history, and had highly symbolic meanings in the nationalist ideology. Mt Rudnik, a hundred or so kilometres south of Belgrade, was an important insurrectionary stronghold in the early nineteenth century; Topola was the village in which Karađorđe Petrović, the leader of the first Serbian insurrection of 1804, lived, and there, on Oplenac Hill, the Church of St George was erected, as the mausoleum of the Karađorđević dynasty; in World War II, Ravna gora was the HQ of the royalist and Chetnik movement. In the Ottoman period, all three areas were *haiduk* mustering places.

The first *haiduk* gathering after wintering was actually held somewhat earlier, on Lady Day, 7 April, when those present would agree on the real meeting for St George's. In the meantime, they had to get their weapons and equipment ready, confess and take communion, and for the last week to refrain from sexual intercourse 'if you want our trooping (*četovanje*) to go well and for us to return home safe and sound' (Vrčević 1890: 81). Many St George's Day customs – the slaughter of the sacrificial lamb, the gathering of plants, washing with spring water – derive from a pre-Christian cult of the forest gods, waters and animals. The cult flower was the lily of the valley (called *đurđica*, or George's plant), the first spring flower, symbol of light and purity, which was picked on the eve of St George's, woven into wreaths and placed on roofs and doors 'for it to be a flourishing year' (Čajkanović 1985: 271).

And it was actually on St George's Day in 1950 that in various parts of

Yugoslavia peasant revolts either broke out or were planned to break out because of forced purchases and the general regime of repression the peasantry was subject to: in Macedonia, in Banija (foiled), and the greatest among them – in the Cazin area of western Bosnia and in neighbouring parts of Kordun, Central Croatia. There were several Serbs in the leadership of the revolt, and several Croats joined in, but the vast majority were Muslim Bosniaks. But this had no effect on the ritual perception of the day of the uprising, because this popular feast-day was recognised by Muslims as well as by Orthodox and Catholics. These cases of traditional peasant revolt were not coordinated; rather, those taking part spontaneously adopted this traditionally powerfully marked day (Kržišnik-Bukić 1991).

The fact that the insurrections, although simultaneous, were not in any way linked organizationally bears witness to the power of the traditional memory that spontaneously links such decisions to certain dates. The Serbian anti-communist émigrés, mainly Chetniks, at once recognised the symbolic potential of these disturbances in Kordun, and in their discourse the disorders are always called the St George's Day Insurrection of the Serbs in Croatia. Local Chetniks and members of the regular ranks of the Knin and Banja Luka Corps of the JNA who took Kotor-Varoš on 11 June 1992 wore on their chests badges with lilies-of-the-valley, quite openly drawing on the *haiduk* tradition, while the fact that it was a badge 'which looked like the TO [regular Territorial Defence] insignia' suggests mass production, in other words well-prepared symbolism.[1] As Peter Burke points out, continuing the previously cited opinion, 'of course riots and rebellions are not just rituals; they are attempts at direct action, not symbolic action', but their instigators, leaders and participants 'employed ritual and symbol to legitimise their action' and the history of Early Modern Europe is full of examples when revolts, including massacres, 'took place on the occasion of major festivals' – the massacre in Basel on Shrove Tuesday 1357, and Londoners remembered 'the evil May Day' of 1517, which turned into a riot against foreigners, the great revolt of Catalonia began on the day of one of the greatest of Spanish festivals, Corpus Christi, etc (Burke 1978: 203–204).

It is, therefore, unrewarding to succumb to the temptation of linking the destruction of religious buildings to the symbolic days of the *haiduk* life, although in many cases ritual features have been recorded. If for no other reason, then because the Serbian paramilitary destroyed so many mosques and Catholic churches that there is hardly a day in the year on which there was no such act. For example, up to mid-1995, in the See of Banja Luka eighty-one

---

1. [They roasted the killers a lamb], *Behar*, 2, September–October 1992; evidence of an exiled Croat woman from the town, officially recorded in Zagreb on 25 July 1992.

churches, monasteries or rectories were knocked down, and in the area of the Mufti of Banja Luka, which covers more or less the same area, 205 mosques. But precisely in the example of Banja Luka there is good reason to take into account this additional element because the SDS and the JNA took power according to a plan, not meeting any resistance capable of delaying the capture and then sacking of a town or village. A Catholic church or a mosque was thus knocked down precisely at the time that the destroyer chose.

Of sixteen mosques in the town of Banja Luka, the two most famous, the oldest and most valuable – the Ferhadi and Arnaudi mosques – were the first to be destroyed with explosives, almost simultaneously, in the night between 6 and 7 May 1993. They were followed by all the others in sequence, up to 8 September of the same year. In 1995, on the night between 6 and 7 May, the great Catholic church on the hill in Petrićevac, which dominated the area, was blown up, and the Franciscan Monastery was set on fire. For this reason, it would seem, it may be concluded that these buildings, essential parts of the local architectural and urban identity, were destroyed ritually, that the attack on them was a kind of culminating point of the whole evocation of the *haiduk*-St George's Day symbolism in the Serbian great-state project. And even if it were not, the Banja Luka Bosniaks and Croats perceived the destruction within this frame of reference, as they were induced to do by the overall behaviour of their Serbian fellow citizens, primarily by the noisy celebration of St George's Day and the invocation of *haiduk* symbolism. And this certainly remains a relevant fact of psychological reality.[1]

The haiduk *criminal and the* haiduk *avenger*

'But is there any other cave in the vicinity?'
'There is down there, about a kilometre below the ruins of the castle. No one knows how long it is ... It's where the haiduks *sheltered.'*
'And you can tell us anything about the haiduks?'
'Who doesn't know about them? Who doesn't know about Mitar Drača and Jovan Kutlača?'
'Well tell us then.'
'Oh, haiduks, *like* haiduks, *until they'd done* haiduk*ing, and it got them hanged in Zadar.'*
(Tresić-Pavičić 1906: 44; conversation with a miller on the Kličevica brook, Bukovica)

When Mirko Jović, on behalf of the SNO, and Predrag Mijailović in the

---

1. cf. Amir Osmančević, [*Banja Luka – a time of vanishing*]. Zagreb, 1995: 76. Zvonimir Komarica: ['They can drive us out, but not drive us away for good'], *Vjesnik*, 6 June 1995.

Assembly of the Socialist Republic of Serbia described the sentries on the Knin barricades as *haiduk*s, it might perhaps appear to be some kind of external appropriation of terminology. But the words of the vice-chairman of the SDS, Dušan Zelembaba, in civilian life an X-ray specialist, who unlike his two compatriots from Serbia lived in the actual area and played a leading part in the local movement, show that what was involved was a complete and unique explanatory framework for an activity conceived of as complete and unique. His answer to a journalist's question about what was happening in Knin at the end of August 1990 and what his role in it was is thus extremely relevant:

> 'I came to Knin to help my Serbian people, and to defend myself. Because whenever someone attacks me, I shall defend myself as long as I can. But I won't attack anyone. And if you want my definition of Dr Zelembaba, I shall tell you: I am a *haiduk* in pursuit of *haiduk*s. My *'haidukery'* is louder.'
> 'Louder?'
> 'Louder ... is heard further of f ...'
> 'Do you think the people won't give back their weapons?'
> 'No, they won't. I don't know who the order [from the Croatian government that all illegally armed groups must be disarmed] applies to concretely ... I think that the order does not apply to the people. Let these gentlemen come and let them disarm the people.'[1]

Zelembaba's statement is based on a recognisable quote from Njegoš's *Mountain Wreath*. The Montenegrin Prince-Bishop and poet inherited his idea of *'haidukery'* from the patriarchal value system and promoted it in the context of the position of his country at the time. Although he would sometimes call *'haidukery'* 'disgraceful heroism', he always made sure to say, either in his own person or through his characters, that it was the Turks who taught the Montenegrins 'their *'haidukery'* and all their outrages'. His view about this kind of violence was put perhaps most pithily in the episode when Selim-Pasha tells the Montenegrins to submit peacefully to the stronger side and thus avoid casualties, and they retort that he could vanquish them only on the battlefield, but not with gifts and promises. Selim's envoy then calls Vuk Mićunović a 'self-willed infidel *haiduk*' who does not know how to behave with a vizier, to which he receives the answer:

Are we both not haiduks *of the mountains?*

1. Srdan Španović, ['Emperor Dušan and his county (interview with D. Zelembaba)'], *Start*, 574, 19 January 1991.

Of shackled slaves, he remains the haiduk,
A better one, surely, since he seized more.
I'm a haiduk *that hunts other* haiduks.
My 'haidukery' *is louder far.*
I don't lay waste to land or people,
But many of those evil tyrants
Have fallen on their face before me.[1]

Mićunović's admission that he is a *haiduk* has a dual meaning: it is a self-conscious declaration of belonging to the right side. But at the same time, he is accusing the government that its unreasonable violence has produced an equally violent response in the people. The Pasha was the *haiduk*-criminal who harried the powerless and was only better to the extent that he had the power to seize more, while Mićunović was the *haiduk*-freedom lover and the *haiduk*-avenger, a ruffian only to the extent that he had to persecute the 'fiery-hearted tyrant' and thus really ethically superior. In the play *Lažni car Šćepan Mali (The False Emperor Steven the Little)* Njegoš's tone is still more convincing, more direct, because 'haidukery' is justified not only by the oppressed but also by Mullah Hassan, who, although he is a member of the establishment, is nevertheless able to discern its injustice. While his interlocutor calls for a merciless settling of accounts with the Montenegrins, whom he sees as criminals to a man, Mullah Hassan shows understanding for their actions. It is true that they are criminals, but this is only half the truth. One has to be honest, and admit that they were driven to evil by the unjust and cruel Ottoman government, while

> *to do ill, defending himself from ill*
> *here there is no crime.*
> (Njegoš 1851: V, 178–182).

It has already been mentioned that the father of the murdered Branka Ðukić defended himself in court by reference to this episode (see page 58). Various Serbian politicians also used it as legitimation of the repression of the Albanians, the economic boycott of Slovenia and the armed aggression against Croatia and Bosnia-Herzegovina. This was done most systematically by Vuk Drašković, in Nova Pazova at the assembly of the SNO, the party that

---

1. cf. Njegoš's lines 1188–1195. The attribute 'louder' (*glasnija*) the 'haidukery' clearly confused the journalist talking with Zelembaba, because he understood it in its contemporary meaning, but the vice-chairman of the SDS explained it in the same way, and it would seem that he himself did not know the original significance. In the original, that is nineteenth-century meaning which is actually precisely quoted, louder would mean more human, fairer, more honest.

he then belonged to, when he openly announced:

> We have to start making lists of our enemies! We have to pay back
> every injury ... To do ill defending oneself against ill, there is no
> ill-doing here, as Njegoš advises and orders us! (*Start*, 548, 20
> January 1990).

It was just these lines that were chosen by a young theologian, D. Kalezić,
later Dean of Theology of the Serbian Orthodox Church in Karlowitz
(Srijemski Karlovci), who had since his student days dealt systematically
with a theological interpretation of Njegoš, in order to explain why the evil
that was perhaps done by 'a hero in his constant struggle against the evil in
the world' is nevertheless not seen that way. In his interpretation, 'a criminal
is, essentially, an abnormal creature: he commits unjust acts, because he has
lost the concept of justice; evil – for he has lost the concept of good'. For this
reason he 'must be made to see sense – even by force – and everyone is called
to do this, and it is considered a supreme duty' (Kalezić 1966: 62), or, put in
terms of Njegoš's words: 'the most sacred human duty'. For the communist
ideologue Dušan Nedeljković, in an interpretation that was supposed to
harmonise Njegoš's meaning with the new post-1945 ideological paradigm,
Mićunović's admission that he was a *haiduk* was a 'summons to open,
revolutionary struggle against all conquerors, plunderers and oppressors'
(Nedeljković 1973: 79).

The common people's consciousness sees that the world is unjust and
that society is in constant conflict, and provides various responses to this.
The ills and injustices of the world are not the consequences of mistakes in
the social order, rather in human nature, in the 'abnormality' of the criminal
mentioned by Kalezić. For this reason it is permissible to act against them
wherever and however one can. This kind of attitude is embodied in the
figure of the avenger, the *noble outlaw* who strikes at unjust and wealthy
individuals, and helps the poor and deprived, 'without trying to reform the
social system' (Burke 1978: 174). From this point of view Njegoš's literary
character Mićunović and the contemporary political leader Zelembaba were
noble outlaws, the first with respect to the Ottomans, and the second to the
contemporary government in Zagreb.

After these insights, it becomes clear that the two politically opposed
communities, Croatian and Serbian, and their political elites, found an
interpretation that has in formal terms precisely the same vocabulary in two
different legal systems and sets of experience, older and more extensive than the
contemporary conflict. For the phenomenon of *'haidukery'* exists in parallel in

history – as the past reconstructed by experts – and in tradition – as the past experienced by members of society. In principle, the protagonists of Croatian discourse took it from the first source, and the protagonists of Serbian from the second. In themselves, the two approaches are complete and, as systems of signs, if considered apart from their social and cultural context, equal.

There is something else that is equally clear, that is, that these two ways of understanding the past determine two ways of understanding national politics or national virtues. Nedjeljko Mihanović, HDZ, MP, later President of the Croatian Parliament, spoke at the beginning of 1993 in the church in Šestine, a Zagreb suburb, at a commemoration of Ante Starčević. On that occasion he described Starčević's political thinking as characterised by 'awareness of the country's identity as a state and its sovereignty', by the 'endeavour to raise Croatian reality to a higher level of thought', and in general rationalism, modernism and the logic of Cato, features compatible with European intellectual trends of the second half of the nineteenth century. He contrasted this with the 'chaotic and opaque Balkan Serbian-Bulgarian reality, in which everything at that time reeked of '*haidukery*', of irregulars, of terror, of vendetta' (Mihanović 1996: 206). But where the literary historian Mihanović sees a disgrace, possible only among the Serbs, entirely incompatible with the Croats, the Serbian novelist Dobrica Ćosić, ideologue of the contemporary Greater Serbian project, practically in the same profession as Mihanović but on the other side, sees the greatest virtue of the Serbian people. What is more, Serbian problems actually began when this virtue was in decline, except that, as he said in his Budva speech of 9 June 1989, it was a mystery to him how it could happen that 'a nation marked by revolts and '*haidukery*' could allow itself to be transformed in Yugoslavia into a 'subservient rabble' (Ćosić 1992: 244–245).

But three weeks later, in front of several hundred thousand enthusiastic people attending the commemoration of the sixth centenary of the Battle of Kosovo, his chief supporter Slobodan Milošević was to announce from the rostrum at Gazimestan that the Serbs 'were in the wars again, and facing wars. These are not armed wars, though such are not yet ruled out' (*Politika*, 29 June 1989). A year later, in no small part thanks to Ćosić – not to mention Milošević – rebellious '*haidukery*' returned in a big way.

But the story had only just begun, and confusion followed confusion. The next came when distinguished figures in the Serbian discourse started complaining about the names they had been called by Croats. At a rally in support of the Serbs in Croatia, in Kula, Bačka, the SDS Vice-Chairman Branko Marjanović, angrily picked out the term *haiduk*, among 'various insulting names' which the Croatian government had used to refer to the

Serbs (*Politika ekspres,* 10 February 1991). A Benkovac man, Dušan Starević, chairman of the Prosvjeta Serb Cultural Association, pedantically listed to a Belgrade journalist 'the monstrous dictionary of evil': sixty 'words of untruth and defamation' used by the Croatian media and politicians in connection with the events in Knin, which included *haiduks* and *'haidukery'* (*Politika ekspres,* 14 May 1991). The president of the local government in Knin, Risto Matković, went so far as to send the Internal Affairs Minister Boljkovac in Zagreb a letter in which he mentioned *haiduks,* as one of the impermissible 'epithets for the Serbian people' (*Vjesnik,* 23 May 1991). While the protest against terms such as *terrorists* and *extremists,* and especially *bandits* and *highway robbers,* can be understood, the inclusion of *haiduks* is confusing, because that is exactly how those involved in the Serbian movement presented themselves, with unconcealed pride, and through the mouths of their most prominent protagonists.

In part, this misunderstanding can be explained through Njegoš. When he heard that the Skodar vizier, a Bosnian, called the Montenegrins *haiduks,* in a pejorative sense, he replied to him that 'this name is not in the least disgraceful' because '*haiduk* means Chevalier (Ritter)', knight in other words, and that it applied not only to Karađorđe and Kraljević Marko, but also to the vizier's countryman Alija Đerzelez, the greatest Bosniak Muslim epic hero (Krnjević 1980: 215). Vuk Karadžić too, writing about the Serbian insurrections, suggested that those who called the South Slavs *haiduks* should in German use the word *Helden,* heroes, and not *Räuber,* robbers (Karadžić 1947: 37).

However, another example of terminological dispute is historically closer and the more interesting in that it came into being precisely where evocations of *'haidukery'* were being powerfully renewed in 1990–1991. The Kordun Serbian partisan poem 'Samovolja Rade' (Opačić 1971) speaks of a bold and praiseworthy but headstrong combatant, prone to act individually, whom the political commissar decided to penalise for this kind of behaviour. To the commissar's explanation that

> *we are no band of* haiduks,
> *self-willed highway robbers,*
> *rather fighters led by the Party*

one soldier protested, because only

> *tyrants of all flavours*
> *set us down as highway robbers,*

not wishing to see the difference between robbery and *'haidukery'.* And then he went on to explain to the commissar:

> *You've got something mixed up, brother,*
> *And have insulted us all a bit.*
> *Don't hang robbery around our necks,*
> *And don't mix* haiduks *up with them ...*
> *This is not some peaceful Pauria,*
> *Rather the bloodstained Krajina.*[1]

In the face of the oppression of the one-time Ottoman viziers, agas and beys, then the Krajina *Jerry sergeants*

> *whoever had a bit of heart and brain*
> *then went as outlaw to the mountain*
> *as we are doing today,*

for now too, in the Third Reich, or the NDH, the common people, the *rayah*, were suffering once again under the state *zulüm*, the Turkish word for reign of terror. For this reason the soldier proudly finishes his moral lesson:

> *Now our Partisan troops*
> *Tramp the same damned mountains.*
> *Once the Turks, and now the Hitlerians*
> *The same hunters of men.*
> *We are outlaws from the state*
> *as once the* haiduks *in the mountains.*
> *These our woeful canyons,*
> *are always the champions of freedom ...*
> *No wonder that the foe is angry,*
> *When we have stopped his roads*
> *Around Kordun, Banija and Lika,*
> *And they call us highway robbers.*
> *But our people long since knew:*
> *Woe to him the enemy lauds.*

---

1. Pauria is an imaginary land – and northern parts of the then Croatia under civil administration as well – where the land is tilled in peace (from *paur*, Germ. *Bauer*, farmer, peasant). Here it is nice to recall how the poet and essayist A. G. Matoš contrasted the temperament and manner of political operation of the two leading Croatian politicians of the second half of the nineteenth century: Ante Starčević was 'a rampart mountain, closed, full of wolves and Lika *haiduks*', while J. J. Strossmayer was 'a soft and rich Slavonian plain' (Matoš, Collected Works, IV, 25–26). In other words, they embodied Krajina and Pauria respectively.

Marjanović, Starević and Matković are today then actually saying what this combatant said to the commissar: yes, we are *haiduks*, but not in the sense a tyrannical government, no matter whose, understands it, or ignoramuses like the commissar who always 'get things mixed up', as bandits in other words. We are *haiduks* the way we understand it ourselves, based on our experience and traditional value system: that is to say, fighters against oppression, freedom lovers and righteous avengers. The *haiduk*, as he says of himself in one of the epic songs, does not attack 'the shepherds in the hills' and does not rob 'the countryman in the country' but 'robs the city dweller in the town / who robs the countryman in the country' (Andrić 1939: 126). This was exactly Dušan Zelembaba's explanation to the journalist using two parallel discourses: in the contemporary vocabulary in that call to the 'gentlemen' to come and disarm 'the people' if they dared, and in the traditional vocabulary through the evocation of the literary model of Njegoš. That this was no simple accidental, one-off occurrence was shown at the same time, with the same quote from Njegoš, in a signed article in another paper by Petar Štikovac, from the leadership of the SDS, a teacher by trade, responsible in the party for cultural affairs: the Serbs in Croatia don't wish to be 'subjects of the Ustasha junta' Tuđman-Špegelj-Boljkovac, and when their freedom is jeopardised, then they 'are bolder than the *haiduk*, for they themselves are '*haiduks* who pursue *haiduks*'.[1]

And this is precisely the point where the short-circuit occurs. The newspaper commentator Joža Vlahović was perhaps the only figure in Croatian public discourse to have sensed this relatively early on. Seven and a half months after the first barricades went up, and only two days before the Plitvice conflict, when the first Croatian policeman was killed, he was protesting about the activities of the 'bandits' that the police forces of European countries registered as 'dangerous and undesirable criminals' and their own children were ashamed of. In the peroration he asked whether they 'were at all aware that they were terrorists? They very likely imagine that they are some kind of heroes, worthy men or at least *haiduks*' (*Vjesnik*, 30/31 March 1991).

The assumption was, as we have seen, quite accurate, with the proviso that the words 'heroes or at least *haiduks*' was expressly corrected by Zelembaba into 'heroes, that is, *haiduks*', because in the conception he was putting forward and by which he was inspired, the hero was a man of the people who responded to every act of injustice. 'Psychologically understood, he never attacks: he never comes across as a highwayman, greedy for booty, but always

---

1. Petar Štikovac, ['Looking into turbid water'], *Duga*, 443, 16 February 1991.

as defender, either of himself or of someone else – in each case he acts in defence of violated justice', as the theologian explained (Kalezić 1966: 61).

In Croatian discourse, just as in the case of the Partisan commissar, there were two juxtaposed terminological sequences. *'Haidukery'* very often appeared in phrases that in various different ways linked it or identified it with banditry or, in more contemporary terms, with terrorism. Phrases of the kind *'haiduk* terrorism' do not allow for any possible semantic distancing and there is thus no doubt what value the speaker places on the activities of the *haiduks*. Put more picturesquely, the Croats speak as though they were reading the Ottoman, Venetian, Austrian or Ragusan state records, where the *haiduks* are ruthless looters, sometimes a mercenary army, mainly ruffians who reject every human law. Official Venetian discourse called them *banditi*, in the Military Border they were *Räuber*, in northwest Croatia the Hungarian loan word *tolvaj* (thief, crook) was used, and in Latin sources the terms are *latrones* or *praedones* (Pandžić 1979: 108), meaning 'robbers, bandits'. The Serbs use the categories of vernacular tradition, where everything is the other way round: the *haiduks* are 'the subject of popular history', and if they are not present in some period, that can only mean one thing – that the people agreed to submit, that they had become so tame and wretched 'that their white teeth no longer showed' (Begović 1986: 230).

For this reason the terminological conflict may also be seen as a surface-level manifestation of a deeper social and historical conflict between codified and customary law, between legality and legitimacy. The Serbian protests do not refer to the term itself, rather to the type of discourse, which derives from a worldview in which the term has negative connotations. They subject to criticism the culturally and historically shaped and ideologically and politically conditioned communicational context in which *'haidukery'* is identified, directly or indirectly, with brigandage rather than with the right of a free man to have the world arranged according to his own measure. When one takes into account this kind of deep-level intonation of the Serbian political movement and psychological profiling of its leaders, it becomes still more evident that the conflict in the early, unarmed phase could not have been settled productively in the categories of modern legal and political theory and that it was not exacerbated by offensive statements of members by the Croatian political elite, however worthy of condemnation. The Serbian side had determined its internal logic and its perceptual and cognitive categories, even while the rigid pro-Yugoslav communists were still in power in Zagreb, and when the overwhelming majority of the Croatian public – not to mention the Bosniaks – were watching television broadcasts of the 'happening of the people' in fear and bewilderment.

After August 1990, the protagonists of Croatian discourse spoke from the perspective of backing up state authority which was in principle considered lawful and legitimate, *ours*. The protagonists of Serbian discourse, meanwhile, participated in communication from a perspective that denied that same authority, held it in principle to be unlawful and foreign, illegitimate and alien. Possible individual objections in the first case, or qualities in the second, do not cast doubt upon these fundamental points of view, as is shown by the answer of the leader of the Sinj Croatian Party of State Right (HSP), Luka Bitunjac, to the HDZ accusation that the HSP did not respect the rules of democracy: 'We are not *haiduks*. We are state builders, we are a parliamentary party that is ready for talks' (*Vjesnik*, 28 December 1992).

Not to be, and not to want to be, a *haiduk* means to be for the state, regardless of what one thinks of a particular party or an individual in power. To be a *haiduk* means to be without hesitation against the state. To put into practice, in reality or in words, the appropriate epic formula means symbolically to declare oneself a political Serb. This is particularly clear in the case of an individual such as the writer Iso Kalač, who comes from a historical and cultural circle that was unacceptable. He described himself as a 'Serb of Islamic spirituality' and supported Milošević's policy with respect to Bosnia-Herzegovina and sought not only declaratively but also substantially to overcome or annul his being a *Turkish convert*, as something accidental. In order to present himself as a true Serb in a substantial, almost predestined, manner, Kalač likened his moving from Sarajevo to Montenegro only a little before the Greater Serbian aggression to plunging into an archetypal situation, 'going off to the *haiduks* on St George's Day' (*Vjesnik*, 4 November 1991).

There are even more telling examples in the writings of Milan J. Četnik, journalist of Radio Knin and correspondent of *Politika* and other Belgrade papers. This young political science graduate (his degree adds additional spice) regularly reported on the events in his area, the self-styled Republic of Srpska Krajina, and after the war collected his articles in a book, where his terminology can be more precisely analysed. As might be expected, he too was angry and insulted when, in November 1990, the Croatian vice-president Vrdoljak called the illegal vigilantes on the roads by the same name that other members of the Croatian political elite had used, claiming that this was 'a poor and incomplete picture' aimed at 'foisting onto Knin a caricature about *'haidukery*'. At the same time the journalist himself used this very term for the leaders of the revolt and members of the armed units. However, his usage had a markedly positive and traditionally permissible meaning, for they had risen up against the Croatian government. The leaders were 'the last generation of Serbian *haiduks*', 'real Krajina *haiduks*' who despised the 'wretched scribblers' mise-en-scenes' (i.e. the negotiations with Zagreb offered by the international mediators). The 'sources of defiance and insurrection were in the villages', those 'reservoirs of the *haiduk* spirit and the epic tradition', the 'Serbian *haiduks* chased off the Croatian police like a covey of partridges', the surroundings of Knin were full of the traces of the 'Serbian blue-blooded *haiduks*' and so on (Četnik 1997: 133–134, 167, 168, 177).

And then, suddenly, in a report for *Politika* on 26 October 1992, he mentions certain unpleasant circumstances in the area of the RSK: looting, arson, theft and murder, and then describes a specific case:

> One classic case of *'haidukery'* is recorded. A few days ago (somewhere on the boundaries of the Knin and Grahovo municipalities), in broad daylight, two hooded men halted the car of senior officials of the Krajina Defence Ministry, beat them up and robbed them (Četnik 1997: 113).

Croatian politicians and the public had from the outset called masked men who attacked cars and robbed travellers *haiduks*, and the same journalist was then angry, because for him it was inaccurate and insulting, since the *haiduk* was an exemplary figure. Yet now he was calling them *haiduks* himself, in a context in which it was clear that he thoroughly condemned them. There is one key difference, however: as long as the armed Serbs were undermining the alien, Croatian government, they were *haiduks* as freedom fighters. In the second case, they were undermining their own state, the Krajina, and the term *haiduk* was translated as robber and bandit. In other words the Knin journalist was here drawing on the Austrian, Venetian and Ragusan state archives, without realising it.

Simultaneously, from the outset – for it could not have been otherwise – Serbian discourse linked another group of evocations with the figure of the *haiduk*. And it is only in this interaction that the presentation of contemporary political relations on the template of traditional memory can be fully formed. As soon as there is a *haiduk*, there has to be his opponent, in order for the totality and authenticity of the authentic historical situation evoked to be reproduced terminologically. The implied and contextually recognisable 'evil state' must be made explicit at the same level, in a parallel terminological series, which means that the semantic void has to be filled with terms from the social and political life of *haiduk* times, above all military and administrative life, for it is these spheres that can give rise to state violence against the people.

Thus one report in a Belgrade paper about a current ideological dispute among the communists of Bosnia-Herzegovina is a real throw-back to that time, conveying a mood of pre-insurrectionary tension: from Sarajevo, although the 'Ottoman Empire vanished a century ago', the *agas* and *beys*, even the *grand vizier*, that is a member of the Central Committee of the League of Communists of Bosnia-Herzegovina, came on the 'well-trodden road' to Banja Luka, 'city of the wretched *rayah* in revolt', *firmans* were even written, and the silken cord (*gaytan*) was sent out against the disobedient, i.e. against the Serbs in the leadership of the Communist Party who did not agree with the views of the Bosniaks in the same leadership.[1]

Nothing stopped the second aspect of traditional culture, its other core motivation – revolt against the upper-classes (*gospoda*) – being used as an evocational template for Yugoslav discourse. In their own regions, Serbian and Montenegrin Partisan and communist leaders found ways of evoking anti-Ottoman epic motifs, more or less modified. Meanwhile, the Croatian and Slovene leaders, in line with their own local traditions, privileged the second group of motifs – feudal peasant revolts. Evocations of both aspects were bolstered, in addition to the mere fact that the vernacular culture was effectively alive, by nature itself, that is the geography of World War II, particularly in the first two years, when the chief operations were carried out in the mountainous regions of Croatia and Bosnia-Herzegovina. The insurgents, that is the Partisans, operated in the hills and the countryside, and their adversaries, 'the Turkish gluttons' and the 'glittering *gentry*' alike, were holed up in the cities, from where they sent out punitive expeditions and directed military operations.

As a structure, this reproduced the spatial relationship deeply inscribed into the traditional texts, whether Višnjić's 'Beginning of the Revolt', where the usurpers, *dayis*, had their seats in the towns, setting out from there to cut down the Serbian village headmen because the '*rayah* was the real master of the cities' (having control of food supplies), or the tradition of the peasant and popular revolts, where the peasants rose up against the castles of the lords. It was this attitude that was preserved in an article by Jakov Blažević, a long-term member of the communist political elite in Croatia, when he expressed his support for the pro-Milošević rally against the agricultural policy of the Belgrade federal government. Such peasant rallies, he wrote, 'enrage those whom the people keep disturbing beneath the windows of their bureaucratic towers', 'day after day the working people are going out onto

1. Rajko Đurđević, ['No way, but there is Neum'], *Duga*, 411, 25 November 1989.

the streets all round the country', that is the people were coming together 'to drive the power-holders from the windows of their bureaucratic towers. 'Burn and blaze Mujo of Udbina, your tower too will see its end'. (*Vjesnik*, 30 August 1989).

The lexeme *tower, kula* in the original, evokes at the same time both peasant revolts and the heroic-*haiduk* epic, where this is perhaps the most frequently mentioned building. The 'tower', a typical term in the vernacular poetry for any kind of substantial building, is accompanied by fixed epithets such as *tall, slender, white,* all conveying the sense of admiration with which the common man looked upon this tall, frequently mysterious building on an eminence, dominating the region, and mostly inaccessible to him. The tower, as seat of the Christian heroes who met in it and set out for action from it, and also the residence of the alien master, was therefore the target of *haiduk* and insurrectionary attacks. Towers are always rich and, along with weapons, horses and robes, the most impressive manifestation of power and social position. They always contain an abundance of treasure, of *scintillating sequins* and *golden ducats,* while the captive will frequently promise to give so many *towers of treasure* in exchange for his freedom. Hence the vernacular poet quite often does not aim at any realistic description of a specific tower, rather 'cares more to create a vivid and plastic image that will work powerfully upon the emotions of the listeners' (Mimica 1988: 132–133).

Given all of this, Blažević's image of the insurrectionary peasants in front of the strong towers is powerfully evocative, founded on the suggestion of a topos from the vernacular consciousness. It is actually a reworking of the extremely common formula of communist discourse concerning the 'towers and fortresses of bureaucracy', that is, the seats of foreign, aristocratic rule, or the 'towers of alienated capital', where the dominant idea is of a mysterious place full of inaccessible treasure, also easily readable in the traditional expressive repertoire.

In parallel with, or complementary to, Blažević's image of the peasant revolt is the image that one Belgrade reporter built on the foundation of a series of protest meetings in Nevesinje, the reasons for which were alleged to be a series of embezzlements of funds meant for victims of the earthquake. The reporter used these pro-Milošević public gatherings of the Serbian population of eastern Herzegovina as a spur for the construction of a metaphor still more complex and suggestive than Blažević's. His description of the way they came together reconstructs the archetypal situation of the siege of a fortress.

The demonstrators, 'the naked *rayah*', 'dashed at' the town hall, seeking 'justice and freedom', but in vain, for the authorities were protected behind 'the walls of their towers (*kula*)' where they 'sat on the sofas of their new duties'. The spirit of the debate held in the Central Committee of Bosnia Herzegovina in Sarajevo a few days earlier is suggested by the author in the words that he puts into the mouths of its members, Bosniaks: *besbelli*, naturally, and *vallah*, of course, or by the Lord.[1] These, like the 'sofas', originally *sećija*, from the Turkish *seki*, have a wide range of cultural, historical and political connotations. For every averagely educated recipient of the message they have the associative power to suggest the centuries of Ottoman rule. They are a linguistic device for the recreation of atmospheric colouring and are hence used in the same way that elsewhere, for example, it was rhetorically asked what was 'heralded' (using the word *telal*, meaning a Turkish town crier) at the session of the local communist committee in Srebrenica (*Intervju*, 220, 10 November 1989). Politicians who criticised the proceedings of the Knin Serbs were said to be the 'heralds' (*telali*) of the Croatian government (*Duga*, 429, 4 August 1990). This Bosnian lexical provincialism, Turkish-derived, contains not only the denotative information about news having been disseminated, but also, connotatively, conveys the additional suggestion that the news is spread, shouted aloud, in a disgusting and ugly way, and, moreover, that the one giving the information does so at the order of the government, as its lackey.

All these Ottomanisms indicate a frivolous and contemptuous attitude on the part of the government to the demands of the people from Nevesinje. The frequency of the Turkish linguistic elements, as well as the hints at the interiors of traditional Muslim houses, suggest a merging and identification of two realities. The people of Nevesinje are not just *like* the one-time Christian *rayah*, but they *are* the *rayah*, just as the government is not just *like* the former Turkish government, but it *is* Turkish. Its endeavours to hush up the embezzlement and the abuse of power failed miserably for the same reason that similar attempts by the former authorities, identical from the point of view of religion and culture, also failed because the '*rayah* got to hear of it and started to revolt and rebel all over *dünyaliks* and *beyliks*[2] – the first term meaning the world, the whole country, and the latter the bey's estate. Both, of course, clearly reconstruct the Ottoman administration and suggest that nothing much has changed over the centuries.

As might be expected in political discourse, the most frequent terms are those that evoke social relations: members of the political elites and leading

---

1. Rajko Đurđević, ['Testing out the national nerves'], *Duga*, 404, 19 August 1989.
2. ibid.

figures in the administration in general are given the attributes of *aga* (big landowner), *bey* (noble, both a civilian and military title in the Ottoman organisation), *pasha* (dignitary with the rank of general) and *subaşi* (steward, bailiff on the estates of beys and agas). Then come terms from the administrative and military organisation of this hated state: *beylerbey* (supreme military and civilian commander of a major district), *vali* (governor of a province, *viláyet*), *çavuş* (junior Janissary commander, and a lower court herald), *seymen* (member of a kind of Janissary infantry, also a policeman), and *seyis* (groom), which is not only derogatory, for the very word groom itself is, but also evocative of a precisely defined type of servitude, particularly degrading, for it implies grovelling to the master, while Janissary itself is synonym for a national traitor, someone who has switched religions.

For example, the members of the Montenegrin government deposed in a rally in January 1989 are regularly called 'socialist *beylerbeys*'.[1] As such, they allied with the 'Bosnian *valis*' against Milošević (Nebojša Jevrić, *Duga*, 412, 9 December 1999). Tito's *seyis* and *çavuşis* persecuted Serbian intellectuals in Bosnia-Herzegovina (Rajko Petrov Nogo, *Duga*, 407, 30 September 1989), and Milošević's opponents in Vojvodina sent their own *çavuşis* to compromise the supporters of Milošević, as a reader's letter to *Politika,* 11 January 1990, warned, showing that the terminology could be a two-way street, from top to bottom and vice versa, in total coincidence of evocation and reference. At a meeting of the SPO in Novi Pazar, the party leader Vuk Drašković promised that very soon the '*seymens* of Broz would disappear and no one would any longer halt the revival and resurrection of Serbian glory' (*Svet,* 220, 19 September 1990). At the founding assembly of the NS, one of its leaders, Momir Vojvodić, spoke of Tito's Montenegrin *seyis,* who carried out the orders of their 'aga' Hamdija Pozderac (*Nedjelja,* 25, 12 August 1999), a Bosniak politician who because of his persistent defence of federalism was the first to bear the brunt of Serbian populism. This terminological and situational catalogue of the archetypal system of repression cannot but recall Kačić-Miošić's epic description of the deployment of the Turkish army:

> up jumped pashas and kadis,
> alay-beyis, agas and sipahis,
> the Janissary Turks hurried off
> and after them the başas and seymens.

Since the media do not act only to inform, but also to give value and

---

1. Momir Vojvodić, NS (*Duga*, 420, 31 March 1990), also Nebojša Jevrić in *Svet,* 222, 17 October 1990 and *Duga* 444, 2 March 1991.

to motivate, individual terms contain a certain message, even a whole topic. A catalogue of key symbols is not just a set of isolated parts, but the significance of each new element carries on from meanings already formed, and creates a larger whole in the recipient's consciousness. By the end of the eighties, through this kind of accumulation of meanings, Serbian discourse had formed a system of evocative terms that can most accurately be called an *absolute terminological reconstruction* of the Ottoman period and hence of the oral heroic epic, or vice versa: of the epic, and hence of the historical period that was preserved in it. And all the semantic gaps in the text of the publication of the final wartime shoot-out were filled in by these terms, which fitted into revived images of the *haiduk* epic and of the anti-Ottoman insurrections of the preceding centuries, suffusing and mutually illuminating each other, completing the reconstruction of the semantic space in which the war was to take place.

Of course, whether the evocation would be used as the symbolic disqualification of this or that particular government depended on the context, but it is indisputable that it would be most effective as communication and most emotionally rousing when it was directed against authorities who, even if they were communists, included those who had inherited the culture of Islam, that 'consequence of the six centuries of Turkish aggression – these unhappy Muslims', as they were defined by Bishop Atanasije Jevtić. In concrete terms, this is Kosovo, where the Albanian *zulümkârs* (Ottoman tyrant) take their *harç* (tribute) from the Serbian tradesmen and their own pro-Yugoslav fellow countrymen (*Politika ekspres*, 24 September 1990), and particularly Bosnia, this 'dark *vilâyet* of *haraçlis*', the collectors of *harç*, as one newspaper subheading put it (*Duga*, 410, 11 November 1989). But in a figurative sense, Croatia was not excepted either, for there too the Serbs today 'pay their tribute in blood', that is, they leave the predominantly Serbian rural areas and go off to the predominantly Croatian cities, there 'changing their faith' and becoming 'Janissaries', as was early on claimed by a leader of the SDS (Petar Štikovac; *Duga*, 407, 30 September 1989). And here everything features precisely as part of the absolute terminological reconstruction of the mythic time of suffering and loss: 'tribute in blood (*danak u krvi*)' is a colloquial synonym for the Turkish expression *acami-oğlan*, a procedure whereby the special Janissary officials or soldiers took healthy, bright Christian boys from the conquered lands and brought them up in the spirit of Islam, training them for military and other kinds of service in the Empire.

Since the communication included Bosniak Muslim social and historical memory objectively, if passively in the early phase, the analysis needs expanding to this national discourse as well. At least ostensibly paradoxically, the Croatian discourse, calling the Serb rebels *haiduks*, put itself in the position that was once occupied by the Ottoman government as opposed to the Christian *haiduks*, Serbian (Orthodox) and Croatian (Catholic) alike. In the Bosnian Muslim folk songs, '*haidukery*' is consistently negatively evaluated, because they were produced in a historical context and a social setting in which, because of their religious identity and privileged position in the system of government, that part of the Bosnian population felt close to the Ottomans, or at least experienced some solidarity with the government that was thus threatened. The *haiduk* intercepted and robbed the 'Turks', in fact, most frequently local traders and landowners. Muslim *haiduks*, who also existed – Celebi states that in the neighbourhood of Bitola there were even many *softas* (Islamic school pupils) living as *haiduks* – were the enemies of the system, and non-Muslims were also the enemy of Islam. The Bosniak epic song in general shows the Muslim ruler as tolerant and caring, not at all as a tyrant, and its heroes are at least as important state-builders as the contemporary HPS member of Sinj, Omer Hrnjica, who 'beat *haiduks* in the field' since they were for him just common robbers and abductors. While Omer Blažević led a posse in pursuit of a *haiduk* whose existence was a 'disgrace' for the Lika *âyan* (local government official) Mustaj-bey, that is, someone in authority and a member of the system that the singer considered lawful, legitimate and his own.[1] The expressions the Muslim epic heroes use for the *haiduks* show very clearly what they think of them: for Alija Novljanin they are 'swine', and for Nuka Bayraktar the name of one of them 'stinks'.

This kind of social memory informs the interesting experience of Avdo Humo. He was a member of the PK KPJ for Bosnia-Herzegovina and organiser of the insurrection in Herzegovina, president of ZAVNOB-H and a senior official in the government after the war. He was also the nephew of the poet Hamza Humo, one of the few communist leaders to be born and brought up in a cultivated city milieu, in Mostar in 1914. The prosperous family used to read the Hörmann collection of Muslim epics, which, according to a National Government questionnaire, was the best-read book among Muslim men on the eve of World War I. In school the Muslim boy 'thrilled to' the

---

1. Sometimes a Christian narrator will also portray '*haidukery*' without any idealisation: he will deprive it of the justification that it is all a consequence of the Ottoman reign of terror. It is then reduced to the mere vending of slaves, and shows the *haiduk* as ruthless to women as well, threatening them with rape (Buturović 1976: 129–130). There are some Christian songs that clearly state who it was that suffered on both sides: 'On the one hand the Turks lay on / on the other from the hills the *haiduks*:/ for the poor there was no salvation' (Nazečić 1959: 6; Popović 1930: 156).

haiduk and Uskok epic, 'to the moral greatness of the heroes who dealt out justice and died for it'. But at home he asked his granny whether she liked such songs too:

> she would reply – they are fine, but they are not ours. This answer would disappoint me, and I went on with my question: Why would ours be better than theirs? – Because our heroes are better than theirs, she replied confidently ... What kind of folk song is it that sings of the theft of the sheep of Ljubović-bey? Theft is a sin, and God will punish it. And who is it that steals? she would ask me. Hungry layabouts, impious idlers. Heroes are real men, they are brave and honest. – Here I would fall to thinking ... and then my earlier admiration for every kind of folk epic song would be shaken (Humo 1984: 35).

On the basis of such an inherited memory, combined with a positive attitude towards the legality and legitimacy first of the Croatian state and then of their own when it was equally at risk, the Bosniaks considered those who disputed them brigands in just the same way as the Croats did. In an election speech in Vitomirica, the head of the Kosovo branch of the SDA Numan Balić was shocked by the '*haiduks* in SAO Krajina' (HTV News, 26 May 1991); the political scientist Fuad Muhić by the '*haiduk* and Uskok-style impulse' of the SDS of B-H to destroy the sovereignty of Bosnia-Herzegovina (*Večernji list*, 14 January 1991); while the journalist Ibrahim Halilović excoriated the Serbian authorities in Mrkonjić-Grad as 'former communists, thieves and *haiduks*' (*Eurobosna*, 26, 17 September 1993). And the lawyer Rešad Mujkić urged that criminals in Bosnia-Herzegovina should be tried as the only way of 'stopping forever Greater Serbian '*haidukery*' (*Vjesnik*, 2 October 1994). Such language, either in the media or the speech of the political elite, could not change the whole course of the war, and at the beginning of 1995 the senior SDA official and Presidency member Ejup Ganić was to say that the establishment of a regular government meant the 'coming of a state of law', 'the establishment of democracy and the end of '*haidukery*' and arbitrariness' (*Večernji list*, 3 January 1995).

Finally, when the creator of the modern Bosniak ideology of national integration, in his account of Bosnian history, came to the reaction of the Serbs west of the Drina River to the Karađorđe insurrection, he found it quite natural to write that they started to 'go to outlawry' and 'to disturb the peaceful population with their '*haidukery*' (Bašagić 1900: 122). It is easy to guess how the same events would have been described by, for instance,

Dušan Zelembaba, while, in connection with events in Knin, the Croatian president Franjo Tuđman would readily have subscribed to the century-old formulation of the Herzegovina bey Bašagić.

Thus, because of the identity of their contemporary political interests, the value coding of *'haidukery'* in Bosnian and Croatian discourse was the same, although the discourses were opposed in their narrative traditions, while it was opposite in Serbian and Croatian discourse, although in their traditions it was identical. The Croatian discourse was to be 'Turkified' or 'Ottomanized' in other relevant elements as well, because the recoding of a single element entailed the recoding of all or most others that were related to it intellectually or contextually. Thus, for example, the actions of the Serbian paramilitary forces were described as *'haiduk zulüm* (terror)' (*Vjesnik*, 3 June 1991), an impossible combination in Christian mouths in the epic, but quite natural in the Muslim epic, as when the Sarajevo traders complained to the Sultan of the *'zulüm* of Mijat the *haiduk'* who blocked the roads and robbed the trading caravans (Andrić 1939: 178).

FOUR

Haiduks in Dictionaries

'But isn't it the same if they went off to be robbers or to be haiduks?*'*

'You're mistaken, sir. Since the time the haiduks *disappeared, from that time there has been no justice for us unhappy poor folks.'*

This bright peasant's answer pleased me a lot. Especially the distinction between haiduks *and robbers. Our people are still aware that there was a noble aim behind '*haidukery'. *And truly, if we are sincere and just, we have to admit that when there were no more* haiduks, *then there was indeed no more justice for the poor.*

(Andrović 1909: 90; conversation with a peasant in Ravni kotari)

Lexicography, culture and politics

In his major four-volume work *Etymological Dictionary of the Croatian or Serbian Language (Etimologijski rječnik hrvatskoga ili srpskoga jezika;* JAZU, Zagreb 1971) the Croatian linguist and Romanist Petar Skok describes the word *haiduk/hajduk* as a Balkan Turkish loan word of Hungarian origin – *hajdú*, pl. *hajdúk*, the original meaning of which was 'mercenary soldier on the Turkish frontier against the Turks'. The Turkish form was *haydud*, the Albanian *haidút*, the Roman and Bulgarian *hajdúk* alongside *hajdútin*, and the Macedonian was *hajdut*.[1] There is also the popular etymology according to which the word was created from the imperative *ajd, hajd*, and the expression *uk*, or 'require something by force', in the sense that the oppressed had nothing else left but to call on their fellow-sufferers to *go, let's get something by force*, that is, to out into outlawry in the hills and thence fight against the rule of the oppressor (Stojanović 1984: 32–33). For a long time *hajduk* must have meant what it was etymologically, a borderer or border guard, but in time the basic meaning spread to outlaws in the Balkan lands

---

1. For a review of earlier opinions, see Popović 1930: 95–97.

during the period of Ottoman rule, and then to all outlaws and rebels.

The associative field that a certain concept evokes does not in itself have any value content but becomes what it is in relation to the complex non-linguistic context in which it is formed and accepted. The same field can be extremely variable, changing its value sign from one individual, social group or communication system to another. When this kind of discord appears, when in a functionally united communication area two differently valued associative fields exist at the same time, it is primarily the consequence of a clash between two totally different semantic spheres (Lešić 1975: 106). Semantic spheres, of course, derive from historical and social experiences and circumstances.

The depiction given so far of the evocation of *'haidukery'* in the associative fields of Croatian, Serbian and Bosniak discourse shows that what is at issue is a distinctly *culturally marked* word (as was to be demonstrated far more vigorously, with the outbreak of the Croatian-Bosniak war in spring 1993, when, together with military and political action, there was a semantic readjustment within these two previously stable discourses). For language does not exist in some kind of vacuum, but is implanted in human culture and reflects the beliefs and feelings of the linguistic community to which it belongs: it is a cultural and social product. It is true that in reality only a minor part of the vocabulary possesses a distinctive culture-specific content. The elements of a segment of the vocabulary so marked are called culturally marked lexical items, and are defined as

> all the words of a language the real understanding of which implies knowledge of certain socio-culturally specific features of a particular language community, or knowledge of a given minimal segment of the cultural context (Bratanić 1993: 28).

For this purpose it is worth looking at the way the concept of *haiduk* has been defined in some important South Slav dictionaries in the modern period, particularly during the period of the second Yugoslavia.

In his study of *haiduks* Dušan Popović lists with unconcealed disapproval the authors who in their dictionaries or similar works defined *haiduk* as thief (Belostenec), robber, brigand, even whoremaster (Ančić), drunk, tramp, ne'er-do-well (Bogišić), murderer, thief, highwayman (Voltić), thief and brigand (Stulli). Something of the reasons for this kind of disapproval lie in the fact that all those named are Croats, or, in a more appropriate formulation in this context, they belong to a social and cultural area of which one of the foundations is Roman law, and they are thus inheritors of the political

155

tradition created in the framework of Habsburg and altogether West European historical legitimism and the political ideologies based on them. On the other hand – whether he was conscious of it or not – Popović, a Serb, drew strength from a different kind of framework of standards and values and political thought, including the national integration ideology and the pertinent political imagination developed out of a different set of historical conditions. Still more eloquent is information concerning the occupations and services, and the place of work, of the said lexicographers. Then it will be seen that this kind of definition of *'haidukery'* did not come into being only 'mechanically, by transmission from old to new dictionaries, or from local into foreign dictionaries', while 'that was not the way our people thought'. This is borne out in the account of a Catholic vicar from southern Croatia in the mid-seventeenth century, who mentions 'fine heroes', and in the memoirs of an Orthodox priest from insurrectionary western Serbia at the beginning of the nineteenth century, who distinguishes 'good' and 'proper' *haiduks* from evil ones (Popović 1930: 97). This difference is the outcome of a complex evolution within the contexts of two intellectual traditions and perspectives on values and standards that inevitably left their mark on the lexical items as well.

In an ideal case, a dictionary is the work of a trained philologist and lexicographer, fully aware of the purpose and importance of the job being undertaken, capable of objectifying phenomena and observing them from a certain critical distance. He or she is aware of the distinctions between colloquial language and written sources, as well as marks of style and jargon, the expressiveness and functional demarcation of given individual words. In cases when this ideal is not entirely fulfilled, the claim still holds that each dictionary 'reflects and interprets a given cultural universe or at least the content of it that is expressed through language'. By definition, a single-language dictionary necessarily 'interprets' this cultural content largely 'from within, for members of the same cultural and linguistic' community and it is at the same time 'a kind of coded text from which the relevant message of the civilisation and culture may be read' (Bratanić 1991: 18, 110). And that is what is essential here.

Two priests whose views Popović quotes as trustworthy on this topic can be placed among 'the vernacular clergy', that is, the lower clergy, often without any particular theological or pastoral education, completely at one with the small local community that they serve. These were men who were advisors and assistants in a mass of everyday practical matters, from medicine to the composition of official and private letters, in fact everything that impinged upon people's survival in uncertain times and still more uncertain lands, rather than spiritual shepherds and guides in the subtle matters of religious truth. They shared good and evil with their parishioners, worked in the fields like them, and in the event of threat often took up arms. One such Orthodox priest, M. Nenadović, was one of the leaders of the Serbian insurrection of 1804. He took part in almost all the battles, was a supplier of arms for the insurrectionists, many of whom had been *haiduks* only the day before, and he acted as a negotiator with the Turks and Russians.

By contrast, the five authors criticised, although they were with one exception also members of the clergy, derived from a markedly different ambience. This was one that, despite being on the border of the empires, and also exposed to the military power of the Ottomans, nevertheless lived a more settled life that was not reduced to the everyday struggle for survival but also enjoyed many of the gains of modern cultural, economic and legal development. Two of them, the Varaždin Pauline Ivan Belostenec (*c.* 1594–1675) and the Istrian Josip Voltić (1750–1825) came from 'peaceful Pauria', as that Kordun partisan would have said. The next two would have been characterised without hesitation by the vice-chairman of the SDS Dušan Zelembaba as those arrogant 'gents' who sought to disarm the 'folk'. Joakim Stulli (1729–1817) was from Dubrovnik, a highly educated Franciscan and polyglot, while Baltazar Bogišić (1834-1908), from Cavtat, was a lawyer with a doctorate from the University of Vienna, a professor at Odessa University, a scientist in Paris and writer of disquisitions on the history of law. When Prince Nikola of Montenegro wanted to reorganise his patriarchal country along the lines of modern European states, it was Bogišić whom he invited to be his minister of justice and to draw up a General Property Code, to create, in other words, the formal conditions for the state to be able, among other things, to put a stop to '*haidukery*'. The fifth, the Franciscan Ivan Ančić (1624–1685), was not marked with the brand of undesirable origin, from either a social or a geographical point of view: he was born in the rural area of Duvno, home of the *harami başi* Mijat Tomić, whose contemporary he was. But as a vicar and preacher, and particularly as a writer of theological and liturgical books with moral lessons for the common people about how to live decently and piously, he could certainly not have praised *haiduk* conduct.

Popović took the names of these authors and their lexicographical entries from the *Dictionary of the Croatian or Serbian Language* (*Rječnik hrvatskoga ili srpskoga jezika*; JAZU, Zagreb 1887–1891), where they are cited as older sources. The dictionary itself also gives its own definition: *hajduk – latro* [Lat. robber], *a man who is armed and lies in wait for travellers on the highway and takes their property by force*, and makes a cross-reference to the entry for *robber*, which in itself speaks volumes. Among the references are quotations from vernacular songs and tales, among which there is a quote from Kačić-Miošić's *Pleasant Conversation*. Further on, the entry cites those parts of Vuk Karadžić's interpretation from the *Serbian Dictionary* which state that people went off to be *haiduks* because of Turkish violence. This suggests that, even when it deserved condemnation, there were elements in '*haidukery*' that did not justify it but did help in a proper understanding of it. This addition, that is the perceived need for it, contains the key for both understanding Popović's disapprobation and resolving many other misunderstandings.

Neither Vuk Karadžić nor Petar II Petrović Njegoš had – and, in the circumstances in which they lived, they can hardly be expected to have had – emotional distance from '*haidukery*', or at least the academic reserve of the professional lexicographer. It is true that they were aware that '*haidukery*' was not a simple phenomenon and they were ready to state that a *haiduk* was sometimes a robber. But they would at once add that he was in no way just that, not even mainly that, rather a laudable person who fought for the freedom of all his oppressed and embittered co-nationals and co-religionists. Neither of them had any illusions about the *haiduks*, but the reality in which they lived did not permit them – particularly Njegoš, the ruler of a theocratically organised patriarchal mini-state that only just managed to survive in conditions of permanent war – to unravel all the contradictions inherent in this context, neither ethical nor political, and hence certainly not lexicographic. Karadžić did endeavour to distinguish, as Popović would have it, bad and good *haiduks*, common robbers and self-sacrificing idealists, through the formulation that the 'real *haiduk* would never kill a man who had done nothing to him unless he was persuaded to by some friend or harbourer'. Whichever way you look at it, this appears to suggest that the only (not very great) difference lies in the degree of submission to friendly persuasion.

After all, Vuk Karadžić did not create a work of lexicography in the standard sense of the word but rather a kind of personal cultural and ethnographic interpretation of his own times, recording the way of thinking of the people with whom he was deeply at one and with whose value system he identified. His *Serbian Dictionary (Srpski rječnik)*, in both his first edition and in the enlarged 1852 edition, is shot through with verses and proverbs, digressions and associations. In it the 'two opposite tendencies: lexicographic discipline and the epic impulse of vernacular narration' are constantly at loggerheads (Popović 1983: 154). The definitions of *hajduk* and priest, village, serf and landowner (*pop, selo, kmet, spahija*) are actually a sociological view, a 'living picture of Serbian society under the Turks' that 'belongs at once to scholarship and to literature' (ibid. 182). A poignant example of the way his style turned into a suggestive literary image is to be found in the description of the *haiduk*'s apparel:

> They most of all wore homespun blue *čakšires* [trousers with a long backside and narrow leggings that fastened at the side], on their feet socks and *opanaks* [a kind of peasant leather footwear, fastened around the ankle with one or more narrow straps, often with a turned up toe], on top a homespun *dečerma* [a kind of waistcoast] and a *koporan* [a kind of short coat, made of coarse cloth], occasionally a *dolama* [robe with sleeves, down to the knees or even longer, over which a belt was placed], blue or green, and on top of all this a bought *gunj* [woollen three-quarter-length overcoat]; on their head either a *ćelepoš* [a light shallow cap of knitted cotton that was often worn under a thick wool cap] or fess or decorated silken cap, from which the silken tassels [plaited at the top and hanging free at the lower end] hung from one side down the chest.[1]

The enormous influence of Karadžić's lexicographic and ethnographic work, which has continued to this day in Serbian culture, has had the effect that, partly unconsciously, and without doubt partly for ideological and propaganda reasons, the definition of *haiduk* has taken on certain non-dictionary features. This quotation of his, which the JAZU *Dictionary* uses to supplement and also actually in a way to mitigate its own lexicographically cold definition, is a good example of this kind of influence, and in this specific case is probably a kind of compromise between the demands of the discipline and the spirit of the times – because Part 3, which included this entry, was printed in 1887–1891, when the freedom-loving figure of the *haiduk* was an important symbol in South Slav liberation ideology, particularly of Croatian and Serbian rapprochement on the basis of the traditions of resistance to Ottoman conquest and rule.

Not even the *Dictionary of the Serbian-Croatian Literary Language* (*Rečnik srpskohrvatskog književnog jezika*; Matica srpska, Novi Sad 1976) could manage without such a supplement, but with a much greater degree of idealisation, which coincided temporally with the enhanced ideologisation of

---

1. *Haiduks*, and in particular *harami bašis*, kept up to the very end this tradition of dandified dress (embroidered shirts and waistcoats, silver buttons, chased belts and weapons, sterling silver caps).

Yugoslav society after the reform movements in Slovenia, Croatia, Macedonia and Serbia at the beginning of the 1970s had been crushed. This gives, as the second and third definitions of the entry for *haiduk*: *outlaw, robber*, or *cunning fellow, trickster*. But the first and basic definition indicates its clear testimony of the epic character of the popular avenger and protector: *Outlaw from Turkish rule and member of the groups that protected the people fighting against Turkish violence*. In one sense, a comparison of this definition and the *Dictionary of the Croatian Language (Rječnik hrvatskoga jezika)* of Vladimir Anić (Novi Liber, Zagreb 1994), where *haiduk* is value-neutrally explained as *outlaw from Turkish rule, one of a band that was outlawed*, bearing witness not only to the professional discipline of the author, but also to the fact that the lexical wealth of the language in many ways reflects the worldview of its speakers and that it is impossible strictly to delimit the lexical and cultural significances of a word.

The topic is further explained by the depiction of the origin and criteria used in another important lexicographical work – *Contributions to Croatian Legal Historical Language (Prinosi za hrvatski pravno-povjestni rječnik)*, which the legal historian Vladimir Mažuranić published in ten volumes from 1908 to 1922. In conjunction with the Law Faculty of Zagreb University, the Yugoslav Academy in Zagreb started systematically printing the medieval statutes of Dalmatia, to which was appended, for the sake of improved understanding, a dictionary, including terms from legal documents from the whole of Croatia. As could be logically expected in the nature of things, *haiduk* is defined from the perspective of a settled legal system organised by local or central government, while semantic changes that the term underwent over time are shown exclusively through the evolution of the organised, regular military and administrative structures, hence: *latro, praedo, robber*, but the first meaning is *a kind of soldier* [city watch, watch supervisor], *volunteer, man-at-arms* [from the fourteenth century the name for a member of the city police service], *servant of the landowner*. For additional explanations, the user was referred to the entry for *grabež* (plunder), which is again eloquent in itself. The sources from which the references are taken are the *Poljica Statute*, which codified public and private law in that self-governing territory in the fifteenth century; and various legal documents and files published in a scholarly archival journal (*Vjesnik kr. hrvatsko-slavonsko-dalmatinskoga zemaljskog arkiva*), and various *urbars*: collections of regulations used in Croatia, Slavonia and Vojvodina to govern feudal relations, i.e. the mutual obligations of landowner and serf. Traditional vernacular poetry was not, of course, a relevant source in this section, and so neither was the vision or evaluation of the *haiduk* it enshrined.

Finally, it remains to observe how the same lexical unit is defined by two dictionaries created in the communities against whose members the *haiduk* bands were seen as protecting the people. These are *Turkish Loan Words in the Serbian-Croatian Language (Turcizmi u srpskohrvatskom jeziku)* edited by Abdulah Škaljić (Svjetlost, Sarajevo 1979; 1957) and the *Dictionary of the Characteristic Lexis of the Bosnian Language (Rječnik karakteristične leksike u bosanskom jeziku)* compiled by Alija Isaković (Svjetlost, Sarajevo 1992). Since here too the dictionary is seen as an interpreter of social and cultural differences among societies, and the words are explained from the point of view of their cultural marking, it is no drawback but rather an advantage that neither of the two authors is a professional lexicographer. Škaljić started compiling his dictionary in 1950 when he was an associate of the Folklore Study Institute, later the Spiritual Culture Department of the National Museum of Bosnia-Herzegovina in Sarajevo, while Isaković is a writer, anthologist and essayist, and a public figure in the widest sense of the word. As the names given to the language in their titles indicate, both dictionaries are products of their times and the states in which they were printed – Bosnia-Herzegovina as a federal unit of Yugoslavia in the first case, and independent Bosnia-Herzegovina in the second. To this extent the definition of the concept that we are interested in here is bound to differ.

Škaljić defines *haiduk* as *an outlaw from government; a highway robber, thief* and, by way of tribute to the current social and political moment and the official Yugoslav political imaginary, he gives the kind of addendum that we have already met: *In the time of the Turks, among the South Slavs (particularly the Serbs) also: fighter against Turkish rule for the liberation of the people.* For Isaković, who had always been a champion of the national independence of the Bosniaks and their right, within Yugoslav language politics, to affirm their own linguistic identity and heritage, and hence the legitimacy of their own historical memory, *haiduk* was ascetically defined as *outlaw; highway robber*, with no additions and particularly no politically motivated concessions to other and different socio-cultural contexts (with the proviso that, of course, this procedure was in itself not only a lexicographic but also a political fact of the first order).

One further difference is also not without significance. Škaljić, by way of reference, quotes lines from a vernacular heroic song, but one where it is not possible to discern any value placed on the phenomenon ('thirty *haiduks* fell upon him' and 'so the lad went to the *haiduks* / to the *haiduks* in the green hills'), while Isaković refers to archival sources, thus to the view of the state administration and its officers, and to an anonymous Turkish-Bosnian dictionary of 1836, in which the explanation of the word can easily be imagined. Certainly, it seems far closer to Belostenec, Voltić and Stulli than to Vuk Karadžić or the final phrase of Isaković's compatriot Škaljić. And anyway, the author whose criticisms of Croatian lexicographers began this review at the end had to admit that in the Turkish dictionaries the word *haiduk* was simply robber, because this meaning was actually 'closest to what the *haiduks* actually were – at least for the Turks' (Popović 1930: 97). And that is what they were not only for the Turks, but for all loyal subjects of the Ottoman state.

At the beginning of the foreword to his pioneering dictionary, Isaković drew attention to the importance of cultural and historical experience, which is always to some extent also political experience: 'The Muslim Bosniaks, as a separate cultural layer in the centuries-old Bosniak society, acquired in time an experience different from that of their neighbours' (Isaković 1992: 6), that is, the Serbs and Croats, not only those in Bosnia-Herzegovina, but those in Serbia and Croatia as well. It is necessary here only to supplement his definition of cultural distinctiveness with a mention of legal and political diversity, that is, to add the datum that in the theocratic Ottoman system the subjects of the Islamic faith were privileged, and only they could take part in matters of government. As members of this faith, they were ineluctably identified with the Ottoman state and with its ideology, and considered the defence of it to be their duty. During the course of the aggression against Bosnia-Herzegovina, the Bosniaks as an historically produced social and national community were to experience a profound identification with the Ottoman period of their history. This was in part a continuation and elaboration of their own long-since established – though occasionally stifled – tradition, and partly a reaction against the propaganda that represented them exclusively as the heirs of all the negative aspects of the Ottoman period.

After the war two Bosniak authors, Ahmet Kasumović and Ćamil Huseinbašić, published their *Encyclopaedic Dictionary of the Defence of Bosnia-Herzegovina (Enciklopedijski rječnik odbrane Bosne i Hercegovine)*, which we shall cite here in its second, expanded edition (Sejtarija, Sarajevo 2000). This is not a standard work of lexicography like that of Škaljić and particularly Isaković: in its macrostructure it is perhaps most like Karadžić's *Serbian Dictionary,* because many of the definitions are expounded in small essays, in line with the new conception of the ideology of national integration. Here of course the most interesting things are the definitions relating to the history of Bosnia in the Ottoman period, the description of which in other dictionaries has already been presented and which have remained alive in the colloquial language until today. In the 1990s these terms became activated in political discourse as well: the *haiduk* was an *outlaw, a robber, a looter, spy, terrorist*, while a *yatak* (harbourer) was *a person who concealed the perpetrator of an offence*, or, put in a completely modern criminal and judicial register, *an accomplice, a person who concealed a fugitive*. It is worth adding that in the eyes of the Christian population two other figures became, with very good reason, symbols of violence and usurpation. The *haračlija*, Turkish *haraçli*, is defined in brief as a tax-collector, thus in factual, formally precise terms, with the addition that his period of office, authorised by the vizier, lasted a year, which does not form part of a lexicographic description; however, such a function clearly suggests the orderliness and regularity of the system in which he worked as well as his legality. The janissary was neutrally, thus again formally precisely defined as *keeper of the public order in the settlements as part of the garrison*. This cool neutrality hides an extremely powerful value charge; it says more perhaps than any explicit comment, more than any positive-sounding definition.

The times of sentimentality and romanticism have clearly ended for ever, that is those in which Škaljić had to be very cautious in framing his formulation and illustrating it from the vernacular epic songs. Then it was taken for granted that it was essential to back up the neutral legal definition of the *haiduk* with the specific significance and associative field that it had acquired in the Serbian setting (and which in a functionally united area of communication was not at all contentious), but not with equivalent semantic categories from the Bosniak Muslim milieu. The implicit message of such a change, announced as early as Isaković's dictionary on the eve of the war, is that the heritage of the Ottoman period in Bosniak or Bosnian Muslim history is not – in principle – any less legitimate, real or valuable than the heritage that was left in the Serbian and Croatian historical memories by the Christian empires to which their states belonged. And this heritage naturally assumes the specific cultural history and legally inherited evaluation of social and military processes and their protagonists. It also includes, particularly in times of great political tension, the ideologisation of this heritage and its instrumentalisation in the current rivalry for social power.

If the one-time definitions of *haiduk, haraçli* and janissary ignored the historical memory of one side, now Kasumović and Huseinbašić were ignoring the other side. This is a helpful and to some extent desirable establishment of a balance, but with the proviso that the title of their work covers the whole of Bosnia-Herzegovina, and yet in it the Bosniak memory does not exist alone, and nor did the Bosniaks alone act in its defence. However, the new ambiguities and contradictions that derive from this will be discussed in the following chapters. Here we would only repeat that all the problematic phenomena and processes are described in a cold legalistic language, very similar to the language of Mažuranić's dictionary of legal history in the Croatian case, consistently from the perspective of a legitimately organised central government administration and its armed forces. Also logical is the use of the concept of *terrorist*, adopted from contemporary legal and political discourse, as a synonym for the *haiduk* of yesteryear; President Tuđman and other protagonists of Croatian public discourse acted in just the same way with reference to the Serbian paramilitary forces.

In the dictionaries, all the historically created differences between the Muslim Bosniaks on the one hand and the Christian Croats and Serbs on the other can be seen clearly and incontestably, but the Croatian and Bosniak political discourse at the beginning of the 1990s demonstrates that these diverse experiences, otherwise a stumbling block to communication, can be very successfully suppressed, under the impact of changed relations of political power and newly acquired experience, for a shorter or longer period, spontaneously or according to a programme.

FIVE

Croatian Controversies
and the War with the Bosniaks

*'Oh, not if it were never so, I don't intend to be a robber,'s houted out
Little Marijan ...*

*'Go on, don't be an idiot, Little Marijan!' snapped Mijat. 'We shan't
rob just anyone, but only those who steal from the wretched common
people. We shall take from those who themselves take ... We shall fight
for justice, against the bullies and the leeches, we'll fight against all the
foreigners that swagger around the country as if it were their own.'*

(Horvatić 1982: 21)

The dual loyalty of Mijat Tomić

In addition to the conflicts that take place at the level of the encounter
between the two ethnic, culturally and historically conditioned discourses,
there may also be clashes within a single discourse. These too derive from the
cultural marking of language and hence show that no culture is homogeneous,
but is composed of diverse and sometimes conflicting values and elements.
The profound value and category realignment that took place in Croatian
discourse around the concept of *haiduk*, when the current political valuation
drove out the traditional one, led to the conclusion that the blame for this
should be attached to those members of the new political elite who as a result
of a long period of absence from Croatia did not know its history. Such men
were the head of the Presidential Office under President Tuđman, who
had lived in France for some twenty years, and the President's advisor, who
had been educated at foreign universities. It is no surprise that this kind of
protest should have come from Dubravko Horvatić, very well acquainted
with the traditional culture and the heroic epic, a writer who wrote a novel
for children about the *haiduk* Mijat Tomić, fighter for 'national justice, and
not just for mere booty', 'based on the old songs and traditions' (Horvatić

1982). When he was travelling in Herzegovina twenty-two years later, this fact saved the author from lengthy scrutiny of his documents. Hearing who he was, a policeman from the Livno Brigade of the HVO said that he had read the book several times, 'we started talking about it, and at length we set up a friendly conversation'.[1]

Deploring the use of what he felt were inappropriate terms for presenting the reality of war to the public and in the media in Croatia, Horvatić warned:

> The word *'haidukery'* sometimes used to indicate the Chetniks of Knin and elsewhere contains in essence a positive connotation. President Tuđman used the word on several occasions, fairly ill-advisedly, but it is clear that it does not come from him, because Dr Tuđman is a historian and hence knows its meaning. I believe that it has been uttered by someone such as Hrvoje Šarinić or Mario Nobilo who, judging from their public pronouncements, know nothing whatever about Croatia and its history. The word *'haidukery'* is not used, then, as a euphemism, rather as the consequence of lack of knowledge.
>
> In the Croatian past *'haidukery'* was used to mean resistance to foreign rule, and still today in the area of Duvno or Livno the *gusle* singers sing of individual *haiduks* such as Mijat Tomić, the most renowned figure of the Croatian traditional songs. Fra Luka Ibrišimović in Slavonia was a *haiduk*, and in Lika the priest Marko Mesić went off a-*haiduk*ing. The poem 'The Nymph of Velebit', which was written by the Orthodox Party of State Right member Danilo Medić, refers to that 'Lika *haiduk*'.[2]

Horvatić, then, in intra-Croatian relations, made explicit the same misunderstanding that Joža Vlahović had sensed only four months earlier in Croatian-Serbian relations. His intervention demonstrates vividly that differences among members of the same ethnic community, even declared members of the same political and ideological trend, can at times be so great as to frustrate perception of the message or at least essentially to re-semanticise it. Not cancelling out and not reducing what is common to them, recipient and transmitter cannot deny their affiliation to diverse, profoundly historically and socially shaped cultural patterns. The recipient will always spontaneously slot the message into the conception that he is used to, that

---

1. Dubravko Horvatić, 'Nađoh pustoš na policama knjižnica' ['I found a wasteland on the library shelves'], *Vjesnik*, 24 April 1994.
2. Dubravko Horvatić, 'Ratni rječnik - lažno zrcalo zbilje' ['War vocabulary – mendacious mirror of reality'], *Vjesnik*, 2 August 1991.

exists in his own cultural experience or that, in his opinion, best corresponds to the particular case.

Two levels of the formation and perception of a message emerge here: the political and the poetic.

The political is expressed as the speaker's view about a given topic or theme, whether it is formed independently or under the influence of an external political authority. Horvatić is not wrong in his complaints and criticisms. He simply overlooks the altered political context of the communication, that is, the fact that the positive views of the *haiduk* were created in a historical context in which their creator was in opposition to a government, or a state, which he did not consider his own, and the *haiduk* was a handy symbol of resistance. This kind of *haiduk* is functional even when there is a government that is formally local but negatively valued. The Croat Jakov Blažević was morally condemned by another Croat, a former Partisan and a disillusioned communist, precisely through the evocation of the epic scheme: as a powerful member of the communist political elite, Blažević was equivalent to a despotic pasha, and the wartime leader of the Croatian communists Andrija Hebrang and the Archbishop of Zagreb Alojzije Stepinac, as victims of this kind of totalitarianism, were *haiduks*, who even 'dead did not let him sleep peaceful – Oh, *haiduk* ashes baneful – me in my dreams do threaten'.[1]

These lines come from the poem 'Three Haiduks' ('Tri hajduka', 1886) by the Serbian romantic patriotic poet Jovan 'Zmaj' Jovanović. The wicked pasha imprisoned or rather immured three *haiduks* in an underground dungeon, without food and water, but, long after they had died in torment, they would appear to him in his dreams:

> *Three years they're mould'ring*
> *Oh,* haiduk *ashes baneful*
> *There's still no peace to have*
> *Me in my dreams they threaten.*

---

1. Zvonko Ivanković-Vonta, 'Po uzoru na idola', *Vjesnik*, 1 December 1990. At the beginning of the same year, and on the same polemical grounds, the same author said of Blažević that 'like Feruz Pasha he could never get away from Hebrang and Stepinac (Oh *haiduk* ashes baneful – Me in my dreams they threaten). Cf. Zvonko Ivanković-Vonta, 'Destrukcija Jakova Blaževića', *Iskra*, 82/83, March 1990. In the seventies Ivanković proved that a number of documents on which the official claim that Hebrang had been an Ustasha spy in the ranks of the Partisans was based were the fabrication of the Yugoslav secret police. For this reason he was exposed to threats and police harassment, which must have had Blažević's tacit consent if not his direct instigation.

Although this is not actually an epic song, the lines do inherit the epic expression, its motifs and values in the spirit of national romanticism. The example also shows that the Serbian association of the term does not preclude its use in Croatian discourse, if it makes possible the formulation of appropriate political messages or analogies. The tyrannical Ottoman pasha is equivalent to the communist strongman, and the cruelly murdered *haiduks* are ethically equivalent to Hebrang who was arrested and killed, without doubt on Tito's orders, and then buried in an unknown grave. And also to Stepinac, who was prosecuted by Blažević in the show trial at which the archbishop was condemned to sixteen years in prison.

In this and in the Horvatić example tradition overlaps with political position, because it enabled criticism of communism to be expressed – or emphasised – by the evocation of the *haiduk* as freedom-fighter. After 17 August 1990, the political and legal situation shifted: there was a spontaneous change in the value system, because the speaker felt that the epic tradition could no longer give shape to the message required by the moment.

Poetically, the message was framed as a quotation from a traditional text, to which President Tuđman and all the other protagonists of Croatian discourse, giving the lexeme *haiduk* negative connotations, denied its old cultural sense. For this reason the recipient of the message had to learn new rules, behave as required by the authoritative shaper of political discourse, learn the rules of his original game of quotations, break through to the meanings that he produced in the clash of quotations between his 'own' and the 'foreign' word, his own and the foreign text (Oraić Tolić 1990: 45–46). But there are also situations when the realignment takes place unconsciously and with no resistance at all, because the political position completely absorbs the perception. This happened spontaneously precisely where the process might have been expected to be hardest, had the categories in which vernacular culture functions been forgotten – that is with the vernacular poet and *gusle* player Mile Krajina.

On the eve of the Greater Serbian aggression, in his songs from the national past, he sang quite naturally of the freedom-loving Croatian *haiduks*, the popular protectors and avengers who 'from the hills did threaten the foe / when they did ill, they took vengeance on the Turks' (Krajina 1990). And yet no more than a year or two later, again quite naturally and without the slightest sense of contradiction, he sang songs with themes from the homeland war, in which, since the 'Chetnik *haiduks* rose' against Croatia, he celebrated the Croatian soldiers who rose 'to resist the Serbian *haiduk*', the aggressor that he alternately but synonymously referred to as 'dire robber band' and 'Chetnik *haiduks*' (Krajina 1994). Unlike such an undistanced, authentic and original inheritor of vernacular culture, the aware connoisseur will find it far harder to get used to the new rules – as shown by Horvatić's newspaper intervention – regardless of whether he has otherwise a *proper* political judgment about the events concerned.

Supposing that Šarinić and Nobilo really did know nothing of Croatian history, they were anyway speaking from a position of authority in which this ignorance was clearly seen to be irrelevant or at least innocuous. It is not difficult to assume that Franjo Tuđman, as a popular writer who had studied South Slav history for decades, knew what Horvatić had said, but here he was not speaking as someone who knew history more or less well, rather as the president of an endangered state.

What is more, it is precisely his popular writings that offer an ideal example of how a change in the political optics or the ideological paradigm takes for granted a spontaneous revaluation of the phenomenon of *'haidukery'* – including Mijat Tomić himself. He wrote an extensive study on the *Partisan War in the Past and in the Future*, as a member of the Yugoslav military and political elite. The first edition was written in the early fifties when he was colonel of the JNA and head of the Organisational Section of the Personnel Administration of the SSNO [Federal Ministry of Defence] in Belgrade. The second, expanded edition appeared some fifteen years later, when he was a retired major-general of the JNA and director of the Zagreb Institute for the History of the Working-Class Movement, founded under the immediate patronage of the CPC. In this work, he consistently treats *'haidukery'* in keeping with the official ideological interpretation of Yugoslav history and the model of the traditional epic as an unassailable authority.

As the book says, *haiduks* were 'led by the most conscientious men' who 'adhered to principles of justice in their struggle'. *Haiduks*, those 'national insurrectionists, protectors and avengers' were characterised by 'unbending moral strength'. The first Serbian insurrection in 1804 was 'a successful example of the transformation of the *haiduk* and partisan struggle into a general national insurrection and then into liberation war', and the *haiduk* epic 'always means a revolutionary war cry to join the struggle against violence, slavery and inhumanity.' Among the most exemplary *haiduks*, forerunners of Tito's partisans, are Starina Novak, whom no enemy can escape, and Mijat Tomić, who went into outlawry 'to the green hills / from the tyranny of Bey Ljubović'. Motivation and decisiveness of this kind are the best demonstration of the 'partisan characteristics of the *haiduk* struggle'. If 'there was here and there some distortion of the objectives of the *haiduk* struggle into selfish and ignoble purposes', then it was an exception, an outrage by an individual 'inclined to vice' and the *haiduks* themselves 'extirpated such phenomena that tarnished the fame and reputation of the *haiduk* struggle', that is, 'they carried out the judicial function' and 'judged robbers and murderers, and also traitors severely' (Tuđman 1970: 73–74).

To depict *'haidukery'* in this kind of idealised tone was to an extent to rationalise, synthesise and make theoretical sense of what was already an important component of the official political imaginary. That is, the Partisan war, and particularly the communist seizure of power at the end of the war, was seen as a sequel to the earlier rebellions and insurrections, in other words, the logical pinnacle and ideal end to long-lasting historical processes, interconnected through the meaning attributed to them. In this way, if they did not have democratic legitimation, the communists were able to ensure themselves powerful symbolic legitimation. The apologia for *haiduks* and Uskoks was supposed to arouse a positive political and emotional response among the not inconsiderable section of the population and the officer corps of the JNA that still had a lively feeling for this tradition.

Only in this way is it possible to explain Tuđman's marginalisation of the feudal peasant revolts (Gubec was mentioned only in passing) that in World War II had been the foundation of the symbolic legitimation of the Croat and Slovene Partisans. In this context, when it was necessary to stress not so much ideological correctness as military success they actually could not function as model, because the rebellious serf, tied to his family and his land, was militarily inferior to the *haiduk* who had washed his hands of all such connections and whose 'rifle was both father and mother' to him.

Considering the later communist idealisation of *'haidukery'*, the hints that some of the Partisans were already resisting the cult during the war are of considerable interest. The dissonance between the chaos of *haiduk* life and a disciplined army of the kind that the Partisans were endeavouring to build was as a rule felt by men who, however much they knew and loved the heroic epic, themselves came from non-epic regions or who had during their education developed a critical distance from the culture of the *haiduks*.

Vladimir Nazor saw the Partisans as the heirs of the old outlaws, but also discerned in them a 'new impulse' that led them, a 'consciousness' that was 'broader and deeper' than the Uskoks and *haiduks*, because the 'sense of being Slav and Croat welled out from deep, long since filled-in springs' (Nazor 1977: XVII, 130). This idea implies that Nazor, however much he admired the *haiduks* because of their individual courage and resilience, nevertheless saw them as warriors without a plan or discipline, unreliable and therefore fickle and unconnected individuals who saw nothing broader than their own immediate interests and were motivated by nothing more than an urgent desire for vengeance and their own mere survival. The same sort of sense is found in the reproof uttered by one Belgrade woman communist in 1942 at a seminar of the Valjevo Partisan squad. Dissatisfied that the squad had evaded making open attacks on the Germans, she said that she had not 'gone off to the *haiduks*', that is, to hide, to be satisfied with the mere fact that she was out of reach of the enemy, endlessly lying in wait for some kind of allegedly favourable moment for an ambush. Rather, she had 'joined the Partisans', i.e. to fight, with organisation and discipline, with a long-term thought-out political programme, to wage war against the occupier and the collaborators (Martinović 1979: 348).

A Romanija man, Mlađen Šarenac, said to his men, as soon as he was appointed commander of a unit, 'that he was not a commander of *haiduks*' but of 'partisan combatants' whose 'aim was to fight for freedom' (Krsmanović 1988: 151). Although he came from the same patriarchal rural surroundings as his fighters, he differed from them in that he had loved to read since a lad and 'by his nineteenth year, thanks to his reading, knew a lot about distant lands, customs, other towns and cities, the secrets of nature' (ibid. 143). He had worked as a mechanic in Belgrade, Kragujevac, Herceg-Novi, Divulje (Trogir), Vodice, Šibenik and Zenica, returning to Romanija at the beginning of the war, when he had joined the leader of the insurrection Slaviša Vajner. In connection with these views it is worth recalling the song 'Wilful Rade' ('Samovolja Rade') concerning the same kind of misunderstanding between the ordinary peasant fighters and their commissar, a clearly organised and to some extent educated urban communist.

When he became president of the Republic of Croatia twenty years later, Franjo Tuđman explained in a lengthy autobiographical interview that he had written his book as a challenge to the Serbian and Montenegrin generals and military historians who had not understood the essence of the Partisan war in Yugoslavia and its 'political meaning' and that the 'Partisan army had to be the army of each individual nation'.

> They went for a unitary army to be detached from the nation, and thus argued for a unitary Yugoslav state, with a predominance of Serbs... For me, to be frank, insistence on the specific features of the Partisan war was just an excuse for my main message: that it was necessary to create the conditions (a system of territorial defence) in which each nation in Yugoslavia, and therefore the Croatian nation as well, would be armed! (*Globus*, 311, 22 November 1996).

There is no question that many Serbian and Montenegrin JNA generals were Yugoslav unitarists or else covert Greater Serbians, but it is still unclear how they could be shaken in this view or outwitted through an apologia for 'haidukery', when it was precisely they, as the war of 1990–1995 showed, who were deeply identified with the *haiduk* tradition, when even without theoretical interpretation they felt themselves and their troops to be heirs of that tradition, and when they were all the more profoundly identified with the JNA precisely because at the heart of its imaginary was the myth of the *haiduk* avenger and the mountain refuge. The apologia for 'haidukery' could not but additionally confirm them in the belief that, as descendants of Starina Novak and Bajo Pivljanin, they were militarily and humanly superior to the inhabitants of non-*haiduk*, servile 'Pauria', i.e. Croatia (and Slovenia), not to mention the 'Turks' of Bosnia.

Just as he had once unreservedly idealised the *haiduk*, so later, adopting another paradigm, as head of a state that was symbolic heir to the legality of the medieval kingdom, Franjo Tuđman unreservedly demonised him, not only in his public pronouncements but, for example, in the confidential official letter to the Presidency of the SFRY when in line with the current constitution he sought help from the federal government against the 'armed rebels and *haiduks*' in Knin (Jović 1995: 228).

Mijat Tomić, who figures prominently in the work of Horvatić, was a historical figure. He was born around the beginning of the seventeenth century in Brišnik in Duvno Polje, where even today the peasants point out the remains of his house in two different places. The first archival record concerning him dates from 1637, and legend – which is most succinctly summed up by the song 'Mijat Tomić went a rebel to the haiduks' ('Mijat Tomić odmeće se u hajduke') – says that he became an outlaw because of the violence of the deputy of the Bosnian pasha, that is, because the Duvno *kadi* Suzica had stolen part of his patrimony, a meadow known as Jabuka. When the *kadi* sent the mowers, Mijat opposed them, putting his life at risk:

> Stay your hand, mowers, don't mow the meadow!
> Jabuka's a part of my patrimony.
> As long as I am left alive,
> Let's see, who dares to mow it.
> (Mijatović 1969: 10)

Mijat emerged as victor in this conflict, and people still point out the grave of the *kadi's subasha* Murat whom he cut down at the time. But he could no longer stay in the village.

Mijat Tomić, as portrayed by the painter
Karlo Mijić in about 1930.

Before that, as a lad, he had looked after sheep for Bey Kopčić, who had sincerely loved him for his diligence and honesty. When he married, Kopčić conferred on Mijat the honour of carrying his wedding banner, although he was a Christian, and Mijat went in his stead to a duel and defeated the *Black Arab* who had terrorised the bey. After he became an outlaw, he mainly dwelled on 'the peak of Vran, above Duvno plain / below the rocky faery cave', where the *haiduks* used to gather, because the mountain had some forty large caves, suitable for longer sojourns. He also spent time on neighbouring Ljubuša and Kamešnica mountains near Livno, and over-wintered, among other places, with Bey Kopčić and the *kadi* in Rama. According to one song, the vizier had the Livno *kadi* executed when he found out that he had harboured Mijat's band for the winter. Mijat's constant companion and most faithful friend was his nephew Marijan, son of his sister Manda, known in the songs as Mali Marijan (Little Marijan), or sometimes Mandić (Manda's boy).

He perished after being betrayed by his *kum* (best man, godfather, here close friend) Ilija Bobovac in Doljani between Jablanica and Vran, according to some researchers in 1642, and to others between 1656 and 1659, and by others again not until 1662. Contemporaries recorded that the news of his death was greeted with great joy in Sarajevo. The common people in Croatia and their songs record that the traitor had been bribed, or Mijat had been fatally wounded, by some Arab – which is very likely a corruption of *azap*, soldier or sentry – Hadžizukić from Konjic, where the family still lived on the eve of World War II (Džaja and Draganović 1994: 94). He breathed his last under Sovićka Vrata on Vran, where even today the part of the field where his grave is meant to be cannot be ploughed. At the initiative of the friars, on St Elijah's Day in 1937, on the Doljani grave, as the inscription reads, the 'Croatian people' and the Croatian Culture Society Napredak unveiled a monument to him – a *stečhak*, found not far away, washed down from Vran, and on it Mijat's portrait in enamel with lines from a vernacular song, 'Well I shall go to seek justice / in the chasms and the narrow canyons'. The portrait was made by Academy-trained painter Karlo Mijić, and during the war it was hidden in a nearby house, where it burned together with thirty civilians who had been shut inside it by the Chetniks of Herzegovina and Montenegro when they were marauding in the area in the autumn of 1942. But the monument still stands.

Today there is still a legend there that says the forerunners of the current inhabitants descended from the mountain under Mijat's protection and settled in the valley of the Doljanka River. Fra Filip Grabovac, in *Flower of Conversation (Cvit razgovora*; 1747), claims that after him 'there was no real *haiduk*, nor will there be one', while the priest and politician Mihovil Pavlinović records in 1979 that 'in Herzegovina and the Littoral much was sung and told of Mihat' and that 'he was a great favourite with the people, because he was one of those *haiduks* who had nothing of the *haiduk* about him apart from his hero's freedom (*junačka sloboda*)'. The first song about Tomić to have been recorded is in the Erlangen MS, and memories of him are still preserved today in many of the place names on Vran Mountain and around it (Mijat's Cave, Mijat's Pothole, Mijatuša Fountain, the grave of Ilija Bobovac), as well as elsewhere (Mijat's Cave on Mt Treskavica near Sarajevo, Mijatovac Spring near Fojnica).

Tomić became known in the broad area inhabited by the Croats. Even today, people in Vareš call the Jukić-Martić collection of traditional songs *Tomićkes*, although among the fifty songs there are only seven about him. His popularity was enhanced in 1931 with the Sarajevo Napredak collection edited by Ivan Rengjeo. It was extremely well received by the common people with a living epic tradition – for the peasants it cost five dinars, and for all others twice as much.[1]

That the people in Herzegovina and in particular in Duvno were 'especially proud of their hero Mihovil Tomić' and linked him in a particular way with another tradition, that of the coronation of King Tomislav in Duvanjsko Polje, was shown in the summer of 1924 by the Zagreb deputy mayor and

---

1. For Tomić see Mijatović 1965, 1969, 1974, 1975, 1985; Rubić and Nuić 1899; Banović 1933.

writer of historical novels, Milutin Mayer, when he travelled there to prepare for the opening of the votive church dedicated to the celebration of the tenth centenary of the kingdom of Croatia. In the middle of Duvanjsko Polje, beside a great meadow that they called Jabuka, the peasants told him that 'their old folks had recounted that it was precisely on this meadow that Tomislav was crowned the first king of Croatia' (Mayer 1924: 62). The folklore collector Stjepan Banović proposed some time later, in 1931, to the Braća Hrvatskog Zmaja, a society that looked after Croatian antiquities, that it should do 'a noble deed' and dig up Mijat's grave and transfer 'his martyr's bones' to the votive church in Duvno, known today as Tomislavgrad (Mijatović 1985: 36).

The next powerful impetus to interest in Mijat Tomić, as well as to a stormy debate about the nature of *'haidukery'* in general, was the eighth volume of *Croatian Traditional Songs (Hrvatske narodne pjesme)* edited by Matica hrvatska (Croatian Heritage Foundation) in 1939, with eleven complete songs about him and notes about thirty-four unknown variants. In his foreword with the significant title 'Concerning Croatian Spiritual Individuality' the editor Nikola Andrić stresses Mijat's 'unique character', first of all his willingness to forgive. It is not crucial whether he was 'in truth as magnanimous as depicted in the songs, what matters is that this is how the Croatian vernacular listener wanted to have him and preserve him in the collective memory'. To the view that Mijat Tomić was the 'prototype of Croatian national heroism and the representative of a very particular national individuality' (Andrić 1939: 20) the Zagreb Catholic weekly *Nedjelja* retorted that it was not possible, on the basis of 'certain' epic heroes, to draw conclusions about 'our spiritual individuality'. Particularly from the poems about Tomić 'we cannot possibly gather any decent impression' because everything there 'teemed with the unnecessary and in fact criminal shedding of blood'. In the epic, it is true, there are examples of 'high ethical awareness, Christian forgiveness and nobility' but there are many more that show the morality of our people 'in a very bad light'. For this reason, the author fairly resignedly concludes:

> Unfortunately, even the school collections of the traditional epic songs which should also be an extremely important factor in the aesthetic and ethical education of school-age children are full of wine-drinking, carousing, swearing, cursing, unfaithfulness, casting down from towers, head-splitting, destruction, blood and so on.[1]

---

1. C. Okrimov, 'Nešto o 'kršćanskom praštanju i plemenitom značaju Mijata Tomića, junaka naše narodne pjesme', *Nedjelja*, 48, 1 December 1940.

Another influential Catholic intellectual layman between the wars, Petar Grgec, wrote in a similar spirit. It used to be believed, he says, that the voice of the people was the voice of God, and so the people, like God, could do no wrong, but such 'adoration of the people cannot be accommodated by Christianity'.[1] Although persistent in the belief that the vernacular songs 'best suit our national being', in a number of articles for the general public Grgec warned that because of many 'moral fallacies' they should be read only at 'a certain age and in a critical selection'.[2] In the same spirit, he also argued for the omission of certain songs from school readers:

> Here too one should take to task all those who would perhaps like
> our traditional oral poetry to be the only teacher of the people,
> and see bellicose customs, which are full of the remains of savagery
> and superstition, as worth more than the Gospel.[3]

It is interesting that this concluding section, which was actually the point of the whole discussion, was omitted when the piece was reprinted in a book of collected essays (cf. Grgec 1940: 74). The reason was surely not unconnected with the fact that the first publisher was the St Jerome Croatian Cultural Association, which brought together all socially engaged Catholics and worked in harmony with official Church policy, while the second was Matica Hrvatska, which had just printed Andrić's collection of songs.

The foundation of the NDH meant the continuation of endeavours to develop the national and political cult of Mijat Tomić, along the lines of Andrić's thesis, particularly in connection with the Serbian epic which was the source of the mystical St Vitus Day ideology of the Kingdom of Yugoslavia and the theory of the superiority of the population of the Dinaric areas, i.e. above all Serbs and Montenegrins, that was formulated in the first decades of the twentieth century by the Serbian anthropologist-geographer Jovan Cvijić. Working in the footsteps of the Romantic idea of the extra-historical national soul, expressed in poetry, the continuity of the soul of a nation, as its innate character, he claimed that in this patriarchal, mainly pastoral, cultural zone, there lived a tall slender race of people with 'hawk-like eyes', brave, 'with a tough highland morality', with chivalric characteristics, a deep sense of self-sacrifice and a willingness to make any sacrifice for the sake of

1. 'Ćudoredna vrijednost narodnih pjesama [Moral values of folk songs]' in: *Kalendar sv. Ante* VII, Sarajevo 1932: 105.
2. 'Narodna pjesma i historijski roman [Folk songs and the historical novel]' in: *Napredak - hrvatski narodni kalendar za 1936. godinu,* Sarajevo 1935: 124.
3. 'Shvaćanje rata u Ilijadi i našem narodnom pjesništvu [The way war is understood in the Iliad and in our folk poetry]' in: *Almanah Selo i grad,* 2, Zagreb 1930: 50.

freedom. Their spiritual characteristics included the finest epic songs, sorrow over the battle of Kosovo, the Orthodox religion, sincerity, intelligence. This man of the Dinaric type was deeply connected to his national forbears, including the *haiduks*, and with deep empathy 'took part in their sufferings, those of which the songs tell', even having a vivid sense of the wounds of the Kosovo heroes, and 'to kill many a Turk means for the Dinaric man not only to avenge his forbears, but also to assuage their pain'. His motto was *sacred revenge*, summed up in the proverb 'He who takes no revenge has not dedicated himself (*Ko se ne osveti, taj se ne posveti*)', and it was along these lines that 'the Serbian national idea' was expressed, 'and it was [from such people] that *haiduks*, Uskoks and avengers arose' (cf. Cvijić 1987).

On the contrary, wrote one author, it was precisely the example of Tomić that showed that the Croatian traditional songs 'in all their beauty not only do not lag behind Vuk's so much celebrated songs, but particularly surpass them in their ethics'.[1] A second author compared the songs about Tomić created among the Catholic Croats with those created 'among the Greek-Orthodox along the border with Montenegro and in Montenegro itself, where people also sang of Mijat', and concluded that the first were far more ethical. In them, he 'was not the *haiduk* the bully, the blood-sucker, he was not licentious', but 'a man of his word, of honour and probity'.[2]

Unlike the politically desirable Serbian *haiduks*, Mijat Tomić was, for the government established after World War II, if not exactly an Ustasha, then without doubt a suspect *counter-revolutionary element*. The fact that he was ideologised in the discourse of the NDH was not the key cause, because the Ustashas had also put Matija Gubec into an ideological frame, and this did not stop the Zagorje peasant rebel becoming the most prominent Croatian traditional figure in the Partisan and communist Pantheon. The difference between the two of them is that among the Partisans there was no critical human mass which would have included Mijat Tomić into this discourse, as the Slavonian and Zagorje Partisans had done with Gubec, because the only section of the population that could have done this creatively – the Croats of western Herzegovina and central Bosnia – not only did not accept the Partisan movement, but fought against it.

Despite attempts to make him into a more prominent pan-national symbol, the strongest and actually the only systematic cultivation of legends

---

1. 'Hrvatska narodna pjesma - izražaj duha hrvatstva', *Hrvatski narod*, 240, 12 October 1941. Cf. also N: 'Hrvatska narodna samobitnost očitovala se i u našim narodnim pjesmama', *Hrvatski narod*, 230, 2 October 1941.
2. Ivan Renđeo, 'Mijat Tomić. Prototip hrvatskog narodnog junačtva i predstavnik osebujne karakterne narodne individualnosti', *Spremnost*, 125, 9 July 1944.

about Tomić was in the relatively restricted area of western Herzegovina and the Duvno-Livno area, where even today if a newborn boy is of robust build he is said to have the 'back of a Mijat'. There are in fact a lot of sayings about him preserved in common speech. Croatian civilians took refuge en masse on Vran mountain from the collective revenge of the new authorities, and a few years after the war, there were still anti-communist guerrillas at work there – the last Ustasha and regular Croatian troops (*domobrans*). One of these groups spent the winter of 1945–46 in the extensive Mijat Cave, thoroughly at home in the symbolism of such a position: while the mountain was being searched by KNOJ and OZNA patrols, they encouraged each other by retelling the 'legends of this fighter of bygone days' (Tovilo 1970: 61). The cave, said Tovilo, had many entrances and 'some people claimed that in the depths below the earth you could get as far as Duvno, though the captain did not believe this' (ibid. 61). Such passages are a common motif in legends and traditions – and in *haiduk* tales too: according to one of them, it was possible to go underground all the way from Mijat's Cave to Travnik (Rubić and Nuić 1899: 276), and according to another, the band of Starina Novak had a back-up hiding place in a cave near Konjic, from where they could go underground right the way to Romanija (Palavestra 1991: 80).

Nevertheless, the basic conditions did exist for the Duvno *haiduk* to enter the new Yugoslav pantheon, because the Partisans were happy wherever possible to identify with the freedom-loving aspect of '*haidukery*', although the Serbs did so to a far greater extent and more systematically than the Croats. Indeed, Mijat turned up in Tito's army, both as a fighter with weapons, and as moral support. First, the Partisans of the Duvno Battalion, founded in mid-1942, took the name – what else – of Mijat Tomić, and when parts of it were incorporated into the Tenth Herzegovina Brigade in the spring of the following year, it helped this unit to become a unique case in the Partisan army, by having, at least then, an equal composition of Croats, Serbs and Bosniaks (Marijan 2000: 522–3). This was no small thing for Bosnia-Herzegovina or the official Tito ideology of *brotherhood and unity*.[1] And then, in May 1943, in eastern Bosnia, Vladimir Nazor wrote his poetic prose Partisan diary

1. In the neighbouring area of Livno in 1942 there was a Serb partisan unit called *Starac Vujadin*, also named after a *haiduk* (Orthodox), a hero of the epic tradition. It is worth repeating that the original epic culture did not perceive the Christian characters as Serbs or Croats in the modern sense of these concepts. But in the competition of military and political forces for the symbolic resources of popular culture such definitions were later ascribed to them. Or perhaps participants in that culture transferred their own ethnic and national identification to them, when they were overtaken by modern national integration processes in the mid-nineteenth century.

Underground Bosnia (Podzemna Bosna) – an obvious imitation of Dante's journey led by Virgil. An enigmatic old man, reminiscent of 'Greek, Illyrian, Bogumil, Turkish and Austrian times', leads the poet through the whole of Bosnian history. He is in fact the Genius of Bosnia, a land that in the current war of liberation was undergoing the awakening of all its dammed-up social energies, its historical apotheosis and the final, organic synthesis of all its components, contradictions and oppositions. On their way of course they come upon the heroes of the folk epic, decked out in their *toke*, ornamental breast-plates of metal, 'with bright arms, upon horses proud'. More precisely, they meet the three most celebrated in verse and the most symbolically potent: alongside the Serb Mali Radojica and the Bosniak Alija Đerzelez, it is the Duvno *haiduk* Tomić who embodies the third, Croatian ethnic and historical component of Bosnia (Nazor 1977: XVII, 188).

One event not long after the end of the war bears witness to the way the new government had in principle nothing against the glorification of the Duvno *harami başi* as part of the general build-up of the cult of heroism and the *haiduks* as their own historical forbears. In Zagreb there was a General Review of Seljačka Sloga, the pre-war educational association that was part of the Croatian Peasants Party, which the new authorities tolerated in the first few post-war years in order to get closer to the peasants. At the Review, the *gusle* player Petar Efendić Perkan from the vicinity of Sinj performed one epic song about Mijat Tomić and a new one about Tito, while in the first row, among the VIPs, were Tito's personal envoy General Arso Jovanović; Andrija Hebrang, who was minister for Croatia in the federal government; the prime minister of Croatia, Vladimir Bakarić; the omnipotent chief of police Ivan Krajačić and other members of the communist elite (*Vjesnik*, 23 September 1946).

But this was clearly too little, and the collective local burden of guilt too great for Mijat to be granted political favour. Somehow and somewhere he got lost along the way. While his pro-Yugoslav and pro-revolutionary Serbian and Montenegrin fellows (or at least those of them who had been smart enough to present themselves as such in good time) built careers in the army, entered the Party, and enjoyed veterans' privileges and a good social status, the Croatian separatist and counter-revolutionary Mijat sank into official oblivion. The Mijat Harambasha, or Mijat Tomić who could be found in post-war anthologies, was not the Catholic from Duvno, rather his namesake, an Orthodox man from the Montenegrin Drobnjak clan. Songs about him had been included by Vuk Karadžić in his anthology, and were then incorporated in new selections. It was this politically acceptable Mijat that Franjo Tuđman was thinking of when he listed the exemplary forbears of the new nomenklatura: this is shown by the reference to his having gone into outlawry because of the 'violence of Bey Ljubović', a man from Nevesinje, a neighbour of the Drobnjaks and the main target of their attacks. In the songs about the other Mijat, it is the beys or *kadis* of the Duvno area that are, quite logically, blamed for his fate. The two Mijats lived separately *at the base*, as the communists would say: in the Livno village of Kablići today there are a dozen Tomić families, originating from Duvno, who are said by tradition to be the descendants of Mijat, and consider themselves as such (Mijatović 1985: 30). In Drobnjaci, meanwhile, at least up to the war, there was a Tomić clan that stated with pride that they derived from that other much-sung *harami başi* of the same name and surname (Luburić 1930: 78–83).

If anyone from the nomenklatura or among the anthology writers even remembered the first Tomić, he would have been seen above all as a kind of proto-communist, opponent of class exploitation – a revolutionary theme that had to be explained 'through the scientific postulates of Marxism-Leninism' (Kaštelan 1949: 91) – but not the Croatian hero in the way in which, in the same Marxist interpretation, Starina Novak could remain a Serbian hero. Unlike Novak, Bajo Pivljanin or Starac Vujadin, who could not fail to achieve the glory of victory, for their names were borne by Partisan and Chetnik units, often in the same regions, Duvno Mijat had not been so provided.

He could console himself with the fact that he shared his fate, for the same reasons, with an eighteenth-century *haiduk*, Ivan Bušić alias Roša, a *harami başi* from Gorica near Grude, on the Herzegovina-Dalmatia border. In 1977, a scion of Roša's line, the journalist Bruno Bušić, the most influential ideologue of the younger generation of Croatian political émigrés, interpreted the life of his *haiduk* forbear, in terms in which Mijat Tomić would certainly have recognised himself:

> Indeed, the life of Ivan Bušić-Roša was in many ways like the life of today's Croatian oppositionists. From the first day when he went to the *haiduks* he was exposed to Venetian, Austrian and Ottoman pursuit squads, the tricks of accusers and enemies, as well as the twists of the lowest drives of some of the *haiduks* from his own band. Spied on by Vlach informants, respected by Muslim heroes ... *Harami başi* Roša sometimes had to leave the Croatian forests and go abroad. Like many Croatian political refugees, he too did the rounds of cities and countries ... but nowhere found peace, because he was everywhere persecuted by paid killers and

unease about his own homeland ... For the Croatian warrior and oppositionist, then as now, there was neither understanding nor mercy in any part of the world, in any country (Bušić 1983: 566–9).

With or without an ideological undertow, in Mijat's home country his memory was not eclipsed even in the new Yugoslavia. Indeed, the disfavour into which he had fallen made him a still more powerful national symbol and ultimately strengthened his connection with Tomislav's coronation assembly. In fact, it made him quite the equal of the first Croatian king. If he did not become a rabid anti-communist in this kind of context, it was clear that he had a poor opinion of the communists, and it was not without irony, or logic, that in such a conceptual position he ended up as the protagonist of a profession that the communists celebrated as a cult, and the proprietor of a curriculum vitae that the communists actually experienced as the ideal anticipation, almost a prefiguration, of their own mission.

It is even less illogical that Mijat was to persist as a powerful political motif in the work of two Croatian poets who were imprisoned in Tito's Yugoslavia not only because of their origins in the Herzegovina / Duvno region, but, perhaps more importantly, because of their political views, and who were prevented from publishing and harassed in a number of other ways. Thus the circle closed by degrees: to start with, Mijat Tomić, as a figure in the traditional epic, did not succeed in entering into the official imaginary of heroes because he personified a region that was on the whole against Yugoslavia (although many of its inhabitants were not Ustashas in a deliberate ideological sense but were simply – or so it seemed to them – patriots who were fighting for an independent state of Croatia). Secondly, as a result, in that area *haiduk* Mijat grew into a still more vigorous and politicised symbol, not only of Croatian ethnic identity, but also of anti-communism. Thirdly, semantically complemented and brought up to date, he was able, as motif and metaphor, to enter into poetry that did not draw on the traditional epic, either poetically or in spirit, and nor did it try, as complex and intimate lyric, to communicate to an audience with traditional aesthetic preferences. Fourthly, in the nature of things, such authors found themselves bearing the brunt of politically motivated repression, which only backed up and confirmed the new symbolism of resistance, and thus through feedback proved the communists right in their view that Mijat – and all that he personified – had been quite correctly put in quarantine.

Thus in the poem 'Duvno Field' ('Duvanjsko polje'), from a lyric cycle published at the beginning of the 1980s, just after Tito's death, Vladimir

Pavlović saw Tomić as a symbol of national survival in

> *bad times*
> *from Tomislav to Mijat,*
> *from Mijat right down to my fate*
> *when my fate makes me stop before him.*

But he was also a sign of the man's inseparable connection with his home country. A young man whom poverty had driven to work in Germany, like so many others in the seventies, and who had been killed there, was buried precisely in this field 'filled with epic unease':

> *And Mijat's black soil*
> *is sprinkled on his forehead.*
> *(Oh cursed land Germania).*
> (Pavlović 1981: 1056)

For the other poet, in a vision of longed-for national revival, it is this *haiduk*, far more than the medieval king, crowned according to legend on the same field, who is a guarantee that an independent Croatian state really will be born from new efforts in the days of the continent-wide break-up of communism, and that finally 'the Tomislav votive stone' will be 'redeemed'.

> *Mijat's shade over Jabuka errs....*
> *at one more parliament, people, gather*
> (Vučemil 1990: 32)

A year or two later the poet's wish was granted, although not exactly on the meadow on which both vernacular tradition and deliberate symbolic production had brought together as equals two representative figures divided by seven centuries: a king and a *haiduk*.

For between 2 and 7 July 1996, a series of events was put on, at the instigation of the HDZ Youth of Zagreb, in Tomislavgrad (formerly Duvno), under the joint patronage of the Assembly of the Bosnia Herzegovina Federation and the Parliament of the Republic of Croatia under the title of *Croatian Sabor* ('Parliament'). As the leaflet of the programme explained, these events 'casting light on hidden but fundamental historical events' were supposed to make the youth of Croatia 'aware of their national tradition' (*Slobodna Dalmacija*, 5 July 1996). The *Sabor* was held in front of a church dedicated in 1925 in honour of the thousandth anniversary of the Croatian kingdom, under a symbolic royal crown. The oratorio *King Tomislav* was performed, and there was a stage show of *The First Croatian Parliament*. The oratorio was inspired by the reliable fact that in 925 a papal letter included the title *rex Croatorum* alongside the name of Tomislav, as well as by the highly unreliable supposition that his ceremonial coronation took place on Duvanjsko Polje. The second performance was inspired by the legend that the Croatian Parliament was formally founded at the same time, in 753. In a session lasting twelve days it determined the boundaries of the state, the internal administrative order of the country, and the relations between Church and state.

After the choir had sung the Croatian anthem, the chairman of the Municipal Council, Mijo Tokić, in his opening words from the official dais, gave the event a powerful, three-layered symbolism:

> Here on Duvanjsko Polje, where the sword of Mijat has always guarded us from Turkish and alien might; here on Duvanjsko Polje, where Tomislav obtained the right to a state in a free and equal Europe; here on Duvanjsko Polje, where for the first time the Croats assembled, as a free and sovereign people, to say what they wanted, and how they wanted it, and for all the citizens – commons, clergy and nobility – to create and organise their own Croatian state.[1]

Not even the chairperson of the Constituent Assembly of the Federation of Bosnia-Herzegovina, Mariofil Ljubić, omitted to mention Mijat Tomić – although, considering the very large and quite legal celebration of Tomislav's coronation in 1925, he did not exactly need to start his speech with the peroration that 'twelve centuries had to pass for us to be able, in freedom and freely, to refresh the memories of these great events and the people in those events'. Indeed, it was as if he made a particular effort to keep Tomić under the lights of the opulent stage setting, 'in the shade of the votive basilica':

> Tomislavgrad has two great names, names a thousand years distant from each other – Tomislav and Mijat. Of course, there are all kinds of differences. But we Croats have transmitted Mijat's name from generation to generation, as well as Mijat's native soil, as symbol of resistance and the quest for freedom.

---

1. This and the next quotation from the speeches are cited according to the direct transmission of Channel 1 of HTV, July 1996 (the author has a video of this).

However much Ljubić himself privileged Mijat Tomić, in the imagery of the celebration and its official interpretation, the doughty *haiduk* had to give way before his established state-creating rival, the royal founder of the state that had so recently risen again after centuries of denial. And the *haiduk* band that dealt out justice from the 'green hills' had to cede precedence to the decisions of the political magnates. For, as a guest from Zagreb, Vladimir Šeks, vice-president of the Parliament, said: 'In the thirteen-century-long history of the Croatian people, it is the Croatian parliament that most directly expresses the idea of national independence' (*Državnost*, 59, 12 July 1996), stressing that he had brought gifts from the parliament to 'the secular and the spiritual arms, equally'.

One way or another, it was an undoubtedly interesting meeting of two different social memories, and two imaginations structured within a single people split by a state line: in the imaginary of the Bosnia-Herzegovina Croats, where the most vivid historical substance is the *physical violence* of the Ottoman government, the *man who resists with his rifle* dominates, the highland *haiduk* who rebels against an unjust government to overthrow it by force. In the political imaginary of the Croats from Croatia, on the other hand, where the central image is the *legal violence* of Austrian, Hungarian or Venetian power, it is the *establishment that resists with legal knowledge and political and diplomatic skill* that predominates – that is to say, the parliamentary representative who remains in the system in order to prove to it its own lack of legitimacy, invoking the old charters and citing the legal provisions, and then winning the right to a state. Put differently, Tomislav symbolises resistance and self-confirmation with institutional resources, with the power of historical and legal legitimacy, while Mijat does so by extra-institutional means.

In the light of all this, it remains to be seen how the main figures of this story fared after the collapse of communism in 1990, when the ethnic-nationalist parties, victors at the first free elections, everywhere started the systematic renaming of streets and squares, sometimes with good reason, restoring the names that the communists had changed, sometimes with an ideological violence equal to that of the communists before them. When it took power in this majority Croat area, even before war broke out, the HDZ of Bosnia-Herzegovina restored to Duvno its name of Tomislavgrad, which it had adopted in 1925 and which the communists had done away with in 1945. It did so following a legal procedure through the Bosnia-Herzegovina Assembly.

But what is particularly interesting here is the change of the names of almost all the streets and squares, the whole city *architexture*. This term was coined by the Israeli anthropologist Maoz Azaryahu, to denote the whole complex of urban architecture and the text that labels it. This text, that is the selection of monuments and names of streets and squares, is actually a kind of narration, a symbolic statement of an ideological and political programme. Every change is always a battle to drive out one memory and install another, a sign that a new government has taken control of the space. The subject in which Azaryahu was interested was the architecture of Berlin and the phases of its development – from the united city and capital of a united Germany, through the Nazi period and the two subtexts that were created in the Western and Eastern parts of the city while it was divided, up to the changes that followed in the former East Berlin after the fall of the Wall. These were not, as one might have imagined, an unambiguous deletion of the communist and a mechanical restoration of the pre-communist architexture (Azaryahu 1992).

As in other cities and villages in the area of the HDZ's para-state of the Croatian Community of Herceg-Bosna, and elsewhere in the post-communist countries, all names linked with communism, Tito, Yugoslavia and its catalogue of exemplary figures and events were immediately removed, to be replaced by those that symbolised the Croatian past and Croatian statehood, from the medieval royals to politicians of the last half of the nineteenth and first half of the twentieth century. They included also the names of the medieval Bosnian rulers, who in this ideological interpretation were also unambiguously Croats and Catholics, as Bosnia was still then exclusively 'Croatian land'. In the second phase, when the policy of the HDZ had become more radical, and gradually slid into open conflict with the Bosniaks, these traditional names too were removed, as they recalled the Ottoman period of Bosnian history. The new architexture of Tomislavgrad, which up to the war had a 10 percent Bosniak population, did not after all become exclusively Croatian, as happened elsewhere in areas controlled by the Croatian Community of Herceg-Bosna. Although the Bosniaks were on the whole degraded to the rank of second-class citizens, there was no systematic destruction of Islamic religious buildings or mass expulsions or murders.

It is not unexpected that the *haiduk harami başi* Mijat Tomić should have figured in this kind of context in the company of princes, kings and members of the Croatian aristocracy, along with politicians, writers, priests and a cardinal, but it is to some extent surprising that he outdid them symbolically. For he got the central, broadest and longest street, which runs through the whole town, and in such a way that one named after his nephew and faithful comrade Mali Marijan (Little Marijan) runs into its main, southern entrance. In the overall architextural situation, then, it is as though the symbolic figure of the unsubdued *haiduk* seizes the town in a belated but nevertheless real victory, and marches through it in triumph at the head of his band all the way to the monumental King Tomislav basilica at the northern exit. It is not quite monosemic, however, for on the way he meets the street of one good old acquaintance, neither Croat nor Christian, not even a victim of either Muslim or Yugoslav repression, nor a person who is in any way underprivileged, in fact quite the reverse, a member of the ruling religious, political and social elite of Mijat's time. For a hundred or so metres before the royal basilica, *Ulica Bega Kopčića* (Kopčić-bey Street) runs into *Ulica Mijata Tomića*.

A whole epic history is thus retained and retold through precisely coded architexture, the bey's presence preserving what was not preserved elsewhere under the HDZ: the message that no age, not even the Ottoman period, can be understood in black and white images.

The Ottoman Empire once again in the Balkans

> In Herzegovina too in all the nooks and crannies the 'fine days of Aranjuez' are fading. And there too, modern life with its gospel of science and its new ideals has begun to make itself at home. The proud Čengićes and Ljubovićes, the heroic Tomić and the marvellous Pecirep, the haiduks, *are being replaced by teachers, surveyors and writers. What a marvellous opportunity these contrasts offer some profound poet. Where is this Herzegovinian Cervantes ...?*

(Antun Gustav Matoš: *From Herzegovina*, 1897).

The Greater Serbian assault on Bosnia-Herzegovina, which started in Herzegovina, with the destruction of the Croat village of Ravno at the beginning of October 1991, as part of the attack by the JNA and its allied squads of Chetniks on Dubrovnik, inevitably revived the smouldering symbolism of *haiduk* resistance and self-defence. When the Serbian aggression against Bosnia-Herzegovina began, the Croats from Doljani and Jablanica founded, inside the HVO brigade called Herceg Stjepan, a battalion that bore the name of Mijat Tomić. And nor was the *harami başi* forgotten in the other, northern part of the country: one member of the 101st Bosanski Brod Brigade of the HVO compared himself, in an interview with a reporter covering the war in the summer of 1993, precisely with Mijat: 'while you snap your fingers, he's off, no one can catch him' (Tunjić 1994: 134).

This shows that the way the *haiduk* was valued in the discourse of the Bosnia-Herzegovina Croats was essentially different from the image promoted in Croatia. When at the end of 1992 the Croatian-Bosniak conflict began to be stirred up and hence a new adversary emerged, still greater cracks, in fact a real rift, appeared. The discourse in Croatia continued to preserve the concept of *haiduk* as criminal, and apply it exclusively to the Serb paramilitaries and thus, whether this was acceptable to it or not, they remained in a terminological coalition with the Bosniaks. Despeite the war between the HVO and the AB-H, for this discourse, the RSK president, Milan Martić, would remain what he had always been, a person who had 'rebelled and gone to the *haiduks*, the highway robbers' (Ivica Marijačić, *Vjesnik*, 9 April 1994). His fellow-thinkers at all levels would fare similarly: the member of parliament Miroslav Kutle (HDZ) did not believe that the rebel Serbs in Slavonia would consent to an agreement with Zagreb, because he knew that 'for the *haiduks* that run the game there, the leaders of the rebellion, their prime terrorists, there was no going back' and that '*haiduks* could not be negotiators' (*Večernji list*, 11 June 1995).

On the other hand, the discourse of the Croats in Herzegovina, and to a lesser extent also in Central Bosnia, initially organised and controlled by the HDZB-H, and later, through the logic of events and social memory, also spontaneous, would establish the concept of *haiduk* as just avenger, and apply it to itself, its own units, and those who were once again defending themselves against 'Turkish *zulüm* (violence)'. Its protagonists would thus, to this extent at least, enter into a kind of terminological coalition with the Serbs.

The first mention of *haiduk* in the new sense occurred in a letter from Mate Boban, president of the HDZB-H, to the archbishop of Zagreb, Cardinal Franjo Kuharić, who in mid-May 1993 published an appeal that everything possible should be done to halt the increasingly ferocious armed conflicts of the HVO and the AB-H, that is, the Croats and the Bosniaks, and to revive their collaboration in resisting Serbian aggression. In the introductory part of Boban's letter were the following sentences:

> Your Grace, I shall not make use of *Beggars and Sons* by the late Ivan Raos, but it makes many things clear to me. Such as the scene when the *haiduk* makes his confession to his Don Pavao but does not obtain absolution until he comes to the [Franciscan] guardian in Imotski. The *haiduk* is defended in his attitude to his enemies by God's attitude to his own enemies (Lucifer and his entourage).[1]

---

1. Mate Boban, 'Nismo željeli rat [We didn't want war]', *Slobodna Dalmacija*, 27 May 1993, p. 2.

This part of the letter was printed in a regional paper that maintained close ties with the Boban circle, but not in the two national circulation dailies – Zagreb's *Vjesnik* and *Večernji list* – although they too were under the control of official state policy. There, this short fragment, together with some other historical and poetic reminiscences, was removed. The editors evidently thought it was an insignificant decoration, a picturesque comparison without any relevance to the main political message, and hence a good chance to save space. However, if you look at the novel *Beggars and Sons (Prosjaci i sinovi)* by Ivan Raos, and find the reference that Boban indicated so precisely, it is easy to see that it is arguably the most important part of the letter – by no means coincidental decoration or emotional overlay, but a way of encoding a far-reaching message. It is certainly one of the most highly worked-out examples of the inclusion of the epic moral code and its terminology into contemporary political communication.

The invitation to the cardinal to read the episode clearly expresses the conviction of the writer of the letter that then he, Kuharić, will himself have many things explained to him, the misunderstanding between them will disappear, and they will become of like mind. The episode in question describes Don Pavao Čikeš, vicar on the troubled Ottoman and Venetian border in southern Herzegovina, in the Imotski-Grude-Posušje triangle, writing his memoirs in 1878, the year of the suppression of the revolt of Herzegovina Serbs against the Ottoman administration and the entry of the Austro-Hungarian army into Bosnia-Herzegovina. Although he had heard the confessions of many people in his lifetime, he admitted 'I shall never forget the day when I heard the confession of my first *haiduk*, a day in which my enthusiastic youthful soul was first touched, and then shocked.' This gigantic *haiduk*, 'a rock of a man', was 'weeping and groaning' and could not forgive himself for having roughly pushed a widow off the road and not given alms to some beggar. The priest was moved by someone suffering over such venial sins, to which few would pay much attention, but then, as 'a matter of custom', asked him whether he had killed anyone. Then they had the dialogue from which Boban directly derived his argumentation:

> 'I am ashamed, Father, to admit, lest you should think I am boasting and bragging ... Well, then, yes, a bit ... Well, thirty or so, what with Turks, what with gendarmes and any other kinds of stinking cattle.'
>
> And when I told him that these were sins, mortal sins, he almost sucked me in with his huge, sincerely astonished eyes. 'What's up with you, Father? What kind of sins are you talking

of? The Turks, man, are our enemies, our religious adversaries, and the gendarmes are blood feud enemies. Shall I perhaps take a feather to the bottoms of our enemies?'

I said: 'Peaceful Turkish merchants are not men of violence, and the gendarmes are the government, and every government comes from God ... The Lord said: Love your enemy as yourself.' (Raos 1971: 148)

Further on, the *haiduk* invokes the fact that in the Bible God dealt decisively and ruthlessly with his enemies – Lucifer and his entourage – a formulation imported directly into Boban's letter, and cast them into hell. And when the priest will not even then give him absolution, he casually concludes: 'Never mind, Father, I'll be off to the friars; they've been longer with us here, and they know better what's a sin here and what's not.' In the memoirs he wrote subsequently, the priest admits that he later heard the confessions of many *haiduk*s and absolved them, because he had soon 'learned what was a sin here' and what was the law of collective guilt and revenge (Raos 1971: 149). Using this literary model, Boban presents the *haiduk* as an exemplary extra-temporal figure, morally unquestionable, even implicitly raised to a divine level, because in his attitude towards his enemy he simply reproduces the Divine attitude towards Satan. Now, in the war with the Bosniaks and the AB-H, he was the mythical avenger of all the 'Turkish tributes (*harçs*) that we had to give', who would at last see justice done in relation to everything perpetrated by the Ottoman conquerors against the 'Croatian Catholic people in Herceg-Bosna'. 'We were impaled, our skin was flayed,' he wrote, 'male children were torn from their cradles and turned into Janissaries', or they 'brought in the *ius primae noctis*' for some agas really did demand that on their wedding night Christian brides should first of all be brought to their bed.

But the whole work makes it clear that Raos's literary picture of *'haidukery'* in southern Herzegovina and the Imotski *krajina* [borderland] was complex, just as it was in reality in those two centuries of 'all kinds of horrors at the electric eel of a border' of the two empires (Raos 1971: 91). On the one hand the *haiduks* were tragic, 'like the Son of Mankind: they had no stone upon which to lay their head', 'pursued by the Turks, pursued by the Venetians and their lackeys', 'damned with slavery and blessed with freedom' (Raos 1971: 147). While on the other their moral relativism and generally every degradation of the idea of resistance to the oppressor into common criminality was worthy of disgust and the severest condemnation. The writer clearly demythologises many among them as those who 'found a hundred heroic tricks for their dishonourable practices' and actually realised that 'it is easier to live from blood than from blisters'. During the Cretan War (seventeenth century), for example, they would capture healthy young men, mostly Christians, and sell them for a high price to the Venetians as galley slaves, and it was even worse for the Christians than the Turks, because the latter 'were threatened with danger only by the Christians, while the Christians were often more deadly to the Christian common people than the Turks' (Raos 1971: 91).[1]

Boban, or whoever wrote his letter, read selectively, as ideologues and propagandists tend to do, seeking only whatever was capable of supporting a judgment framed in advance. The message is clear: Kuharić is like the young Čikeš, raised in the seminaries and theological colleges of the city, far removed from the harsh reality of the border area and its coarsened people who for centuries 'had had knives sharpened on their ears', and in his idealism, or naivety, or stupidity, he does not understand the world and thinks that it is possible to live in it according to Christian ethical principles. But with time, like Čikeš, he will understand his errors, add some 'amendments' to the Decalogue, that is accept and bless the right to revenge, and thus become 'one of us', a priest of the people, like the friar who will give the *haiduk* absolution. (In a still broader vision Kuharić is like Belostenec, Stulli or Ančić, educated priests alienated from the people, who, in their comfortable offices, surrounded by books, compile dictionaries in which the *haiduk* is defined as robber, giving unfair advantage to formal legalism over vernacular moralism).

Not long after Raos's unnamed – but to that extent more representative character – an authentic epic figure with a name appears in the discourse. A newspaper commentator who does not agree with the advocates of the Croats and Bosniaks reaching an agreement, even at the price of certain concessions, but maintains that it is only the Bosniaks who are to blame for the conflict, quotes his constant interlocutor, his cousin Ćipa, representative of popular wisdom and common sense. Thanks to just this kind of traditional memory, he had from the beginning doubted the sustainability of the alliance:

---

1. The leader writer of the church paper was appalled by the letter that had 'gone beyond all standards of common sense', particularly by 'playing with the familiar witty scene from Ivan Raos's novel *Beggars and Sons*, where several centuries ago a Christian *haiduk* from the border area with the Turkey of the time would not accept the confessor's idea that it was a sin to kill 'Turks', but had rather sought another confessor 'who knew what was sin here and what was not'. We did not expect a message of moral relativism from circles that usually pride themselves on a firm and strict orthodoxy.', 'Pismo koje bi vrijedilo zaboraviti', *Glas Koncila*, 23, 6 June 1993.

> I remember the words of my cousin Ćipa at the height of the
> election campaign and the firm Croat-Muslim coalition. He
> asked in amazement: 'What would our '*aiduk* the late Mijovil
> Tomić have to say about all this?'[1]

That of course cannot be known. Dead mouths do not speak, tradition
has its ways and politics its own. Mijat's character was introduced into
contemporary political discourse in one way, but it could have been
completely different. This Herzegovina *haiduk* was a fighter against the
Ottoman authorities, that is, in one aspect, *via facti*, against the followers of
Islam, but his band contained, as well as the majority Catholics, also Muslims
(and Orthodox). Even a contemporary children's novel will note with
approval that Mijat never discriminated against people of other religions, and
so several Muslims joined his band 'and fought with it against the violence
of the Turks' (Horvatić 1982: 61, 55). Not long ago, among the Bosniaks
near Konjic and Jablanica, a tradition was recorded showing Tomić in a good
light, as a man of probity who kept his promises and had no prejudices about
the Muslims (Đogo 1931).

Both traditional memory and a contemporary children's novel that
slotted harmoniously into the tradition obviously make possible a different
set of metaphors than that of the journalist. For instance, this could be the
kind that was suggested by Bruno Bušić in the liberal political atmosphere of
the Croatian Spring 1967–71 when he wrote in 1969 that it was 'necessary
to revive and give new force to the ethical principles of Mijat Tomić and his
'*haircut godfatherhood (šišano kumstvo)*' (Bušić 1983: 82). Originally inspired
by the principles of Ante Starčević's Party of State Right, Bušić did not fail
to point out that there were Muslims in Mijat's band, just as in the article
about his distant *haiduk* forbear he mentioned that *harami başi* Roša was
also respected by the Muslims' heroes and that in his band, as well as thirty
Catholics, there was one Muslim who was described by a contemporary of
these events, a Franciscan chronicler of central Bosnia, as 'not a bad man
either' (Benić 1979: 261). More important, though, is the mention Bušić
makes of 'godfatherhood'.

As distinct from the baptismal godfather, which, of course, was possible
only among Christians, in Bosnia-Herzegovina, as in Serbia up to the 1804
Insurrection, the idea of the haircutting or shaving godfather developed as
a form of ritual kinship among Muslims and Christians, something that
overcame religious differences and strengthened bonds of friendship among

---

1. Petar Miloš, 'Alija - guja u njedrima [Alija – viper in the bosom]', *Slobodna Dalmacija*,
   8 December 1993.

those of different faiths. A godfather would cut a lock from his godson's hair and thenceforth protect him even at the cost of his own life. In some regions of Bosnia-Herzegovina the Muslims considered the 'haircut godfather' (*šišani kum*) as more important than similar relations contracted at marriage or circumcision. It is mentioned in *The Mountain Wreath*, when Arslan-Aga Muhadinović asks Vuk Mandušić, whom he appreciates as a hero, to be the godfather of his son. Vuk, however, refuses because 'there can be no godfather but a Christian godfather', in other words the two of them can have such relations only if Arslan-Aga is converted to Christianity (Njegoš 1987–1043).

Bušić, of course, was not thinking of this scene, rather of the song 'The Haircut Godfatherhood of Tomić Mihovil' ('Šišano kumstvo Tomić Mihovila'), or 'Tomić Mihovil and Tešnjanin Alija', as it was entitled in 1861 when it was first printed in Zadar. In this song, the Duvno *haiduk* becomes the haircut godfather of the firstborn of Tešnjanin (in some versions Biščanin) Alija. It is precisely by the evocation of this motif that Bušić argues for the collaboration of Croats and Bosniaks in resisting Serbian political hegemony in Yugoslavia. In this Bušić was no exception, rather part of a trend in Croatian political life that used this epic and its real-life motif to address the Bosnian Muslim milieu for the purpose of rising above old hatreds and old mistrust. In 1931, the folklore collector Stjepan Banović wrote a libretto for an opera based on this song.

A decade later, a Mostar Muslim, the teacher Husein Đogo (Dubravić), a journalist and writer, made use of the same theme for his play *Mijat Harambasha and Tešnjanin Alija*, also with a clearly discernible political tendency deriving from the Party of State Right ideology. In the play, the little son of Tešnjanin Alija, nameless in the epic songs, receives a name: Adem, after another Tešnjanin, Đogo's political fellow-thinker, the politician and later assistant head of the NDH Adem-Aga Mešić. The godson thus becomes a symbol of the two religions of the Croats, and the relationship is a ritual that reconciles and unites not just two families but also the two wings of a single nation: Croats of the Catholic and Croats of the Islamic faith. Mijat accepts the relationship, saying that they are all 'of Croatian speech and Croatian kind', irrespective of religion, because 'God is one' and Alija replies that now they are 'just one family' which is 'quite right as we are Croats'. In the end the Catholic *haiduk* and the Muslim merchant agree that the main culprit for all their woes is 'in the East', that is, Belgrade (Đogo 1941).

A chapter in Horvatić's novel about Tomić is dedicated to the same theme, also with a message that does not fit in with the political insights of cousin Ćipa: the protagonists become friends, because Alija has understood that Mijat 'became a *haiduk* out of distress, and not out of wickedness or the desire for plunder', while Mijat recognises that Alija is no greedy tyrant, but a worthy and hard-working merchant, who has become rich only by 'careful stewardship in his shop' (Horvatić 1982).

But when, twenty-four years after Bušić's article, and eleven years after Horvatić's novel, the *haiduk* Mijat Tomić was evoked with different connotations, it was inevitable that the protagonists of that trend in Croatian political discourse should also redefine the current adversary – the Bosniaks and the AB-H. Alija Izetbegović became the Grand Vizier (Josip Jović, *Slobodna Dalmacija*, 30 April/1–2 May 1993), his official diplomatic representatives were 'Alija's *telals* [Ottoman town-criers]' (Željko Olujić, *Slobodna Dalmacija*, 27 January 1994), and the summons by some local Croat clubs to a protest in front of the Embassy of Bosnia-Herzegovina in Zagreb ended with the statement that they did not want to be subject to Greater Serbia, but not to any 'new Agas and Beys either' (*Slobodna Dalmacija*, 1 March 1994). The priest Anto Baković, retired, but still very active in public life, writes that after an attack on the Croat villages in Neretvica the AB-H is called by 'its one and only proper name today – Ottoman' and he 'begged' Croats to accept the term (*Vjesnik*, 17 June 1993). In his writings up to the end of the year Baković persevered with this, but without many followers in Croatia itself. The newspaper columnist Srećko Jurdana wrote of the 'Ottomans in Bosnia' and the 'Ottoman refugees' taken in by Croatia (*Slobodna Dalmacija*, 24 June 1993), and a marginal party, HDSP, issued a communiqué about an attack by the 'Ottoman hordes', that is, the AB-H, on Vareš (*Slobodna Dalmacija*, 8 November 1993). The most persistent local promoter of the ideologeme about the 'new Turks' and about the Turks having come again, the parish priest of Mate Boban's birthplace, his personal friend and, it would seem, the real author of a good many of his public statements, Fra Ante Marić, published countless articles in the 1991–3 period crammed with the most naturalistic and disgusting accounts of the violence of the Ottoman regime: impalement, the roping of Christian peasants to horses' tails and so on. These were all clearly ideological and intended to mobilise opinion, in an attempt to portray the current military and political conflict as a continuation of the former clash between Christianity and Islam. Collecting them all into a book, he gave it the title *Stay Your Hand, Mowers*, evoking the classical epic words of Mijat Tomić when he found the *kadi*'s people on his meadow (cf. Marić 1994).

Wielders of memory

The Ottoman conquest of Bosnia, that is, the collapse of the medieval Bosnian kingdom in 1463, left a profound mark in the collective ideas, historical consciousness and oral traditions of all three ethnoreligious communities. This watershed is in some sense a focus of all later thinking about the various aspects of social and political reality and a frequent source of fatal partiality. In schematic terms, it can be said that on the Croatian and Serbian sides, the chaos, the reign of terror and the arbitrariness of the local rulers during the last two centuries of Ottoman rule were attributed to the first two centuries as well, when conditions were in fact relatively settled. Among the Bosniaks, on the other hand, the picture is reversed. The entry into Bosnia of an empire that was at the peak of its power, and effectively organised militarily, financially and administratively, is interpreted as liberation, the basis of the country's prosperity. And the major achievements in architecture and art of the Ottoman period were taken as a sign that the society was in all its aspects, and for all its members, subject to practically impeccable governance. In both cases the result is a distorted and deeply ideologised image – at once the demonisation and the idealisation of one and the same polysemic and complex situation, conditional upon the working of both internal and external factors.

Such memories, which are transmitted through family and social contacts and printed testimonies, constitute an important component of the collective awareness and exist latently as transhistorical criteria for the assessment of current events and relations of social power. But objective conditions and external stimuli still determine whether these memories will be activated, and to what extent, as real social and political power. At one time they may be invoked by one side, as a spontaneous self-defence mechanism, just because the other side, following its own internal political and psychological needs, has instigated the idealisation or demonisation of a given historical situation.

At another time the collective traumas are objectively revived by a social situation that is inaccessible to the direct influence of either side. During the serious Croat-Bosniak conflicts in central Bosnia, Fra Ljubo Lucić, a sincere Bosnian patriot, a very decent and well-meaning man, recalled one such situation. In World War II, there were considerable numbers of Bosniaks – whether out of conviction, escaping from Chetnik massacres, or according to the logic of the call-up – in Ustasha and regular Croatian army units (*domobrans*), or in rural militias that were part of the military system of the

NDH. But in central Bosnia, where the numerical relation of Croats and Bosniaks was on the whole balanced, for various reasons Bosniaks

> were mainly among the Partisans, which cannot at all be said for the Croat population of this part of Bosnia ... After the war the Muslim section of the population occupied many more senior positions in the new government than the Croatian population, so that in some parts of central Bosnia it was said that the 'Turkish *vakat* (era)' had come again. This fact should not be overlooked when the causes of the current misunderstanding are analysed.[1]

Then again, enduring collective notions were programmatically awakened and instrumentalised by organised political forces. At the end of 1992 and the beginning of 1993 the discourse of the HDZ and HDZB-H aimed at just this kind of psychological mobilisation, shifting after a period of alliance with the Bosniaks to a policy that would give rise to the massacre of civilians, concentration camps (Dretelj, Gabela, Mostar Helidrome), the expulsion of the Bosniaks from many areas ruled by the HVO, and the systematic destruction of cultural and religious monuments, as well as whole city centres (Mostar, Stolac). The evocation of the *haiduk* was just a part, if an important one, of a state of mind thus created. Complementary to it is the systematic propaganda evocation of traditions enshrining the historical memory of the Christian peasantry from the final chaotic period of Ottoman rule. The task was not a difficult one, because these 'oral tales and memories' amounted to a relatively narrow circle of topics: the violent abduction of young Christian women to the landowners' mansions and the insistence on the *droit de seigneur*, which in these patriarchal communities was the 'worst of crimes and an insult to human dignity' (Palavestra 1991: 75). To them we can also add the punishment of impalement, for the evocation of which a scene from the novel *Bridge on the Drina* by Ivo Andrić could be drummed into service (Žanić 1996c), and the establishment of a *devşirme*-system, the boy-tribute which supplied the membership for Janissary army, and 'was the most important method for drawing people from Christian Europe into the machinery of the Ottoman state', including of course their conversion to Islam (Malcolm 1994: 45–46).

Mate Boban's letter to Cardinal Kuharić is an exemplary specimen of such a procedure. After the introductory evocation of the *haiduk*, which functions as cognitive core and symbolic skeleton for the whole text, there is a pedantic listing of everything the Catholic Croats suffered under the Turks,

---

1. Ljubo Lucić, 'Hrvati i Muslimani', *Svjetlo riječi*, 124, July 1993.

ergo Bosniaks: 'we were impaled, our skin was flayed', the Turks took their tribute and raised male children as Janissaries, a list that repeated that of his ideological fellow-thinker in his newspaper columns with still more morbid details, returning with particular delectation of the motif of the 'aga wanting to sleep with the bride the first night' (Marić 1994: 169). Hence it is hardly accidental, historically, ideologically or politically, that, for example, the Serbian general Ratko Mladić was happy to tell foreign envoys and journalists, referring to the Bosniaks, that the Serbs had to 'submit their brides to their agas', that they would be impaled or that the Serb boys were taken off to the Janissaries 'later to be employed against their very own people' (Janjić 1996: 76, 101, 120). There was an easy concurrence between the HDZ and the Serbian discourse in other motifs, e.g., that the AB-H 'took Croatian maids and mothers who had been arrested off to their Muslim *harems'* (Stipe Puđa; *Slobodna Dalmacija*, 5 August 1993), and in terminology, notably that the Herzegovina Croats were at war with the AB-H in order to prevent the incursion of 'Turkish converts (*poturice*)' into the south of Croatia (Marko Semren; *Slobodna Dalmacija*, 7 July 1994).

A leading article in a Bosniak paper close to the SDA expressed outrage with good reason first at Serbian and then at Croatian worn phrases about the 'new Turkish invasion', and concluded: 'They are forever fighting new battles of Kosovo and Siget; they always have the Middle Ages in their heads' (*Ljiljan*, 55, 2 February 1994). At the same time, its editors and journalists embarked on a terminological reconstruction of its own exemplary age: at exactly the time when Boban was evoking Raos's *haiduk* as a model for the political behaviour of Croats, an AB-H soldier had become 'our *asker'* (Rifet Hasković; *Ljiljan*, 21, 7 June 1993). In an article by a militant party ideologue, the AB-H itself was called the 'Bosnian *nizam'* (Nedžad Latić; *Ljiljan*, 29, 13 October 1993): the term used for the regular army of the Ottoman Empire, as established in 1826. The message was clear: just as once the soldiers in the service of the lawful and exemplary Ottoman government had fought those rebelling against it, and, as the traditional epic said, 'thirty *askers'* had fought against 'thirty *haiduks'*, so today the legal *nizam* was fighting against two para-*nizam*s, Karadžić's Serbian and Boban's Croatian forces. The processes were interdependent: anyone who made use of the *haiduk* legitimised the employment of the *asker* and vice versa. One historical identification give rise to another, because semantic voids always tend to be filled, and ideological and terminological reconstructions to be brought into equilibrium.

The manner in which the Bosniak evocation system was promoted leads to the conclusion that it was not just a matter of the stylistic figures of the individuals concerned, but deliberate editorial tampering. For example, the article on the foundation of the AB-H Officers' School in Zenica, written in a neutral style, almost like an official report, is headlined in the style of a hymn 'A Bosnian *asker* am I!' ('Bosanski sam asker ja!') (*Ljiljan*, 41, 27 October 1993), while an unsigned weekly review of battlefield events, also written in dry officialese, obtained the title 'Bosnian askers – stronger than Geneva!' (*Ljiljan*, 46, 1 December 1993). The hymn of the 504th Muslim Krajina Brigade, celebrating its *askers*, was not the only song to use such terminology.

Terms are always as much a reflection as an instigator of political relationships and attitudes, inseparable and indistinguishable from them but, once borne along by their own internal logic, they endure. And even when the circumstances that originally gave rise to them change, they find their way into increasing numbers of newspapers and thus become a relatively widespread system of references. Two years later, in the summer and early autumn of 1995, after the Washington Agreement, the *haiduks* of the HVO were once again allies of the *askers* of the AH, and were able to devote themselves with all their might to that other, Serbian, *haiduk*, who had started it all, when in spring 1992 he attacked areas and people who were neither militarily nor terminologically prepared for such a course of events. In the meantime both factors had changed: in the 'fierce battle' for Donji Vakuf the VRS had a disastrous encounter with the *askers* of the 77th Vrbas Division of the AB-H (Džemal Sefer: *Bošnjak*, 20, 8 August 1995); the Bosnian *askers* of the 5th Corps soon entered Ključ (Edhem Ekmeščić; *Bošnjak*, 32, 31 October 1995); and the *askers* of the 2nd Corps pushed deep into Ozren (Fuad Halilović, *Zmaj od Bosne*, 99, 21 September 1995).

Some ten months after the end of the fighting, as part of the campaigning for the first elections after 1990, the HDZB-H arranged a huge meeting in Tuzla, at which, as the reporters said, the following impassioned words of the party leader, Ivo Andrić Lužanski, received the biggest ovation:

> I want to tell the great pasha Selim Bešlagić, a man who never misses a chance to spit on the Croatian people, that his pashalik is breaking up. The Croats are no longer the *rayah*... but a nation that is master in its own land.[1]

Least important of all here is that it was the liberal mayor of Tuzla who was proclaimed a 'pasha who oppresses the Christian *rayah*' [non-Muslim

---

1. B. Ćurković, 'Nismo raja ni 'sečeno cveće'', *Slobodna Dalmacija*, 8 August 1996.

common people]: he was a member of the Social Democratic Party, who, with a civil patriotic programme and in the difficult circumstances of war, managed to preserve relatively good inter-ethnic relations in the city, to keep religion apart from politics, and prevent Bosniak radicalism. As a result, he suffered constantly from the gross attacks and ploys of the SDA, whose ideologues could not come to terms with the fact that the second largest Bosnian city was beyond their political control. What is more, in the Tuzla region there were no Croat-Bosniak armed clashes at all, and the local HVO brigade had participated in the defence of the town the whole time as part of the 2nd Corps of the AB-H.

More interesting is the Croatian politician who is unable, or unwilling, to frame the most common or garden public criticism of his political rival, whether or not he has any grounds for his criticism, in any way other than by the mechanical reproduction of a few universal images and terms, aiming at the most superficial associations and banal of analogies. And most interesting of all are those who rewarded him with ovations, although they had for four years during the war been living witnesses that it was this man proclaimed pasha who had been among the rare leading Bosniak politicians to have opposed the idealisation and political manipulation of the Ottoman period and the Ottomanisation of the Bosniak socio-political identity, whose rhetoric was consistently civil and democratic. Decades of repetition of one and the same explicatory scheme seem to have destroyed the capacity to think in different categories and to have produced a real live Pavlovian reflex.

Half a year later, in the south of the country, in Mostar which had come out of the war devastated, divided into a western section ruled by the HDZB-H and an eastern section ruled by the SDA, there was a serious conflict. On February 10 1997, on the west bank, a provocative carnival was organized, deeply offensive to the Bosniaks, the climax being the burning of Alija Izetbegović in effigy. Meanwhile on the east side a group of Bosniaks had set out to visit the Muslim cemetery in Liska Park. They were intercepted by Croat police, who insulted them and drove them back, striking the Mufti of Herzegovina himself in the process. This scandalous behaviour angered not only the Bosniak public but also the international administration in the city, and in an extensive report in an influential SDA-controlled weekly, the author defined it vividly as

> the resurrection of Stojan Janković – who committed a vile crime in this very place at the end of the seventeenth century – in the person of the commander of the police of the western part of

town, Marko Radić Make, and the 'mourning' members of the special police.[1]

Stojan Janković was an Uskok *serdar* (commander) from northern Dalmatia. During the Venetian and Ottoman wars in the second half of the seventeenth century, as a soldier in the service of the Doge, he often made incursions into Herzegovina with his squad, looting, burning and carrying the Muslim population off into slavery. The incursion he made into Mostar in 1687 was particularly bloody: he surprised and murdered the faithful at their prayers in the mosque. This event remained deeply seared into the social memory of the Mostar Muslims, right up to the beginning of the twentieth century, as may be seen in the memoirs of Avdo Humo cited above (cf. p. 152). He writes that his deeply traumatised grandmother had related the story to him, concluding bitterly:

> Look now, you're going to read in school about the hero Stojan Janković. You can well see what kind of a hero he was. Why didn't he attack the Turkish army and show his valour there, and not against innocent people. (Humo 1984: 38)

It is not easy to say how much recent generations knew about it, but two things are certain, and a third very probable. First, in post-war Yugoslav school textbooks there were epic songs, Christian of course, about the fearless hero Stojan Janković, as part of the promotion of the *haiduk* and the Uskok cult. Secondly, the Yugoslav communist establishment, to which Humo actually belonged for a long time, saw nothing bad or inappropriate or one-sided in this. Thirdly, it is likely that in the grey zone of passive anti-communism, among the population more closely tied to tradition, particularly among the local Islamic religious ministers, memory of the crime continued to live on in some form (although probably not always with the awareness that Muslim squads, that is Herzegovina Muslims, had made incursions into the Venetian area with identical intentions and consequences).

And so if it is not possible to know everything that was said in February 1997 in ruined East Mostar, it is nevertheless possible, newspapers in hand, to decide that just 310 years after the Janković massacre, which really did happen in today's Liska Park, there was an author in an influential Bosnian newspaper who recalled it all. He immediately connected the two events and their participants, and offered this analogy to his readers as a worthwhile

---

1. Enes Ratkušić, 'Nakon karnevala koji je vodio Mijo Brajković (...)', *Ljiljan*, 214, 19 February 1997.

explicatory scheme, with the suggestive message that in the meantime nothing had changed. As for Make Radić himself, an arrogant troublemaker and bully who was able because of the chaos of the war and perfidious political patrons to attain legitimacy in no less a form than that of chief of police, the analogy is not so bad: it is bad only that it continued the vicious circle of political manipulation through traumatic memories and allegedly unsettled accounts.

Some wise and honest granny such as Humo's would probably have been able to utter some bitter comment in connection with this as well. And perhaps she already has. Only we have to wait until her grandson grows up, and in his disappointment writes the memoirs of his own generation.

Churches and the heroic epic

The peaks were overgrown with juniper scrub that gave the grey undercoat of the mountain a still darker expression. Such is Vran in its entirety: grey, gloomy and archaic. Even if there were no national tradition concerning the haiduk *Mijat Tomić, whose life and deeds are so closely connected with the name of this mountain, the very appearance of Vran would leave an impression with us of majestic reality... Nature created this mountain, this pyramid either for the* haiduk *for his defence or for the heart of the mountaineer, who is able to appreciate this beauty.*

(Fleger 1935: 226–9)

The site of Mijat's downfall, the parish of Doljani (950 inhabitants, 1991) is a story within a story. The good relations between the two ethno-religious communities from the time of their joint resistance, when a good number of Bosniaks fought in the HVO, were ruined by incidents involving an increasingly strong and almost entirely Bosniak AB-H in Jablanica. In the end, on 28 July 1993, Bosniak units fought their way into the village and murdered forty-three civilians, incarcerating another 200 in Jablanica. A year later a visitor would meet people in Doljani who remembered with bitterness both this tragedy and the massacre of 1942, when the Chetniks in the Rama area systematically killed all men over the age of sixteen. Then the *haiduk* whom local tradition 'sang of as representative of the struggle of the people for their rights' must have been recalled, with an epic quotation about how the 'Turkish tyranny oppressed the commoners (*rayah*)', protection was nowhere to be found, and so Mijat went off 'to seek justice / in the chasms and strait ravines' and 'himself to teach the Turks to judge / the best was

Suzica the *kadi*.[1]

After Kupres fell to the Serbs in April 1992, the HVO pushed its way over Vran – with its highest peaks of Veliki Vran (2,074m) and Mali Vran (2,017 m) – to the Road of Salvation (*Cesta spasa*), the only link between central Bosnia and the south. The road ran through the basin between Vran and Čvrsnica, that is, precisely where, as an old friar who lived in this almost entirely depopulated area explained to a journalist, Mijat Tomić 'awaited the columns of the unrighteous, punished them, protecting his own people, property and religion' (*Slobodna Dalmacija*, 7 October 1994). And he is not the only reason that these mountain areas are deeply implanted in the consciousness of the Croats of western Herzegovina. Here, during the first Yugoslavia, when the state monopoly run by the government in Belgrade systematically destroyed the cultivation of the tobacco that was the mainstay of their existence, they smuggled tobacco on their backs all the way to Slavonia. Here to this day the lowland stockbreeders entrust their herds during the summer droughts to the mountaineers, the herdsmen who look after them on the mountain grazing grounds.

Naturally, when the Croat-Bosniak conflict ended, the use of such evocative epic terms and motifs for the purpose of the moral, historical and political legitimisation of the quarrel also ceased. Although it unfolded methodologically according to the same pattern as the Serbian discourse, in the whole of the Croatian equivalent it did not come anywhere near the scope and comprehensiveness of the Serbian. There were several reasons for this, some of which touch very deeply on cultural and political history.

The open Croat-Bosniak war lasted a little more than one year, a shorter time than the Serbian aggression against Bosnia-Herzegovina. It was opposed from the beginning by most of the Croatian public – all the relevant opposition parties, a relatively powerful current in the HDZ itself, including the presidents of both of the houses of parliament, Mesić and Manolić, the Catholic Church in Croatia and Bosnia-Herzegovina, the most highly respected cultural institutions such as the Croatian Academy with its president Ivan Supek and Matica Hrvatska (Croatian Heritage Foundation) headed by Vlado Gotovac, a fairly high-circulation part of the press that had retained its independence, above all the Split weekly *Feral Tribune* and Rijeka's daily *Novi list*, and the non-HDZ political forces among the Croats in Bosnia-Herzegovina. These groups all championed an alliance of the two victims of Greater Serbian expansionism, the preservation of Bosnia-

---

1. Marijan Karaula, 'Rijekom Ramom nizvodno', *Svjetlo riječi*, 135, July 1994. The quotation is from the epic song 'The Death of Mijat Tomić' ('Smrt Mijata Tomića') (Mijatović 1985).

Herzegovina within its internationally recognised borders and the pursuit of an agreement with the Bosniaks about the decentralisation of the country.

What is more, the figure of Tomić, like the whole of the *haiduk* epic, was poorly known in Croatia proper, and there was no experience at all of the tradition being put to political use. This is indicated in a way by the fact that in 1992 Mijat Tomić was not mentioned where he might have been expected – in the book of the Ministry of Defence, *For Croatia (Za Hrvatsku),* compiled by Ivan Tolj from Herzegovina, which discussed exemplary figures from national history, people who had made their names in warfare and resistance to alien rule. Nor does he appear in the later similar but far more extensive and ambitious *Manual for Croatian Officers, NCOs and Soldiers (Priručnik za hrvatske časnike, dočasnike i vojnike),* among those heroes in the battles against the Turks, where there were such moral and patriotic examples as Marko Mesić, liberator of Lika, whom Horvatić too mentions in the letter quoted here against the 'erroneous' use of the concept of the *haiduk,* and the Uskok *harami bașis* Vuk Mandušić and Ilija Smiljanić (Vukasović 1995). This omission is the more unusual in that the relevant chapter about 'famous Croatian men – models, patriots' was written by the history professor and journalist Anđelko Mijatović, who had in fact dealt very systematically with Tomić, had personally spent years visiting the places connected with him and prepared several volumes of songs and material about him and his times.

In Serbia similar military handbooks without *haiduks* are simply unimaginable. One reason is that the Serbian Orthodox Church (SPC) admitted many of the elements of Serbian vernacular culture and the mythical consciousness of their congregation into its political ecclesiology, including the liturgy, even strengthened them, creating a kind of theological aura around them. In this 'vigorous symbiosis' of Church and commoners, the former assumed the political and the latter the psychological initiative (Džaja 1992: 98). Under Ottoman rule, the ancient popular rituals, beliefs and traditions were revived. Although the already assimilated layers of Byzantine Christian culture were not expunged, this 'economically and spiritually impoverished milieu' was incapable of accepting theological learning and other higher forms of feudal culture (Popović 1983: 109).

It was only in the 18th and at the beginning of the nineteenth century in southern Hungary, under Western influences, that the Serbian Orthodox Church began to wage a more vigorous campaign against ancient popular beliefs, while Western Christianity had managed more or less to deracinate traces of the polytheistic cults in the European nations by the sixteenth or seventeenth century. As a result, the Catholic Church in the South Slav lands was far stricter and more selective: it systematically suppressed songs containing drastic examples of superstition, debauchery, cruelty and violence generally. Its pre-war intervention in the attempt to bring about an uncritical idealisation of Mijat Tomić was just part of this continuous educational effort. Thus, for instance, in 1727 Fra Lovro Sitović of Ljubuški, in his 'Poem about Hell' ('Pisna od pakla'), attempted to replace with religion the world that was offered to the people in 'futile songs' about warfare and red wine, against true Church morality. Similarly in 1736, Fra Toma Babić pragmatically called upon the people to sing religious songs instead of those about *haiduks*.

Disagreements did sometimes occur in this connection. At the end of the 1930s Fra Gašpar Bujas, professor for a long time at the Franciscan Colleges in Sinj, Makarska and Zagreb, a theological writer and researcher into popular creativity, responded to the accusations of some people involved in culture (Kukuljević, Jagić, Vodnik, Prohaska) that the Church in general outlawed traditional poetry. Citing the views of the Franciscan and Jesuit writers under attack, Bujas concluded that they actually deserved recognition because 'they had carried out an admirable cultural mission by prosecuting the disgraceful and corrupt traditional songs'. He claimed that it was no longer possible to think romantically of the intellectual inventions of commoners, such as Vuk Karadžić or Ivan Kukuljević, because the times had passed in which the traditional song 'was looked upon as something almost divine, without questioning whether it contained, perhaps, elements that certainly could not be to our honour or pride' (Bujas 1939: 23).

Among the Orthodox, the Phanariot (Greek) senior clergy were divorced from the lower clergy and the commoners, and this pushed the junior clerics ever deeper into vernacular culture. The people got out of the habit of attending church, often took communion without confession, and religious life was reduced to the celebration of the family patron saint (*krsna slava*). As early as the sixteenth and seventeenth centuries the Franciscans were being educated in Italy and Hungary or sending novices to their convent schools in Slavonia, which produced a number of outstanding individuals such as Matija Divković, the writer of the first Bosnian printed book in the vernacular in 1611; Ivan Starčević, founder of the first elementary school in Bosnia-Herzegovina; and Mato Nikolić, first graduate physician in the country. Meanwhile, the Orthodox parish priests were unable to keep the registers until 1850, and even then rarely and irregularly. Right up to 1878, education was 'insignificant', as was theological literature, for religious education was 'poor' (Davidović 1931: 42).

The work of the Catholic Church described had, of course, its other side and cannot be observed outside the complex reality of its time. Its interventions against the 'negative' ancillary manifestations of traditional culture always contained a greater or lesser amount of moralism, and the secular love lyric and ballads also came under attack. What is more, in the seventeenth and eighteenth centuries, the Franciscans 'extirpated' 'haircut godfatherhood' because it threatened Catholics with the danger of the loss of their own confessional identity, by enabling stronger inter-confessional syncretist communication (Džaja 1992: 179). Still, on the basis of the aspects that concern us here, it is not wrong to conclude that the critical attitude to the *haiduk* cult, particularly of the Franciscans of Silver Bosnia Province, played a long-term positive educational role that was not without effect on contemporary events. Aware on the one hand of how deeply the figure of the *haiduk* protector was embedded in the popular consciousness, and on the other of how many apologias for violence and revenge were filtered through it, they endeavoured to maintain a delicate balance. This involved preserving the figure of the *haiduk* as aspiration for the preservation of religious and national identity, freedom and social justice, and at the same time removing from it all the components that encouraged the hyperbolised cult of force, autarchy and asocial conduct.

A good many articles along these lines can be found in the monthly periodicals of the Franciscan province of Silver Bosnia. One leading article sharply condemned the settlement of central Bosnian Croat refugees in areas from which the Serbian population had been expelled instead of helping all refugees to go back to their homes. The idea of mass resettlement could be arrived at, said the writer, only by the '*haiduk* mentality that is learned from the *gusle* songs, while '*haidukery*' should not be a catechism for those who call themselves Christians and Europeans of the twenty-first century'.[1] Of course in this kind of context it is impossible to avoid the figure of Mijat Tomić, so deeply implanted into the awareness of the Croats of Bosnia-Herzegovina. As so often before, the whole problem was reduced to the selection of the epic situation or song that could be taken as a paradigmatic model for framing the current political message. Protagonists of the exclusivist policy of the HDZ chose what they chose. The Bosnian friar, a long-term teacher at the Franciscan high school in Visoko chose what so many earlier advocates of rapprochement between Catholics and Muslims had chosen, irrespective of their different ideological points of departure and their objective historical adversarial positions. His article showed conditions in Mijat's time in a

---

1. Mirko Filipović, 'Bosanski Hrvati nisu cigani-čergaši', *Svjetlo riječi*, 152, November 1995.

balanced way, relativised all extreme interpretations of his activity and, as expected, on the basis of the motif of 'haircut godfatherhood' and some similar situations, concluded:

> It is useful at this time when criminal *'haidukery'* has taken control in our region to give an example of the honest *haiduk*, a *haiduk* who is a noble man.[1]

When he mentioned 'criminal *'haidukery'*', the friar was thinking also of what took place precisely on Mijat's mountain. In the fierce year-long battles with the AB-H, the HVO had kept control of Vran, but after the Washington Agreement, which meant the conclusion of that war at the beginning of 1994, groups of bandits kept operating in the wooded foothills, along Salvation Road, *'haiduks* in HVO uniforms' who disgraced the Croats in Bosnia-Herzegovina and their army, as the fraternal leader wrote in the same article.[2] They intercepted convoys and buses, robbed lone drivers and charity consignments, and did not draw the line even at murder. The European Administrator of Mostar, the German Hans Koschnik, says in one interview that he had been told that 'a long time ago there had been some *haiduks* who were sometimes liberators, and sometimes robbers' (*Slobodna Dalmacija*, 13 August 1994), but personally, he admitted, he was powerless to control these criminals. Apart from a police and government test, this was for Croats without doubt a moral test. What was being tested once again was the relation between the terminological code that had functioned in a stable manner in Croatia for four years and the one that in Herzegovina, at the beginning of 1993, struck off from it and opposed it.

But the leaders of HDZB-H, until the nineties almost without exception local communist officials, were accustomed to listening to orders from party committees. They obediently followed the orders of their new patron from Zagreb when in Široki Brijeg he required from them 'determined steps' against 'the *'haidukery'* that is occurring here' (*Hrvatski list*, 61, 22 June 1994).[3] When soon the Croatian ambassador in Sarajevo, Zdravko Sančević, also stated that the events on Vran were *''haidukery'*, the most common kind

---

1. Ignacije Gavran, 'Plemenit hajduk', *Svjetlo riječi*, 163, October 1996.
2. Mirko Filipović, 'Otkud hajduci u uniformama HVO-a?', *Svjetlo riječi*, 135, July 1994.
3. It was rather striking that this section of the presidential speech was omitted by the three main dailies in anti-*haiduk* Croatia, all of them more or less under the control of the HDZ, but not by a weekly from '*haiduk*' Herzegovina. Clearly, the speaker's political authority was stronger than local tradition and its predominantly positive understanding of the *haiduk*.

of '*haidukery*', as once upon a time in the Turkish empire' (*Dani*, 23, 15 July 1994), there would be a confirmation that there had been no value changes in the discourse of official politics in Croatia – the *haiduk* was still a bad guy. A month or so later the Bosniak member of the Presidency of Bosnia-Herzegovina Ejup Ganić explained from his side in the highest-circulation pro-government paper in Croatia how he saw Washington and the decision to federalise the country: 'The establishment of the Federation means the coming of a country of law and order, a Federation means the establishment of democracy and an end to '*haidukery*' and tyranny' (*Večernji list*, 3 January3 1995). Such a terminological correspondence on points where he had not expected it must have greatly puzzled fictitious cousin Ćipa, but however well he knew that words are not without importance, he persisted in the conviction that something else would be decisive, notably the so-called situation on the ground.

The rehabilitation of Andrija Šimić

I was a sinner, but never an outlaw. I did not cause grief to the poor, I helped the pauper, and I always esteemed female honour ... I took from those who had, and gave to those who had not.

(From an interview with the *haiduk* A. Šimić printed by *Pučki list* in Split, after his release from jail in 1902; Milas 1972)

Mijat Tomić was not the only Croatian *haiduk* who suddenly found himself in the paradoxical reality of war. Even before Washington, at the beginning of 1994, a convoy had passed along Salvation Road, over his Vran Mountain, bringing aid to the besieged Croats in Nova Bila near Travnik, and to the whole population of central Bosnia. As a journalist observed, at the end of the road Slavica Bilić from Imotski promised the central Bosnian Croats that, if it were necessary, help would come again, either 'through the normal channels or along the paths over Vran that were trodden by Andrijica Šimić' (*Vjesnik*, 23 February 1994).

Andrija Šimić, also known as Andrijica or Little Andrew, because of his small stature, was a real character and lively memories of him are preserved in Herzegovina and the Imotski region, as the last Croatian *haiduk*, a 'hero with exceptional physical features, brave and intelligent' (Milas 1972: 12). Born in 1833, into a very poor family in Alagovci, near Grude, he became an outlaw when the Turkish tax collectors robbed his father, and the *kadi* to whom he appealed refused to intervene and rather practically arrested him too. He did most of his *haiduking* in the Imotski-Vrlika area and hung out on Mt Kamešnica, where today his cave may still be seen. Sometimes he would go as far as Kupres, Glamoč, Duvno, Mostar, even Sarajevo and Travnik. When he was residing on Vran, Čvrsnica and other Herzegovina mountains, around 1870, and attacking the Turks, the people, particularly the Muslims, began to believe him to be invulnerable, possessing supernatural powers to help where needed, and in their tales his exploits were magnified to miraculous proportions.

There is no doubt that his biography is typically *haiduk*, but it is so actually mainly because it is far from unambiguous, and both he and his antagonists constantly avoid any attempt to push them entirely into the moulds of either ideological historiography or practical political journalism. The fact is that, if we accept for a moment the categories of vernacular morality, Šimić did not rob just the rich beys, but also prosperous Catholics. But justification could somehow be found, and with a bit of special pleading, this could turn into a struggle for freedom. It is also a fact that he killed. Another fact, however, is that it was he, when his band intercepted the rich Dervish-Bey Kopčić in 1869, who prevented the other *haiduks* from killing him, at no small risk to himself. The bey himself decently testified to this three years later at the court in Split, and charged only the members of the band, refusing to say a single word in accusation of Šimić. This Dervish-Bey was one of the same line of Kopčićes, masters of Duvno, whom we have already met in connection with Mijat Tomić, and about whom Don Federico Maroli wrote that in 1710 they had given protection to the bishop of Makarska, whose secretary he was, so that he could freely carry out visitations to the local Catholics, and that they had 'proved to be the most humane and most merciful people we have ever heard of or met' and that they were 'amicable and kind to the Christian folk' and on good terms with the Catholic priests and monks (Šimčik 1933: 50–1). This does not of course gainsay the fact that there were many violent and ruthless beys who ill-treated the Christian commoners every day.

Outlawed and with a price on his head, Šimić was captured in the spring of 1878. The Austrian government condemned him to life imprisonment and incarcerated him in Koper, but after a number of appeals he was pardoned in 1901. The bishop of Mostar, Fra Paškal Buconjić, petitioned for him, stating that the 'people had always held that he, Andrijica Šimić, had gone to the *haiduks* out of sheer adversity'. Returning to his homeland, he aroused enormous interest – everyone assembled to see him, and in the *harami bași* outfit, with his *tokas* on his chest, he went round the places of his campaigns, visited his former *yataks* and related tales from his life in the taverns. He died not long afterwards in 1905.[1] While visiting Duvno twenty years later, the

---

1. Cf. Milas 1972; Džaja and Draganović 1994: 99–100; Palavestra 1991: 82.

Andrija Šimić, 'the last Croatian *haiduk*', photographed at Sinj in 1902 (left), and his grave at Runovići (right). (Jukić 1995)

Zagreb deputy-mayor and historical novel writer Milutin Mayer saw how the commoners revered him as 'heir' of Mijat Tomić, because he had 'protected the *rayah* from the *zulüm* [violence] of the Ottomans and mercilessly routed the Turkish tyrants' (Mayer 1924: 57).

Since, like Tomić, he was not in Tito's Partisans, and nor did he have a very good opinion of the communists, after 1945 he had to be satisfied with a similar outsider position and a semi-legal, opposition life in the tales of the local population. He was compensated for this, just as Mijat was, after the disintegration of Yugoslavia, on the ninetieth anniversary of his death. He had a street named after him in Imotski, as well as the former Ive Lole Ribara Street in the 'royal town' of Knin, during the symbolic transformation of the city *architexture* after the liberation. He got a street in Duvno/Tomislavgrad, not a very big one, but in an important place: just in front of the memorial basilica of King Tomislav's coronation, it joins up with the main street that bears the name of his great predecessor and model in the same profession Mijat Tomić. Two indomitable *haiduks* thus came to honour the royal founder of the state for which they had themselves, in their time and in their own way, fought and made sacrifices. In Imotski, a memorial plaque was placed beside the wall where he was taken ill, with the inscription: *In this place on 5 February 1905 the Croatian haiduk Andrija Šimić died,* and a conference devoted to his life and times was held on 11 November 1995. A TV documentary was shot in which the actor Ante Šućur, in *haiduk* gear, spoke Šimić's selected thoughts, recorded during his trial in Split or after his release, including his belief that he was not guilty because he 'took from those who had too much and gave to those who had nothing' (Jukić 1995).

The writer Jure Ujević said that 'the Robin Hood motif' was inherent in Šimić. And the physician Mijo Milas, who had researched the *haiduk's* life for years, recalled that after the crushing of the Croatian Spring, during the time of increased repression against the Croats, 'one old woman had said to him: Oh, if there were only three Šimićes they would soon settle everything'. He added that he was particularly glad that today the Croatian soldier acted like Šimić, and 'did not loot and did not commit arson' but 'made war morally' (Jukić 1995). At the Imotski conference many of the papers gave scholarly accounts of conditions in Šimić's time and various aspects of life that impinged on the phenomenon of outlawry. But of course it was impossible to avoid the idealisation of this 'Croatian Robin Hood' (*Slobodna Dalmacija*, 24–25 December 1995).

All in all, the way things go, and had gone with Mijat Tomić more than half a century earlier over the issue of Andrić's collection of traditional songs, once again that same unquenchable conflict between vernacular tradition and scholarly truth appeared on the horizon: between legitimacy and legality, the vernacular value system and the legal principles of contemporary civil society. Prompted by newspaper reports of the conference, an old Franciscan from Imotski wrote about it in a church paper. He recalled that in Šimić's day Turkish power was already on the wane and the *haiduks* of the time did 'not fight against the Turks, but robbed their own people'. Quoting descriptions of Šimić's assaults, extortions and robbery in the court records, he concluded:

> It would be more useful if such symposia were held for more noble causes. It is not very nice to promote our national vice, of which we ought to be ashamed. It is particularly not very nice to celebrate before later generations a man who was the leader of a gang of thieves. [1]

Not long afterwards, one more voice, a Franciscan again, that of Špiro Marasović, professor of Catholic Theology at Split, expressly linked the 'moral chaos' in Croatian society, the criminality surrounding privatisation and 'unlawfulness that is sometimes very similar to the mafia' with 'the decasyllabic, epic mentality that was able to present every instance of its

---

1. Vjeko Vrčić, 'Zaštitnik obespravljenih?', *Glas Koncila* 7 January 1996. It is amusing to mention that the author of this warning was at the time the Guardian of the Imotski Franciscan monastery, that is, someone who performed the very same duties as the figure in the novel of Ivan Raos who gave the *haiduk* absolution with no questions asked, because he did not consider the murder of Turks a sin. But Mate Boban was not one to bother himself with the distinction of real and novel reality or conditions and relations in the mid-seventeenth and the end of the twentieth century.

own '*haidukery*' as merit'. For this reason 'the destruction of this myth has been a major test for the Church up to now, and will be an even greater one henceforth.' (*Novi list*, 23 August 1997). But until that moment much time had passed and a great many events had occurred, not only the military about-turn in Croatia, which gave birth to the defeat of the Chetnik rebellion and the liberation of the country, but a whole other war in Bosnia-Herzegovina, so far mentioned only marginally, but in its scope, in the material devastation and human losses far more terrible than the aggression against Croatia. What is more, there was not just one but three wars: the original war, resulting from the Serbian expansionist programme, and the two subsidiary, no less cruel or ruthless ones – first the conflict between the two victims, the Croats and Bosniaks, whom the Greater Serbian programme had consigned to expulsion and extirpation, and their armies, HVO and AB-H, which had defended the country together during the first war of the year. And then the inter-Bosnian conflict in the far west of the land, between the forces of Fikret Abdić and those loyal to the lawful authorities in Sarajevo, within a people which suffered extreme human losses and the destruction of their cultural and historical heritage, and which was brought to the verge of extinction.

As in Croatia, so too in Bosnia-Herzegovina, at the beginning of the tragedy, the self-confident figure of the mountain *haiduk* appeared, convinced of his own superiority, invincibility and his right himself to determine, according to his own criteria, what was justice, and then to mete it out by his own methods: by friendly persuasion or preferably by force.

SIX

The Attack on Bosnia-Herzegovina

Romanija Mountain is very large; wheresoever one passes, there is a walk of about five hours to cross it. From the Sarajevo side there are terrific canyons, so that even the hardiest man should not climb it, until he has dined well. Along by the road hangs one cliff resembling an overhanging roof; there, they say, Novak's, Radivoj's and Gruica's sentries lay in wait. And if a traveller did not give them a gift of some kind, they would take him prisoner. Turks would be killed without mercy. They were mighty heroes, and they resided in caves on Romanija. Sarajevo people moved against them several times with soldiers, particularly Ağa Djerzelez, but they beat the army each time, because Romanija is inaccessible from that side. And so even today, if any bushes should chance to grow on Romanija, the Turks immediately set fire to them out of fear that the haiduks might be concealed in them. Or so I have heard tell.

(Mažuranić 1842: 34-36)

The haiduk *standard on Romanija*

Romanija is a limestone plateau in eastern Bosnia. However, the people often use the name to refer to the whole area that stretches north as far as the Bioščica River, and in the east and south to the mountains along the valley of the Drina and its tributaries. The highest peaks are Dijeva (1573 m), Lupoglav (1,569m), Orlovina (1,629m) and Velika Stijena (1,617m) in the central part, at the watershed of the Gračanica and Mokranjska Miljacka rivers. Since it is exposed to strong winds, and often shrouded in fog, covered during the long cold winters with deep snow, densely clad in conifers with just the occasional patch of pastureland, there are settlements only on the lower areas round the rim, up to about 1,000m. From time immemorial, the population has been engaged in animal husbandry: rearing sheep, goats, pigs and horses. In the 1970s and 1980s, a few industrial plants were established. The area was populated in the time of the medieval kingdom of Bosnia, when it formed part of the estates of the Pavlović family. In 1244, the episcopal estate *Pracha Biscupnya* is mentioned as being in Sjetlina, south east of Pale. And in two places stećci bear witness to the presence of the heterodox Bosnian Church. Important remains of prehistoric cultures have been unearthed on Glasinac.

According to the 1991 census, the population of the two municipalities that cover the major part of the Romanija area had the following ethnic structure: of the total population of Pale of 16,310, 69 percent were Serbs, 27 percent Bosniaks; in Sokolac, the 14,833 population was 69 percent Serb and 30 percent Bosniak. The municipality of Rogatica, which covers the smaller eastern parts of the plateau, had 21,812 inhabitants, 60 percent of them Bosniaks and 38 percent Serbs, while in the municipality of Goražde, which in its western part covers the south-east cisalpine side of Romanija, the population was 37,505, 70 percent Bosniaks and 26 percent Serbs. In the whole area there were also a few hundred Croats and a small number of 'Yugoslavs', or people with no declared ethnic affiliation, and others. The Bosniak population had on the whole settled here before the Ottoman period, while the Serbian inhabitants derived from migrations caused by Ottoman incursions in the sixteenth century, and from later individual migrations, mostly in the eighteenth century, from Montenegro and Herzegovina.

But Romanija is also *something more*. It is an important part not only of physical geography, but also of an imaginary traditional geography, a space that resides not only in historical time, but still more intensely in epic time, rich in its diverse meanings. It is a distinctive form and vision in the landscape, and has inspired many visitors and travellers to poetic descriptions and suggestive contrasts.

In 1925, the Serbian poet and novelist Miloš Crnjanski wrote a series of reports for the Belgrade weekly *Vreme*, attempting to analyse the cultural and political reality of Bosnia, and to find an explanation for the social tensions in (among other things) the impact of the climate and the mountain landscape on the psychology of the population. In one article, entitled 'Pictures and Conditions around Sarajevo' *(Slike i prilike oko Sarajeva)*, he actually paused on the dismal impression that the view of the majestic surrounding heights made on the people in the valley:

> In the distance, over the hills, the black and blue forests, the *haiduk* heights. This is Romanija, and below it, the blue and green hills, absolutely empty and silent. (Crnjanski 1990: 429)

Twenty years later, in 1944, a similar impression overcame the Croatian poet Frano Alfirević, when in a fairly short travelogue he described the

The Romanija massif as seen in 1857 by the Russian consul in Sarajevo, Alexander Gilferding.

mountains above Sarajevo, contrasting the breadth of Jahorina, up which 'we climb gently, as if on carpets, in a gentle walk', a mountain of 'idyllic silence with undulating foothills', full of green pastures and tall firs, at the top of which 'we arrived as easily as if we had been long strolling through a lovely park, intoxicated with the strong scents', and Romanija, which was

> Dark, long, harsh, mightily gloomy, having in it something serpentine and cold, as if a vast dragon were sprawled out in front of our eyes. This is not a mountain for excursions, fun in the snow, with houses where the singing and playing of cheerful young people ring out, as on Jahorina; this is the legendary mountain of *haiduk*s and the quarrelsome, like Mijat Tomić, spectrally cold in its wild caves and terrible gorges, with sharp edges to the cliffs that rear up like fantastic teeth.[1]

Such fascination with visual details and unpleasant recollections clearly cannot be ascribed simply to the poetic melancholy of the Mediterranean Alfirević or the Central European Crnjanski, brought up in the Hungarian plains and vibrant Vienna University at the turn of the century. Probably

---

1. 'Likovi Bosne', *Vijenac*, 9, 28 April 1994, p. 5.

every foreign travel writer, wherever he came from and whatever the true purpose of his journey to Bosnia, has accorded this mountain a special place among his impressions, without concealing the sense of unease and alarm that he has felt passing this way. At the end of May 1658 the French traveller Sieur Poullet saw on 'terrible Romanija' some thirty fresh graves and not far from them an empty smashed-open chest – traces of a recent *haiduk* ambush. He went peacefully by only because his strong entourage had driven the *haiduks* back into the dense forest with which the mountain was 'clad' (Skarić 1985: 119). Although Bosnia was filled with the Ottoman army, which was preparing for a crucial push against the Habsburg Empire and the conquest of Vienna, these were the years in which the *haiduks* from what was also Ottoman eastern Herzegovina and the Venetian domains in the hinterland of Boka Kotorska had made forays all the way to the first houses in Sarajevo and liaised with the *haiduks* on Romanija. The Sarajevo people did not dare leave the immediate surroundings of the city, even digging defensive trenches in some places around the town.

As soon as the historian and philologist Alexander Gilferding arrived in Sarajevo as Russian consul to Bosnia-Herzegovina in May 1857, he set off to get to know the land where he had been posted. Although it was high summer, mid-July, Romanija had a 'kind of terrifying and gloomy appearance'. He listened to Serbian stories about 'the exploits of the famed *haiduks*, heroes who had for ages been the living protest of an oppressed people against their Turkish masters', but also stated that among its cliffs the 'recalcitrant' Sarajevo Muslims would often hide their wealth lest it be stolen by the Sultan's officials and the military units that came to this border country from other areas of the Empire (Gilferding 1972: 92).

The journalist Heinrich Renner, a correspondent for newspapers in Vienna and Berlin, knew Bosnia-Herzegovina extremely well, and would go there even before Austro-Hungarian rule was established there in 1878. He too, of course, reminded the reader that 'at one time the traveller had passed through Romanija in fear and trembling', where, as he remarks, backing up his account with numerous quotes from the heroic epics, Starina Novak and his *haiduk* band would often sojourn. There were still *haiduks* there in 1882, but 'today it is all peaceful and calm, everyone goes his way without any hindrance, and the barracks in Podromanija, the sentries in Glasinac and up in the mountain remind one that the authorities are keeping a sharp eye open and not allowing the old times to return' (Renner 1900: 255–256).

The Finnish archaeologist and ethnographer Sakari Pälsi, writer of several classic works of children's fiction, travelled with his wife through Dalmatia,

Herzegovina and Bosnia in 1929. On Romanija he was impressed by the height of the firs that had just been felled and were being hauled by horses to the sawmills, and when he made the ascent by bus from Sarajevo, at Mokro he did not fail to recall that here 'in Turkish times the famed *haiduks* had lived' (Pälsi 1996: 102).

Much later, but still in a watershed time, when in Yugoslavia as everywhere else in southeastern and eastern Europe communism was irretrievably imploding, between the first and second rounds of multiparty elections in Croatia, this mountain became an important motif in political communications in a very distinctive way. Even after the first round it was clear that the HDZ, Croatian Democratic Union, led by the former communist dissident Franjo Tuđman, was going to win. In this triumphant mood, on 4 May 1990, the party organised a meeting in the Zagreb neighbourhood of Peščenica. The conference was entitled *Days of the Croatian Standard*, and a member of the leadership, someone who had already been elected to Parliament, Šime Đodan, coloured his speech with the exclamation:

> We know where the border of the ancient Croatian state was. It will not always be on the Una River. We tell this not to the communists, because there aren't any, but to the Chetniks. We are not afraid of anyone's threats, not even those of [federal PM] Ante Marković and [federal defence minister] Veljko Kadijević (...) Within these five years, this standard of ours will wave on top of the mountains of Romanija. (...) Bosnia is Croatian, belonging to our ancient people (...) What is ours, we shan't give to anyone. (*Večernji list*, 4 May 1990).

It is hard to say whether the anyway vociferous and rowdy Đodan, in the grip of his emotions, came upon the association with Romanija, a kind of symbol of Bosnia, spontaneously, as an improvisation, or whether it was part of a carefully devised piece of rhetoric, and its well-moderated peak. Whatever it was, the reaction from Bosnia-Herzegovina, where free elections were to be held in just six months, came the very next day. The local branch of the League of Communists in the municipality of Sokolac, on Romanija, 'energetically' protested against the 'appropriation of SRB-H and Romanija' and declared that Romanija 'communists and other citizens' were dedicated to the 'freedom-loving traditions' of their area and to 'a united and democratic Yugoslavia' (*Oslobođenje*, 6 May 1990). Not many people cared a jot for their declaration: the spirit of ideological orthodoxy already sounded completely outmoded, the invocation of Yugoslavia still more so, and clichés about 'freedom-loving traditions' of this or that area had long since been relegated to the empty rituals of Party officials. In this day and age, the reactions of other political and ideological orientations were more important.

As for Croatia itself, Đodan's message, mediated by the octosyllabic formula 'on top of Mt Romanija (*navrh gore Romanije*)', actually its rhetorical core, soon developed into a symbol not only of the speaker's public personality, but of the whole HDZ policy vis-à-vis Bosnia-Herzegovina, at times mocked for its absurd enthusiasm and immersion in anachronistic medieval categories, at others condemned for its calculation, its poorly concealed expansionism and therefore its disastrous consequences for the interests of Croatia, which just then, exposed as it was to the menaces of Milošević, had a vital need of all and any democratic allies, particularly in Bosnia.

A year after the Peščenica meeting, the independent journalist Viktor Ivančić assessed a conciliatory speech by Đodan in the Parliament as 'the quite unexpected' transformation of 'a man who in a pre-election epic had verbally planted the Croatian standard on Romanija' (*Slobodna Dalmacija*, 1 June 1991). Three and a half years later, the opposition MP Mladen Vilfan (HSLS) observed, with marked irony, in a speech during a parliamentary debate about HDZ policy towards Bosnia, that the party had gone a long way 'from the standard on Romanija to the seven Herzegovina municipalities that Šešelj had offered us at the outset' (*Večernji list*, 6 September 1993), that is from the ambition of hegemony over the whole of Bosnia to controlling, after half a year's war with the Bosniaks, only a few impoverished communes (or municipalities) on the borders with Croatia. Almost exactly four years after the speech, another opposition politician, Igor Dekanić (HNS) recalled, with equal irony, that 'HDZ promises about standards on Romanija are further off than ever' (*Vjesnik*, 9 April 1994), and just a year after that, the Committee for the Celebration of the 50th Anniversary of the Victory over Fascism in Dalmatia was to condemn both the Greater Serbian designs on Croatia and Bosnia-Herzegovina and the conception of 'Croatia as far as the Drina with that celebrated standard on Romanija' (*Slobodna Dalmacija*, 24 April 1995).

Clearly, Šime Đodan had made use of an utterance with exceptional imaginative resonance, one that was suggestive and easy to remember, and although he was not the first to activate the Romanija symbolism, he had made it overnight common property, an almost colloquial slogan, whether or not it was really understood. He actually provided an ideal point of departure for penetrating the deep structure categories of political communication in the successor states of SFR Yugoslavia, just when it was extremely dramatic, into the bargain. It would soon be a year since Milošević had openly brandished his weapons in Kosovo, the non-communist parties had already won in the Slovene elections, and the dogmatic military supremos in Belgrade saw political pluralism as 'counter-revolution' that had to be quashed at all costs, and they were flirting increasingly openly with Milošević.

Two semantic layers need first to be distinguished in the symbol of Romanija. The first includes the general, universal symbol of the mountain heights, where the divine revelation occurs, heaven and earth are conjoined, which is not only the residence of the gods, but the aim of human aspiration. Since the mountain expresses the concepts of constancy and unchangeability, mastering it means to prove oneself stronger, and in this alone Đodan had opened up stimulating levels of understanding. The popular belief was that nymphs (*vila*) called *nagorkinja* or *zagorkinja* (-*gor*- being a root for mountain or hill) inhabited the mountain tops. At night, they sang and danced in a ring in the moonlight.

The mountain, in reality or in imagination, has an important role in traditional culture all over the world, representing values opposed to the lowland and the urban, a subset of the ancient nature-culture antinomy. Just as in the Latin West of the early medieval period, the move into the desert is experienced, in St Jerome's words, as a second baptism, so in the heroic culture of archaic Balkan society the departure for the mountain, to the green hilltops, *u goru zelenu*, is experienced the same way.

The other semantic layer, however, is concerned with Romanija itself. Like many objects and localities, mountains have particular characteristics in the South Slav traditional songs. Šar-Mountain (*Šar-planina*) or Šara on the border of Macedonia and Kosovo is a stereotypical name for a mountain in the context of pastoral themes. Kunara, or Kunor, Kunarica, Kunovac or Kunovnica, is a favourite site in epic songs about Uskoks and Muslim heroes. Some see this mountain as a symbol that cannot be located in reality, a point on the cultural, fictitious map that covers vast imaginary areas, while others hold that the *Kunara mountain high* of the Bosnian, Herzegovinian and Dalmatian songs corresponds to Mt Kunovac (631m) in Lika, by the source of the Una River. This is the much-sung spot where the bands gathered and there were deadly battles between Mujo and Halil Hrnjica, Mijat Tomić, Stojan Janković and other Christian and Muslim heroes.

On this map, Romanija is without doubt the archetypal mountain of the *haiduks*, *the haiduk bride (hajdučka nevjesta)*. It was this mountain – together with Vran, the Herzegovinian equivalent in epic topography and mythopoeic awareness – that the Croatian poet Tin Ujević put in his sonnet 'Wolves and *haiduks*' ('Vuci i hajduci', 1935), using the stylistic devices of the heroic epic, as a kind of catalogue of the traditional culture of the poet's homeland on the borders of Dalmatia and Herzegovina and in general of bygone times, of vernacular beliefs and typical *haiduk* life:

> *Tonight nymphs touch the branches*
> *visions of Vran and Romanija mountains,*
> *while the rebels take their ease on silk*
>
> *and count out the gold the troop has won (...)*
> *and their comrades are the* bauk[1] *and the wolf*
> *as long as there is the song and the* haiduks.

For all these reasons, in Đodan's utterance, Romanija is not a fact of geography, rather an image, for 'facts of themselves do not produce a powerful impact on the vernacular imagination, but rather the manner in which they are presented and classified'. In fact the image arouses 'the marvellous and legendary aspects of events', 'its compactness suffuses and fascinates the spirits' (Le Bon 1989: 73). The material for shaping the image and the framework for its understanding are provided here by the folklore matrix, that is the texts of traditional culture. This procedure transforms them into a base of legitimacy for the statement that a certain territory is 'ours' as opposed to 'theirs', in this case Croatian rather than communist or Chetnik.

The legitimisation of a political system entails the reproduction of the substance of a worldview according to which the members of a given society accept the social, legal and political system as proper and just, and not only out of habit, fear or individual interest, but also through belief in its validity. In a broader sense legitimisation covers all the processes in which the basic consensus of values in a society are produced and reproduced, and hence, also, the inclusion of appropriate traditional motifs – traditional connotations – into political discourse.

This was the procedure employed, for example, by Soviet propaganda between 1948 and 1950 to back up its demands for the Karelia region – and justify its later annexation – using the theme and quotations from the Finnish national epic *Kalevala*. Like many works of folk poetry, *Kalevala* depicts the fight between Good and Evil as symbolized in the struggle between the hardworking and friendly people of Kalevala and Pohjola, the home of wicked sorcerers. In the Soviet interpretation Kalevala appears 'as a country

---

1. *Bauk* – a bogeyman.

with a classless society where a kind of primitive communism existed' and is 'thus almost a forerunner of Soviet Russia itself' (Kolarz 1952: 103).

When the Athenians had a mind to annex Salamis, by way of legitimation they quoted a passage from the *Iliad* that says that twelve Salaminian ships were put into the line 'where the Athenian forces were', thus suggesting that it was a united army, and hence a united state. If it was so then, it should be again. And they made their claim good, thanks precisely to these lines, because the fifth and sixth century Greeks 'treated [the Homeric poems] as an account of real events and real people and appealed to them as an authority on matters of past history', showing them respect as 'repositories of information' (Bowra 1978: 508).

But for a motif to become effective as legitimation within one's own discourse, and against competing discourses, certain preconditions need to be fulfilled. The so-called ideal recipient is always a historical recipient and the message always enters into a specific social context. The protagonist of the discourse thus has to recognise the communicational situation as appropriate for a given evocation and the potential recipients must be motivated as social beings and ready to accept this perception. Therefore, every element of the message can be treated as an assignment handed to the recipient, a call upon the recipient to complete its semantic field, supply the missing elements, fill up the voids. In every part of the text, at each moment of reading or listening, the recipient is at the intersection of several currents of information that link characters and themes (Balcerzan 1974).

Đodan's Peščenica utterance implied as many as four ideal recipients: *Croats*, as members of the speaker's community, with whom programmatic and value solidarity was to be established; *Serbs* and *Yugoslavs*, perceived in the ideological conceptions of Chetniks and communists, as members of rival communities, which must be unambiguously demarcated; and *Muslims* or *Bosniaks*, as members of a community that was objectively interested, since Romanija was located in Bosnia-Herzegovina, but also as Croats of the Islamic faith (or at least, an unquestioned Croatian ally) because of the speaker's ideological conception that the Bosnian Muslims were historically members of the Croatian nation. Since the overall semantic field of the Peščenica image thus included, and implied its extension into, four traditional systems, it becomes crucial to establish what kind of a response the speaker could expect from the implied recipients of his message, and what information was conveyed by the legitimating contents of Đodan's image.

Although it was his use of the image that caught the attention of the Croatian public, Šime Đodan was by no means the first to mention this mythical mountain with its political connotations in the then still united Yugoslavia. Quite the contrary, he was already well to the rear of the field, by at least seven and a half months. The Romanija motif had been purposefully activated in Serbian political discourse on 13 August 1989, when the Holy Virgin Monastery was dedicated at Knežina. A mass and requiem for the victims of Kosovo were held at the opening, beside three graves the central one of which was dedicated to six Serbs killed by the *Schutzkorps*[1] in 1914. According to the controlled Serbian media, the event was attended by between 50,000 and 100,000 people, which must be fairly exaggerated, although photos show that there was mass attendance from various areas, including twenty-three buses that had brought Serbs free of charge from Kosovo.

Although the bishop [*vladika*] of Zvornik and Tuzla, Vasilije, admonished those present to respect the service, there was an atmosphere of debauched popular fiesta, with girl singers of so-called newly composed folk songs and loud music from the PA system not only after but also during the liturgy. Three or four processions wound through the crowd. They were each set up in the same way: at the head were two persons with SPC [Serbian Orthodox Church] and SFRY standards; then a person with a standard depicting a cross; and then one with a picture of Milošević. On one, with the inscription 'To Milošević, the Serbian Obilić', his image was encircled with icons. This is how it was on the 'meadows of Knežina, on the mountain of Romanija, where the last *haiduk*s were the purveyors of refreshments from Sokolac', 'while the sun warmed the people's heads, and the wind fluttered the Serbian flags' as the subheading of the article by Belgrade reporter Z. Bogavac put it.[2]

Bogavac's text starts with two legends. The first concerns Kraljević Marko, or Prince Marko, whose brother had 'established a monastery, and to be absolved of his sins, finished it with a golden cross' in Knežina itself. The second says that 'in the time of the crescent' the cross was taken away, the monastery set on fire and torn down, and its stones were incorporated into a mosque, and then in his sleep, 'some *khoja*' was told by God to find the chains on which the monastery bells had been suspended, and if they should

---

1. *Schutzcorps* – in the Austro-Hungarian army squads that protected the flank or rear of the attack units; in eastern Bosnia in WWI these units were on the whole composed of local Muslims. This example shows how systematically Milošević's propaganda exploited all historical traumas that might stir up feelings of vengeance among the Serbian population and incite it to war: it is most often events from WWII that are evoked, but WWI is not forgotten, and both are consistently worked into the interpretive context of the mythic tragedy of Kosovo.
2. Zoran Bogavac, 'Bela tačka u planini', *Duga*, 404, 19 August 1989. For the iconography, typical of any number of psudo-religious gatherings at the time.

be 'let down the minaret' 'the face of the heavens over Knežina should clear', that is the hail that had almost ruined the peasants would cease.

Incidentally, Serbian vernacular tradition ascribed even the foundation of the Old (Orthodox) Church in Sarajevo to Marko's brother Andrija, who obtained permission for its construction from Husrev-Bey (1480–1541), a successful general and Ottoman governor in Bosnia, who built a monumental mosque in Sarajevo and made a major impact on shaping the new identity of the town. There are no historical grounds for this, but such motifs regularly express the yearning of a certain population – in this case the Sarajevo Serbs – that 'as a kind of gauge of their own independence and long continuance' they should connect important legendary or historical personalities with the area in which they lived (Smailbegović 1986: 125). For if a personality as powerful as Husrev-Bey had found time to concern himself with the construction of a little church, this implicitly indicated that Andrija was able to communicate with him from a position of equality, or that he himself was at least taken seriously, as well as the community on whose behalf he was acting, even though they belonged to a 'hostile religion'.

So, once the article had set the two religions and ethnic traditions against each other through a precise choice and deployment of symbols, the general framework was worked out and filled in with an extensive range of contrasts. Typical symbols appear always in pairs: one pair consists of a Muslim woman in her baggy trousers, *dimi*, serving the Orthodox priests in their robes; another is the mosque from which the muezzin's voice was not heard, and the monastery from which the 'bells tolled, weak and muffled'. Thus the two communities are confronted not only at the level of their legends and other traditional narratives, at the level of their historical memories, their soul, but also at the level of externals, their appearance and clothing, just as their territories are marked by the characteristic religious edifices from which come the characteristic sounds – the voice or the bell.

These contrasting pairs are matched by three other antinomic pairs: in space, the mosque is 'down, below the hill', and the monastery is 'up, on the mountain,' 'on the hill'; in time, the former is 'one of the oldest in Bosnia', while the latter is 'the youngest in all the lands where prayers are addressed to God and people cross themselves with three fingers'[1] and, again, the mosque 'looks older than it is', and the monastery remains 'the youngest Serbian monastery'; in visual terms, the former is 'in the dark', while the monastery

---

1. While Catholics, who crossed themselves with the whole hand with fingers together, the Orthodox do it with three fingers, folding two into the palm, and extending the thumb, index and middle fingers. In the 1990s, Belgrade propaganda made this formal difference a symbol of things Serbian.

is 'white'. But the fact of beauty unites and symbolically reconciles them; 'lovely is the mosque', but 'and the monastery too is handsome', just as the two introductory legends unite the motif of sin and redemption, or rather penance.

In the expressive fabric of the story there is a high degree of deep-level unity, and what appears to be a mere sequencing of fragments emerges as a firm structure built on regular parallels: the two worlds, the two religions, are sometimes closer, sometimes further apart. At the end, 'in the dusk', the monastery is reduced to its 'snowy white, almost innocent walls', like 'the still empty pages of an album of future sufferings' and, when darkness finally falls, it becomes completely dematerialised, just clear colour, 'a single small white spot' against the 'dark forests of Romanija', in a world that is reduced to relationships of light and dark:

> 'God will grant that it is good,' one of the bishops present concluded his talk.
>
> The Serbs went off to their homes, along the roads that in various ways wind through the dark forests of Romanija.
>
> *'Which mountain, Ivan, which mountain, brother Ivo, has no conversation?'*
>
> When darkness falls on Romanija, in the distance, on the top of Knežina, only a small white spot can be seen ...

The scene breathes serenity, as well as mystery, founded on both the contrast of light and dark, and on the rhythm of the two quotations: the bishop's words that annunciate good, bring hope that 'future sufferings' will be evaded, and the graphically highlighted words that reawaken anxiety. These are the introductory lines of the traditional folk ballad 'The Gravely Wounded Brother' ('Teško ranjeni brat'), where to the repeated question the only reply is the ritual triple reiteration of the name of the mountain:

> *Which mountain, Ivan,*
> *Which mountain, brother Ivo,*
> *has no conversation?*
> *Romanija, Ivo,*
> *Romanija, Ivan,*
> *Romanija, brother Ivo.*
> *Come then, brother Ivo,*
> *Come then, brother Ivan,*
> *Come then, brother, brother Ivo,*
> *and have some conversation.*

This is a song of 'stifled sadness, an unclear but deeply experienced memorial to the losses on distant and dangerous battlefields' (Delorko 1963: 14), its rhythmical lines 'are like a vast pendulum that swings in my breast and in my gut', as a future Croatian political émigré wrote in a youthful text (Bušić 1983: 56). It is the more universal in that it is detached from precise factual indication of anything but geography, suggesting that it is a metaphor, an image, rather than a testimony.

The anonymous call to the hero with no surname to put life into the numbed world in Bogavac's article is evoked with exceptional power. The suggestiveness of the ballad is used in the same way as it was by the Croatian writer Ivan Raos in his novel *Beggars and Sons (Prosjaci i sinovi)*. An Imotski draper, Matan, is returning to Yugoslavia after the assassination of King Alexander in Marseilles. But when he sees that everything Croatian is being ruthlessly suppressed and a state reign of terror is gathering momentum, he decides to leave again, because anything is preferable to being in that land of persecution and menacing silence. In the train

> all the way to the border he hummed a new ballad sung in its
> unsungness:
>> This land, Mate,
>> this land, my Matan,
>> there's no conversation in this land.
> (Raos 1971: II, 275)

In both these texts, by Bogavac and Raos, the vernacular lines powerfully evoke the doom that has afflicted the land and the people, the unjust accusations against them and their inability to offer any defence against them. For both of them the point of the quotation, or rather the paraphrase, is to raise the ethnic problem to the level of the mythic. And that was precisely how Bogavac's article gave real substance to the key elements of a topic treated highly metaphorically in the Serbian tradition, one which was opened up between 1989 and 1995 to many new meanings and interpretations. All these are texts in which, through the traditional motif, the ancient idea of the mountain as a chthonic place of transition from this world to the next is manifested, a place of a dangerous, alien and demonic presences where impure forces gather and the border of which is also the border of the settled world of the living and the unsettled natural world of the dead. The most marked characteristic of this kind of world is precisely the *absence of voices*, which is nothing but the absence of lives. Romanija, like *The Wailing Mountain, Lelej-gora* or *Lelejska gora*, from a South Slav fairytale, is a place where bells do not toll and cocks do not crow. In the mountain people do not die a natural death: the cause of death of the epic figures is either supernatural (a curse, a malediction) or violent, mostly cruel. In the oldest traditions the inhabitants of the place are demonic creatures, dragons and giants, and then mountain spirits (nymphs), both demonic and yet vulnerable and mortal beings, sometimes good, sometimes evil. In the later songs with a *haiduk* theme, the mountain spirits are replaced by the *haiduk harami başı* as ruler of the mountain, and in the mythopoeic consciousness he does not entirely lose his connection with the mythic creatures (Detelić 1992: 56).

Đodan's evocation of Romanija succeeded in surprising if not actually confusing a large part of his Croatian audience, because it is a place name that does not mean a great deal to the average member of the public in Croatia, being simply 'some mountain or other' in Bosnia. The reference was unable to arouse any particular associations apart from the general idea that this was actually just a colourful way of saying that Bosnia belonged to the Croats. The Serbian audience, on the other hand, was far more profoundly initiated into its meaning and symbolism.

One reason, as was soon to be seen, is that the symbolism of the mountains, and of Romanija in particular, was from the outset an important part of the political discourse of Milošević's populism. The second is that in the eighties the writer Vojislav Lubarda, a member of the extreme nationalist group around Dobrica Ćosić, published a cycle of novels in which he built up a cult of Romanija as the stronghold of freedom and the Romanija Serbs as a kind of ethnic elite, the most Serbian of the Serbs, the most constant in their ethics and the hardiest in their convictions.

The cycle consists of the novels *Transfiguration* (*Preobraženje*; 1979), *Repentance* (*Pokajanje*; 1987) and *Assumption* (*Vaznesenje*; 1989), which all received the highest Serbian literary prize in the year of their publication, as well as a vast amount of publicity in the media and cultural institutions in Serbia that had already been seized by Milošević's men. The author was presented as one of the many Serbs who had had to flee from Bosnia before the rising tide of Islamic radicalism, concealed behind the mask of communism. The trilogy was printed in a single volume in 1991, and again in 1995, in relatively large print runs, and was rapidly sold out.

The novels set up the same spatial opposition, understood as an opposition at the level of values and ethics, as the report from Knežina. The Serbian village of Uzgor was located in the 'upper world', on the mountain, the site of heroism, of sincerity, constancy in the faith and in readiness for sacrifice, while the predominantly Muslim city of Čaršija is in the 'lower world', in the valley, the site of moral decline, hypocrisy, religious and all other kinds of betrayal. The Orthodox Serbs of Uzgor were 'born for glory', wanted good-neighbourly relations with the Muslims, but their goodness and charity always worked to their disadvantage. Because the Muslims always allied with everyone: with the Turks in Ottoman times; with the Croats, Austrians and Hungarians in the First World War; with the Germans and the Croats in the Second. The Muslims' hatred was irrational. The psychoanalytical explanation was that they were aware that their forebears had been Orthodox believers who had converted to Islam for the sake of economic and political privileges. And if they hated their neighbours the Serbs, this was because their presence was an daily reminder that there had been no need to convert, that, what is more, those who had not converted had become so much the better people, for they had preserved their souls, their individual soul as well as the collective soul transmitted by tradition.

In other words, the Muslims actually hated *the Serbs in their own selves*, and by killing them, they were actually attempting to kill their own pangs of conscience, to rid themselves of their internal pain and envy, to emerge, finally, from their humiliating position in the 'space below' and to attain the honour that lay in the 'space above', which was its *genius loci*.

The narrator's ancient forebear, Toko, founder of Uzgor and progenitor of a numerous local Serbian family, had moved to Romanija from Montenegro, from where he had been forced to flee after he and his brothers had slain a wanton young aga, in self-defence, to save himself from humiliation. This distant event was the foundation of the family's identity and passed down to later generations. The material symbol of this genealogical and ethical line of continuity was located in the *gusle* that Toko had personally acquired from the blind Abbot Stefan, before his flight. This was the very *gusle* to which Stefan had 'invoked vengeance on Christmas Eve', that is the legendary massacre of the Montenegrin Muslims that is the theme of Njegoš's poem *The Mountain Wreath*. This reveals the eschatological mission of Uzgor: its inhabitants are grateful to the 'blind old man' for having advised their forebear to take refuge precisely on Romanija, 'on straight Glasinac, so that here too, as in Montenegro, the murrain should be eradicated from the sheepfolds for ever and ever' (Lubarda 1987: 163).[1] In this vision of things, Romanija is a kind of new or extended Montenegro. To the sound of the old *gusle*, the family often sang the epic songs of Kosovo, the Serbian revolts and the *haiduk* campaigns,

1. Cf. line 673 of Njegoš in which Vladika Danilo announces the decision to set out on the extirpation of the Muslims: 'Let's drive the murrain from our sheepfolds'.

and heralded the time when all the Serbs should be united. The narrator's father in particular, who regularly outwits the government authorities, 'as Starina Novak', speaks almost entirely in quotations from Njegoš's poem and the heroic epic, and will immediately find a parallel in them for every situation in life.

Thus with respect to attitudes to the Muslims, a direct symbolic link, or rather an identity is established between the historical situation in Montenegro in the eighteenth century – or the way in which it is depicted in a work of fiction – and in eastern Bosnia right up to the 1960s. Time is stopped in the ancient moment of primary evil, the coming of Islam to the Balkans, and everything that has happened since then and is still to come is just a reproduction of the relationship between Good and Evil established and frozen at that time, right up to the final settling of accounts the outcome of which would be the disappearance of one or the other.

All the wars of Starina Novak

Whenever I hear or read the words Romanija or Glasinac, the names of the regions to which the destiny of my forebears has been linked for close on two centuries, I feel joy and exaltation, as if I had received a rare and precious gift (...) As a child, by my father's side, and then as a young journalist (...) I was in the habit of wandering the tracks and canyons of Starina Novak and his haiduk *comrades Deli-Radivoje and Dijete Grujica, to listen to the echo of the legends and to imbibe the harsh call of the* gusle, *the first and most important education for every man of Romanija.*

(Lubarda 1993: 17)

A guest at the Great Assembly of the SNO at Oplenac (see p. 133), Žarko Gavrilović, head of the Serbian St Sava Party, recalled that 'it was from here', that is, from Karađorđe's native village of Topola nearby, 'that once before a lamp of freedom for the Serbian people had been lit', going on to develop the fundamental symbolism of the current political meeting as a functional and substantial equivalent to the gathering of the *haiduk* band after it had seen out the winter. Just as then the mythical leader, the *harami başı*, would ritually announce the beginning of a new cycle of wars, so his heir or reincarnation, the contemporary political leader, exactly on St George's Day, when *haiduks* traditionally gathered, announced the equally ritual initiation of his followers, leading them into an archetypal epic time: 'Such a lamp has been lit today too. Like a new Starina Novak, I say unto you that Serbia has been resurrected' (*Borba*, 7 May 1990; *Vjesnik*, 7 May 1990).

Coincidence would have it that this happened on the very same day as the HDZ Peščenica meeting. Then a month after these two meetings, the SPO president Vuk Drašković gave the main Zagreb daily an interview about the political conditions in Yugoslavia. Since he had been voicing warmongering views about the non-Serbian peoples in Yugoslavia for several years, and stated that in this country the Serbs had been systematically exploited, it was natural for the journalist to ask him what he meant when he said that in the event of a break-up of Yugoslavia the borders between the republics would have to be redrawn. This was his reply:

> Bosnia-Herzegovina is mine, and not Mr Tuđman's (...) Put a Croatian flag on Romanija? In the name of all that is holy, where is that Croat hero who would be able to get past Starina Novak, Dijete Grujica, Deli Radivoje on Romanija, pass by them in peace, and get to the top, to plant an alien standard there? (*Vjesnik*, 10 June 1990).

When Drašković said that he would not permit such statements 'out of any electoral principles whatsoever' he showed that he understood the political context – the Croatian electoral campaign – in which Đodan's evocation had been given shape, and he returned to it twice more in a single year. At a press conference in Sarajevo he referred to those 'maniacs' who 'were even now talking about a standard on Romanija, without knowing that even if they got past Stari Vujadin and Dijete Grujica at the foot of Romanija they would have someone waiting to greet them at the top' (*Oslobodenje*, 27 February 1991). Then, at a press conference of his own party in Belgrade he briefly remarked that the 'demand for a Croatian standard to be hung over Romanija' was also leading to war (*Vjesnik*, 11 April 1991), deliberately forgetting that it was he who some five or six years earlier had stated that the western border of Serbia was in the suburbs of Zagreb, and that the communists had seized from Serbia what rightfully belonged to it – the whole of Bosnia and more than a half of Croatia, and that the time had come for the Serbs to take back these areas, one way or another.

His depiction of the Romanija *haiduks* waiting, one after another, for the intruder, the 'Croatian hero with the alien flag', is a reference to the Serbian epic song 'Starina Novak and Deli Radivoje', in which 'they drove one on the other' the ambushed Turks, and:

> *What Deli Radivoje missed*
> *Young Tatomir greeted;*

What got past young Tatomir
Dijete Gruica waited for,
What Dijete Grujica let slip,
Starina Novak held fast.
They cut down thirty Turks.[1]

Using the same epic situation, sections of the other two Bosnian religious and ethnic communities, Muslim and Croat – and through them whole units of the Bosnian epic tradition and the common vernacular historical experience – also metaphorically expressed criticism of certain political procedures. Or, to put it more precisely, this experience and this vernacular culture, as repository of themes, motifs and characters in which certain typical social situations are condensed, are not susceptible to division by ethnic or confessional criteria, but they do diverge as to the moment when these situations start to be interpreted from an individual point of view and individual experience.

Even before Đodan's evocation of the 'standard on Romanija' and Drašković's polemical rejoinders concerning the invincible *haiduks* of Romanija, a Bosnian sociologist and member of the more liberal Bosnian communist elite had written a newspaper article analysing the mechanisms of Milošević's appropriation of power. He showed how Milošević had first of all dismissed the leadership in Kosovo and forced upon it the faceless Rrahman Morina, former member of the secret police. Then he settled accounts with his political rivals in Vojvodina and placed his toady Nedeljko Šipovac in power. Then he set about taking control of the League of Communists. Here too the same mechanism was set in motion: first of all, Milošević came up with some general statements about being the defender of equality and democracy, and pushed his obedient allies into the foreground to start the final political shoot-out: the discrediting, not only political but also moral, of all those who thought differently, while he himself waited behind the scenes for the new balance of forces to be established. This kind of allocation of roles reminded the author of:

a metaphorical line from the Serbian traditional epic: 'What Starina Novak missed, Dijete Radojica caught, and Deli Radivoje settled'. Wasn't it in just this spirit that the 14th (so-

---

1. This 'classic' and best known image has a number of variants, such as when Starina Novak deployed his companions in such a way as to be sure that Alija Đerzelez would not give them the slip: 'thou, Grujica, at the foot of Romanija / I shall wait at the end of Romanija / and thou, Rade, in the middle of Romanija' (Milutinović 1990, 149).

called extraordinary) congress of the League of Communists of Yugoslavia was held according to the vision of the new-born child from Vojvodina for whom Starina Novak left this dirty bit of the business, in the expectation that if it failed the whole thing would be settled by the folklore-armed Deli Radivoje? The scenario didn't work out.[1]

In another example, a Croatian historian made use of the same epic situation. He was Professor of Medieval History at Sarajevo University and a fierce critic of HDZ policy in Bosnia and of the anti-Bosniak propaganda on Croatian TV during the time of the Croat-Bosniak war. For him, the foundation of the Croatian para-state structure of Herceg-Bosna under the official patronage of Zagreb was just as criminal as the separatism of the Bosnian Serbs, while the rhetoric of the Croatian media, which were promoting the anachronistic categories of the heroic epic and showing the Bosniaks as latter-day Osmanlis, did not essentially differ from Serbian propaganda. When Radovan Karadžić called his ally Mate Boban to set off together to 'erase the name of the Turk', one from the north and one from the south, the author gave this parodic version of the *haiduk* ambush:

> *what Ilija Guzina missed*
> *Smiljko Šagolj would wait for,*
> *what youthful Šagolj let past,*
> *Sloba Lovrenović would slit the throat of,*
> *whatever beasts Sloba let through,*
> *Milan Zorić would stab to death ...*[2]

In the this case, the names of the epic heroes have been replaced by the names of contemporary figures: Milan Zorić was the editor of the Banja Luka section of Serbian Televison, while Ilija Guzina was the editor at Pale; Smiljko Šagolj was the Croatian TV correspondent from Bosnia, and later head of its studio in Široki Brijeg, while Slobodan Lovrenović was a columnist for the paper *Hrvatski list* in Mostar, and a mouthpiece for Mate Boban. But the structure, style and lexis have been adopted without alteration, and have convincingly reproduced the original epic situation and diction.

This and the previous example are one-off and uncharacteristic examples in the discourse of both Muhić and Lovrenović, who worked from democratic

---

1. Fuad Muhić, 'Balkaniziranje ustava', *Danas*, 425, 10 April 1990.
2. Dubravko Lovrenović, 'Prilog za biografiju Mate Savojskog', *Eurobosna*, 24, 3–9 September 1993.

positions and within the categories of rational political communication. What is more, both of them had a powerful ironic dimension, and in the case of Lovrenović, elements of the grotesque and caricature. It is clear that the authors approach vernacular culture critically: it serves them as a vehicle for criticism and irony about those who have no distance from it. It is a means of creating special rhetorical effects and making discourse more dynamic, and not an authentic basis in terms of expression and motivation for constructing their statements. The premise for this kind of thing, of course, is that they are emancipated from the mythic consciousness and clearly understand two differences.

First, the heroic epic always gives a filtered and reduced image of reality, and if this picture does in some elements correspond to the facts, in general it is considerably at variance with what critical historiography understands them to be and can be accepted as historical only if it is confirmed by extra-poetic discourse. Most of the heroic epic

> has an element of the fabulous in it, and though this does not necessarily discredit the other elements, it raises doubts about the reliability of poets as witnesses to a real past. There is nothing to prevent a poet inventing if he wishes to do so, and in a non-scientific age the lack of critical spirit makes such inventions more likely than not. The poets may honestly believe that they are telling the truth, but their idea of truth may not be the same as ours (Bowra 1978: 510).

Secondly, put quite simply, the two authors know that they are living in a historic time, in an ongoing and multifaceted process of social and all other kinds of changes, in which contemporary relationships cannot be mechanically, unambiguously and entirely derived from those of long ago. History helps, to a greater or lesser degree, in understanding the roots, objective and subjective, of current events and relationships. But the crucial categories for comprehending contemporary matters can be provided only by that same contemporaneity, looked at objectively and analysed critically in all its aspects.

Awareness of these two differences is the reason why Muhić and Lovrenović used the epic evocation only once. They know that irony loses its point if it is repeated, that it becomes banal, turns into cliché. By contrast, the absence of any such awareness is why Vuk Drašković, for example, can endlessly repeat the idea of the three *haiduks* stopping the Croatian standard being placed on Romanija, and it is never a cliché, either for him or his target audience.

For neither he nor they understand the category of ironic distancing. What is more, for the mythic consciousness, a humorous vision is blasphemy, and they are deadly serious: Starina Novak is their contemporary (or they are his, it is all the same). For a modern consciousness, the evocation of an epic situation is a functional rhetorical supplement to discourse, making it more vivid, while the discourse itself is really grounded in analytical categories. For the pre-modern awareness, this evocation *is* the discourse, its source and confluence, for it is founded on the very same non-analytic categories. They are consubstantial, for they believe the pertinent realities – poetic and realistic, once and present – to be consubstantial.

The actual syncretic figure of the *haiduk harami başı* Starina Novak 'is one of the most enigmatic poetic creations of the *haiduk* series of songs' (Stojanović 1984: 146). As one post-war school anthologist wrote in exaltation: 'on the imperial highway, with his sabre that let no one past, he acted as divine vengeance' (Đurić 1954: 12).

The epic of Starina Novak absorbed many of the older oral (not only *haiduk*) traditions, and wrapped him in a cloak of mythic layers. In his figure, the traditional song actually immortalised Baba Novak, commander of the *haiduk* troops in the Danube region at the end of the sixteenth century, who was sung of over the whole South Slav area, as well as in Romania. There he is described in the traditional songs and textbooks as a national hero who fought against the Ottomans at the end of the sixteenth century, in concert with the powerful medieval prince Michael the Brave of Walachia, Transylvania and Moldavia. Baba Novak had transferred to him what was known about the century-older Debelić Novak, who according to tradition had defended Serbia together with Prince Marko. But through this figure one can also discern still older traditions from the seventh to the tenth centuries, when the Slavs in Thrace or Romania entered Byzantine military service as border guards fending off the incursions of Arabs and Bulgars, and in lieu of payment received lands along the border. Hence the unusual phenomenon that in a song about the *haiduks* there are also elements of the pre-*haiduk* traditional songs of the Middle Ages, characteristics of feudal chivalry. According to this interpretation, the name Novak Debelić is actually a vernacular corruption of the name *novus debellator*, new victor, as this kind of soldier was called in Balkan medieval Latin. And in one aspect of him, Starina Novak was the vernacular personification of the Byzantine *stratiot* (Stojanović 1984: 152).

The vernacular imagination gave him the occasional characteristics of the pagan supreme deity Dabog, who was for the Serbs 'in the ages concealed in the dark' the creator of all life, bound both materially and morally to raise the people that he had created (Cvetanović 1988). Also to be seen are Novak's similarities with the Indo-European Thunderbolt Bearer, and his ur-Slavonic derivation Perun (e.g. the mythic power of the voice which makes the boughs bend and the leaves fall, marriage to a sprite who bears him a son), and according to the way motifs are grouped, it is reasonable to conclude that Novak and Grujica are personifications of the Moon and Sun. Although *Starac* (Old Man) was a kind of patriarchal title attributed only to the wisest and best among the old, given the mythological components of the character of Novak, his attribute of *Starina* need not be identified with the current meaning of the word *starac*, old man, but rather linked with the expressions *starati se* (look after, care for), and *starosta*, guardian, leader, head of the band (Radenković 1988). This Novak then would be a mythical polytheistic forbear, a progenitor who never ceased in his protection of his descendants.

This line of argument helps to explain what is at first sight the confusing fact that Vuk Karadžić's *Serbian Dictionary*, which gives an exhaustive picture of the patriarchal village, does not contain the word *predak* (ancestor, forebear) although it has thirty-one derivations from the root *sta-*. As the Balto-Slavic *star* meant 'what had stood a long time, what stood firmly', this 'actually gets us closer to the idea of the original ancestor', the protector and progenitor (Popović 1983: 84). In this context it is important to recall that the Soviet newspapers called the president of the All-Russian Central Executive Committee Mikhail Kalinin by the pseudo-folk name of 'all-soviet *starosta* (senior)' (Elbaum 1991: 722). Whether directly linked with this or not, Tito's (second) nickname of Stari – which he received in his early forties! – is undoubtedly connected with the same ancient vernacular concept.

All this goes to show how far Starina Novak departed from the realistic events of history, how much he was immersed in myth and appeared as the protector of a whole nation and its collective idol – which seldom happens with the *haiduk* (Cvetanović 1988: 207). At the end of the nineteenth century the following proverbial expression was recorded among the Serbs of Bosnia: *Ever since Starina Novak*, signifying the very distant past, in some unfathomable Primordial Time (Kasumović 1911: 137).

In the songs he was usually joined by his son Grujica and his brother Radivoje, and sometimes his other son Tatomir is mentioned, all of them together being referred to as Novak and the Novakovići. There are signs that the epic Grujica was formed by merging the traditions of two historical *haiduks* of the seventeenth century: one from Perast, in Boka Kotorska, and one from the village of Zubci near Trebinje, in eastern Herzegovina, which was the starting point for many *haiduk* forays against Dubrovnik. As late as the second half of the nineteenth century there was a still living tradition that in their old age Novak, Radivoje and Grujica left Romanija and went to live in peaceful retirement on the coast (Nazečić 1959: 15–25).

All these interwoven traditions and the historical facts behind them cannot be entirely reconstructed, but in this context it is not irrelevant to recall that the SDS *governor* of eastern Herzegovina, Božidar Vučurević, came from Zubci. In his public speeches he regularly expressed his pride in coming from an area that had produced such famous *haiduks* and rebels. In this whole area there was a powerful cult of the *haiduk* who attacked not only the Turks, but also Dubrovnik, and particularly in the songs about the *harami başı* Bajo Pivljanin of the seventeenth century, hostility towards this city is very 'clearly and definitely' preserved, even 'emphasised' (Nazečić 1959: 190–1).

The songs about these *haiduks* open the third, and perhaps the most popular, volume of Vuk Karadžić's *Srpske narodne pjesme* [*Serbian Folk Songs*]. The first is the best known of them – 'Starina Novak and Headman Bogosav' ('Starina Novak i knez Bogosav'), with which many other anthologies or collections also open, for it is a kind of paradigm of and key to understanding all the *haiduk* epics. The typical *haiduk* biography and basic definitions of the *haiduk* worldview are depicted through the words of Novak, but it is also possible to discern the complex relation of historical fact and its vernacular interpretation, as well as the confusion of figures and periods.

When Headman Bogosav asks Novak what has driven him to 'break his neck, walking the hills / in the *haiduks*, in an evil trade', the *haiduk* replies that in his youth he spent three years 'day-labouring' for Jerina, building the walled city of Smederevo. Jerina, or Irene, Irina, the *damned Jerina* of song and legend, is actually a historical figure, the wife of the Serbian despot Đurađ Branković (*c.* 1375–1456). She is still cited today as a cruel ruler not only in Serbia, but also in the area of Bosnia between the Drina and Bosna rivers, although she never held sway there (Palavestra 1991). As he did not earn enough for 'sandals (*opanci*) for his feet' and still had to pay taxes, Novak decided to flee to Bosnia. At the foot of Romanija, he met up with a Muslim wedding procession. The 'Turkish bridegroom' came out and attacked him out of sheer waywardness. In self-defence Novak killed him and took his clothing, arms and horse:

> *Behold it is forty years*
> *I have grown used to Romanija hills*
> *Better, brother, than my mansion,*
> *For I hold the way between the mounts,*

Await the Sarajevo youths,
And seize their gold and silver,
And fine homespun, velvet,
Dress myself and my band,
And know full well to reach
And keep my own in awful place:
I fear no one but the Lord.

In the eighteenth century Romanija became one of the main *haiduk* resorts of the western Balkans, and the operations of the epic Novak were transferred to this mountain. The peasant imagination felt the powerful presence of Novak over the whole region where the Serbs lived – from the Morava area to Herzegovina, as shown by the many place names and local traditions, but in the epic, Novak became closely connected with Romanija. He and the mountain are practically synonymous and even today the people know Haiduk Cave (*Hajdučka pećina*), once the haunt of Novak's band, near the village of Mokro, as well as Novak's Rocks (*Novakove stijene*) and Haiduk Spring (*Hajdučka vrela*), a spring that is also linked to his band.

The literary and educational paper *Bosanska vila*, launched in Sarajevo by Serb intellectuals a few years after the establishment of Austro-Hungarian rule, systematically encouraged readers to collect ethnological material and write down the traditonal songs and customs. From the invitation and questionnaire that was published for the purpose it is easy to see what kind of a position the figure of the *haiduk* was to occupy in the national integration ideology and the catalogue of exemplary national figures and moral examples, which was just acquiring its final form.

Geographically speaking, Starina Novak was to represent Bosnia as one of the programme's Serbian lands, and was to be the incarnation of the fighter for its freedom. From a temporal perspective, he was supposed to become a symbol of the post-Kosovo era battle against the alien conqueror and a kind of counterpoint to St Sava, as an already established symbol of the pre-Kosovo golden age of national independence and religious homogeneity. The paper had already carried out a successful campaign of collecting materials about St Sava, who represented 'the time when the Serb freely enlarged his power' and yet lived in peace. But now, writes the editor, it is time to explore personalities from the time when, after the Kosovo catastrophe, the Serb could exist only if he was 'powerful and energetic in his misfortune', and did not meekly bow to his fate. Like St Sava in his time, Starina Novak was the most noteworthy in the period 'when the heroes hid in the caves and in the thick oak forests, defending their golden liberty and honoured cross with their swords', 'as an initiator' of 'that great chivalric and unequal combat'.[1]

Among the letters that arrived at the editor's office from the field it is worth highlighting a legend from the Zvornik area about how Novak's band came upon the monastery of Tavna that the Turks had burned down in 1463. Realising that this was a 'Nemjanić foundation', that is, an edifice from the time of the medieval kingdom of Serbia, the *haiduks* cleared the overgrown walls and repaired them 'in such a way that the walls, the dome and the altar could be seen from afar'. Novak often crossed over into Serbia to collect contributions from the people and the lower clergy for the monastery.[2] The legend is interesting because it shows how the people sees its hero not only as a fighter against the foreign master, but also as a conscious guardian of the cultural and religious heritage, a person who understands the importance and value not only of the vernacular but also of the elite state culture, almost like some 'state-building' politicians.

The editorial board also published as a supplement an unsigned drawing of Starina Novak, which evokes precisely this kind of image: there before the reader is not so much the leader of a band of wilful highland robbers but more the well-presented and cultivated magnate who would have led an organised state army or presented national political programmes in the Viennese Imperial Council (see illustration on page 236).

This 'ethnographic' campaign of the Serbian middle class in Bosnia, which became a modern political force after the end of Ottoman rule, set out an ideological and political interpretation of Starina Novak, laid the foundations for his cult beyond the borders of vernacular culture and determined his place in the Serbian political imagination. What the popular culture had previously felt only inchoately now received a conscious interpretation and was accepted into the political plans of the younger middle classes.

But the exclusive definition of epic heroes of the kind that nationalist ideologies aim at cannot always be fitted into the original vernacular culture or indeed into any ideological and political conceptions. The Franciscan Ivan Franjo Jukić (1818–1867) was an ardent supporter of the Illyrian movement, which stood for the ethnic, linguistic and cultural unity of all the South Slavs, while respecting historical state and political identities, including not only Croatia and Serbia but Bosnia as well, as the successor of the medieval *Regnum Bosnae* in accordance with the legitimist conceptions of European political theory of the time. He endeavoured in the liberation resistance

---

1. Vid Vuletić-Vukasović, 'Starina Novak ili početak borbe 'za krst časni i slobodu zlatnu'', *Bosanska vila*, XIII, 1, 1 January 1898.
2. Vasilije Ćuković, 'Starina Novak ili 'početak borbe za krst časni i slobodu zlatnu'', *Bosanska vila*, XIII, 18, 30 September 1898.

Starina Novak, as portrayed in 1898
by the anonymous artist of Bosanska
Vila.

to homogenise all the Slavs, including the indigenous Muslims, always
distinguishing them clearly from the Osmanli Turks who were foreigners,
the subjugators of Bosnia and the parties chiefly guilty for the sufferings of
all Bosnians, whatever their faith. Hence as he puts it the *haiduk* was not
primarily a Christian rebelling against Muslim rule, but rather a symbol of
pan-Bosnian resistance to all intruders. Here the fact that some of the local
Slavs had with time assumed the religion of this intruder was of secondary
importance, and irrelevant as a possible reason for being politically or
emotionally less loyal to a homeland that was shared with the Christian
Croats and Serbs.

When the Ottoman pacifier of Bosnia Omer-Pasha Latas had him
arrested and deported to Istanbul, the 'sad and wretched' Jukić, while crossing
over Romanija, recalled Novak's son Grujica 'lying in wait for the Turks' and
concluded: 'if there had been more Grujicas in Bosnia, I would not now be
being escorted by the Ottomans; there would not be such wastelands, such
wretchedness'.[1]

This is just one example that shows very clearly that it was the Ottomans
who were the real enemies and really to be blamed for the backwardness
of Bosnia, just because theirs was a foreign government, and not because

---

1. Cf. I. F. Jukić, 'Putovanje iz Sarajeva u Carigrad god. 1852', *Bosanski prijatelj*, XII/
   1881, vol. 3, pp. 71–91.

its protagonists were Muslims. For Jukić used the common name for all the inhabitants of Bosnia, 'Bosniaks', to refer to the local Muslims of Slav origin, together with Catholics and Orthodox. At the same time he avoided the term 'Turks', because in vernacular usage, as well as in the epic songs, this meant anyone who was a Muslim, a member of the Turkish faith, just as in the Balkans all Catholics were called Latins or Romans, and all the Orthodox were called Greeks, irrespective of their ethnic or cultural identity. The name 'Turks' actually erased the whole distinction that Jukić thought of key importance, aware that to ignore it would have great and very dangerous political consequences. By contrast with Jukić, all those who have wished to produce precisely such fatal results, down to modern times, have always made use of this same vernacular expression, implying that the Muslim population in Bosnia is a foreign element, and that it is proper to behave towards them precisely in the same way as towards the Ottoman government in the land.

Speech in the mountains

The Sarajevo summer of 1991 was marked by a great shortage of petrol (...) One Saturday, putting my trust in luck (...) I headed off in my Volkswagen towards Pale. Two kilometres before the entrance to this impoverished village at the foot of Romanija, there was a petrol station belonging to Zagreb's INA Corp. (...) On a wooden chair leaning against the glass window an oldish man was sunning himself.

'Is there any petrol, boss?'

The man squinted out of one eye, as if aiming into the sun or as if he had seen an idiot. He shook his head and perhaps said a 'jok' [no] but I didn't hear him. I returned with a mournful expression on my face and engaged first gear, and I had only just moved off when he shouted after me:

'But this is no longer an Ustasha station, this is the first station of SAO Romanija.'

(Miljenko Jergović, 'Last Trip to Pale', *Svjetlo riječi*, 142, January 1995)

A few days after the first Drašković response, loaded with epic evocations, a woman journalist asked Đodan 'What happened to that standard on top of Romanija that you kept bothering people in Bosnia-Herzegovina about?' There were no such references in his answer:

I was completely misunderstood. It had nothing to do with carving up the borders, as has been imputed. Why shouldn't the Croatian flag flutter in Bosnia-Herzegovina, even with a five-

pointed star? If Bosnia-Herzegovina is the state of the Croatian
people too, why should they be forbidden to carry Croatian flags
at their meetings? At the same time, however, the Serbian flag was
allowed to flutter at rallies in Sokolac, Šipovo and Drvar (*Večernji
list*, 16 June 1990).

Neither facts nor logic can be marshalled against this argument, but it
would be very possible to discuss whether Đodan had chosen the right image
to express it. In other words, the right of the Bosnian Croats, and the Bosnian
Serbs as well, to display their national and political emblems over the whole
of their country was not in dispute and could be exercised in a hundred ways
and with reference to many localities, symbolic or literal, but then, it was
specifically Romanija that Đodan had chosen, thus putting his hand into a
kind of referential hornets' nest. It seems to me that he was not aware of the
power of his image and all its layers. But not two months later anyone at all
interested had a chance to learn an excellent lesson from extremely competent
lips. In mid-August, in that so significant place, the SDS president, Jovan
Rašković, made a number of speeches that could perhaps most appropriately
be defined as *Everything You Have Always Wanted to Know about Romanija
But Never Dared to Ask*.

On 12 July, St Peter's Day, the SDS of Bosnia-Herzegovina was founded,
sister organisation of the same party in Croatia. The choice of date was charged
with symbolic significance. Despite the dissolution of traditional forms of life
and the extended families that had been the basis of society for generations
of Romanija shepherds and herdsmen, on this mountain, as well as in other
traditional stock-rearing areas, the feast of St Peter was still an occasion to get
together in the open air. Then the better-off families would take their second
breakfast collectively around the church *sofra* [low wooden table], with tables
and benches, food and drink, they would sing and dance; the grown-ups
would fire guns and the children torches called *lile* (Đukić 1976). It was in
this setting of a popular gathering that the SDS president, Jovan Rašković,
founded local parties in Sokolac and other places on Romanija. It is more
than likely that the enthralled listeners included many of those dissembling
communists who had even at the beginning of May expressed their shock
and horror at the very mention of any possibility of carving up the borders
of Bosnia-Herzegovina and then overnight they had become 'ethnically
aware' and from being nationally disinterested communists who defended
brotherhood and unity, Tito and Yugoslavia, they had turned into militant
nationalists who damned Tito for having been the downfall of the Serbs, and
they had begun to intimate the creation of Greater Serbia.

This then is what Rašković said on these occasions at the meetings on Romanija, to people who were already well prepared for such messages, not only by the official media propaganda from Serbia, but also through a succession of informal but tightly networked channels from *gusle* tournaments and the distribution of audio tapes at meetings such as that at Knežina which were only ostensibly ecclesiastical.

> I am personally very pleased to be here in these wonderful clearings on Romanija. There are no finer hills than these. There are many absurd things about the Serbian people. One of these is that I, who go tramping round the world, should have been in Hong Kong four times, but only came to Romanija for the first time a month ago, and here I am again. No more Hong Kong for me, I know where I am going to come, and where I'll relax. Your sacred Romanija!
>
> Tuđman promised that here on Romanija the Croatian flag (*barjak*) would fly. There'll never be a Croatian flag here; everyone knows whose Romanija is. We came here before the Croatian flag, and that is our pride. And it is not hard to get here before that flag, because it actually never will come here. Everyone knows whose Romanija is, and whose flags can fly on it (...)
>
> The mountains are Serbian gathering places, Serbian refuges and resorts, nests of heroic freedom and monuments of the Serbian people. But Romanija is even more than that. It is a mythic mountain that sets afire the imagination of boys reading Vuk's poetry or listening to the Serbian *gusle*.
>
> Romanija is an outpost of peace and liberty in Bosnia-Herzegovina and so in Yugoslavia as well. As long as there's Romanija, both Bosnia and Herzegovina will be peaceful and free. Romanija holds the keys to our liberty. Anyone who thinks he's going to nail his flags on top of Romanija has got another think coming. If he really did nail it in, that would be a nail in all our heads. (...) We can remember all those killing fields where innocent people died. We can remember the rivers and the pits, although our historians have forgotten the ford over the Drina, where a thousand lasses were driven into the river before the hordes of the bloodthirsty Ustasha Francetić (...)
>
> And today too, forty-five years after the war, the Croatian state-builders cherish the vain hope that they are going to create a 'Greater Croatia' and that this Croatia will encompass both Bosnia-Herzegovina and with them Romanija. (Rašković 1990: 260–3)

239

The semantic field covered by the speech develops on six levels. On the first level, the mountain is valued rather generally in the category of the aesthetic, as something that in this too exceeds the external world and is demarcated from it. At the second, this separateness and specialness is determined by the phrase 'sacred Romanija' in the category of the sacred, as a consecrated spot.

At the third level the utterance is linked to the current occasion, to the aspiration of a competing community to appropriate the space for itself. Rašković stated that it was Tuđman who had promised this, although Tuđman had never even once evoked the motif, rather than Đodan, who really had, and whom the Croatian media consistently identified as the speaker, whether or not they thought him Tuđman's mere mouthpiece or an independent politician. This was no oversight on Rašković's part, but a way of equating the status of the utterer of the threat and the substance to which it referred. For just as Romanija represented their own Serbian community, to which Rašković and his audience belonged, so Franjo Tuđman, as president of the state of Croatia and of the ruling party, and as 'president of all the Croats', as he liked to say of himself, and hence superior to Đodan, was representative of the competing Croatian community. To put it another way: for the message to achieve its full impact, the subject had to have the symbolic, political and all other kinds of force equivalent to its object. Through Đodan, it was perhaps just a few Croats who were speaking, or perhaps only he himself, but through Tuđman, all the Croats were speaking, just as any planting of the Croatian standard in some other place would concern only some Serbs, while displaying it on this very Romanija would concern all Serbs. It embodied its people just as Tuđman embodied his.

At the fourth level the meaning of the mountain is defined in the traditional system of each community, by being merged in two of its central texts.

The expression that the mountains are the 'nest of heroic liberty' is a quotation from the section 'The Kolo' in Njegoš's *The Mountain Wreath*, lines 710–13:

> *Thou Mountain-Nest for Freedom's Quest!*
> *On thee God's eye hath kept a constant guard;*
> *What sufferings hast thou not endured;*
> *What victories yet brings Time as thy reward!*

Njegoš started developing the image of the heroes' nest, surrounded by enemies, which has an important role in his vision of history, as early as 1833 in the historical poem 'The Voice of the Highlander' ('Glas kamenštaka'), in which mountainous Montenegro is the fortress of freedom, the 'Serbian nest', the 'falcon's nest', 'nest of old Montenegrin fame / woven in the midst of the Turkish empire' which had always, ever since Kosovo, been able to defend itself against the Turks. While the surrounding Balkan Christian states succumbed, sooner or later, the little community in the high mountains remained an oasis of liberty and faith, a model to the enslaved and herald of liberation.

It is possible that Njegoš inherited this image, which in the 1830s became a commonplace of national romanticism from the poem 'The Serbian Girl' ('Serbianka') by his teacher and friend Sima Milutinović, in which Montenegro is the 'lee and nourishment', the 'refuge' and – as a sum of all these metaphors – the 'nest' (Aubin 1989: 82). This motif contains the legend that the surviving Serbs found refuge there after the debacle of Kosovo, 'to continue here with the battle against the Ottoman Empire, / to preserve the Serbian faith and identity', 'just as Njegoš put it in *The Mountain Wreath*: 'What is not bound in chains / will flee to these mountains" as the former boxing champion Miodrag Perunović, member of the pro-Serbian Montenegrin NS and one of the more important figures in all the pro-Milošević rallies in Montenegro, explained to a Belgrade journalist (*ON*, 22, 10 October 1990).

The mention of this motif and in general the symbolism of the mountains, the *haiduk green hills*, constitute a point at which it is worth making a somewhat lengthier digression in the analysis of Rašković's political imaginary.

SEVEN

Birth of the *Haiduk* Cult

The massif extends in a southeast-northwest direction. Climbing up it, at the beginning you come upon stunted and sparse pines, and then upon denuded white stone. There is an unusual appearance to the cliffs that grace the mass to the left of the road. It is, in effect, a vast serrated complex of stones the tops of which have a particular form and represent now a pyramid, now a regular thick ridge, sometimes a thin trunk, and something like a split hoof. This complex is known in the vernacular as the Romanija Cliffs [Romanijske stijene]. To the right stretches an uninterrupted, straight and yellowish chain of cliffs that, as they say, is a five-hour journey long.

(Gilferding 1972: 92)

The decadent West and Balkan Arcadias

Travel literature about Bosnia-Herzegovina – along with that describing Greece – must be one of the most abundant in Europe, in view of the size of the country and the number of inhabitants. The travelogue itself is a genre in which the transmission of meaning from one culture to another is exemplified even more clearly than in dictionaries, all the more since it is this literary genre that is used, often consciously and more or less covertly, to express political views and ideological platforms.

On the eve of the Congress of Vienna, the Englishman Arthur Evans, the future celebrated discoverer of Cretan Minoan culture, then a twenty-four-year-old passionately interested in archaeology and cultural anthropology, travelled through Bosnia and Croatia. As soon as he came to Syrmia he heard plenty about the 'brigands' hiding in wooded Fruška Gora and about their 'increasing brigandage', and coming closer to Zagreb, in the Banija region, learned that a group of sixteen 'Hajduks, as the Croats called them' were operating in the area of Petrinja. In the note at the bottom of the page he explained that *hajduk* is 'the usual word for brigands etc in Eastern Europe' (Evans 1876: 62).

However, the editor and commentator on the translation, the Bosnian Serb folklorist and literary historian Vlajko Palavestra, considered Evans's note susceptible of another interpretation, and he wrote the following addition:

> It is necessary to explain and correct Evans' statement that *haiduk* is the common name for brigand. At the time when Evans was in our lands, the *haiduks* were called outlaws, but earlier, under Turkish rule, *haiduks* were fighters of the national movement for the struggle against Turkish tyranny (Palavestra, 1973: 104).

But the Serb was a bit hasty in his intention to correct the Englishman's alleged misunderstanding. Just before the disputed quotation, Evans himself had pointed out that 'these Croatian highwaymen [...], however, had hitherto conducted the business of the road on the most gentlemanly principles' (Evans 1876: 62). Furthermore, right after the note that led to Palavestra's criticism there are sentences that might have been written by any ideologue of romantic Yugoslavism (or Serbian or Croatian Romanticism of the second half of the nineteenth century). And the commentator on the translation might have signed them himself, as might many compilers of school readers in both the Yugoslavias:

> Nor let us judge too harshly of their profession, for in this old-world East of Europe the Hajduk is often a gentleman in his way. 'Tis Robin Hood and his merry men who still live on, roughly redressing their wrongs in a vicarious fashion against that society which refuses them legal requital, but capable none the less of much tenderness to women and children, and discriminating their friends from the class that oppresses them. Across the Turkish frontier the cause of national freedom hopelessly lost centuries ago on the battlefield, has been championed from generation to generation by the Hajduks of the forest mountain, in achievements not unsung by Sclavonic bards; and, likely enough, these Croatian brothers are striving too for the ancient liberties, as they understand them (Evans 1876: 63).

In fact, there is no disagreement at all. If the expression *brigands* escapes him as a tribute to his education in austere Harrow and still more strait-laced Oxford, where he learned to think in terms of legality, formal legitimacy and legal procedures, Evans was, nevertheless, in the 1870s, with his predominantly romantic view of *haiduks*, particularly the comparison of them with Robin Hood, quite a long way from the lexicographer Joakim Stulli of the beginning of the nineteenth century and from Ivan Belostenec two centuries before that, and very close indeed not only to Palavestra, but also to Vuk Karadžić and Njegoš. And Evans's *haiduk* who was a *gentleman in his way* precisely corresponds to Njegoš's desideratum of *Ritter and Chevalier*, just as his 'society which refuses them legal requital' is identical to the concept of heroic liberty, to be discussed below.

It is true, the low density of population and the relative powerlessness of central government made outlaws viable longer than in the west. And in the east, the oppressed and impoverished peasantry was readier to make common cause with the outlaws than the freer and more advanced peasants in western societies. But it is also true that the stereotypes and generalisations, of the kind that the western media and mouths of the political elite were full of during the 1990–1995 war, lead nowhere. Someone like Belostenec, living practically beside a field of permanent battle with the Ottomans, 'at the edge of the world', surrounded by despairing refugees who crowded in every day from Slavonia, and the various armies and mercenary squads that were deployed along the border, was closer to the modern concept of law than Evans was, two centuries later. He was a member of the establishment, of the prosperous upper middle class of an effectively organised and governed state at the height of its power. Neither, of course, was 'typical', but both of them show that every society and every time is a complex, often inherently contradictory entity. (And who can say what it means to be *typical* or *representative* of some socio-cultural milieu?)

After all, even the legends of Robin Hood, that prototype of many of the world's *noble criminals* or *gangsters with a heart of gold*, a kind of 'international paradigm of social banditry', as Eric Hobsbawm defined him, are not without cruelty and callousness, especially the earlier cycles. Nevertheless, English popular traditions shaped him into a symbol of the struggle for the 'olden rights' against the Norman aristocracy, made him into a righter of wrongs, taking from the rich – not all, only those who abused their position and oppressed decent people – and giving to the poor. Evoking him and his *merry men of Sherwood*, which is nothing other than a Nottinghamshire version of the Balkan *haiduk* band in the green hills, the rich Oxford student Evans is no less romantic in his views than his poor, uneducated South Slav contemporaries. Apart from that, the 'Croat friends' who interpreted local conditions for him were a very timid trader and civil servants from the towns of Sisak, Petrinja and Zagreb, and when he went later to Bosnia, he was accompanied by Muslims, Ottoman police, or *zaptiyes*.

Given their own official, social position and immediate experience, neither of these two groups could have expressed different views about *haiduks*. Evans's fellow traveller in the train to Zagreb, a trader who was afraid for his money, certainly could not. There are two inimical worlds at issue here: just as, naturally, no policeman in the world, Christian, Muslim or whatever, wants to risk his life chasing armed fugitives who will stop at nothing, so the fugitives themselves do not like those who wish to bring them to justice. The commoners take sides emotionally and intuitively, from the narrow horizon of their insecure everyday life, and in its system of values, and its cultural model, the civil servant – who counsels the ruler or executes his orders – is an odious figure.

In connection with the group of *haiduks* not far from Zagreb, Evans finds out that they 'had taken to outlawry to avoid (...) military conscription' (Evans 1978: 62). Later in northern Bosnia he saw two graves that the *zaptiyes* told him belonged to *haiduks*, and Evans tried to find out what their fate had been. 'Had they turned brigands? – to redress, perhaps, some wrong unutterable? or were they rather the victims of some outrage?' (Evans 1878: 101). It cannot be denied that *haiduks* came into being for all these reasons, but something is missing which would make the picture complete: common theft, extortion or the criminal's pleasure in violence. But when *haiduks* were considered a priori and in principle to be freedom fighters or unhappy wretches who had had no luck in life, then this last element simply did not come to mind.

In a still wider cultural and historical perspective, the Croat, Serb and Montenegrin *haiduks* are joined not only by the British Robin Hood, Captain Cook and Rob Roy, but also by the Slovak outlaw Juro Jánošik, the magnanimous Andalusian bandit Diego Corrientes, the Catalan Joan de Serralonga, the French smuggler chief Cartouche, the Neapolitan Angiolillo who protected the chastity of maidens, the Russian Stenka Razin, who hanged the tyrant governor on his own gallows and proclaimed the equality of men, the Cossack rebel Emelian Pugachev and Oleksa Dovbuš in the Carpathians. These are important figures in popular culture, particularly in the eighteenth century, bold outsiders without whom no picture of society is complete. Their life and work are very favourable material for myths that 'satisfied repressed wishes, enabling ordinary people to take imaginative revenge on the authorities to whom they were usually obedient in real life' (Burke 1978: 166).

Then again, the South Slav or pan-Balkan *haiduk* geography, this parallel legendary map, in a certain way also hallowed, on which the war of 1990–1995 was for many participants waged in a more authentic way than on the secular one, is part of a lengthy and uninterrupted sequence of Arcadias that humankind has created, its ideologies always recurring and being put to new use in political projects. When at the beginning of the seventeenth century French, English or German travellers started to describe the Balkans with many Arcadian elements, and two of the key topoi of the genre – *simple customs* and *the noble savage* – it was just another episode in the long search of European social thinkers, ethnographers, folklore collectors and poets for a lost golden age of general harmony and peace.

Intellectuals longed for the utopia in which the primitive was equated with the good, for a happy people of pure and natural simplicity who knew nothing of government, industry, agriculture or writing, but nor what plagued contemporary European spirits – mendacity, treason, vanity, hypocrisy, envy and cupidity, not even having expressions for these concepts in their languages. They kept their freshness and strength and could be savage only in the same sense as the savage or wild fruit which nature produces regularly and quite of its own accord, as Montaigne wrote of the Brazilian Indians. They had a land that they loved, were heroes in a fight, bold and resolute in their speech, and free, while Europeans did not even know what the word *freedom* meant, as Voltaire wrote of the peoples of America and Persia (cf. Cocchiara 1981).

A key role in the recruitment of Croatian, Serbian, Montenegrin and Bosnian regions in the eighteenth century view of the customs of so-called natural or innocent peoples was played by the Italian natural historian Abbot Alberto Fortis. In his *Voyage to Dalmatia* (*Viaggio in Dalmazia*, 1774), particularly the chapter 'On the Customs of the Morlaks', the elite European public in its 'rapture for the poetry of the primitive and the noble savagery of uncultivated peoples' found everything it needed: the bold *haiduks* whom pitiless misfortune drove to the green hills, an ethical understanding of revenge, blood brotherhood and sisterhood, superstitions and original music (Bošković-Stulli 1978: 247).

When the Serbian oral poetry became known in the west at the beginning of the nineteenth century, first of all in Germany, Jakob Grimm and other German Romantics were particularly delighted with the heroic songs. According to the already established model of Greece as a land of immortal ancient heroes, Romantic literature was easily able to create the idea of one more Arcadia, on a fictional map of the Balkans. The new Homeric land, now Slav, was Serbia, and very soon the Montenegro of Prince Nicholas (Nikola). The establishment of equivalence between the heroes of Kosovo and the *haiduks* on the one hand and ancient Achilles on the other hand was all the easier since Vuk Karadžić himself readily compared the Serbian epics with the Homeric poems. (A century and a half later the 'awakened' Serbia of Slobodan Milošević fitted impeccably into such Arcadian projections of 'heroic simplicity' or 'simple heroism', particularly the 'epic' Republic of Srpska of Radovan Karadžić and Ratko Mladić. Day after day images were supplied to culturally prepared TV viewers in the west of the archetypal noble savage, who had perhaps done something that in the allegedly civilised world was considered a crime, but was nevertheless also a hero who would rather die than give up his freedom and his land, which was perhaps technologically backward, and yet was blessed with innocence and populated by a folk possessed of an indestructible freshness of spirit.)

This is how Fortis describes an important and common feature of the social life of the countryside in the hills in the Dalmatian hinterland, whether they were Catholic or Orthodox villages:

> The Morlacchi have their rustick assemblies, especially in houses where there are several young women; and in these the memory of ancient national stories is perpetuated. A musician always attends these meetings, and sings the old *pisme* or songs, accompanying them with an instrument called *guzla*, which has but one string, composed of many horse hairs. The tune, to which these heroic songs are sung, is extremely mournful, and monotonous (...) Their poetry does not want strength of expression, but the smallest ray of imagination rarely appears in it, and the little that is attempted is seldom happy. Yet those songs have a great effect on the minds of the hearers, who are at pains to get them by heart; and I have seen some of them sigh, and weep at a passage, which did not appear to me the least moving. Perhaps the force of the Illyric words, better understood by the Morlacchi, might produce this effect; and perhaps, as seems to me more probable, their artless minds, little stored with ideas, might more readily be affected with any turn of expression that appeared to them extraordinary (Fortis 1778: 82–83).

It would be unfair, however, to accuse Fortis of prettying-up the image of these 'rustick assemblies' for 'he described them faithfully, but what he saw was the dimension that impressed the foreign traveller' – singers who sang of the heroic past to the accompaniment of their bizarre instruments

(Bošković-Stulli 1978: 248). Fortis was a connoisseur and fan of the poems of the third century Scottish bard Ossian, which had actually been invented in 1760 by James MacPherson. With their dense melancholy and love of wild nature, they had an enormous effect on the development of European Romanticism, and it is not unimportant that MacPherson and Fortis were financially assisted by the same Maecenas – Lord John Stuart.

On another mountain range on the edge of Europe, a thousand-odd miles away from the Celtic one, Fortis found – or thought he had found, or was intent on finding – 'Illyrian' Dalmatia, and drew the same conclusions dictated by the dominant spirit of the age, that is, that there too, among the local population, 'innocence, and the natural liberty of pastoral ages are still preserved (...) or at least, many traces of them remain in the places farthest distant from our settlements' (Fortis 1778: 64–65).

Unlike Fortis, who was perfectly at one with the intellectual climate of the second half of the eighteenth century, when Enlightenment and Romantic ideas intertwined, some 170 years later, the English writer Rebecca West gave a personal, ideologically coloured interpretation, or rather characterization, of the South Slavs. She completed her lengthy meditative travelogue through Yugoslavia on the eve of World War II, *Black Lamb and Grey Falcon*, during the Blitz. Her 'fixation on the Serbs', as Brian Hall with good reason summed up the dominant impression of the work, came from her personal distaste for the spirit of appeasement of Western governments in the face of Hitler, or rather an obsessive search for a nation that she could use as a metaphor for the defence of liberty at any cost. She found it in the Serbs, or in the myth of Kosovo, and in its message that it was better to die with honour than to live in conditions of moral ambiguity. Thus she created an idea of the Serbs as the incarnation of the Good that, innocently like Christ, sacrificed itself to put down Evil, once Turkish, now German. By contrast with the Serbian heroes, the Croats, since they had for centuries lived under the Habsburg crown, were a nation contaminated by the worst possible cultural influence – that of the Germans – while the Bosniaks were an anachronistic Turkish survival and a blind alley of history, a kind of living dead. This was to be a 'remarkably attractive approach, for writer and reader alike, because it was comprehensible' and 'we all want history to be comprehensible' (Hall 1996: 41).

West's way of thinking and the figures that fascinated her are well depicted in the scene of market day in Sarajevo. Although you can see both Muslims and Christians in the town, her attention was most drawn to the Serbian peasants who came down from the neighbouring mountains, for they were 'nearly all of the heroic kind'.

The finest are the men, who wear crimson wool scarves tied round their heads and round their throats. This means that they have come from villages high in the mountains, where the wind blows down from the snows (...) These men count themselves as descendants of the *Haiduks*, the Christians who after the Ottoman conquest took refuge in the highlands, and came down to the valleys every year on St. George's Day, because by then the trees were green enough to give them cover, and they could harry the Turks by brigandage. They reckon that man can achieve the highest by following the path laid down in the Old Testament. I cannot imagine why Victorian travellers in these regions used to express contempt for the rayas, or Christian peasants, whom they encountered. Any of these Bosnians could have made a single mouthful of a Victorian traveller, green umbrella and all. They are extremely tall and sinewy, and walk with a rhythmic stride which is not without knowledge of its own grace and power. Their darkness flashes and their cheekbones are high and their moustaches are long over fierce lips. They wear dark homespun jackets, often heavily braided, coloured belts, often crimson like their headgear (...)

Although they may eat only after their men have finished their meal, and labour arduously every day, even during pregnancy,

their women do not look in the least oppressed. They are handsome and sinewy like their men (...) But I will eat my hat if these women were not free in the spirit (...) In some sense these women had never been enslaved. They had that mark of freedom, they had wit (West 1993: 326 –328).

The many journalists who wrote of the collapse of Yugoslavia and the war in Croatia and Bosnia-Herzegovina referred to her travelogue, using quotations from it as the epigraphs of their books or in some other way revealed how much they had been affected by her image of the Balkans as a nightmare in which for six centuries, from Kosovo on, nothing had changed, and in which it was best not to meddle. Coming into the war-torn areas, they often saw only what they had been prepared for by this fifty-year-old book. What is more, a copy of it, much the worse for wear, marked *UNPROFOR use only*, cruised the UN HQ in Sarajevo, and only reinforced the prejudices the officers had brought with them to Bosnia: 'they bought into this idea that the Serbs had been our allies in two world wars' (Simms 2002: 179–180).

The preface to David Owen's memoirs, after the London conference on the former Yugoslavia at the end of August 1982 appointed him as one of the two authorised peace mediators, suggests that he read *Black Lamb and Grey Falcon* for the first time in the 1970s, when as British Foreign Minister he was concerned with what was going to happen with Yugoslavia after Tito died. Like Rebecca West, he, of course, knew that nothing in the Balkans was ever easy, and that there 'history pervades everything and the complexities confound even the most careful study' (Owen 1995: 1). Thus, as soon as the fighting started at the beginning of the nineties, he 'had dipped into, rather than re-read' her travelogue and 'on every page (...) had found a labyrinth of history, weaving a complexity of human relations that seemed to bedevil the whole region' (Owen 1995: 6). He took the book up again for the third time after he had been appointed mediator, just before his first journey to Zagreb, Belgrade and Sarajevo, 9–12 September 1992.

At more or less the same time, in the BBC London studios, the director Paul Pawlikowski and his team were editing material shot in the mausoleum of the Karađorđević kings at Oplenac in Serbia, at Gazimestan (Kosovo) and on Romanija, among Serb peasants and soldiers who were laying siege to Sarajevo. Their documentary film *Serbian Epics* (Pawlikowski 1992), even if it is not directly inspired by the images and interpretation of Rebecca West, nevertheless gives the impression of being a screening of her work. The pictures of tanned highlanders in the mountain clearings, lambs turning on spits as the bottle of brandy goes from hand to hand, to the sound of the *gusle*, evoking the heroic past and the struggle with the Turks, no doubt partially catering to the public's taste for the unknown, the unusual, the heroic and the unspoiled, for a distant and exotic area where Christianity and Islam, West and East, Europe and Asia meet in such an interesting and indeed fateful manner. This is a benign interest, like that of an airport novel, and it contains no political stance, ideological alignment or social awareness. These exist only in the creator of the film, as they did in Rebecca West.

While the soundtrack gives the *gusle* player chanting about the Serbian people as being 'habituated to war', scenes of rural life start to unfold in front of the viewer: one family is collecting plums in front of a modest house, and then the householder, after his son or perhaps grandson has brought him a shirt, climbs into a tank and goes off through the leafy forest to battle, while the others continue with their jobs as if there was nothing particularly untoward. It is soon seen that the grey-headed tank crew member is in fact a *gusle* player, who entertains the soldiers when they are off duty. While he sings, the tank is at rest in the shade, under the branches of trees some fifty metres off, children are climbing over it and swinging from the gun. A

Romanija massif, summer 1992: between two mortars trained on Sarajevo, Serb peasants and soldiers (still in JNA uniforms) listen to a *gusle* player's song about the battle of Kosovo. (still from Pawlikowski's film *Serbian Epics*, 1992)

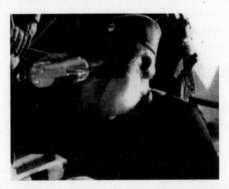

Romanija massif, summer 1992: roast lamb and a circulating bottle of brandy are accompanied by two *gusle* players singing on the Serb front line: 'Hey, pretty Turkish maiden, our monks will baptise you. Sarajevo in the valley, we Serbs have you surrounded ...'

little further off a ten-year-old boy with a rifle in his hand watches a mower, indeed, looks after his gun while he cuts his meadow in a respite from the fighting, and a black-haired woman, one of those that in Rebecca West's book 'had that mark of freedom', skitters around the soldier bareback on a restless horse that otherwise runs freely through virgin nature and just tosses its mane slightly when it catches from the distance the muffled sounds of artillery fire (see illustrations above).

This is a world of the heroic patriarchate, in which the frustrating laws of contemporary civil society are not valid, but rather those of natural morality. It is the idyll of paradise lost, an island on which men have preserved their purity of character and emotions as they have the purity of nature, a kind of *merry men of Mount Romanija*, as opposed to the vicious *sheriff* in the Balkan version of Nottingham, Sarajevo. Half a century earlier, West had written that 'these men could have made a single mouthful of a Victorian traveller, green umbrella and all'; now all could see that they could do just the same with every Croat, and particularly with every Bosniak.

They have no motor thresher or reaper, but thresh with horses and reap with a sickle, but at the same time, in a contrast that is as exotic as it is natural in this world from another world, they handle their tanks adroitly, set complicated sights on mortars and fire from sniper rifles. While everything on the mountain is rippling with life, sunshine and the luxuriant colours of summer nature, in the valley lies the city that shows all the evil of contemporary civilisation: it is desolate and grey, wreathed in fog and smoke that can hardly be identified as coming from the tank shells from the hills or from the pollution produced by industry and traffic. Minarets and monotonous housing blocks with geometrical forms file past the viewer's eyes, and the close-ups of the yellow Holiday Inn and the two black, fire-ravaged skyscrapers of UNIS Co. additionally enhance the impression that this is a spectral lifeless shell from some unspecified cataclysm, rather than the effect of a very concrete crime, more the agonic megalopolis from a post-catastrophe film like *The Day After* or *Mad Max* than a place where human beings live.

The camera does not show a single casualty, or fire, or shell from the hill, or explosion, as if somewhat unusual, perhaps also in a way frightening, but undeniably romantic mountain warriors were shooting at a mere model, at a town that had long since been abandoned. As if, indeed, they were carrying out some unusual ritual of their own in which the Evil of the City was being buried and the Good of Life celebrated.

Radovan Karadžić shows Sarajevo to the Russian poet Eduard Limonov and explains to him that the city was built on Serbian land. When the Turks came – 'whose descendants the Muslims are' – he says, the Serbs who did not want to renounce Christianity and be converted to Islam had to leave the fertile land in the valleys and trek to the free hills and mountains. Thus he taught his Russian guest the very same thing that fifty-five years earlier the Serbian writer Stanislav Vinaver, the cicerone of Rebecca West, had taught his English lady guest, and she had enthusiastically written it all down, for it had been ideologically and politically necessary for her that the unvanquished Christians 'after the Ottoman conquest, took refuge in the highlands'. This is after all an ancient myth of many peoples, among other things it is the classic motif from *The Mountain Wreath*, about the Serb heroes who would 'not be shackled in chains' but instead after the defeat at Kosovo withdrew into the mountains of Montenegro to preserve the 'heroic pledge, the name of hero, and sacred liberty', and it is also the evocation of the concept of *heroic poverty*, from the value system of patriarchal societies, as much as it is the message of Rebecca West from the perspective from which she experienced her own times and her vacillating Western contemporaries, with whom she was deeply frustrated because of the years of climbing down in the face of Hitler's demands. A really brave people will always make the decision to live free but in poverty, rather than change their faith, or betray themselves merely to preserve their lives.

All these scenes reverberate with the Romantic views of a happy natural state and virtue instilled into the soul of nature, the symbol being the Serbian highlanders of Romanija, or alternately with an image of civilisation as thwarting and perverting mankind, the symbol here being Sarajevo with its mosques and standardised concrete tower blocks. This attitude, however, is not a feature only of Western Romanticism, but also of its ideological and intellectual contemporary in the east of the continent, Russian populism. Out of fear for the capitalist 'inflammation' destroying the rural communities, during the 1870s a radical group advocated the seizure of political power through conspiracy and violence. After seizing political power, the party will use the power of the state to renovate society and, by transforming the commune where they use shared tools of production and carry out common labour, will lead the society directly into socialism. The less militant populists did not concern themselves so much with concrete plans, but shared the same cultural animosities and affinities, and searched in Russia itself and elsewhere in the Slav world for a Utopia to show them that their dreams were feasible.

The image that was mediated to the Western public by Rebecca West in her book and Pawlikowski in his film is comparable to the picture that, also in the travelogue genre, was mediated to a different audience by the Russian consul to Sarajevo in the mid-nineteenth century, the historian Alexander Gilferding. Like all Slavophiles and advocates of pan-Slavism, he too was convinced that the Romanic-Germanic civilisation of Western Europe was alien to the Slav world, and Catholicism and Protestantism its main adversaries. Like Pawlikowski in Romanija, he found a land in Herzegovina 'that to this very day (...) was unspoiled and virtuous', and like Pawlikowski in the Romanija rural highlanders as opposed to the Sarajevan urban Orient he found in the Orthodox peasants around Trebinje, a majority Muslim town, a Christian 'purity of conviction' that 'was as yet unsullied by egotistic plans and uncertainties' (Gilferding 1972: 33).

Although he had come practically half a century earlier, with a different motivation and from a different historical and cultural background, Gilferding shared one further point with Rebecca West. As servant and joint-creator of the Russian policy of assistance to the Orthodox Balkan Slavs, he was in principle reserved towards Bosnia because of the powerful presence of oriental forms of life there. As proponent of the Romantic Slav ideal, he felt antipathy to the beys and the Bosnian Muslims in general, who cared less about their Slav origin than he thought they should. As a vigorous campaigner for a single language for all Slavs, he found it hard to tolerate the many Turkish loanwords in their vernacular.

In the mountains, not only was all this absent, but they were an effective contrast to the lowlands and the cities that developed in them. The city or lowlands, the *space-outside-the-mountain*, since it was less valuable, was more an object of contempt than of hatred. Since geographical relations were indivisibly linked with religious and ethical ones, the antithesis of 'up' and 'down' powerfully recalled the dualism of the medieval worldview in which the heavenly, what was up there, was linked with exaltation, purity and the good, and was opposed to the earthly, to what was down there, over which baseness, impurity and evil cast their shadow.

Karadžić's minion Božidar Vučurević seemed to have sprung fully armed from the pages of Gilferding's book. He grew up in the villages around Trebinje, and with the help of the JNA organised, in 1992, the expulsion of the Muslims and the destruction of the Islamic architectural heritage in the town. He was particularly voluble and indefatigable when he was explaining what lay behind the destruction of another city – Croatian and Catholic Dubrovnik. On this occasion it was possible to make out the model just mentioned in which parts of geography are distinguished according to their degree of sacredness. The people of Dubrovnik, he warned, 'must know where Herzegovina is, and Herzegovina is always above them' (Mihović 1993: 131). In this town on the coast, as he elaborates his idea in another place, 'life was always whorish; nothing above sea level – a nothing kind of people', or 'people are like climate – where the climate is softer, so are the people, and where it is harsher, the people are tougher'. The inhabitants of Dubrovnik, which stands here as a symbol of the city in general, were used to swarming around the moorings, the exchange offices, the customs and in recent times the Dubrovnik gentry came out of their salons and hired them out together with their bedrooms to ne'er-do-wells from out of town. In this hiring, they spared neither themselves nor their women and children (Mihović 1993: 41–42).

In other words, the tourist industry that enabled Dubrovnik to develop, set up international links and become wealthy was just another word for prostitution. Someone who was willing to hire out his house or rooms for money was no better than a pimp who by that very act was selling himself, his history, honour, soul and body, whether in reality or symbolically. For this reason he compared the role of this or any other town in the life of a given people with the function of the spleen in the human organism: just as in it the erythrocytes that have performed their life cycle are broken down, which make it 'the graveyard of red blood cells', so Dubrovnik is the 'spleen of this area, the Serbian spleen', because every Serb from Herzegovina who had moved to the town had experienced there both moral collapse and loss of identity, his blood, vehicle of vitality, was turned into water. This also means feminisation, for war is the only context in which virility is maintained and renewed. In Vučurević's village, people will say, with a special kind of pride, of their own house that 'it was burned down in both world wars' while 'our neighbour Dubrovnik never went to war', and hence it is 'good for them to have a house or two burned down' (Mihović 1993: 84).

Before he collected his thoughts into a book, Vučurević developed them in a number of interviews, and one allegedly urban writer who was overnight translated into a national ideologue, Momo Kapor, worked on the same set of motifs. He did, he admits, regularly spend the summer in Dubrovnik, except that at the beginning of the eighties he suddenly noticed that no one was reading anything except instruction manuals for machinery and church newspapers – Catholic, of course. 'The wealth acquired overnight had created the mentality of a people without spirituality or compassion', 'a Sodom and Gomorrah' of vice, greed and 'spiritual prostitution'. The antithesis of such a world was the Herzegovina hill country behind the city, where he met 'slender, tanned lads with guns in their hands, with drawn and dusty faces, serious in their mission at the borders of two aged empires, the Eastern and the Western, the Catholic and the Orthodox', where men recalled the ancient wars and heroisms to the sound of the *gusle*.[1]

---

1. Momo Kapor, 'Predeo spržen mržnjom [Area scorched by hatred]', *Pogledi*, 100, 17 January 1992.

Long before, Rebecca West had felt the same ideologically based antipathy towards Dubrovnik, although from very different cultural premises. For she too saw in a racially conceived nationalism a bulwark against the chaos of a weary Western civilisation and felt disgust for the same nations as Vučurević and Kapor – the Germans, Italians and Turks, and also for those who had imbibed their cultural and political influences, the Croats (and Slovenes), that is, and the Bosniaks. The difference is only that this intelligent and well-read Englishwoman managed to frame her travel-writing with a deal more sophistication and finesse. But they all did the same thing, and for all of them, and for Gilferding as well – there was only one Slav people in the Balkans that was graced by characteristics worthy of respect and admiration, only one that lived, at least predominantly, in the exalted, numinous setting of the mountains.

And in the *haiduk* poems too, *the green hills* were not just a background to the poetic picture, not just a setting or framework for the action, rather the traditional poet regularly attempted to make them into a kind of fellow combatant or ally of the *haiduk*, a sharer in the battle against the outsider 'with a certain active attitude and benevolence towards the heroes' (Stojanović 1984: 55). The motif of the *haiduk*'s farewell to the hills exists in all the songs of the Balkan peoples, the *haiduk* frequently expressing his gratitude to the mountain for all it has given him, and the mountains often grieving for him when he is killed. The symbolism and apotheosis of the mountains were hence from the beginning an important sub-system in the metaphors of contemporary Serbian *'haidukery'*.

A month and a half before the first round of multiparty elections in Croatia, the mountain area Petrova gora underwent a process of acquiring great symbolic value. On 3 March 1990, a major Serb rally was held, demanding that the federal authorities arrest the leaders of the non-communist parties. Although in the nineteenth century the mountain was a refuge of the *haiduks* and had a generally important place in the geography of the epics, on that occasion the fact that the Partisans had been very strong there in World War II was in the foreground, and the accent was placed on a kind of ritual 'de-Ustasha-ing' of Croatia. In Lika, symbolism was from the outset developed along the epic line of the mountain cult. As the local SDS leader explained, the Serbian people 'were built in freedom in these mountains' which maintained them in freedom. The mountains had been 'since time immemorial inhabited by snakes, wolves, hawks, the occasional *haiduk*,' and when the Serbs found their freedom endangered even there, as was happening in the 'infernal décor of Croatian democracy', then they

1. Audio cassette 'The tragic demise of Branko Đukić' by the *gusle* player Božidar Đukić. (1985)

2. Audio cassette 'Twilight of the gods at Žuta Greda' by the *gusle* player Vojo Radusinović.

3. Audio cassette 'National *gusle* player – Ranko Mastilović'.

4. Audio cassette 'Killing of a federal law officer in Kosovo in 1981' by the *gusle* player Slavko Jeknić.

5, 6 & 7: Audio cassettes – 'Fourteenth emergency congress of the LCY' (1990), 'The enthronement of Dr Franjo Tuđman' (1990) and 'O Herceg-Bosna, you are lost to me' (1996) – by the *gusle* player Željko Šimić.

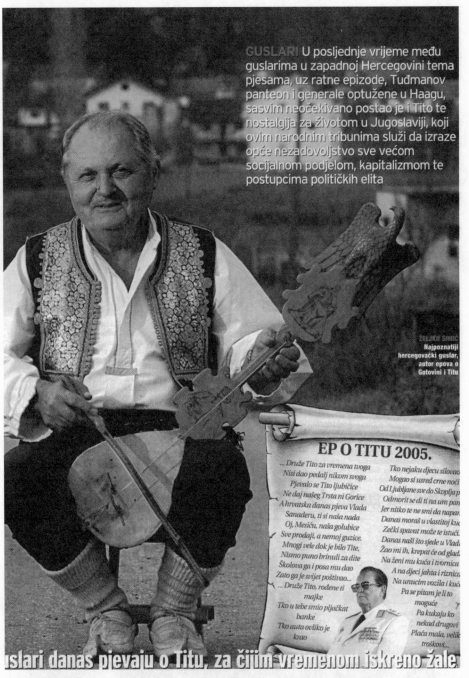

GUSLARI U posljednje vrijeme među guslarima u zapadnoj Hercegovini tema pjesama, uz ratne epizode, Tuđmanov panteon i generale optužene u Haagu, sasvim neočekivano postao je i Tito te nostalgija za životom u Jugoslaviji, koji ovim narodnim tribunima služi da izraze opće nezadovoljstvo sve većom socijalnom podjelom, kapitalizmom te postupcima političkih elita

ŽELJKO ŠIMIĆ
Najpoznatiji hercegovački guslar, autor epova o Gotovini i Titu

EP O TITU 2005.

... Druže Tito za vremena tvoga
Nisi dao pedalj nikom svoga
Pjevalo se Tito ljubičice
Ne daj našeg Trsta ni Gorice
A hrvatska danas pjeva Vlada
Sanaderu, ti si naša nada
Oj, Mesiču, naša golubice
Sve prodaji, a nemoj guzice
Mnogi vele dok je bilo Tite,
Nismo puno brinuli za dite
Skolova ga i posa mu dao
Zato ga je svijet poštivao...
... Druže Tito, rodene ti majke
Tko u tebe smio pljačkat banke
Tko auta ovliko je krao

Tko nejaku djecu silovao
Mogao si usred crne noći
Od Ljubljane sve do Skoplja p
Odmorit se di ti na um pan
Jer nitko te ne smi da napar.
Danas moraš u vlastitoj ku
Zečki spavat može te istuči.
Danas naši što sjede u Vlad
Žao im ih, krepat će od glad.
Na ženi mu kuća i tvornica
A na djeci jahta i riznica
Na unucim vozila i kuć
Pa se pitam je li to moguće
Pa kukaju ko nekad drugovi
Plaća mala, velik troškovi...

uslari danas pjevaju o Titu, za čijim vremenom iskreno žale

8. The Croat *gusle* player Željko Šimić from western Herzegovina, photographed in 2004; on the neck of his instrument, figures are carved symbolizing two central traditions of Croats in that region: the mediaeval king Tomislav (top) and the seventeenth-century *haiduk* Mijat Tomić. (photograph by Tom Dubravec)

9. Metropolitan Amfilohija Radović, the most ardent supporter of the Great-Serb policy and of Radovan Karadžić in the hierarchy of the Serbian Orthodox Church, performs as a *gusle* player in 1999 at a church

10. The Croat *gusle* player Mile Krajina performs in 2002 on the central square in Zagreb, at a rally organized in support of General Mirko Norac, indicted and later convicted for war crimes.

OSNIVANJE SDA: Na osnivanju središnje muslimanske stranke u Velikoj Kladuši sudjelovali su i kasniji najveći Izetbegovićevi politički protivnici Fikret Abdić i Muhamed Filipović

11. Screen bearing the image of Mujo Hrnjica behind the stage at the founding conference of the SDA at Velika Kladuša.

12. Restored fortress of Mujo Hrnjica on a hill above Velika Kladuša, the official residence of Fikret Abdić; rusty German howitzers, Partisan trophies from the Second World War, have been placed along the approach road.

13. Performance of the *moreška*, a mediaeval Mediterranean dance, in an authentic setting on the island of Korčula in about 1960. This original war dance, the core of which is a duel between white and black king for a beautiful maiden, spread in the thirteenth century into Spain, Italy and Corsica, while variants were popular also in northern Europe (Flanders, England). However, Franjo Tuđman proclaimed its performers a combat unit, a precursor of the Croatian army.

14. The Mijat Tomić *Haiduk* Troop – 'a historic formation of the Croat people in B-H' – poses in 2001 at Doljani, beside the restored tombstone of the *hajduk* after whom it was named.

15. The Mijat Tomić *Haiduk* Troop photographed on the occasion of its foundation in September 1999, in front of the memorial basilica of King Tomislav at Duvna/Tomislavgrad.

16. Front row centre: a Bosniak in the garb of an Ottoman warrior and brandishing a scimitar, as a symbolic member of the Mujo Hrnjica *bölükbaşı* detachment, at the founding conference of the SDA in Velika Kladuša.

17. Idealized mediaeval Bosnian knight as exemplary precursor of the modern Army of B-H – cover illustration of the book *Historija bosanske vojske* [History of the Bosnian Army] by Enver Imamović.

18. Iconography of the Army of B-H when it defined itself as exclusively an army of Bosniaks, and reduced the tradition of Bosnia to its Islamic component: Alija Izetbegović and generals Rasim Delić and Sakib Mahmuljin in a position of prayer, behind them the official poster with a mosque and Moslem tombstones.

became 'more cunning and stronger than the wolves, faster and prouder than the hawks, bolder than the *haiduk*' (Petar Štikovac, *Duga*, 443, 16 February 1991).

In Bosnia-Herzegovina it was Romanija that was to experience its most complex and in a way most creative apotheosis, of which there will be more later. Ozren too is a mythic mountain. It was addressed especially systematically by the Belgrade journalist and painter Dragoš Kalajić, the ideologue of the pro-fascist New Serbian Right (Nova Srpska Desnica). While the poisoned cities were decaying in the lowlands, on Ozren there lived warrior folk whose faces 'were burned by Sun and fire', and whose songs were 'pure as the mountain springs and adamant as granite'. Or as one member of a tank crew said to a visitor from Belgrade:

> Everything that you can see lit up by the Sun – this is Serbian. And everything that is covered in fog and smog and pestilential vapours – that is Muslim.[1]

If such a vision seems like a synopsis for Paul Pawlikowski's film, the conclusion from an earlier article by Kalajić seems no less convincingly to have been taken from Rebecca West. When in the middle of the war he arrives on Ozren for the first time, Kalajić meets there 'one of the rare oases of preserved beauty, goodness and truth' in the midst of 'a defiled, perverted and polluted Europe', the 'resort of the most freedom-loving and most indomitable Serbs to whom the Muslims had given a wide berth', a place where the Serbs defended 'the honour of their forebears who had perished that we might live' and 'had opened a new cycle of civilisation with their struggle for freedom'. Mount Ozren, says he, had been 'excommunicated [by the communists] from their programmes of modernisation, urbanisation and industrialisation', and had thus 'unwittingly preserved the virtues and values its people.' In the mountain hamlets he came upon the same kind of people that the English writer had also searched for, the same kind that had thrilled her at that fair in Sarajevo. Although they had for a time fallen victim to modern civilisation and gone off to live in the cities of Tuzla, Doboj or Maglaj, the Ozren people had at the onset of war returned to their homeland and now they

> bear on their faces the gleam of a happiness it is hard to find in the cities (...) They have no regrets, but rejoice in this fortune in

---

1. Dragoš Kalajić, 'Na sunčanoj strani Bosne [Sunny side of Bosnia]', *Duga*, 1613, 15 April 1995.

misfortune, that they have returned to the life of the cultivator (...) Ozren is an oasis of the natural hierarchy of virtues and values where reputation is invisible and honour is determined by usefulness.[1]

However obvious it might have been that such ideas were in line with the standard repertoire of modern right-wing ideologues, for the purposes of our theme it is more appropriate to look at them from the point of view of cultural anthropology and to consider them together with the views transmitted by the *haiduk* epic, bearing in mind that the model of space is one of the basic cultural categories. For with the appearance of the *haiduk* themes in the epic poems an essential change occurred in the status of the mountain as numinous space. And there was a general revolution of values in two basic spatial oppositions: *house – woods*, and *own – alien*. In the earlier, chivalric model of the epic, created in Serbian feudal society, the city was a cultivated space that afforded protection, and the house was a place of intimacy and safety; while danger lurked in the mountain and forest. By conquering Serbia and occupying the cities, the Turks created a sharp discontinuity in the traditional understanding of geography: the city became a jail and a place of suffering, and the mountain was transformed into a new home, the *haiduk* dwelling-place, a secure and protected place where the heroes on the run from the city created a new and different kind of family. The *haiduk* in one such song introduces himself: 'My home's a stony cavern/ Romanija my heritage / my brothers are the mountain *haiduks*'. In the new *haiduk* model of the epic, the city is perceived as a place of threat that has been occupied by foreigners, and with this transformation, a series of new themes related to it enters the songs: the danger of going into the city and staying there, imprisonment and escape from the town, and its encirclement, devastation and even total destruction (cf. Detelić 1992).

After the first anti-Ottoman insurrection in the nineteenth century the cities were restored to the Serbs. But not even then did the epic songs describing this change of government give the fact anything like the importance that it had, objectively speaking. For the insurrectionary leaders themselves the cities were a secondary objective of the war, for both they and the imagination of the epic poet 'at least at the beginning' saw all the complex and dramatic events in insurrectionary Serbia as 'universal 'haidukery', guerrilla war in which the whole people partook'. Under the 'terrible pressure' of several centuries of awareness that the cities were alien, Turkish, the Serbian epic had lost

---

1. Dragoš Kalajić, 'Zemlja etičke čistoće [Land of ethical purity]', *Duga*, 513, 23 October 1993.

all notion of the holy city, although it had long been a favourite
epic theme in the Christian world (...) During their lengthy period
of servitude under the Turks, the Serbs – as Orthodox – had the
necessary conditions to build their own urban culture, since
Eastern Christianity offered the prototype of the old, developed
cities of the Levant. But they remained entirely without this
support (...) Here and there Constantinople appeared as a holy
place, but soon afterwards it was transformed into Stamboul.
From that time on, silence reigned (Detelić 1992: 207).

Historical experience and social memory were thus interwoven with
the fact that outlawry or *'haidukery'* had existed since ancient times in the
surrounding border mountains between the Raška region and the Sava-
Danube lowlands, Macedonia and Albania, Thessaly and Epirus and the
population had lived in what were virtually patriarchal mountain republics.
Back in the mid-nineteenth century, the Russian consul in Bosnia noticed
that the Ottoman government had no authority at all in Drobnjaci and
Piva, in the northwest of Montenegro, although these tribes were formally
within its borders. While elsewhere 'the Christians trembled and bowed
before the *müdür* [county administrator], here they were good friends with
him'. The Ottoman government in the cities was content to receive its taxes,
and did not interfere elsewhere, while the clans collected them themselves,
making sure the burden was shared equally. This equilibrium was destroyed
irretrievably in the middle of the century when the Ottomans brought in the
Albanian *başibozuks*, armed squads of formally demobilized soldiers, who
started to terrorise the autarchic highlanders (Gilferding 1972: 293–294).

Vasa Pelagić too, participant in and ideologue of the Bosnian Serb anti-
Ottoman insurrection of 1875–76, depicted a similar mood in the 'six good
small republics', i.e. the six Herzegovina tribes from between Sutorina and
Durmitor. They possessed complete self-government, independence in fact.
They themselves chose their headmen and settled their disputes, were exempt
from military service, and lived without any contact with the government or
the Muslims in the towns. Although they did give certain tributes, this was
in principle refunded to them by the fee that the Ottoman government gave
them as a kind of garrison on the border with Montenegro. Since they were
satisfied with this kind of life, they did not want to join the insurrection,
in spite of calls for them to show solidarity with their Christian brothers;
they were only finally moved to join by threats from Montenegro (Pelagić
1953: 69–73). Without knowing of such lengthy historical experience as
this, it is impossible to fathom how, in the spring of 1942, the Ustashas and

Chetniks in Bosnia – in spite of the exclusivism of their official ideologies, their previous bloody showdowns and the reprisals carried out by both sides against civilians – managed nevertheless to achieve an identical compromise with relative ease.

For at the beginning of 1942 the government of the NDH realized that they did not have the power to crush the Serbian revolt, and they negotiated with eight Chetnik squads on Ozren, Manjača and other mountains of western and northern Bosnia. The deal recalls irresistibly the coexistence of the Christian tribes in the hills and the Ottoman, Muslim rulers in the towns described above. The Chetniks formally recognized the NDH, and accepted the prescribed taxes, and in return they could bear arms and organize local self-government in their own region the way they wanted it. No one, not even an Ustasha unit, was allowed to enter the mountain 'peasant statelet' without permission, and they themselves collected tax and carried out all other matters of administration (Vrančić 1985; Topalović 1964). In such cases, of course, natural and psychological elements, ideas that made up the social memory and the actual configuration of the terrain are indissolubly and interdependently interwoven.

For Bosnia consists geographically of spacious, ramified and forested mountain massifs, separated from each other by cliffs or lowlands. Before the great resettlements caused by the Second World War, the spatial distribution of the population, particularly in the Bosnian Krajina, could be essentially reduced to a diagram: in the mountain villages, the Serbs; in the flat land at the bottom and the river valleys, the Croat and Bosniak villages; and a bit further off the city, mainly inhabited by Bosniaks. In the event of attack or danger, the population of the Serbian villages from the lower slopes would draw back onto the plateau or the high forest, where they had the huts they inhabited during the summer transhumance. They were reached by narrow, barely passable tracks, little more than gullies, known only to the locals. Such a mountain with its twenty or thirty villages constituted a 'geographical as well as a spiritual and defensive unit' and was on the whole economically self-sufficient, in both Ottoman and Austro-Hungarian times, as well as in the NDH. After the collapse of the first Yugoslavia and the proclamation of the NDH, on every such mountain

> a common Chetnik squad was formed from armed village groups. This squad was independent of that of its neighbours. Its mountain was in fact its state (...) The main thing was that no Ustasha foot nor Croatian government should step onto their mountain, that the mountain should be only 'ours, Serbian'.

Whatever government sat in far-off Sarajevo or Zagreb was not a crucial issue for us. The mountain and the Serbian settlements on it remained the same through the ages, while on the plains and in the cities governments would come and go – Serbian, Croatian, Bosnian, Venetian, Hungarian, Yugoslav, Croatian and so on (Topalović 1964: 36–37).

Half a century later, the sociologist Ozren Žunec wrote, according to an analysis of the behaviour of the military and political leadership of the RSK, that 'states that are menaced by guerrillas might be given a not entirely cynical piece of advice: put the guerrillas in a ghetto – attempt to persuade the guerrillas to proclaim their own state, and then force them to fight for its borders, and the problem will soon be settled' (Žunec 1995: 9). For the 'state' that the Serb rebels proclaimed in Croatia was neither that nor was it a guerrilla stronghold. It best corresponded to Topalović's description quoted above of the attitude of the highland Serb villages in Bosnia in World War II. With the exception of the lowland areas along the Danube and some parts of western Slavonia, they contained in essence a fairly clearly expressed dualism of spatial ideas. Expelling or killing the entire Croatian population in the area under their rule, and extending to the very suburbs of Sisak, Karlovac, Zadar and Šibenik, but not entering them, enabled the inhabitants and soldiers of the RSK, through the objective fact of the spatial deployment of forces, to experience every day, more or less consciously, the stable semantic structure of two sharply distinguished worlds: the world of 'up' and the world of 'down', the world of the Serbs and the world of the Croats.

This split into a sacred and a profane space was still clearer or more compact in perception in the spatial binomial of Trebinje and Dubrovnik; here it was put into effect in a far smaller area, and with a far stronger contrast of altitudes. But the purest model of a highland republic, or *haiduk* state, was achieved on Romanija, that is in the spatial and value dualism of Romanija and Sarajevo.

Both members of this binomial retained in a still more marked form all the necessary psychological, natural, social and perceptive premises. Unlike the Croatian towns, Sarajevo had a markedly Islamic semantic aspect, both demographically and architecturally, and Romanija a long *haiduk* tradition, the experience of economic self-sufficiency (which the far smaller, lower and on the whole stony mountains of Croatia did not). Then it had a high degree of religious and ethnic compactness, which was, outside the cities on the rim, in fact total. Then it had a potent epic culture as a source for schemes of mobilisation and motivation. And, finally, it had a perfectly intelligibly

261

disposed value dualism of ideas of 'up' and 'down', mountain and lowland, the way that Vojislav Lubarda had so suggestively and tendentiously stated it in his trilogy of novels on the centuries-old, fateful tension between the Serbian village of Uzgor and the Muslim city of Čaršija (see pp. 224–6).

In an interview, Radovan Karadžić formulated this irreconcilable dualism precisely and on an essentially accurate historical model: not only in Ottoman and Austro-Hungarian times, but in the time of Yugoslavia as well, the Serbs and things Serbian were driven into the villages, and in the cities, which were formed 'during the time of one occupier or another' and hence exposed to 'bogus foreign influences', there was 'such coercion that only the brave and the bold would expose their soul and their spiritual affiliation'. In the cities the Serbs 'were by their very inheritance mercenaries'. By contrast, the village lived 'a far greater plenitude of popular and religious life'.[1] The city, then, is specifically identified with the occupation; it was by definition the work of the foreign invader.

In short, this time both the Mountain and the City beneath it were large enough to be able at any time to recreate convincingly that bygone moment when the epic intervened in the understanding of geography. This time, far more clearly than in the war in Croatia, the city was seen as a space of danger under foreign rule, and the mountain as a place of freedom. The archetypal image of Chaos and Cosmos was at work again.

---

1. Dragan Stamenković, 'Vaskrsenje šćućurene duše (razgovor s R. Karadžićem) [Resurrection of the huddled soul (interview with Karadžić)', *Svetigora*, 35/36, March 1995. (This monthly is published by the Metropolitan of the Cetinje Serbian Orthodox Church.) This part of the interview got a lot of publicity in the Serbian media, and it was published, for example, by the Belgrade weekly *Svet* (86, 4 September 1995) under the title 'The Holy Ghost always whispered to us what we were to do, of which I was personally convinced'.

EIGHT

World War II

We went to school [in the Romanija village of Dobrodoli in 1938–1941] all together, boys and girls, Serbs and Muslims. The teacher was called Ilija, the son of a teacher in Sarajevo, Milorad Pejinović (...). We had religious instruction on Thursdays, and the Muslims on Fridays. But although we had different religions, we got on well together and didn't feel any differences between us. A great deal of the credit for this has to go to the teacher, who didn't allow any discrimination among the children, either because of religion or because of class.

(Krsmanović 1988: 27)

Marking the mountain – Dangić, Vajner and Francetić

The concept of *heroic liberty (junačka sloboda)* in Jovan Rašković's Romanija speeches is conceptually related directly to the mountains, for they are the *nest* in which such liberty is generated and maintained. The pre-war Montenegrin politician and journalist Sekula Drljević in his study of conflicts in the Balkans also interpreted this liberty in terms of Njegoš's literary image. In his understanding, the concept of *heroic liberty* 'was to the concept of middle class liberty in the Western 'democracies' as truth is to falsehood'. For while 'bourgeois liberty was the illusion of unarmed people that they were free', heroic freedom was 'the right of the armed hero to use arms against anyone in the defence of his honour, even against the organs of the state in the performance of their duties.' (Drljević 1944: 169).

The persistence – and a contemporary echo – of this idea is not hard to recognise in the interview which the vice-chairman of the SDS Dušan Zelembaba gave half a year after Rašković's powerful performances on Romanija. It shows clearly that this party systematically included the categories of traditional culture in its public discourse. To start with, Zelembaba expressed his incredulity that it could occur to the 'gents', i.e. the authorities in Zagreb, to disarm 'the people' in Knin, and at once he stated quite explicitly: 'I believe that only an armed people is a free people.' (*Start*, 574, 19 January 1991; see p. 136).

The word freedom does not appear at all in the Catholic and Muslim songs, and is rarely mentioned in the Orthodox ones, and then almost exclusively in those Montenegrin songs that speak of eighteenth century battles with the Turks. They do not convey a single one of the meanings that the concept has in the medieval, pre-Ottoman literature and legal documents, where it means: a) privilege, economic immunity; b) the merchants' freedom to trade in the state; c) courage; and d) personal freedom. From this point of view, the lands of the South Slavs were in complete harmony with the European political and economic context of the time. But in a patriarchal society, in the social regression brought about by the Turkish conquests, by the collapse of the medieval states and enduring wars, no concept of personal freedom developed, for there was no need for such an idea, or for the concept of national freedom and independence, because such a society had no concept of the nation. Thus not even in the epic songs does the concept of liberty have any particular substance; since it came into being in the context of the religious and ideological struggle against the Turkish conqueror, and can be understood exclusively within this context, it is used 'only in the sense of 'freedom from the Turks', i.e. freedom from Muslim suzerainty in general, and outside the epic songs it was used as a religious and ideological symbol' (Brkić 1961: 168).

The word *sloboda* (freedom) in the sense of the French *liberté* was included in the 1852 edition of Vuk Karadžić's *Srpski rječnik (Serbian Dictionary)*. It was not in the first edition of 1818, for at the time of the insurrection and immediately after it, such terms and cognate political ones – *otadžbina* (fatherland), *buntovnik* (rebel), *ustanak* (insurrection) – were only just making their way into the vernacular. If he knew them, Karadžić did not think of them as inherent in the popular speech and accepted them only in the highly politicised atmosphere of revolutionary 1848 'when they became incorporated into the living organism of the language' (Popović 1983: 139).

For the purposes of comparison, at about the same time, a dictionary of legal and political terminology was compiled, on the basis of the Central European historical legal tradition and the German language of the original, edited and printed for the South Slav peoples of the Empire in Vienna. It distinguishes as many as seven kinds of liberty in a civil society that was moving towards modernisation, in some places faster and in others more slowly. Of course, this terminological system recognised freedom of belief

(*Glaubens-Freiheit*) and of religion (*Religions-Freiheit*), as something self-evident, as a general principle, not as opposed to someone or something else, distinguishing, however, between the inner conviction of the person and the outward practice of that conviction. Then came the concepts of freedom of learning (*Lehr-Freiheit*), freedom of speech (*Rede-Freiheit*), freedom of the press (*Press-Freiheit*), of trade (*Handels-Freiheit*) and 'freedom of movement' (*Frei-Zügigkeit/der Personnen*), that is, freedom for the individual to settle and live where he will.[1]

It can thus be seen that two parallel societies were established, societies with different conceptions of the essential category of public belief, the watershed being – it is essential to underline – not ethnic but political. The division was between members of the same ethnic, national and religious communities: Croats into those in the Habsburg Monarchy and those in Bosnia, under the Ottomans; the Serbs in the Monarchy, and those in the soon-to-be-independent Principality of Serbia south of the Danube (and, also, those in Turkish Bosnia). Thus the only relevant distinctions would be how large the group of Croats and/or Serbs was, how deeply it was involved in the process of developing institutions of formalised law, or how far it persisted in the concepts of folk morality. This border was, however, extremely fluid and dependent on which part of a given community, in the complex, unpredictable and sometimes externally influenced patterns of power, was going to acquire social and/or political power, and attempt to impose its own worldview as the only legitimate conceptual framework on the whole community.

Both Yugoslav states cultivated the epic culture of liberty and statehood acquired through war and sacrifice. Just before the outbreak of World War II, the historian Ferdo Čulinović published a substantial volume in which, according to material drawn from the traditional songs and proverbs, he systematised the legal ideas and knowledge that were supposed to be the basis for the development of an independent and indigenous legal system, that is, of 'laws in harmony with the way the people think', in accordance with the state ideology of unitary Yugoslavism and Serbian war victimology, as opposed to modern European legislation. According to him, that is, written law derives mainly from 'learned legal scholars', it 'has always been created by people from towns', while 'the understanding of the bourgeoisie was mixed with alien elements and did not reflect the people's thinking about law'. For this reason it 'had the mark of the few' rather than of the

---

1. Cf. *Juridisch-politische Terminologie. Deutsch – kroatische, serbische und slovenische Separat-Ausgabe.* Vienna 1853; quoted from Mamić 1992: 110.

many, that is 'it did not accord with the collective sense of justice'. By contrast with bourgeois or written law, popular, traditional or unwritten law 'derives from popular feelings about law and justice', it is 'an expression of the whole', one that is preserved in the rural society 'where foreign influence has not yet penetrated, or at least not so far, bringing in the alien and destroying the native' (Čulinović 1938: 8–9).

Within this categorical framework, a start was made on the elaboration of individual legal concepts, including, of course, liberty. 'The people', avers Čulinović, 'calls freedom 'heroic', for it is attained in the affray, and is not a gift', which he supported with two more late-19th century proverbs: 'No deliverance but with blood (*Bez krvi nema spasa*)' and 'Nothing shed, nothing won (*Bez prolića nije dobića*)' (Čulinović 1938: 30). It is worth mentioning here the elaboration of the concept of the state, that is, the attempt to give it a theoretical basis in the categories of the heroic epic, so as to see the deep roots on which the ideology and political mythology of not only the first but also the second, communist, Yugoslavia, were founded, and their consequent enduring and irremediable democratic deficit. The author does, indeed, state that the traditional songs do also mention agreement 'as a manner of founding law, and hence the state' but at once goes on that there are 'many traces of the state arising by force', what is more, this is 'the most common and it would appear to us closest to the way of thinking of our people'. The state reposes upon the sword and 'heroic combat' and victory is 'the source of authority and position' in a state so created (Čulinović 1938: 53).

Since this is the way things are, this concept should be followed, formalised and promoted by all the institutions of government/state, from the educational system down to the mass media – this is the message of the book. It is this ideologically motivated and propagandistic selective approach to the complex value system of popular creativity that has promoted the ethical and 'legal' criteria formed in a segmented and autarchic peasant and warrior society in the sixteenth and seventeenth century into a universal social model and the ethical and legal foundation for a twentieth century European state.

The other important motif in Rašković's Romanija speech was the mention of 'Vuk's songs' and the 'Serbian *gusle*' as the medium of transmission of the epic song. They open the semantics of the speech not only in the direction of the general concept of the 'heroic liberty/freedom' of the ethically and legally autonomous armed individual but also towards the concrete motifs of the Romanija *haiduks*, the more so in that the speech ends with the cry: 'I fear no one save God' (Rašković 1990: 269). This is the formulation with which Starina Novak concludes his confession in the epic song: 'I fear no one but God!' Such a formulaic expression of self-confidence occurs in other epic songs too, including one by the Croatian vernacular poet and *gusle* player Željko Šimić, who puts them into the mouth of the recently-elected President Franjo Tuđman, as his programmatic utterance on being ceremonially inducted into office:

> *As long as I'm a Croat by birth*
> *I shall fear nobody save the Lord.*
> (Šimić 1990b)

The explicit and direct quotation, as in Rašković's speech, or, alternatively, its indirect inclusion in the depiction of a temporary political leader, as in the second case, establish and confirm the ultimate identification of past and present, at the level both of typical situations and representative personages.

At the fifth level, Rašković evokes the Independent State of Croatia (NDH) and the Ustasha movement, first through two images of suffering as a transition to an explicit evocation of events of half a century earlier. In the first, the reference to 'a nail in the head' indicates a form of torture employed by the Ustashas and which in the post-World War II press became a kind of shorthand for the Ustashas. It was particularly powerfully imprinted on social awareness by the film *The Occupation in 26 Scenes (Okupacija u 26 slika)* by the Croatian director Lordan Zafranović (1978). The scene of bestial violence, lasting a full seven minutes, was made with such unsparing naturalism that many adults were unable to watch it and left the cinema. Thousands of elementary schoolchildren were forced to watch it, taken in groups to screenings as a form of teaching about WWII.

As a result, this appalling scene was seared into the subconscious of much of the population of Yugoslavia (and when the film had been largely forgotten, TV Belgrade showed it, at peak viewing time, in the autumn of 1991, at the time of the all-out assault on Croatia). Since the mountain itself was anthropomorphised in Rašković's image, for the potential contemporary Croatian standard stuck in its head corresponded to the one-time Ustasha, ergo Croatian, nail in the head of its inhabitants, the identification of the symbolic space and its inhabitants was complete: man is mountain, mountain man. They are one in good and evil: not only a hero, the denizen of the mountain is also a victim and a martyr; not just a place of freedom, the mountain is a site of suffering for freedom and because of freedom, a point at which 'all the sites of our executions', of all times and spaces, are symbolically conjoined.

In Rašković's next image the 'mass burial pits' are evoked as Serbian sites of execution, as well as parts of the wider symbolism that suffuses the utterance. Since they are the world beneath, the world of death and darkness, at the general level of symbolism they are opposed to the mountain as world above, the world of life and light, place of health and freedom. Prepared by the dramaturgy of such images, Jure Francetić's reference to the 'hordes of bloodthirsty Ustashas' marks the final introduction of Romanija into the sixth level of meaning: into the set of meanings that the mountain acquired in the social awareness of its Serb inhabitants during World War II, the concretisation of that Evil and its foundation in a dualism of space that the images of the 'nail in the head' and the 'pits', however suggestive they may be in themselves, merely indicate in outline.

In the last 150 years, in addition to *'haidukery'*, many real battles have been fought by organised armies on Romanija. Some claim that it was at Pale in 1832 that the Bosnian autonomist Husein-Bey Gradaščević was decisively beaten by the Sultan's army (according to another interpretation of unclear historical sources, it was somewhat to the east, near Vitez, in central Bosnia). It was on Romanija, around Mokro and Han Pijesak, that the forces of occupation of the Austro-Hungarian Empire fought in August and September 1878 with the Muslims who resisted the occupation of Bosnia-Herzegovina. In the first months of World War I, the advance squads of the Montenegrin army pushed as far as the southern parts of Romanija, as far, even, as Rogatica, and were dispersed only in October, after they had perpetrated a series of crimes against the Bosniak population. In World War I many Romanija Serbs fought as volunteers in the army of the Kingdom of Serbia, while the Bosniaks were recruited into the Austrian army, as well as constituting the major part of the *Schutzkorps*, the volunteer squads organised by the Austro-Hungarian authorities, which also have crimes against the Serbs to their name. (In the Austro-Hungarian army there were, of course, many Bosnia-Herzegovina Serbs, conscripts, and their conduct during the time of the conquest and occupation of Serbia was on the whole not very different from that of their co-combatants, Croats, Bosniaks and others. Yet after 1918, this aspect of the war was subjected to total social oblivion, both spontaneous and organised.)

On the northern slopes of Romanija, near Han Pijesak, the Kingdom of Yugoslavia constructed a complex system of fortifications and underground chambers where, in the event of a second world war, the king, government and military command were to have been located. (The second Yugoslavia enlarged these fortifications until they became a real underground city, and this was in turn inherited from the JNA by Ratko Mladić and the Army of

Republika Srpska in 1992.) In this 'state' the Romanija Serbs felt the inviolable masters, a kind of select set of guardians of the Crown and Yugoslavia, a *de facto* Greater Serbia in the dangerous 'Turkish' environment, on the front lines of the defence of a beleaguered Christian faith and fatherland. On the one hand, official Belgrade – in a manner that made a particularly powerful impression on these villagers – supported them in the belief that they were destined to fulfil a special national and historical mission: most of them did their military service in the elite Royal Guard (Krsmanović 1988: 134). On the other hand, no one was particularly concerned about the fact that most of the population was illiterate: there was just one primary school in Sokolac, and another in Dobrodoli, opened only after 1938. But then, rulers have always known that praetorians have always been better and more devoted the less they have known and the less they have used their own heads.

When King Alexander was killed in Marseilles in 1934, a pamphlet issued by the Belgrade weekly *Seljačko pravo* over the whole of its front page, wins a special place among many similar reactions in that it located the occurrence within a whole system of traditional references. Defining Alexander as the 'third [murdered Serb] emperor' after Dušan and Kosovo's Lazar, the editor summoned a kind of epic pantheon, where every name called was assigned a special symbolic task at a crucial historical moment. In the catalogue in which meaning-laden localities address personages that had become semantically identified with them (Lovćen to Njegoš, Kosovo to Obilić), it was impossible to leave out the famed mountain of the *haiduks*:

> Blackly trumpets Romanija mount and calls on Grujo and Novak:
> *Come quickly my protectors to serve as a model to the living!* (*Seljačko pravo*, 14 October 1934)

On the morning of 6 April 1941, after the German bombing of Belgrade, it was at Han Pijesak that King Peter II Karađorđević took refuge. On 9 April the government of General Dušan Simović arrived on Romanija, taking up residence in the Catholic Convent of the Society of the Daughters of Divine Love. Founded in 1911, on Kalovita Brda, a little outside the town, it had a primary school attended by both Orthodox and Muslim children, as well as a sanatorium. On 13 April the government held its last session and continued on its flight towards Montenegro, leaving the Staff of the Supreme Command in the convent, authorised to sue for peace with the Germans. A day or so later the Germans arrived in Pale, and on 18 April the Kingdom of Yugoslavia signed unconditional capitulation.

After this, in order to defend the Sarajevo-Višegrad railway, a regular

NDH army (*domobrans*) garrison was installed in Pale, and held the place until the end of the war. (The *domobrans*, literally the home guard, was in fact a regular army recruited according to the conscription law, unlike the Ustashas, who were volunteers.) If considered from just one point of view, events in the general area of Romanija to the end of May of the next year could give the impression of being a deliberate and purposeful process (thus serving as the basis for the cult of Romanija). But from a broader perspective, there is nothing but an infinitely tangled web of general chaos, anarchic and egotistic commanders, surprise attacks in the style of feudal peasant revolts, revenge for ancient grudges and private justice, robbery and massacre. But while the Croat and Bosniak Ustashas attacked the Serbs, and the Serb Chetniks attacked the Bosniak and sparse Croat population, while the peaceable neighbours of yesterday turned on each other, there were also frequent examples of people protecting and helping each other, even at the cost of their lives. In this nightmare,

> some went to the Chetniks, some to the Partisans, and others again to the Ustashas. But hardly anyone knew what he really wanted. For the ideology of their movements was remote from them. They were caught up in a sad time, when there was nothing for them to do but kill each other (Krsmanović 1988: 344–345).

Here perhaps it will be enough to mention the main facts and figures about what in the glossary and political imagination of Tito's Partisans was called the 'Second Enemy Offensive', and by the Ustashas the 'Romanija Project'. From early summer, Romanija was the scene of operations by the Chetniks of Major Jezdimir Dangić, Draža Mihailović's deputy for Bosnia, who carried out wholesale slaughter of the Bosniak population. In mid-summer, on 28 July, the Romanija Partisan Troop was formed. It had forty-seven members, mainly Romanija Serb peasants armed with blunderbusses, flintlocks, hunting carbines and French three-round Mannlicher carbines dating from WWI. The commander was a Sarajevo communist, the thirty-eight-year-old Slaviša Vajner, aka Čiča, who a day earlier slipped out of the city onto Romanija disguised as a mountaineer. The epic song 'Insurrection on Romanija (Ustanak na Romaniji) describes the crucial moments:

> *Oh Romanija, long and broad (...)*
> *Thou cradle of young partisans,*
> *Refuge from the days of blood.*
> *You stand proud like some spirit,*

Hide the feeble from the tyrant (...)
Your fame is not yesterday's alone
Your glory comes from days of yore.
You've remembered Grujo, Novak (...)
It was July the twenty-seventh
When Ante [Pavelić] had his fastness shaken
Čiča came to Romanija's midst
And called all the vital people ...
(Orahovac 1971: 21–23).

After the event had been celebrated round the campfire ('and there was a *gusle* player there to sing songs about the heroes of old times', Krsmanović 1988: 275), the troop embarked on its first, unsuccessful action: an attack on the police station in Žljebovi. It grew rapidly, becoming a squad in which there were also several Sarajevo Jews and Croats (Vajner himself was of Jewish-Czech-Croat descent, born and brought up in Croatia) and a group of Bosniaks. This group soon grew into a separate company with sixty members, and then into a battalion commanded by the Romanija peasant Mujo Hodžić, but they fought under the Serbian flag with a red five-pointed star. Hodžić had rejected the suggestion of some of the communists that it would be useful to design a special symbol to show that Muslims too were joining the uprising, and thus to deny the Ustasha claims that the resistance was exclusively Serbian and Chetnik.

Vajner proved to have exceptional organisational abilities and courage, but his identity was unknown, and so in the Serbian villages it began to be rumoured that it was something to do with the enigmatic Prince Đorđe Karađorđević, the older brother of King Alexander 'which suited these royalist peasants down to the ground. Some of them knew that Đorđe was a good deal older, and warned: 'Tut, man, it can't be Prince Đorđe, but it has to be someone important', but who, they were unable to say, and just shook their heads sagely' (Čolaković 1977: I, 453). He was also respected by the Muslim population, whom he protected from the Chetniks, as in general he attempted to oppose all attempts at mass reprisals against civilians. Sometimes he succeeded, sometimes, alas, he did not. When on 29 October 1941 the Chetniks and Partisans together attacked Knežina, about 150 local Ustasha Bosniaks surrendered the village without a fight, with the proviso that the inhabitants were to be spared. Nevertheless, what ensued was looting, arson and 'the Turks being scattered to the four winds'. The Serbs from Knežina, who were among the insurrectionists, took part in this action while Vajner tried in vain to stop it (Čolaković 1977: I, 441–459). Vajner was killed in

271

Pjenovac, on the Olovo-Han Pijesak railway line, on 21 January 1942.

The Partisans, of course, evoked the Romanija *haiduk* Starina Novak elsewhere as well, because he was known all over the area. For example, when they surrounded Bileća in January 1942, the Operations Staff of the People's Liberation Movement [NOP] squads for Herzegovina issued a proclamation to the local Serbs and the *domobran* garrison, saying they could join them without fear 'as their brothers, the descendants of Obilić, Starina Novak (...) all your glorious forebears' (*Zbornik NOB* IV/3: 104). It was clear, though, that the evocation of Romanija itself was emotionally the most suggestive, the most extensive in its propaganda effect, the most fully worked-out in its interpretations. Thus Slaviša Vajner was sung of as 'the best of heroes / comrade Čiča – Starina Novak', and the rebels were in general perceived, or presented themselves in their songs, as a perfected, revived Novak, who had 'recovered from his wounds'; Grujica, 'who had completed his schooling'; and Radojica, 'who had served his time' (Čubelić 1966). In the autumn of 1941, Rodoljub Čolaković, a prominent figure among the Partisans in eastern Bosnia, heard this song, with its initial line 'Make merry Mt Romanija,' from his guide, an 'elderly peasant from Glasinac' (Čolaković 1977: I, 560). At the beginning of the next year it was used as the epigraph of the first Partisan Songbook, printed in the forests of Romanija by the press of the Regional Committee of the Communist Party of Yugoslavia for Bosnia-Herzegovina.

In addition to these new songs, based on traditional motifs, but set to music, and sung in several parts, or in harmony, the classical epic *gusle* songs were also sung on Romanija. A participant in these events, a member of one of the most numerous Romanija fraternities, recalls the way the Serbian population experienced the establishment of the NDH and the Ustasha reign of terror:

> as if we had gone back to Turkish times. I recalled the popular songs, which I had learned before the war from our teacher. They sang of the heroism of the *haiduks* and the brutality of the Turks. Times like that had returned to Romanija. Many were to become heroes in songs. While Uncle Mladen and I were returning from Pale to Bijele Vode, I compared the Romanija rebels with the *haiduks*, and the Ustashas with the Turks (Krsmanović 1988: 108).

This perception was the more possible because in the general area of Romanija, by virtue of the composition of the population, it was Bosniaks that composed most of the Ustashas, domobrans and servants of the new regime.

In the forest, where the people found refuge, you could constantly hear the '*gusle* players singing about the *comitadjis* and the *haiduks*' (Krsmanović 1988: 150), but in more peaceful days too, in the houses, during work in the fields or with the animals, it would often happen that 'a sycamore *gusle* appeared from somewhere or other, and a song rang out according to the old traditions' or 'a story was told' about '*haidukery*' against the Ottomans and *comitadji* actions against the Austrian government (Krsmanović 1991: 110). This was the continuation of the long *gusle*-playing tradition, now additionally backed up by the war's daily provision of new topics and unlimited scope for merging, interweaving and connecting subjects ancient and modern. In the judgement of one folklore student, it was Romanija that had 'the most talented epic poets', both during and after the war. One of them, Tomo Đukić, published his first poem entitled 'The Downfall of the Former Yugoslavia' ('Propast bivše Jugoslavije') in the bulletin of the Romanija Partisan Squad, and after the war his works were the most performed, and the most often included in the collections (Rodić 1982). Thirty years later, during a military celebration in eastern Bosnia, the JNA general Vlado Šegrt recalled that in his brigade there was a *gusle* player, Radovan Vuković, from Romanija. After fighting the whole day long, at night he would take up the *gusle* and 'sing the of day that had passed. He sang of those that had been in the morning and by nightfall were no more' (*Oslobođenje* 4 September 1971). He was killed in the autumn of 1943.

But Vajner and his squad and Dangić and his Chetniks were not the only ones to connect themselves with the *haiduk* tradition in these months, whether they explicitly identified with them or whether they were seen as such by the terrified Serb peasants, or, from its own perspective, by the government of the NDH.

A certain Neđo Borovčanin from one of the local villages led an armed robber band from whom not even the Serbs were safe. Although they also had beards and wore the cockade, or the white eagle, the crest of the Serbian royal house of Karađorđević, they wanted to distinguish themselves from the Chetniks, and so they called themselves the Green Corps (*Zeleni kadar*). (This was the name taken by those who in 1917–18 had deserted from the Austro-Hungarian army or had refused to answer the mobilisation summons and fled to the woods, supported there by the local population and their relatives. Some of their armed bands embarked on *haiduk*-type raids against government institutions and wealthy individuals.) The local population also made a distinction: they called the Chetniks, who had some kind of political agenda and organisation, *Đikans*, and the Borovčanin group '*Greenies*' *(zelenaši)*. Their main hideout was in Novak's cave, but they were liquidated in May 1943 by the Ustashas, when Serb peasants informed against them, unable any longer to put up with their reign of terror (Krsmanović 1991: 142–6). Some of the Chetnik groups on Romanija and around Kalinovik were led by the gendarme general Ljubomir Novaković, from the end of 1941 up to May of the following year, when all trace of him was lost. He refused calls to join the Chetnik military organisation and would not recognise Draža Mihailović, instead claiming that he himself was the Chetnik Commander-in-chief. He presented himself as Starina Novak, and his soldiers called him only this, particularly as on the whole they did not know his real identity (Zečević 1968: 136–8).[1]

Unlike such groups, Vajner's Partisans and Dangić's Chetniks acted in a more or less organised fashion, attacking Ustasha and *domobran* strongholds and police stations, and from 1 September to 1 November had a joint operations HQ and organisation of government in the towns they controlled. Their first major success was to capture Sokolac on 25 August, thus taking control of a fairly large area. This Chetnik-Partisan agreement was formally dissolved in Vlasenica on 17 November the same year, when the communists realised that the Chetniks were not only avoiding direct fighting with the Germans and the Ustashas, but were even collaborating with them, while still carrying out mass reprisals against the Bosniaks following Ustasha atrocities – all of this under the epic motto of fighting *for the honoured cross and golden freedom*. Or, as Dangić's envoys openly told the Partisan negotiators at one meeting, they intended 'to slit the throats of the Turks, except for any pretty Turkish ladies' and 'screw down the Croats so hard that they wouldn't dare for a thousand years to look at a Serb askance' (Čolaković 1977: I 476).

They carried out this kind of screwing-down on 11 December, when they looted and burned the convent at Pale, and took five nuns – two Croats, two Slovenes and one Austrian – over Romanija to Goražde, where on 15 December they perished tragically by jumping out of a window to avoid being raped.

---

1. In areas with a strong *haiduk* tradition, on Romanija and in Serbia, at the beginning of the war there were individuals who behaved strictly in accordance with the old laws of *'haidukery'*. No matter which organised army or ideology they belonged to, they would go off to the woods, with rifle and bag with a little food, set ambushes for the Ustashas or Germans on their own initiative, and occasionally go back home to rest, change their shoes or carry out work in the fields (Krsmanović 1991: 182; Vučković 1980: 223). This is matched by the example mentioned above of the Kordun Partisan from the song 'Samovolja Rade', and the already quoted report about the unnamed Serb of northern Dalmatia going off to the *haiduks* in August 1991. Cf. pp. 115, 140–1.

In a string of battles from August 1941 to February 1942 the combined forces of the Germans, Ustashas, *domobrans*, local Muslim militia and one Italian unit pressed the rebels hard. In the second half of January 1942, the *domobrans* took Sokolac itself, the strongest rebel fastness. The *domobran* Antun Miketek composed a song about it in octosyllabics, later to be printed by the NDH military authorities in a pocket book of military poets:

> *Romanija, our pride and joy,*
> *was full of rebels*
> *who burned and looted*
> *our homeland dear (...)*
> *our darling domobrans*
> *wiped out the foeman.*
>   (*** 1944: 11)

The rebels had some successes in their counter-assaults. So, on 31 March, the Black Legion (*Crna legija*) of the then Lt Col. Jure Francetić had to move against Romanija from Sarajevo. This elite Ustasha unit with about 1500 soldiers took all the major Romanija settlements, inflicting particularly heavy casualties on the rebels at Sokolac, and on 3 May entered Višegrad, from where a symbolic bottle of water from the Drina River, 'border between East and West, watershed of civilisations', was sent to the *poglavnik* Ante Pavelić in Zagreb. The Serb population – whose villages had been burned and looted, and who had been subjected to general persecution and massacre – fled in panic across the Drina into Serbia. This was the time of the creation of the song in which the symbol of the conquest of the mountain is mentioned from the Croatian point of view:

> *On the peak of Mt Romanija*
> *the Croatian standard flutters.*
> *Unfurled by youthful lads,*
> *Francetić's volunteers.*
> *The small print on it says*
> *the Chetniks are long gone.*[1]
> (Rojnica 1969: 111)

A memoir writer, who had been a relatively senior Ustasha official, writing as an émigré after the war, mentions that 'the Partisans appropriated and

---

1. For all these events, from the viewpoints of the different participants, see Vrančić 1985: II, 176–220, 248–260. Čolaković 1977: I, 441–459, 511–618; Dedijer 1981a: I, 77–85, and Tomasevich 1975: 157–162, 206–207.

modified this popular song (...) as they did some other Croatian war songs'. Another Croatian author, a journalist at the time of the NDH, mentions it as a popular (folk) song, only quoting a slightly different version, which is natural and inevitable in such cases. In it the fourth line goes 'all the Ustasha volunteers' and the sixth 'the Partisans are long gone' (Dujmović 1976: 417–8). This last difference shows that neither official NDH discourse nor that part of the Croatian population that accepted it for one reason or another made much difference among the rebels: for them Chetnik and Partisan were synonyms. And after all, until Tito arrived on Romanija, and even after that, the rebels themselves did not on the whole differentiate one another: they saw themselves primarily as *haiduk*-avengers, those who were fighting *against* something – the Ustashas – not caring much about differences in motivation, agendas, symbols or behaviour.

Since, from a military point of view, the Black Legion had achieved a major success against the 'cursed rebel' because of whom 'all Bosnia wept bitterly' and since Francetić had shown remarkable personal courage, other vernacular poems also celebrated him:

> *Francetić, come join our round dance*
> *spend time with friends below the village,*
> *Francetić, the standard's waving,*
> *you planted it atop Romanija.*
> (*** 1943: 25)

But the remaining Chetniks held out in the almost inaccessible parts of the mountain, which had not lost its symbolic strength for them. In September 1942, Major Dangić wrote a report on conditions in his area of responsibility, stating that the 'new Chetnik songs have already sung of our new heroes and national leaders'. One of these songs, sung after a massacre of Bosniaks at Foča, in which the Chetniks from Pale took part, told the 'scum' Pavelić that now 'the Chetnik moved against Sarajevo', and in fact that

> *Romanija leads the round dance,*
> *to set all Bosnia free*
> (Dedijer and Miletić 1990: 197)

The Chetniks of course understood this liberation as the total destruction of the Bosniak (and Croat) populations. But even if they did not accept the Chetnik ideal or even fought against it, 'many people of Romanija found it hard to understand the political disquisitions of the Partisan leaders' who were opposed to reprisals against civilians and explained that no people could bear collective guilt for the crimes of some of its members. 'They respected them, but they didn't understand them at all' (Krsmanović 1988: 61). When Vajner's charismatic authority was gone, there was no personality capable of keeping their passions to some extent in check and, in the longer term, remodelling their deep immersion in the epic traditions and legends.

In fact, the only dam against the Romanija Serbs' total acceptance of the Chetnik cause was its nature – the crimes against the Bosniaks and even against Serbs who kept their distance from them, the looting, carousing and evasion of combat with the Germans and Ustashas, repelled some of those Serbs who were otherwise not the least inclined to the anti-monarchist Partisans.

A conversation between the main spokesman of the Communist Party of Yugoslavia in the area and Serb peasants in a village at the foot of Romanija close to Goražde shows vividly what this kind of meeting with the terrified and embittered people must have been like. Čolaković explained to them how criminals had to be distinguished from the rest of the people, and that not only could they cooperate with the Bosniaks, but in the common interest they must do so. Then an old man interrupted him, asking with candid amazement:

> You tell me, how can we possibly live together in brotherhood with the Turks? Isn't it better either for them or for us to move out?

Čolaković was moved by this kind of attitude to reflections that, although expressed in simplified categories of communist ideology, with some admixture of the author's own stereotypes, reveal good intentions and correctly perceive the fundamental problem:

> I observed their farm-labourers' faces; all older people, all prematurely aged from their hard life and cares, from the arduous and uncertain struggle for their daily bread. Their fathers must surely have been serfs, perhaps even some of them themselves, and the Bey was a 'Turk'. Through the ages, the hatred of the serf for the Bey piled up in the spirits of the commoners (*rayah*), and was transmitted from generation to generation. And the Serb exploiters, who grew away from the commoners with the development of capitalism, calculatingly transformed this justified and lawful class hatred for the feudal Bey into hatred of the Muslim

in general, into an ugly feeling of chauvinism. Old Yugoslavia not only did nothing to change this feeling, but its rulers cultivated it among the Serbian peasants of Bosnia-Herzegovina. Then came 1941 with all its monstrous explosions of chauvinist passions [and] Bosnia swam in blood (Čolaković 1977: I, 652–653).

Fifty years later, Jovan Rašković and Radovan Karadžić felt absolutely none of Čolaković's anxiety when they stood in front of the sons and grandsons of those peasants, in whose spiritual outlook and cultural model very little had changed. What was to blame was the political system that had been brought in by force and the social mainstream that had been systematically promoted by this same Čolaković and his sacrosanct party for forty-five years. They were so precise in seeing where their forebears in power had gone wrong, and so incapable when they had a chance not to repeat their historical failure. They had been so convincing in their condemnation of the Chetnik and Ustasha mass reprisals, and so ready to do the same thing themselves in their arrogant post-war triumph. Čolaković did describe the guilt of those who manipulated the historically conditioned 'class hatred' but at the same time he called this 'hatred' 'lawful and justified' as long as it remained a 'class' phenomenon in the sense in which social differences and divisions were understood by assiduous readers of Stalin's *Short Course of the History of the All-Russian Communist Party (Bolshevik)*. Political discourse, after the war, changed its target and its appearance, but not the nature and the core of the evocation. When Slobodan Milošević began to grow to maturity on this spiritual soil and the Chetnik spirit began to awaken under this aegis, it was of no concern to the archetypal *Turkish bey* whether he had been murdered by the archetypal *haiduk* because he was a *bey* or because he was a *Turk*.

In his Romanija performances, Jovan Rašković had no need of any old men to ask him 'how can we be with them'. With the authority of a highly educated man who was friends with the Belgrade academicians and the alleged *Serbian Tolstoy* Dobrica Ćosić, he himself gave any potential questioners clear answers to any doubts they might have on this question. He himself came in time to thrust them ever deeper into the conviction that epic and historical reality were one and the same thing, and that time was at a standstill, halted for ever and ever 500 years back at the Battle of Kosovo. So that there should be no mistake, at the end of his speech he summed up all the previous evocations into a single united archetype of the Enemy: the *Turks* from the epic reality of Vuk's and Njegoš's works, and the *Ustashas* Frančetić and Tuđman from historical reality.

Thus the two historical situations were as categorically equated, and

Romanija was singled out as opposing them, as a kind of omnitemporal, universal sign of freedom, defiance and persistence, a refuge first for Novak's *haiduks*, then for Vajner's Partisans and Dangić's Chetniks, today for Jovan Rašković himself, or Radovan Karadžić, tomorrow for yet another, and in fact, always one and the same archetypal *Serbian freedom-lover*.

It is possible to define the precise moment when the Mountain and the City below it were irrevocably located within the coordinates of the epic image of the world, or when it was clear that Rašković's speech was not just the one-off grasping of an individual at suggestive symbolism, but part of a chain of programmed evocations. In front of Novak's cave on Romanija, inheriting the folk tradition of the St George's Day (*Đurđevdan*) waking and washing in spring water, as well as the symbolism of the *haiduk* bands gathering again on this day after the winter period, the SDS of Bosnia-Herzegovina and the SRS, on 6 May 1991, held a rally which included, among several thousands, also the chairmen of the two parties, Karadžić and Šešelj, the latter giving the main speech. He reminded those present of the local *haiduk* traditions and called on them to finish the age-old battle against the Turks. He even expressly named two Bosniak villages that had to be the first to be destroyed.[1] In addition to direct political agitation, the meeting also contained a number of ritualistic elements such as collective washing. The poet and political pamphleteer Rajko Petrov Nogo described, about a month later, the new spiritual birth that he had undergone when he washed his face 'in the highland spring and the native tongue on Romanija. And while we were looking at ourselves in the spring, we grew Starina Novak moustaches' (*Duga*, 2 August 1991, after Čolović 1993: 130–131). Thus this poet's thick black whiskers, thought by many before the war to be Nietzschean, turned on that miraculous highland morning into something fairly different – unless the *haiduk* Starina Novak is understood as a Serbian variant of the philosopher's Superman.

In this text, the 'clear outlines' of the initiation ritual appear: the holy mountain and its spring, the place of contact with the lower world and

---

1. After this the persecution, murder and looting of the Romanija Bosniaks began. In the trial of the leader of the Bosnian Serbs, Momčilo Krajišnjik, held in the ICTY in The Hague, evidence was given about all this by Sulejman Crncalo, a Bosniak from Pale. Cf. hhtp://www.un.org/icty/transe39/040902IT.htm – Šešelj came with an armed escort of Chetniks and in the next years regularly arrived on Romanija on St George's. In the early morning he would talk on the plateau in front of Novak's cave, and next in nearby Knežina in front of the monastery, in the presence of the priest, he would name the new Chetnik leaders, mainly the commanders of the local paramilitary units, but in 1993 he also named the vice-president of his own party and MP in the Serbian parliament in Belgrade, Tomislav Nikolić.

original purity, the symbolic day, the ritual purification in spring water, and in language too, similarly mythically pure, which wells up from the depth of the national soul like the water from the depths of the holy mountain. During the ritual the initiates established a supernatural contact with their heroic forebears and were miraculously transfigured. For the moustache was 'a sign that they had obtained the status of mature and virile men, and since these were not ordinary whiskers, but *haiduk* whiskers, obviously they must have at the same time become warriors' (Čolović 1993: 131). The whiskers were also to be found in another evocation of the *numen* of the mountain, when a war reporter described a large innkeeper at Pale, at whose place the Serb soldiers had met to talk over the events of war, as 'a fellow getting on in years with whiskers like Starina Novak's' (Jevrić 1995: 142).

According to the ideal that the epic song shapes and transmits in its image system, the *haiduk* has to be healthy, very powerful, handsome, and – the crown of it all – to have particularly fine and luxuriant whiskers, 'dark whiskers from ear to ear' (*mrka brka od uha do uha*) or 'a moustache down to the shoulders' (*do ramena brka*), which is not just a decoration, but a partner in a dialogue, a fellow combatant, because the *haiduk* will often 'twist his dark whiskers' (*suče mrke brke*) as if he were talking to them or taking counsel before making important decisions. *'Haidukery'* is of course an act of manliness. That is, Serbian populism from its very beginnings, at one not unimportant level, had been a rebellion of the suddenly aware but previously unacknowledged male, an announcement of his unquenchable, untameable and inexhaustible sexual potency.

Quite a lot about this could be gathered from the manner in which the relationships of Serbs and Albanians in Kosovo were presented in the politically controlled media and in the *gusle* songs. On Romanija, this demonic aspect of the Greater Serbian imaginary was concretised in the Slaviša Vajner Čiča Elementary School in May 1992: twelve Bosnian girls were imprisoned in it, systematically raped, and then released in September, in a state of advanced pregnancy when a safe abortion was out of the question.[1]

'Tito moves across Romanija'

The short winter day was drawing to its close when we came out onto the edge of a broad, rolling plateau covered with snow where the tiny settlements could hardly be made out. Someone said: 'So here we are

---

1. Mirsad Tokača, 'Rapes and Forcing on Prostitution', *WHY* – A publication for Human Rights and Peace, Sarajevo, 6/1995, p. 5.

at Glasinac' (...) In front of us, on the western edge of the plateau a leaden grey mountain stretched ahead. Again, somebody said: 'Look, Romanija, Čiča's Romanija'. To the left were the bald sugar-sprinkled caps of Mt Jahorina.
(Nikoliš 1980: 363)

The very nature of guerrilla warfare *in the forests and on the highlands* gave mountains a powerful symbolic charge in the Partisan (i.e. Yugoslav) discourse, which became connected with the old motifs of the heroic epic, interpreting it within its own worldview. On the one hand this occurred within the general framework of the traditionally sanctioned idea of the mountain as 'refuge of my tribe', of 'mother', that 'in the hardest days / guards our Partisans', as the vernacular poet addressed Petrova Gora, and on the other through the inscription of the contemporary struggle within the ethics of *'haidukery'*. In the case of Romanija, there was the opportunity to make not only a general identification of the two historical situations, but some very concrete and individual mergers of identity. Josip Broz Tito and the Supreme Command of the Partisans (NOVJ) arrived there on 24 December 1941 after the Germans had put down the revolt in western Serbia and at the end of November taken Užice, the capital of the Partisan 'republic'. The main force of the Partisans nevertheless managed to get out and cross into Bosnia, where on 22 December, in the town of Rudo, they founded the First Proletarian Brigade, the first non-territorial, mobile unit of its planned regular army. Then they went on towards Romanija and met up with Vajner and the local leaders of the revolt.

Tito's arrival in the area, first of all in Rogatica, then Bijele Vode, then the village of Ivančići, 'our new Užice' (Dedijer 1981a: I, 81) where he held a council with the local communists, led to the composition of a number of poems that were no longer exclusively Serbian, but placed the overall Partisan struggle, or all the Partisans, irrespective of their ethnic or regional origin, in the semantic field of *'haidukery'*, and linked the communist ideology, reduced to a popular revolt against unjust rule, to the powerful, and long-since unambiguously characterised symbolism of rebellious, indomitable Romanija. A typical example of the motif of the conquest of the mountain with a flag was the song:

On top of Mt Romanija
the red flag is waving.

Let it wave there, let it,
it should have done so sooner.

On the flag, a sign or three:
hammer, sickle, five-pointed star.

On the flag a letter, two or three
the letters of Comrade Tito.
(Jovičić and Jastrebić 1977: 140)

The Serbian nationalist politician Vuk Drašković, who at the end of the eighties set in motion a campaign to rehabilitate the collaborationists of Mihailović and was the first in Serbia openly to propagate Chetnik ideology, claims that the Partisan version was borrowed from the Chetniks:

On the top of Mt Romanija
the Chetnik flag is waving;
Let it wave there, let it,
it was brought for us from Serbia.

He goes on to claim that the Partisans got to know it in the summer of 1941 when 'the people around Romanija rose up in arms and when there was still not war between the members of the movement of General Mihailović and Broz's people', rather they 'were singing in the same house, in the same positions, the same song, with slight variations' (*ON*, 32, 1 March 1991). This claim might be accurate, and probably is, like Rojnica's previously quoted assertion that the Partisans 'appropriated' the same song from the Ustashas. After all the rhyme *vije/Srbije* (fly, wave/Serbia) is just as motivating as the *vije/Rusije* which is at the core of several other Partisan couplets, as in:

From Kordun (from Banija/ from the Balkans) to Russia
the people's (the red) flag is waving,
on the flag a golden letter,
that's the name of Lenin.
(Dedijer 1981b: 371, 373)

What is important here is the fact that most of these songs, particularly couplets, existed in all three versions, for in all three armies – Partisan, Chetnik and Ustasha – parts of the same type of rural, oral culture existed in the dominant social composition, and it was easy, within the common structural and expressive framework, to switch the names of the heroes. For example, in the couplet *White nymph lady, tell it truly (pravo) / is — really healthy (zdravo)?*, the Partisans in Bosnia inserted the name Pero Kosorić, the Chetniks Pavle Đurišić, and the Ustashas Ante Pavelić (Dedijer 1981b: 109) – each of them having five syllables. The name could change even within the same army, depending on which enemy was in the foreground at any given moment. Among the Partisans, after the Chetnik massacre of the Croats in the village of Gata in Dalmatia on 1 October 1942, in a round dance this was sung: *On the top of Mt Romanija / the Chetnik's skin is waving*, and there was another version in which it was *the Ustasha's skin waving*, but both of them were – as a former Partisan testifies – officially repressed as inhuman and crudely vengeful.[1]

It is worth mentioning that even the mythical *Red Flag (crveni barjak)* acquired a real and substantial meaning. When in the autumn of 1941 Vajner's insurgents took control of Romanija, they raised the red flag at a place called Red Rocks (Crvene stijene), where it could be seen from a long way off. At the end of January 1942, when the Germans and Ustashas crushed the insurgents, they took it down, but in the same place a certain peasant hung out a large red Romanija-style shawl, like the one Rebecca West mentioned in her book. The Germans from Mokro and Pale directed artillery fire at the pole, but during the night the peasant put up a new, undamaged one. The game of nerves lasted for some time (Krsmanović 1988: 137–8). Although the communists made the song one of the mainstays of their political imaginary, it is doubtful that the Romanija peasants perceived the red flag as an ideological sign, either before or, particularly, after Vajner's death. It is more likely that for them, especially when the real communist flag was replaced by a local shawl, it was a symbol of a trans-ideological and apolitical resistance grounded in traditional identifications – simply, a sign for 'heroic liberty'.

A similar case, prompting a similar question and suggesting an identical answer, occurred half a year earlier near Knin. After the Ustashas massacred some fifty civilians in the Serbian village of Polača below Mt Dinara, on 29 July 1941 a hundred or so peasants attacked the police station, waving a red flag. The Italian garrison in Knin was aghast that the patriarchal Serbian highlanders were acting under the communist symbol, while the Communist Party later explained the event as proof of its strength and the rapid penetration of communist ideas 'among the broad masses of the people', all the more so since the commander of the rebels was a candidate for membership of the party. However, in fact the flag had nothing to do

---

1. Cf. Ante Nazor, 'Tragom kanibalske poezije', *Vjesnik*, 11 March 1990, p. 10.

with communism: when the outraged peasants came together and seized any kind of weapons for their revenge, one of them ran into a local church, and grabbed a church banner, which happened to be red, and carried this into battle (Plenča 1986: 232). Not even there, then, was the identification ideological or political, rather quite the opposite, it was traditional and religious, and entirely local. And it could hardly have been otherwise in these first few months of a universal reign of terror and chaotic guerrilla warfare, until the few communists managed to force themselves upon the resistance movement as its leaders.

But for the moment the most important thing to have in mind is the fact that all three armies announced their presence, by identical poetic means, in the same momentous locality in the Romanija region in the course of the first year of the war. And they assigned particular significance to the mountain in their motivational imaginative sets and a relatively distinct position in the consecrated map of the war the ending of which could not yet be discerned.

The Partisan leader himself was included in the new sign system by means of songs on various topics, in which the first two lines were almost always the same. Indeed, the best known – for it was included as a matter of course in elementary school reading books – is the following:

> *Tito moves across Romanija*
> *and leads his divisions.*
>
> *When Tito came to Serbia*
> *he set up the people's army.*
>
> *Women comrades, let's plant flowers*
> *wherever Comrade Tito's army goes.*
>
> *The country no more will be a slave*
> *For the army of Comrade Tito walks on it.*
> (Cvitan et al. 1967: 118)

In the second commonest version the third and fourth lines go: 'When Tito moved across Romanija / he founded the people's army' (Crindrić 1969: 20). Neither in fact corresponds to the truth, for Tito did not go into Serbia via Romanija, rather, the other way round. He did not found the 'people's army' after marching over Romanija, but came there at the end of 1941, after the First Proletarian Brigade had already been founded in Rudo. Tito was in Romanija again in June 1943 after the battle of the Sutjeska, but even then he did not go into Serbia, rather into Herzegovina, to the south, and then to the west. He did not return to Serbia, where there had been no armed anti-fascist struggle in the meantime, until the end of 1944.

But these divergences from reality show the power of the vernacular imagination and its aspirations to make an 'illogical' sequence of events seem 'logical'. Tito's advent in Serbia, in Belgrade, the capital of the new Yugoslavia, and the founding of the true 'people's' army were far too significant events not to be preceded by the symbolic initiation of the hero. These events, particularly the second, were not a step towards the peak of heroic action, they were the actual peak, and hence only a tried and tested hero could perform them. And for the authentication of the hero, his transition from the world of the profane into the world of the sacred, there was hardly a better place than Romanija.

The song quoted above is actually a sequence of four roughly linked couplets that were all, including the first, incorporated into other Partisan songs, either individually or in various combinations. It was first printed in a collection entitled *Naše pjesme* (*Our Songs*), published by the Culture and Art Department of the Propaganda Division of ZAVNOH, the Croatian wartime anti-fascist parliament. It was sung in regions under Partisan rule in Croatia and western Bosnia, where 'everybody knew it' in one of the very numerous versions (Zlatić 1975). In the reader quoted from here – and it is not very different in the others – it is illustrated with a photograph of an unnamed but quite large Partisan unit lined up for review, beside the famous monument to Tito in Kumrovec by Antun Augustinčić, his determined stride lending credence to the song.

The war ended at last. Vajner had been dead for some years, and not long after him Francetić was killed in Croatia, and the third 'king of Romanija', Jezdimir Dangić, was arrested and condemned to death at a Sarajevo court-martial as a war criminal. But for a few years after this, in fact up to the mid-fifties, Chetnik groups were still operating on Romanija. They killed representatives of the new regime and terrorised the populace, finding harbourers among Serb and Bosniak peasants, embittered by the communist policy of forced purchase and collectivisation and the violence of the secret police. Among these Chetniks there were local people as well as groups from Serbia, the Semberija region and Montenegro who in the later stages of the war and even after its formal end sought refuge from the victorious JNA in the forests of this age-old *haiduk* centre. As chance would have it, the largest of these groups, from Herzegovina, arrived on Romanija on the eve of St George's Day, 5 May 1945, and this, as well as their general situation, contributed greatly to their identification with the *haiduk* tradition (Krsmanović 1991: 169).

After the war, Yugoslav ideology systematically nurtured its own Romanija cult, by totally controlling the symbolic space and channelling its semantics. Although Tito was at the centre of Partisan activity, and thus occupied the central place in the symbolic geography of Romanija, at different times, the mountain became the locus for various leading figures of the movement, later party bosses, ministers and generals, Serbs, Montenegrins, Bosniaks and Croats: Aleksandar Ranković, Đuro Pucar, Svetozar Vukmanović, Rodoljub Čolaković, Osman Karabegović, Avdo Humo, Kosta Nađ, Franjo Herljević, and the non-communist Croatian anti-fascist Ivan Ribar, the first Speaker of the newly convened federal parliament, as well as the eminence grise of the second Yugoslavia, and its main ideologue, the Slovene Edvard Kardelj, and the Jew Moša Pijade, a Belgrade painter whom Tito had befriended during his imprisonment, and the author or co-author of some of the most important wartime and post-war documents.

In this way, Romanija, more than any other mountain, turned out to be a kind of Olympus of the Partisans, and a sojourn upon it, or even a brief passage over it, gave each individual a certain aura in his wartime biography, contributing to it an additional episode rich in associative power. The combatants of the Fourth Krajina Brigade thus sang of Moša Pijade while they danced a round dance:

> *Off goes Moša from Serbia*
> *over Mount Romanija,*
> *his army beats the Krauts.*
> (Zuković 1988: 331)

This particular example really shows the power of the epic imagination and its cultural codes. Pijade was a shortish, somewhat weak, middle-aged man in poor health, prematurely grey, who always wore spectacles, he was born and brought up in a town, unaccustomed to physical labour, and, apart from having a pistol at his waist, he never bore arms at all, let alone led men into battle. But since he was the whole time at the side of Tito and other authentic 'descendants of Starina Novak and Miloš Obilić', popular song turned him into what he ought to have been: a strong hero at the head of a victorious army.

The few local communists mainly perished at the beginning of the war, but they obtained the status of pan-Yugoslav 'people's heroes'. They had barracks, schools, streets and squares named after them on Romanija itself, as well as in Sarajevo and elsewhere in Bosnia, and the wartime poems created on Romanija were reprinted in schoolbooks and popular compilations. Pero Kosorić, from Sokolac, on Romanija, was celebrated, for example, as a synthesis of two renowned *haiduks*:

> *His white heroic face*
> *Was like the face of Grujica.*
> *And his sword cut as light*
> *As the sword of Novak.*
> (Orahovac 1971: 95)

Another, Slobodan Princip, whom the vernacular rhymer presents as a 'young chap of the Obilić mould', came from western Bosnia, but brought with him to Romanija – or embodied – at least one important set of symbols. His uncle was one of a series of symbolic successors of Miloš Obilić: Gavrilo Princip, the man who assassinated the Austro-Hungarian Crown Prince, Franz Ferdinand, thereby precipitating World War I.

Of course, during the post-war decades new *gusle* players and other vernacular poets continued the Slaviša Vajner cult, as a rule linking him with the one-time Romanija *haiduks*: thus in one image of Žarko Šobić's, Vajner 'sewed a golden tricolour / for Novak and for Grujica' (Radovanović and Lovrenski 1985: 63), and in a series of picture books about the most important battles and figures of 1941–5, the one devoted to Romanija, 'hill of heroes', also set up the triune symbolic continuity of Novak – Vajner – Tito (Hozić and Pašić 1983).

Tito's crossing of the mountain was portrayed as a march into the very heart of the enemy: 'Tito went across Romanija / and comrade Stalin across Germania', was sung in post-war Yugoslavia, according to one testimony, until the break with the USSR in 1948 (*Vjesnik*, 15 September 1994). And besides, in the reader mentioned above, the song 'Tito went across Romanija' is part of a thematic unit entitled *Lenin's Truth*. The unit starts with a Belarusian folk-tale about an event from Lenin's life, and goes on with a description of Bolsheviks' capture of the Smolny Palace in St Petersburg and Lenin's arrival in it. The mere presence in this context of the poem about Tito crossing Romanija implicitly suggests that the mountain is a kind of Yugoslav Smolny, in which the leader of the revolution symbolically masters the heart of the foe's resistance, setting up his HQ there and then departing for the ultimate victory (see Cvitan et al., 1967: 118).

In August 1946, all the ethnic cultural and educational organisations in Bosnia-Herzegovina were abolished, including the Croatian Napredak

Association. And the Imperial Cinema in the Sarajevo building belonging to the association was renamed Romanija. When this happened, there were many in the city, particularly among the Croats, who were quick to recognise an important political message in the act. The contours of Romanija were included in the central field of the new coat of arms of the Socialist Republic of Bosnia-Herzegovina, and at the entrance to the Lapišnica Tunnel, which runs from Sarajevo to Pale, red letters were used to write in relief *Tito went across Romanija* ... Naturally, Uprising Day in Bosnia-Herzegovina could not be celebrated without an evocation of the mythic mountain. And so, in his report for a Croatian newspaper, a Sarajevo journalist exaltedly linked the Romanija place name of Red Rocks (Crvene Stijene) with the colour of the flag of the victorious ideology:

> Romanija awakes, the Red Rocks bristle. The same flag. Čiča rides on a white horse. Slaviša Vajner enters over the Romanija field into history. Black kerchiefs wave after him, for the troops, for the army, for the avengers, the freedom-lovers of the Romanija hills. And it is not without reason that the people think: 'Romanija of the high peak / where Čiča recruited his men ...'[1]

A mosaic with a picture of the Partisan columns entitled 'At the Turning Point of the Ages (Tito goes over Romanija)' *(Na prekretnici vjekova / Ide Tito preko Romanije)*, 5 x 3 m, the work of Joko Knežević, of Omiš, a former Partisan, was placed in a setting that has no connection whatever with Bosnia, on the quay at Omiš, in Dalmatia, and the lengthy vicissitudes surrounding it are not uninteresting. The artist made it in the mid-fifties, with the ancient Roman casein technique, that is, with lime, fresh cheese, and sand. Although of very great value, for some years it 'hung round terraces and museums' for no one wanted to put it anywhere. It was only when Knežević removed from the foreground a figure who had in the meantime fallen into political disfavour and replaced it with a local *People's Hero*, that the mosaic was placed in the new square of Omiš, very well fitted into the setting, leaning against the wall of an old stone house, with running water in front of it and two stone slabs with the names of the fallen Omiš Partisans on either side (Knežević 1996: 285).

And there the mosaic stood, as a symbol of the 'bloodstained struggle for the liberty of the peoples of Yugoslavia in the National Liberation War of 1941–1945', until the next political watershed. On 15 December 1992, in the now independent Croatia, the Omiš town council charged the

---

1. Ramo Kolar, 'Vječna mladost Titovih kolona', *Vjesnik*, 27 July 1986.

town's Culture Centre to remove it and store it in the museum, because its symbolism and 'subtext (...) in today's context of the Croatian Homeland War, was, to put it mildly, very questionable as an ideological and historical anachronism.' But the centre did not carry out this decision, and the mosaic was not touched by the Omiš men returning from the war in September 1994 when they removed two neighbouring memorial slabs, 'irritated', as they explained, 'by the five-pointed star which had been worn by the Serbian and Yugoslav and Communist aggressors' (*Slobodna Dalmacija*, 9 September 1994). And yet the work was removed two years later, just before President Tuđman was due to visit Omiš. Since the protocol for the day envisaged the guest dropping in, after the Festival of Dalmatian Close Harmony Groups, for a drink on the very square where the mosaic stood, it was removed as a possible cause of offence (*Globus*, 296, 9 August 1996).

Tito went over the mythic area for the last time when he was already an old man, visibly sick and infirm. In eastern Bosnia he was present at the celebration of the 35th anniversary of a battle in which he had been injured in a German air-raid, and then set off by car for Sarajevo through Goražde and Romanija. At the pass, on both sides of the road, stood pupils from the Slaviša Vajner Čiča Elementary School of Sokolac, singing 'at the top of their voices' the 'song that during the war, and afterwards as well, became the freedom-loving symbol of this area,' – what else but 'Tito Goes Over Romanija'? (*Oslobođenje*, 7 July 1978).

Less than two years later, the mighty emblematic picture of the hero's passage over the legendary mountain achieved its creative peak, and a kind of emotional catharsis. Just as, some fifty-six years earlier, King Alexander had not been able to leave the world without a symbolic set of Romanija baggage and a guard of honour of Romanija *haiduks*, neither could Tito, who for half a century had been inseparable from Romanija in the Yugoslav political imaginary, at least as much as Starina Novak was in the epic imagination. What is more, he made its symbolism, previously in the political discourse more or less exclusively Serbian, supra-ethnic, pan-Yugoslav.

At the news of the death of his friend, the great writer Miroslav Krleža stated that it was more than just a place name of epic geography, however imaginatively resonant it might be: it was a vision of the fatal border between two incompatible worlds, the world of the dead and the world of the living.

> Tito is going after a long column of his dead divisions – over Romanija. He is going far off, into the immense fields of popular song, from where he might well have come (*Vjesnik*, 7 May 1980).

Irrespective of Tito and Vajner, Romanija existed in the set of Yugoslav symbols also at its own original level, as a *haiduk* mountain. To this extent it can be said that in the panoramic synthesis, along with all the other references, Tito himself also appeared in the guise of Starina Novak. Thus it is neither strange nor unexpected that at a time of new political ferment at the transition from the eighties to the nineties, the Romanija motif was dusted off and reactivated in the discourse of those who, even at the time of the fall of the Berlin Wall, imagined that Yugoslavia could remain an isolated island. At a rally for the defence and preservation of Yugoslavia held in Belgrade on 16 March 1991, organised by the ideologically rigid League of Communists – Movement for Yugoslavia, there was a banner bearing the inscription *On the Top of Mt Romanija ...* (*Duga*, 446, 30 March 1991). Since this was just five days after Drašković had once again evoked the symbol of the ethnic banner on Romanija, the pro-Yugoslav demonstrators at Ušće, in Belgrade, countered both his and Đodan's ethnic evocations, with their own evocation of the non-ethnic (supra-ethnic) banner in the unuttered – but implicitly universally readable second line: *The red banner is flying ...*

General Đerzelez

> *Among the last came Đerzelez. The song preceded him (...) He was greeted by silence, full of admiration and respect. He bore the glory of many conflicts and a power that caused a chill of fear. All had heard of him, but few had seen him, for he had ridden away his youth between Travnik and Stamboul.*
>
> (Ivo Andrić: 'Đerzelez in the Caravanserai', 1920)

For all Starina Novak's domination, even the Catholic *haiduk* Mijat Tomić had some connection with Romanija, even if only marginal. Their encounter was the fruit of one of those frequent epic contaminations that bring all the essential characters at least once to all the essential places of traditional geography, and in mutual contact. In one song, the Duvno *haiduk* with his band at Vran, Ivan-planina and Romanija digs a well and spreads out his cape,

> *when the Bosnian merchants pass*
> *let them throw a grosch or ducat*
> *so we'll have some easy profit*

and before winter comes he asks his band who will go to Romanija for the takings. Up pipes Mali Marijan, carries out the task, and happily returns.

In another song, Mali Marijan takes part in a duel in the place of his now infirm uncle Mijat, and since the road goes over Romanija, he calls on Starina Novak and his band. They recognise his voice 'singing on Mount Romanija' and return the greeting, and the same thing happens on the way back.

But it can be said that in the context of the Đodan-Drašković polemic about the right to traditional symbolic capital, Mijat Tomić was not a suitable Croatian conqueror of the peak, the 'Croatian hero' who would plant his banner on Romanija. Even if Đodan had really had him in mind, it would have been difficult for him to have responded with rhetorical effectiveness to Drašković's provocative question. First of all, Mijat was actually a friend of someone whose embittered adversary he should have been, i.e. Starina Novak, because both of them were members of the same social group, had inherited the same system of values and standards, and had been driven into outlawry by more or less the same motives; this it is why they greet each other so cordially in the song. Secondly, only three months after Đodan's Peščenica speech, the Serbian rebellion in Knin and Lika began, and the concept of *'haidukery'* assumed completely negative connotations in Croatian discourse. Thirdly, the planting of the standard would have to mean the establishment and proclamation of a state, and in the new Croatian imaginary this was not and could not be a task for a *haiduk*. Fourthly, it is hard symbolically to legitimate the presence of a Croatian Catholic in a place where there was in fact hardly a Croatian population at all.

Rather than Tomić, it was the greatest traditional hero of the Bosnian Muslims, Alija Đerzelez, who would have had a far better chance of opposing Starina Novak. Very far from being – like all such figures – unambiguous, Đerzelez had, in truth, become blood brother to another symbol of the Serbian cause, Kraljević Marko, but at the same time he was quite capable of thrashing the Romanija *haiduk*s and sending them packing. In Novakuša Cave near Nevesinje, in eastern Herzegovina, the peasants still point out Novak's fireplace and the bed where he lay after one clash when Alija Đerzelez drove him from Romanija (Cvetanović 1988). On another occasion he was even more magnanimous. Starina Novak and Grujica had spread a cloak on Romanija, as was their custom, and on a fir tree had hung a *kürde*, a large curved sabre with a double edge, which every traveller had to bow to and endow with ducats. But Đerzelez would not have been who he was if he had not sworn to his miraculous horse that he would cross Romanija on the morrow, but 'we shall not bow / nor shall we give to the *kürde*'. When on the morrow Novak saw how the 'Turkish lad so young' came out of the city onto Glasinac, he turned to his band and said:

List here, my brothers dear,
a Turk wends over Romanija,
for us, both loss and shame.

They decided to intercept him, but Đerzelez easily mastered the overconfident *haiduks* and drove them, bound, before him over the mountain. In their terror they begged for mercy, and he let them go after receiving their promise that they would never again attempt to forbid or impede his passage (Delorko 1964).

The conflict of Đerzelez and Novak is the most common motif of the epic songs in Bosnia-Herzegovina; sometimes one side wins, sometimes the other, sometimes it is a draw. Like Starina Novak, Alija Đerzelez too is a later compilation of the common people's imagination from the folk poems, a product of poetic work in the seventeenth and eighteenth centuries, based on a complex historical foundation and borrowings from the epic material of earlier times, particularly about two historical personalities of the second half of the fifteenth century: *gazi* Gerz-Elias and General Alauddin Ali-Bey Mihal-Oglu, scion of one of the most celebrated branches of the Empire. The Bosnian Muslims adopted him and made him the protagonist of their heroism as opposed to the heroes of the neighbouring Christians, seeing in him their protector and defender against the Christians at a time when after two and a half centuries of warfare the balance of military power had changed to the disadvantage of the subjects of the Sultan. Here the inhabitants of Sarajevo were in the lead, and the urban legends even gave him a special quarter, a *mahalle*, and a house, where he apparently lived with his mother and sister Ajkuna.

At the end of the nineteenth century it was said that his mace was kept in the dervish *tekke* at Bistrik, right behind the large barracks in which the Austro-Hungarian army of occupation was housed. This was a coded but nevertheless clear message (to those who knew) to the representatives of the new, Christian rulers that they could not feel safe or welcome. The Ottoman historian Ibn Kemal (1468–1534), discussing the annals of war in Bosnia in 1480, mentions the important role of Gurz Ilyas as *sipahi* and *akinci* warror, his services in the defence of Sarajevo at the time of the Christian counter-offensive. According to this chronicler, Ilyas 'gained fame among the people' and 'filled this country with his bravery and the awe accorded him'. From the depiction of his heroism, which was under the very strong influence of the epic tradition, it can be seen that this personality was the subject of legend and poetic reworking as early as the end of the fifteenth century.

Thus for the Muslim population of Bosnia, Đerzelez's time remained 'a never to be forgotten era of glory and victory, which was never repeated in such brilliance in the history of the Turkish Empire'. In other words, he endured in more or less the same way as in the Serbian national memory the Battle of Kosovo survived as a turning point in which a powerful army, as well as a religiously homogeneous and socially secure medieval state, were destroyed (Olesnicki 1933: 37). Many songs in which Đerzelez appears are built on the motif *there's no hero but a Bosniak*, or 'are a part of the Muslim tradition dominated by the idea that no Bosniak hero could be replaced by any hero from any other part of the Empire' (Buturović 1992: 461). He is a symbol of the Bosnian Muslim participation in the Ottoman wars. In one song he is even crucially important for the conquest of Baghdad. He has a horse with marvellous wings that carries him in an instant from battlefield to battlefield, sometimes wearing the emblems of Mohammed's son-in-law Ali, sometimes, as vanquisher of a dragon, coming closer to the Christian figure of St George or showing himself as one more Balkan derivation of the mystical serpent-slayer Heracles, in a sequence including Miloš Obilić from Serbia and the Greek Digenes Acrites.[1]

In other national traditions too there was an awareness of what a standard this figure represented for the Bosnian Muslim identity, and of his enormous propaganda potential. Thus the Christians' vernacular consciousness exalted him to such a level that it recognised in him a worthy opponent of its greatest heroes – Prince (Kraljević) Marko, Sibinjanin Janko [János Hunyadi] and others. In the episode in *The Mountain Wreath* where the wedding guests, Muslims and Montenegrins, compete in singing about their own heroes, two pairs of figures are formed. The Muslim wedding guest calls up 'Gergelez, wing of a falcon' and his sword, for 'the ears of the Vlach had rebelled', while the Orthodox wedding guest invokes Starina Novak and his thunderous calls from 'the top of Klisura' for the 'Muslim's ears had gone deaf', that is, they ignored the rightful Christian aspirations for freedom.

But the panoramic figure is far from being exhausted in such mutual intolerance and exclusivism. There was a different, parallel process going on at the same time: when one community noted that the competing community had created a powerful symbol that affected its identity and social self-awareness, it could react in one of two ways. One was to attempt to destroy it, which was impossible without major conflicts and open repression, and if that rival community was stronger, politically and demographically, in any

---

1. Cf. Balić 1973: 29–30; Buturović 1976, 1992; Lord 1974; Murko 1951; Olesnicki 1933; 1934.

case impossible. The other way was to attempt to appropriate it for yourself, to include it in your own repertoire of identity, and thus endorse your own part in the hero's virtues and successes, thus neutralising your own current social and political inferiority. This was what the Bosnian Christians did with the invincible Muslim hero: they invented a Christian origin for Đerzelez. In parallel with the songs in which he was an implacable enemy of the Christians and a symbol of Ottoman dominance, legends and epic songs were created in which he was born from a secret liaison between Dijete Grujica (or some other Romanija *haiduk*) and a Sarajevo Muslim widow.

Just what the supreme Chetnik commandant Draža Mihailović thought about Đerzelez as symbol of Muslim Bosnia and its golden age may be seen in his intention, at the end of the war, to reorganise the Royal Yugoslav Army in the Homeland, as the Chetniks were formally named, into four ethnic armies, or corps. He understood that he could not match the Partisans and their programme of federalism and ethnic equality with an exclusively Serbian conception. Therefore, on 1 December 1944, on the anniversary of the creation of the Kingdom of Serbs, Croats and Slovenes (Yugoslavia), he issued a decree founding a Serbian, a Croatian, and a Slovene army, and a Group of Muslim corps. They would all be under a single command (of Mihailović himself), while the four individual commanders were to bear 'nationally symbolic names'. The Muslim commander, whose real name was never established, 'and perhaps no one was ever selected for the job' (Tomasevich 1975: 436), was known conspiratorially as *General Đerzelez*; the Croatian part of the army was to be commanded by *General Gubec*; the Serbian by *General Marko*, and the Slovene by *General Andrej*, after Count Andrej Auersperg of Turjak, a general and participant in a number of anti-Ottoman campaigns in the sixteenth century, who was also included in the warriors' pantheon of the first Yugoslavia as representative of the Slovene military tradition. Thus the two generals, Alija and Marko, in new political conditions, in the new Chetnik imagery that followed a change in their ideological paradigm on the eve of inevitable defeat, were symbolically to reproduce the epic blood-brotherhood of the greatest heroes of the South Slav Muslims and Christians.

Anyone who wanted to separate the two traditions could not manage without Marko or Alija, just as anyone wanting to reconcile them could not. It was only necessary to choose, in the overall epic tradition, the motif that was in line with current political needs. Ideological treatises and political disquisitions had a style and expression that prevented them from reaching the ordinary people, but an image based on topics and figures known to all, on the inextricably interwoven tradition could easily transmit the desired political message and produce a powerful effect.

At one time, the Muslim poet Musa Ćazim Ćatić announced that he was a Serb and – logically – in his poem 'Srpski ponos' ('Serbian Pride', 1899) he expressed this symbolic synthesis of his own two identities with the message that he celebrated equally Marko Kraljević and Miloš Obilić and 'brave Đerzelez' (Ćatić 1968: I, 4–5), while the Serbian novelist and journalist Vojislav Lubarda used them to express just the opposite message, notably his own idea of the incompatibility of the two traditions and the two ethnic and religious identities. As he says, in the Romanija town of Rogatica before World War II there was a stifled but unpleasant tension that was felt by both Serb and Bosniak children, through whom 'Marko Kraljević and Musa Kesedžija, Alija Đerzelez and Starina Novak were still fighting each other' and 'the dull thumps of ancient maces resounded and the vengeful swords flashed' (Lubarda 1982: 161).

Although there is a site with the alleged *türbe* (Muslim covered grave) of Alija Đerzelez in Kupres, legend has it that he was actually killed not far from Šipovo, in the village of Prhovo, subsequently Gerzovo, where his *real* grave is. However, two local traditions assign his death to different places and causes: according to the Bosniak tradition, he was cut down by fraud while he was saying his prayers at a place called Ploče, fifty metres from the grave; while according to the Serbian tradition, he was killed in a conflict between Serbian and Bosnian wedding parties in neighbouring Krstovi (Niškanović 1978). This difference implies two value conceptions or messages to the competing communities. For the Muslims, the message is that their hero was invincible in a fair fight, and could be bested only in some underhand way, at the time when he was praying, that is, at a moment that any true hero should respect. For the Christians, the message was the opposite, the hero was beaten on a fair field, by an objectively stronger, cleverer and better adversary. Epic situations are always a reflection of the real situations, desires and rivalries of social groups.

There is an apparently exotic contemporary variation of this other tradition, but one that is quite legitimate in the commoners' culture and their cult of the ancestor. It was sung by the café singer Mirko Pajčin, alias Baja Mali Knindža of Knin, who was the most popular performer of what were known as newly composed war songs in the RSK and RS in the 1991–5 period. Asked about his origins in an interview, Pajčin replied as follows:

> In the *Zemaljski muzej* (National Museum) in Sarajevo I found out that I come from the Daničić clan of Montenegro. But when my clan killed Alija Đerzelez in Šipovo, they fled to below Dinara

mountain, between Grahovo and Livno. We are from the village
of Gubina, and we took our name from a certain Paja (*Nacional*,
1, 24.11.1995).

From the end of the nineteenth century, a *dernek* (village fair) was held
beside the Gerzovo tomb, on St Elijah's Day, or Aliđun, as the Muslims
had it, to which both Bosniaks and Serbs from the local villages came, and
also from Jajce, Mrkonjić-grad / Varcar-Vakuf and Šipovo. The first would
gather around the tomb and kneel, while the second group would attend
mass on a hillock beside the Orthodox church. In the afternoon, all would
get together round Alija's tomb, and then the secular part of the event,
together with trading, would begin. Since the fun was carried on separately,
and the lads who were competing at running or tossing the *küskü*, an iron
bar, competed as Serbs and Bosniaks, not as individuals, but as members of
the given communities, it could be described as two parallel meetings at the
same place. Still, because of its multi-ethnic nature, this *dernek* was 'a special
feature in the overall picture of traditional popular gatherings on Ilindan (St
Elijah's Day)' (Niškanović 1978: 166).

Initially the grave was cared for by the Bosniak Dizdar family, and when
they moved away, it was neglected. From that time on Gerzovo was an
exclusively Serbian village, and after World War II, the villagers repaired and
maintained the grave. It is worth recording that the local Orthodox priest
made a contribution to its upkeep. At the beginning of World War II *derneks*
ceased being held, and the tomb burned down in the war. At the beginning
of the 1970s, a Bosniak from the neighbouring village of Lubovo erected a
new one, and also maintained it. One night in October 1991, while Vukovar
was disappearing under the Serbian siege and JNA shells were destroying
Dubrovnik, Chetniks from nearby Šipovo blew up the grave. This symbolic
murder of the greatest Bosniak epic hero, the only one whom Kraljević
Marko recognised as a greater hero than himself and made his blood brother,
heralded the Chetniks' next war aim.

Because of the connection of the epic figure of Alija Đerzelez with Sarajevo
and of Starina Novak with neighbouring Romanija, on which his band lay in
wait for 'the lads from Sarajevo', it can be said that in the mainstream of Bosniak
folklore there was a fertile semantic framework for a response to Drašković's
question as to which hero was capable of putting up a 'hostile banner' on the
peak of the mythic Serbian mountain. This did not, it is true, happen, either
in reality or symbolically, but Đerzelez was nevertheless to appear later as a
significant evocation, only at a different semantic level. He would not, that

is, be a symbolic legitimation and traditional base for the appropriation of Romanija, but an element in the construction of the traditional legitimation for a contemporary political leader, or rather a supplementary base for and consolidation of his charisma. In this process it was not the occupation of contentious geographical space that was so important, rather the continuity in the mystical significance of the name itself. After the war, the Bosniak sculptor and SDA activist Alma Suljević announced that the bridge she was designing in Sarajevo would bear Alija's name. Asked which Alija she meant, she replied that this name 'referred to all the Alijas who were important for our people and our land, from Đerzelez to Izetbegović'. For, she went on to explain, a name was not obtained by accident, and anyone who bore it 'bore all the gravity of the meaning of the name. It is not by accident that the word Alija means – high, exalted' (*Ljiljan*,152, 13 December 1995).

But Alija Đerzelez was not the first hero of the Bosnian Muslim epic to be evoked by way of counterpoint to the Serbian *haiduk* imaginary. Nor was Alija Izetbegović the first Bosniak political leader to be treated metaphorically according to a motif from the traditional culture of his ethnic and religious community. And this is why another fairly extensive digression is required.

NINE

The Bosniak Internecine War

I shall bear you a son, not one, but many sons, who shall be heroes like Hrnjica. And when at Bairam you go with all your sons to the mosque, everyone will turn to look at you and your children, at our children; everyone will envy you our riches.

(Alija Nametak: *Trava zaboravka [The Forgetting Weed]*, 1943)

The battle below Hrnjica Tower

Immediately after the signing of the truce that halted the fighting in Croatia at the beginning of January 1992, the writer Ivan Aralica, whose novels about the protracted fighting on the Ottoman border and the complex relations between Christians and Muslims President Tuđman called his favourite reading matter, wrote in the Zagreb government-controlled daily *Vjesnik* long political analyses and essays about the collapse of Yugoslavia, endeavouring to predict the stance of the various figures in the conflicts. It was clear that after Slovenia and Croatia, Bosnia was to be the next target on the Greater Serbia agenda. In one article, Aralica stated accurately that the leaders of the Serbian rebellion in Croatia had 'acquired their propensity to create states by reading the traditional epic songs', rightly observing that they did this selectively, focusing only on their own heroic epics and ignoring the Bosniak ones. For otherwise they 'would have to see that in the heart of the [Bosnian] Krajina in Kladuša there lived someone whom the *gusle* players said had to be watched out for – little Mujo, the viper of Krajina (*mali Mujo od Krajine guja*)'. His remark that 'today those who have no inkling whatever about the traditional songs know about Mujo Hrnjica of Kladuša' and 'his modern incarnation', Fikret Abdić, called 'our *Bábo*', from the Turkish word *baba* for father, and in the Bosnian Muslim vernacular meaning any affectionately viewed paternal authority figure.[1]

---

1. Ivan Aralica, 'U Krajini serhat', *Vjesnik*, 23 February 1991.

The only thing that Aralica, like many others, could not have guessed was Abdić's later destiny, which was full of U-turns, contradictions and actions that are hard to explain without delving once again very deeply into the categories and value system of the traditional culture in a rural, patriarchal milieu.

Just four years earlier, at exactly the time when the previously anonymous Milošević was starting his rise to power, Mujo Hrnjica had been recalled by another writer, a Serb this time – Vuk Drašković, also up to his neck in politics, and also brought up in a region with a living epic tradition. While Aralica came from Promina, near Knin, a sparse Croat oasis in a predominantly Serb environment, Drašković underwent his initial socialisation in the predominantly Serb eastern Herzegovina. In the second half of the eighties, backed by some of the senior clergy of the Serbian Orthodox Church, he launched a virulent anti-Muslim campaign, first of all against the Kosovo Albanians, and soon after that against the Bosniaks.

So, in a place and on an occasion crammed with national symbolism, on 6 December 1987, in a speech at a *parastos* on the 170th anniversary of the death of Karađorđe, the leader of the first Serbian insurrection, in the Church of the Archangel Gavrilo [Gabriel] in Zemun, Drašković accused the political leaders of Serbia of high treason for having stood by watching passively while the Albanians were, in demographic terms, taking over Serbia, while in Bosnia 'a vampire Mujo Hrnjica stretched from the Drina to the Krajina' (Drašković 1989: 69). The message was clear: the Muslims were taking control in the whole of Bosnia, and the symbol of this unrestrained, ruthless power was Hrnjica who, like the undead, had risen from the grave, although it seemed that at the beginning of the nineteenth century Karađorđe had dealt a death blow to non-Christian rule. Thus he too identified the same figure in the epic tradition of the Bosnian Muslims as the symbol of that bellicose spirit that might spike the guns of the revived Serbian *haiduk*, who – as Drašković himself said while he was still a compliant and ambitious member of the communist youth movement – was a *man of a special mould* who needed to be taken seriously and resolutely opposed.

Quite recently, a tradition was recorded in Sarajevo about a villager from Rogatica taking oats to sell in Sarajevo, on the eve of World War II. On Mt Igman he encountered a stranger 'in Bosniak dress' with a 'notebook under this arm'. The mystery man unlocked a steel door in the rocks, and took him into a cave where, covered in green homespun, three of the great heroes of the Bosniak epic tradition – the brothers Mujo and Halil Hrnjica, and Alija Đerzelez – were sleeping. Inside were their horses too, 'like three red nymphs tied together', and a cauldron into which blood dripped from a sabre hung from the ceiling of the cavern. The unknown man, who took care of the horses, told him that the heroes would wake when the cauldron was filled with blood, and yet the peasant saw that the blood was dripping very slowly. Then the unknown man said to him: 'There'll soon be a war, and it will flow fast, they will wake up' (Smailbegović 1986: 195–196). The story does not venture to say what happens next, but it is easy to imagine, since the tale features the international motif of the hero or mythic king sleeping on a mountain, who will wake at the right moment and deliver his people from mortal danger.

Still, Mujo Hrnjica was not destined to serve so much as a central symbol for the Bosnian ethnic tradition as opposed to the other, competing ones, rather to embody Otherness, and then the open schism inside the Bosniak tradition itself. Hrnjica could not forestall the war, because decisions about it were made not in Bosnia but in Belgrade. And he did not even spend the war years on Igman, where he and his brother Halil and Alija Đerzelez would have been roused by the rumbling of the Serbian artillery firing at Sarajevo. Nor was he elsewhere in the Sarajevo theatre of war, face to face with Starina Novak and the other Romanija *haiduks*, perhaps in the same Bosnian Army unit as a young Kladuša man, 'a genuine *gazi*' in whom at the moment of the attack on Bosnia 'his Bosnian Krajina blood boiled over, that same blood that had flowed in the veins of his forebears Gojeni (*Stout*) Halil and Mujo Hrnjica,' as a Bosnian war reporter wrote in enthusiastic vein (Bajro Perva; *Ljiljan*, 59, 2 March 1994). Throughout the three and half difficult years, he remained in his native region, in the far west of Bosnia, in Velika Kladuša, surrounded by two Serbian para-states, one in Croatia, one in Bosnia, face to face with his own fellow-countrymen, torn between two trends in Bosnian politics that were bitterly opposed to one another. He was, in short, more a prisoner of war than a hero.

But the imaginary stage on which, like a parallel history, all the later events were to be mirrored, had long since been set, and was only waiting to see which one of the possible scenarios would be played out, which epic poem would be the first to be read. And as always in such circumstances, there was no shortage of contenders.

According to one of the songs, Mujo Hrnjica had no reason to pay any heed to the excitable Vuk Drašković, because he had long since shown that he was able to cope with threats of that kind: in one clash, he had defeated, single-handed, a trio of the most celebrated *haiduks* of Romanija – Starina Novak, Deli Radivoje and Dijete Grujica (Murko 1951: 257). True, the

Romanija team was then playing away, at Udbina, in a region that Mujo knew like the back of his hand, and where he had been active for years with his Kladuša troop; but it is also true that Mujo was two men down, and at the end there was nothing left for Novak to do but turn towards the east and cast a mournful, loser's glance in the direction of Romanija. If however a different song is taken as the starting point, then Hrnjica had good cause to be concerned, if not earlier, then at the latest in those muggy August days when Jovan Rašković was making his fiery speeches at Pale and Sokolac and reminding the Serbian peasants of the eternal, mythic power of Romanija, which would shatter all Serbian enemies. That is to say, the Bosniak song 'The Two Hrnjicas and the Sixty Haiduks' ('Dva Hrnjice i šezdeset hajduka', Hörmann 1888–1988, XLIII) might remind Mujo Hrnjica that when he was seriously wounded after a conflict with a *haiduk* band, he had hardly managed to crawl along 'in the middle of Romanija'. And had his faithful white horse not brought 'three mountain nymphs (*vilas*)' to work their miracle cure on him, Romanija would have been his grave. According to a third epic song, there was even more reason for caution: at a melee on Livno Polje, Grujica, the son of Starina Novak, killed him, and later converted his sister Ajkuna to Christianity, married her and had a goodly crowd of children with her (Andrić 1939: 15).

There was always, however, that selective reading that Aralica referred to, not himself immune to this awkward habit, and the even more awkward custom of being able to recognise it more easily in others than in oneself. For Croatian politics, once it had decided to read the heroic epic, imagining that absolutely everything was explicable and predictable through its categories, nevertheless read only selectively, and in a distorting mirror.

Mujo Hrnjica, Mujo of Kladuša, together with the most famous of his brothers, Gojeni (*Stout*) Halil, belongs to the same set of Muslim Krajina heroes as Mustaj-Bey of Lika, Tale of Orašac and Osman Tanković. In the vernacular epic Halil Hrnjica is an imperial *meydanci*, or champion, a hero who has deserved to do combat on behalf of the Sultan with the most celebrated of opposing champions. As the anonymous vernacular poet says, when he defeated the famed Christian hero Filip the Hungarian (Filip Madžarin), Halil 'brightened the face of Bosnia' and received the greatest of honours in the imperial capital, for the like of such a hero, except, of course, the incomparable Alija Ðerzelez, had not been seen since the Ottomans conquered Constantinople.[1] In the same song, the tower belonging to Halil's

---

1. The epic Filip the Hungarian was in fact Filippo Scolari (1369–1426), an Italian nobleman from Florence who served the Croatian-Hungarian king Sigismund of Luxembourg. He made his name in the fighting against the Venetians, and also

brother Mujo is proudly said to be the most elegant of all the twelve towers in Kladuša, and to outdo them all in height (Hörmann 1888–1889: XXXII).

The extensive epic cycle concerning the Hrnjica brothers came into being during the constant fighting on the borders between the two empires, whether as part of the major military operations set in motion by the distant imperial capitals; or as part of the ongoing *small war*, as it was called, when the Austro-Hungarian generals encouraged the borderers in the Croatian Krajina to make guerrilla and looting incursions into the Bosnian Krajina; or whether the Bosnian beys incited the Muslim borderers to make raids across the border into the Croatian Krajina, for just the same purpose. The epic Mujo Hrnjica – his first name appearing in the variants: Mujaga, Mustafa and Mustafaga, and his surname as Hrnjina, Hrnjetina and Hrnjadin – was formed on the historical model of the Bosnian Krajina warrior and aga Mustafa Turčalović, who was involved in a movement of the Muslim Borderers (*Krajišnici*) against the decisions of the Sultan in the first half of the seventeenth century. To this extent, then, the epic tradition of the Hrnjicas – which sees the representatives of the Krajina as fighters for the interests of Bosnia as against the 'traitorous agas' who curry favour with the Sultan or the central government – preserves the Bosnian Muslim population's enduring idea that Bosnia has a very special position in the Ottoman Empire (cf. Buturović 1992, 1991).

According to legend, Mujo Hrnjica was a commandant of the Ottoman border troops, that is a *bölükbaşi*, similar to a sergeant, and raided, with his brothers or alone, all the way to Šibenik, Zadar, Karlovac, Sisak and even Zagreb. He was sometimes involved in larger operations, but far more often acted on his own initiative. He was the subject of poems and songs over the whole of the western Balkan epic area, including northern Albania. Of course, the epic image of Hrnjica is no less ambiguous than other such images: just as there are songs about collaboration and blood-brotherhood (*pobratimstvo*) (or blood-sisterhood, *posestrimstvo*) with the Christians, so there are also those that 'narrate a great deal that is little to the honour of a real hero' (Lopašić 1890: 158). Such songs show that among the border Muslims there was a lot of '*haidukery*', that is, that the Hrnjica brothers worked hand in hand with the Christian *haiduks* and themselves had the

---

against the Ottomans, in the area of today's western Bulgaria. Because of the time when he lived, it is clear that he could not have had any contact with the Bosnian Mulsims, because Bosnia was to be conquered only forty years after his death. But this case too shows how the epic song ignored historical time and joined otherwise incompatible heroes in order to provide for the representative of the community, and via him itself as a whole, the maximum amount of symbolic legitimacy.

character of the *haiduk*: they were much given to plunder, and were hard not only on their military opponent but also on Christian girls.

Like all the epic heroes, Hrnjica too can be read as a symbol of collaboration and friendship, but also as a symbol of irreconcilable enmity. From the Croatian angle, it was like this: a song from Ljubuški says that on Mt Lipet, south of Konjic, on the Mostar to Sarajevo road, Mijat Tomić killed Mujo Hrnjica who 'had done Christendom much harm' (Mijatović 1975: 30), but the balance seems to be restored by a song from Dalmatia in which Mijat calls upon Mujo to join him in plundering the caravan of the trader Vojin, to which Mujo happily agrees, bringing his thirty men from Kladuša, and the two bands, Christian and Muslim, fall on the caravan in concert, kill Vojin, split the loot and part good friends (Mijatović 1985: 81–84).

It is no different when read from the Serbian angle: it was clear to Vojislav Lubarda, writing in the summer of 1992, what the denouement of the Yugoslav crisis was going to be because, at the end of the eighties, preparations began in Kladuša to erect a statue to the 'Turkish criminal' Hrnjica, and in the cafés people sang about how the Hrnjica boys had 'lopped the head off the Serb' and 'captured *giaour* slaves'. The Serbs, he said, could not forget that the song celebrated 'highway robbery and the mass murder of the Serbian common people (*rayah*)', which was being repeated by the 'current descendants' of Mujo and Halil Hrnjica (Lubarda 1993: 103–4), by which he meant members of the Army of Bosnia-Herzegovina. Not surprisingly, the Serbian writer forgot that in the years before that, in other cafés, they had been singing, just as vociferously, other epic songs, no more civilised, about the removal of 'Turkish heads', and failed to mention which song about Hrnjica he was referring to, although it is not really crucial, because the choice is very wide. There was no shortage of blood, but then again, if he had wanted, he could have used the one written in Travnik, about the nuptials in Ravni Kotari, above Zadar, at which select heroes from both sides of the border had spent a week in mutual fun, from the Orthodox Christian Stojan Janković to the Muslim Mujo Hrnjica, while Mohammed's green flag and the Christian one 'crossed' (*krstali barjaci*) and fluttered ecumenically in the breeze (Hörmann 1888–9, XXII).

And of course, there were potential readings of these and many other songs being opened up on the Bosniak side.

In Velika Kladuša, in the hamlet of Kulište, there are stones that are said to be the remains of Mujo's tower. The place where his house stood is known. There are place names such as Hrnjica's Spring (*Hrnjičino vrelo*) and Hrnjica's Well (*Hrnjičin bunar*), and beside the track near it is the grave of his mother and son Omer, with a *türbe*. Beside the Grabarska stream, people point out the location of the stone pillar in which he ground powder, and on the city hill there is a stone tablet with traces made by Mujo's spear and the shoes of his miraculous and invincible horse. When a white horse, or *đogat*, appears in the Muslim songs, it is usually Mujo's horse, and it is clearly a very special and magical horse, like Prince Marko's piebald (Šarac), which reveals the extent to which the ancient mythical ideas were incorporated into the figure of Mujo. Mujo's grave is shown at Petrova Gora – where he was treacherously killed in an ambush by his blood brother (*pobratim*) Meho Katarica with a round moulded from gold, since he had slyly winkled out of Mujo the detail that he could not be killed with lead, but only with such a bullet.[1]

In the seventeenth century in Bosnia there was a very strong conviction that Islam was invincible, so that the loss of Slavonia and Lika in the great Austro-Hungarian counter-offensive resounded dolefully in the consciousness of the Bosnian Muslims, as may be seen in many traditions and songs, and for the first time cracks appeared in their earlier self-confidence. The fact that the Muslims driven out of Lika settled along the Una River, from Bihać to Kladuša, created an important condition for epic continuity, and it was precisely here that the memory of former glory and greatness was preserved most insistently (Schmaus 1953). One of the finest of the Muslim epic poems 'Filip Madžarin i Gojeni Halil' ('Filip the Hungarian and Stout Halil', Hörmann 1888–1889, XXXII), indicates that the Krajina had its feudal immunity, as a *serbest* area, where the soldiers were free of feudal duties in return for military service, and that for outsiders Mujo Hrnjica, as local war lord, was a 'greater and fiercer force' than the Sultan himself (Buturović 1992: 595). In the *serhat*, the border area, the organisation and purpose of which was similar to that of the Christian Krajina, almost all the Muslims worked own their land, having obtained it as Ottoman borderers at the westernmost outpost of the Empire.

It was there, in the 1980s that the *Agrokomerc* socialist agribusiness developed, bringing considerable progress to what had been an impoverished and backward region. In 1987, the founder and CEO Fikret Abdić, aka Bábo, winner of the highest federal award – the AVNOJ Prize for Economics, member of the Communist Party of Bosnia, and delegate to the Federal Parliament in Belgrade, was accused, in unclear circumstances, of manipulating bills and dragged into court. There were numerous indications that the Serb-dominated Yugoslav secret police was behind it. They wanted,

---

1. About Hrnjica, see Buturović 1976, 1991, 1992; Lopašić 1890; Maglajlić 1988; Mijatović 1985; Murko 1951.

and managed, through Abdić, to bring down his political patron Hamdija Pozderac, a tireless crusader for federalism and Bosnian political autonomy within Yugoslavia. But the average Kladuša Bosniaks were still not aware of the far-reaching implications of these backstage games, rather they saw Abdić primarily as their saviour, the real and symbolic father, *bábo*, who had grown up in their milieu and had never distanced himself from it even when he attained political power. For them he was the personification of the whole area and to condemn him meant to condemn them all, to defend him meant the defence of that whole predominantly Muslim region from the alienated, corrupt and remote central government – be it in Stamboul, Belgrade or even Sarajevo.

And Abdić was very well aware which category he had to slot his case into if he wanted to leave the right impression on these confused people, in fear for their livelihood, and yet deeply bound to their region and its traditions. When it got around that he had fled abroad, on the eve of his expected arrest, he gave an interview in which he said: 'Flight is for the coward, and there are few of those among the inhabitants of Krajina' (*Vjesnik*, 4 September 1987).

The comparison of the two ages and two realities, the Ottoman and the Yugoslav, would be made in just the same way, against the same background, by Fikret's brother, the manager of the *Agrokomerc* office in Karlovac, himself a vernacular writer. The time of Mujo Hrnjica and the time of Fikret Abdić

> were exactly the same in many ways, particularly in their fear and in their attitude to the government. Mujo was just as afraid of the Turkish Sultan whom he served as Fikret was of the Prime Minister of Yugoslavia Branko Mikulić, and how much Mujo feared the emperor, was expressed by the vernacular poet in this way: *God a bit, the sultan not a bit / and the vizier like his Đogat (white horse)* (Abdić 1992: 82; original italics).

It would be fruitless to attempt to establish conclusively from whom the initiative to equate Abdić and Hrnjica derived: from him and his associates, from *on top*, as a deliberate strategy to curry favour with the populace for the sake of political manipulation and to create a cult of personality, or from the grass roots, *from below*, as the spontaneous craving of a closed patriarchal society for an authoritative leader. As in all such cases, both processes interweave and supplement each other, first one and then the other coming into the foreground. But the effect was remarkable. In this exhausted, neglected region, in the second half of the 1980s, a hundred years since the Croatian historian Radoslav Lopašić, seeing indescribable hunger and want, concluded 'anyone who could see them today could not for a moment imagine that they were the descendants of the bold Mujo Hrnjica' (Lopašić 1890: 149), powerful emotions coalesced around the figure of Abdić, resulting in an identification of the current political number one with a figure from the tradition for whom there is no parallel in recent times in the South Slav epic space.

On the one hand, the promptings derived from the warrior tradition of which the epic time of Hrnjica was only the beginning. After him came one event after another that left deep traces in the collective memory and profoundly affected the formation of the local identity: first the rebellion against the central Ottoman government in 1848–51, put down in blood by Omer-Pasha Latas; then resistance to the Austro-Hungarian occupying army of 1878, when Kladuša, although on the very border and bearing the brunt of the attack, the last Bosnian stronghold, surrendered on 20 October; and finally the Second World War and the actions of the Muslim militias of Husein Huska Miljković, who was the only real government in this area, in 1943–4, a line of defence between the Germans, Partisans, Ustashas and Chetniks.

It is putting it mildly to say that Miljković, the first twentieth century reincarnation of Mujo Hrnjica, was a controversial figure. His warpath with his de facto private army was just one more piece of evidence showing how far from reality is any straightforward, black and white interpretation of the events of war in the Yugoslav space, whether it is the official version of history imposed after 1945 by the communists, victors of the war, or some version propagated by various émigré factions.

In the 1920s, Husein Miljković aka Huska had been a delegate to the Yugoslav Parliament in Belgrade, and still sided with the government after the assassination of the Croat opposition leader, Stjepan Radić. A few years later he became a member of the proscribed Communist Party, even a member of the District Committee of the Communist Party of Yugoslavia for Karlovac, and after the Nazi occupation he was one of the organisers of the revolt among the Serb population in Kordun. The Serbs respected him for his courage, and his common-law wife was a Serb. He rose in the party and in the Partisan military hierarchy, and then in 1943 left the Partisans and founded his own army of about 3,000 men, mainly illiterate Muslim peasants, who carried through their independent policy with the single aim of preserving the Muslim villages from destruction, and meanwhile collaborated in various ways with the Ustashas and the Germans. After about a year, he crossed again with the whole of this 'army' over to the Partisans, under the direct area of responsibility of the Main Staff for Croatia, and through Tito's express order was promoted to colonel. Soon afterwards, he was killed in an ambush, in obscure circumstances, by two of his previously close adherents, turned against him, apparently, by the Germans. In response, some 200 of his soldiers once again reneged from the Partisans, and fought quite independently against all and sundry – robbing the Muslims themselves – not only until the end of the war, but for several years afterwards.

In his HQ Miljković had two judges – one from the civil courts, one for shariah law – an executioner and two men who administered floggings, for in his army an official punishment, alongside the death sentence, was the lash. When they were asked what they were fighting for, Huska's soldiers said that they were fighting for the *din*, that is, for Islam, and even their official greeting went: *Za din spremni*, Ready to defend the faith, a clear echo of the Ustasha equivalent *Za dom spremni*, or Ready to defend the home[land]. On their caps they wore a star and a crescent, and, as in all the armies, they had their own songs. Many of these celebrated Huska, quite often in the standard image of the hero on horseback leading the people, and a particular favourite said that wherever Huska went, 'there was no Russian [communist] land, but a Turkish [Islamic] land / all for the faith, all for the faith' (Čolaković 1977: II, 674).

On the other hand, the emotions that clustered around Abdić were fed on the traumas of the first decades of the post-war period, above all on the brutal suppression of the so-called Cazin Revolt of 1950, a muddled one-day uprising brought about by compulsory purchases, to which the government responded with mass imprisonments, death sentences and the relocation of several hundred families, as well as the Cazin Plague of 1958–68, an enigmatic epidemic of jaundice that took many, especially children's, lives, without the government doing anything to put it down, or react in any way to the warnings of the local doctors. It is hard to avoid the impression that such callousness was a kind of collective penalty imposed upon a region that was 'politically unreliable'.

There, however, as well as lively recollections of the bold and irrepressible Huska Miljković, in whose 'army' Abdić's father served, right until the present time there were still vernacular expressions connected with his symbolic predecessor: a man who does things *like Hrnjica* is a man who is strong and audacious, can do a lot, eat a lot, just as all heroes since the times of Homer have eaten vast quantities of 'flesh of the lamb' and drunk 'wine from six-gallon flagons'. The two last characteristics at least fitted Abdić, a tubby workaholic, to a tee. Between 1969 and 1987 he transformed his *Agrokomerc*, once a struggling rural cooperative, into a powerful firm producing poultry, eggs and confectionery, with a labour force of 13,500, more than 6,000 in Kladuša alone. This success became more than an economic fact, not just the first more or less up-to-date and stable source of income, but also a balm for all the traumas and a source of self-confidence and pride, and many Bosniaks recognised the murky circumstances in which the financial scandal erupted in an article in Belgrade's daily *Borba* on 14 August 1987 as an ominous sign.

A kind of pepper named after Mujo Hrnjica, in a ten-gram packet with a picture of him on horseback, was absolutely the first such use of a figure of the Muslim epic tradition in Yugoslavia, and when the pepper had to be withdrawn and the remaining stocks destroyed soon after the scandal broke, to statements that it was scandalous so to glorify a 'Turkish thug (*zulümkâr*)' it was clear that the exposure of the alleged financial offences of Abdić was just a part, and perhaps not the most important part, of a much more comprehensive political project. Another theme that the media made extensive use of was the restoration of the neglected seventeenth century tower on the hill over the city (219m), in which, Abdić claimed, there were to be a local museum, an inn and restaurant. The works started in 1986, according to a planning order from the Urban [Town and Country Planning] Institute of Bosnia-Herzegovina. What was at the centre of the political and media campaign, however, was not, as one might have expected, accusations of conspicuous expenditure, but an ideological interpretation, aimed at the fundamental and irreversible political disqualification and moral de-legitimation of a local tradition, although in its poetics, social functioning and in the historical conditions in which it was created it did not differ at all from its non-Muslim equivalents.

In Zagreb, even in journalistic circles, there appeared an anonymous vernacular poem called the 'Kladuški deseterac' ('Kladuša Decasyllabics'), suggestively calling Abdić, who was in fact a remarkably authoritative figure, a pasha, aga and bey, and ending with the lines:

> *Fikret built both towers and çardaks*
> *for World Bank notes of hand (...)*
> *From his tower Fikret called more tribute*
> *still from Yugoslavia or there would be worse!*
> *Five hundred years the Turkish* zulüm
> *and so much will be Fikret Bey's rave!*

In the great hue and cry after Hrnjica no account was taken of the complex

Fikret Abdić speaks from a decorated truck in front of a screen depicting the Kladuša fortress of Mujo Hrnjica.

relationship between poem and reality, the world of the historical epic and the historical reality in which this poetry was created and in which it had its life. This could sometimes have been ignorance, but sometimes also, it would seem, political malice. Instead, there was a string of accusations concerning the so-called historical guilt of the Islamised South Slav population. According to one of the most vociferous accusers, an associate professor at the Political Science Faculty in Belgrade, Miroljub Jevtić, 'the acceptance of Islam was betrayal' although 'today's Muslims can hardly be burdened with the evil of treason perpetrated by their forebears'. However, if any Bosnian politician should attempt to speak in any different way of this 'treason' he too would start to bear 'the stamp of the traitor to the same extent as a Mujo Hrnjica' (*Duga*, 412, 9 December 1989). What was to become a real media trial of Mujo Hrnjica for crimes committed several centuries earlier included not only journalists, but also politicians and scholars.[1]

It is only apparently paradoxical that this assault on a vernacular legend occurred precisely at a time when the Serbian heroic epic had already been evoked in its most bellicose motifs and established in all essential elements as the semantic backbone of official media and political discourse. The message of the ideologically orthodox Sarajevo daily *Oslobođenje* was that

---

1. For a review of this campaign see Maglajlić 1988; Bošković-Stulli 1995; Žanić 1993a.

Mujo Hrnjica had to remain in the traditional songs, because as a figure who did 'everything he did (...) on behalf of the government he served, on behalf of the *din*, and against the cross', he 'could not symbolise any glory, rather our differences and our crucifixions, our dissensions and our schisms'.[1] This need of a Muslim journalist to excuse himself for the fact that his particular community had a sentimental or positive attitude towards figures from its own vernacular tradition is intriguing, and tells us much about the predominant, ideologically-induced social atmosphere. In the meantime, protected by an ideologically endorsed position in an unassailable Yugoslav symbolic imaginary, Starina Novak was taking giant strides out of the traditional song and had already assumed positions, unhindered, for the war that was to follow. And it was not exactly advisable to draw attention to the way he and his Christian *haiduks* had symbolised the same 'dissensions and differences', at least as much as Hrnjica had, just from a different angle, for everything that he did, he did 'on behalf of the cross, and against the *din*'. Ideology once again created a closed system from which it was impossible to establish a dialogue.

The trial of Abdić lasted two years. During this time his brother Hasan was exposed to systematic media and political demonisation and political repression, and he committed suicide. The Croatian economist Hrvoje Šošić, a close friend of Tuđman, printed a number of newspaper articles, and three books, in which he developed the idea that Abdić was a man with a special mission and inspiration, a successor of Hrnjica and Miljković, 'the third in a line to complete the Kladuša Trinity'. When he was finally acquitted, at the end of September 1989, Abdić drove from the remand centre in Bihać to Velika Kladuša in a white Mercedes – the modern equivalent of the white horse on which Mujo Hrnjica rode, and he was given a welcome fit for a hero and indisputable national leader. When political parties started to be founded in Bosnia-Herzegovina as well, including the Bosnian SDA – accompanied by the song 'Good Lord, who would have said last year / the Muslims would have had a party too' (*Vjesnik*, 30 October 1990) – it seemed quite natural that the man who of all the Bosniaks had the greatest aura of being done-down by the communists and proponents of Greater Serbia should become a member. It was still more natural that at the big SDA meeting in Velika Kladuša on 15 September 1990, the first anniversary of Abdić's acquittal, his epic alter ego was also be symbolically rehabilitated along with him.

On a screen that stretched behind the whole of the large stage there was, as Fikret's brother Muhamed Abdić recalled, 'the figure of the Krajina saint, the

1. Muhamed Nuhić, 'Neka Muje u narodnoj pjesmi ...', *Oslobođenje*, 3 October 1987.

legendary Mujo Hrnjica, on his *magic Đogat*, which was as it should be, for Mujo was the first citizen of Velika Kladuša, and perhaps even older than the town' (*Zapadna Bosna*, 12, 25 February 1994; original italics). In front of this image, face to face with 200,000 people who cheered him in delight, Fikret Abdić stood proudly surrounded by Alija Izetbegović and the other leaders of the SDA (see colour plate 11). In the front row were men in Ottoman costumes, wearing the fez, and bearing *kuburs*, old-fashioned blunderbuss-style pistols filled with powder, and *yatağans*, long crooked daggers at their waists. Thus the picturesque figures that had strutted at rallies in Serbia and Montenegro for several years already, symbols of the heroic epic tradition and ethnic and confessional identity, with their *haiduk tokas* on their breasts and also with their *kuburs* at their waists, acquired a symbolic counterweight at the visual level as well.

In the introductory part of the programme, the actor Amir Bukvić from the Croatian National Theatre in Zagreb read seventeen lines from the song 'Hrnjičić Omerica' (Hörmann, 1888–1889, XL). It would be hard to imagine a better and more suggestive metaphor for the current events and political relationships. Mujo, or Mustafaga Hrnjica, after twelve years in prison in a foreign country, is pining for his homeland, believing that the whole Krajina, left without his protection, is 'enslaved, burned by fire', and when his son Omer at last finds him, the following conversation ensues between them:

> *My Omer, light of my eyes.*
> *Is the Krajina still where it was before?*
> *Is the* meykhane *there by the town gate?*
> *Do the Krajina Agas still sit in session?*
> *Do they drink the wine in the* meykhane*?*
> *Is my tower still standing upright?*
> *Has my darling remarried?*
> *Is my mother still alive?*
> *And Omer Hrnjica said then to him:*
> *'Ah, my* bábo, *serdar Mustaf-Aga,*
> *the Krajina is where it was before,*
> *and the* meykhane *by the city gate,*
> *the Agas of the Krajina sit in session,*
> *they drink their wine and talk of you,*
> *and your tower is standing high,*
> *and your darling has not remarried,*
> *and your mother is living still.'*

Once set free from the dungeon, Mujo Hrnjica really does find in his homeland a reality in which all the constitutive elements have been preserved, particularly those testifying to the constancy of social relations and traditional values: people have not been set at loggerheads, but live in harmony, he has not been forgotten, neither have his loved ones betrayed him. There must have been a particularly symbolic echo in the mention of the tower, which remained standing although they had wanted to destroy it, really and metaphorically, and neither can Omer's filial address to his *bábo* have been heard without reference automatically being made to Abdić's nickname.

After the elections on 18 November 1990, Abdić became a member of the Presidency of Bosnia-Herzegovina, and at the same time one of the most controversial figures in the months when the JNA and the Serbian militias that it backed began their conquest of Bosnia-Herzegovina. On 22 April 1992, Bosanska Krupa was attacked and laid waste; in June daily attacks on Bihać began, and a week or so later, Abdić left Sarajevo for good in a Canadian air force plane, flying via Zagreb to Velika Kladuša. During a one-day stay in the Hotel Esplanade in Zagreb, surrounded by associates and politicians, he enjoyed hearing the vernacular poet Muhamed Škrgić reading his decasyllabic lines about the trio of Krajina heroes, i.e. Hrnjica, Miljković and Abdić himself (Biščević 1993: 27). This was something entirely different from what he had written a short time before, as an influential member of the SDA, in his agenda leaflet. Then he had opposed both those 'who shuddered when Mujo Hrnjica was mentioned, that figure from the oral tradition and the popular song books' and those 'who would glorify him' and 'in fact, one should have a normal attitude towards both history and legend', with everyone being 'free to mention' their own heroes 'without such mention bothering anyone else' (Abdić 1991: 106). This conciliatory and balanced approach, which had nothing in it to object to, has been replaced by planned instrumentalisation of the psychological and mobilising potential of the tradition.

Nevertheless, that idealised Abdić who at the end of the eighties symbolised Bosniak resistance to the Greater Serbia agenda was not forgotten even after he had become irretrievably mired in political dirty tricks and mob-tainted black-marketeering. Acknowledgement for what he had done in the eighties, when he had revived the economy of his region, was given by a fierce political opponent, himself a *krajišnik* (borderer) from Sanski Most, on the sixth anniversary of the *Agrokomerc* scandal:

> Once upon a time Mujo Hrnjica lived in the Krajina, a kind of Krajina Robin Hood. He did not give a hoot for the Vlachs or the Padishah, worked a bit in concert with the Serbs (he chased

Christian girls round Ravni Kotari with Stojan Janković), and protected the commoners [*rayah*]. His brother Halil was more of a hero, but there, the people set Mujo down in their oral tablets (...) And then, Huska Miljković lived in Krajina. One of my favourite heroes, I have to admit. During the second war, Huska Miljković waged his own war, had his own army (when the KPJ had 5,000 members, Huska had 3,000 horsemen) and saved his people. Huska defended Krajina from everyone: from the Germans, the Ustashas, Chetniks, Partisans ... Up to 1944 Huska was a small island of freedom in enslaved Europe. Then he was betrayed by the Partisans.

Today in the Krajina there is Bábo. His great-grandfather was Mujo Hrnjica whose father was Huska Miljković. Fikret Abdić is a typical *krajišnik* [borderer]. Short, eccentric, adamant, and courageous to the core. In the Agrokomerc scandal he was unbent, almost indestructible. I recall the *cenaze* [Muslim burial] of his bother, when Abdić [brought from prison under escort] was greeted by 30,000 insulted and humiliated people, who kissed their Bábo's hands, and had Bábo given just a wink, a new Krajina insurrection would have broken out ... Fikret Bábo Abdić was the only man in the SFRY whom UDBA [Yugoslav secret police] couldn't stitch up with embezzlement charges. Bábo thus became a legend, and not only in Krajina. Bábo became the Bábo of all the Yugoslav Muslims.

Since Abdić now began increasingly openly to do deals with the Chetniks, the author warns him that 'there is no end that can justify this collaboration, even hungry Krajina mouths', the more so since his two famous predecessors had shown that 'both pride and the stomach could be satisfied without such cooperation'.[1] The comparison of Hrnjica with Robin Hood shows that the Ottoman *bölükbaşi*, just like the Christian *harami başi*, could be perceived in their own milieu within the framework of the European paradigm of protector and avenger of the dispossessed or the common people, not only Christian, but quite often Muslim too.

Hopes that Abdić would not break off finally with the central government came to nothing. On 27 September 1993 he proclaimed the Autonomous Province of Western Bosnia in Velika Kladuša and part of the municipality of Cazin, attempting unsuccessfully to include Bihać as well. There, however, the lawful authorities remained in power. Fighting every day, completely surrounded, relying on such assistance as could be airlifted from Croatia,

---

1. Zilhad Ključanin, 'O, mojne bábo!', *Ljiljan*, 26, 14 July 1993.

by the end of the year the Fifth Corps of the AB-H had come into being in Bihać, around the spontaneously assembled squads and units of the Territorial Defence. Meanwhile in Kladuša, Abdić had created his own private army, the People's Defence of Western Bosnia (*Narodna Odbrana Zapadne Bosne*), which signed a non-aggression pact with the rebel Serbs in Croatia and Bosnia.

'Did' and 'Babo'

The deep political schism, the quarrels and the bloody war were, among other things, a battle for the heritage of Mujo Hrnjica. The vernacular poet Tahir Ključanin directly called on the epic hero to leave the Chetnik collaborator Abdić and stand shoulder to shoulder with the Fifth Corps, which 'trampled, and did not forgive'.

> *Now we're standing on our two feet*
> Krajišniks *are afraid of no one*
> *Arise, Mujo, defend the Krajina*
> *Your Fikret's on the Chetnik side.*
> (Mujičić 1995: 109)

In the competition all the traditional means were at work, and thus the song linked cursing the city, a common motif in the vernacular tradition, and the most terrible traditional punishment for the perpetrator himself, the bane of his race:

> *Ah, Kladuša,*
> *burn in the fire,*
> *what an idiot*
> *you have nurtured*
>
> *Expunge for us*
> *the name of our Mujo*
> *let God provide*
> *his seed will be extinct.*[1]

In the free, Bihać part of the Krajina, Abdić acquired a new nickname – Todor, a typical Serbian name that clearly indicated how his policy was assessed. For his supporters, and for him himself, of course, he remained the untouchable Bábo, and it was quite natural that there should be a poster

---

1. Bećo Mesić, 'Četnik', *Ljiljan*, 59, 2 March 1994.

in the centre of Kladuša with the stylised figures of Mujo Hrnjica, Huska Miljković and Bábo himself (Biščević 1993: 12). But in these months another Bosniak political leader won a familiar family designation, for the SDA party activists and the media close to the party media started pushing the nickname of *Djed* or *Did* – Grandfather – for Izetbegović. And there are important nuances to this. The first version belongs to the standard language, and is somehow a *terminus technicus*, while the second is dialectal, and is preserved in the vernacular speech of the Bosnian Muslims, and has an additional emotional, associative and symbolic value in that it suggests age, simplicity, and familiarity with righteous folk, particularly in the countryside, where in large families the grandfather was still an authority respected by the entire household.

At one level the nickname suggests a genealogical status pushed one generation back, emitting a clear symbolic message to the renegade Abdić: the father was an authority, yes, but each father had his own father over him. At another level, particularly in its archaic vernacular form, *Did*, the nickname was a clear reference to the name of the head of the medieval Church of Bosnia. Official SDA policy interpreted this church as the forerunner of Islam and thus as a crucial part of its project for a Bosniak national integration ideology. In this interpretation, the Bosniaks were the direct descendants of the Cathars (or *bogumils*) who converted to Islam of their own free will, thus creating continuity between Ottoman and pre-Ottoman Bosnia and its statehood, with no connection to Christianity. This had nothing whatever to do with the facts.

The Church of Bosnia was a heterodox Christian church, and in its hierarchy *Djed* or *Did* was the equivalent of a bishop. He had an exceptional place in public life in pre-Ottoman Bosnia. The public documents were kept at his residence, his reputation meant that he was called upon by Bosnian governors (*ban*), kings and lords in the most delicate social and political disputes, he mediated in conflicts, and, as counsellor and chief witness, placed his signature on royal charters. And it is important to recall that the documents of medieval Bosnia were frequently written in the Ikavian dialect, so called from the use of the vowel *i* where contemporary standard Serbian employs *e*, and standard Croatian – and contemporary standard Bosnian – *ije*, as can be seen in variants *Did – Ded – Djed*.

The real rivalry of the two political and military leaders thus received two symbolic terms of comparison: in the metaphor of the people as one big family, the testy, unreliable and flighty father had to face the wise, consistent and constant grandfather. And in the mythopoeic world of the revived tradition it could be sensed that when faced down by the rise of the Sarajevo incarnation of Alija Đerzelez, the one-time pan-Bosnian Hrnjica would have to retreat to the local framework of his own Kladuša, without much likelihood of his maintaining his position even there.

Croatian official politics, on the other hand, was playing a two-faced game: it was helping to deliver aid to the Fifth Corps of the Bosnian Army in besieged Bihać, and at the same time flirting with Abdić, giving him almost unlimited propaganda backing and considerable support in materiel. He was a frequent guest on state television, which, like the other media, was controlled by the HDZ, and attempted to present him as a 'sensible' European Muslim as opposed to the allegedly Middle Eastern-type fundamentalist Izetbegović. He had his big moment on 17 November 1993 when he moved into his new residence, the finally completed Hrnjica Tower in Kladuša. But there was no longer any trace of the former intention to restore the original setting of Bosnian Ottoman architecture, nor was there anything of the once incorruptible Bábo, who in the show trial had defiantly stated that he feared no penalty, as he was fighting for a just cause. The tower was surrounded by bunkers and armed guards, the garden and the interior were embellished with tropical plants, everything was lined and panelled with leather and imported wood, the bathrooms had Italian sanitaryware and the vast conference room was all in glass (see colour plate 12).

And out of oblivion a monument to Mujo Hrnjica suddenly emerged – accompanied by verbiage all too appropriate from the one who had paid for it to be made. Everyone who remembered that six years earlier the editor of communist TV Sarajevo, Smiljko Šagolj, had tried to find a camera angle to make the 30cm model look like a monument a full three and a half metres high, and hence a key piece of evidence of Abdić's *folie de grandeur*. They could only laugh wryly at the information that the Kladuša sculptor Zlatko Dizdarević had used eight tons of plaster to make the final version of Mujo, on horseback, with a hawk on his wrist – eleven metres high and fifteen metres long (*Zapadna Bosna*, 19, 15 April 1994).

In the spring of 1994 plans were afoot to cut the monument up, take it to Zagreb and have it cast in bronze, and finally to erect it in Kladuša. But things turned out differently from the way the client had imagined. On 21 August, Kladuša was captured by the Fifth Corps under General Atif Dudaković, and Abdić, his People's Defence of Western Bosnia and several thousand civilians fled into the part of Croatia occupied by Serbian paramilitaries. While *Did* called on them over Sarajevo Radio to go home and to understand that 'not every *bábo* was a good *bábo*' because 'this *bábo*' had turned his guns against his own people and made an alliance with those who had killed our brothers' (Izetbegović 1995: 115), they preferred, hungry and exhausted as they were, to cheer Babo when he came to visit them in the company of Milan Martić and members of the Serbian paramilitaries, or addressed them from a truck, standing in front of a vast canvas with Hrnjica's Kladuša tower on it, and a portrait of himself, in the exemplary manner of socialist realism (see illustration p. 309).

On 26 December 1994 banner headlines in the biggest circulation Croatian weekly *Globus* proclaimed: *Fikret Abdić and 1200 soldiers renege to Serb haiduks*. The paper thus determined precisely, at the level of the traditional imaginary, the new perception of the Kladuša governor for the Bosniak and most of the Croatian public.

Although Abdić and his supporters managed to go back to Kladuša on 16 November, and even to proclaim the Republic of Western Bosnia there, his political adventure was inexorably drawing to a close. Not even those with whom he had made overt or covert alliances were able or willing to change the fate of the self-styled reincarnation of Mujo Hrnjica: neither the president of the RSK, Milan Martić, a former local policeman, whom the *gusle* players of Bukovica had sung of as an incarnation of the Uskok *harami baši* Stojan Janković, Hrnjica's fiercest epic adversary, but actually a good friend with whom he would sometimes genuinely make merry and get drunk at weddings; neither the president of Republika Srpska, Radovan Karadžić, that new Starina Novak on Romanija; nor the patron of them all, Slobodan Milošević, President of Serbia, leader of supernatural origin, since a name so significantly symbolic could only have been given him by a nymph: 'from *srf* [victory, fight] and *sloboda* [freedom]'. As far back as the Gazimestan celebrations, a *gusle* player had sung to this new deity in whom the very heart of the national destiny had been embedded: 'Slobodan his sacred name,/ Milošević from Miloš, / Obilić from Kosovo' (Mastilović 1989).

And this kind of reading of Milošević's surname is a vivid proof that in the archaic consciousness the name of the hero was never an accident, but always a sign of his overall value, a shop window of the bearer's features and the characteristics of his life, a reflection of his reputation, his feats, battles, duels and *meydans*. For this reason behind the semantic value of a name – as already shown with the example of the two Alijas, Đerzelez and Izetbegović – there is always or a more or less covert *hero story* that those in the know will reveal to the uninitiated.

When one adds to this the fact that in the meantime the contemporary Croatian incarnations of Mijat Tomić were having to forget, in the Washington

Agreement, the song about how Mijat had it out with Mujo on Mt Lipet and recall, if not the one about his *haircut godfathership* with Tešnjanin Alija, then at least those about the *alliance de convenience* of Mijat's and Mujo's bands against the Serbian trader Vojin, it is clear that Fikret Abdić no longer had a chance. It was only a question of time before the threat from one of the wartime Bihać songs recorded on cassette, 'Oh, Todor, traitor to your race' ('Oj Todore, izdajice roda'), would come true:

> Pack up eggs and chickens,
> pack up turkeys, rabbits,
> for you and the Chetniks
> we've got some assault troops ready ...
> The Fifth Corps of a knightly army
> will drive you to the end of Serbia.

In a series of operations from early 1995 the forces of the HV and HVO pushed from the direction of Livno, across the Dinara mountain above Knin. The Croatian Army (HV) made a strike and in two days broke the RSK, and on 6 August, at the border near Tržačke Raštele, joined up with the Fifth Corps of the Bosnian Army. And on the evening of 7 August 1995 its soldiers entered Velika Kladuša, and hung the military and state flags of Bosnia-Herzegovina from Mujo Hrnjica's tower. Abdić was forced to flee across the border into Croatia for a second time. The next day, on his birthday, Alija Izetbegović arrived in Kladuša, and held a victory press conference in the luxury Abdić hall in Hrnjica Tower, while a day later the inhabitants of Bužim greeted him with the song: '*Did* Alija, cock your beret, / never fear while your Bužimites are alive' (*Ljiljan*, 171, 24 April 1996).[1]

---

1. The previous chapter told how in WWII various armies used the same versification and thematic outline, just changing the names of the protagonists. This is just another example of the same procedure. Thus, for example, at a rally in Žabljak, celebrating the overthrow of the Montenegrin leadership, adherents of Milošević sang the couplet: 'Slobodan, cock your *šajkača* [traditional Serb rural hat]/ while your Durmitorites are alive' (*Pobjeda*, 14 January 1989). In WWII, among the Partisans of the Bosnian Krajina they sang: 'Comrade Tito, cock your Tito hat/ all your proletarians are alive' (Jovičić and Jastrebić 1977: 232). One Partisan couplet gave Tito the same *šajkača* that Milošević got a half-century later: 'Tito, cock your *šajkača* / many of your proletarians are alive' (Cindrić 1969: 35). The couplets are connected not only by the poetics, but also by the cap motif, as key to the symbolic identity of the addressee – anyone who wears a *šajkača* is a true Serb, while Tito, bold and decisive as he was, could well be considered a symbolic Serb, at least as long as he fought Germans and Ustashas. Thus the continuity of vernacular literature goes beyond religious, ethnic and ideological boundaries. A cocked cap is a universal visual indicator that someone is happy and carefree.

Since there was no way of doing it gently, the deranged family hierarchy had to be re-established by force: *Did* faced down *Bábo*, and Mujo Hrnjica was incarnated in a new hero, the victor of the war.

Atif Dudaković was promoted to division general, becoming thus the most senior officer in the AB-H. Over the whole of the last page of a weekly that had been launched by the former editor of *Ljiljan* and one of Abdić's most disappointed admirers, Zilhad Ključanin printed a greeting to the victor and his soldiers:

> What the *gazis* [heroes] of the 5th Corps endured under your brilliant command will go down in history [...] You have shown the whole world how the descendants of Mujo Hrnjica fight and win. And show their borderers' (*krajišniks*) defiance. Stubbornness. Honour. Dignity. Their borderers' wrath [...] *Aferim* [bravo], *gazi* of the Krajina![1]

But Abdić's many years of endeavour were not without reverberation among his most embittered antagonists. Since he wanted so much to be the new Mujo Hrnjica, and since all such traditional figures are so unavoidably ambivalent, it was not difficult to find an interpretation that would not diminish the authority and authenticity of the new incarnation of Mujo, i.e. Dudaković, nor forgive the old incarnation all the ill he had caused, but at the same time would not prevent him being recognised in the role in which he had so passionately immersed himself. The new relationships were explained, in the spring of 1996, to the Czech social anthropologist Radan Haluzík by a middle-aged Muslim peasant from near Bužim:

> Hrnjica was just as big a traitor as Fikret. He took one group of the commoners there, and another back; the way the wind blew. Hrnjica and Fikret, the same Mob. Hrnjica had his autonomy just like Fikret; Hrnjica also ran with two sides. Fikret went with the Chetniks, and we paid for everything.[2]

Ever since the district attorney in Bihać had called in 1994 for an investigation of Abdić for war crimes against the civilian population of Bihać, Bosnia-Herzegovina had sought his extradition in vain. Living in Croatia, in Zagreb and Rijeka, Fikret Abdić once again got onto the front pages after

---

1. Zilhad Ključanin, 'Aferim, gazijo!' *Bošnjak*, 21, 15 August 1995.
2. I am grateful to Haluzík for having let me listen, during his stay in Zagreb, to the recordings he made on his field trip.

the Croatian police arrested five Bihać men on 4 April 1996 on suspicion of having plotted to kill him in a fairly spectacular way: with a rocket launcher and cumulative armour-piercing grenades from an ambush on a bend in the road above Rijeka where he often passed in his car. The Croatian authorities suggested that the Bosnia-Herzegovina authorities were behind it, while Bosnian official circles claimed it was all a put-up job, the more so as there were two former members of Abdić's para-army among the suspects.

Everything was unclear and contradictory. The first version of the indictment spoke of an 'act of international terrorism', which was changed into 'an act of preparation for an act of terrorism', and everything ended two years later with two of them being set free, two of them being sentenced to a year in prison, and one to a year and a half. But the alleged target of the alleged assassins, talkative and bouncy as ever, at once went public with his own explanation of events. In a big interview to a pro-government Zagreb weekly, Fikret Abdić ultimately revelled in his role as heir of Hrnjica and Miljković, adding what was the only thing missing for his curriculum vitae – in which he himself could perhaps no longer discern what was fact and what fantasy – to be fully rounded off. This was of course the final chapter, concerning the killing of the hero in an ambush, by the blood brother who had sold out to the enemy. Although the fabula had not been fully effectuated in this case, the very framework of it was enough to concoct a tale driven by its own internal dramaturgy:

> They decided on an assassination when they saw they couldn't shift me in any other way [...] Dudaković had even openly stated before this: 'His own men are going to liquidate him.' Now in the Bosnia-Herzegovina Embassy [in Zagreb] they claim that it is Abdić-ites that have been arrested. They had planned in advance whom they were going to shift the blame onto. They were obviously thinking of the fact that Mujo Hrnjica had been liquidated by a local man, that it was the same with Huska Miljković, so it seemed to them simplest to explain that the same thing had happened to Abdić as well. (*Vjesnik*, 4 April1996)

There was in fact nothing left for Abdić, without any contact with reality, than to go on fabricating his own role in life, at the same time showing to the public that it was similarly fabricated by others, by his friends and enemies alike. This is, after all, at least half the truth: the editor of the paper had actually taken his claim – *They wanted to kill me like Mujo Hrnjica* – as the sub-headline and thus given it the main importance. And if he did not actually die, his final comparison provided a perfect image of his political end, and closed the now totally empty shell of a construct that had once been so vital. In reality, irrespective of the weird proceedings of official Croatian policy, the epic Krajina hero had already had new life breathed into him.

At almost the same time as the Abdić interview, on 21 April in Bihać, in the same 'hardcore Krajina' a spectacular parade of the Fifth Corps – 'the Krajina *gazis*' (Mustafa Borović, *Ljiljan*, 171, 24 April 1996) took place, and at the end of the summer three Bosnian Army generals from the Bosnian Krajina inherited the heroic epic tradition. In electing Atif Dudaković, Sakib Mahmuljin and Mehmed Alagić to the Executive Committee, the SDA 'respected, endorsed and reaffirmed this tradition', maintained the 'continuity of the memory' and 'testified to the people' that in Dudaković, Alagić and Mahmuljin the Bosniaks had their own contemporary Mustaj-Bey of Lika, Mujo Hrnjica and Osman Tanković (Mustafa Spahić, *Ljiljan* 192, 18 September 1996). And in stating that through this act the SDA 'had politically verified the universal people's trust in these generals and their reputation', he himself symbolically endorsed them with traditional legitimacy, naming their equivalents in the epic poetry.

This symbolic reaffirmation no longer had the power of that mass rally at the constituent assembly of the SDA in Velika Kladuša. It could not have, for in the meantime the relationships had been fundamentally changed. In the summer of 1991, the epic Mujo Hrnjica was a message to the other communities, primarily the Serbian one. Six years later the circle closed with a message to an outcast from their own community, not to those who had threatened it from outside, but to him who had besmirched 'the name of our Mujo' from within. Still, in reality, underneath the once again stabilised official imaginary, raised to a new level of meaning, there was a deep schism – the population long set irreconcilably at loggerheads, often inside the same family, traumatised by the destruction of the war and post-war reprisals. Two years after the military defeat of the Abdić project, on the eve of local elections in the autumn of 1997, his followers sent an anonymous message to a leading local supporter of the central government: 'We are Bábo's, you are Did's [...] We are Bábo's Muslims, and you are the mujaheddin of Did the Schnozzle' (*Dani*, 60, October 1997), while at the elections for the central government a year later the unofficial slogan of the newly-founded Abdić party, DNZ, was in the form of a question addressed to the local populace: 'What's the point of a stepfather [Izetbegović] when you've got a living Bábo?' (*Feral Tribune*, 677, 7 September 1998).

Towards the end of the 1990s, in Sarajevo, two editions of an *Encyclopaedic*

Dictionary came out in a relatively short time, the aim being, in the context of the recently ended war and in the new military and political establishment, to systematise the historical, contemporary and traditional material on which the Bosniak national ideology and its catalogue of exemplary figures were to be founded. In it, as expected, there were the many figures of the epic tradition of the Bosnian Muslims: Alija Đerzelez, 'protector of the poor, guardian of maiden modesty, defender of the faith and bold *meydanci* [dueller]', 'proud and magnanimous to the defeated' (Kasumović-Huseinbašić 2000: 120) and the Hrnjica brothers, who even got a fairly long entry. These 'Krajina *gazis*' lived 'extremely modestly while operating in the defence of justice and the poor in Velika Kladuša', they were all 'fearless, skilled and self-sacrificing', and in particular the *bölükbaşi* Mujo 'defended the borders of Bosnia against aggression from Croatia' (ibid. 135). In these formulations it is not difficult to recognise the politically motivated idealisation and the influence of the universal Robin Hood motif, or the suggestive substitution of the modern concept of 'aggression' for the essentially different and far more complex conditions on the restless Ottoman-Habsburg border in the seventeenth century.

Full circle has been reached: after years of wandering and hesitating, after many had snatched at him in an attempt to seize something of his fame, the complex epic Mujo Hrnjica ended up, like so many of his Muslim and Christian companions, in the sterile ambience of a party publication. This is not surprising in itself, but it is fairly unusual that he was renounced by the very same person who had dragged him out of the vernacular tradition and brought him into political discourse in a big way at the end of the eighties.

After the final collapse of his political project and the affair of the alleged assassination, Fikret Abdić started to try to renew at least some of Agrokomerc's activities, from Croatia, as well as to organise in a political sense his supporters in the Kladuša area, of whom there were still quite a number. But he was constantly dogged by the events of the war. As early as 1994, the report of UN civil rights commissioner Tadeusz Mazowiecki had drawn attention to the fact that there were concentration camps in the area under his control, in which the inmates were tortured, and that his army attacked civilian targets and looted humanitarian aid convoys. Soon an indictment was filed in Sarajevo and extradition was sought, but since Abdić had dual citizenship, Croatia itself organised a trial in Karlovac, where, three years later, in the summer of 2002, a sentence of twenty years was handed down to him for violations of the Geneva conventions, i.e. for war crimes against POWs and the civilian population.

Just as twelve years earlier, the eloquent and self-possessed Abdić turned the courtroom into a political platform, and in the autumn of 2001 the media transmitted the statement of his agenda, as it was in a way, in which he put himself in a different interpretative framework from that which he had followed the whole of his life up to that time. The judge, that is, warned him to refrain from long addresses that had no connection with the subject of the trial, but he refused, insisting that all his words should be put down properly in the official record:

> I am not only an innocent man, but also a saint. Matija Gubec was tried in the same way, and he's long gone, but the record of the trial has remained. I am interested only in the court record. (*Feral Tribune*, 842, 3 November 2001).

Kladuša's Bábo no longer identified himself with Mujo Hrnjica, but with the leader of the anti-feudal peasants' revolt in northwest Croatia of the sixteenth century. This great manipulator knew well that symbolic messages, just like verbal ones, needed translating. When he addressed his Muslim followers, he presented himself as a revivified figure from their own tradition; when his target audience was the Croatian public, he built his symbolic identification on a figure from the Croatian tradition – a serf who rose up against the feudal powers and perished in the unequal struggle. Abdić clearly understood that his career was at an end, that he had definitively lost the battle for symbolic capital among the Bosniaks at the national level, but that nevertheless his cult had its own interior dynamics at the local level, and that it was not a bad idea to give it a parallel line of development inside the Croatian political imaginary as well.[1]

A wily politician will always be able to straddle fences and have a line of retreat in two reference systems, and so the general, ahistorical message of the bold fighter for social justice and the protector of the weak is coded in two historically-shaped contexts.

---

1. For the symbolic importance of the figure of Matija Gubec in the Croatian social and political imaginary.

TEN

The Siege of Sarajevo

At the beginning of October 1992 in Sarajevo I set out on a practically frenzied search for food. Some of my friends discerned a certain political optimism in this – for if I did not believe in the future, if I did not see the end of the war or at least the possibility of making it through the winter, I wouldn't have bothered so much about laying in supplies. Whenever I could, I confirmed such an assumption:

'It'll settle down soon, it has to. St Demetrius Day [Mitrovdan] is in the offing, the haiduk farewell.'

(Jančić 1994: 21)

Real and symbolic geography

Everything presented so far shows that for an evocation to communicate effectively it must function as a certain perceptual pattern incorporated in the culture (cf. Hymes 1974). That is, it must fit into a pattern of understanding, explaining and selecting contemporary events and persons by analogy with particular models. To function in this way, each new evocation must on the one hand be coordinated with other elements already evoked in the given discourse, and on the other be open to potential future evocations. It fits into a system of relationships and thus becomes part of a broad network of reciprocal relations between those segments of an utterance that bear meaning, whether its intention is to oppose or to appropriate them. Thus a dynamic system of meanings is created that *lives* in the communication and each of its shaping elements is constantly recreated and reconfirmed.

The communication process of which the semantic core is the evocation of Romanija Mountain started with Đodan's speech at Peščenica. Before then it is possible to speak of more or less systematised evocations of the location and the traditional range of meanings linked with it in Serbian discourse and in the construction of the Serbian political imaginary. If any reactions occurred in other communities in connection with this process, they were expressed in the non-affective terminology of ideological discourse, and few paid attention to them. The fiery and eloquent HDZ chief was the first – consciously or not, with previous preparation or spontaneously moved by the heated atmosphere of the campaign meeting – to respond to the protagonists of the Serbian national discourse in their own symbolic style, in the same semantic categories and with the same epic connotations. And their brisk and evocation-rich reactions show persuasively that they easily recognised him as a relevant competitor.

From the point of view of the sociology of knowledge, socially accumulated knowledge about Romanija as an especially important locality existed in all the relevant communities to a varying extent and defined in different ways, grounded in various historical or fictional facts. But it was on the whole only in the Serbian community, that is among some of its social and political elite and in a large part of its public, that it was systematised at a high functional level. There was not, then, any common semantic universe, rather 'socially segregated sub-universes of meaning'. And each of them emerged, 'like all social edifices of meaning' borne by 'a particular collectivity' that is 'by the group that ongoingly produces the meanings in question and within which these meanings have objective reality'. Between such groups there is often conflict and competition because each one endeavours 'to establish itself and to discredit if not liquidate the competitive body of knowledge' (Berger and Luckman 1971: 103).

The collapse of Yugoslavia, then, was a breakdown not only of common institutions, charged with formal and explicit administrative and political control, but also with the production of shared, integrated meanings and universally binding knowledge that drove out all other, particularist knowledge. Inevitably, this assumes the breakdown, at least formally, of the 'stable symbolic canopy of the *entire* society' (ibid.: 103). At this moment a two-fold battle was engaged: on the one hand, for the symbolic resources, which had up to then been drawn in under this common canopy, but which now each group wanted just for itself, defined according to its own criteria, and on the other hand, for the restoration of legitimacy to those sub-universes that had been partially or completely delegitimised, ignored or even explicitly politically proscribed.

Since the central institutions were now too weak to control the common canopy by repression, the public space was breached by increasingly vigorous competition among the sub-universes of meanings. Heterogeneous and increasingly autonomous attitudes to the whole of society appeared, each one seeing it from the point of view of the given sub-universe. And these were in the main defined in terms of ethnos and religion, that is, the competing sub-universes were socially structured by the criterion of traditional culture and tradition mediated by historical and social experience, and they were produced as exclusive ethnically and religiously based knowledge.

From the point of view of communication theory, at the beginning of this process each of the four communities possessed an appropriate system of meanings capable of being activated by its discourse, but not necessarily having to be. It always depended on the decision or the skill of participants in the political communication to select sign systems which were based on a specific kind of code. A code is worked out through use, and as it develops it creates its own tradition as a data bank. A participant in political communication is thus to an extent in the position of the writer at the outset of the writing project: before the real readers or listeners appear, they are there only hypothetically, that is, there is *a project of a recipient*. This project is given shape in relation to the hypothetical recipients' familiarity with the theme to be discussed and the way in which it is to be done, with respect to their ability to understand the author's idea to the maximum extent. Because everything that is outside the perception, that does not strike a chord in the totality of the recipients' life experience – the only relevant experience here – is automatically ineffective, outside the message (Balcerzan 1974).

The Greater Serbian ideology was the only one that already had, several years before the war, a fully elaborated project of recipients modelled on the content of the vernacular culture – above all in relation to the Bosniaks (and Albanians) as 'Turks'; but also to the Croats as 'Latins, tricksters of old (*Latini, stare varalice*)', as one Belgrade journalist heard in Bukovica 'a hale and sensible old man' say (*Duga*, 425, 9 June 1990). Even more importantly, this ideology had a precise project of recipients within its own community: it knew to whom it was appealing, with what meanings, on whom it could rely. All the others created their projects (both inner- and outer-directed) in the course of the war, built either on the contents of the traditional matrix, or on some other model, but they were regularly merely a reaction either to the Serbian project or to the events of the war.

As for the codes themselves, one does not mean just those that were directly, consciously and purposefully brought to life in agreement with the participants in the communication but above all those that had become stabilised in the social consciousness of specific groupings during the lengthy practice of mutual communication. Such use makes a given motif more or less recognisable to members of the community, and every time it is given new currency it stirs associations with its previous use. As such, it receives reciprocal endorsement and explanation along with other such motifs in a unique and simultaneous communication situation.

If, with respect to the motif of *acquiring and controlling Romanija,* the Serbian and the supra-ethnic, or non-ethnic Yugoslav codes are among the most highly elaborated, then Đodan's evocation of traditional culture was condemned from the outset to real inferiority as communication compared to the competing Serbian discourse – however impressive or even shocking, but most often frivolous and misplaced it might have seemed to the Croatian public. In the Croatian social memory there was simply no substance capable of supporting it effectively or making it anything other than a symbol of the eloquence and hastiness of a not particularly highly valued politician.

The Bosniak social memory, however, did possess potential within which it was possible to create an evocation at least by way of suggestion. For suggestion is a part of the full meaning of the sentence, but we do not feel its presence as central or fundamental, the way we do with primary meaning on which it is never dependent. This is to do with secondary meaning, a measure of meaning that is given implicitly, by suggestion and connotation (Beardsley 1967: 291–293). In political discourse, the percentage of primary and explicit, of secondary and implicit meaning, depends on the level, the extent and the criteria in selecting the expressive resources with which the transmitter of the message has drawn on the traditional and vernacular matrix, either his own or the competing one.

It is this kind of evocation, at the level of suggestion, that was activated in Bosniak discourse, seven months before the Yugoslav evocation of Romanija in the demonstrations at Belgrade's Ušće, but four months after Đodan's and three months after Drašković's first reply. The Sarajevo independent Bosniak youth paper *Vox* published an apocryphal *Agenda for the Immigration of Bosniaks from Turkey (Program doseljavanja Bošnjaka iz Turske),* allegedly an official document from the Parliament of Bosnia-Herzegovina. According to this, four million 'Bosnian, Herzegovinan and Sandžak Muslims lived in Turkey'. Those who had fled 'under the assaults of the Latin and the Greek cross' were to be returned at government expense and over ten years planted in the homeland according to a plan, so that Bosnia, 'without having to rely on natural increase', should reach a population of ten million.

Then the phases of the programme were set out in twenty points, making a complex network of satirical allusions, banter and parody of the symbolic loci and procedures of the three main ethnic parties in Bosnia-Herzegovina. Thus, for example, it was announced that the fifth wave of immigrants would wash over the Bosnian Krajina, and then a Muslim Krajina State would be formed, an ironic pastiche of the Serbian SAO Krajina, which had already been proclaimed in Croatia. And the little town of Duvno would be renamed Duhno: this was a parody of the pointless claims of some Muslim linguists that Muslims were distinguished from Serbs and Croats because their vernacular had retained the (Turkish) phoneme *h* while the others had lost it or replaced it with *v*.

Two points, with reference to settlements on the mountain, come directly into the referential sphere of the *acquisition and control of Romanija*:

> 6. At Sokolac, a Sokolac Colony will be created and here, on the top of Romanija, the green banner will wave (*vioriti zeleni barjak*)!
> 15. A second branch of the Bosniak Institute will be founded in Knežina.[1]

The alleged future Sokolac Colony was a subtle word play from the same root. On the one hand it was an allusion to Sokolović-Colony, a Sarajevo neighbourhood mainly inhabited by Bosniaks from Sandžak, who were considered particularly tough. And on the other, it was a declaration that a kind of mirror image of this rather dangerous settlement, with a provocative green flag to boot, would be built precisely in the little town of Sokolac in Romanija considered in local political mythology to be most authentically Serbian (and most authentically 'Romanijan'), and where the series of 'patriotic' speeches had begun.

Particularly notably and subtly worked out were the waves of alleged immigration and the localities where branches of the Bosniak Institute were to be set up. This institution, actually a museum and documentation centre, was set up in the sixties in Zurich by the rich Bosniak political émigré Adil Zulfikarpašić, with his own capital. He was a former Partisan and post-war senior communist official who defected, disillusioned, to the West in the early 1950s. Over the years he collected a large and extremely valuable collection of documents, books, manuscripts and items of material culture connected with Bosnia and its past, and in the days of the collapse of communism announced that he would take the whole collection to Sarajevo and donate it to his homeland. Although in a political sense he always acted as a liberal democrat, in his elaboration of the term Bosniak Zulfikarpašić was often inconsistent and ambiguous, and so it is not surprising that many

---

1. *Vox*, I, 6, September 1990, p. 3.

Croats and Serbs could have imagined that the name was intended to extend to them as well. Propaganda, particularly Serbian, was quick to back them up in this fear, and depicted the Institute as one of the chief instruments for the implementation of the perfidious Islamisation of Bosnia.

And so there is nothing surprising in the unruly young satirists, clearly highly versed in the local identity myths and political imaginary, choosing Grude and Knežina as the places where the branches of the Institute were to be established.

According to Point 9, the fifth wave of immigration would cover western Herzegovina and 'the first branch of the Bosniak Institute would be established in Grude'. This region had an absolutely dominant Croat majority in any case, but Grude itself was something quite special: the population was literally 100 percent Croat, which was without parallel not only in Bosnia-Herzegovina but also in Croatia itself. Hence from the beginning it had a very special symbolic status in the political myths of the HDZ, particularly the rightist, extreme nationalist wing of the party, for in World War II the local Croats were almost to a man involved in the Ustasha movement. After the war they long suffered this collective stigma and were subject to communist repression for even quite harmless, romantic expressions of national (ethnic) identity, although, in truth, they had nothing at all against open, pro-Ustasha, anti-government acts of provocation. As a result, a powerful local identity was created: Grude was 'the heart of Croatianness', the 'most thoroughly Croat place in the world', inhabited by the 'best, most stubborn and purest Croats', in addition, on paper at least, they were unwavering Catholics. But now it was supposed to be colonised by 400,000 Bosniak returnees from Turkey, double the population of this impoverished region, and a mint of money was to be spent, in addition, on the construction of the Bosniak Institute, while all knew that in forty years of communism, because of the collective stigma that burdened the area, central government had invested practically nothing in the economy and infrastructure! This was a nice specimen of the *Vox* authors' good sense of the way the chauvinist rhetoric of the time could be inflated to the level of the absurd and the grotesque.

The previous, fourth 'assault wave' of colonists, according to Point 7, would cover Nevesinje and Gacko, also impoverished little towns, but this time in eastern Herzegovina, where the majority population consisted of Serbs – and not just any Serbs but, like those on Romanija, the 'best, most stubborn and the purest' and in addition unwaveringly Orthodox. In World War II the Partisans had had no foothold there either because the Serbian population had mainly joined the Chetnik movement. The local ethnic imaginary had two more handholds however. In Nevesinje in the last years of Ottoman rule an insurrection had broken out that remained fixed indelibly in the memory of the local population, forming one of the backbones of its ethnic and religious identity. The other was the young anarchist Bogdan Žerajić, from Nevesinje, who had carried out the assassination of the Austro-Hungarian military governor in Bosnia in 1910, and then killed himself so as not to fall into the hands of the police. These two myths were nurtured by all the governments, and after 1945, the communists also made them part of their own political imaginary. They were useful in giving them legitimacy as the heirs of the 'ancient freedom-loving tradition of the area', sidestepping the awkward circumstance that in World War II it had been Chetnik through and through, and allowing it to be symbolically integrated into the Yugoslav political imaginary.

At the end of the eighties, it was precisely the Nevesinje Serbs, under the aegis of the Milošević agenda, who were the first in Bosnia-Herzegovina to initiate public protests with the usual claims that the country was being 'Muslimised' and that the Serbs were endangered and being systematically exploited. The leader of these local protests lasting several months in 1989, Borislav Žerajić, derived a good deal of his symbolic legitimacy from the fact that he came from the family of the one-time assassin who had 'sacrificed his life for Serbian liberty'. He regularly invoked him, convening meetings in front of the monument to his forebear in the centre of town, and adding that his action was also the 'second Nevesinje insurrection', just to increase the number of enemies – the Muslim Sultan in Istanbul and the Catholic Emperor in Vienna. He claimed that the communists had the same ancient 'conspiracy' focused on Nevesinje as they did towards Serbia itself, because Nevesinje was nothing but a prefiguration of an authentic Serbia in Herzegovina, a kind of advance guard, and when the town was laid low, Serbia itself would be automatically threatened, as in the motto 'A weak Nevesinje, a weak Serbia' (*Borba*, 18/19 November 1989).

The predominantly Serb town of Gacko had a similar local mythology and past. This was enhanced by the fact that Vuk Drašković was born there, at the time the most vociferous Serb nationalist, particularly suggestive when – with the authority of the learned man and writer – he convinced the Serbian population that it had been the victim of its Muslim neighbours 'since time out of mind'.

The chapters to come will contain more of the historical and traditional background of this myth, and as for the announcement that the second branch of the Bosniak Institute would be founded in Knežina, on Romanija, the reader of this book already knows the reasons. The authors of the *Agenda* clearly remembered that a provocative Serbian church ceremony had been held there a year earlier, the first event in the psychological and political mobilisation of the local Serbs, the inauguration of the Milošević cult in Bosnia and an ominous herald of the ever-closer tempest of war.

The young satirists did not need to wonder for long which point to take next for their imaginary map: when the *Agenda* was being drawn up, hardly a month had passed since Jovan Rašković had given his inflammatory speech to the local Serbs, and everywhere around they were able to see with what systematic aggression the myth of the impregnable and indomitable mountain fortress of the Serbs was being renewed, to see the way in which under the onslaught of creators of the new/old symbolic universe, from moment to moment, the concept of the Partisan and Titoist Romanija with which they had grown up was vanishing, and that the Yugoslav flag on the mountain was already being replaced by the Serbian one, indeed, even the Chetnik one, and it was difficult to resist the challenge, in the context of the general establishment of this dialogic and paradoxical attitude to competing sign systems, to start a symbolic polemic with the central symbol of the *Flag on the Mountain over the City*.

Since this could no longer be the communist flag of Bosnia-Herzegovina, a red field with the inserted Yugoslav flag, because its time had clearly passed, the alternative occurred of its own accord. To be precise, it was defined and imposed by those who had raised the alarm in Romanija because of the 'vampire Mujo Hrnjaca'.

However, before we move on to a motif that is a kind of central figure in this book – a prism in which far wider processes and the constellations of political power can be read – it is worth discussing the origin and the fate of the satire discussed. Its story is one of almost incredible manipulation, revealing the channels through which the social and political elites, as part of their all-embracing indoctrination, spread disinformation to the public and their rivals in the processes of negotiation and decision-making.

Vox was founded with private capital in Sarajevo in the spring of 1990, at a time of turbulent political events, hopes, expectations and fears, when all kinds of media outlets flourished everywhere, in the euphoria of the newly attained freedom of speech. They were mainly short-lived, with bombastic titles. In Serbia Milošević was at the height of his power; democratic elections had been held in Slovenia, and were just being held in Croatia; in Bosnia-Herzegovina and in Macedonia they had been announced for November. The editorial board was made up exclusively of very young, urban people, students and even secondary school children, punks and members of other subculture groups, not burdened by ethnic and religious divisions or stereotypes. Although formally defined as *Bosniak*, the paper had some Serbs and Croats on the editorial board as well and the editor-in-chief was a Croat. Thus *Vox*, somewhat anarchic and unkempt as it was, was a true scion of the guerrilla youth press that in the second half of the eighties had broken the ideological shell and opened up space to pluralism of ideas and social criticism.

The humour was often rough and even morbid, and the authors acknowledged no taboos or sacrosanct authorities. Almost every issue would excite some scandal or other and anger some toffee-nosed bigwig. Eventually a proposal was made – actually by a Bosniak, an SDA MP in the Assembly of Bosnia-Herzegovina – to the public prosecutor that it should be condemned and the editors were called in for interviews with the police. And then something happened that could be described as absurd, or in the logic of later events, quite logical and predictable. After the war two of the editors, Nihad and Sead Kreševljaković, recalled that they were aware that 'there were some very tasteless jokes in that issue' but what amazed them was that the police did not mention that as a reason for the ban, not even the *Agenda for the Immigration of Bosniaks from Turkey*, stating instead that they were 'put out by some quite unexpected detail, for example, that in that issue we had called Milošević a dictator'.[1]

However, accusations that the paper was programmatically chauvinist and anti-Serb were not true. Looked at quantitatively, Serbs were indeed the most frequent *Vox* targets, but only because Karadžić and Milošević and their satellites had earned such a status by their actions and claims. When they pushed themselves forward with their own doltish arrogance – which was not infrequent – Tuđman and the HDZ, the federal prime minister Ante Marković, the communists, the JNA and the SDA and Alija Izetbegović in person, with whom they had been on a war footing from the outset, all came in for their share of criticism and mockery on the pages of *Vox*. Not even the leadership of the Islamic community was spared when it interfered in political processes.

Even in cases that were pushed too hard or that were quite tasteless, *Vox*'s constructions contained enough elements for anyone who approached them with minimal common sense to be able without any difficulty to realise that this was satire, in other words, an imagined reality that criticised the real

---

1. Paula Bobanović, 'Tekst iz našeg satiričkog srednjoškolskog lista (...) [Text from our satirical secondary school paper ...]', *Nacional*, 178, 14 April 1999, p. 56.

reality. Thus its many agendas and declarations are readable, undoubtedly witty, identifiable ironic commentaries on real agendas, actions and declarations by the political figures of the time, particularly Karadžić's SDS of Bosnia-Herzegovina. The fictitious *Immigration of Bosniaks from Turkey* was perhaps the best joke of all, because it pithily encompassed all the essential points of the Bosnian political map of the time, including the stereotypes, prejudices and obduracies that were current even among the Bosniaks.

The Bosniak diaspora in Turkey that the *Agenda* mentions was created after 1878. Coming under the rule of Austria-Hungary, a Christian state, was for the Bosnian Muslims a major turning point, a shock to their civilisation that aroused a sense of threat, driving many into emigration. But there were also particular pressures and there was a lot of perfidious propaganda. The Muslim exodus was encouraged by the political leadership of the Serbs in Bosnia-Herzegovina (sometimes also by the Catholic clergy), the aim being to buy up exiles' land at rock-bottom prices and to settle their own people from overpopulated areas on it. There were even Muslims who urged their own people to move out in order to make a profit by acting as middlemen in the buying and selling of land and houses. And there was encouragement from the Ottoman side as well: their propaganda showed the situation in Austria-Hungary in the darkest colours, while glorifying Sultan Abdul Hamid II and his rule. The introduction of universal conscription on the European model in 1881 also considerably speeded up the emigration: for traditional Muslims it was inconceivable to serve as the soldier of a Christian emperor.

When the Turks were disastrously defeated in the Balkan wars of 1912–13, and their European possessions were reduced to the area immediately around Istanbul, the religious and political leadership of the Bosnian Muslims, who had long cherished the illusion that it was possible to go back to the old ways, finally told its people openly that the only way out was to keep a tight grip on their land and to accept the non-Muslim state as a political reality.

In the new homeland, many of these incomers made names for themselves in fighting for Kemal Atatürk, which helped them in gaining a reputation in social life as loyal citizens of the modern Turkish Republic, particularly in the army. Since they often tended to group together, there are even today compact villages in which Bosnian customs, songs and language have been preserved.

It is very difficult to calculate how many Muslims moved to Turkey in the forty years of Austro-Hungarian rule, for the official statistics of the time are neither complete nor reliable, but serious estimates do not exceed

120,000–130,000. Looked at proportionally, this is a not insignificant number, for when Austria-Hungary took over Bosnia-Herzegovina, the Muslim population was about 450,000. And it is still more difficult, in fact impossible, to estimate how many of their descendants there might be in present-day Turkey, the fifth or sixth generation as they are now. But one thing is very clear: four million is a gross exaggeration, although of course exaggeration can have a number of different motives. Someone might be pouring scorn on someone else's megalomania and obstinacy, and someone else might be egging people on in their collective psychosis and paranoia. The *Vox* journalists were not in the second group – on the contrary.

The general idea in the *Agenda* of the organised return of the diaspora was easily recognisable as a skit on the theme of statements that were being made practically every day at this time by various political leaders. The most numerous and most bombastic claims made were in Croatia, which is hardly surprising, for the Croats were by far the largest group of economic and political exiles from the former Yugoslavia. In the euphoria following the collapse of communism and its own electoral triumph, the HDZ's leadership announced the return to Croatia of hundreds of thousands of expatriates and the influx of billions of their dollars (here again Šime Đodan achieved short-lived fame with the statement that in just a year or two exiles were going to bring in $20 billion – many laughed at this obvious nonsense, but there was no small number of believers). In Serbia too there was talk of the return of rich Serbs from the USA and other western countries. And some Bosniak people in public life started talking about Bosnian Muslim exiles in Turkey and grandiloquently counting up all the distinguished Turkish businessmen and, in particular, senior officers of Bosnian descent.

The parodic intent was clear, but the times were not inclined to humour, or to people with a sense of it. A different kind of person had risen to the surface. As soon as the *Agenda* was published, Karadžić's party activists photocopied it in hundreds of thousands of sheets and distributed it to Serbs throughout Bosnia-Herzegovina, and in Serbia, Montenegro and Croatia as well, as an authentic document. The media controlled by Milošević, which means practically all the media in Serbia, and the Banja Luka *Javnost*, the paper of the SDS of Bosnia-Herzegovina, reprinted it, seriously analysed and discussed it, and referred to it as a key piece of evidence that annihilation was secretly being prepared for the Serbs, who must therefore close ranks around the SDS and defend themselves with all means at their disposal. In a number of fantastic and inaccurate reports about the situation in Bosnia-Herzegovina that Radovan Karadžić regularly sent to the Serbian leadership and higher echelons of the JNA in Belgrade there were standard propaganda chestnuts about repeats of the Ustasha massacres being got ready for the Serbs and the like. Space was very soon found for a report that the 'leadership of the Muslims had illegally founded a Ministry for the Immigration of Turks into Bosnia-Herzegovina.'[1]

This was an entirely recognisable replay of the *Vox* satire, but in the universally deafening warmongering, Vuk Drašković, leader of the extreme nationalist Serbian Revival Movement (SPO), at the All-Serb Assembly of 9 September 1990 in Novi Pazar, centre of the of the majority Muslim-populated province of Sandžak in Serbia, bordering on Bosnia, chose to refer to it even more directly. This great rally was announced as the Serbian response of self-defence to the creation of 'armed formations of Serbocides' in Croatia and 'Serbophobe headquarters' in Macedonia that were in alliance with the Albanians (he called them Arnauts, a derogatory term), and the 'Islamic fundamentalists' in Bosnia-Herzegovina and the 'de-Serbed Montenegrin renegades'. In front of 20,000 to 30,000 people, among whom there were a good many with Chetnik emblems, and with firearms not concealed from the eyes of the police, he told all Muslims in Yugoslavia that the SPO would 'at its own expense' put up signs pointing the way to Turkey and cut the arms off anyone 'carrying Asian and Ustasha flags over the Serbian land of Raška'. At the end he revealed to the mass, now quite beside itself, the dramatic news that he had 'just got hold of' a resolution from 'a secret meeting' of the SDA in Sarajevo at which it was decided that on 31 December the Islamic Republic of Bosnia-Herzegovina would be declared, under the rule of a Council of Beys in Travnik (*Svet,* 19 September 1990; *Vjesnik*, 11 September 1990).

However, there was no such conspiratorial resolution; rather it was one more product of the joking – and politically naïve – lads in *Vox*. In conjunction with the *Immigration Agenda* they had printed, in the form of a leaflet, a *Declaration of Independence of the Islamic Republic of Bosnia-Herzegovina (Deklaracija o nezavisnosti Islamske Republike BiH)*. One of its eight points, for example, was that the currency of the new republic was to be called *bukva,* or beech; *Vox* regularly printed its price not only in legal Yugoslav dinars but also in the fictitious *bukvas*. The joke was clear to anyone with half a brain: it referred to the proposal that the currency in Slovenia be called the *lipa*, linden, because this tree in Slovenia had the status of national symbol, and *bukva* would be the Bosnian equivalent. This irony, or self-deprecation, for the word *bukva* in the South Slav lands metaphorically

---

1. Karadžić's talk with JNA generals was bugged by the Bosnia-Herzegovina Counter Intelligence Service and published in the independent weekly *Slobodna Bosna*, 2, 4 November 1991.

means thickhead, and there are versions such as *bukvan*, blockhead, and the very common colloquial phrase 'thick as a *bukva*', implying someone rather slow, good-natured and harmless, a likeable fellow in fact, as well as a number of other phrases and proverbs. This widely known and basically benign folklore was referred to in Point 5 of the *Agenda*, which said that in the second wave of the return 'sylvan-minded Bosniaks would colonise the beech-forest rich Šekovići' – actually, an impoverished mountain commune in northern Bosnia.

There was also broad joking in the second point of the *Declaration* according to which in this kind of Bosnia the Serbs and Croats would be minorities and the 'constitutive' nations would be the 'fraternal Muslims and Bosniaks'. At precisely that time, just before the census, there were public debates concerning the ethnic name of that part of the republic's population: some were for keeping the religious name, Muslims, as stipulated in Yugoslav law, while others advocated the term Bosniak, which in the Ottoman period had a long tradition although not in any particularist sense, rather as a label for all the inhabitants of Bosnia regardless of religion. The ironic variation, then, of the long-term official Yugoslav ideological formulation of the 'fraternal nations' was aimed at the absurdity of these polemics within the Muslim/Bosniak elite, the more manifest at the time because there had been a dramatic rift between two leading politicians, Alija Izetbegović, who favoured the name Muslims, and the rich returnee from Switzerland Adil Zulfikarpašić, who even in exile had persistently promoted the term Bosniaks.

The formulation that the last communist prime minister of Bosnia-Herzegovina, Obrad Piljak, and the 'government in exile in London' were still forbidden to return to the country is also a parody of one of the key sentences of the political mythology of Tito's Yugoslavia. Of course there were no runaway Bosnian politicians in London, but as literally everyone who had been at least to elementary school in Yugoslavia knew, after the capitulation of the Kingdom of Yugoslavia in 1941, the king and government fled to London. This government had formal legitimacy in international law, but in the country, because he was leader of the anti-fascist resistance, real power was in the hands of Tito, and in time he started to demand political recognition from the western allies. For this purpose in 1943 the leadership of the anti-fascist movement, a kind of wartime parliament called AVNOJ, which included many non-communists, made a decision that King Peter and the 'government in exile in London' were forbidden to return to the country until the issue of legitimacy should be settled at elections, after the war.

Finally, the satire mentioned the introduction of a two-chamber parliament, in which one house would be the 'Chamber of Beys' in Travnik, as mentioned by the overexcited Vuk Drašković to his equally overexcited audience. He was not of course the only one to alarm his Serbian co-nationals by warning of perfidious and deadly plots. The same satirical, self-satirising *Declaration* was published as a facsimile at a carefully selected moment, just two days before the elections in Bosnia-Herzegovina by the Belgrade weekly *NIN* with banner headlines warning that this had to be 'taken seriously' because 'in Slovenia everything had started with the louts in *Mladina*' (*NIN*, 16 November 1990), i.e. with critical texts concerning the situation in Yugoslavia that had been published by the youth weekly *Mladina* in Ljubljana from the mid-eighties on.

This well-planned and by now unstoppably frenzied madness completely drowned out voices that pointed out that this was merely a piece of humorous and satirical writing.[1] That it could not possibly be a serious document, or a least that there was something fishy about it, was, after all, obvious at an entirely technical level: this number of *Vox* was printed in September 1990, while in the preamble to the *Immigration Agenda* it says that the Parliament of Bosnia-Herzegovina had 'voted it in on 15 September 1991'. It was, then, post-dated a whole year, but with time, this date too came and went: those who had previously believed continued to do so, and from then on the business of convincing people became at least in one way easier. More freely treated variations then appeared, more and more somnambulistic and increasingly unstoppable. The organised madness triumphed.

In January 1992 one SDS member of parliament said in the still joint Assembly of Bosnia-Herzegovina that he had learned 'from his own sources' that Izetbegović and German Chancellor Kohl had officially agreed that Turkish *gastarbeiters* in Germany – whom the Germans had tired of but who would not go home – would be settled in Bosnia-Herzegovina. And some ten days later in a Belgrade fortnightly the fascist Dragoš Kalajić announced that Turkey, in agreement with the USA, planned to send four million Turks to Bosnia-Herzegovina to create there 'the first *Jamahiriya* in Europe' (*Duga*, 1 February 1992). The *Agenda* was pulled out every time Serbian propaganda needed to stoke up the anti-Muslim mood: on the eve of Mladić's Goražde

1. There was an explanation in an independent Belgrade weekly, in the form of a letter to the editor, stating how and where the document had been created, and attention was drawn to the dangerous way it was being manipulated. As the author said 'with this kind of ongoing frame-up, they [Drašković and other Serb propaganda makers] are continuing with the dissemination of the psychosis of fear, deliberate persuasion, synchronised war-mongering propaganda'. Safet Bandžović, 'Vakat i obraz', *Vreme*, 179, 28 March 1994.

offensive, Belgrade's *Politika ekspres* of 15 March 1993 published as a sensation that it possessed 'a secret plan for settling four million Muslims in the territory of the former Yugoslavia'. At one time it was Turks involved, at another time 'just' Muslims, sometimes they were coming alone, at other times they were being brought in by the western states, but there were always the same terrifying four million – a mystical figure that long resounded in the ears and blocked out all possibility of thought, a number that blinded, that was nourished by its own energy.

The satire of these Sarajevan punks very quickly made it to the highest international level. To widespread consternation, in the spring of 1991 President Tuđman had a private meeting with Milošević in Karađorđevo, in Serbia, and a short while after that, on 15 April, in Tikveš, on Croatian territory. It has never been reliably confirmed what their talks were about. Milošević never volunteered, and Tuđman reported hazy phrases about having attempted to negotiate so as to avoid the war that was looming with increasing menace over Croatia, but there were indicators enough that the most important topic of their talks was the possible partition of Bosnia.

Tuđman returned from Tikveš to Zagreb by helicopter, together with his most trusted associate, Hrvoje Šarinić, head of the President's Office. At a certain moment, Tuđman took out a sheet of paper written in black ink, saying that it had been given him by Milošević. It stated that the Muslims were the greatest danger for peace in the region, and that caution was needed to prevent them linking up along what was called the 'green transversal' from Turkey to Bosnia, through the parts of Bulgaria and Macedonia inhabited by Muslims. The proof was that 'they had already placed a green flag on Romanija' (Šarinić 1999: 41–2).[1] Šarinić was not convinced of this, but Tuđman said: 'there must be something in it'.

One must ask whether the two presidents truly believed in the existence of such a plan. At one level, in Tikveš Tuđman was clearly the victim of a con-trick on Milošević's part, although he did not perhaps completely fall for it, at least not at once. But clearly his deep personal animosities towards Bosniaks and Islam in general, and his conviction that, unlike Croatia and Serbia, Bosnia was not an authentic and indigenous political and historical formation, prevented him from rejecting the text as a manifest fabrication. Milošević's case was clearer: he was a cold and rational manipulator, who knew what he was doing, and expertly manipulated the political naivety, megalomania and prejudices of his partner in the dialogue. It is interesting

---

1. Šarinić repeated this as a witness at the trial of Milošević at the ICTY on 21 January 2004. Cf. http://www.un.org/icty/transe54/040121ED.htm (pp. 31266–7).

that the text was written by hand, clearly written, then, by Milošević himself during their conversation, or as he prepared for it, by way of a memo. And when senior government leaders write by hand in such cases, they do it when it is something really important, presenting it in condensed bullet points, and noting only what is essential. From Milošević's point of view, it is clear that here the identification of the 'greatest danger to peace in the region' and the unmasking of the transcontinental strategic plan for making a land bridge among the Muslims fell within this category. These were, without any doubt, major, vitally important and far-reaching matters that every interlocutor had to be informed of, with all available proof presented.

But did a flag on a mountain in Bosnia really come into the category of relevant evidence and did it really have enough weight to be picked out from the mass of potentially far stronger proof, which there surely must have been if such a terrible international conspiracy really existed? For when invention is resorted to, then in principle there is no limit, and Milošević's presidential fountain pen might have been employed to write something hotter, with objectively greater gravity, such as spy tapes of secret political negotiations, confidential information about unannounced military exercises, data about suspect cash flows ... In objective reality, it would have been logical to expect any of these, but here we are not dealing with real, rather with symbolic reality. And in that, there is little, if anything, that has greater weight and greater suggestiveness than an ordinary green flag on a mountain that is far from being ordinary. And indeed it is irrelevant whether Milošević was being rational when he wrote the memo, knowing that he would impress his interlocutor who was weighed down with historicism and political myths, or whether perhaps he had simply fallen victim to the machine for the production of manipulation that he had himself set in motion: in his consciousness, too, the idea of the flag on Romanija resounded with infinite associations.

One way or another, we are once again on the lines and in the focus of our basic analysis.

Looked at theoretically the announcement from the *Immigration Agenda*, that 'the green flag would wave on the top of Romanija' is a suggestive model for shaping a Bosniak variation of the formulaic song, recoding the key locality. Because the satirical reworking contains all the essential elements of the ideal evocation: the name of the locality, the colour green, which is unambiguously identifiable as a symbol of the relevant religious identity, just as in Yugoslav Partisan songs red was universally recognised as symbol of that ideology and political agenda, and, finally, the obligatory stylistic lexeme *barjak*, that is, flag, standard or banner.

The languages in the central South Slav area have two words for the concept of flag: *zastava*, or flag, which is of ur-Slav origin, and exists in other Slav languages as well; and *barjak*, which derives from the Turkish *bayrak*, and came in with the Turkish conquests of the fifteenth century. The first word is an unemotional, associatively neutral, unmarked word that belongs to the standard language, while the other is clearly stylistically marked, has the ring of antiquity and tradition and markedly poetic, rather grand, connotations, that are derived from the fact that it is only used in the vernacular poetry of the Croats, the Serbs, Bosniaks and Montenegrins. Thus quite literally all the songs about Romanija, including those quoted hitherto, and the many that have not been, use this word *barjak*, sometimes translated here as *banner*. At the same time, since it is two-syllabled, it also determines the metrical structure of the line, and cannot actually be replaced by the three syllables of *zastava* – and so in all versions and pastiches and reworkings, from Ustasha to Chetnik songs, from Đodan's speech to Drašković's replies, from the *Vox* satire to Milošević's memo, there is nothing but *barjak*: this word is in most people's consciousness part and parcel of the line, which is unimaginable without it. Today in everyday talk, not only in the city but also in the country, *zastava* is the only word used, but when Romanija is to be sung of, ironically or seriously, there is no question: *barjak* has long been the word of choice.

How powerful such connotations can be is seen in a case not connected with the Romanija story. When in the autumn of 1990 there was a debate in the Croatian Parliament on the *Coat of Arms, Flag [zastava] and Anthem of the Republic of Croatia Bill*, the HDZ member Davor Aras, a former political prisoner and member of the hard-line nationalist wing of the party, asked for the word *zastava* to be replaced by *barjak*, which he claimed was 'an old Croatian term' (*Vjesnik*, 4 October 1990). As we have seen, *barjak* is not a Croatian word at all or, compared to the Old Slav *zastava*, even an 'old' word. However, Aras obviously perceived it as special and solemn, and hence appropriate to such an important and emotion-laden text as the law about the symbols of a state that was just coming into being. He was in error in his choice of categories, which could not possibly be philological. But he rightly saw what was really behind it all: not philological but psychological – or sociolinguistic – categories, associations and emotions, epic and solemn moods evoked by the word, connotations of the vanished world of the heroic epic, considered by every nationalist to be authentically traditional and the guardian of the national soul.

And thus the urban Sarajevo punks, many of them still teenagers, who certainly never used the word *barjak* in everyday speech, had felt quite intuitively that their parody had to use, not only the political reference but the precise lingustic reference, although their *Agenda* was not written in verse, and therefore there were no versification obstacles in the way of their using *zastava*. Yet there was a cultural and psychological obstacle, and one that was insurmountable. Choice of the wrong word for the same concept would have ruined the joke. As it was, by writing in prose that it was a *barjak* that was going to be waving on Romanija, they enabled the recipient – whether he or she belonged to the same or a different political worldview and cultural mainstream – spontaneously to construct an exemplary verse model of the message: *Navrh gore Romanije / zeleni se barjak vije*; *On top of Mt Romanija / the banner green is waving*.

This model appears as suggestion in a context that sets up a manifest relationship with the important constituents of the competing catalogue of symbols – here primarily Serbian – already familiar to the reader of this book: the place names Knežina and Sokolac, both of them on Romanija. The second line (*zeleni se barjak vije*), constructed here according to positive contextual and metrical premises, is confirmed more or less at the same time inside the same national discourse. The lines

> *The banner green is waving, long live the SDA*
> *Herceg-Bosna make merry, Alija is our leader*

were regularly sung and performed from audio cassettes over PA systems at SDA election rallies in the autumn of 1990 as a kind of party and indeed ethnic anthem (*Vjesnik*, 30 October 1990) and they cannot be denied some traditional resonance, for the Bosniak epic, just like the Christian one, was thoroughly naturally imbued with scenes in which the green banner waves over the ramparts of a captured city or when an army or a wedding party musters below it.[1]

Šime Đodan himself returned to the great polemic about quotations two years after the Peščenica meeting, when he was asked by the journalist Marko Barišić:

---

1. It is worth mentioning that in this context and in this period it was not unusual for Bosnian Muslims to use the term Herceg-Bosna. It occurred on the Croatian political scene at the end of the nineteenth century, as shorter and more practical than Bosnia and Herzegovina, with certain connotations of familiarity and affection, and regularly referred to the *whole* of the country. Thus it was spontaneously adopted in the Muslim milieu too. It began to acquire negative connotations, particularly for the Bosniaks, only during the war, at the end of 1992, when the extreme nationalist wing of the HDZ appropriated the name for the *part* of Bosnia and Herzegovina which they controlled and which they wanted to annex to Croatia.

341

'Finally, I must ask you about the banner on Romanija. What about it now?'

'The banner was on Romanija. Eighty Muslims joined the HDZ, they sent Stipe Mesić [then the secretary general of the party] their membership fees, bought a flag – and the banner is waving there now! The banner waved in Foča, and in Višegrad ... The Croatian banner will wave wherever there are Croats and wherever they are willing to sacrifice themselves for that banner. Because, today the banner has to wave in Sarajevo. [...] And Romanija is a mountain near Sarajevo. I said then that it would be five years before the Croatian banner waved on Romanija, but not a fortnight has passed, and it was already waving! (*Slobodni tjednik*, 106, 01 April 1992)

In this quotation 'banner' is used in the place where the speakers used *barjak*, and 'flag' where they used *zastava*, and the 8:1 ratio shows the extent to which the discourse is impregnated with epic associations and stylised under their influence. The speakers simply could not avoid it; if they changed the term, they would no longer be talking about what they were talking about. And it is no accident that the only Đodan use of the term 'flag' is associated with the trivial and emotionally neutral verb 'buy', that is, in a situation that does not exist in the epic culture, or one that is typical of profane and desacralised modernity, where everything, including the national symbols, are mass-produced for the market, and can quite normally be obtained in the appropriate shops for the appropriate sum of money. However, when it is to do with bearing the object, or dying for it, actions that the traditional culture experienced with great intensity, 'banner' is used instinctively, inevitably bringing with it the expressively marked verb 'wave' – *viti* – as in the songs. In other words, there can be a 'flag' anywhere, but on Romanija only a 'banner'.

Đodan repeated the same story a year and a half later, at the height of the Croat-Bosniak war, also responding to a direct question from a journalist, Tomislav Dujmović, which shows once again that the Peščenica declaration had remained deeply etched into the memory of the Croatian public. Whatever the concrete occasion, the topics and circumstances of the interview, an encounter with him simply could not end without the issue of the banner. While he had previously found some way of getting out of trouble and manoeuvring so as to prove that he was not ignoring the existence of the Bosniaks or the autonomy of their political will, this time he could conclude triumphantly:

'I want to say quite frankly that it wasn't Šime Đodan that raised the banner (*barjak*) aloft on Romanija, but that others did it at my bidding, and that it was actually our Muslim brethren.' (*Danas*, 49, 14 December 1993)

Clearly the story had taken an unexpected turn, but anyone who thought that Đodan had the fatal *Vox* satire in mind would be mistaken. At the same time as he gave the interview to the sensationalist *Slobodni tjednik* quoted a little earlier, and announced for the first time that some kind of Croatian flag really had been put on Romanija, another journalist, the war reporter Željko Garmaz, was interviewing, for another Croatian weekly, the very organiser and leader of the action, a personage very different from the student punks from Sarajevo.

His name was Vezir Muharemović and, as may be seen from the interview, he considered himself an ethnic Croat who was a Muslim by religion, and he championed political alliance and the closest possible links between Croatia and Bosnia-Herzegovina in the battle against Serbian aggression. In World War II, the Chetniks had slaughtered many members of his family. Hence his obvious warm feelings towards the Ustashas, whom he saw exclusively through this prism, as he did those who had defended Muslims against the massacres in the Drina valley. On the eve of the war he founded a Muslim-Croatian association called Drina, its task being to investigate Chetnik crimes in eastern Bosnia. He was one of the organisers of the big demonstrations in front of the Bosnia-Herzegovina Assembly (Parliament) in the late summer of 1991, requiring the JNA, which had just started the aggression against Croatia, to let draftees from Bosnia go home.

Muharemović was, he said, convinced from the beginning that the Yugoslav crisis could not end peacefully and that Milošević was going to attack Bosnia. He participated in arming and preparing Bosniaks for its defence and attended many of the party meetings on the eve of the first free elections. He became disillusioned with the SDA and the HDZ, of which he was initially a member, and joined the HSP, which resolutely urged the indivisibility of Bosnia and the collaboration of Croats and Bosniaks. On St George's Day [*Đurđevdan*] 1991 he organised a party meeting of the HSP in Goražde, as a counterweight to the alarming Serb congregations on Romanija, and the ritual at the cave of Starina Novak already described (see p. 279):

> Šešelj was on Romanija, and we were on the Drina at the same time. That had a very encouraging effect on the population – they could see they had not been left on their own and that someone was looking after them!

A year later, during the Serb offensive and the massacre of Bosniaks in eastern Bosnia, in March 1992, he took part in the defence of Goražde with a unit of his own. Still, what he was most proud of was another episode, and he was always pleased to talk about it, so the event can be precisely reconstructed:

> 'Vezir, you really do keep on about that detail from your bio to do with that banner on the Drina and on Romanija!'
> 'After Mr Đodan's speeches, I pondered for some time about writing to that gentleman, because as he talked about it, I decided to be active in that way as well. I even have photos. I waved that flag [*zastava*] about as freely as I wanted. They were different times, of course. I have to say that we unfurled the banner in Goražde, for the first time in forty-five years.'
> 'Which one?'
> 'Why, the Croatian one, of course ...' (*Nedjeljna Dalmacija*, 1092, 2 April 1992)

This interview had clearly been read by the journalist Jelena Lovrić, at that time one of the fiercest critics of the HDZ, particularly of its calculating and fickle Bosnian policy. President Tuđman had recently announced that for the sake of the common defence of Croatia and Bosnia-Herzegovina he would found a confederation, but her view was that there was no sincere and strong view about the political equality of the two attacked countries behind this, it was simply a manoeuvre through which Croatia could de facto suck in Bosnia and thus expand its territory. She concluded:

> True enough, in this case the border on the Drina works like that boast of Đodan's when he recently said that the banner (*barjak*) had after all been planted on Romanija. Some scouts or a party of trippers did have an unfurled Croatian flag (*zastava*) on this Bosnian mountain for a few hours. Of course, this was nothing but electioneering and manipulation (*Danas*, 536, 26 May 1992).

There is no doubt that the sequence of replies from the moment of the first evocation of *the Banner on the Mountain* motif can also be called manipulation, but this does not remotely exhaust the meanings of this great war of quotations, in various genres, with its series of participants with differing intentions and varied social and political backgrounds. Nor can the category of manipulation as a rational activity be used to explain the complex system by which a large number of vernacular traditions and expressive elements of the traditional epic culture became involved in the communication, afterwards themselves emitting their own independent meanings. Conscious manipulation can first of all be laid at Đodan's door, because he actually defended himself the whole time and endeavoured to find a coherent explanation for his bombastic Peščenica statement that later got completely out of control but could still never be separated from his person and his public activity, still less from the intense symbolic connotations that had for decades accumulated around the rhetorical figure.

This last episode with Muharemović's action is only additional confirmation. It is of no particular importance here that he did not take the Croatian flag to the very top of Romanija,[1] but only to the eastern edges of the highland area, near Goražde, because what was important was not a real but a symbolic reality.

The Croatian political imaginary and social tradition were chronically short of the figure of the symbolic hero-mountain-conqueror. But then it was finally supplied, through the action not of a symbolic person, but a real one, and it was irrelevant that he was entirely anonymous and objectively speaking politically unimportant. Muharemović expressly states that he was spurred to hang the flag – both as object and as term, i.e. 'banner', which is just as important – by 'those speeches of Mr Đodan's'. And Đodan accepted the authenticity of his act in relation to his own evocation of the motif, that is he accepted it as the embodiment of his verbal adumbration. The legitimation was thus total and mutual. In that world Muharemović and his group of fellow-countrymen were no trivial scouts or trippers, but epic heroes on a serious and important quest. In this world it was irrelevant that they held the flag there for just a few hours, because as soon as it was there, it stayed there forever – a mythical act is not measured in transient human hours.

Thus the implied couplet *On the top of Mt Romanija / the Croatian banner waves*, shaped at last on that foundation, can be considered in value terms equivalent to the other traditional texts, and Muharemović is equated, in terms of function and category, with the other figures of the epic tradition. After all, when they came into being the epic hero was initially a historical figure, who was then stylised through the process of the artistic

---

1. If he had tried to then, it is easy to see how he would have ended up at the top, and what the consequences would have been. In that case there would have been the premises for the creation of at least two authentic political myths with a realistic base: a Croatian, even a composite Croat-Bosniak, myth concerning a national hero who sacrificed himself, and a Serbian one, concerning the defence of the sacred national ground against a specific enemy. As it was, a tragicomic and sometimes farcical performance occurred, a battle for symbolic capital, in which some participants really could not, and some did not want to, differentiate reality from fiction.

transformation of reality and in line with the horizon of expectations of the social context. Consequently, it is irrelevant whether or not this mythic couplet was produced in historical reality, in the sense that someone sang it, for it is enough for it to exist as latency with backing in a falsifiable real event. From then on it was capable at any moment of being recognised as based on reality, and not the product of mere wishful thinking.

Thus completed, the evocation at last corresponds to the value principle. This means the relationship between message and value system of individual, group and society as a whole, that is, the system that directs and channels their behaviour, determines what is good and what is bad, creates the criteria for the desirable and the undesirable. These dominant values, behaviour norms or cultural standards are the unavoidable framework within which every propaganda effort must be located. Any message which departs from this framework, is in opposition to the contents that make up the 'referential value commitment', is condemned to failure from the outset (Šiber 1992: 29). An excellent example is precisely Đodan's own evocation of Romanija at Peščenica.

The Ustasha Jure Francetić, who, as the only genuine Croatian flag bearer on Romanija, needed no additional metaphorical treatment, was at that time considered by the great majority of the Croatian public ideologically, politically and above all ethically compromised, even for the most radical nationalist discourse, and if Đodan or anyone else was thinking of him, he could not possibly have said so explicitly out of political considerations, with respect to his local listeners, the Bosnian and the international audience. (Which, as we have seen, did not remotely impede just such a reception of the evocation among Serb recipients, or at least the encouragement of such a reception by Jovan Rašković. For him the evocation of the Croatian flag was extremely welcome so that he could at once accuse Croatian politics of being explicitly Ustasha and persuade the Romanija Serbs that they were once again in mortal danger.)

The Partisan and communist Josip Tito Broz was not very suitable either, although his conquest of the peak could well have been appropriately recoded, not only because of the considerable Croatian participation in the anti-fascist Partisan movement but also because of the manifest anti-Chetnik significance of his arrival on Romanija. And it was precisely thanks to him and the red banner (*crveni barjak*) he brought with him, that in 1942 the dissipation of the Romanija Partisan squad was halted, after its members had been increasingly frequently crossing over to Dangić's Chetniks. However, the radical nationalist discourse of the HDZ refused to perceive Tito as a Croat, or to acknowledge the Partisan movement as an integral part of Croatian political emancipation in the context of World War II, which it really was historically, irrespective of the later communist usurpation of power and the crimes that this army committed. Autistic anticommunism and political immaturity unambiguously called Tito a 'bad Croat', even a Croatian traitor. And, although the Chetniks had catastrophic defeats inflicted on them in the war by Partisans waving Tito's red flag, that flag was deprived of all political moral legitimacy, perceived as an anti-Croatian, indeed a Serbian flag.

The Bosniak Alija Đerzelez was the only possible candidate. This would not have been without precedent, because he was precisely the hero invoked by the writer Enver Čolaković in 1950, in his poem 'Đerzelez Ale', as the mythical liberator of Bosnia from the communist rulers. Like the already quoted Sarajevo tradition of Đerzelez and the Hrnjica brothers who slept on Mt Igman on the eve of the other war, so Čolaković, a Bosnian Muslim who considered himself a Croat and lived in Zagreb out of favour with the new government, presents his hero as a sleeping redeemer who at the crucial moment will awaken or be aroused. The poem was written at the beginning of the 1950s, when it could not have been imagined that another war would break out or that at the end of the sixties there would be a degree of political liberalisation, in which the Muslims would be emancipated as a political nation and Bosnia would become a federal unit.

The poem was published on the front page of the Zagreb Party of State Right (HSP) magazine. Its appearance, at a time quite different from that in which it was written, in the autumn of 1991, during the hardest weeks of the Greater Serbian aggression against Croatia and the concluding moments of the preparation for the assault against Bosnia-Herzegovina, gave it programmatic importance and prophetic drama:

> *Saddle the fastest steed,*
> *buckle the sharpest sabre*
> *speedily bid your mother adieu*
> *and move out, Đerzelez Ale.*
>
> *Shake the dust from your garb*
> *and brush your tousled hair*
> *from eyes long dead,*
> *rapidly ride out of the grave*
> *and strive for the life of Bosnia!*
> *Draw your mace and your sword*
> *And hurtle through dusty Bosnia*

and look, and do battle, Ale.[1]

But if in the contemporary war the true Đerzelez was not actually invoked, his and Hrnjica's symbolic equivalent was, a kind of champion, a previously anonymous HSP member from eastern Bosnia, a member of the same religious and ethnic community, whose act in the total communication context thus achieved epic nature and meaning. Đodan's discovery of this kind of *functional* Đerzelez at the same time deflected a political conflict with the Bosniak community, which would certainly have been provoked by the appropriation of the *real* Đerzelez. But it also avoided a conflict of principles of value within the speaker's (Đodan's) own community, the majority of whom did not share his view that the Bosniaks were actually Croats of the Islamic faith who had not yet realised this or did not want to admit it.

Therefore, after a long period of seeking and wandering, the Peščenica speaker finally found a figure that he could place at a site that was semantically empty, having been made so through political calculations. Thanks to the minor and not at all epic circumstance that the agile and determined Muharemović had been reading the Croatian papers at the time and learned of his suggestive rhetorical figure, the constructional error in the system was repaired. Urged more by intuition than rational political knowledge, he moved fast. After that the message was no longer compromised nor did it conflict with the value principle of Đodan's community in which nobody, whatever they might have thought of Francetić or Tito, could in principle have anything against a Bosnian Muslim counting himself a Croat and carrying the Croatian flag wherever he wanted in his own Bosnia, as long as he did so of his own free will.

So at last the time came when the Croatian public, which had insistently sought a rational explanation for a bombastic and politically dangerous statement, and also Vuk Drašković, who had asked in outrage who it was that was capable of coming with a Croatian flag onto a Serbian mountain, could finally be informed, with personal details, and with the precise date and precise account of the circumstances, of the Croatian hero who had performed the unimaginable: passed straight by the Serbian *haiduks* and placed the *barjak* on the mountain peak. There is no reason to doubt that Đodan personally felt a great sense of relief and satisfaction, but he clearly did not notice one very important thing: that for quite some time he had been addressing neither his Croatian critics nor his Serbian wartime adversaries, but exclusively himself.

---

1. *Ognjište*, II, 3, Zagreb, October 1991.

New Armageddon

At just the same time as Đodan and Muharemović were telling the Croatian public of events on the southeast slopes of Romanija, the symbolic focus of this mountain area shifted to the southwest. So far, the principal point had been Sokolac, where the series of speeches by Rašković and the Serbian political rituals had begun and from where, on the eve of the assault on Sarajevo, the Bosnian Metropolitan Nikolaj had been moved for safety. Henceforth it was to be Pale, located at the place where Romanija was already beginning to merge into Jahorina.

In this Sarajevo resort, at 900 metres, dating from as early as the time of Austro-Hungarian rule, the Sarajevo psychiatrist and ambitious poet Radovan Karadžić had built a second home in the mid-eighties, with the help of his good friend Momčilo Krajišnik, director of a civil engineering firm. And, since this job seems to have entailed embezzlement and theft, they both spent some time in remand prison in 1987. Afterwards, of course, they pronounced this proof that the Serbs in Bosnia were subjected to persecution. Now they set up their political and military headquarters at Pale, for unlike Sokolac, Pale was a stone's throw from Sarajevo.

Novak's Cave, the imaginative centre of the mountain, was more or less the central point between Rašković's Sokolac and Karadžić's Pale. The collapse of communism allowed the general public to learn about the Chetnik crime committed against the nuns of Pale, after half a century of enforced silence. Romanija 'had seen and known everything', Turks and *haiduks*, 'all kinds of armies, ferocious and bloody battles and forced marches', but that five-day sixty-five-kilometre progress of the five nuns along the snow-covered road 'below Novak's Cave' was something quite new: 'Romanija, in all its history, had not known the like', wrote a cleric who, as a boy, had been present at their tragic ending in Goražde and now asked himself bitterly, in a clearly identifiable allusion: 'Where is the vernacular poet now ready to fiddle in despair on his *gusle* a new song: "The Nuns Cross Romanija"?' (Baković 1991: 126).

Just before the war, the editors of Sarajevo Radio Television decided to replace the main titles which had been composed, in communist times, according to the musical motif of the song 'Tito Crosses Romanija' ('Ide Tito preko Romanije'). The Bosnian rock singer Goran Bregović composed a new motif at their request for the *frula* player Hamdija Salković, but the Serbian part of the editorial board found it 'a bit too Muslim'. Soon most of them had gone to Pale, and the tape was destroyed (*Nacional*, 11, 2 February 1996). For weeks, regular units of the JNA, together with Chetniks, had been coming into Bosnia-Herzegovina from Montenegro singing all the while: 'Sarajevo and your mosques / Romanija's lads will smash the lot' (*Duga*, 09 May 1992).

However, when in September 1991 Serbian volunteers from Pale went to make war on Croatia, they 'were not considered any kind of heroes by those who were left behind, and it even happened that the mother of one of these youngsters cursed the leader of the group in which her son had gone,' the Pale vicar Josip Baotić remarked afterwards. As late as March 1992, he was celebrating Catholic masses for the *conversion of the criminals* without anyone stopping him, saying openly that he was thinking of 'those who in Croatia had destroyed or seriously damaged many churches'. He was in for Pale the last time on 5 April, when the leadership of the Serbian Democratic Party (SDS) of Bosnia-Herzegovina, led by Radovan Karadžić, had already taken up quarters in the Hotel Panorama. The panic-stricken vicar described the situation when he reached Sarajevo: 'People, there is a watch up there, they don't let you go up on the hill, there are tanks and guns up there, they say there are a thousand officers from the JNA in Croatia,' but they all replied: 'Oh go on, you're making it all up' (*Dani*, 11, 28 March 1993).

In the afternoon of that same day, the JNA opened fire with heavy mortars on the police school at Vrace, and the next day Serb snipers shot at civilians in front of the Bosnia-Herzegovina Assembly building from the Holiday Inn while the JNA and Chetniks took over all communications around the town. Their plan to cut it off was frustrated by sections of the special police loyal to the authorities led by Dragan Vikić as well as by spontaneously formed and poorly armed civilian units. At the beginning of May the leader of one of these units, Bosna 84, a pre-war petty criminal and debt collector, Jusuf Prazina aka Juka, ceremonially smashed the sign with the name of the Romanija Cinema in the main Sarajevo street. 'No room for Romanija in Sarajevo any more. Now it's far off ... at Pale!' (Ivanković 1995: 23). Not long afterwards the name Imperial was officially restored to the cinema.

During these days a car drove round Pale with a powerful PA system from which 'Serbian traditional songs' rang out, 'particularly those accompanied by the *gusle*' (Vuksanović 1996: 30). Even earlier, when he had gone at the beginning of March to the JNA barracks at Lukavica at the other end of Sarajevo to see whether he could get the Serbian street barricades removed peacefully, the Bosnian Territorial Defence commander Hasan Efendić saw that the soldiers were spending a lot of time listening to *gusle* songs (*Dani*, 98, 20 March 1999). During the most ferocious Serbian shelling of Sarajevo during the first months of the war the voice of the Romanija *gusle* player

Kosta Plakalović rang out from powerful loudspeakers on the surrounding hills, singing his song about 'Francetić Jure' who 'nine and nine times more [...] garbed in black the mother of the nine Jugovićes'.[1] The following song was created at the time in the glory of revenge:

> *What's the thunder, what the lightning*
> *above the town of Sarajevo?*
> *These are Serbian avengers*
> *Ratko Mladić and the Chetniks.*
> (*Duga*, 533, 6 August 1994)

The evocation of Romanija in the Yugoslav (communist) discourse remained marginal in the whole transition period and disappeared at the beginning of the war, because the social and political premises for the existence of this discourse had been removed. Up to the beginning of the war, the Bosniak evocation, which had a traditional basis for development, had not developed as part of the political discourse, neither in the sense in which the Serbian evocation developed in a sophisticated and ongoing way, nor in the particular sense in which it appeared in public communication in Croatia. Even if it had appeared, as in the case of the *Vox* satire, it would probably have been incomplete, because it did not name a specific representative person as banner-bearer. (This could not, of course, be expected in the genre, because it did not wish to enter into the polemics of political discourse and contest it in its own categories and terms, rather it mocked and denied the point of all such discourse in principle.)

But the Bosniak public discourse clearly conveyed the consciousness of the representativeness of the locality: the journalist who wrote of the defence of Gradačac made the heroism of members of the AB-H metaphorical in his pronouncement that 'when the time came, they would ride off to Romanija' (Enes Arslanagić; *Ljiljan*, 18, 26 April 1993), from which it is easy to conclude that the mountain was perceived not only as a military centre for the adversary but also a symbolic one. The soldier Murat Šabanović, recuperating in Zagreb after being wounded, announced his departure for besieged Sarajevo in clearly symbolic words: 'I'm not afraid of them. I am coming right over Romanija', which the editor turned into a headline,

---

1. In the eighties Plakalović was one of the most active members of the Filip Višnjić *Gusle* Players' Society and took part in many tours. His most successful songs were 'Čiča [Slaviša Vajner's nickname] from Romanija' and 'Balkan Wars', and he was particularly appreciated for his exceptionally powerful voice (Radovanović and Lovrenski 1985: 39). He is the grey-haired *gusle* player singing on the meadow in Pawlikowski's film.

recognising the symbolic charge in the name (*Nedjeljna Dalmacija*, 1094, 16 April 1992).

In time, both military and patriotic songs were spontaneously created in which the description of new things took over completely the well-known motif and versification model of World War II with a concretely named hero – a liberator who carried the flag triumphantly. And at last and entirely logically the flag had a colour that represented his religious and ethnic community:

> *The banner green waves out,*
> *over the hills of Romanija*
> *it's carried by some youthful lads,*
> *Naser's band of volunteers.*[1]

As it goes on, it says that this invincible army, that gave 'its all for Alija' will liberate Foča, and Kladuša and so on. The person at its head was police special forces member Naser Orić, commander of the defence of Srebrenica, who for Bosniaks grew during the war into an authentic and charismatic hero. And since the road from besieged Srebrenica to surrounded Sarajevo really did go over Romanija, the song not only had a powerful symbolic connotation and readily identifiable reference to its predecessors in various armies but it could also be concretely situated in real geographical relations. It can be said that it brought a whole collective participant into the battle for symbolic capital, capital that had so far been missing from the Bosniaks' religious, ethnic and ideological repertoire during the twentieth century.

To this extent, then, the motif is more effective and diversely alive in Bosniak discourse than in Croatian, where no songs were created, because there was no basis for them, and where the motif appears exclusively in internal political communication in the formulation *Đodan versus the Rest*, and is exclusively connected with his name, with lasting ironic overtones, sometimes weaker and sometimes stronger.

That is, Đodan did not notice that he was not communicating with the Serbian community and political elite, but defending his metaphor, later understood as a statement of fact, inside his own Croatian public space, and that in this context no one required him to justify the statement, to legitimate it within the categories of traditional culture, as a symbolic substitute for reality, but rather in reality, i.e. in the context of the current military and political conditions.

---

1. I bought the cassette of martial songs without any indication of authorship or performer from a street seller in Sarajevo in 1999.

In Croatia the statement itself was taken quite literally, as the expression of illegitimate territorial claims and unfounded political ambitions, and it was always seen this way, and it did not actually hamper or limit Serbian symbolisation of the mountain. Nor is there any sign that it had any echoes among the Bosniaks. In short it was, and remained, an exclusively intra-Croat matter, and not even Đodan's *deus ex machina* in the shape of Vezir Muharemović was a message to the Serbs but primarily, if not solely, to political adversaries and competitors among the Croats. They, like Mladen Vilfan of the HSLS, never tired of reminding the 'standard-bearer (*barjaktar*) of Romanija' of the awkward fact that he had not long since been a very senior official of the Communist Party (*Nedjeljna Dalmacija*, 1275, 6 October 1995). Or like the satirical journalist Tanja Torbarina, who wondered, when the Romanija Serbs greeted the Russian battalion of UNPROFOR with delight, whether Đodan had gone to greet 'them with the Croatian banner (*barjak*). Having planted it in Zagreb' (*Globus*, 168, 25 February 1992).

The Osijek news journalist Helena Puljiz was the last person to ask Šime Đodan, who had even served as Minister of Defence some time in the summer of 1991, about 'all that shouting about banners waving on Romanija'. He reminded her at once that the statement was not unfounded at that time. First of all, since the police of Bosnia-Herzegovina had arrested and 'beaten the daylights out of' some youths in Herzegovina because they had been carrying the historic Croatian flag, he had wanted to convey the message that Bosnia-Herzegovina was not the 'backyard of the Greater Serbian secret police, but that it was also Croatian land, and that the Croatian banner would wave over the whole land of Bosnia-Herzegovina, including on the peak of Mt Romanija'. Secondly, he repeated the already well-known and quite accurate story that, inspired by his speech, 'a group of Muslims, some forty of them, I think' really had unfurled the Croatian flag on Romanija and that, accordingly, his statement had some basis in reality.

But new conditions, above all the Washington Agreement between the Croats and Bosniaks, the revival of the alliance of the HVO and AB-H and its first concrete result: the joint liberation of the Kupres plateau – all this enabled Đodan to interpret his ancient image for the first time in the context of a realistic constellation of forces at the front. In other words, to break free of his dependence on polysemic and shifting elusive symbols and a more or less anonymous person, Vezir Muharemović, and give everything a far more serious dimension that it was possible to define rationally:

> This is not now impossible. [...] Now the army of the Republic
> of Bosnia-Herzegovina is within reach of Pale. Romanija is no

longer a problem, because in spring the forces of the AB-H will probably break out onto the Drina and the Sava, the AB-H is suddenly getting stronger, and the Croatian army, the HVO is very strong. Accordingly, a banner on Romanija is not out of the question. (*Glas Slavonije*, 20 March 1995)

From this new perspective, bringing the Flag onto the Mountain is no longer the isolated action of a single local politician, a caprice, spurred on by someone else's idea, but the logical consequence of far broader and deeper processes in which whole armies were taking part. If it had not been for Đodan's statement at Peščenica, it is very possible that Muharemović would not have had the idea of carrying a flag up Romanija, and no one would have been concerned. If two armies of liberation now brought this flag up onto Romanija, then it would be a matter of different categories: it would be the legitimate act of a state establishing its lawful authority over part of its territory. And this was no game any more – legal armies of recognised states were doing it or not doing it, according to logic and law which was no longer dependent on what kind of rhetorical figure might be used by some exalted speaker at a political meeting.

But since Đodan nevertheless did use this figure of speech, it now needs to be understood in a new light: he said what he said not as a quirky politician or, heaven forbid, a provocateur, but more as a visionary who had foreseen events years in advance. With this to sustain him, at least in his own eyes, Đodan soon retired, and then the Croats left him in peace. Drašković and Rašković had already said everything there was to say from the Serbian side and there was nothing that needed any response.

From the outset, Serbian discourse had a far superior command of the Romanija motif. It was capable not only of activating it for its own propaganda but of making use of all the shortfalls in the competing discourses, whether brought about by external or internal reasons. It was, of course, this discourse that controlled the motif, adapted it to new conditions and was able to emphasise it in the appropriate way. At the same time, this national discourse was the only one to establish a direct relationship with the way the Romanija myth had been handled in Yugoslav discourse, partly absorbing and partly exploding this level. For example, Vesna Mališić's report about the election campaign in Bosnia-Herzegovina – where at the party meetings of the reformed communists, the new Social Democratic Party of Bosnia Herzegovina, they carried Tito's picture and, when the party leader Nijaz Duraković appeared, they chanted *We are Tito's, Tito's Ours* – was headlined in a Belgrade nationalist magazine with the recognisably parodic: 'Nijaz moves across Romanija (*Ide Nijaz preko Romanije*)' (*Duga*, 435, 26 October 1990).

On 20 February 1994, a Sunday afternoon, some twelve hours before the deadline for the NATO ultimatum to the Bosnian Serbs to move their artillery twenty kilometres away from the Sarajevo battlefield, the Russian battalion of UNPROFOR arrived in Pale and was greeted with vociferous enthusiasm, with a real popular celebration and acts of ritual hospitality: the men gave the soldiers in their APCs bottles of brandy after having taken a nip themselves, a traditional sign of sincere welcome, the women carried bread and salt on platters, also an ancient Slav way of honouring a valued and honoured guest, preserved in Russian vernacular culture, while on a clearing oxen were roasting on spits. The local Serb population, that is, did not see in these soldiers so much international peacekeeping forces under the blue UN flag, rather members of the 'fraternal Russian people', and of the Russian Orthodox Church, with which the Serbs were tied by strong emotional and historical bonds. In a mood of revived nineteenth-century ideas about Slav togetherness and mythologemes about a Muscovite Third Rome, they were the saviours from 'Western menaces' and a report on local Serbian TV began with a triumphant motto: 'The Russians move across Romanija (*Idu Rusi preko Romanije*)' (*Vreme*, 175, 28 February 1994). This was not mere parody, but the final act of annulment of the Yugoslav aspect of the Romanija myth. While the system of governance that Tito had built was still strong, there would have been no chance of the lines concerning his mythical crossing of Romanija being parodied in public discourse, with someone else's name instead of his. The advent of Russians on the holy mountain of Serbianness must have driven Tito's Partisans from it forever, and made it a kind of Armageddon of the global confrontation of civilisations.

With time, it was to acquire one more global dimension. Some on the Serbian right, intellectuals such as the novelist Milorad Pavić, the association called Nova Vizantija (New Byzantium) and the protagonists of official politics developed the concept that Serbia, or the Federal Republic of Yugoslavia, was the 'legitimate heir of Byzantium' as the writer Milovan Vitezović (SPS) put it in a parliamentary debate to vote in the Coat of Arms Law (*Republika*, 79, 1 November 1993). The painter Milić of Mačva, a kind of official state philosopher in Republika Srpska and a regular guest at important assemblies organised by the SDS, was quick to incorporate Romanija into this somnambulist conception as the place where time could be brought full circle. Unlike America, which through the Bosniaks and the Albanians was aiming at restoring the Ottoman Empire, and the Vatican, which manipulated the Croats and dreamed that the Russians and Balkan

Orthodox nations would be converted to Catholicism, he advised that by 'accelerated actions', without waiting for Serbia itself to mature, the New Byzantium should be created at least in the area of Republika Srpska and Republika Srpska Krajina. The alleged heir to the Byzantine crown, Prince Peter III Palaeologus, direct heir of the last Emperor, Constantine XI, living in Italy, 'was preparing to visit Pale and to lay the foundations of a Byzantine Empire'. And soon afterwards, he concluded, 'I see the army of Mladić under the walls of Constantinople'.[1]

So, in one aspect at least, the myth of Romanija sank into a thick fog of historical mysticism and fantastic pseudo-political constructions, but there is no need to doubt that such fables made a powerful impression at least on some of the initiated, enhancing in their minds a sense of providential election, invulnerability and superiority.

The lame wolf

> On a winter evening, by the blazing fire, when I had only just learned my letters, Granny Milica, my father's mother, told me quietly, as if she were seeing a vision, the tale of the terrible Romanija wolf Mrkonja, who laid waste to a dozen sheepfolds in Glasinac. [...]
>
> 'When at last he came to the end, when they caught him in a trap, Mrkonja bit off his own leg with those same teeth to free himself.'
>
> 'That's terrible,' I shuddered, appalled.
>
> 'That's strength, my son.'

(Lubarda 1993: 116–17)

The wolf is particularly connected with Europe, and is an animal that since the Neolithic age has undergone complex and manifold symbolisation: from the most familiar, that the founders of ancient Rome, Romulus and Remus, were in fact sons of the wolf-god, to the wartime initiation rituals in which the wolf has a central role, for it links the secular and the divine. In pre-Christian Greek, Roman, German and Gallic beliefs the deity of the lower world is first of all imagined in the form of a wolf. In many nations the wolf is analogous to the warrior because of its strength and ferocity in battle. In vernacular constructions of the European Middle Ages warlocks most often appeared in the shape of wolves, and witches wore garters of wolf skin.

One of the standard epithets for the *haiduk* is *mrk*, or gloomy-grey, or perhaps dun, just as it is for the wolf, with which poetry frequently and gladly

---

1. Milić of Mačva, 'Satana u košu', *Javnost*, 227/228, 5 August 1995. The painter argued this idea in several accounts in this and other papers. On the alleged prince and talks of his arrival, see T. Burzanović, 'Rađanje nove Vizantije', *Javnost*, 223, 1 July 1995.

compares the *haiduk*. Few poems on the *haiduk* theme can pass by the chance of this comparison or indeed the rhyme *vuci/hajduci* – wolves/*haiduks*. The typical image is a mountain or spring in the woods that is 'never alone/ without either a wolf or a *haiduk*'. It exists in all the songs and poems on the theme, old and new, and as poetic image and poetic resource it additionally deepens the identification of the former and the current warrior when it is present in new verse, in a new, easily recognisable version from World War II:

> *Clouds stream along the sky,*
> *Red banners over Romanija.*
> *Romanija, you're never alone,*
> *Without a wolf or a partisan.*
> (Orahovac 1971: 102)

In the war half a century later, in the Army of Republika Srpska there were plenty of units with names such as: the Drina Wolves (*Vukovi s Drine*), who sacked Višegrad under the leadership of the Obrenovac licensee Milan Lukić; the White Wolves (*Beli vukovi*) on Jahorina and around Kalinovik; the paramilitary Grey Wolves (*Sivi vukovi*) from Serbia, who were found in Bosanska Posavina. The best known among them, Vučjak Wolves (*Vukovi s Vučjaka*), Vučjak being *Wolf Mountain* in northwest Bosnia, was founded on 2 July by the local smuggler and trader Veljko Milanković. First of all they robbed and terrorised the Bosniak population in Prnjavor and its surroundings, and then joined the JNA in the attack on Croatia, and looted western Slavonia, in the area between Jasenovac and Okučani. When a Sarajevo paper wrote of them, their actions were defined as the usual 'highway robbery', 'Bosnian Krajina "*haidukery*"' as carried out by 'Veljko and the three and thirty *haiduks*' (*Slobodna Bosna*, 18 November 1991).

By contrast, the reporter of a Belgrade fortnightly at once took pains to point out that it was not for nothing that Milanković had the 'old *haiduk* name' of Veljko, which had a direct association with one of the best known *haiduks* in Serbia, who joined the insurrection against Ottoman rule in 1804 and became a figure in many heroic songs. Milanković, the reporter went on, was born on Mt Vučjak, where 'people who communicate with wolves live' and who often call their first-born by 'wolf or *haiduk* names'. It is believed that children 'born at the crack of dawn in winter, while the wolves howl from the snowy heights of Vučjak, are gifted with particular strength and pride' and 'everything there has something wolfish in it' (*Duga*, 24 October 1992, after Čolović 1993: 129–130). The cult of the *Vučjak Wolves* had a certain religious aura in Republika Srpska as well, because they crossed the

Sava River into Croatia on Orthodox Assumption Day, 28 August 1991, celebrated every year as part of the fete in the village of Mlaka near Okučani (*Glas srpski*, 30 August 1994), on occupied Croatian territory.

The Republika Srpska Army Major Tihomir Janjić is described as a mythical warrior fighting against 'tyrannical violence (*zulüm*)' and it was said that it was no accident that he was born in a marked, numinous place, in eastern Herzegovina, in the 'hawks' nest', where the place names themselves – Mt Vukodlačica (Wolf Fur) and Vučja Bara (Wolf Pond) preserve memories of 'ancient times, which are like those of today, that in the area near Nevesinje *haiduk*s and heroes live' (Tihomir Burzanović; *Javnost*, 218/219, 3 June1995).

As in many other things, Romanija is in the forefront in this symbolic aspect of Serbian political discourse. Here it is not just the people but also the wolves that are different, as in Lubarda's recollection of childhood quoted at the beginning of this section. What is more, in the referential framework it undergoes as it were a genuine semantic explosion in which all the relevant motifs from various different imaginative currents meet and merge. At the end of the summer of 1994 one of the most productive contributors to the Serbian wartime political imaginary came to Romanija, after visiting the battlefields at Vinkovci, Dubrovnik and Bihać, and there, of course, he found a fearless 'nation from the traditional tale, this people from the mountains' who rejected with contempt the Contact Group's peace plan, preferring to die rather than 'accept any *ferman* [decree] of the Sultan'.[1] This spirit of the mountain and of its inhabitants would never be understood (at least not in the way they were by Rebecca West) by foreign journalists, 'those fat-arsed big-headed gents with their pagers' who 'burped at receptions' and mooched around 'Pale, where Starina Novak once shared his supper with the wolves', trying to find out why the Serbs knew no fear.

Somewhat later, in a hut on 'Ravna Romanija, where Starina Novak had once shared his supper with the lame wolf', there was a conversation in which the hosts attempted in vain to explain to these foreign journalists where they were and what was really going on in this place. Afterwards they split up: 'We are going along Ravna Romanija. The wolf-team is pulling us'. The unnamed narrator, 'he from whose hands the wolves breakfast on Mt Trebević', told an amazed London journalist that 'the English had Excalibur and the Serbs had the sword of Starina Novak'. The journalist asked where the sword could be found, and was given this explanation:

---

1. Nebojša Jevrić, 'Gde je zakopan srpski Ekskalibur [Where is the Serbian Excalibur buried?]', *Duga*, 536, 17 September 1994.

'There are three peaks on Romanija,' he was told by the one who is now called Novak on Romanija (Romanija has never been without its Novak). 'Once in a hundred years, it happens that the shadows of the three peaks, of which one is to the west, a second to the north and the third to the east, will touch. Whoever is at that place has to light a fire. And spend the night by the fire. In the morning he has to kill the animal whose tracks he will see in the ash, and spatter the ashes with its blood. And then he must start to dig. There he shall find the buried sword of Novak from Romanija. If this is not how it is done, the sword will turn into cinders. If he does do it, at a depth the same as his own height, he will find the sword of Novak of Romanija, with which he defeated all his adversaries.'

When the *Daily Telegraph* reporter Michael Montgomery asked whether anyone had ever experienced this, the narrator, 'he whom on Romanija they call Novak (Romanija has never been without a Novak)', which is a repetition of recognisable allusions to Radovan Karadžić, replies that it was precisely he. He did everything the way it is laid down in the tradition, ready in the morning to kill the creature whose trace he should find in the ash:

> 'And in the morning, in the morning, my dear sir, I found the print of my own foot in the ash. Such is our fate, dear sir from the *Daily Telegraph*. Only those who have drenched Romanija in their own blood can find the Serbian Excalibur.'

This interweaves motifs from the Old French legend of King Arthur, typical situations from the *haiduk* songs and syncretic legends of St Sava, the founder of the autocephalic Serbian Orthodox Church in the thirteenth century, and the universal motif of hidden treasure buried at a depth equivalent to the height of the one who digs.

The sword is a concept unknown in *haiduk* songs, for *haiduks* do not have them. They fight with the sabre or the Turkish *yatağan*, the long curved knife. Nevertheless, it is a universal symbol of the soldier's calling and the virtues that accompany this vocation – fearlessness and strength. In Christian traditions the sword is a noble weapon, belonging to knights and heroes, and is often given a name in the heroic lays, where the swords of the most renowned heroes have names, an indication of the personalisation of the weapon. The name Excalibur, together with the motif of the sword that brings the chosen one the power to rule and invincibility, is adopted from the legends of King

Arthur and the Knights of the Round Table. This is the name of the vast sword meant for the one who is the true king of the whole of England. The sword was stuck in an anvil from which it had to be extracted, which feat many great men and knights attempted, but which only the fifteen-year-old Arthur could perform. The young man who had not hitherto known of his noble origin because he had been taken from his mother at birth was thus recognised as the chosen one and crowned, becoming a great conqueror and victor over many armies.

As this enigmatic narrator rhythmically repeats, this new Novak on Romanija, with his company, 'drinks the ruddy wine in secret (*pije rujno vino u potaji*)'. This is a quotation from 'Old Vujadin' ('Stari Vujadin'), one of the best-known *haiduk* songs, included in all the relevant anthologies, Yugoslav textbooks and readers. In the song, the Ottomans had managed to capture a group of *haiduks* and their leader, the eponymous hero, knew what awaited them, and told his sons to endure all the Turkish torments, and not to betray their *yataks*, harbourers, or the band, or 'the tavern girl young / with whom we drank the ruddy wine / the ruddy wine in secret'. This universally familiar image takes us into the second semantic circle of this important and clearly very subtly composed piece of propaganda in the form of a report. It has associations with the important councils held by legendary heroes on the eve of crucial battles, including the association with the recently introduced evocation of the councils of Arthur and his knights, as well as one aspect of Starina Novak and his band that is not so incompatible with the Old French–English legend as might at first glance seem the case.

Although the songs about Novaks range typologically in the framework of the usual epic themes, there is one in which an enemy comes to 'the Novak mountain, the court of Novak (*Novakov dvor*)', and in it Novak and the band are not shown as *haiduks*, rather as the rulers of the land (Radenković 1988: 225). Through the thick layers of Jevrić's report it is precisely such a Novak that can be seen: on the one hand he is a ruler like King Arthur, on the other he is protean, metamorphic and elusive, always embodied in someone or other, for 'Romanija is never without a Novak', as is suggestively repeated. And the sword is not incompatible with such a Novak: when he finds it, he has the right to carry it, not only as warrior's weapon, but as emblem of ruler, a means by which peace and justice are established and maintained.

At the third level, through the image of the 'wolf team' and the 'lame wolf', the secret Romanija Novak is revealed as the very founder of the nation – St Sava. The pre-Christian Indo-European wolf was, as ruler of the lower world, lame in one leg, and kept this characteristic even after anthropomorphisation.

Lameness is also a mark of being chosen, the one who embodies the ancestor of the clan and has supernatural power. According to old vernacular beliefs, St Sava was *the patron saint of the wolves,* or the *wolf shepherd,* which means that in Serbian pre-Christian beliefs there was a wolf god whose functions were later transferred to Sava. In the Serbian tradition wolves are his constant companions, his hounds and his comrades (Čajkanović 1941). Even more concretely, in Jevrić's image that on Romanija Starina Novak 'shared supper with the lame wolf' it is possible to retrieve a legend widespread in many Serbian lands – an ancient one, known in other Slavonic nations as well as among the Estonians and Latvians – concerning St Sava who on his own day called all the wolves on the mountain and assigned them food for the next year, that is, sent them to various folds, and told them what to slaughter and devour. At Christmas time he would leave the wolf supper at the crossroad. By association with the lame wolf, Starina Novak, or he who embodied him on Romanija, became equivalent to St Sava in his aspect of progenitor who looked after his nation as a good shepherd his flock (Čajkanović 1941; Matić 1972: 58–95; Kulišić et al. 1970).

Whoever may be concealed behind the mysterious Romanija Novak, whether it is Radovan Karadžić or someone else, this *haiduk* mountain now rose one more degree in its transformation into the numinous space of national revelation, in its growth into a cosmogonic point from which a new time was to begin, a new, corrected history.

ELEVEN

At the Core of the Epic Map

All the Drobnjak clan chiefs were waiting at the Drobnjak borders for the Lord [the Montenegrin prince, Nikola, on the occasion of his progress to the tribes annexed in 1858/59] to escort him through the clan. The people gathered in suitable assigned places, especially where breakfast, lunch and tea had been set. As one passed through the villages of Pridvorica and Petnica, where the father of the famed Vuk Karadžić, Stevan, had been born, a large cavern could be seen in the hill. Some of the Drobnjak clansmen used to hide in it when the Turks campaigned against them, which was quite often. Thus Milovan Mimović Karadžić with 15 of his selected comrades shut themselves up in it during the Turko-Montenegrin War of 1852/3. But in the end they had to surrender to the enemy.

(Dučić 1893: 331)

Radovan Karadžić – the leader as sign

In extreme Serbian nationalist circles, there was increasing dissatisfaction with the policies of Slobodan Milošević, who was accused of having passed up the chance of achieving a final and total military victory in Croatia and Bosnia-Herzegovina in 1991–2, and also of having remained, in ideology and mentality, a diehard communist, who had never fully understood national aspirations and traditions, or the 'genuine Serbian soul'.

The greater this dissatisfaction was, the more rapidly and vigorously Romanija was transformed into a symbol of genuine Serbianness, which was no longer only in conflict with the external enemy, but also with the traitors within, with the 'bad Serbs' or 'second-rate Serbs' in Belgrade, and in this political discourse this very same city, until so recently adored and idealised as the 'capital of all the Serbs', was turned into an amoral swamp, a source of lurking danger and a place where genuine patriarchal virility rotted without redemption, just like Dubrovnik and Sarajevo. 'Here, in the forest [on Romanija], I can yell out loud as far as my throat will carry my voice. I can be absolutely at liberty, while people in the middle of Belgrade simply cannot be,' announced the prose writer and minister of information in the government of Republika Srpska Miroslav Toholj (*Telegraf* according to *Republika*, 103, 1 November 1994). 'The artillery from Romanija resounds in Serbia and shakes it to the core,' wrote a poet and president of the Association of Serbs from Bosnia-Herzegovina (Udruženje Srba iz BiH) in the anniversary number of the Serbian daily paper, with the message that the differences of the two political leaderships, that on Romanija and that in Belgrade, must not be allowed to become differences between 'the Serbian East and the Serbian West' (Gojko Đogo, *Oslobođenje*, 6 January 1995).

Radovan Karadžić himself, in the extensive and programmatic interview already mentioned, pointed out that the archetypal historical situation had turned upside down, suggesting in a familiar way that he was aware of the role he was to play in the new relationships:

> Fate would have it that the centre of events and convulsions and also of the revival of the Serbian people should move here to us. Once upon a time it was in Serbia, once in Montenegro, once in Kosovo, once upon a time in Vojvodina. It moves, but it is in the same body, and the part of the body in which the centre now lies is Republika Srpska and Republika Srpska Krajina [...] Once I [...] said that it was probably not meant to be that the Drina should be crossed from the right to the left bank [from Serbia to Bosnia]. This was tried before Karađorđe, and by Karađorđe, and after Karađorđe. It is clear that the Drina could be crossed only from the left to the right bank.[1]

The vernacular poet also recognised the situation in the same way, from his own point of view, of course, and in his own rural phraseology and poetics. According to him, Milošević was a traitor and a 'ram' who would sell out and sacrifice all the Serbs to the west of the Drina, just to curry favour with the world and the rich politicians of the west. But this treacherous and perfidious intention was frustrated by an insurmountable obstacle:

> *All would be easy were there not in Bosnia*
> *The giant figures in the heart of Romanija;*
> *Standing at the defence of Serbian honour*
> *'After the war, they'll come into power'.*

---

1. Dragan Stamenković, 'Vaskrsenje šćućurene duše', *Svetigora*, 35/36, March 1995.

[...]
The ram must vanish as soon as may be
While still the sun from Romanija warms.[1]

Milošević's Belgrade, which at the beginning of the war was definitely seen as the incontrovertible centre of Serbianism, was gradually acquiring the negative features that in the epic social consciousness usually belong to the inimical Muslim and Catholic cities. By contrast, the symbolic significance not only of Romanija but also of Pale itself rose until it could be stated explicitly that it was Pale that had become 'the current Serbian Cetinje – the capital of the Serbian struggle for continued existence and a united state', for peace 'in which [the Serbs] are not to become the *rayah* of the newly mobilised *Bosancheros*, the agas and beys, who'll be served by the *subaşis* and *başas* [Janissary soldiers]' (Momir Vojvodić, *Javnost*, 218/219, 3 June 1995).[2]

This new mythic capital, this *Non-Belgrade* or *Anti-Belgrade*, is ruled by a person in whom all that is most authentic in national history is embodied and condensed, a person, then, just as Milošević had been judged to be at the end of the 1980s. Here, as notorious Nebojša Jevrić suggestively repeated, is 'he whom now on Romanija they call Novak (Romanija has never been without a Novak)', this new insurrectionary leader, the 'big fella, Karadžić – the trans-Drina Karađorđe' (Milić od Mačve, *Javnost*, 211, 8 April 1995), and, indeed, a new Njegoš, a priest, a statesman and national poet all rolled into one. And so the old Montenegrin highlander expected Radovan Karadžić, who was already both statesman and poet, to be sworn in as prince-bishop in Bosnia, as a new Njegoš, for there 'he was driving the Turks hither and yon (*razgoni Turke na buljuke*)' and 'finishing off what neither [Montenegrin king] Nikola nor [Serbian and then Yugoslav king] Alexander had finished, the business

---

1. Dragan M. Gavrilović, 'Azman', *Glas Srba* (Vienna), 153, 1 September 1995. after *Vreme International*, 255, 11 September 1995.

2. *Bosancheros* (*Bosančerosi*) is a sneer aimed at Bosnians, independently of their ethnicity, which suddenly spread round Yugoslavia in the mid-1960s as a reworking of the title of the popular Michael Curtiz movie *The Comancheros* (1961). The film tells of a large group of outlaws that existed in the 1830s in West Texas, around the Comanche Indians, trading with them and raiding on both sides of the border. That despicable bunch, made up of Mexicans, Spaniards, Indians, blacks and gringos of various ethnic origin, was 'trusted by none and loved by few', as the publicity had it. An associative link was spontaneously created in the popular mind between their 'multi-ethnic multiculturalism' and Bosnia, together with the stereotype that Bosnians were slovenly and unreliable, and this was confirmed in the newly-minted slang expression. However, this journalist was obviously restricting its meaning only to the Bosnian Muslims.

of Karađorđe and Njegoš. The extirpation of the Turkish converts, *istraga poturica*' (*Duga*, 1612, 1 April 1995).

Here, at Pale, in one and the same person, at last there ruled a scion of the 'house of Karadžić' who was an 'heir of the [royal] Nemanjić' line. Thus, after the mythic *haiduk* who under Ottoman rule had preserved the memory of former greatness and the spirit of resistance, after the leader of the insurrection from which, at least in part of the ethnic territory, a contemporary nation state had arisen, and after the prince-bishop who had understood that the presence of potentially disloyal inhabitants of another faith could be settled only by a radical act, by extirpation, here is a fourth, with whom the mythic series naturally concludes: the reviver of the one-time state in all its power, greatness, glory and – last but not least – religious homogeneity, the utopia of harmony and unity that was devastated by the fatal battle of Kosovo Field.

This is precisely the way Radovan Karadžić was hailed, as heir to the medieval Nemanjić dynasty and founder of a new ruling house, by the popular vernacular poet and *gusle* player whose formulations always precisely anticipated events or interpreted them in the right key, and who this time too must be believed to have known what he was talking about. This was the most distinguished of the Vasojević *gusle* players, Božidar Đukić, whom we met at the beginning as a most important participant in the Masters of the *Gusle* tour of the end of 1986, with which a great many things in Bosnia-Herzegovina began, and also as the author and performer of the 'Tragic Death of Branka Đukić' and 'Extinguished Hearths of Kosovo', epics that started a very great deal in Kosovo as well. Once again, his epic vision of reality is crystal-clear, and its messages are extremely cogent:

> *Novak cries from out his cave,*
> *And begs from Grujica Child,*
> *On, Grujo, tell Radovan*
> *The Turkish truce invalid,*
> *While male heads on shoulders sit,*
> *Only by the musket can we deal with the Turks.*
> (Zagorac 1996: 112)

The idea voiced by the old peasant from the former Montenegro-Herzegovina border about Radovan Karadžić as a new Prince-Bishop Njegoš, and the idea that the experienced *gusle* player built up about Nemanjić-Karadžić continuity were not merely general phrases drawn from the depths of the epic and narrative heritage, just as they were not merely an echo of well-worked propaganda or a mere mechanical conjoining of the relevant points of the national imaginary and its pantheon. They derive from the strong internal logic of the overall imaginary and the category of epic reality, and however strange it might sound, they are not without support in the real biography of Radovan Karadžić. The existence of such support is, after all, the basic condition for appropriate ideas to be able to come genuinely alive and be effective as communication. The political myth is never a total invention, but rests upon at least a modicum of facts that it then highlights and interprets in the mythic manner. Its core is not inaccurate, it is just placed under special lighting, and coincidences or formal similarities are given the meaning of deep historical logic and strong structural and substantial connections.

Karadžić was born on 19 June 1945 in the village of Petnica (or Petnjica) below Mt Durmitor, in Drobnjak country, which was the origin of the already mentioned famed *gusle* player of the Balkan Wars, Tanasije Vućić. We have considered the importance and systematisation of the support already shown for the reference system within which the symbolic legitimation of the Greater Serbian campaign against Croatia and Bosnia-Herzegovina were built. And we have seen the motivational system of *haiduk* revenge and the struggle *for golden freedom and the honoured cross (za krst časni i slobodu zlatnu)*. In that context, it is no exaggeration to say that precisely this point, this detail reveals the very core of the mythopoeic fable concerning the symbolic life of a boy from a poor family who started off in life looking after goats, sheep and lambs:

> Little Radovan was a shepherd to a little flock, big Radovan became, several decades later, a big shepherd to another, big flock (Zagorac 1996: 27).

It is not this comparison alone, but the overall manner of his birth that evokes biblical images and a Christological set of motifs, presenting him as a long-awaited and finally arrived Messiah. The future president of Republika Srpska was born in a setting like that of Bethlehem, literally 'in a scene like that from the Bible: like Jesus's coming into the world', in a humble stable on Durmitor, surrounded by cattle, sheep and two horses, 'the first witnesses' of this significant event. And then, like so many mythic heroes, he was almost ritually bathed with water drawn from Barčica, that 'healing and miraculous spring' that never dries up and to which he constantly returned. As a child he was 'full of strength' – 'every day, several times, he would come to the Barčica Spring, and this water seemed to pump into him the strength of a geyser as if for the whole of his life' (Zagorac 1996: 25).

These are, of course, the standard and not even remotely original motifs of every cult figure and cult of personality, and they need not be accorded greater importance than they have. The essential things came later, but they would certainly work more suggestively and symbolically with this kind of introduction. Radovan Karadžić was a relatively anonymous member of the public, an ambitious but not very talented poet, constantly suspected of being a Yugoslav secret police informer. And yet, he became the leader of the SDS of Bosnia-Herzegovina when much to the surprise of a majority of those taking part in the St Peter's Day constituent assembly of the party, he was proposed for the position by Jovan Rašković, who had in turn been prompted by Dobrica Ćosić. This was enough for him to have received 221 votes out of a possible 222 – one vote being counted spoiled.

At this moment, however, something came into focus that was not at all the standard prop of any personality cult or a mass-produced more or less adroit panegyric. And to this, which is not his middle-class figure, it is hardly possible to give as much attention as it deserves. One can speculate as to whether his two influential proposers really knew that their favourite had something that the others did not, but the fact is that he did have it, and he was well aware of it, even if others were not. That is, Radovan Karadžić was not a politician but a sign, clearly and powerfully resonant in the consciousness of those who were most important in the whole story and who were meant to bear the main role in the project that was shortly to start. These were, of course, those mountain peasants, unspoiled by civilisation, who in Paul Pawlikowski's film were so naturally and innocently at one instant whetting their scythes on the meadow, and at the next skilfully driving tanks over the *mountain green* and firing shells at the helpless City in the valley.

Origins – tribe, clan and individual

In a social milieu in which a standard politician, however skilled and well-trained, would have remained an outsider, Radovan Karadžić was among his own folk, a figure who had literally come out of a song and dropped down to earth to take his place at the head of his people. With Slobodan Milošević, there was a good deal to be invented and adjusted and if by chance he had not had the name and surname that were as if made for the imaginative resonance of their symbolism, because they were etymologically derived from the concept *sloboda*, freedom, and the name Miloš, the name of the hero of the Battle of Kosovo who had killed the Sultan, the whole process of constructing the myth would have been at least slower, and that might have saved a few lives.

But with Karadžić nothing needed to be added or brushed up: many may have thought that he was just a bewildered provincial chap from the waterless karst in the back of beyond, below Mount Durmitor. But the only important people, those who were to make up the major part of the army that would set off to conquer and commit genocide, accompanied and tutored by the tireless *gusle* players, knew that the truth was just the opposite, that the chosen one had an elite origin.

The first set of people, the alienated and feminised city gents, looked for his birthplace on the wrong map, where railways, airports and motorways were marked, where the important things were modern educational establishments, great ports or industrial centres, where the major settlements were those with the largest populations, where relationships were expressed in quantitative or material terms, where somewhere as small as Petnica could hardly be seen at all, and Sarajevo and Zagreb and Belgrade were marked with large circles and big letters. But in the epic map, the categories are different, and Petnica is the capital, Zagreb, Belgrade and Sarajevo are unimportant backwaters, or inimical foreign territory.

The Drobnjak clan inhabited the area between the Piva and Tara rivers, today part of Montenegro, but in the traditional terminology of Old Herzegovina, on the former border between Montenegro and Ottoman Herzegovina. With the Kučis (Kuqi in Albanian) and the Vasojevićes they were one of the three most important Dinaric clans. As the ethnographer and Serbian language reformer Vuk Stefanović Karadžić, himself a Drobnjak by origin, wrote, not without pride, they were 'among the most important and most courageous of the Herzegovinan clans [...] and often killed Turks, cut off their heads and took them to their homes' (Karadžić IV: 396). One of the main sources of this pride is the fact that in this autarchic and isolated clan no one had ever been converted to Islam.

They are mentioned in the archives for the first time in 1285, and tradition has it that they got their name from the fact that on St Peter's Day one of their ancestors had split open the *drob* or guts of a 'Turkish Pasha', that is, the Bosnian governor Gazi Husrev-Bey, which is in line with historical facts. This competent Ottoman general, a descendant of Sultan Selim I on his mother's side, under whose administration Sarajevo became a powerful trade centre with a well-developed artisan sector, really was killed in a campaign against the Drobnjaks in 1541 (Luburić 1930: 11–12) and a tradition concerning the way he was killed and the origin of the Drobnjak tribal name lived on even among the Bosnian Muslims (Bašagić 1900: 33).

Living for generations within the Ottoman Empire, as a kind of independent mountain republic, the Drobnjaks, like the Vasojevićes, became part of the Principality of Montenegro only after the Berlin Congress of 1878 (actually the bit of the Drobnjak area including Petnica, but without Durmitor itself, was added somewhat earlier, after the Montenegrin victory at Grahovo in 1858). Hence they knew nothing of the traditions of Montenegrin separateness and statehood identity. Instead, they were deeply immersed in the world of the Kosovo epic and the tradition of the glorious medieval state of the Nemjanić dynasty. And they considered themselves to be in some sense the *purest and highest quality Serbs*, 'Serbian Spartans', and aspired to unification with Serbia, with which they had traditionally strong personal links, for many of them had settled there (cf. Banac 1984: 270–6; Cvijić 1987).

When in the 1840s Njegoš compiled the book *Ogledalo srpsko (Serbian Mirror)*, his personal selection of the national epics with the ideological and political aim of combining the key sites, events and personalities of Serbian and Montenegrin history and providing a comprehensive notion of the struggle for freedom, the Karadžić clan of Petnica were included in this representative catalogue with the epic poem called 'Kula Karadžića' ('Karadžić's Tower'). It sings of the military campaign waged in March 1812 by the Zvornik *sancak beyi* Zulfikar-Pasha Čengić, known as Pasha Miljevina, and his cousin from Gacko, Smail-Aga Čengić, against the Drobnjaks, who had refused to pay their annual tribute. As recalled by Zulfikar-Pasha's great grandson, Adil Zulfikarpašić, the influential Bosniak politial émigré of the Yugoslav period, the 'great heroism' of the time, on both sides, 'was sung by Muslims and Orthodox' (Djilas 1994: 12). According to the song from the Njegoš collection, in its first assault on the 'Drobnjaks, frenzied heroes' the Bosnian army was met with 'bursts of fire' and repulsed, but in a new push, all the Drobnjaks were 'incinerated by fire'. Only *vojvoda* (General) Šujo Karadžić survived, besieged in his 'white Karadžić's Tower'. From there he replied to Smail-Aga's calls to surrender:

> *never shall Šujo yield to you*
> *while his head is on his shoulders*
> (Njegoš 1951: 49).

The heroic epic songs suggest that as early as about 1655 'all the Drobnjak stores' were in Karadžić's Tower (Luburić 1930: 158), that is, the Drobnjaks kept their weapons, military equipment and loot there. When in one of the songs about 300 *haiduks* anxious for *şikâr* or booty assemble, their leaders debating in which direction to go, Bajo Pivljanin, the most sung-of *harami*

The traditional stone house of the Karadžić family at Petnjica, celebrated in many heroic ballads.

başi from the Herzegovina-Montenegro border, says that

> *In Drobnjak, mighty tribe*
> *In Petnjica little village*
> *'neath Karadžić's white tower*

there was a lot of livestock and 'all the Drobnjak stores in keeping'. This was a clear suggestion where the desired booty could be found, which, incidentally, once again shows that in the actual traditional song it is possible to find that even the most idealised *haiduks* were not exactly altruistic fighters against Ottoman rule. But the other *harami başi* were against this, not wanting 'to strike our brothers' who had themselves suffered from the Turks, and so in the end the *haiduk* army moved against the tower of Bey Ljubović near Nevesinje (Milutinović 1990: 86).

In another song, the roles are reversed. They tell Bajo that

> *In Petnjica, Karadžić's Tower,*
> *there's the store of all the Drobnjaks,*
> *here'll be* şikâr *for the band*

but he refuses, and also leads the *haiduks* 'to the white Ljubović tower / at Nevesinje's white town's end' (Karadžić VII: 48; Luburić 1980: 158 recorded a version a hundred years later in Drobnjak country). The Karadžićes themselves knew a song about how Bajo did after all steal from them, but they sent a posse after him that caught up with him and retrieved the booty (Zagorac 1996: 16).

With this kind of origin, confirmed by Njegoš and Bajo Pivljanin, Radovan Karadžić was able to set out on a journey on which practically the whole traditional memory and political imaginary of his people would be encountered, on which the dividing line between epic and historical reality, between the real and the imagined, past and present, customary and civil law, modern categories of political action and ancient vernacular concepts of the conflict between Good and Evil embodied primarily in (Orthodox) Christianity and Islam would be entirely erased.

When he presented himself as a descendant of Vuk Stefanović Karadžić in the documentary film *Serbian Epics* (Pawlikowski 1992) and in a series of public appearances, many thought it was just a case of propaganda mystification or the usual kind of megalomania based on an accidental coincidence of surnames. But not even the scene when Radovan Karadžić played the *gusle* in the birthplace of Vuk Karadžić sitting on his bed could in fact be said to be 'extremely bizarre', as the Croatian journalist Jasna Zanić Nardini put it (*Vjesnik*, 18 December 1992). And nor did he, by proclaiming himself Vuk's descendant, cheat the English who 'do not know that Dr Karadžić is by origin from Durmitor, and not from Tršić or from Romanija mountain', as the freelance Serbian journalist Miloš Vasić wrote (*Vreme*, 113, 21 December 1992). Everything was accurate and understandable in the experiential perspective and cultural knowledge or basic cognitive associations of those whom Radovan Karadžić was actually addressing.

With the collapse of the traditional patriarchal, extended family, the cult of the forebear also vanished: the modern middle-class family rarely knows anything of its predecessors further than the second or perhaps third generation back. And if they do know, they do not pay much attention to them, nor do they arouse any particularly strong emotions. And so it was quite logical for the Serbian journalist Vasić, a Belgrader, to state that the two Karadžićes could not be related, for Radovan was born in Petnica, on Durmitor, and Vuk in Tršić, in southwest Serbia, by the Drina River, in 1787, and hence – considering the great difference in time between the two events as well – to draw the conclusion that there were two different families involved, as would be the case within the categories of bourgeois society.

But the components of patriarchal vernacular culture are experienced and measured very differently. Every clan, including the Drobnjaks, considers itself a natural community created by consanguinity. It is not just a military and political group but also a kinship unit, and the proof is the legend that all members derive from a single common ancestor. The cult of the ancestor and the feeling of kinship are so strong that many, even children, know their ancestors by name back to the twentieth generation and are able to describe in detail their characteristics, the main events in their lives and the reasons that sometimes forced them to leave their original domicile (Gesemann 1968; Cvijić 1987). For, in traditional social thought all authority is vested in the ancestors, who are significant as points of either genealogical unification or differentiation. Though living persons do have authority in some matters,

> it is never absolute. It is either the authority of parents, which is part of the same pattern of relationship as that of ancestors, and always limited by the authority of ancestors, or it is authority given by assumed devolution from ancestors. The authority of living persons is partial and subject to challenge; that of ancestors is pervasive and absolute. Ancestral authority is the key to [...] the reproductive capacity of the society (Calhoun 1980: 304).

According to such criteria, and from such a perspective, it is not just Radovan's and Vuk's family, but many others as well, no matter where an individual happened to be born, that are forged into a tight unity.

There is indeed something theatrical in the scene in which Radovan Karadžić lights a candle in front of a portrait of Vuk Karadžić in the house in which the latter was born in Tršić. There is also irritating banality in the scene showing that he and his son have the same dimple on their chin as Vuk. And yet such actions can only be properly understood if they are put into their original social and cultural context and judged by its categories. The 'bizarreness' perceived by the Croatian journalist is a quite relative category: some people find the *gusle* bizarre, some the electric guitar, but there is no universal objective criterion by which to judge such a dispute.

From this perspective, Radovan Karadžić's own statement in the film that St Michael the Archangel, vanquisher of the rebel angels, revered by both the eastern and the western churches, is 'the patron saint of our family' (Pawlikowski 1992) is probably crucial: he is referring to the Karadžić clan's *krsna slava*, or occasion on which the patron saint is celebrated. It is above all else a holy day in honour of the ancestors, and among the Orthodox it is the biggest holiday after Christmas and Easter. It does not change; individuals do not select it according to some affinities of their own, rather it is handed down through the family, or rather the clan or tribe, and is thus 'perhaps the most profound pivot of the entire familial tradition' and guarantee of its identity (Kalezić 1989: 52). According to the traditional song, Archangel's Day, 21 November, was the *krsna slava* of Emperor Dušan Nemanjić himself, and the cult of the saint is particularly developed in the pastoral mountain country for the sake of protection against wolves. Only he could close the jaws of the wolves, hold back the lame wolf and lead them into the wild country where there were neither cattle nor men (Antonić and Zupanc 1988: 160). Thus he had his cult on Romanija, and the Vasojevićes held him the patron saint of their whole clan.

This is the clue that needs to be followed in order to be able to understand the frame of reference in which the BBC film presented Radovan Karadžić and thus not to overlook the fact that the seemingly unconnected dots traced by the filmmakers create a robust sign system. Although he was performing for the sake of foreigners, the whole performance contains no hint of stylisation that might be offered as a concession to an audience of a different social and cultural background. There is, therefore, no reason not to believe that Karadžić was presenting precisely the semantic field in which he sees his own person and in which, clearly, a considerable number of his followers also see him. And, as we have seen, a great many industrious propaganda experts and authors in the media under the control of Karadžić and Milošević went to great pains to increase this number.

Some of the traditions are partially or entirely susceptible to historical verification, and some are not, but it is always important to bear in mind that they are authentic for those who follow them, and that their own image of themselves and historical events is enshrined in them. Thus the Karadžić clan tradition says that they came from Mt Karadžica in northern Macedonia. After the battle of the Marica River in 1371, when the Ottomans inflicted heavy losses on the Serbian feudal army, the Karadžićes moved away, not wishing to submit to the Turks. This means that their 'warring and dangerous wrestling' with the Muslims lasted almost six and a half centuries, as calculated significantly by the biographer of the president of Republika Srpska (Zagorac 1996: 11). First of all they settled in Vasojević land, in the area of Lijeva Rijeka, in the village of Lopate, which gave Radovan Karadžić one more important mark and created another connection, an extremely important one for patriarchal culture.

Apart from being the most numerous clan in the Brda region of northern Montenegro, the Vasojevićes have to this day preserved the greatest internal compactness of all the Dinaric clans. The cradle of the clan is this very area of Lijeva Rijeka, and its core consists of three brotherhoods deriving from the three sons of the original ancestor Vaso, whom clan tradition places at the Battle of Kosovo. The branch founded by the eldest son, Radoslav or Rajo, is known as the Rajevićes, to which the Milošević brotherhood belongs (Vešović 1935). Simeun and Svetozar Milošević, Slobodan's father and grandfather, were members of this brotherhood. The leader of the first Serbian insurrection, Karađorđe Petrović, came from one of the Vasojević brotherhoods, from the village of Kralje, and so of course did the subsequent Serbian reigning house, the Karađorđevićes (the epic formulation of the *gusle* player B. Đukić, who also derived from the Vasojevićes, that the Karadžićes were in a sense a predestined ruling house, should be understood in this light). From here too comes Miroslav Šolević, leader of the Kosovo Serbs, and organiser of all the essential rallies that formed part of the so-called anti-bureaucratic revolution at the end of the eighties.

It has already been stated that the singer Mirko Pajčin, alias Baja Mali Knindža, proudly identified himself as descendant of the hero who cost Alija Đerzelez his life (see pp. 295–6). The life of Simo Dubajić of Kistanje, too, retired lieutenant colonel of the JNA and organiser of the first pro-Milošević rally in Knin, 28 February 1989, gains its authentic significance only when it is said once his forebears in the Bosanska Krajina, western Bosnia, 'liquidated a Turkish bey' and then, 'for Turkish justice not to extend to them', they fled across the border to Venetian Dalmatia, to the area of Knin. Then the Belgrade journalist can present him with admiration as an indomitable hero in whose 'veins flows the blood of these forebears and also of [the seventeenth century uskok *harami başis*] Stojan Janković, Vuk Mandušić and Ilija Smiljanić' at the mention of whom 'the Turks filled their knickers' (Dragan Barjaktarević; *Duga*, 395, 15 April 1989).

These are actually two bloodlines: the first is realistic, founded on a number of real forebears and transferred by the natural route of the human gene, while the second is symbolic and founded on the circumstance that Dubajić now lives in the same area in which the former famed *harami başis* lived. It is transmitted through the mystical route of the gene of space, or *genius loci*, but both are equal, and complement each other, merging inextricably into the being of the national hero.

Perhaps it is Šolević's account of his origin that is the most impressive example of the tenacity of such traditions, as well as of the self-awareness and social status derived from them. It also shows the manner in which temporal levels are interwoven, long past and contemporary events semantically enhancing each other and merging in a creation in which such diverse categories as astrology and Yugoslav ideologemes about Tito's *historical no to Stalin* in 1948 can coexist:

> I was born on 14 August 1948 in the village of Sekirača, municipality of Kuršumlija, on the old Serbian-Turkish border, that is, the current border between Serbia and the province of Kosovo. I was born in the sign of Leo and in the year when Tito said No to Stalin. My family came here in 1878. My grandfather was six years old when they brought him here from Montenegro, and here they were given the surname Šolević. From the old surname, Đujević, of Montenegro, they made three surnames – Šolević, Jovanović and Vuksanović. My people took the name of Šolević, from a great-grandfather Šolo, and they moved here from Lijeva Rijeka [...] That is a little valley surrounded by very steep and craggy mountains with very little cultivable land, and the precise location of their *savardak* [circular hut] is known. The ruins are still there, and, look, they say to me, here was your great-grandfather Radisav's *savardak*. (Doderović 1990: 8)
>
> My people moved in here 110 years ago from Montenegro, from Lijeva Rijeka. And Lijeva Rijeka, you know, is where the father of Slobodan Milošević comes from. Here are the Vasojevićes, and in him it's a real Vasojević heart that beats. (Hudelist 1989: 310)

In Vasojević country every year, on 28 August, Orthodox Assumption Day, a traditional clan assembly is held, attended by clan members who moved long ago into the cities or even abroad. When they were visited by a reporter from Belgrade, prompted by the report that Milošević's forebears hailed from there, they showed him exactly where Karađorđe was from, in which village Milošević's male ancestors were born, and in which those of Radovan Karadžić.[1] Also interesting is the information that at the St Peter's Day assembly of 1993 this clan made the decision to annex itself to Serbia should Montenegro leave the Federal Republic of Yugoslavia. This shows that there was still a lively awareness, at least in part, that the clan was not only a kinship but also a political community.

This sense of connection and solidarity at the political level is very strong even today, and Miroslav Šolević described in great detail how crucial clan links were during the organisation of many of the rallies, particularly in Vojvodina, where after World War II a large number of Serbian and

---

1. Zoran Marković, 'Zapad će platiti odštetu Srbiji', *Duga*, 536, 17 September 1994.

Montenegrin families from the mountain areas were planted on the estates of expelled Germans and Hungarians. Keeping in touch with their kin in the old country, they and their descendants were quick to respond to all calls and took part in all the campaigns with 100 percent reliability (cf. Hudelist 1989; Doderović 1990).

It was in Andrijevica and other Vasojević places that the first *happening of the people (događanje naroda)* occurred, and it was from there that the strongest and most militant columns of demonstrators set off during Milošević's putsches against the Montenegrin leadership in 1988–9. It was from there that their couplets spread with the aim of acquiring for the top man of the Serbian communists the traditional legitimacy of a non-communist, authentic national leader: 'Oh Slobodan, mountain wolf / *cevherdar* [rifle embellished with mother of pearl and precious stones] of Montenegro' (*Pobjeda*, 17 January 1989); 'Montenegro Slobo gives birth / to set Kosovo free' (*Danas*, 363, 29 August 1989) or 'Slobodan, mountain spirit / Montenegrin is your line' (*Vjesnik*, 29 May 1991).

This insistence on the Montenegrin origins of Milošević confused the middle-class urban public, which thought of Milošević as a Serb, but for the traditional worldview this was a key legitimating point – for only with this kind of origin could he be an ultimately authentic Serb. When the vernacular imagination finds a suitable semantic point of origin and manages to integrate a leader into the stable schemes of its historical memories and categories of its worldview, and then, following an authentic traditional sign, acknowledges him as its own, it no longer even notices that in the meantime certain contradictions have developed between his bourgeois personality and the original collective identity.

The fact of the symbolic origin is in itself powerful and suggestive enough to legitimate him as leader, even to make of him – as the *gusle* player sings – a symbol of the faith, however much he showed every day that he was an atheist of the Bolshevik type:

> *Son of mothers both*
> *Montenegro and Serbia*
> *symbol you are of holy Serbdom*
> *crossing with the fingers three.*
> *Every thought of yours is pure,*
> *Christ is shining in your heart.*
> (Mastilović 1989)

It is of relatively little importance whether the subject of the song personally promotes such an origin, or even cares about it at all. From all accounts, unlike Karadžić, Milošević did not care about it at all, at least not in the categories of vernacular culture, nor did he incorporate this element into his political image. However, it was essential that he was perceived in this way by his followers, and that the chiefs at operational levels of decision making were fully aware of his significance in their political work, as Šolević demonstrates persuasively. The fact that, unlike his brother, Slobodan Milošević maintained no links at all with other Vasojevićes, and never visited his father's home country, does not prevent members of the clan experiencing him as a member and telling vivid stories about him.[1]

The Karadžićes moved out of Vasojević country into Drobnjak country in about 1630. But one family, from which the Drobnjak Karadžićes sprang, remained in Lijeva Rijeka, in the village of Lopate. This family was 'close kin' to the Miloševićes of the Vasojević village of Uvač. Three centuries later there were fifty-eight Karadžić houses in Drobnjak country, of which twenty-eight were in Petnica. According to the tradition that lives among them, they all derived from three brothers, mentioned in the traditional songs: not only the Drobnjak Karadžićes but also those in Serbian Drina country, where Vuk Karadžić was born, are considered to be related to each other. They all share the *krsna slava* (patron saint day) of St Michael the Archangel, and they also celebrate St George's Day, *Đurđevdan*. Both Vuk and Radovan are descended from this family (Luburić 1930: 156–67; Zagorac 1996: 11). In his memoirs Vuk Stefanović Karadžić says that his grandfather had moved away from there in about 1739, but in the Drobnjak country they state that Vuk's father was born in Petnica, in which all the Drobnjak Karadžićes lived until 1835 (Luburić 1930: 164).

But this kind of hair-splitting chronology of profane or rationalist bourgeois history completely misses the point of sacred or traditional history or living vernacular consciousness. The contemporary Drobnjak vernacular poet precisely identified what the Belgrade liberal *Vreme* journalist M. Vasić would not see, and could not, when he thought that the life of each

---

1. Cf. the previous note. Jovan Plamenac, editor of *Barske novine* of Bar, which was the most militant supporter of the politics of Milošević and his Montenegrin satellite Momir Bulatović, dealt systematically with the question of Milošević's origins. His articles were reprinted in many papers in Serbia, even in Bosnia-Herzegovina. They gave particular publicity to the precisely elaborated genealogy, abundantly seasoned with quotations from the epic songs, according to which Serbia's strongman was in the eighth generation a direct descendant of Miloš Markov, Vasojević hero, one of the greatest of the *çetebaşis* (commander of armed clan troops), who was killed in 1735. Cf. *Nedjelja* (Sarajevo), 35, 21 October 1990, and *Novosti 8* (Belgrade), 524, 12 April 1990.

individual was a thing by itself, one that began with the date of his birth. But the vernacular poet, author of the epic poem 'Epic Halo for Vuk Karadžić' ('Epski oreol za Vuka Karadžića'), knew the full truth and said that God had 'toasted / Drobnjak and the village of Petnjica', where 'the divine hand had painted / the habitat of Karadžić Vuk' (Šobić 1987: 43). Irrespective of what it might say in his documents, in this world an individual is born long before the formal date of his birth, and in the place where his oldest ancestors were born, and only that is his real home country. Put another way, he can have two birthplaces, even very far apart from each other, one where his forebears were born, and the other where he himself was born, but it is clear which is the authentic and legitimate place.

Migrations were a permanent phenomenon among the clans of the Brda area, densely settled on an impassable and infertile soil, constantly at war with the Turks, and with other clans over pasture. People moved to the more fertile lowland areas of Serbia, and to Romanija too, where a large section of the Serbian population originates precisely from these migrations. In many brotherhoods they still sing to the *gusle* about the primogenitors who hid from the Turkish *zulüm* or reign of terror, and it is known 'exactly from which place they set off towards Romanija' (Krsmanović 1988: 35). If they did not keep up direct links with the branches that had gone that way, these brotherhoods knew of them as well as of those that had stayed in the old land.

The Čvoros, the most numerous Romanija clan, recall that they came from Nikšić country, after their *haiduk* ancestors killed some Ottoman *bölükbaşi*, at the end of the eighteenth century. The primogenitor of the Gluhovićes came from Drobnjak country in the mid-nineteenth century, and the Krsmanovićes, also Drobnjak by origin, say that they were forced to emigrate after one member killed an *aga* on Durmitor with a hoe (Krsmanović 1988, 1991). Two branches of the Kosorićes, the most famous of all Drobnjak groups, which produced eleven *vojvodas*, moved to Romanija at the beginning of the nineteenth century. Some of them settled near Rogatica, others near Sokolac. They produced the student Pero Kosorić, leader of the communist insurrection of 1941, also sung of along the same epic lines as Slaviša Vajner, that is, as symbolic heir of Starina Novak and his fearless *haiduk*s. In the neighbourhood of Romanija, the brotherhood of the Divljani underneath Mt Jahorina, famed as *gusle* players, were a branch of the Drobnjak Karadžićes (Luburić 1930).

Among the Drobnjaks too the main brotherhood particularly cultivated *gusle* playing. As one student of that influential Serbian human geographer Jovan Cvijić, also a Drobnjak by birth, wrote, 'the people believed that the

Radovan Karadžić plays the *gusle* in the house where Vuk Karadžić was born at Tršić near Loznica. (still from Pawlikowski's film *Serbian Epics*, 1992)

Karadžićes suckled every child at the *gusle*' (Luburić 1930: 164). The Slovene folklore student M. Murko met on his travels several Karadžić *gusle* players, such as the trader Miro in Žabljak and the wealthy boss Rašo, whose forebears had moved in the nineteenth century from Petnica to the surroundings of Žabljak, and who was specifically said to be from the family of Vuk Karadžić (Murko 1951: 139). Radovan's father Vuko (Petnica 1912–Nikšić 1987) was also a well-known *gusle* player; however, the son had a more modest talent – he grew up in the world of the heroic epic, enjoyed *gusle* playing, but his voice was considered too thin.

He himself clearly had a different opinion, because he played the *gusle* in front of the former American president Jimmy Carter when he came to Pale to negotiate peace, as well as for the special envoy of the Russian president Vitaly Churkin. One publication with pretensions to be the official lexicon of the leading personalities of Republika Srpska called the SDS leader 'a successful *gusle* player' born 'into a famed *haiduk* and *gusle*-playing family' (Miletović et al. 1995: 11), while another hagiographer had nevertheless to admit that Radovan was not up to the level of his forebears, and yet said that the mark of destiny could be seen in it, that is, his predetermination to be a *continuation of gusle-playing by other means*: 'The father sang of Serbia to the thin voice of the *gusle*, the son does it now to the thundering voice of the cannons' (Predrag Milojević according to Zagorac 1996: 112).

Not hiding how much he cared that the scene should be solemn and packed with significance, Radovan Karadžić posed for the cameras sitting on the bed in the birth house of Vuk Karadžić and stated that he would sing a song 'that was preserved in the memory of my family through the generations' (Pawlikowski 1992; see illustration above), and started:

> *Thirty captains drink the wine*
> *in the wide mountain of Romanija,*
> *in an icy cavern,*
> *among them Captain Mitar ...*

The most exhaustive index of South Slavic epic figures contains no mention of any Captain Mitar (Krstić 1984) and yet among the Drobnjak Karadžićes there were actually three famed Mitars who might be considered. The first is one of the three brothers who were the primogenitors, who according to tradition came from Vasojević country, and whom the song calls a *ban*, governor. The second was a chief or *vojvoda*, that is, the head of the whole clan in the second half of the eighteenth century, remembered in epic song as an ally of Džafer-Bey Čengić, with whom he led a joint attack on the town of Kolašin (Karadžić VIII: 56). And once again it is worth pausing for a moment over this interesting and realistically presented Christian-Muslim alliance, of the kind that modern exclusivist ideology has completely wiped out of existence, and formed instead a phoney black and white image of former times. The third was a village headman or *knez* from the middle of the nineteenth century, a brother of *vojvoda* Šujo and also a participant in the important enterprise that will be discussed in the chapter to come. The title of *knez* which he bore corresponds to the later name of *kapetan*, because the Principality of Montenegro organised the newly annexed clans administratively in line with its own legal system, that is, the division into captaincies, the concept of which corresponded to the old concept of the self-governing *knežina*, or rural community that, as a collective, communicated with the Ottoman rulers (Dučić 1874).

Thus the epic 'Captain Mitar' or 'Mitar *kapetan*' proudly sung of by the leader of the Bosnian Serbs might have been this *knez*, village headman, Mitar Karadžić. However, it is not really necessary to insist on the identification of either personage or song. It is sufficient to note that Radovan Karadžić, in a powerfully symbolically marked place, in the birth house of Vuk Karadžić, selected lines with an equally strongly marked motif – the heroic band that, drinking wine, ritually assembled at an important consultation *in the wide mountain of Romanija*, where the cameras had previously shot him, and where they would continue to record him after his trip to Tršić. It is even more important – since in the Vasojević country the *finger of Fate* had linked him with the Miloševićes and with the Karađorđevićes themselves – that in the Drobnjak country he derived from the same blood as Vuk Stefanović Karadžić. On the way to perfection, which is neither an inappropriate nor too sentimental expression, he needed just two more encounters.

The first would be with the only remaining figure from the very core of the national pantheon: the man whose incomplete extirpation of the Muslim converts he was supposed to complete. And the second, with a 'Turkish' enemy commensurate with a person of his aura.

At this point all the epic and historical motifs would receive their final dénouement and become inextricably merged – all the typical situations and all the representative persons who were listed by his political patron, Jovan Rašković, in his programmatic Romanija speeches on St Peter's Day in 1990. We are still to see, then, how Radovan Karadžić met the Montenegrin Prince-Bishop Petar II Petrović Njegoš, and Smail-Aga Čengić, the *müsellim* or steward of Gacko.

The second death of Smail-Aga Čengić

As a border town, under Ottoman rule, Gacko was the scene of constant *'haidukery'* and raids – battles over pastures, folds and cattle-stealing. Livestock, the most accessible product of the rural economy, was the target of raids by the rural population over the whole of the Austrian-Venetian-Ottoman area, and the basis of the border economics of plunder. Cattle theft had a dual function for this population: an 'economic (the redistribution of resources) and a cultural one (competition over honour and power)' (Bracewell 1992: 100). Thus in the Gacko area, both sides took part in the raids, because under despotic rule, the poor Muslim peasants suffered just as much as the Christians, with whom they often felt solidarity. At the turn of the century songs about taking and defending livestock were sung with some adjustments in both Christian and Muslim environments, and they were even the Muslims' favourite genre. Sixty years or so later, a Sarajevo folklore student found that, while they were still fresh in the memory in this area with its lively epic tradition, such songs were sung quite reluctantly and only within a closed circle (Buturović 1976b: 205).

The reason for this could be the tragic experience of World War II and a kind of spontaneous social censorship for fear of provoking new conflicts with their Serbian and Montenegrin neighbours. During the war, serious massacres were carried out in this area by both sides. Significant in this context is Vuk Drašković's recollection that in the Serbian villages in the 1950s 'at weddings, and funerals, patron saints' days, and gatherings' the *gusle*-singing was 'almost exclusively about people having their throats cut and about [mass burial] pits', that is, the Ustasha massacres. Hearing one *gusle* performance on a winter evening in 1950, full of naturalistic descriptions of mutilated victims, during which the men were sombrely silent and the women gnashed their teeth, wailed and cursed aloud, the then four-year-old was so traumatised that in the night he imagined he saw Ustashas and took up a hammer 'and laid about me at the visions until my arm went limp' (Drašković 1989: 96). Still, as soon as he learned how to write, he copied the song down from the *gusle* player and learned it by heart. The government, he said, had forbidden such songs and punished the *gusle*-singers who performed them. Some ten years earlier, an envoy of the Comunist Party of Yugoslavia, Uglješa Danilović, reported to his superiors that in this area, in September 1941, after a spontaneous Serbian uprising against the NDH, the Chetniks had tried to encourage the rebels to eliminate the Muslims 'in a war of the Cross against Islam'. They were easily successful because in this area 'looting and arson [directed against] the enemy (the Muslim) was a tradition' (Zbornik NOB IV/1: 445).

Half a century later, some of the commanders of the Army of Republika Srpska openly invoked and glorified this tradition, as did leaders of paramilitary groups, Nebojša Jevrić and some other Serbian journalists who published reports from the battlefields in Croatia and Bosnia-Herzegovina. The writer Dragoš Kalajić attempted to give it a new theoretical justification. In his travels through Republika Srpska he once happened to be in 'Serbian Sarajevo', at a lunch in honour of a certain officer of the Army of Republika Srpska. The wine that was served, he learned, had been looted.

> The knowledge that I was drinking wine that was the booty of war made it even more tasty to the palate. The bourgeois in me resisted a bit, but the genes of the Krajina Uskoks were incomparably stronger, and shut up all my moralising. Of course, at some imaginary court of justice both sides should be heard, the middle-class indictment of looting and the Uskok defence.

According to the thesis that was then developed, contemporary bourgeois civilisation, particularly the Western variety, did not have the moral legitimacy to be able to condemn the taking of war booty, because it was itself based on 'war booty of global dimensions', that is the exploitation of the colonies, and on the multinationals.[1] There is no need to mention that from the other point of view, that of the Bosniak, everything is the opposite, and that this interpretation irresistibly recalls the conversation that the

---

1. Dragoš Kalajić, 'Ukus ratnog plena', *Duga*, 1614, 29 April 1995.

young Avdo Humo had had some seventy years earlier with his grandmother about the ethical contents of the traditional heroic songs (see p. 152). For the commentators of a Bosniak weekly, everything that the Serbs and Serbia had acquired through the centuries was nothing but '*haiduk* acquisition':

> The normal person's hair stands on end today at such an *economy*, but for the decasyllabic cadets of *Haiduk*-Stanko or *Haiduk*-Veljko it was for centuries the most profitable way to make a living [...] In the last century the Serbs ambushed caravans on Romanija or in eastern Herzegovina, and at the end of the 1980s, Belgrade simply raided the vaults of the then federal national bank.[1]

Naturally, he too forgot – or never knew, because he could not have learned it from the official Yugoslav interpretation – that there were the most diverse alliances in these raids, and that among the *haiduks* there was no small number of Muslims, just as among the merchants there were plenty of Christians, including Orthodox Serbs (one was Vojin, whom, according to the song, the Muslim Mujo Hrnjica and the Catholic Mijat Tomić had robbed in concert; see p. 303)

The leader of the Montenegrin pro-Milošević NS, Novak Kilibarda, was himself a fiery agitator among the Serbs in eastern Herzegovina and in the hills above Dubrovnik in 1990–1. Later, after the obvious downfall of the Greater Serbia project, when he had sobered up a bit, he attempted to find some understanding and justification for the mass looting of Konavle and the surroundings of Dubrovnik in the autumn of 1991.

> Recall the Montenegrin heroic songs. They speak of heroism and of heroes' loot [...] Now it's very easy to pronounce these men looters. But the same men had been taught, like their fathers and grandfathers before them, that a glorious hero had driven off a herd of oxen and sheep from the estate of Bey Ljubović, and then turned the whole lot into a lovely girl. (*Duga*, 1609, 18 February 1995)

Historically speaking, this is a realistic view of things, but in Kilibarda's case it is pure hypocrisy, because he himself played an important role in the educational system that celebrated '*haidukery*' and among the politicians who 'taught' 'these men' at the end of the eighties and roused them to war with high-sounding quotations of epic phraseology. For example, it was he

---

1. Hadžem Hajdarević, 'Ekonomija i hajdučija', *Ljiljan*, 209, 15 January 1997.

himself who told the Montenegrins a day or two before the barricades went up in Knin that, as always, they had to 'march with all force against two bitter enemies, Catholicism and Islam' (*Nedjelja*, 27, 26 August 1990). And the stolen livestock he mentions on this occasion was from the land of the same Nevesinje Ljubović beys who in the sixteenth and seventeenth centuries had furnished a number of distinguished men for Ottoman Bosnia. It was the land also of the same *haiduk*s and Uskoks, Bajo Pivljanin above all, of whom the old Mostar grandmother had told stories to her grandson Avdo Humo, when he was confused by what he had learned in school about Ottoman times.

As for the other, still more famous and powerful Muslim line of the Čengićes, in the middle of the sixteenth century, they came from Asia Minor, settled in eastern Herzegovina, and with time extended over the whole of Bosnia-Herzegovina. Making a name for himself in 1809–10 in the quelling of the Karađorđe revolt in Serbia, Smail-Aga Čengić was appointed district governor (*müsellim*) in Gacko, and was killed on 5 September 1840, at Mljetičak, not far from Petnica. The attack was ordered by the Montenegrin Prince-Bishop Njegoš himself, in revenge for the death of his younger brother and some other relatives in a fight with the Bosnian army, in which Čengić had been serving, at Grahovo in 1836. Two hundred of the Drobnjaks took part in the vengeance, the final council of war being held in Karadžić's Tower, and the leaders were two prominent members of the brotherhoods, already mentioned here: the Petnica headman Mitar and the *vojvoda* (or clan chief) Šujo, whose full name was Vasilije (*c.* 1788–1858), mentioned as a hero in the Muslim songs as well, and also a famed *gusle* player.

The Čengićes and the Drobnjaks sometimes fought each other, sometimes worked together, sometimes they just tolerated each other. Šujo's biography is the best indication of all the changes and reversals that took place on that endlessly troubled border. Smail-Aga himself tried several times to kill the rebellious and violent Šujo, but their relationship was not that simple. Since the tribe was formally at least under Ottoman sovereignty, Šujo was named the Drobnjak chief by the Bosnian vizier in Travnik in 1806. Thus, he was actually a reliable and authorised representative of the Ottoman government in his clan, and of his clan to that government. But the newly appointed chief and a group of the Drobnjaks crossed over into Serbia that same year and joined Karađorđe's counter-Ottoman insurgents, taking part with them in the capture of Belgrade. The years went by, and in 1832 Šujo was working as an ally of Smail-Aga Čengić, and on behalf of the central Ottoman government he crushed an autonomist rebellion of Bosnian Muslims led by

Husein-Bey Gradaščević. And eight years later, as a man in whom Čengić had no doubts, led him into the fatal ambush at Mljetičak, and, as Njegoš's personal friend, took his head, weapons and horses as a gift to the prince-bishop at Cetinje (Šišić 1908). The story is rather confusing at first sight, but it is far from being untypical of the complex times, and not so very different from what the modern age likes to call good political instinct.

The death of Smail-Aga Čengić, about which popular songs were at once composed, resounded powerfully on both sides, among the Muslims, of course, very painfully, both because of the death of a distinguished man whom they particularly valued but also because of the manner of his death. Adil Zulfikarpašić says that there was actually 'a chivalric relationship between the Čengićes and the leaders of Montenegro' and that they formed godfather/godchild relationships with each other. After the Austro-Hungarian annexation of Bosnia-Herzegovina in 1878, the Montenegrins offered to let Smail-Aga's grandson, an enemy of the new government, take refuge in their country. But the death of Smail-Aga left a feeling of 'special bitterness' because it was prepared in 'an unchivalrous manner', one that 'in my family is considered a Montenegrin disgrace'. For Smail-Aga Čengić was not killed 'in a duel, in open battle', like Njegoš's relatives at Grahovo, rather in 'a sneaky attack', Zulfikarpašić confided to his friend, the best-known Yugoslav communist dissident, the Montenegrin Milovan Djilas (Djilas 1994: 22).

According to Zulfikarpašić, Smail-Aga was a 'great hero, just and generous, and no tyrant' (Djilas 1994: 16). If a little sentimental, this conclusion is not historically inaccurate. The grandmother of Djilas, who was forty years old at the time of Smail-Aga's death, remembered him well as a particularly honest man and, for the conditions of the time, a just steward (Djilas 1958: 101). And after all, even the first Karadžićes, who started to abandon Petnica around 1835, settled on a not very distant estate, a *čiftlik*, of Smail-Aga's (Luburić 1930: 165). It would seem that in the popular memory it was a case of hatred drawn upon himself by his arrogant and cruel son Rustem being transferred to the father.

The greatest Muslim poet at the turn of the century, Safvet-Bey Bašagić, Smail-Aga's great-grandson on his mother's side, sharply denounced the organisers of the ambush, telling them in his verse:

> *Do heroes fight and break their word ...*
> *Is break-faith heroism called?*
> *Cower before the brighter face*
> *Of the knights of Herzegovina!*

This poem could not be printed during the first Yugoslavia 'for national [state-building] reasons' (Balić 1952: 28); it is not hard to work out which and whose. It militated against the official, state-ideology-supported version of the event as a heroic act of liberation by the idealised *haiduks* of the *green mountain*. The young Bosniak journalist Ahmed Salihbegović recognised much later in the manner in which Karadžić ravaged the Bosnian towns a continuation of the 'tradition of the terrorists who killed Smail-Aga Čengić' (*Ljiljan*, 177, 5 June 1996), showing once again that in the Bosniak social memory the ambush on Mljetičak remained as a symbol of dishonour, a paradigm even in the new/old political imaginary after the tragedy of the war of 1992–5. And it may also be noted that the same contemporary political term, *terrorists*, was used for the armed Drobnjaks that was employed, in parallel with and identical to '*haidukery*', by the Croatian authorities to refer to the Knin barricades.

But the ambush had its sequel. In the following year Ali-Pasha Rizvanbegović of Stolac organised a campaign of vengeance against the Drobnjaks and the neighbouring Moračans, inflicted a severe defeat on them and decorated Čengić's grave, his *türbe*, at Lipnik by Gacko, with 120 of their heads.[1] The Čengićes gradually moved out of Lipnik, and after 1875, Smail-Aga's turbe was maintained by a neighbouring Orthodox family, and it was finally destroyed by the Chetniks in World War II (Hasandedić 1990).

Among the Montenegrins, of course, news of the successful revenge at Mljetičak was joyfully received and celebrated, and immediately numerous epic songs were created about the event. Vuk Karadžić, who, as a Drobnjak, was himself interested in the event and attempted to meet chief Šujo, described in the commentary to the fourth volume of his collection *Srpske narodne pjesme (Serbian Folk Songs)* how the action went and included three songs about it, with the observation that there were four more, only 'on the whole similar to the first' (Karadžić IV). In the eighth volume he printed a song that in a broader review of raiding along the Montenegro-Herzegovina border, also contains a relatively ample account of the attack on Smail-Aga Čengić.

Like the other songs, it shows the events from Njegoš's first letter to Šujo Karadžić, 'chosen *vojvoda*, / knight and governor (*ban*) from ancient

---

1. One might draw attention to the poem 'Mir' (Peace) from the first collection of poems of the then Sarajevo medical student Radovan Karadžić (*Ludo koplje/Mad Spear*, Svjetlost, Sarajevo 1968, pp. 11–12). The naturalistic image of 'piles of lopped off heads / the long hair of the Drobnjak chiefs / slaughtered in the stony heights' is an incontrovertible reflection of events of about a century and a half earlier and one more indicator that the author know his clan history.

times', asking him to help him avenge his relatives, to the final scene at Cetinje, when Njegoš thanks the leaders of the action and rewards them. He
confirmed the chieftainship (*vojvodstvo*) of Šujo, and thus the title that he
had been given by the vizier became truly legitimate, for it was endorsed by
a Christian ruler, although formally speaking it was neither necessary nor
possessed of any foundation in law, for the sovereignty of Montenegro did
not extend to the Drobnjak country; but the concept of borders and laws at
the time was somewhat different from today. In so doing he addressed him
with the words: 'Blessed be thy right hand! / Able so to put Turks to death'
(Karadžić VIII: 61).

In his epic 'The Poet's Dream on Lola Mountain' ('San pjesnikov na planini
Loli') the productive contemporary vernacular poet also gives his vision of
Drobnjak history, and does not forget to highlight Šujo Karadžić and evoke
the scene when, after the ambush on Mljetičak, the 'three great Drobnjak
chiefs' – Šujo, Novica Cerović and Mirko Aleksić – played triumphantly
with the head of Smail-Aga Čengić (Šobić 1983: 25).

The song concerning Čengić's death at Mljetičak was often sung at *gusle*
competitions in Republika Srpska, and in performances for special occasions
in Banja Luka's Army Centre and at the main St Vitus Day celebrations
at Sokolac. In the words of Radomir Lakić from the Banja Luka Janković
Stojan *Gusle* Association in the show *Open Screen* of 14 May 1995, on Banja
Luka Serbian Radio Television, the young members of the association were
keenest on learning to perform this song. And he himself had performed it
many times in barracks or at the front, at the express request of the soldiers,
who knew that there was talk in it of 'the forebear of our president'. He then
performed the song in the show, after the anchorwoman had explained that
it contained an important event 'in the eternal struggle of the Serbian people
against the incursions of Islam into Europe', and that 'the famed Drobnjak
vojvoda Šujo Karadžić had taken part in it – the forebear of Dr Radovan
Karadžić and a great friend of Prince-Bishop Njegoš'.

In the version performed, it is Šujo who is shown as the most determined,
the boldest and most self-sacrificing among the Montenegrins, and when at
a certain moment the other two leaders propose putting off the attack, he
retorts:

> *Ignominy, Mirko and Novica*
> *Or I shall morrow strike the Aga,*
> *Or I shall lose my very head*
> (Karadžić IV: 57).

When after Dayton it began to be said that the international military and police in Bosnia-Herzegovina would have to arrest Radovan Karadžić as a war criminal and surrender him to the ICTY, there were frequent mass protests in Republika Srpska, and many political leaders and ordinary folk announced that they would not permit it, at the cost of renewed war. In this reaction, there was some awareness that a trial of Karadžić would open up all the murky background to the war, the real system of command and the broad network of commanders, finally demonstrating that this was not spontaneous Serbian self-defence against a revival of the NDH and the creation of an Islamic state in Bosnia-Herzegovina, rather a classic war of conquest and a long-planned war of genocide and culturecide against the Croats and Bosniaks.

But, also, the so-called man in the street certainly had some idea that the arrest of Radovan Karadžić also somehow entailed the arrest of Petar II Petrović Njegoš and of Vuk Stefanović Karadžić, in fact, of their whole history and the whole of their world, and that it would be a kind of revocation of the *extirpation of the Muslim converts, the revolt against the dayis,* the ambush on Mljetičak and all the *haiduk* ambushes on the *green mountain,* all of them events in which – through his paradigmatic origins – their current leader had taken part and was actually embodied. The banner *An Attack on Karadžić – An Attack on the Serbian People,* displayed at such meetings, was indeed a standard populist line, but at another level, concealed from outside eyes, it was a truth that many of the protestors really felt, deeply and sincerely, with unassailable logic.

Karadžić himself, and his political comrades and patrons, knew that this truth, so profoundly implanted in the spirit of their subjects, would protect them at least as much as their bodyguards and the underground bunker in Han-Pijesak, or any other shelter. The aura of the first among them, and the aura of the first among the mountains, were equal in value and merged into an image that concealed all other realities. A snigger, then, would be the last and worst manner of reacting to the news that in the summer of 1997, at Pale, after the international community had forced Radovan Karadžić to withdraw from formal politics and formally renounce his duties, the story spread that he had taken refuge in Novak's Cave on Romanija, planning a big comeback. As the nationalist ideologue and poet Matija Bećković wrote, there was no Serb who would be willing to guide the international military forces 'through the mountain of Romanija to show them where the cave of Starina Novak was' (*Nedeljni Telegraf,* 11 November 1998).

Very soon the ICTY issued a formal indictment for war crimes against

Blind *gusle* player forming part of a monument to Prince Lazar and the heroes of Kosovo erected at Kruševac in southern Serbia in 1889, on the occasion of the 500th anniversary of the Battle of Kosovo, which subsequently became the model for all similar sculptures.

Karadžić and he, along with General Ratko Mladić, became the most wanted person in the territory of former Yugoslavia, which in the categories of the traditional patriarchal culture could only enhance his cult and the epic aura that enveloped him. Independently of where Karadžić was really hiding and whether he was actually in Bosnia, for this section of his followers (and for those who regularly fed them with mythic ideas and epic references) it was quite clear where he had to be. For Karadžić was not guaranteed safety by the secrecy of his refuge, precisely the opposite, by the fact that the location of his hideout was known to all, which meant for all of them that in its very nature it guaranteed that he was untouchable.

One among the many songs that celebrated Karadžić – and General Ratko Mladić – in the well-known frame of reference, issued on audio cassette in Serbia at the end of 2001, elaborated this idea very precisely in the expected value categories, and with the epic motifs and expressive models:

Tell us, brother Radovan,
do the nymphs of Romanija feed ye,
Romanija, if you are a mountain,
Radovan must be guarded ...
In a cave of Mount Romanija
Rašo and Ratko drink the crimson wine.
(*Dani*, 244, 15 February 2002; Rašo is an affectionate diminutive
for Radovan)

After the announcement of the indictment, they started holding 'defence meetings' in Petnica, not, it is true, with many people taking part, compared to the ecstatic rallies that had preceded the war, but it is not unimportant that they received great publicity in the nationalist media, and that they were attended by the high representatives of the Serbian Orthodox Church. At the first, in the summer of 2001, the oldest male member of the Karadžić clan ritually greeted all those who were present in front of the village church, and then talked of the national hero who was again compelled 'to go off to the *haiduks*', with the proviso that all Serbs in all the Serbian lands were Radovan's 'harbourers (*yataks*)', the *gusle* players were performing new epics with lines about the green Romanija fir trees concealing Karadžić from the 'damned country of America' and about how for 'ten full summers' he had been walking this mythic mountain. At the end, the church choir sang what they called a song in prayer:

Who's fighting the bitter battle for Serbian Bosnia?
Oh brother, it's the Serbs from Mt Romanija.
While Romanija exists, the Serbs fear not,
while Romanija is, the Serbs exist.
Romanija, mount of mountains,
keep safe our brother Radovan ...[1]

In the meantime, in this mosaic, both marvellous and morbid, just one more element was missing.

---

1. Srđan Janković, 'Spasavanje ratnika Radovana [The saving of warrior Radovan]', *Monitor*, 563, 03 August 2001. Ibid., 'Ko brani Radovana Karadžića', at http://www.aimpress.ch/dyn/pubs/archive/data/2000107/10730-005-pubs-pod.htm

TWELVE

The Dayton Agreement

*[If the NATO planes escape the standard ground to air missiles] we'll be
waiting for them at another, higher level of defence: we'll invade their
electronic systems and block them for so long that they will collapse. After
that second level, there are still three more levels of secret defence the
last of which is unknown to me too. Put quite simply, our AA system is
like the old technique of Serbian warfare from the song 'Starina Novak
and Deli Radivoje': 'What Deli Radivoje misses, will be met by young
Tatomir, what gets past young Tatomir, Child Gruica is waiting for;
and anything Child Gruica lets through, Starina Novak is there for ...'*

(Dragoš Kalajić: 'Odbrana izvora/Defense of the Sources', *Duga*,
546, 17 September 1994.)

The three Kosovos, three Novaks and three Serbias

These were the words used by Major Novica Stojanović, at the AA batteries
of the Republika Srpska Army above Teslić, to describe the defensive system
to a visitor from Belgrade in the days when NATO attacks on the Bosnian
Serb positions were expected, at the end of 1994. The admiring visitor, a
journalist, the right-wing ideologue Dragoš Kalajić, at once recognised in
such a concept a marvellous combination of contemporary technology and
the 'eternal tradition of noble minds'.

A year later, during the combined liberation operations of Croatian
forces and the AB-H, with American support, this undoubtedly innovative
approach to military theory collapsed overnight in ruins, but at the time of
the interview, Serbian self-confidence was intact, the cult of the invincible
haiduk was at its peak, and the symbolic structure of the whole military and
political project – with Romanija its topographical and semantic core – had
been further elaborated and practically rounded off.

All the essential elements of both the spontaneous vernacular imagination and the organised job of symbolic branding converged at this one point. Romanija had indeed become an Olympus, just as once, in sixteenth and seventeenth century Greece, after the country had fallen to the Ottomans, the ancient aura of divine Olympus had been strengthened and revived. In the context of resistance to Ottoman rule some other mountains had greater military importance and more suitable attributes for insurrectionary activity, and were hence important hideouts for the Greek *haiduk*s, the *klephts*. But it was Olympus that the Greek national *aiodos*, the singer of heroic songs, celebrated as the last resort of freemen, the haunt of freedom that was embodied in the *klephts* as a kind of 'sacred *klephtic* mountain' in which wounds would be healed of their own accord (Stojanović 1984: 50–3).

Actually, there was one thing still on the to-do list for Romanija, much-sung habitat of *haiduks*, refuge of virility and primordial virtue as opposed to the perverted and feminised cities: it had to become a new Kosovo, the *Peak of the Land*, the core around which the organisation of the symbolic space would be completed, the place where in a renewed act St George would kill the primeval Dragon. As Radovan Karadžić argued to the university professors of Banja Luka, dissatisfied that their city was neglected although it was the largest town in the area controlled by the Serbs, it was Pale, and not Banja Luka, that had to be the capital of the Serbs in Bosnia because the 'serpent [the Bosniaks] must never be held by the tail, but by the throat [Sarajevo]' (*Glas srpski*, 19 October 1994).

On St Vitus Day (*Vidovdan*) 1995 in Sokolac a St Vitus Day Assembly was held, that is, a *spiritual and intellectual* commemoration. It was attended, along with Karadžić, Mladić and Krajišnik, by the bishops of the Serbian Orthodox Church, the Sarajevan metropolitan Nikolaj and the Serbian Patriarch Pavle. Six years earlier, at Gazimestan, at the 600th anniversary of the Battle of Kosovo, Milošević had announced that in the resolution of the Yugoslav crisis 'not even armed battles could be ruled out'. There were only two Kosovos then: the original, primary Kosovo, where six centuries earlier the national calamity had begun – and at last, under Milošević's leadership, the awakened nation was starting to recover from this disaster. The second was in Croatia, near Knin. In each place there had long been a church (known as *Lazarica*) dedicated to St Lazar, the prince who had led the Serbian army into its fatal clash with the Ottoman conqueror. The third of them, on the mythical pan-Serbian Olympus, joined at just this time.

Reporting from Romanija, a journalist from the chief weekly of Republika Srpska was thus able to say that on that symbolic day at the door of the Romanija *Lazarica*

Symbolic heart of the Republika Srpske Krajine: bronze statue 'The *Gusle* Player', work of the sculptor Đorđe Jovanović, ceremonially installed outside the memorial church to Prince Lazar at Kosovo near Knin, on St Vitus Day 1994, as a gift from the city of Novi Sad.

> three Kosovos met: the old one, Lazar's, which shall last as long as there are Serbs; the picturesque and indestructible Dalmatian Kosovo, and the new, Romanija Kosovo, risen from blood and ash, defended with heart and mind. One St Vitus Day, in three Serbian states.[1]

The third important guest from the Church hierarchy, Bishop Irinej of Bačka, explained that 'not even Kosovo Field itself' was merely a geographical or territorial concept but rather a spiritual one (*Vreme International*, 247, 17 July 1995). And before the final blessing Patriarch Pavle called upon those present 'here in this Romanija Kosovo' to join in prayer 'to the sainted prince who with his brothers and sisters, with our forebears, went out to Kosovo, not to crush others' freedom, but to defend their own, not to wrest others' land from them, but to defend their own' (*Javnost*, 224, 8 July 1995). Indeed, in spite of the solemn atmosphere, from the speech Radovan Karadžić contributed for the occasion, it could be sensed that events in this other reality, this profane reality, and on this other map, the real map, were developing in a very awkward manner, and that the Serbian army was no longer as successful as it had been at the beginning of the war, when it confronted only terrified

---

1. A. Đ., 'Svi kao jedno srce' *Javnost* 225/ 226, 22 July 1995.

civilians and a lightly armed territorial defence:

> Surely today on Romanija's Kosovo, more of the people would
> have been here, had the best and most knightly of them not been
> on the borders and if the best and most knightly of them had not
> been wounded or had not been killed. (*Pravoslavlje*, 680, 15 July
> 1995)

By a trick of fate, the third Kosovo found itself at the centre of three
key points of a real political project, as well as at the numinous site of the
imaginary national space, almost identically distant as the crow flies from
Knin to the west and Gazimestan to the southeast. The newly built Lazarica
in Romanija's Sokolac appeared then as a pivotal place of parallel geography
and a keystone in a firm and well-considered symbolic edifice, and with it
Republika Srpska became the one true authentic Serbia, more Serbian than
Serbia itself.

Of course, the central geometrical position of Novak's Mountain,
Romanija, in the broader area (also) inhabited by Serbs is a coincidence. It is
a coincidence that near Sokolac there had long been a little place, a hamlet,
named Kosovo, and in the Sarajevo district at the end of the nineteenth
century there had been a village of Kosović, which was later abandoned.
What is more, in Croatia, Bosnia and Serbia there are dozens of similar place
names, because people everywhere always give a name to any special feature
associated with a river, plain, mountain or other point in their surroundings.
If they see that blackbirds – *kos* – gather in a place particularly often or in
particularly large numbers, it is quite logical that it should be called *Kosovo
polje*: *kos* + *-ovo* (suffix denoting the possessive) + *polje* (field) > *Kosovo* for
short. There are plenty of other examples: *Kosovski potok* (Blackbird Brook),
Kosov lug (Blackbird Grove), *Kosovo brodište* (Blackbird Ford) and various
derivations such as *Kosovac* (two villages, quite unconnected, one Croatian,
in Slavonia, one Serbian, in Šumadija); *Kosovnica* (a village on the island of
Krk in the far west of Croatia); *Kosova* (a village near Banja Luka, which
shows that even in Republika Srpska there is toponymical rivalry); as well
as *Kosovica, Kosovača, Kosović* ... In Croatia alone there are at least a dozen
such place names; some are mentioned in documents from the twelfth
century, translated into Latin as *campus merularum* (*campus* – field; *merula*
– blackbird).

All these are quite ordinary fields (plains) that did not differ from one
another in any way until the moment in 1389 when on one of them, in the
southwest of medieval Serbia, a relatively marginal battle was fought between

the Ottoman and the Serbian, or Christian, armies. Both commanders were killed: Prince Lazar and Sultan Murat I, both armies suffered major losses, but as far as can be gathered from contemporary sources, the outcome of the actual battle was inconclusive. Plenty of sources close to the time go so far as to speak of a Christian victory. However, from a historical perspective the Turks came out the winners because at that time they were the stronger and more organised force, on the way up, and Serbia was a state on the downward path, riven by internal conflicts. In fact, the medieval Serbian state managed to struggle on for another seventy years or so, but over time it was the battle of Kosovo that came to be associated with the national downfall.

Thus a single Kosovo came to be highlighted as different, as more important than all the others, marked in a particular way and exceptional in its meaning; one toponym became a symbol. Put another way, the possibility was created for a single coincidence to become a law, primarily, naturally, wherever Serbs lived. The subsequent spontaneous vernacular interpretation or organised ideological action of social elites began to inscribe a broader traditionally mediated system of signs of identity into a trivial local reality, to link this local physical fact with its more than merely geographical namesake, and thus to reinterpret, sanctify and legitimate it in new categories. According to one interpretation, in general in the traditional literature, Kosovo became 'the archetype of battlefield, a scene of slaughter, and then an assembly ground for debating all the important questions of our national life', a 'synonym for chivalric warfare and lost empires, for shameful betrayal, honourable death' (cf. Reðep 1987: 71).

The first Kosovo outside Serbia itself that was formally treated according to this new semantic key was the one near Knin, that is, Dalmatian Kosovo, as it is regularly called in Serbian sources. This is a lowland region consisting of seven villages more or less like all other villages in the area. During the permanent war and devastation of the area after Bosnia fell to the Turks in 1463, the old Croat population disappeared completely, some were killed, some fled. Since no rulers like empty spaces, the Ottoman governors, and after them the Venetian government, offered the abandoned land and houses to village headmen, either in Bosnia or in the neighbouring Dalmatian areas, both Catholic and Orthodox, if they would only settle there.

In the sixteenth and seventeenth centuries, Orthodox Serbs from Bosnia, mostly from the region of Glamoč, settled in Dalmatian Kosovo. They themselves believed that they had come originally from the first Kosovo after the defeat of 1389. When the Orthodox priest Savo Nakićenović was recording local traditions in the 1920s, he went further, as one who stated the tradition and then fitted it into wider systems, adding his own conclusion that the Serbs had settled this valley 'because of its similarity with their own old cradle', giving it its name for the 'sake of the grievous memory of Kosovo' (Nakićenović 1990: 43). Something crucial had occurred: the tradition of the fateful importance of the battle of Kosovo and the cult of Prince Lazar, which had been kept alive by the Church, had in the meantime become a mainstay of the political agenda of the young Serbian state.

In 1882 the Princedom of Serbia proclaimed itself a kingdom, and at once began extensive preparations to commemorate seven years later the fifth centenary of the Battle of Kosovo, making it a fundamental framework for their state ideology, iconography and legitimating discourse. The government in Belgrade announced that the fifth centenary had a double meaning; on the one hand it meant 'a memory of bygone Serbian glory' and 'the exemplary virtue' of the Kosovo heroes and, on the other, it was a manifestation of 'resurrected Serbian independence'.

On St Vitus Day 1889, all Serbian churches held a *parastos* or memorial service for the memory of Prince Lazar and those who had perished at Kosovo. A series of events was held in Belgrade and elsewhere in Serbia, the main one taking place in Kruševac. This city was the centre of the feudal domain ruled by Prince Lazar Hrebeljanović, and it was from there that he set out for the fatal battle. Kruševac was decorated ceremonially: arches were placed over all the roads into the town, with various, mainly patriotic, slogans such as *Concord Alone Saves the Serbs (Samo sloga Srbina spasava)*, as well as *Serbia – the Old Serbia, Bosnia-Herzegovina – Macedonia – Zeta* and *Syrmium, Croatia, Banat, Bačka, Dalmatia, Slavonia* – an agenda of lands and areas that were held to be Serbian and that were to be assembled under the mace of the Serbian dynasty into a single united state. The celebrations were attended by delegations of Serbs from Zagreb, Syrmium (Srijem), Dalmatia, Bosnia-Herzegovina and Old Serbia, i.e. Kosovo, which was still under Ottoman rule. On the base of the monument to Prince Lazar, leaves and flowers were placed from 'all the regions of the old Serbian empire', as the papers put it – laurels gathered at the foot of Lovćen (Montenegro), palms and immortelles from Dalmatia, and holly from Bosnia.

Although logically the Austro-Hungarian government did not look with any fondness at programmes put on as manifestations of national unity in Serbia and Bosnia-Herzegovina, for example in Mostar and on Romanija, the most important celebration outside Serbia proper was actually held in Dalmatia, at Kosovo near Knin, where a church was consecrated to the memory of St Lazar, the first one outside Kruševac. This meant the establishment of the cult of 'Saint Prince Lazar the Martyr of Kosovo' and the foundation of the Vitus Day tradition in this area. Up to that moment, for most of the population the concept of Serbianism expressed only their *religious* identity as Orthodox. Henceforth they would begin to voice particular Serbian *political* demands and manifest a Serbian national consciousness in the modern sense.

With this celebration, the Kosovo legend was not only expanded to but actually territorialised in northern Dalmatia, transmitting two messages in perpetuity: one of the former golden age and the lost national state, and the other of the necessity of national concord when the state was renewed. From the outset the Serbian Orthodox Church had officially referred to this locality by the name Dalmatinsko Kosovo, Dalmatian Kosovo, and in Serbian journalism we can also find the pair Little Kosovo and Big Kosovo. This kind of language shows what importance a small and seemingly distant and unimportant region had taken on in the Serbian ideology of national integration and in the political agendas shaped in Belgrade. This Little Kosovo was actually envisaged as the core of a wide-ranging symbol-creating project, a kind of parallel and no less valuable Serbia that in the foreseeable future would be not only symbolically but also really united.

The church consecrated to Prince Lazar in Dalmatian Kosovo was a permanent site of political rituals at St Vitus Day celebrations. It was made the central point of the political imaginative set of the local World War II Chetnik leader Momčilo Đujić, who as a priest and man with a developed sense of the epic culture managed to arouse in the local Serbian population suggestive and practically mystical ideas about their mission on 'the western border of Serbdom', here 'in Western Kosovo'. Beside the Lazarica, with Italian patronage and assistance, Đujić organised reviews and parades of his troops, gave fiery speeches, celebrated liturgies in which he glorified the 'revenge of Kosovo' and heralded an all-Serbian state with no Catholics or Muslims. He located his court martial there at the end of 1942, and in 1943 his 'central prison', actually a camp in which he tortured and murdered Croats and those Serbs who held out against the Chetnik ideology.

Half a century later, in 1991, the celebration was again coloured by the expected creation of Greater Serbia, this time on the ruins of Yugoslavia, and Knin was proclaimed the central point of the project, because 'Serbianism is undertaking its most difficult examination just here, in the area where the bells of the Lazarica can be heard' as an ideologue and writer, sometime minister of culture in the self-styled government, was to claim in the main speech.[1] Two years later, in a celebration at the Lazarica, a message was read out from *vojvoda* Momčilo Đujić (who had fled after the war and gone to live in the US), saying that there were two Kosovos – the original one, and this one in Dalmatia, 'both sprung from the battle and the blood shed for the freedom of Serbdom'.[2]

Today it is impossible to determine the origin of this toponym in the neighbourhood of Knin. When there are identical or similar place names based on climatic and other objective features over a broad area covered by the same language, and this is the case with 'Kosovo', it is possible that some migrants did accidentally come upon a name in their new domicile that they remembered from before, and then ascribed particular significance to this coincidence. It is also possible that over time such a similarity is forgotten, and the colonised community starts to believe that it had named the locality itself. There is also a third possibility. Since even before the Battle of Kosovo in 1389 reference was made in the documents to a locality near Knin called Kosovo, where there were as yet no Serbs, the newly arriving population, Catholic and Orthodox alike, might have been moved in their naming of the locality by the very same stimulus as the previous population, that is, they might just have seen a lot of blackbirds in the plain, not thinking at the time of an analogy with any other Kosovo. And there is a fourth, too: that some more educated Venetian official or scribe from one of the coastal cities might have known what the place was once called, and informed the Serbian incomers when they were allocated their land.

Nor is it possible to discount a fifth possibility: that the Orthodox settlers really did bring the toponym Kosovo with them. Migrants often take place names from their homeland with them and transplant them into the colonised area, as can be seen throughout North and South America, both full of place names that the settlers brought from Europe, sometimes with the attribute New, Nouvelle or Nuevo, sometimes without. Such an explanation is in complete accord with the way in which the cult of Saint Prince Lazar spread. For example, during the Serbian migrations to the north, a group of monks from Ravanica monastery in the south of today's Serbia, where Prince Lazar was originally buried, brought his relics with them and gave the name of Ravanica to every place at which they were kept in memory of the original church, claiming that there was no interruption in the working of the Lazar foundation, *zadužbina* (Mihaljčić 1984: 210). This was how they named their first stop near Buda in Hungary, and then Vrdnik, on Fruška Gora, in

---

1. Jovan Radulović, 'Vidovdan – ispit ponosa i viteštva', *Istina*, 8, December 1991.
2. 'Pozdrav Srpstvu vojvode Momčila za Vidovdan 1993', *Istina*, 9–10, December 1993.

Vojvodina, where they moved in 1697.

But such a transfer of place names undoubtedly contains the root of the self-awareness and identity of the local Serbs in the hills of northern Dalmatia, and such self-awareness is authentic as a psychological reality. It is, therefore, also beyond dispute that such a transfer in itself does not erase other possibilities or other kinds of self-awareness, and in particular does not contain significant implications for state's rights. What is not accidental, however, and implies modern ideological pretensions is the decision that the traditionally verified point should be formally and officially sanctified by the construction of a church in memory of Prince Lazar, thus declaring to the world not only that Serbs live here, but that there is or will be another Serbia.

All that has been said of the second Kosovo and the second Lazarica near Knin in Croatia also holds good for the third Kosovo and the third Lazarica on Romanija, in Bosnia. With respect to the similarity of place names, later interpreted in terms of ideology, indeed of a kind of national theology and eschatology, *both* from the point of view of the reproduction of state ideology, through the reproduction of its central symbolic point, *and* from the point of view of that social force, the Church, that thought up and carried through the programme of the territorial plantation or multiplication of Serbia. The fact that the third Kosovo or the third Serbia was formally institutionalised only a hundred years after the first and the second is only a technical difference: the semantic currents that flowed towards Romanija over the centuries clearly went in this direction and created a firmly networked base. It depended only on the relationships of political forces when this complex and historically ripened dynamic was to acquire its final formal crown.

Romanija had anyway long been a highly symbolic space, and, with the collapse of communism and the rise of Milošević, it might have embarked on the great finale of its final formulation as core of the new political imaginative set and canny elevation to ever higher and more complex semantic levels. There, it would become a place for the total vision of national history, a point from which at last the end of the road to the Promised Land and the fulfilment of the prophecies could be discerned. With the dedication of the Church of St Lazar on Sokolac it really did become an encyclopaedic aggregate, to use a phrase of Northrop Frye's from his theory of the mythical mode. In principle, each episode of some social memory or culture can be a germ from which such a concatenation of motifs will start 'if the culture is sufficiently homogeneous', after which its elements 'have a strong tendency to stick together and form encyclopaedic aggregates' (Frye 1971: 55–6), but it is not illogical that the germ out of which the encyclopaedic form developed should have been precisely a mountain overlooking Sarajevo.

Serbian vernacular culture with its central ecclesiologically formed motif of the fatal defeat at Kosovo, the epic heroic songs and cult of the avenging *haiduk* and liberator was undoubtedly homogeneous in the Frye sense, and Romanija contained references to all the relevant episodes of this culture. In this context, suddenly not even its geographical position in the centre seems a mere coincidence or its Kosovo belated. Quite the reverse, it is able to be the centre precisely because it is the third, and only that which is third actually becomes the first, since it is the centre of abstractions and unknowns if the edges are not first of all defined: the first Kosovo and the first Lazarica in the east; the second Kosovo and the second Lazarica in the west; then the third Kosovo and the third Lazarica, it could be said, spring up of their own accord, through the internal development of the myth. In this dynamic pointing towards Romanija, stimulating imaginative lines of force had long since met, and the war of 1990–5 was just the closing chapter of this deep-level course of sacred history and the ending of an internal logic determined by the said lines of force at least as much as by the social and political processes of profane history in the eighties.

But *profane* history alone cannot give an answer to the question of why the top brass of the Serbian Orthodox Church (SPC) had gathered together on the occasion of the consecration of a little, architecturally modest, and essentially rural church on a highly inaccessible mountain.

As with the liturgy at Sokolac the 'three Serb states' – Serbia, Republika Srpska and Republika Srpska Krajina – were equalised in value terms within the categories of the Kosovo myth, so they had been identified even earlier and equalised in the categories of their central exemplary figure. Just as Republika Srpska had obtained the only thing that it lacked compared to the other two members of the national trinity, its own Lazarica in its own Kosovo, so Republika Srpska Krajina obtained what it alone had been deprived of, compared to the other two territories: its own archetypal *haiduk* in its own 'nest of heroic freedom'.

This was indeed not a mountain like Romanija, because Republika Srpska Krajina, although a mainly upland territory, did not have a real mountain furnished with meanings and symbolic potential capable of being more or less compared to those of Romanija. The *haiduk* tradition had been lively on the Slavonian mountains of Papuk and Psunj, as it had in Kordun and Lika, up to the early twentieth century, but it did not have powerful, individualised characters, defined in a complex manner in the vernacular culture, particularly none whose significance could rise above their region and serve as a symbolic link with Republika Srpska or Serbia itself. Such a figure had to be imported, just as it was necessary to find a substitute for the appropriate elevated point in space with the closest value-equivalent, and it did this in an extremely logical manner. Its *haiduk* became Starina Novak, and the fortress on the hill above Knin became its Romanija. Thus the three Kosovos and the three Lazaricas were matched by the three Novaks.

As early as the autumn of 1991, comic strips and pulp fiction were created in which this imaginative set was structured consistently and rounded off. The previously unnamed *haiduk* from the declaration of Dušan Zelembaba and other SDS leaders received his name and surname – Starina Novak. The Romanija *haiduk* appeared in them in the unexpected but not illogical role of *gusle* player who sang to the members of the Serb paramilitaries in the Knin fortress, in the lulls between the military actions in which he took part as a kind of consultant and expert in commando skills, a representative of the 'glory of the old Uskoks, and the exploits of their descendants the *kninjas*', as these soldiers were colloquially called. Among them were two whose names stressed the symbolism additionally: Grujica, almost a boy, but no less capable and courageous than the others, as the contemporary incarnation of Dijete Grujica, Novak's son from the epic poem, and Radojica, the most adroit and highly trained of them, as a contemporary version of another famed *haiduk*, Mali Radojica, Novak's brother (and Grujica's uncle), Deli Radivoje, who sometimes appears in the epics under this name.

It was inevitable that in such a semantic framework the motif of the height taken with a flag should appear at the outset. The image of the banner that waves at the highest point of the sacred ground thus determines not only its national political affiliation but also its central importance in the religious map. The action of the comic strip has a clear and unambiguous framework: according to a decision of the Croatian state leadership on 10 April, the day on which the NDH was declared in 1941, a group of Ustasha commandoes was supposed to raid Republika Srpska Krajina and put up the Croatian flag on the Knin fortress. However, they were foiled by the Serb *kninjas*, in a fable that contains all the features of the action genre. The Yugoslav and Serbian flags continued to wave over Knin, and the Croatian 'chequerboard' flag (*šahovnica*) was seized; Grujica decided to give it to Starina Novak, because 'the old one he had captured in '41 must have rotted away by now' (Đukić and Katić 1991; see illustration on page 402).

Thus, again quite logically, the Romanija *haiduk* was presented in a new role, adapted to the social memory of the new audience and the frame of

Romanija *haiduks* in a 1991 cartoon strip: Starina Novak as a *gusle* player on the Knin fortress, Grujica and Radojica as *knindže* [word play on ninja warriors] who will repel the assault upon Knin of Croatian commandoes.

references in which the Greater Serbian propaganda presented events in Croatia in 1990. While in Bosnia or on Romanija and elsewhere Starina Novak protected his people from the Turks, in Knin, or in Croatia in general, where such symbolism had a very slender historical basis and none at all in reality and was thus functionless, he was transformed into the leader of resistance against the NDH redivivus and protector of the Serbian *rayah* from the Ustasha *zulüm*. Thus Novak and the Novakovićes were put 'under the aegis of a summarily indicated epic tradition', that is, the 'symbolic ethical and patriotic value that this tradition has for us today' were successfully transferred to Knin (Čolović 1993: 77).[1]

The allocation of characters in the trashy novel *Demoni dolaze* (*The Demons Are Coming*) is a little different, but there too the fundamental prototype is taken from the same segment of the folklore matrix. The main character among the 'terrible *kninjas* who knew no fear, weariness or obstacles', and trained under the mysterious Captain Dragan, a returned expatriate, 'a grey-haired lad of military bearing', is called Sava, and with him is a girl, Milica, who is determined to take revenge on the Croats since she had once been raped by her then boyfriend, a Croat, with whom she had been much in love, and his tipsy chums. Thus this important motif of the assault on female honour appears in the imaginative set that was to give an interpretation of the attack on Croatia (as the reader will know, this was very important in the anti-Albanian propaganda in Kosovo, when in the statements of the political elite and in the *gusle* songs it was claimed that the Albanians raped Serb girls according to plan. When the aggression against Bosnia was launched, this would soon be activated in this context as well).

But when, in September, the select *kninjas* organise an important action, which as motif is not only an essential part of the convention of such novels but in the new context a clear copy of the epic *haiduk* ambush of the Turkish caravan in the deserted canyon, the group includes a Radojica, a Grujica and a Novak, 'a greying moustachioed fellow'. This kind of definition suggests age, of course, in the epic sense discussed here, but at one point he is called more exactly 'old Novak', while Captain Dragan, addressing him, calls him 'old man', *stari*. He is, in fact, the leader of the group and at the end of the action is debriefed by Captain Dragan, who is all the time in contact with another real-life figure, the leader of a Serbian paramilitary organisation, Željko 'Arkan' Ražnatović. In the performance of the action there is some of the much-sung *haiduk* initiative, that is the manner in which warfare was understood by, for instance, Samovolja Rade from the Kordun Partisan song. The participants in the ambush, experienced commando-*haiduk*s, do not obey Captain Dragan's strict order, based on the formal criteria of military science, but they succeed all the same, or rather, precisely for that reason they succeed, with relatively low-powered hand-held launchers, in routing an incomparably stronger column of armoured vehicles, vans and buses full of Croatian police. On another occasion, after an attack on Šibenik, also successful, in yet another copy of the stereotyped epic situation about a mountain as refuge of freedom and the lowland or coastal city as source

---

1. I am grateful to Dr Ivan Čolović, an anthropologist from Belgrade, from whose book I learned of the existence of these comic strips, for having provided me with a photocopy of them.

of evil, the contemporary *haiduk* band returns to its indomitable republic 'along the mountains, to Krajina, steadily uphill' (Krajišnik 1991).

But the moment in which the symbolic peak is achieved in the construction of the tripartite synthetic Greater Serbia was at the same time the moment at which its actual dissolution began. At the outset, it would seem, some of the new *'haiduks'* and those who backed them perceived their work as a kind of drama, as the harmless staging of epic motifs that in itself would have a magical impact on reality and channel events in the desired direction. A few days after the first Croat fatality, the Croatian policeman Josip Jović, in a clash between the Serbs and the regular police force at Easter 1991 in Plitvice, a Serb from a nearby village called Jezerce seemed to have sobered up for a moment, and perhaps become anxious, when he admitted to a Belgrade journalist: 'The shots shattered our illusions. Without the *haiduks* the romanticism and the *"haidukery"* all vanished' (Vujasinović 1995: 67).

But there was hardly any drawing back, and the logic of events was determined by those who had activated the traditional conceptual machinery and thus at the beginning prevented the coming conflicts from being settled in terms of rational political categories.

The SDS leaders and their intellectual and political patrons in Belgrade, agents of legitimation who were officially entrusted with the definition of the newly nascent reality, created a symbolic universe that in principle excluded the categories of political negotiation and rational compromise among the proponents of the competing political agendas. The roles, priorities and procedures were taken from a real social and historical context, revamped and put into an ahistorical, epic world, and hence legitimated within a different set of concepts and frame of reference. Legitimation is understood here as the process of the production of new meanings 'that serve to integrate the meanings already attached' to disparate processes. Within this process, symbolic universes are created that furnish and define the borders of social reality, that is, they state what is relevant in social interactions. Legitimation explains the order of things and 'justifies it by giving a normative dignity to its practical imperatives', but it is important to see that legitimation 'has a cognitive as well as a normative element'. That is, legitimation 'is not just a matter of "values", it 'always implies "knowledge" as well', it 'not only tells the individual why he *should* perform one action and not another; it also tells him why things *are* what they are' (Berger and Luckmann 1971: 110–11).

As a result, the new political situation – the collapse of communism, the profound economic, political and institutional crisis of Yugoslavia, and the creation of a multi party system and free market – took on another sense, that is, cognitive and normative legitimation were systematised in another way. The dominant Serbian national discourse, like the other national discourses, was at that moment faced with a choice between two conceptual machineries for the construction and maintenance of the selected symbolic universe. And it made the decision not to select this machinery from political and organisational theory, but from vernacular culture and the epic tradition. The social processes were to be entirely excluded from their realistic historical context and integrated on a different, ahistorical level, as a kind of eternal *haiduk* drama with *gusle* songs and shooting, placed in a particular symbolic universe that 'itself does not require further legitimation' (Berger-Luckman 1971: 122). And since it was the first players who were in a position to choose, this to a very large extent determined which conceptual machinery was to be chosen by the others when they were faced with the necessity of choice.

Five years after the '*haiduks* that chased the *haiduks*' had blocked the highroads in Lika and northern Dalmatia with barricades, four years after Starina Novak had shown up in Knin Fortress, and not a month and a half after the epiphanic point of the selected symbolic universe had been established at the Romanija Kosovo, and after it had become more than obvious that it was going to be impossible to settle the conflict in a peaceful way, on 4 August 1995, the Croatian Army (HV) launched a major military operation to liberate the rebellious and seceding regions. The Army of the RSK was shattered in a few days, and on the very next day the Serbian flag was hauled down from Knin Fortress (the Yugoslav flag had, from the beginning of the conflict, been anyway just a comic strip motif and décor for the naive) and the Croatian flag was raised. Almost the entire Serbian population fled to Republika Srpska or Serbia.

At the moment of the total collapse, an anonymous Belgrade reporter was able, with unconcealed nostalgia, to recall his visit to these regions in August 1990 and the 'textbook image' that had deeply affected him at the time. The road over Planičnik Pass on the Zadar to Benkovac road was blocked with a pile of rocks, and a large bulldozer, beside which stood a man

> with a semi-automatic rifle on his shoulder and a low-slung pair of binoculars. That August afternoon, Janko's eyes glittered like the silver plates (*toke*) on the breast of the *harami bašis*, like *haiduk* plasma swirling in archaic Dinaric defiance.[1]

---

1. 'Pijani vremeplov poslednje bune i seobe [Drunken time machine of the last revolt and migration]', *DEM*, 10, 29 October 1995. In this weekly, stories are not signed, rather the authors are mentioned in alphabetic order on the second page. It seems that

During the preceding and subsequent weeks, units of the VRS (Army of Republika Srpska) entered the Bosnian city of Srebrenica and carried out a massacre of several thousand Bosniak civilians, and in a mortar attack on Sarajevo killed forty-one and wounded several hundred citizens. As a result, there were NATO air strikes for two weeks against its armoured and artillery positions, its command and communication centres and its telecommunications systems. In coordinated operations, the forces of the HV, AB-H and HVO liberated large areas, reached the outskirts of Prijedor and Bosanski Novi, and 25 kilometers south of Banja Luka. The VRS collapsed in panic, and 100,000 civilian refugees crowded into Banja Luka and the Posavina corridor to Serbia. There was a morbid irony in the fact that for want of space several hundred of them found refuge in the huts of the former concentration camp of Omarska not far from Prijedor, in which in 1992 some of the greatest atrocities against Bosniaks and Croats were committed, from systematic rapes to ritual murders.

The Croatian-Bosnian offensive was halted by pressure from international diplomacy, and at the negotiations that began on 1 November in the American airbase at Dayton, Ohio, controlled by Richard Holbrooke, it was decided that Bosnia-Herzegovina should be organised as a state consisting of two entities – Republika Srpska on 49 percent and the Federation of Bosnia-Herzegovina on 51 percent of the area. Thus the Serbian para-state, created by crime and genocide, was legally and politically institutionalised as a de facto state within a state. Presidents Tuđman, Izetbegović and Milošević officially signed the agreement in Paris on 14 December 1995. According to the agreement the VRS had to withdraw from the Sarajevo neighbourhood of Grbavica and the suburban municipalities of Ilidža and Vogošća, so they dug up corpses from the local graveyards and transported them in trucks to new graveyards, mainly at Sokolac.

---

the author of this story is Petar Samardžija, whose name is given among the writers in this number of *DEM*. The Knin correspondent of Belgrade's *Politika,* Milan J. Četnik, wrote that in the morning of 17 August 1990 he had visited the recently erected road barricades in the Knin-Obrovac-Benkovac triangle with reporters from TV Belgrade, two reporters from Podgorica's daily *Pobjeda* and the correspondent of *Politika ekspres,* P. Samardžija. At Planičnik they came upon a vast 'trench digger' and its driver, Janko Cvjetan. Across his shoulder he carried a 'semi-automatic rifle and binoculars hung around his neck' and in a superior manner, 'smiling calmly', he halted the upset and frightened tourists and other travellers in cars and trucks, which left a powerful impression on the reporter; Milan J. Četnik: 'Kako je Babić proglasio ratno stanje', *Politika,* 17 August 1990, reprinted in: Četnik 1997: 128–9. It is clearly the same event and the same '*Haiduk* Janko' whom the journalists of several media, including national TV, presented to the Serbian and Montenegrin viewers as an archetypal Serbian hero.

At the same time, the leadership of Republika Srpska announced its intention to build a new city, Serbian Sarajevo, one version saying it would have 100,000 inhabitants, and another 200,000. The project, backed by Radovan Karadžić, was unveiled on 9 January 1996, the fifth anniversary of the promulgation of Republika Srpska in the Bistrica Hotel, Jahorina. The mythical mountain of Romanija was assigned an important role in the project: there was to be an industrial zone in Mokro, and Pale would be the centre of the whole city, with libraries, theatres, department stores and sports halls. But even in the new situation its epic symbolism had not completely evaporated, since this highland Serbian Sarajevo, as the architect Tihomir Obradović explained to the invited audience, would 'be some kind of response to that Muslim or let us say Bosnia-Herzegovina Sarajevo, a defence against the spread of Islam to the east' (*Slobodna Bosna*, 15, 22 March 1996). The Vice-President of the Government of Yugoslavia (Serbia and Montenegro), Nikola Šainović, even officiated at the grand opening of the first stage of the works, on 12 November 1996, and then all sounds of the 'epoch-making' project died away.

Unlike these voices, which at least for the public, at least for a short time, mentioned industry and libraries and sports halls and gave at least some indication that it was the late twentieth century, the other and clearly more important voices, deeply immersed in the past and in the ahistorical categories of the epic, showed no signs of lassitude.

In an article in which he summed up the outcome of the war and mapped out future strategic aims of Serbian policy (also on the fifth anniversary of the proclamation of the Serb para-state in Bosnia-Herzegovina), Ljubomir Zuković, one of the ideologues of Republika Srpska and another professor of traditional literature who put his knowledge at the service of political propaganda, estimated that in the war just finished there were no out-and-out losers or victors. The 'Ustashas' or the 'Latins' had gained a good deal of land, but had paid dearly for it, because they had been driven into a federation with 'the fanatical Islamic fundamentalists'. It was the 'converts to Islam (*poturice*)' that had lost the most, since their original objective had been the establishment of an Islamic state over the whole of Bosnia-Herzegovina, and since they had no chance historically speaking, except that Izetbegović did not seem to remember how his 'forebear and political guide' Fočić Mehmed-Aga from Višnjić's poem 'The Beginning of the Revolt against the Dayis' had ended. Those with relatively the most reason to be satisfied were the Serbs, because they had obtained their Republika Srpska, a state, which had to be developed the way it was. And as for Sarajevo and the one-time majority

Serbian parts of the Bosanska Krajina, they had to be patient, 'fight for time', wait 'even if to the first St George's, until the hills go green, *dokle gora zazeleni*'.[1]

A little earlier, in a paper which cultivated connections with Russian and other East European conservatives and Orthodox fundamentalists, and had moved to Belgrade on the eve of the breakdown of Republika Srpska Krajina, a poem was printed in two languages, Serbian and Bulgarian. The title of this interesting, even programmatic, poem came from the famed *haiduk* mountain overlooking Sarajevo. It is the way it is, and although the introductory part is gloomy, the images are not without an intelligible message: from that of the *gusle* player to that of the winds bearing caps symbolising the two nations, the Serbian *šubara*, a fleecy leather cap, and the Bosniak fez. The kaleidoscope closes with an image in which, on the Sacred Mountain, as the light fades, at the edge of the forest, Alija Đerzelez and the Romanija *haiduks* tussle:

> *Sing out, sister; Romanija, oh*
>
> *From the gas station, a drunk plays the* gusle,
> *By him some kids and a dead crow*
>
> *Two winds wave the murmuring boughs,*
> *one from* šubara *and the other from fez.*
>
> *From the darkling wood, where reigns the gloom,*
> *burst out, viper, Starina Novak.*
>
> *Still it darkens, storm drives the feathers,*
> *Alija and Grujo fly about the glade.*[2]

The order of the epic shoot-out, which was sharply evoked by Vuk Drašković at the very beginning of the whole story, is well known to the reader of this discussion, and still better to the readers of the paper in which the poem was published. Everyone can choose a perspective from which to understand

---

1. Ljubomir Zuković, 'Zlo – i gore [Bad – and worse]', *Javnost*, 245/ 246, 6 January 1996. Fočić Mehmed-Aga, whose job Izetbegović allegedly continued, was one of the four *dayis*, janissary commanders, who in Ottoman Serbia had broken loose from the central governemnt and had caused a revolt with their cruelty. The *gusle* player F. Višnjić left a suggestive epic image of these figures, especially of Fočić, in his poem 'The Beginning of the Revolt against the Dayis' ('Početak bune na dahije'), and allusions to or quotations from it were very often used in Serbian nationalist discourse on the eve of and during the war.
2. Milosav Tešić, 'Romanija', *Zbilja*, 21-22-23, 31 October 1996.

the closing image: as an admission of defeat, or as the announcement of a new settling of accounts through war. For as the archetypal epic songs say, up to the moment in which the Bosniak epic hero and the son of the Romanija Serbian *haiduk*, as if photographed, were caught in a duel to the death, Alija Đerzelez has already mastered the *haiduk* Deli Radivoje, sometimes Tatomir too, and now Starina Novak awaits him. There is as well, as the reader also knows, the Serbian song in which Starina Novak brings victory to the *haiduks* at the end, as there are so many others that on Romanija on various occasions and with various intentions – and in changing alliances – bring in many other epic heroes, from the Herzegovina Catholic Mijat Tomić to the Velika Kladuša Muslim Mujo Hrnjica.

Only one thing seems sure: that the epic duel is about halfway through, only without there being any certainty as to which temporal adverb to apply to the situation: only or already.

THIRTEEN

Social Memory and the Production of Symbols

They say to us, why didn't you stay? If someone had told us to stay, we'd have stayed. I know, the army's the army, no getting round that. When the army comes, hide in the woods, when the army goes, come out of the woods. That's how it was once, and it could be like that now, but some damned way it isn't.

(Old Serb peasant from Western Bosnia, a returned refugee, talking to a Zagreb journalist; *Tjednik*, 40, 28 November 1997).

Haiduks, *peasants,* askers *and heroes of socialist labour*

In both Yugoslavias (the monarchist and the communist states) the idealised figure of the *haiduk* was right at the centre of the ideological image of the world. From 1918 to 1941 the emphasis was on the *haiduk* fighting against the alien conqueror, and from 1945 to 1990 this component was matched, and even to an extent superseded, by one in which the *haiduk* was seen as fighter for social justice as well. In the Kingdom of Yugoslavia the *haiduk* fitted into the official ideology of the integrating Yugoslavism of the centralised state which built its referential core on the cult of the *national dynasty* of Karađorđević that had sprung out of the first Serbian insurrection, and which understood the new multi-ethnic and multi-religious state legally and politically simply as an extension of the Kingdom of Serbia.

The virile and fearless *haiduk* was not, naturally, confined within the borders of the ruling political imaginary set, but found an important place for himself in certain artistic trends such as Zenit(h)ism, a variant of Dadaism and other West European avant-garde movements in the twenties. As opposed to the flabby *Latins,* rotten Paris and London and the swanky new 'European agas and beys', the Zenithists incorporated into the appeal of their programme the Yugoslav or Balkan, de facto Serbian, barbarian genius or 'barbarogenius', imagined as a modern hero of elemental purity and raw, indomitable virility. Since he had preserved his vitality thanks to the resilient power of his *haiduk* forebears, his new task was to cure 'the old whore' of Europe, this 'revamped Turkey of our century'. According to the poems and manifestos of the ideologue of Zenithism, Ljubomir Micić, and his disciples, these '*haiduks* of mankind', the 'Balkan *haiduks*' would 'peck out the brains of Western culture', first of all taking on the Croats, a nation of rejects, 'a sect of people of the Roman Catholic religion' whose 'perverse' culture was the 'bastard brat of the unequal marriage of the trained monkey and the parrot' and so on. The Bosnian Muslims and other communities that were formed in the Balkans under the cultural influence of the Ottomans were portrayed in a similar, or much worse, way.

In some sense related to the Cvijić apotheosis of the Dinaric warrior, the philosopher Vladimir Dvorniković (1888–1956) added another important note to the spiritual setting of the first Yugoslavia. His thinking, synthesised in a large volume on the study of the national character of the Yugoslavs (1939), provided the ideologues of integralism with a lot of material useful for their propaganda, although the basic premises of it were laid down before 1918 and were not originally intended to comprise an effective ideological agenda, and least of all to be material for the manipulation of practical politics. This was largely what they were reduced to, however, particularly after the proclamation of the royal dictatorship of 6 January 1929. According to Dvorniković, character was what gathered individual qualities functionally into a single whole as the 'core of the personality', both in the individual, and in the nation, which is a 'higher-order historical personality'. As a nation, the Yugoslavs are distinguished by their 'fighting strength', which is spiritualised by their 'love of freedom', while the heroic epic is the 'most characterful Yugoslav collective spiritual creation', from which the 'Balkan heroised Yugoslav' speaks out (Dvorniković 1990).

In the communist Yugoslav federation, the *haiduk* motif symbolically legitimated the Partisan struggle and the rule of communism. The figure of the *haiduk*, or the Uskok, figured in the period in two roles: as a kind of founding father of Serbian/Croatian brotherhood and collaboration, and as a forebear of the Partisans and the communists in general, which, of course, did not exclude its previous significance. He was an exemplary and sanctified hero, a fighter *sans tache ou peur*, and this was as a rule a vision that outweighed individual ideologies and political agendas. This may be seen not only in ideological discourse, but also in the historiographic works of influential and respectable historians.

In the standard and extremely popular *Survey of the History of the Croatian*

Nation (Pregled povijesti hrvatskog naroda), a work by the Croatian historian Ferdo Šišić, we find the formulation that the *haiduks* were 'stalwart folks', 'those courageous people who in the Croatian and in the Serbian people, throughout the whole time of the Turkish yoke, kept their sense of freedom and liberation' (Šišić 1962: 312). There is additional interest here – since in just a few decades of the twentieth century Croatia went through a number of changes of power and sovereignty – in the fact that the first edition was published in 1916, while the country was still part of the Austro-Hungarian Empire, the second in 1920, immediately after the creation of the Kingdom of the Serbs, Croats and Slovenes, that is Yugoslavia, and the third in 1962 in communist Yugoslavia. The formulation worked very well in each of these very different systems.

The Serbian historian Vladimir Ćorović, a contemporary of Šišić's, although himself inclined to a romanticised and idealised past, in the given case showed himself a little more critical or at least circumspect. His *History of Yugoslavia (Istorija Jugoslavije)* was written at a time of profound crisis in the Yugoslav state ideology, in the years of the royal dictatorship, when the aggressive cult of *haiduk* heroism was reaching its peak, and the book was supposed to serve the creation of an idea that the South Slav nations were designed by destiny to be together and that the whole of their history actually led in the direction of unification. However, his assessment was essentially more balanced:

> In the Turkey of the sixteenth to eighteenth centuries, the *haiduks*, although they were sometimes just common robbers, enjoyed the approbation of the Christian people, to which they themselves mostly belonged, exclusively because of their assailing the Turks [...] and the people often found its avengers in them. (Ćorović 1933: 308)

Unlike Šišić, who gave his own assessment, Ćorović deftly avoided such a challenge and spoke about the way the 'people' experienced the *haiduks*, which is something very different, for if the people did perceive them in a positive light, this does not necessarily imply that they really deserved it. In addition, Ćorović explicitly stated that this happened in spite of the *haiduks* sometimes being common robbers, and that the criterion for their being seen so positively was 'exclusively' their enmity to the Ottomans. In other words, he suggested that the view was partisan and should not be taken at face value. What is more, the suggestion that *haiduks* 'mostly belonged' to the Christians is nevertheless different from the ideological dogma that they were exclusively Christian: the author's adverb leaves room for the implicit, ideologically heretical but historically accurate deduction that there were some non-Christians, who could only have been Muslims, and therefore that the Islamised South Slavs were not solely tools of the occupier, traitors and oppressors of the Christians. A more precise elaboration or shading would have been hard to expect at that time.

It has already been stated how immediately after the establishment of the NDH, a senior Ustasha official mocked the Croatian Peasants Party (HSS) member Branko Pešelj because his party urged peaceful means of political struggle and an agreement between Serbs and Croats (see p. 68). Two other testimonies reveal an astounding coincidence between the views of two people who were otherwise utterly different. The communist Marijan Stilinović was an urban intellectual, born in northwest Croatia, in *peaceful Pauria*; he studied in Zagreb and lived there until the war, moving in leftist literary circles. After the war he was appointed Yugoslav ambassador to Prague. He spent the war, of course, with Tito's Partisans, and in mid-1942, dissatisfied with their bearing and the combatants' military performance, he wrote in his diary the lapidary conclusion: 'Radić's politics have been the downfall of our people, who are stroppy and always in the mood for a rebellion' (Stilinović 1986: 172). An anonymous and clearly semi-illiterate Ustasha, born somewhere in the *bloody Krajina*, who after the establishment of the NDH was appointed to a senior position in central Croatia, complained in the autumn of 1941 to his interlocutor that the Ustashas had passed up a 'marvellous' chance to settle scores once and for all with the Serbs. All that was needed, he said, was to set things up in just a few places, for example, to kill two or three prominent people in some Croatian village, to set fire to a house in another, and then the Croats, convinced that this had been done by the Serbian Chetniks, would set out in general vengeance against the neighbouring Serbian villages. If they did not respond spontaneously as predicted, an adroit way could be found to get them going. There were not, 'alas', as many such sparks 'as there should have been', for which he blamed Stjepan Radić, the assassinated founder of the HSS. For his 'idea of humanity came back against us at the most decisive moment' for 'in most villages' the Serbian peasant did not raise a hand against the Croatian peasant, or vice versa (Jakovljević 1999: 81).

The Bosnian Serb Vasa Pelagić (1838–99), one of the leaders of the last rebellions in Ottoman Bosnia in 1875 and the organiser of the first working-class 1 of May celebrations in Serbia, was a controversial figure in whom the theologian met the rabid anti-clericalist, the nationalist who considered

Bosnia without a shadow of reserve to be a Serbian land, and a socialist who knew contemporary Russian and Western authors. From the founding of the Communist Party of Yugoslavia, he was an important figure in its catalogue of models, and after 1945 had his place confirmed on the shortlist of officially designated *forebears of the socialist revolution*. His writings were reprinted with state patronage and often with forewords by leading party theorists. In one of his works published in 1879, in which he explained the causes of and the downfall of the insurrections of the Bosnian *rayah*, in the chapter 'Why rebellions occur' *(Sašta se rađaju bune)*, he attempted in broad theoretical lines to explain the reasons for rebellions and revolutions, or to explain 'who drove worthy workers to join the *haiduks*, who drove them to rise up, who forced the poor to kill, to seize and sometimes to steal'.

Quoting a fragment of one of the heroic songs of the *haiduk* cycle, he concluded that

> The masters of church and state should look well and carefully at their reflection in it. They should compare their big salaries and easy work, their luxurious and dissipated lives, with the life of a working man who bathes in his own sweat. Then they would themselves see and admit that they who preserve and maintain the current socially unjust organisation are to blame for all human ills and evils, for all rebellions and revolutions.
>
> What we have said is an eternal moral and scientific truth, which no one who is honest and learned will deny. But in spite of that, whoever is against this existing injustice, whoever rises up against oppression, exploitation and pillage is considered a rebel and an enemy of the state order and system, and is condemned to all kinds of tortures and cruel punishments. (Pelagić 1953: 33)

Such sentences would easily have been signed by not only Dušan Zelembaba but by any orthodox Yugoslav communist, whether he did or did not know that the woes of the 'worthy worker' on which Pelagić founded his conclusions are contained in the first thirty lines of the song 'Starina Novak and Headman [*knez*] Bogosav'. For this song was ideal in that it encompassed both fields of the communist legitimation system. The first part, when Novak in Serbia performed feudal labour on building works, bore the message of social injustice and unbearable exploitation, and the second part, when he fled to Ottoman Bosnia and became a *haiduk*, contained the message of the battle against the foreign conquistador and enslaver. Put a different way, in the first part of the poem Novak was a 'class-conscious' worker, almost a communist or at least a Marxist, and in the second part, an effective revolutionary patriot. In addition, the song symbolically linked two Yugoslav imaginaries – the peasant and the *haiduk*. In other words, Novak's epic *curriculum vitae* embodied two archetypal fates: the fate of the serf who rebelled against the exploitation of the local feudal lord and the fate of the *haiduk* who suffered from the cruelty of the external conqueror.

A lesson in an elementary school reader clearly shows how the idea was worked out and in what manner it fitted into official patterns of socialisation. The unit 'Bright Paths' *(Svijetle staze)* starts with Gorky's lyrical prose piece, 'Song of The Storm Petrel', and closes with a number of themes from the National Liberation War (NOB), and it is given a wider historical context in a piece about the Allied landings in Normandy. Then comes a selection from a Tito interview about the point and forms of the Partisan struggle, and at the end is the lyrical poem 'And freedom ripens' *(I sazri sloboda)* by the Croatian poet Vesna Parun. Thus at the level of composition, a fabula is developed about the route from slavery towards freedom. The song 'Starina Novak and Headman Bogosav' is preceded by an excerpt from *The Communist Manifesto*, under the emblematic title 'Proletarians of the World, Unite', explained as a 'call to communists and proletarians of the whole world to smash the system of exploitation and to set up a different and more just system in which no one will be exploited'. In such a consistent fabulative framework the life of the Romanija *haiduk* shows that 'the feudal violence of the local lords was joined by the violence of the Turkish invader'. Novak then became a typical representative of the 'class of the exploited' that inevitably came into conflict with the 'exploiter class' and in that revolution, as the 'working class' took power and brought freedom to the oppressed (Bukša–Antoš 1966: 113–60).[1]

As well as party ideologues, authors of school textbooks and compilers of popular anthologies, the authors of historical works, given all their different motivations and their positions in the relationships of political power, uncritically promoted the idea of the continuity of resistance 'from

---

1. The song, however, is not given in its entirety: four lines are omitted in which Novak recounts how he lies in wait for and robs the 'youth of Sarajevo'. In addition to basic educational reasons, the omission was also necessary because otherwise such a literal identification of *haiduk* and Partisan, or communist, would suggest that they too would have seized 'both silver and gold, and nice shawls and velvet'. Nor is there the final Novak statement that he fears nobody but God, which is of course easy to explain by the official view downgrading religion, that is, the official state policy of atheism, and also by the cult of *haiduk* reincarnation, in the communist revolutionary, who was afraid of absolutely no one, and therefore not God either, in fact, Him least of all.

the oldest piratical and buccaneering times to the freedom-loving rebels of the National Liberation Movement in our own period' (Stojanović 1984: 11). What holds true for the tradition in general also goes for this: there is no continuity in the organic sense of a conscious and coordinated political agenda that is systematically carried out from generation to generation. But there is continuity in the sense that there are successive layers of perception of a particular phenomenon and its ideological interpretations. It is, like all traditions, at once spontaneous and designed, genuine and spurious.

Sometimes this design is given shape only as a nuance, as a mild intervention into a poem; sometimes it attains the dimensions of caricature, as in a popular historical manual, an officially approved textbook for senior levels of high school and teacher-training schools from the ideologically most rigid decade, the first ten years after the war. As well as the inevitable romantic assessment that the *haiduks* did not attack the poor but only the '*zulümkârs, haraçlis*, traders, and all those who supported Turkish rule', it was added that the *haiduk harami başis* 'best knew the external political conditions of their time' (Slipičević 1953: 288–9), that is, they were sophisticated military and political leaders in the modern sense. If some of these works are to be believed, the *haiduks* and the Uskoks also possessed a subtle vision of home politics. As protagonists 'of that eternal epic heroism of ours, which created the finest and greatest things in our history', they were 'the first in the history of our peoples to have laid the foundations of state power' and on the basis of 'their Christianity, as opposed to fickle Islam, they forged the unity of the Croatian and Serbian peoples in their common fight for freedom against the Turks' (Stanojević 1970: 422, 472).

All these quotations are an example of a kind of school that was susceptible to, or consciously pandered to, the power of the vernacular epic tradition and the exaggerated cult of the *haiduks* and Uskoks. Such authors, simplifying the complexity of historical reality, merging and mixing centuries and modern phrases, were actually doing the same thing as the popular poet, when he generalised so much and transferred modern phenomena to earlier periods, and 'in essence did not give a historical picture of "*haidukery*" either as a whole or in its details' (Nazečić 1959: 8). As a Croatian historian wrote in a polemical analysis of Stanojević's study of the Venetian-Turkish wars of the sixteenth to eighteenth centuries, this kind of

> in essence feeble sociologising and psychologising goes the way of outmoded romantic conceptions, an uncritical line of inappropriate enthusiasm for just one part of the history of the South Slav nations [and] according to this is an example of a

416

narrowed understanding of history that, under the impression of the subject and the pertaining material, neglects a more complex historiographic approach to this social group, neglects the complexity of the whole historical development in three centuries of the Croatian and Serbian peoples, which was manifested in the most diverse forms of the economy, society, civilisation, statehood and military matters, and is in its manner of interpretation unhistorical (Macan 1992: 118).

In the uncritical communist cult of *haiduk* heroism there were some phenomena which cannot be counted politicisation or political manipulation in the original sense, but which nevertheless convincingly show all the traps and contradictions into which the ideologised consciousness will fall. Quite often in a collection of heroic vernacular songs, especially when published for school use, it is possible to find the editor's remark that 'in several place he has softened [...] certain phrases for educational purposes' (Čubelić 1956: 236).

Sometimes it is not hard to identify such interventions in detail. One fertile writer of popular texts about the heroic epic and compiler of popular anthologies says in the foreword to one of them that he left out certain songs that would otherwise be able to claim a place in an anthology 'because this book is also meant for use in schools' (Đurić 1954: 640). Since he gave the titles of five rejected songs, one can see that they are all songs in which a man wreaks his animal will on a woman because of some real or alleged adultery or because he has been rejected as a wooer. There would be nothing to say against the anthologist's educational and humanist motivation if he had not put into his selections poems in which men inflict similar tortures on other men. Apart of course from the mutilation of breasts, the reader is acquainted with the whole sordid catalogue of torture: all kinds of mutilations, gouging out of eyes, flaying, burning alive and impalement, all taking place not in the melee of hand-to-hand combat, but outside it, beside the campfire, after the clash is over, by way of punishment of the prisoner, captive or traitor. Thus little is left of the overt care for the education of juveniles but – conscious or not – transparent hypocrisy.

Another telling example comes from an author of a series of disquisitions on the *haiduks* that did not manage to free itself of the ideologeme treating them as proto-communists or proto-Partisans. This one is a review of a Franciscan chronicle from Makarska, rich in details about the constant warfare on the Dalmatian-Herzegovinan border in seventeenth and eighteenth centuries. According to the reviewer, if the crimes of the *haiduks* who attacked Muslim traders or government officials cannot actually be justified, they have to be understood because of the incontrovertible Muslim reign of terror against the Christian *rayah*. But this, at least to an extent balanced, point of view was to change when it came to the presentation of the life of the *harami başi* Ivan Bušić Roša, who was no better or worse than other *haiduks*. Roša spent a long time as a *haiduk* in Bosnia, and at the end of the eighteenth century returned to his native Imotski region, and fell upon the Orthodox families that had been planted there by the Venetian government. Then, instead of being a proto-Partisan, he suddenly turns out to be a proto-Ustasha. In this phase the reviewer sees Roša as an 'Ustasha-post-war Croatian anti-communist guerrilla forebear' worse than the infamous *haiduk* Stanko Radović Sočivica who 'did not kill even the Muslims just because they were of the "Turkish faith" if he had no other reason for killing' (Grgić 1958a: 86).

This rather large trifle shows very well how strong the ideologeme about *'haidukery'* was, and how, probably sometimes unconsciously, it was not just stereotypes about *haiduks* that were transmitted, but also recognisable reflexes of totalitarian doctrines about peoples and religions of greater or lesser worth.

A third in an inexhaustible list of similar examples may be found in a reader authorised by the Republican Secretariat for Education of the People's Republic of Bosnia-Herzegovina in 1963. In an analysis of the epic song 'Little Radojica' elementary school pupils have their attention drawn particularly to the tortures that this *haiduk* bears in silence: fire is lit on his chest, snakes are placed on his breast and wedges are beaten under his nails (Marek *et al.* 1966: 128). It is easy to imagine how insistence on such images could work on the imagination of children. Even four decades after the war, the literary syllabus for the school year 1985/1986 in SR Croatia promoted the heroic epic to such an extent and manner that it was clear that it was not a matter of standards of literary value, rather the selection of a certain didactic orientation in the teaching. It also included the poem 'Old Vujadin' about a *haiduk* whose eyes were gouged out and bones shattered but still he would not reveal the band's den. Promoted even while the Communist Party of Yugoslavia was operating underground, after 1945 the figure of Vujadin occupied a central place in this segment of the official Yugoslav imaginary as an example of a *man of a special mould*, the communist or Partisan, who even in the greatest agony would not abandon his beliefs or betray his comrades.

A process that started with natural human sympathy for those who had suffered and ended with the ideological absolutisation of a heroism in which the insistence on painful and morbid scenes became an end in itself can be nicely presented in two examples. At the beginning stands a schoolboy listening to what his seniors are saying about the torture inflicted on the communists by King Alexander's police. He starts 'to identify with their fate' and connect them 'with the popular songs', particularly the one about Old Vujadin, where he finds 'many virtues similar to the virtues of the communists' (Humo 1984: 25–6). At the end stands a member of the *nomenklatura* for whom 'the conscious sacrifice' of Old Vujadin 'for comradeship, for loyalty to joint ideals is the eternal and best feature of the self-denial and moral strength of the fighter for justice and freedom' (Tudman 1970: 477). The boy in the first case spontaneously made the connection between the tradition mediated by the song and contemporary events, and, although he could not yet understand the reality around him, this aroused in him an elemental solidarity with people who were suffering torture. The politician in the second case quite consciously built from this connection an ideological paradigm according to which the individual must to the very end and without any complaint subordinate himself to the collective, for the individual is nothing, and the collective is all.

It is true that there were collectors and anthologists who did not fail to mention that 'we should not idealise the *haiduks* too much, at least not all of them' for they often robbed indiscriminately (Mijatović 1969: 228), just as there were folklore students who warned that the over-representation of the heroic epic in teaching and the cult of heroism were educationally dangerous. Such an approach, among other things, created a distorted and one-sided idea about vernacular poetry in general, because it completely ignored ballads and lyric songs. But even the most superficial review of Yugoslav textbooks shows that no one heeded the well-founded warning that *'haidukery'* was not 'the only topic of oral poetry within which there had been major poetic achievements' or that insistence on the powerful emotional reception of a literary work of art 'was not the only or best precondition for understanding and learning about literature' (Perić-Polonijo 1985).

It is hard to say how far it is representative, but the experience of the Croatian poet and student of folklore Olinko Delorko is undoubtedly salutary. In 1950 he was employed in the Zagreb Institute for Folklore Research (Institut Za Narodnu Umjetnost), his task being 'thoroughly to study our oral poetry'. This made him feel 'slightly awkward', because so far he had learned only that part that had been presented in readers and anthologies as 'the best', and he had not found it remotely attractive with its rough warrior rhetoric, its cruel violence and 'monotonous expression'. But as he told his co-worker and collaborator, researching into other, 'forgotten collections', old periodicals, and collecting songs in the field, he made a great discovery, something of a personal revelation: he found oral poetry that 'was not in the previously mentioned textbooks', he found songs of 'extraordinary artistic success' and 'examples of a rarely refined poetry' and published them in two collections entitled *Croatian Folk Ballads and Romances (Hrvatske narodne balade i romance)*. They 'caused a revolution in the way oral poetry was perceived and had a considerable effect on the generation of young poets' who were at the time in Croatia modelling themselves on the poetics of Lorca and the artistic resources he found in the motifs, rhythm and expressive means of the Spanish romances (Bošković-Stulli 2004: 124).

But poets go their way, and ideologues and politicians theirs. The latter still had in mind only the songs and collections that Delorko had found disturbing, while they clearly responded to the belligerent excitement and exaltation. Delorko did not deny the existence of the heroic and rough scenes, the horror and crimes, and did not attempt to mitigate them. But he attempted to find in them 'expressions of the dark depths of the human psyche' parallel to the insights of the great names of world literature such as Dostoyevsky, Poe, Dante and Andrić (Bošković-Stulli 2004: 125), that is to get down to deep human motives, passions, errors, doubts, and link them with Goya's moving drawings on the topic of war, to look for psychological nuances and explain them as a condemnation of war and the pointlessness of slaughter that leaves behind it only human misfortune. The ideologues, meanwhile, continued to see them as propaganda slogans and useful material for an uncritical and autistic culture of warfare that was always in search of new victims.

As mentioned several times already, the merging of communists with Greater Serbian nationalists at the end of the eighties, or the easy transformation of anational communists into fiery nationalists, which so much confused observers of events not only in Serbia but also in Russia, at the turn of the eighties and nineties, was not actually unnatural. Two routes quite naturally led to it, that is to say, two historically formed sets of the collective imagination, not always as different from each other as they sometimes seem. The first might be called the traditional set of rebellion and resistance, and the second the political imaginary of the revolutionary left. In the first the central figure is a generous rebel of the Robin Hood or Stenka Riazin type, and in the second some outsize and muscular factory worker of the kind seen in thousands of socialist-realist monuments in squares from Ljubljana to Vladivostok, from the Baltic to Albania.

In Yugoslav society, and to a large extent in the societies of the new independent states, the central problem was in the continuity that stretched deep into traditional society. While the changes that outside observers of the 'Yugoslav experiment' enthused about, in their fondness for confusing form and content, had an impact only on the ideological cloak of society, not in its deeper layers. In the end communist modernisation proved to be only semi-modernisation and post-Yugoslav societies were quickly and rapidly taken over by a powerful trend of retraditionalisation. The ruling ideological paradigm, which allowed neither criticism nor alternative, supported and promoted, at the level of social relations, perceptual perspectives, social standards and attitudes organised around the central value of the hero, of heroic liberty (*junačka sloboda*) and heroic poverty (*junačka siromaština*), that is, in sociological terms, the heroic code and radical egalitarianism. Such a coincidence of ruling statist ideology and the social matrix that was its mass base, whether or not its participants were aware of it, 'hint at an essential and lasting block to general social change and change in the functioning of social subsystems' such as technology, social solidarity, and political and institutional, value and standard systems (Žunec 1997: 33). Modernisation was to a very great extent a thing of the surface, of the façade.

The Greater Serbian aggression against Croatia and the wars in Bosnia-Herzegovina that followed only enhanced the heroic code, not only, of course, among the Serbs, who activated it consciously and programmatically with great precision as part of the psychological mobilisation for war, but also among the Croats and Bosniaks, in their wartime efforts at defending themselves and in the accompanying verbal and non-verbal production of symbols. Aleksa Đilas lucidly noted that 'a very important and perhaps crucial role' in the communist assumption of power was played by the social and political context of the first and second Yugoslav states. Although the regime of the Kingdom of Yugoslavia

> persecuted the communists, it prepared for the victory of communism not only because it weakened the anyway weak liberal democratic institutions and because it aggravated the anyway poor relations between the ethnicities, but because it accustomed the population to an undemocratic manner of rule. Before World War II, political culture was suffused with authoritarian elements and was unready to resist any kind of dictatorship (Đilas 1995: 21).

Almost exactly the same thing can be said about events half a century later. The claims of Serb ideologues and propagandists that the war of 1990–5 was just a continuation or a replay of World War II – in the sense that relations of

421

power and alliances were repeated, the Croats being once again on the side of an incorrigibly hegemonistic Germany and the Serbs siding with the western democracies – was a mere propaganda phrase that some Western politicians fell for, or eagerly anticipated. François Mitterrand was just the best known for the cynical persistence with which he repeated them.

It is the same with the claim about the irremediable centuries-old hatred among the peoples of Yugoslavia. There were no more instances among them, throughout history, of distrust, conflict and hatred than among other communities, and the tragic paradox lies in the fact that the social reproduction of them was brought about precisely by that same political elite that legitimated itself – internally and externally – by the politics of equality, *brotherhood and unity (bratstvo i jedinstvo)*. One of the best-regarded prose writers of the younger generation in Croatia, Zoran Ferić, recalls what teaching was like in his elementary school in Sisak in the seventies. The teacher read the children a book about Jasenovac concentration camp in which 'there was a detailed description' of how the Ustashas tortured and killed the camp inmates. 'The descriptions of these tortures were truly dreadful and we children were totally shocked.'

Still more important was how the lesson plan of this unit was shaped, and what consequences it had over the long term, apart from the said shock:

> Nothing was said of the fate of the murderers, however. My feeling of injustice that the book did not say how these murderers were punished or killed was so great that I spontaneously started making up stories, very cruel of course and full of similar tortures, about how people in the end punished Luburić, Majstorović, Ljubo Miloš [Ustasha war criminals] and many others whose names I no longer remember. The kids from the class came and listened with great relish to stories about how Luburić was shut up in a hollow tree full of hornets and how they put earwigs in Ljubo Miloš's ears slowly to eat up his brains.
>
> What I didn't spot, of course, as a kid, was that I, in some sense, had been turned into Ljubo Miloš. As children, we sought revenge. Now, as adults, reading about Majstorović, we probably seek an explanation. And both one and the other have been denied us.[1]

The traditional imaginary

The memoirs of Yugoslav communist leaders abound in precise descriptions

---

1. Zoran Ferić, 'Uskrsnuće fra Sotone u hrvatskoj javnosti', *Nacional*, 398, 1 July 2003, p. 64.

of the rhetorical strategies they used in instigating the uprising of 1941 and on all occasions when the peasantry had to be won over. In the villages of eastern Montenegro in the autumn of 1941 Milovan Đilas compared the *Wehrmacht* with the Turks of former times, with the difference only that 'the latter had no tanks or planes' and included in his speeches lines from the folk songs and from Njegoš (Đilas 1990: 189). It was no different in Lika, where 'truths and legends about *haiduks*' were transmitted 'from generation to generation, in song and tale, as powerful expressions of love of freedom and indomitability' and the first insurrectionists used the same caves as hideouts that had been used by the former *haiduk* bands (Jovanić 1988: 19).[1] A volunteer in Spain, member of the Central Committee of the Communist Party of Yugoslavia and the Main Staff of the National Liberation Army (*Narodnooslobodilačka vojska, NOV*) of Croatia, a Croat from the Gospić area, Marko Orešković, experienced the organising of the insurrection in Lika as the assembly of the *haiduk* band under 'the banner', *barjak*, and he was fond of calling himself 'a big old Lika *haiduk*'. His speeches to the Serbian peasants, when 'he could interest and convince them with old-fashioned epic vocabulary', 'as if he had known these people for years', were able in the autumn of 1941 to impress his Serbian party colleague from the same area, the future JNA general Đoko Jovanić (Jovanić 1988: 106–7). The Croatian poets Vladimir Nazor and Ivan Goran Kovačić, who joined the Partisans in the winter of 1942–3, came across a peasant in the Banija region who was already fed up with giving his food to all the armies that swept through. Grumpy and suspicious, he was in a far better mood and entertained them liberally when Nazor started mentioning Uskoks and *haiduks* and 'Goran embarked on a tale about Mijat Tomić, inventing all sorts of connections with the Partisans and weaving in some of his own 'folk' lines' (Nazor 1977: XVII, 116).

Probably the best Partisan memoir writer, and one of the best educated, left a telling testimony about the ambivalent attitude of the Yugoslav communists to such evocations. On the one hand, speeches should reflect the 'party style', and '*Teach*' Vanja, aka Jovan Hadžić, a village schoolmaster from Serbia and fighter in the Kragujevac Battalion, was looked on askance for being 'an outstanding orator' but with a style that was 'considered

---

1. There was a particularly vivid memory of Lazo Škundrić, the last Lika *harami baši* who had been a *haiduk* in the band of Luka Labus for five years, and after Labus's death was its *harami baši* for thirteen years. He made raids into Bosnia, robbing beys and agas. He was captured and for a short time imprisoned in Teresientstadt (now in the Czech Republic), then pardoned and named commander of the anti-*haiduk* posses in Lika, just one more in a long line of *haiduk*s whom governments, this time the Habsburgs, drummed into government service. He died in 1901.

incompatible with that of the party'. On the other hand, 'if it was necessary to talk to the common people, to the peasants, then the Staff was at a loss, and had no better choice than Vanja'. In the summer and autumn of 1941 Hadžić's accounts of rising up 'against Sultans and Kaisers', '*dayis* and *haraçlis*' and his calls to the peasants to drive away the 'janissaries', i.e. the members and officials of the Serbian quisling government, and not to allow the 'Turks, I mean the Germans' to take away their grain (Nikoliš 1980: 306), had the effect of obtaining food for the squad out of the most resistant village, and drawing the most wavering of youths into the Partisans.

The remark that 'in those days when the party line had to be made intelligible to the broadest masses of the rural folk' Hadžić was worth 'as much as a dozen other amorphous, faceless and maladroit members of the party' (Nikoliš 1980: 306) did not apply only to the communists and the Partisans. Such speakers were valuable to everyone, from the Chetniks to the Ustashas and the leaders of Muslim militias in Bosnia-Herzegovina. Nikoliš shows that in some situations what must have always been implicit became entirely obvious, that is, that the common traditional imaginary that cancelled out current differences in ideology and politics and made it impossible at the level of discourse to differentiate armies whose ideologies and agendas were utterly diverse. In September 1941, when the Ibar Chetnik Squad, which was at that time considering cooperating with the Partisans against the Germans, was drawn up on parade, both the Chetnik and the Partisan speakers made almost identical very moving speeches, based on the same vernacular phraseology and imaginary and 'on that day brotherly cooperation between us and the Chetniks reached its highest level' (Nikoliš 1980: 316). It is worth noting that both speakers were village schoolmasters, people who by the nature of their occupations were expert in the epic tradition and the mentality of the people they were addressing.

The communists' reserve towards the speeches of Jovan Hadžić must have had two causes. One of them was undoubtedly their ideological worldview, which could not accept the frequent invocations of Divine Aid and thanks to God for help in various epic situations, as we have seen in the attitude of Yugoslav state ideology to the last line of the song 'Starina Novak and Headman Bogosav' and other epic references to the Divine and Providential aid. The second reason, at least in some cases, was clearly an intimation, if not actual knowledge, that the epic poems could well be a source of conflict – Christians against the Muslim population, and Muslims against Christians.

A first-hand testimony vividly shows what disagreements were constantly in the air. In the summer of 1942, not far from Kupres, in western Bosnia, the local population was addressed by an Orthodox priest from Montenegro on behalf of the Partisans who had just arrived, mainly Serbs and Montenegrins. He cited Njegoš, and although the exact lines are not mentioned, it is not hard to guess from the fact that afterwards the local Muslim cleric quietly addressed the Partisan leadership with the warning: 'Skip the bit about the Turks. It won't go down well with the Muslims' (Dedijer 1981a: I, 255).

The revolutionary imaginary

Nikoliš's remarks about the desired 'party style' takes us back twenty years, to the source of the ideology and discourse that was used by members of the Communist Party of Yugoslavia in fomenting rebellion in Serbia and other South Slav lands. Ironically enough, what they so disliked about the epic was just as much a feature of the discourse of their Soviet models. They too had to face the same difficulties and doubts in their efforts to balance the relations between speaker and audience and find a way of connecting, in their communication, both the educated minority and the uneducated mass, the workers and the peasantry. In 1931, in an article about 'The Russian language after the Revolution', the semiotician Boris Uspenski attempted to settle the problem once and for all by demanding that work should be done on two levels: the teacher 'must master a language intelligible to the object of the education' and the educatee had to 'adopt a language that was capable of being a form of his cultural awareness' (Elbaum 1991: 726).

Two things were observed a few years after the Revolution. On the one hand the vast majority of workers and peasants whom the communists addressed did not read the papers and simply could not understand the language of newspaper reports. On the other hand, for the intelligentsia that had been educated before the revolution, the messages of communist speakers and op-ed writers were a mere ragbag of worn-out and pointless stereotypes. Endeavouring to master the biggest and most important of the two gaps, that with the patriarchal countryside, the new government adopted a discourse that was to a very large extent reduced to metaphor and generally the figurativeness of the language of the vernacular tradition. This pandered to spontaneous Christian Utopianism and its vision of a world without lords or tax collectors. Thus the Revolution was accompanied by a mass of millenarian slogans, such as those borne in Red Square in 1919, in the presence of Lenin: *Long Live Workers and Peasants Whose Empire Will Never Be At an End*. And hundreds of peasant greetings and declarations of support were couched in religious terms, of the 'sinful' Tsarist regime or the new revolutionary 'path of salvation and truth'. The people, that is, had a very fuzzy idea about the nature of the new organisation and structure of government; it understood the Revolution as the 'achievement of the Justice of Good on Earth' and its imagination created the figure of the Bolshevik as a fighter for workers' rights with a beard down to his waist like Stenka Razin or Emelian Pugachev (Elbaum 1991; Figes–Kolonitskii 1999: 127–153).

As the philosopher N. Berdyaev said along the same lines, the Russian Revolution was feasible only if it relied on the dissatisfied peasants and their 'ancient hatred for the nobility, *spahis* and officials'. The peasants were ready to take their vengeance for their grandfathers and great-grandfathers, and the world of the ruling, privileged classes, 'their culture, customs, their appearance, even their language, were something completely alien to the peasant people, who took all this as something that belonged to another race, to some completely foreign people' (cf. Berdyaev 1964).

The social discontents that shook northern Croatia in the autumn of 1918 showed that in favourable circumstances even in an 'un-*haiduk*' area, an area that had never been governed by the Ottomans and thus did not originally know the *haiduk* traditions and cult, the general ancient popular ideas could easily be revived. Local deserters from the Austro-Hungarian army who were hiding in the forests and hills inherited the tradition of the Balkan *haiduk* rebel; the leaders, called *vojvodas* or *harami başis*, were given a green branch with a horse's tail as a symbol of power. The rebels, mainly peasants, acclaimed the republic, but the political substance of this republicanism was mainly the ancient vernacular belief in a new world without taxation or the call-up, without big landowners, traders or officials, townspeople or bureaucrats (Banac 1992). They cheered in just the same way at the end of the eighties at the rallies in Serbia and Montenegro, with the same ancient ideas before their eyes.

In Russia itself, the key creator of revolutionary rhetoric and the communist imagination in general was the poet Vladimir Mayakovsky, who personally, and not without reason, called his works 'party membership cards'. His rhetoric proved to be so powerful and effective that it was later applied by almost all the revolutionary leftist movements. Both verbally and during his work in the ROSTA Agency, visually, on posters and wall newspapers, Mayakovsky created practically all the crucial motifs of Soviet propaganda, just as he anyway provided iconographic models that were later imitated and reproduced. His stereotyped and strictly polarised figures very quickly became commonplaces, two of them in particular: the working man, the proletarian, shown as a well-built, powerful and healthy man, and the bourgeois or *kulak*, shown round like a ball, grotesquely obese, an image later to be transferred to the Soviet bureaucrat. From Mayakovsky too came the motif of the 'razor to be used to slit the fat gentry's throats' and the motif of the 'working-class shock brigades' or the idea of worker as soldier and work as warfare. As well as creating, Mayakovsky also adapted, primarily from biblical motifs and the vernacular epic tradition, and thus in his poems the figures of Ilya Muromets or Sir Svyatogor from the Russian folk poems, *byline* (Polić 1988), could easily be recognised as incarnated in revolutionaries.

In the early twenties, Mayakovsky was already being translated in Yugoslavia, and his life and poetry were written about. He quickly became well-known and popular, and on the eve of the war was the canonical poet of the literary left 'although fairly one-sidedly understood' as a poet of verse that was important for agitation and politics who 'absolutely had to be recited at political meetings and rallies' (Flaker 1968: 416). Something of the power and range of this influence on Yugoslav communists may be seen in the fact that one of Tito's key military commanders, General Petar Drapšin, knew Mayakovsky by heart, and carried his poems in his bag throughout the war (Brković 1990: 145). And, in the winter of 1943–4, among the Slovene Partisans, who also promoted the rhetoric of the Russian poet, Rodoljub Čolaković spent the night reading his favourite work – Mayakovsky's poem about Lenin (Čolaković 1977: II, 652–3).

Some phrases and figures in the first phases of Milošević's anti-bureaucratic revolution, when his agenda was directed towards seizing power in Serbia itself, also testify to this. There, of course, the political and ethical denigration of adversaries could not be carried out in ethical and religious categories, as would be possible later, when it was directed towards external objects, to Albanians, Croats and Bosniaks, but had to be primarily social, i.e. based on egalitarian communist rhetoric. The mood of that phase of mass gatherings, when they were suffused by the spirit of a folksy kind of utopia, can be most pithily summed up by the example of a big rally in Podgorica in January 1989, when, at his second attempt at gaining power in Montenegro, a set of Milošević's political satellites was brought in: *We want a socialism in which we'll all eat white bread* (*Vjesnik*, 11 January 1989).

As for Mayakovsky in particular, there was a fascinating message from the workers of the large New Belgrade factory called IMT to the 'opponents of unity', that is to Milošević's political opponents, that the working class, if things would not work out in a different way, knew ways 'of speeding up the hand of time' (*Danas*, 336, 26 July 1988). This is an easily identifiable topos of Mayakovsky's that revolution is nothing other than an acceleration of otherwise too sluggish historical time. During an attempt at a putsch aimed against the leadership of Vojvodina, in a procession of demonstrators that set out from Bačka Palanka on the morning of 6 October 1988 towards the centre of Novi Sad, a banner was borne bearing the message: *The Working Class Also Likes Pineapple (I radnička klasa voli ananas)*. Though unusual, its basic message still conforms to a series of statements of social protest: *Free the Economy of Excessive Contributions; Our Wages are Twenty Thousand, How about Yours?; The Same Bread for All* (*Omladinska iskra*, 62, 12 October 1988). In this interpretative framework it was in principle clear that pineapple, a fruit that in those years of hyperinflation and profound economic crisis had almost disappeared from Yugoslav shops and was too expensive for ordinary people, symbolised a life of luxury, that it was a symbol of the material and cultural gap between the alienated elite and the people.

But it is also important here that pineapple has a reliably determinable source in a couplet that Mayakovsky printed in a Moscow journal on 24 December 1917:

> *Stuff your pineapple, munch your grouse*
> *Your last day's here, bourgeois louse!*

This soon became a favourite slogan of the Bolshevik revolutionary squads, and was printed on wall newspapers that were shown in shop windows, at stations and in other public places, and the poet later included it in the cult poem 'Lenin', into the scene of the Petersburg working-class demonstrations that seem today like a precise description of the procession that seventy years later poured into Novi Sad. The 'working-class mass flowed' down the streets and recited verses about pineapple as a threat to 'those / that sit in their armchairs' (Polić 1988: 52, 129). The similarity is further backed up by the mention of the armchair (*fotelja*), also a constant symbol of the *anti-bureaucratic revolution*, as shown by the couplet: 'Get out of your armchairs / to show the folk you care ...' from the already mentioned meeting at Podgorica (*Duga*, 389, 21 January 1989) and dozens of slogans against 'bureaucrats in their armchairs (*foteljaši*)' in which an echo of Lenin's calls to a 'war to the death against the rich, the idlers and the parasites' was clearly to be heard.

Just as in the nineteenth century Russian nationalists created the cult of the *muzhik* as representative of the people, in which the deep and unspoiled truth of life was founded, the Russian communists simply transferred this ideal to the proletarian. And the Yugoslav communists did the same thing in their cult of the uneducated peasant people that stemmed from the work and ideology of Vuk Karadžić as well as from the general romanticist mood of the second half of the nineteenth century. Later on, instead of the 'unreliable' peasantry and the 'alienated' intelligentsia, in communist ideology the working class was to become the new messianic social group and was thus very largely to inherit the ancient idea of the noble savage: it had an innate class urge that always directed it on the right road, as Rosa Luxembourg said, that is, an unerring revolutionary instinct that distinguished justice from injustice, truth from lies, its conscience was always good and its intentions righteous, and its very nature and its origin protected it from falling prey to the plots of the so-called social elites or to moral blight.

In fact, the anti-bureaucratic revolution was in spirit nothing but yet another episode of the ineradicable centuries-long idea about the noble savage that was sometimes embodied in a chosen people or in a chosen class, and then, again, in Serbia at the end of the eighties, once again in a people whom history, since it was 'the largest nation in the area between Vienna and Constantinople', had chosen to rule this area and make it conform to the form of historical existence that it considered most appropriate and most righteous.

Western and Eastern imaginaries

Apart from being a primarily political and legal act, the creation of the Yugoslav state in 1918 had profound cultural dimensions, because it brought into close contact many areas that had developed and created their cultural profiles separately for centuries, that had for centuries been parts of states with very different social organisations and stratifications. Unification did in a certain sense also mean 'culture contact' and it is no exaggeration to say that the new state, with its specific qualities, had an effect on some areas that was similar to that of invasion by a foreign power – so strange to them were some of the institutions and procedures. Some features were done away with, some were expanded, and some emerged as dominant in the whole country. The former systems of social organisation, whether or not they had formally, in some institutional or constitutional form, ceased to exist in the last decades of the nineteenth or first decades of the twentieth century, continued to have a profound effect on human relationships. And 'an understanding of the traditional systems is necessary for their remains to be recognised, if one wishes to investigate and understand life and relations in given areas' (St Erlich 1978: 254).

As a result, the merger of the two imaginaries described, the revolutionary (or communist) and the traditional, had a very important specific feature in the case of Yugoslavia. In fact it was achieved against the background of two in some ways similar but in other ways very different central character-signs of the vernacular tradition. That is, within its borders, Yugoslavia included two typologically cognate but different vernacular traditions. The eastern one was dominant in Macedonia, Serbia and Montenegro, and the western, in Croatia and Slovenia, while Bosnia-Herzegovina was the central space for their encounter and indeed friction. It was also the space where the presence of a third, different tradition appeared as a theatre for the reassessment and indeed denial of the eastern imaginary. The border of the Austro-Hungarian and Ottoman Empires, which was in many aspects recognisable throughout the existence of Yugoslavia, left a deep trace, among other things, in the construction and functioning of symbolic legitimating systems.

Throughout central and eastern Europe, the idea of the native peasant oppressed by foreign empires was dominant. From this perspective, folklore is seen as a mirror of the past. Folklore students and the ethnographers, trained and the self-taught enthusiasts who sallied out into the most backward hamlets and recorded the oral heritage, as guardians of the collective memory, were charged with a duty to 'legitimize ideology through their research and their role in cultural programming' (Silverman 1989: 155). But this general framework also contained differences that determined the contents of the prop-bags of political symbols in different countries after the communists assumed power.

Communist legitimation through the *haiduk* and his activity fitted smoothly into the traditions of all the Balkan countries with a strong tradition of brigandry, not only the three eastern Yugoslav republics. The period of Ottoman rule was exceptionally lively in the social memory in Bulgaria as well, and state cultural policy was also founded on the idea that in the period of 'the Turkish yoke' the *haiduk* songs had 'affected the folk consciousness, awakened the will to fight, and strengthened the resistance of the people'. From the establishment of Bulgaria as a state *haiduks* were powerfully promoted in the educational system, and even before 1945 leftist poets used '*haiduk* themes and poetics to illustrate the anti-capitalist struggle', and poems on the model of the heroic epic, using its phraseology, were created about leading individuals, ranging from shock-workers on the agricultural estates to political leaders (Silverman 1983: 55–6. 1989). Some of the basic references were not changed even when, after the collapse of communism, the Bulgarian army once again defined its symbolic identity and the fighting traditions on which it was to rest: the ancient date of the *haiduk* assembly *in the green hills*, St George's, became the official military holiday, known as the Day of Courage.

By contrast, the countries of Central Europe did not have the *haiduk* as a phenomenon, nor the experience of this manner of fighting against the Ottoman invader. In that area it was anti-feudal peasant revolts rather than *'haidukery'* that were subject to pseudo-Marxist rationalisation. Because of the particularities of the Ottoman feudal system – structurally different from the classic European agrarian-estates feudal system – revolts were not known in that form in the Balkans. Every such peasant revolt, particularly if Karl Marx or Friedrich Engels had left any analysis or at least approving note about it, was a potentially legitimating point of origin for the communists. Here, the central and most irreproachable reference was Engels' extensive text 'The Peasant War in Germany', first printed in 1850 in the journal *Neue Rheinische Zeitung*, and after that in a number of editions in book form. Permeating the whole essay is the idea of the necessity of a merciless struggle against the feudal masters, the landlords. Only a radical abolition of all traces of feudal domination, Engels said, could create the most favourable conditions for the success of a proletarian revolution. In this respect Engels was in full harmony with Marx, who wrote to him several years later that 'everything in Germany will depend upon whether it will be possible to support the proletarian revolution by something like a second edition of the *Peasant War*. Only then will everything proceed well.'

It was also natural that the German communists, faced with the necessity of determining how far the peasantry could be relied upon as a revolutionary factor, should have carefully studied the history of the Peasant War in the first half of sixteenth century. Their attention was particularly drawn to its leaders, one of whom was Thomas Münzer. It is characteristic that as early as 1845, in one of his first articles for the Chartist *Northern Star*, Engels called the attention of the English workers to this 'famous leader of the Peasant War of 1525', who, according to him, was a real democrat, and fought for real demands, not illusions. It was particularly natural for the new political elite in East Germany symbolically to anchor themselves to these events of approximately four centuries earlier. The peasant movements were explained as an essential link in the chain of events that from the first such insurrections in the fourteenth century directly and 'lawfully' led to the dictatorship of the proletariat and the establishment of communism of the Soviet type as the zenith of national history. This event, as was regularly emphasised, 'occupied a leading position in the revolutionary traditions of the people of the German Democratic Republic', and in it, as it was always smart to point out, Karl Marx himself had seen 'the most radical fact of German history' (Brendler 1977: 227).

It was on the same prototype that symbolic legitimation developed not only of the communists but of all political trends focused around issues of social justice, workers' rights and agrarian reform in Slovenia, Croatia, Czechoslovakia and other neighbouring countries.

In Slovenia, which was not directly exposed to the Ottoman expansion, there were relatively few popular songs concerned with fighting the Turks. But even those that do exist have no connection with the 'counter-Turkish guerrillas', the *haiduks*, treating instead clashes with the regular feudal armies. In these songs it is mostly the legendary King Matthew (Matjaž) who appears as leader of the counter-Turkish army, based on the model of the historical figure of the fifteenth century, Croatian-Hungarian king Matthew Corvin/ Matthias Corvinus, but he is a ruler, not a rebel or insurrectionary (Terseglav 1988: 540). Instead of the class-conscious *haiduk*, Slovene communists had at their disposal – as did the East Germans – the class-conscious serf, and vernacular traditions and songs about peasant revolts, a black and white image handed down by tradition about a world in which the elite and the folk were in constant, irreconcilable conflict.

A typical example of the way in which this perception of social development was cultivated and promoted was the popular little book by the teacher Lojze Zupanc, published a few years before World War II, with the note that it was completed on St Vitus' Day (*Vidovdan*). This was no accident, because this date, of which there was no tradition in Slovenia, was supposed to serve as symbolic legitimation in the broader context as sign that a particular national history, the Slovene, was actually at the deep level part of pan-Yugoslav history, that it had its own focus, which united the motifs of suffering and resurrection, exactly like the Serbian St Vitus' Day. And, consequently, the Slovene serfs, anti-feudalist in disposition, are identical to the Serbian *haiduks*. The conclusion states this expressly: the history of the Slovene people is most authentically expressed in the peasant insurrections, and experienced its zenith in the creation of 'our free young state', the Kingdom of Yugoslavia, in which the former peasants became 'equal citizens' (Zupanc 1937: 31, 66).

The central topic is the revolt of 1459, when the peasants on the Turjak estates refused to give their dues to the feudal and ecclesiastical masters. The book is dedicated to the 'fighters for the freedom of our language and culture', to the 'resolute and bold peasants who set fire to towns', 'hanged the manorial stewards and yoked burghers to the ploughs' (Zupanc 1937: 1), and with their scythes and pitchforks rose against the imperial army and the feudal armies that were all of foreign origin, mainly German, like the owners of Turjak, the counts of Auersperg.

Among the Slovene Partisans, Milovan Đilas noted 'a special hatred for castles and palaces' and the leaders of the Slovene Communist Party, Edvard Kardelj and Boris Kidrič, often used, in their communication with the ordinary people, the vernacular phrase *Town burns – count flees* (*Grad gori – grof beži*), which had remained in the colloquial language from the times of the peasant wars (Đilas 1990: 339). Finally, an eloquent account of the five-day battle in September 1943 for Castle Turjak was left, by a quirk of fate, by a Partisan memoir writer who stemmed from a typically *haiduk* area, eastern Herzegovina. He clearly knew Zupanc's book and took information from it. This castle was at the time the last redoubt of the anti-communist White Guard (*Bela garda*) in Slovenia, not counting the larger cities with strong German garrisons surrounded with barbed wire and fortification systems, and the Partisans gathered large forces to take it, for:

> Turjak didn't mean just a victory over the White Guardists. An old injustice from the times of feudalism was avenged. Here, in this town, lived the German Count Auerspergs. In his history of Turjak, the teacher Lojze Zupanc writes that the serfs in the fifteenth century resisted the *harç* [tributes] of the Turjak people. 'Many sad memories of the days of that intolerable servitude and oppression, of the violence and ruthlessness of the lords of the manor have been preserved to this day in popular tales in the Turjak hills'. The people talk of Georg von Turn and his steward, against whom they rose and whom they killed in their town of Kočevje [...]
>
> Today it happened that the brigade that stormed the castle walls of Turjak included many descendants of the serfs of Turjak, whose thatched cottages are still huddled below the old town. Sons of peasants, today's Partisans, knew every corner and every wall of the old castle to which their fathers were not long ago taken off to be flogged, their sisters for the counts' seigniorial rights, and the crops from the fields went into the castle storerooms.
>
> The battle was tough indeed, and the enemy held out. Today he didn't have the count's face, but he represented the same forces of alien tyranny and local toadies, backwardness and slavery (Dedijer 1981: 408–9).

Dedijer's 'peasants' sons, today's Partisans' (or in the Croatian version, 'Gubec's sons, today's Partisans') is functionally and psychologically the same as the Serbian-Montenegrin phrase 'sons of *haiduks*, today's Partisans'. In these long-lasting social diagrams in Slovenia (and in Croatia too) we can even find an evocation of the same traumatic material of the vernacular memory, primarily the *jus primae noctis*, which in the areas under the Ottomans was exercised by agas and beys, as well as the Ottoman term for tribute, the *harç*, used for feudal dues. But these Slovene areas were part of the Habsburg Empire, and it was the classical European agrarian-estates feudal system that reigned, where the taxation system was actually handled in a different way, and left for posterity a different terminology and colloquial phraseology. Nevertheless, the use of the Ottoman term shows that this reference system, which in a historical sense was close only to the eastern half of Yugoslavia, had spread to the whole country and became a source of generally applicable terminology for the presentation of social conflicts.

The interesting manner in which, just after the war, one Croatian educational and popular anthology coped with the Slovene handicap of not having had a *haiduk* tradition also shows the functional identity of the two figures – the rebel peasant and the avenging *haiduk* – in the new government's imaginary. As part of the thematic unit *Uskok and haiduk Poetry*, along with the classic epic songs about Starina Novak, Mijat Tomić and Bajo Pivljanin, with special accent being placed on those about the concrete reason for and the manner of their outlawry, there was also a Slovene song, included without regard for literary or social history, but with a deep political logic, called 'Rise, brethren!' ('Zdignete, brati!') about the rebellion of the Gubec serfs (Visković 1947: 223).

The difference between the two types of song can be seen at first glance in the description of the decision to resist: the *haiduk* on the whole does this as an individual, as he comes into conflict with the aga or bey or *haraçli*, and does not call upon the other peasants to join in a general rebellion, rather he flees to the mountain and only when there gradually gathers his band or joins a band already at work, while the rebellions of serfs started with a conflict which from the beginning contains an image of a public mass movement, rather than guerrillas for whom secrecy is a necessary precondition for success. Thus the song referred to, although included with the *haiduk* songs, starts with an image unimaginable in the world of the *haiduk*, but quite natural for the Central European peasant wars: the 'brethren' are called upon without fear to raise the standard and to sing out the battle song with all their hearts.

Croatia was not such a pure case as Slovenia, but does nevertheless belong to the same model, for in its borders – unlike in Bosnia-Herzegovina – the wars with the Turks had faded from memory. As statistics show, of the total of 81 military conflicts with the Croats or in Croatia in which local Bosnian Muslims took part on the side of the Ottomans, five took place in the fifteenth century, 39 in the sixteenth and 31 in the seventeenth, but only six in the eighteenth century, while 12 of the total of 13 conflicts with the Serbs took place in the nineteenth century (Ćerić 1968: 120). What is more, these conflicts were in fact suppressions of revolts from which the modern Serbian state directly derived, and which have a central position in the Serbian national ideology, curricula and social memory. If one takes the epic song as criterion, which one should considering its role in the cultural policy of the Kingdom of Serbia and of the later Yugoslavia, only the songs of Kosovo and post-Kosovo times describe Serbian heroes fighting with real Turks, and to some extent with Arabs, while later songs deal with the battles of the *haiduks* with 'Turks', meaning local Muslims (Popović 1930: 55). To this extent it is logical for them to generate an impression that the main enemy is the local man who converted to Islam and entered into the administrative system of the Ottoman Empire, rather than that empire itself as external force.

Although there were more than six times as many conflicts with the Croats, because of the gap in time they have far less importance in the social memory, they are more distanced, and are less able to be politically mobilised, than those twelve conflicts with the Serbs. On the Bosniak side too, the closer in time such conflicts were, the more they strengthened the feeling of distinctiveness not only as opposed to the central government but also as compared with the neighbouring peoples (Ćerić 1968: 120). And then, the Croatian ideology of state rights and national integration was by force of historical circumstance directed towards a religiously neutral and legitimist manner of proof, and less concerned with being Croatian and being Catholic than was the case in Serbia and with Orthodox Christianity. This was not necessary for the Croatian national ideology because it was shaped by resistance to encroachments by nations which shared the Catholic tradition – Italians/ Venetians, Hungarians and Austrians – and religion was thus incapable of serving as a differentiating element. The Catholic tradition was to acquire importance only at the time of Yugoslavia, in 1918, as a distinguishing element as opposed to the Orthodox Serbs.

The Croatian nineteenth-century Illyrians and the bourgeoisie in general ceased to see the Muslims in Bosnia-Herzegovina as Turks who should vanish together with the Ottoman Empire. The State Rights ideology of Ante Starčević who 'was one of the first Christian thinkers anywhere to express admiration for Islam' (Banac 1984: 108) was an additional barrier in the way of any possible demonisation of the Bosniaks and the Islamic religious and cultural area. The Starčević ideology in particular attracted the sons of the beys who, after the Austro-Hungarian occupation of Bosnia, went to study in Zagreb in greater numbers partly because he wrote of them amicably as 'the oldest and purest nobility in Europe'. Literature too, with writers such as Luka Botić (1830–63) and in particular Josip Eugen Tomić (1843–1906), treated the heroism of the Bosnian beys in the spirit of romanticism, and *Matica hrvatska* (Croatian Heritage Foundation) printed the first local Bosnia-Herzegovina Muslim writers.

There are good reasons to say that this kind of tradition, with all its false starts and ambiguities, and even with the undeniable admixture of political cunning from time to time, was built as a cultural layer into the resistance offered by the Croatian public from the beginning of the conflicts of the HVO and the AB-H at the end of 1992 to tendencies to demonise the Bosniaks. Clearly the ideologeme about Muslims as 'Croats of the Islamic religion' or the 'purest Croats', that had existed in various forms and to a greater or lesser extent on the Croatian political scene up to the end of Yugoslavia, ignored their enduring sense of their own distinctiveness, sometimes stronger and sometimes weaker. By the first decades of the twentieth century it had become entirely anachronistic and politically dysfunctional, and was perceived among many Muslims, with good reason, as illegitimate appropriation. However, it is also clear that such romantic pan-Croatism did not generate hatred for Islam and its followers, and tried to keep religion apart from political life, recognising Muslims historically as a community with the full right to live in their own country, Bosnia.

In such a vision the Muslims were not traitors or 'the worst Serbs' or 'fickle in religion' who willy-nilly had to be reclaimed for Christianity or simply colonists who needed driving back to Turkey as they were – and still are – in the Serbian nationalist ideology. And this is an important distinction, particularly if it is seen in the overall retrospective after the wars of the nineties. In fact, in the first half of the nineties, Franjo Tuđman's Croatian Democratic Union (HDZ) was the first relevant political force in Croatia, after almost 300 years, whose discourse contained defamation of Islam and the Bosnian Muslims.

Croatia's central political imaginary in the second half of the nineteenth century and the whole of the twentieth century does nevertheless belong to the Central European model. In addition to the dominant state rights line of argument and its pantheon of princes, governors (*bans*) and kings who competed with corresponding or parallel figures in external ideological and political pantheons, Croatian politics, like any other that wished to be imaginatively complete and effective in propaganda terms, had also to have a figure who would resist the undesired government from *within* or from *below*. The Croatian incarnation of the oppressed people who rise against the unjust and cruel governors was not the *haiduk* but the serf. This had to be Matija Gubec from Stubica, leader of the rebellion of 1573, as shown by the Montenegrin vernacular poet Žarko Šobić when he summoned him as the representative of the Croats to the fateful counsel of the insurrectionary Yugoslav leaders after the incident at Žuta Greda (see p. 94).

The first documents about the peasant revolt in northwest Croatia were published in 1854 by the ideologue of the Croatian liberal middle classes Ivan Kukuljević. Five years later Mirko Bogović wrote his play *Matija Gubec, Peasant King (Matija Gubec, kralj seljački)*, and with August Šenoa's novel *The Peasant Revolt (Seljačka buna)*, 1877, the cult of Gubec as 'first champion of humanity, the first martyr for equality for all in Croatia regardless of differences among them' as he was called by the political leader of the Croatian peasantry Stjepan Radić, was definitively established. Gubec occupied a central place in the rhetoric of Radić's Croatian Peasants Party, from its foundation in 1904, and in particular in the thirties and World War II, in the sense in which Radić in one of his most celebrated speeches, at Zagreb's Borongaj, on 15 April 1923, warned Serbian centralists that 350 years earlier this 'trampled peasant' represented the indestructibility of 'Croatian national strength' and justice as a principle of human society. The popular myth of the peasant leader asleep underground, preserved among the peasantry in northwest Croatia to this very day, was picked up in the proclamation in which at the end of 1942 the local Croatian Peasant Party leadership in Split called for resistance to Italian fascism, using the formulation that Gubec would sooner or later 'come again' and put an end to tyranny and injustice (Jelić-Butić 1983: 305). It appeared again, somewhat later, in the appeal of the Communist Party of Croatia that the Croat 'should today know that the time has come, that Gubec's beard has wound nine times around the stone table and that now is the right time for a fight for justice and human rights', in other words, for involvement in the war against the German and Italian occupiers (Jelić 1973: 333).

The motif of this 'profoundly social peasant rebellion with its evident revolutionary qualities' (Jelić 1973: 328) was a rallying point for the Croatian communists since the foundation of the party in 1919. And during the war it was woven into the ideological base of the Partisan movement. The Croatian communists and other anti-fascists who were volunteers in the Spanish Civil War called their company *Matija Gubec* and a very strong Partisan brigade would soon bear the same name at home. The Partisans, to the melody of the popular patriotic song 'Arise, Ban!' ('Ustani, bane!') from the beginning of the century, on the model of the first two lines, 'There's no Croat, no hero / the like of Ban Jelačić', sang: 'There's no peasant, no hero / the like of Matija Gubec.'

This became the de facto anthem of the anti-fascists in northern Croatia, and proclamations of the Croatian Communist Party systematically called upon the people to recall this 'great antecedent of our struggle'. The artistic peak of the literary processing of Croatian history through a vision of the position of the peasantry in feudalism and the peak of socially committed poetry between the wars were Miroslav Krleža's *Ballads of Petrica Kerempuh* (*Balade Petrice Kerempuha*, 1936). Just as many Serbs and Montenegrins took with them to the Partisans Njegoš's *Gorski vijenac* or collections of heroic epics, and sometimes the *gusle*, so the Croats, particularly the more educated urban population and those originally from northwest Croatia, had in their knapsacks this poetic evocation by Krleža of peasant resistance and doggedness. Before the war, the *Ballads* were regularly recited at events bringing together young members of the left wing of the Peasants Party and friends of the communists, and the practice continued in the Croatian anti-fascist army (Bošković-Stulli 2002: 166, 183).

The Croatian Peasant Party expanded the Matija Gubec cult all over Croatia, among the Croats in Vojvodina, and to some extent among those in Bosnia-Herzegovina, but it did not completely overlay regional and local traditions. Thus in central Dalmatia, where the anti-fascist movement was particularly strong, from the end of the nineteenth century, when unionism started to develop and modern leftist political ideas began to be disseminated, complementary to the Gubec rebellion, as central evocation of the Croatian imaginary, was the popular uprising of 1510–14 on the island of Hvar led by Matij Ivanić (Anić 1977; Pavličević 1977). The Dalmatian coastal and island peasant society under the government of Venice had a distinct structure, different from that in the areas ruled by the Habsburgs, and different from that in the Ottoman-ruled regions. In a basic and general sense it was able to acknowledge and accept the rebellious serf and the indomitable *haiduk* as symbols of resistance, but could authentically identify itself only with that which embodied the uniquely local historical experience. And this was the semi-free commoner who in the system of the Mediterranean city commune fought for political recognition and better social status.

But there was no cult of Gubec in Istria, although it had a convincing Croatian (and Slovene) majority population, because after the collapse of

Austria-Hungary in 1918 this province had belonged to Italy, and was cut off by the state border from the direct reach of the Croatian Peasant Party discourse at the time when the symbolisation of the peasant leader was attaining its final form. Here, instead, the corresponding role was taken by a fictional figure, the literary hero Veli Jože, *Big Joe*, from the tale of the same name by Vladimir Nazor. Istrian youth under Italian fascism put the tale of this 'good-natured giant' printed in 1908 in the centre of the fight for national emancipation, and its eponymous hero at once became – and has remained – a symbol of the strength and resistance of the Croatian people in general, and of Istrians in particular, as against Italian imperial ambitions on the eastern shore of the Adriatic. The growth of Veli Jože into an important cult of national energy was the fruit of his systematic promotion in the school syllabus and also of spontaneous interest of the political public in the unambiguous non-literary messages of Nazor's tale (Bratulić 1987).

Like Gubec, Veli Jože was a hero who was asleep or was still to be found and who at a crucial moment when the fate of the nation was poised on a knife edge would awaken or be recognised and take over the leadership of the community, unveiling in it and in himself a previously unknown strength and toughness. In the very first number of the Partisan paper *Glas Istre (Voice of Istria)*, in August 1943, his name occurs a few times, among others, in a direct message to his literary creator, who had just been elected president of the Anti-Fascist National Liberation Council (ZAVNOH), the Croatian Parliament in the free territory, that Jože 'slept no longer' but was fighting 'to drive forever the fascist scum from our Croatian soil'. To this Nazor replied with a still stronger concretisation of the fundamental symbolism of his own character: the Istrian 'was coming out onto the Partisan field of battle, putting Veli Jože on his cap, over his forehead, the red badge of glory' (Bratulić 1987: 193–5). In the contact area of central Croatia, the two cults mixed and joined. For example, in the papers of the 13th *Primorsko-Goranska* Assault Division, composed of people from areas that were equally linked to the south with Istria and to the north with the areas where the tradition of the peasant revolt survived, there are evocations of both Nazor's character and the 'celebrated peasant champion Matija Gubec' (Flaker 1981).

Of course, in Ustasha discourse, the 'hero and martyr' Matija Gubec was 'an example of Ustasha consciousness and the Ustasha spirit' (Jelić 1973: 327). For not even the most extreme nationalists would give up Gubec, however close their political imaginaries otherwise were to state-building legitimist aristocracies, because it was only through him that they could transmit the political message that the eastern model had been able to convey through the archetypal *haiduk*. Kings, princes, *bans* and feudal magnates, however much they might have sympathised with aspirations for state independence, should not have to deal with explosives and the burning of feudal castles and leading guerrillas over the forested hills. Such dangerous and dirty jobs should be undertaken by someone of far more modest origin, from the dregs of society. Thus the secret society of young Croatian nationalists who, after the murder of Stjepan Radić, decided on terrorist methods of fighting against the Kingdom of Yugoslavia and adopted the name of Matija Gubec. And, given these methods, it was impossible to imagine the struggle against its communist successor without the rebellious serf. This explains his presence in the list of exemplary 'national revolutionaries' in the introductory, ideological section of the brochure *Avengers of Bleiburg (Osvetnici Bleiburga)*, manual for anti-Yugoslav terrorist actions drawn up in 1964 by the political émigré Adolf Anić in Australia (*Globus*, 197, 16 September 1994).

In short, whoever wanted to achieve political influence among the Croats knew that in addition to the entire pantheon of medieval kings he had also to refer to Matija Gubec, whether mediated through some traditional genre, either through Krleža's artistic transposition, as it was done in Serbia with Višnjić's 'Beginning of the Rebellion Against the Dayis' and in Montenegro with Njegoš's *Mountain Wreath*. Gubec's rebellious peasants and Ivanić's stalwart commoners or the miraculously powerful Veli Jože, all of them were the equivalents, in content, point and function, of the insurrection of the Christian *rayah* and the *haiduk* bands among those with vivid memories of Ottoman rule, including the Croats of Bosnia-Herzegovina. Just as in the eastern regions 'the *rayah* rose up like grass from the ground (*usta raja k'o iz zemlje trava*)' against the Turkish cities, the beys' and agas' towers and *ocaks*, so in every major social crisis in the western areas Gubec's struggle for the *old justice, the old rights (stara pravda, stare pravice)* was evoked, his insurrection against the *lords*, under 'the banner of peasant right / against the lords' wrong', as one of the peasant poets involved in the Croatian Peasant Party cult of Matija Gubec described his revolt (Grabeljšek *et al.* 1974).

This was an imaginary that revived the times

> when the peasants had no land
> but were the lords' villeins,

and it was permeated with images of assaults on feudal houses, castles and forts. In the Dalmatian variant, in a very popular song created on Hvar in 1935, the peasants were reminded that 'they'd always been slaves' but also that even now Matij Ivanić was arising from his grave and leading them in a final victorious campaign against *force and injustice (sila i nepravda)*, against the palaces, villas and towers of the lords.

Functionally, it was comparable with the eastern imaginary and its figure of the highland *haiduk* avenger, but it differed in two aspects that were very important in the Yugoslav political context. First of all, it contained far fewer naturalistic images of violence, mutilation and torture, and secondly, which cannot be ignored after the wartime experiences of 1990–5, it was indifferent to the 'Turks' and had no anti-Islamic semantic potential. Gubec, Ivanić and Veli Jože are in principle very difficult, if not impossible, to manipulate in support of religious feeling, for their oppressors and enemies, the Hungarian or Austrian masters, the Venetian patricians or the Italian bourgeoisie and landowners, shared the same Catholic religion. Consequently in these traditions religion did not and could not play any part.

Since the political action of the Croatian independentist and nationalist parties of 1989–92 was directed towards the national and not the social aspect of liberation, since it promised the establishment of a strongly structured independent and sovereign state, and not an egalitarian popular utopia without masters, tax-collectors or military obligations in which everyone would eat white bread, and pineapple too – there was no place in their discourse for this kind of evocation.

This was not essentially changed by the fact that Franjo Tuđman came from Zagorje, from a village hardly twenty kilometres away from Tito's native village, and both of them were fairly close to Donja Stubica, where the peasants' revolt had started and where since 1974 there had been a monumental statue to Matija Gubec. Hence there were grounds for linking Tuđman with Gubec, just as communist discourse had elaborated this geographical background into the Tito personality cult (Tito himself sometimes slyly remarked that he understood the problems of the 'working people' very well since, among other things, he had from birth imbibed Gubec's message about social justice). The link could at least have been achieved in the form of the most generalised freedom-loving symbolisation such as Nazor's in his 'Message to the Croats' (*'Poruka Hrvatima'*) in June 1943 about the 'two Croats from Zagorje, the two Kaikavian speakers', Gubec and Tito, in whom flared the pure 'longing of the ancient Croatian soul for its ancient freedom' (Nazor 1977: XX, 16).

However, because of his powerfully expressed desire to distance himself from Tito, even this became an insuperable obstacle to Gubec entering the new Croatian imaginary in the 1990s.

Tuđman never mentioned the fact that he came from 'Gubec's region'.

From the beginning he was coded in other categories: as heir or reincarnation of the medieval kings, reviver of long-lost harmony, precondition for the revival of the independent state. In the words that the vernacular poet put into his mouth, he promised his nation that he would follow the ways 'of his great-grandfathers/the kings and the Croatian *bans*' (Šimić 1990b), i.e. precisely those grandees whose souls were cursed in *Gorski vijenac* and against whom popular anger was always directed, whether it was embodied in Matija Gubec or Starina Novak. A song about Ban Jelačić in which the communists replaced the *ban*'s name with the name of a serf who dragged down the feudal *ban*'s government returned fifty years later in its original form, celebrating not only the real *ban*, but also his contemporary embodiment with the same task of reviving the national state.

The motif of the Croatian state as opposed to the previous Yugoslav state was set up easily and spontaneously, for the competing supra-national imaginary, with its idea of Yugoslavia as state that at the same time aggregated and cancelled out all partial state traditions, had already collapsed of its own accord. Without such a frame of reference, all the elements at lower levels of the Yugoslav imaginary became pointless, and new substances appeared in their place.

At an appropriate moment, when Croatia achieved international recognition, this could be explicitly said although there was no real need: 'Vukovar and many other cities are the heroes of its seven offensives, and Banski Dvori [the Ban's, now governmental, palace] is its Drvar'.[1] The new semantic grid completely overlaid the old one: Vukovar, city on the border with Serbia that in the autumn of 1991 for three months resisted the twenty-times superior Serbian forces and thus enabled Croatia to organise its defence, took the place of the official Yugoslav division of World War II into the seven German and Italian offensives against the main body of the Partisan forces. Banski Dvori, seat of the president and government in Zagreb, attacked by Serbian missiles in an attempt to kill Tuđman, took the place of the little Bosnian town of Drvar where in May 1944 the German forces launched a combined land and air attack in an attempt to capture or kill Tito.

But the new attitude could not be so easily established with the elements of the tradition built into the old imaginary, although it was clear that Matija Gubec had no chance of keeping his previous central place, since every imaginary is a transfer of the value system of a given society. Nevertheless, the manner of settling accounts with him was surprising. It was so very different from the mildness with which a year or two later in his own home town, in

---

1. Željko Krušelj, 'Srbija više ne može biti isprika', *Vjesnik* 19 January 1992.

Tomislavgrad (Duvno), an area controlled by the HDZ in Bosnia, the *haiduk* Mijat Tomić was practically begged to let King Tomislav and the grandees from the legendary eighth-century session of parliament occupy pride of place. This was a courteousy to the old *haiduk*, his merits were recognised, in his own time he had done his job of bringing down the alien state honestly and courageously, but now, when the state was being built, it was royal and not *haiduk* skills that were needed. Briefly, he was offered retirement in due time with good severance pay.

Gubec was not so lucky. Without the slightest respect for the efforts he had invested o represent his people in Yugoslav circumstances as best he could and, at least in the communist remake, to be a symbol of its aspirations for liberty, the tormented Stubica serf was proclaimed a common 'vagabond and show-off' who 'fomented a rebellion against the Croatian people, instead of going off and fighting on the Turkish border' as the appointed (i.e. not elected) pro-HDZ MP to the House of Counties (the then upper house) Hrvoje Šošić claimed (*Danas*, 40, 12 October 1993). Communism was dead and the real representatives of the Croatian people were no longer wretched serfs armed with pitchforks and scythes seeking justice, but their most fervent opponents – feudal forces in brilliant armour preserving the state from internal unrest and all who broke the law.

Šošić's colleague in the House of Representatives, Nedjeljko Mihanović (HDZ), extended this condemnation also to Matij Ivanić, perhaps feeling, since he was born in central Dalmatia, to an extent obliged symbolically to reorganise his area and bring order into the interpretation of historical events there. As he wrote in an ambitiously conceived article, the communists maintained that the Croatian nobility had always served foreign interests, and made much of anyone who opposed this nobility in any way. This was among other things a concession to the Serbs, jealous of the Croats for having something 'indigenous, knightly, aristocratic', European, while they themselves had nothing but 'Balkan *"haidukery"*'. The truth is the opposite, however: the Croatian aristocracy was exceptionally democratic, with a powerful sense of national interests and 'clear ideas about our sovereignty and statehood'. It was not then the nobles who acted in an anti-Croatian manner, but rather those whom the communists praised.

> If by some chance the revolts of Matij Ivanić and Matija Gubec had succeeded in their local area, Croatia would have been deprived of its Croatian nobles, without its spiritual and political elite, its Croatian aristocracy, and instead of our own nobles we would

have got some foreign Venetian or Hungarian domination.[1]

Although the two namesakes need not have been so brutally and almost ritually ejected from the national pantheon, at the end of the eighties it was already clear that the messages of their cults were increasingly at odds with the spirit of the times and that it was no longer Gubec that could be – as the Montenegrin *gusle* player-singer Žarko Šobić imagined – a Croatian partner or counterpart to the awakened Serbian and Montenegrin statesmen Prince Lazar, Prince-Bishop Danilo and Emperor Dušan.

Since under communism the political and historical identities of Slovenia and Croatia were identically structured and both countries inherited the same tradition of the peasant revolts, it was natural that after its declaration of independence an identical change in the political imaginary should take place in Slovenia too. This change was formally and ceremonially effected on the model of the same event that was then, in the context of the war between the HVO and the AB-H, the focus of the imaginary of the Croatian political elite. By force of circumstance, because of the large number of Bosniak refugees in Slovenia at that time, it also acquired a strong anti-Muslim tone. This was the fourth centenary of the Battle of Sisak, on 22 June 1593, in which a Slovene squad under the command of Count Andrej of Turjak (Turjački) had also taken part, contributing to the crushing Ottoman defeat.

More than a year before the anniversary, the Slovene rightist populist Zmago Jelinčič had reminded his fellow-countrymen that it was they who 'had defended Europe from the Turkish threat' at Sisak and they were now 'giving way' when faced with the same kind of incursion, that is the refugees from Bosnia-Herzegovina (Kuzmanić 1997: 79). The semi-governmental Ljubljana paper *Delo* published a series of articles about the victorious turning point that had been achieved by Turjački and Baron Adam Ravbar with their Slovene 'aristocratic cavalrymen', and Defence Minister Janez Janša put on a military celebration on the anniversary of the battle in Castle Turjak where he promoted fifty officers of the Slovene Army, presenting them with swords. In the great battle at Sisak 'the flower of Kranjska [Carniola, now central Slovenia], or rather, the Slovene army', led by Count Andrej Turjački, 'inflicted a fateful defeat on the Turks who had for centuries attacked and looted Slovenian provinces', said Janša's cabinet chief.[2] Thus after almost a hundred years of sovereign rule in the Slovene political imaginary, the

---

1. Nedjeljko Mihanović, 'Povijesna uloga hrvatskog plemstva [Historical role of the Croatian nobility]', *Hrvatsko slovo,* 54, 3 May 1996.
2. Svetlana Vasović-Mekina, 'Victory after four centuries', June 28, 1993, *Vreme News Digest Agency No 92*, at http://www.scc.rutgers.edu/serbian_digest/92/t92-6.htm

exploited serfs of Turjak moved deep into the background, giving way to the exploiting counts and barons, who, as aristocracy, were now to represent the symbolic basis of newly acquired Slovene statehood.

An interesting paradox can be observed in all of this: the revival of the cult of the counts of Turjak at the time of independence, their promotion into a kind of nobility that preserved the Slovene state tradition, was in one way just a negation of communist Yugoslavia, which decried the nobility and symbolically upgraded serfs and peasants as the authentic representatives of the national spirit. But in another way it meant a return to the official symbolic pantheon of the first, monarchist Yugoslavia of 1918–41. Then, the counts of Turjak, the Auerspergs, represented the Slovenes, or the Slovene component of the common state. King Alexander Karađorđević gave his third son the typically Slovene given name of Andrej, after Andrej of Turjak, in order to obtain symbolic legitimation with the Slovenes, just as, calling his second son Tomislav, he had made a symbolic gesture to the Croats. The conspiratorial name *General Andrej* that Draža Mihailović had anticipated for the commander of the Slovene corps in the planned reorganisation of his monarchist *Yugoslav Army in the Homeland* (see p. 294), referred to the same most distinguished member of the family of the Turjak counts.

In the ceremony organised by Janša, some other still older meanings of the cult of the Slovene contribution to the Christian victory over the Turks at Sisak were also revived. This event occupied an important place in Slovene schoolbooks under Austria as a metaphor for Slovene devotion to the House of Habsburg (Jelavich 1990). After 1918, of course, this devotion was anachronistic and pointless, but Austria, or really the Habsburg Danubian monarchy in both Yugoslavias, meant for Slovene and Croatian non-communists affiliation to the West and Western Christianity, and was a symbol of Europeanness and of belonging to the Central European cultural area as opposed to the Balkans, that is the eastern part of Yugoslavia.

In Serbia there was no such turning point or major symbolic reconstruction after the fall of the Berlin Wall. Although here too the cults of the medieval kings and the former powerful and territorially far larger state were renewed, in the political imaginary and in the dominant forms of socialisation promoted by textbooks after 1991, the *haiduks* retained their key position as promoters of the values of love of freedom and the incarnation of the virtue of heroism, whether they simply viciously destroyed the enemy, or whether they went singing to their deaths or, like the *haiduk* Mali Radojica, underwent torture without a murmur (Rosandić 1994; Pešić 1994; Stojanović 1994).

For many Ustashas, Chetniks and Partisans in the war of 1941–5, and particularly for many Serbian participants in the war of 1990–5, what Ivan Meštrović said of a guard at the Ustasha prison in Zagreb who sang all night of *haiduk* Mijat Tomić held particularly true: notably, that they 'still lived in the age of the epic popular song, and outside the time they were actually in, and I understood that they were just carrying on with the life of their ancestors' (Meštrović 1993: 307). Since it assigned an independent national state the highest possible value, the official Ustasha imaginary, even after 10 April 1941, could not carry on with what it had done since 1928 in relation to Yugoslavia: call upon the *gusle*, the heroic epic and Matija Gubec as the Croatian version of the *haiduk* who would bring down the state. Posters showed Pavelić as the heir of King Tomislav and King Zvonimir, renovator of a state that was being undermined by the 'foresters' (*šumnjaci*), the Partisans and Chetniks, those contemporary heirs of the *haiduks*. A Romance philologist and writer and official of the Ustasha Ministry of Foreign Affairs complained three years after the war, from exile, that even girls from Zagreb high schools went off to be 'female *haiduks* (*hajdučice*)', Partisans, and thus followed the 'biggest Croatian *haiduk* band (*hajdučka družina*) of all times – named the Yugoslav Communist Party' (Bonifačić 1996: 329).

The central image of the official Ustasha imaginary was *the defence of the city*, and its interpretative model was the monarchist defence of Alcazar in the Spanish Civil War. The first in a series of 'Croatian Alcazars' was Višegrad in eastern Bosnia in the autumn of 1941, and this image was then systematically promoted, during every successful defence, however short-lived. Kupres was the Alcazar of 1942; Livno played the same role several times during the war; Sanski Most and Banja Luka in 1944; the little town of Odžak in northern Bosnia at the very end of the war, in May 1945, and so on. A report about the defence of the Banja Luka Kaštel, the old fort that dominated the town, written by the official war reporter of Pavelić's Personal Guard in the official paper of the NDH shows authoritatively why the role of *the city that is defended* could not be taken over by Siget, as would be expected, considering its important place in the Croatian political imaginary:

> We know many historical fortified and defensive battles, which
> the Croats concluded successfully, and sometimes also tragically
> (like Siget), and we know of the siege of Alcazar from the similar
> Spanish war.[1]

---

1. Miro Gal, 'Hrvatski Alcazar', *Hrvatski narod*, 11 October 1941. For the defence of Alcazar and its mythical treatment in the Francoist political imaginary, see Hugh

For unlike Alcazar, defended by Franco's forces, the Croatian defence of Siget was unsuccessful, the whole garrison perished, if heroically, and the city was taken by the Ottomans. No appropriate symbolism for the positive motivation of an army could be drawn from this. In addition, the battle of Siget suffered from another handicap: a too active use of its symbolism would probably have upset the Bosnian Muslims, that is, in official discourse, Islamic Croats, who had inherited a quite different view of the event – the view of the victors. It is not just that there had been many Bosnian Muslims in the Ottoman army, but its very commander and the victor of Siget, the Grand Vizier Mehmed-Pasha Sokolović, was a Bosnian by birth. He was a markedly positive personality in the social memory and the traditionally mediated self-perception of the Bosnian Muslims, proof of their military competence and devotion to the Sultans. As the creator of the modern Bosniak national integrationist ideology wrote, he 'gave us the prime role in the mixture of nations of the Turkish Empire', in him is 'the source of our great pride, which defied both East and West for three centuries' (Bašagić 1900: 42). In this sense Alcazar was a neutral symbol to which those Muslims who belonged to the armed forces of the NDH, and there were many of them, could subscribe with no inhibitions.

Of course, apart from the official imaginary, underneath the prescribed and standardised metaphors, the vernacular eastern imaginary, as it might be called, lived a full life, which nothing prevented from presenting events the way it had done for generations. The sculptor Meštrović, in the Ustasha jail in Zagreb, was particularly struck by 'a giant from Duvno', who spent the whole night singing 'about the *haiduk* Tomić Mijat, especially about how and why Mijo became a *haiduk*'. He had a very lively feeling for the moment when Mijat said that Jabuka Meadow, which the Ottoman *kadi* of Duvno wanted to cut, was his patrimony, and that no one would mow it as long as he lived 'and at that he would stamp his feet loudly on the floor, as though there were someone opposite him' (Meštrović 1993: 307).[1]

Some Ustasha captured in August 1942 told the Partisans how the commander of a battalion in Kladanj had led them into battle by maintaining that 'some Sixth Brigade and the Sarajevo Yids were coming with a hundred

---

Thomas, *The Spanish Civil War*, Modern Library 2001, particularly pp. 235–236, 311, 397–400.

1. But this Ustasha was also enthusiastic in his singing of the shaven godfathership (*šišano kumstvo*) of Mijat Tomić and Tešnjanin Alija (Meštrović 1993: 307), very much in accord with the State Rights ideology and Ustasha policy of 'Croatian Catholics and Croatian Muslims,' of the single united people that cut across the lines of religious differences.

horses of gold and silver' (Čolaković 1977: II, 76). It is not hard to recognise in the major's image the suggestion of a classical *haiduk* ambush 'in the gorge' and the standard epic picture of a caravan 'with a hundred pack horses' (and therefore it is reasonable to suppose that the mention of the Jews had nothing to do with ideological anti-Semitism, but rather with the vernacular view that Jewish merchants were extremely rich). In the *haiduk* epic 'a hundred horses' is a formulaic image, just as 'a hundred' is a standard number in the whole of the national epic when the large number and importance of a group or action has to be emphasised: a hundred guests come to the wedding, the bride is given a hundred ducats or sequins, a hundred heroes meet somewhere, and a hundred lads lie in wait for someone (Maretić 1902: 27–28). At the same time the major's formula is a numerical stereotype of mythopoeic culture, because numbers in mythopoeic systems are elements of a special code used to describe both man and world. In archaic traditions or cultures they are used in situations to which a religious or cosmic importance is attributed. They are a consecrated means by which man orients himself in the world.

The Chetnik political imaginary did not have to face this kind of dichotomy between the official and the real, among other things because the historical phenomenon of the Chetniks actually derived from the *haiduks*. Since both Serbian insurrections directly carried on from the tradition and experience of *'haidukery'*, an interest in this kind of warfare was continued in Serbia in the nineteenth and twentieth centuries. As a military organisation, the Chetniks were founded in Belgrade in 1903, initially to fight against Ottoman rule in Macedonia. In small guerrilla groups, according to the classic *haiduk* model, they would cross the border, carry out a raid on some small Ottoman unit or most often rob and burn a village and then run back to Serbia. At the peak of its political and organisational strength at the end of the 1930s, it consisted essentially of people from the Serbian petit-bourgeoisie and the peasantry and 'partly for that reason it was never able to develop a politically attractive programme' (Tomasevich 1975: 119–120). Originating in the countryside, the Chetnik movement among the Bosnian Serbs was also traditionally connected with agrarian society and preserved the 'raw peasant patriarchal ideology, that remained alien and incomprehensible to the urban element' (Šehić 1971: 78). So much was admitted, at least during the first year of the war, by Mihailović's close associate and commander of the First Ravna Gora Corps: 'There were no political people in the real sense of the word at that time, only the writer and journalist Dragiša Vasić and two or three "civilians" who helped him "to give some ideological direction to the movement"' (Vučković 1980: 163).

Instead of ideology, they made use of the symbolic system of the *haiduk* fighting tradition and cultivated the memory of the first Serbian insurrection, in other words: the motifs and the phraseology of the heroic epic. Such an imaginary – which governed the language, the perceptive schemes and values of a social group, and the hierarchy of its practice – fixed at the very beginning the empirical order that the Chetniks invoked and in which they found themselves. Among other things, this inevitably gave rise to the view that all Muslims in the area of the former Ottoman Empire were quite simply Turks, aliens.

In this connection it may be said that anyone who wanted to cross over from the Ustashas to the Partisans had to change his imaginary, at the level of ideologically standardised points of identification, from state-building to state-breaking, from King Tomislav, feudal knights and the nobility to the leaders of the peasant revolts. Just as for someone in Slovenia who wanted to leave the White Guard and join Tito's Partisans it was enough to topple the legalistic Turjak count from the top of his private pantheon and put in his place his rebellious serfs. Meanwhile, any Chetnik who wanted to join the Partisans could stay in the same reference system, among the very same *haiduks* and their fearless *harami başis*, with one not at all unimportant exception. This exception of course was the attitude to the Bosniaks and to the general population that had inherited Islamic culture, because the Partisan ideology and practice did not allow of any discrimination in this respect.

However, the conversation previously quoted between Rodoljub Čolaković and the Serbian peasants in Eastern Bosnia shows how difficult it was for ordinary people to get past this obstacle, and that many, even after they had got past it, not just at the formal level, but also in their own minds, still remained slaves to it over the long term. And this was because all the other contents of the heroic and *haiduk* epics, which had their own legitimacy among the Partisans, went on emitting implicit anti-Ottoman, and thus de facto anti-Muslim, meanings. A *haiduk* simply could not be authentic, nor could an epic song about him be authentically evoked for motivational purposes, without his anger at Turkish tyranny and violence, the desire to revenge himself against the agas and beys, the indiscriminate burning of Muslim villages, and contempt for the 'traitors who had taken the Turkish religion'.

Hence in the discourse and imaginary of Milošević's populism the notion that the Islamic world planned 'the conquest of Serbia and the return of contemporary agas and beys to their old hearths' (*Novosti* after *Vreme*,

180, 4 April 1994) was a natural extension of the folklorified Chetnik propaganda, deeply suffused with epic consciousness, and certain elements of the symbolism of the National Liberation Movement, best illustrated by the Bosnian Partisan song about youngsters who 'are not slaves / they're our old *haiduks*' and that in the NDH

> *it's the interest of the Aryan race ...*
> *in the region of the Croatian state*
> *to slaughter everything called Serb*
> *and return the agas and the beys.*
> (Orahovac 1971: 25)

For this reason the appeal to *'haidukery'* as the fundamental symbolic model for the aggression against Croatia and, particularly, Bosnia-Herzegovina, would enable Serbian nationalistic discourse to have a powerful metahistorical, supra-ideological and hence psychologically exceptionally compact mobilisation, stable in its signs and readable in its meaning. Its legal product is the well-known scene recorded by BBC cameras on 21 November 1991 when the units of the Territorial Defence and the JNA came shoulder to shoulder into Vukovar with the names of various Partisan brigades and the red five-pointed star on their caps, with bearded Chetniks with the monarchist cockade on their black *shubaras*, under the name, to boot, of their one-time fierce rivals, Ljotić's White Eagles (*Beli orlovi*), now led by the international criminal Željko 'Arkan' Ražnatović. And all of them were harmoniously singing a cannibalistic Chetnik song from World War II about slaughtering Croats.

For all of them perceived themselves primarily – spontaneously, and under the influence of years of indoctrination – as *haiduks* destroying the alleged new NDH, just as the next day, in Bosnia-Herzegovina, they would be overthrowing an alleged new Ottoman Empire. This is shown by a very popular song that clearly names the adversary: 'hold it, pashas and Ustashas, / don't touch, it belongs to us' (Čolović 1993: 120).

The view of these exalted warriors passes through all modern ideology as though through glass and halts only at distant and intoxicating epic scenes, where a symbolic national reconciliation is taking place and a consensus about reasons, aims and methods is being worked out. They do not act either in the space of history or of ideology, rather in a space of extra-historical and timeless metaphor, in the framework of the poetics of a literary genre. 'These days the Karađorđe insurrection, which has lasted 200 years, is just being completed', stated Radovan Karadžić on 21 August 1994 at the Rally of Serbian Harmony (*Miting srpske sloge*) on Krajina Square in Banja Luka, in front of a crowd of several tens of thousands, the leadership of Republika Srpska and the senior clergy of the Serbian Orthodox Church (*Glas srpski*, 22 August 1994). If someone had not realised that these days marked the anniversary of the important Karađorđe victory at Mišar near Šabac in 1806, where the flower of the then Bosnian nobility in the Ottoman army was wiped out, and that Karadžić always spoke with good cover, he would have been reminded of it by the Deputy Prime Minister of Republika Srpska, Radoslav Brđanin, the next speaker, who referred to the basic ideas in the background of the Mišar battle. Brđanin, says the journalist, 'did not omit to reinvigorate that vow from the Kosovo supper on the eve of the fatal battle' (Anđelko Anušić: *Glas srpski*, 23 August 1994). A supper, of course, the meanings of which, in the Radusinović-Šobić epic of 1989, had been minutely elaborated to take account of the new, and yet actually the same, ancient, unchanging conditions (see p. 94).

Once again the heroic style and the fighting spirit of the Dinaric clans that had known its peak in resistance to Ottoman incursions was activated. Ottoman violence and this heroic spirit were historically conditioned and nurtured, but the core of the problem was that such a lifestyle remained untouched, even after the aims of the anti-Ottoman struggle had been achieved. And it was promoted by the many ideologies that succeeded each other in the South Slav lands, however much they opposed each other, at least ostensibly. Time had come to a standstill, all events were perceived as a replay of the original event, and life became one vicious circle:

> There is an obvious reciprocity between the historical fate of a nation and its dominant values. The values of the nation affect the course of history, while historical events back up the values and the aims that were created earlier. But when we look for the beginning of this circle, we are faced with a riddle (St Erlich 1965: 39).

The Bosniak traditional imaginary

The manner in which the heroic epic was presented in the educational system and interpreted in the political imaginaries of both Yugoslavias could, of course, produce nothing but frustration among the Muslims who possessed some awareness of their own social and cultural-historical identity. All the praise that was lavished on the *haiduks* meant, even when it was not explicitly stated, an equally intense vilification of his opponent the *bey*, and of all who were not only an active part of the Ottoman system of government but were identified with it through religion. The heirs of the Islamic cultural and historical tradition, primarily the Bosniaks, were caught in a trap from which they could not extricate themselves without fundamental, unbiased intervention in the understanding of this same fatal association, its historical conditioning and complexity. But when the Bosniak and other democratic forces – or just reasonable individuals – in Yugoslav society attempted to do this, they were regularly met with governmental repression and dangerous ideological disparagement – as the *Hrnjica case* clearly shows – while the real makers of political decisions and the creators of the dominant ideological paradigm had neither the need nor the will for such an intervention. Quite the opposite.

This fixed and petrified antinomy constantly produced various kinds of conflict. The most widely-admired Bosnian Franciscan of the nineteenth century, Grga Martić, attempted to overcome it in the local categories of vernacular culture by extolling heroism as a common, meta-ethnic and meta-religious human value. His programmatic poem 'First Acquaintance' ('Prvo poznanstvo') of 1840 gives an allegorical image of the history of the South Slavs and the mission of the folk song among them, particularly in connection with themes and heroes related to Bosnia-Herzegovina. Among the leading heroes, there is equal mention of the Ravni Kotari Christian *serdars* in the service of Venice – Ilija Smiljanić, Vuk Mandušić and others, then the 'highland stalwarts', Mijat Tomić, 'the invincible' Starina Novak and 'that reliable chap' Grujica, as well as the 'Turkish *delis* [big heroes]' the Hrnjica brothers, 'from Kladuša, fatal town' and others. In the constant battles sometimes one and sometimes the other wins, 'as luck would have it', and the final message is that everyone should be 'proud of his own heroes' and 'celebrate the glorious homeland' (Martić 1991: III, 113–21).

This conception functioned in the setting of the time – that of authentic, untouched vernacular culture, in the patriarchal, agrarian and stock-breeding society – which, as Murko's fieldwork shows some ten years later on the eve of World War II, was still to a large extent alive well into the twentieth century in a country in which urbanisation and modernisation were belated. But it was dissipated in an age of increasingly marked social stratification and of the ever more powerful inroads of national-integration ideologies, including the Bosniak, in which the social memory of the Ottoman period acquired a practical political dimension.

It is no accident that one may observe in more recent times, precisely among Bosniak folklore students and anthologists, an endeavour to neutralise the historically conditioned contradictions and – in the spirit in which Fra Grga Martić wrote – to draw attention to the chivalric spirit in which Muslim and Christian heroes were united, to the common ground that never quite disappeared from the awareness of the common people.

One such anthologist, for example, deviated from the usual arrangement of songs in cycles, grouping them instead by subject and theme. His anthology included a unit called *Heroic Friendship and Blood-Brotherhood (Junačko prijateljstvo i pobratimstvo)*. As he wrote in the foreword, these songs show that, in spite of conflicts and divisions, 'there were friendships, with blood-brotherhood (*pobratimstvo*) and fraternisation (*bratimljenje*) and honourable respect for chivalric deeds on both sides' (Frndić 1969: XIII). On the other hand, for the Serbian anthologist, the Muslim poems were politically unacceptable, because by singing of the defeats of the *haiduks* and showing the agas and beys in a positive light, they were de facto celebrating exploiters and tyrants (Đurić 1954a: 557) or, put in official jargonese, the class enemy. At the height of the *Agrokomerc* scandal, when the state propaganda merchants were endeavouring to show that the Muslim epic as a whole, and the Mujo Hrnjica story in particular, were embodying and perpetuating 'our divisions and schisms', the Bosniak folklore expert pointed out that the truth was actually the opposite: in its chivalric respect for its adversary, this epic 'often promoted what the advocates of the disputed thesis stood for in principle, and with justification – common values and community' (Maglajlić 1988: 559).

One should of course bear two things in mind: first, that the same thing can be said of the Christian epic, because it contains many examples of interconfessional collaboration, mutual respect and tolerance; and secondly, something quite opposite can be said of both epic traditions, with more or less the same kind of evidence. However, the problem was not in any case this relativity of every general judgment, but that it was precisely this relativity of perspective that was denied by the broad ideologically motivated view, supported by real political power, that one of the epic traditions was generally acceptable and 'truly Yugoslav', progressive, and inspirational for contemporary politics, and the other was politically dubious, backward and historically anachronistic, unusable if not actually harmful.

In parallel with a lasting sense of separateness from the Turkish Ottomans and sometimes open and even armed opposition to the central government, immediately after the conquest of Bosnia in 1463, the local Muslims started to take part in further Ottoman incursions to the west and north, and then in the later defence of the Empire against the Christian *reconquista*.

Statistically, not counting conflicts with the *haiduks*, with the Uskok hit and run raids across the border and the suppression of minor rebellions, up to the middle of the nineteenth century, they fought on the Ottoman side in 241 major armed conflicts, 129 of which were against the neighbouring Slav peoples with whom after 1918 they were united in the same state: 81 with the Croats, 15 with the Montenegrins and 13 with the Serbs, to which may be added 3 with the Slovenes. The other operations were in Hungary, Poland, Bulgaria, Russia, Greece, Persia and Iraq (Ćerić 1968).

After the creation of Yugoslavia, the Bosnian Muslims concealed the many epic songs about these wars, for the adversaries in the wars were their new masters and government (Buturović 1992: 135). The American folklorist Albert Lord was able to make an indicative comparison in this respect, with the same singer and using the example of the same epic song, about the Ottoman capture of Baghdad, in which Bosnian Muslims took part. In a version of 1934 the song contains an ordinary scene in which Alija Đerzelez is in the mosque at the *sabah*, the morning prayer, while this detail is omitted from the version given him in 1951. Lord understood the reason for the reworking: the singer felt that at a time of communist repression of religion any mention of religious establishments and rites, particularly 'Turkish' ones, could get him into political trouble, particularly since in the meantime he had become president of the National Front in Novi Pazar, a pseudo-democratic organisation that the communists manipulated from the wings (Lord 1990: I, 216).

Two examples from a later time, when the Yugoslav federation had actually formally ceased to exist, are typical of the persistent production of systems of social values favouring Serbian national cults and presenting them as the only authentic state or at least the most Yugoslav cults.

At a round-table meeting about traditions that were supposed to inspire the newly founded army of the Serbian-Montenegrin federation, organised at the beginning of 1993 by the military supremos in Belgrade, one participant stated that it was necessary 'to give new value to our insurrectionary tradition, not only the rebellion against the *dayis*, but also all rebellions against domestic *dayis*'. Another laid stress on the national epic as 'an unquenchable source of patriotism and the highest moral national features, real manuals for patriotism, ethics, commitment and heroism' and hence 'a clear point of departure for the spiritual development' of the new generations. A third warned that 'some fighting traditions of the national minorities were opposed to the fighting and freedom-loving traditions of the Serbian and Montenegrin peoples' although there were also examples of 'members of ethnic minorities making their own contribution to freedom' (Đorđević 1993: 20, 76, 85). A young military historian writing about the organisation of the army of the Kingdom of Yugoslavia and its political and symbolic identity could not ignore the facts that show that, while it proclaimed itself pan-Yugoslav, it was predominantly Serbian, although he explains this laconically by concluding that the officers were trained according to 'all the positive achievements of the Yugoslav nations through the ages, their struggle for freedom, which through sheer force of circumstances [...] was greater [...] among the Serbs and Montenegrins' (Bjelajac 1999: 39).

These quotations tell us a great deal. First of all, the new Federal Republic of Yugoslavia (Serbia and Montenegro) explicitly placed the *haiduk* tradition in the centre of its military and political identity, with a particular emphasis not only on the anti-Ottoman but also on the general anti-Muslim tone of the heroic epic of the early nineteenth century, although more than a third of the population of this successor state to SFRY belonged to an Islamic cultural and historical tradition, that is, they were people with a different historical memory (Sandžak, Kosovo, southern Serbia, eastern Montenegro). Such a one-sided apotheosis of the heroic epic makes it impossible for this population first symbolically and then really to be integrated into the army and society as a whole. Ultimately, since it was immersed in nineteenth-century traditions, it blocked the origin of a modern middle-class society that recognised the mechanisms for a tolerant management of diverse views of the past.

What is more, these citizens were expressly rejected, for their 'fighting traditions' were at odds with the Serbian 'fighting and freedom-loving traditions'. This distinction is not uninteresting: the Muslims of Sandžak and Kosovo, for it is they that are meant, had only 'fighting' while the Serbs also had 'freedom-loving' traditions. As a result, it is implied that those who are not Serbs have no interest in freedom, more precisely, that they do not have the right to any kind of understanding of the term freedom or experience of freedom that was different from the Serbian. This is precisely seen in the observations that there are 'examples' of them having 'made contributions to freedom', and the case is quoted of one armed group of Muslims in Sandžak having joined the Serbian insurrectionists at the beginning of the nineteenth century.

The third and most important thing that emerges from Bjelajac's cunning but still quite transparent sentence is that the Yugoslav government had the sincere intention of including the traditions of the other nations in the symbolic identity of their army, but, unlike the Serbs, they simply did not have very many of them. Thus this ostensibly balanced sentence reveals a continuity of ideological thinking that, sometimes openly and sometimes covertly, suggests that the Serbs are, if not the only freedom fighters, then certainly the most convincing and reliable ones; and that their traditions and the political worldview inherent in them are if not the only criterion then certainly the main one by which to judge other worldviews. In short, that only the Yugoslavia that offers a political extension of Serbia is authentic and reliable.

This deeply rooted ideology actually has its origins in the times from the beginning of the nineteenth century when the first military forces came into being in the Balkan countries – in Serbia, Greece, Bulgaria, in Wallachia and Moldova, and later in Romania. All of them derived from the battles of the outlaws (the *haiduks, haiduts, klephts*) against the Ottoman government and the participation of these units in the wars of the European powers and the Ottoman Empire, and from the local Christian units that the Ottomans themselves organised for battle to fight local Muslim rebels who opposed the central government. The first military commanders were recruited among village leaders accustomed to *'haidukery'* (Djordjević 1982). Only later, mostly after 1860, did regular national armies come into being in these countries on the western model. But, as far as Serbia is concerned, it was clear that a century and a half was not enough for even the modest beginning of a critical reinvestigation of the hypertrophied cult of the *haiduk-Übermensch* that sprang from this kind of source.

The image of the world that schoolchildren and all who were exposed, during both Yugoslavias, to the working of this powerful political imaginary often naturally led to the conclusion articulated by one of the leading Yugoslav communists, Rodoljub Čolaković, on the basis of his own upbringing: 'For us [children from Bosnian Serb families] the Muslims were the Turks, the eternal oppressors and enemies of the Serbian people' (Čolaković 1985/6: 33). The memories of Avdo Humo already quoted show what this was like from the point of view of the inheritors of the Muslim tradition, whatever their later ideological profile. He said that he 'never identified with the Turks' but 'then', as schoolboy and young man in Mostar, 'still felt a degree of closeness to them because of the shared religion' and felt very awkward when faced with the hypertrophied cult of *'haidukery'* and the black and white picture of the Ottoman period imposed by the educational system (Humo 1984: 26).

The poet Skender Kulenović, who, paradoxically, declared himself a Serb, was not even that sentimental towards the Turks. What is more, his father usually talked about them with contempt as newcomers to Bosnia, and Skender himself was indifferent to religion, did not care about his aristocratic origin in a family of beys and paid no attention to the irony with which his fellow students, non-Muslims, addressed him in high school in his native Bosanski Petrovac in the 1920s. But there was something that excited and sincerely amazed him: 'There was just one thing I could not remain indifferent to: when someone slipped up and called us Turks, or when they deliberately threw it in our faces. Us – Turks?' (Kulenović 1971: 40–1). Even when there was no malice intended, such misunderstandings could not be avoided even among close political colleagues, just because they derived from far deeper cultural levels, from spontaneously selected or deliberately reworked social memories. In the summer of 1943 the Partisan leadership composed a leaflet calling on the population of Sandžak to join them. An Orthodox priest from Serbia, Vlada Zečević, proposed to the former senator and pre-war member of the main Bosniak party, the Yugoslav Muslim Organisation (JMO), Nurija Pozderac that he 'could write something' laudatory about Turkey, but gave up after Pozderac replied 'amazed': 'But Comrade Vlada, what connections have I got with Turkey and the Turks?' (Zečević 1968: 219).

The picture is not so simple, though, nor is the process of giving shape to the cultural, historical and political identity of the Bosnian Muslims so straightforward. For in parallel with this kind of explicit and cogent rejection of identification with the Turkish Ottomans, not only among intellectuals but also among ordinary Muslim people, the fact remained that, particularly with the latter, a key segment of it, a relatively powerful memory, an instinct with nostalgic emotions about the golden age of Ottoman Bosnia, lived on as a result of their more intense immersion in traditional culture and the heroic epic. This feeling was spontaneously and naively transferred to the 'heir' of the once powerful, vast empire, that is to the secular Republic of Turkey, although an explicit hedge against the Sultanic ideology of this theocratic empire was incorporated into the foundations of its political and symbolic legitimacy.

Thus the proclamations with which both the Ustashas and the communists endeavoured to win this population over to their side and which were aimed precisely at such nostalgic feelings cannot be simply called anachronistic or inappropriate.[1] For example, the Partisan staff in western Bosnia at the end of 1941 told their 'Muslim brothers' that they should not fall for German and Italian propaganda, because the 'whole Islamic and Arab world' was on the side of the USSR, England and the US. And 'the Turkish people was also following the successful struggle of Russia, with which the late Kemal

---

1. The third military and ideological component in the central Yugoslav area, the Serbian and Montenegrin Chetniks, did not even try, because they regarded all Muslims simply as 'Turks', a foreign body that should be removed either voluntarily, by their reconversion to Orthodoxy, or by force.

[Atatürk] had had friendly cooperative relations' (*Zbornik NOB*, IV, 2:167). At about the same time, the opposing side, the authorities of the NDH, judged, not without reason, that the symbolic weight of Turkey in the consciousness of Muslim peasants was very great and that they were at least partially politically oriented towards it. The author of one official military report about the situation in western Bosnia and the area around Tuzla said that the local Muslims 'showed a lot of interest' in the 'attitude of Turkey to the Axis powers and it could be assumed that their overall sympathies were on the side of Turkey', while another report about the battles in Bosnia-Herzegovina in February 1942 says that the Muslims 'were still reserved' but that the 'attitude of Turkey would in every respect have a great effect on the stance of the Yugoslav Muslims as well' (*Zbornik NOB*, IV, 3: 404, 496).

It is hard to say precisely in this complex situation to what extent the Partisan leaders and the communists in general were truly aware of the ambivalence of the epic tradition and the fact that its uncritical and often exalted evocation at mass rallies had a reverse side that was in direct conflict with their official agenda of *brotherhood and unity*. But it cannot be denied that in the perception of ordinary Bosnian people, the dividing line between Partisan and Chetnik could at this point be to a large extent annulled. When they adopted *'haidukery'* as their symbolic or metaphoric model, the communists in the Partisan leadership predetermined the perception of their struggle among participants in the vernacular culture and built an implicit anti-Islamic component into later Yugoslav symbolism. For if, in the official imaginary of his multi-ethnic and multi-confessional state, Tito or some other member of the military and political elite was a *new Starina Novak* or a *new Miloš Oblić* and at the same time was not and could not possibly be a *new Alija Đerzelez* or a *new Mujo Hrnjica* – although these were identical cultural and historical, ethical and semantic categories – it meant that a structural error was built into the political imaginary of the second Yugoslavia from the outset. This was politically very inept and would have long-term negative consequences.

The archetypal Christian *haiduk* was to an extent *Yugoslavised*, recoded into a supranational or anational Partisan or revolutionary communist, an atheist what is more, but still, in his referential roots and dominant interpretation, he remained very much the original Christian and predominantly Serb member of the *rayah* who fought not only against the savage janissaries, the cruel *haraçlis* and the robber-*dayıs*, but against all beys, agas and other Muslims, whatever they were like. Those Bosniaks who were culturally and historically aware not only could not participate effectively in such a semantic field, they were directly opposed to it through the living substance of their own tradition. Those who were not could only look on in confusion and alarm, without really understanding what was going on in Serbia at the end of the eighties, and very soon among many of their Serbian neighbours in Bosnia-Herzegovina. As early as the election campaign of 1990, wishing to show their resistance to Greater Serbianism, some Bosniaks relied naively on the obsolete Yugoslav imaginary: while speakers at the SDS Bosnia-Herzegovina rally in Bijeljina cheered Serbdom, and *gusle* players bellowed from the PA system about fearless, immortal *haiduks*, the local Bosniaks retorted with cries of *We are Tito's – Tito is ours!* (*Večernje novosti*, 11 August 1990). A year and a half later they were mercilessly slaughtered. A photograph of members of Arkan's Serbian Volunteer Guard (*Srpska dobrovoljačka garda*) kicking dead Bosniak civilians on the streets of Bijeljina went round the world.

To some extent traditional culture, like language, is a system that only comes into being through speech, and the speech must be learned in order to master the language, to build the house from the foundations. It is then accurate to say that as a result of a series of handicaps and decades-long Yugoslav cultural policy, the sharers of the Bosniak tradition – with the exception of some of the religious and the non-communist cultural and political elite – had largely forgotten this speech. That is to say, they learned it only during the 1992–1995 war, only after they had been brutally confronted with the Serbian apotheosis of the *haiduk* and '*haidukery*' – and, of course, with its effects in reality – and started to seek and find symbolic equivalents in their own social memory and build them into their own political propaganda discourse.

Still, awareness of this speech and its identical semantic potential was expressed at the very beginning of the Bosniaks' political organisation. At the constituent assembly of the SDA in Sarajevo, a non-party guest, the lawyer Halid Čaušević, shouted three lines that indicated a direct and value-equivalent symbolic retort to earlier Serbian evocations of the substance of the heroic epic and the ideologeme of Dobrica Ćosić or Vuk Drašković that the fateful clash of Christianity and Islam was being repeated in Kosovo and Bosnia-Herzegovina, in the context of the *Agrokomerc* scandal. And that the 'new' arrogant beys and *haraçlis* were again exploiting and persecuting the unprotected Serbian *rayah*, in a new way, through new interest groups and political alliances, but the relationships and motivation were essentially unchanged.

> *Bojičić, are you afraid of God?*
> *God but little, and the emperor not at all*
> *and Ćosić like my own roan horse.*[1]

---

1. *Intervju*, 235, 8 June 1990.

This cry, however isolated at the time, meant in a sense a demand for a radical change of values in political communication. Instead of the often confused defensiveness, passivity and concealment behind the threadbare, dysfunctional rhetoric of Yugoslavism, he announced that Bosniaks too had figures that represented them as a community capable of taking a tough stance, defending itself resolutely and, if necessary, responding with similar self-legitimating categories.

Alija Bojičić, whose surname also appears as Bojčić or Ubojčić, is one of the biggest heroes in the tradition of the Bosnian Muslims: he is mentioned in the Muslim/Orthodox competitive singing at the wedding in *The Mountain Wreath*, as equivalent to the greatest Christian heroes, and the Croatian Andrija Kačić-Miošić in the mid-eighteenth century called him a 'dark wolf, famous hero'. In general in epic poetry when someone is said to be 'a hero like Bojčić Alija' it means he is being accorded the greatest respect. Songs mention him in various places along the Venetian-Ottoman border, but all that is historically verifiable is that he was killed at Zadvarje, southern Dalmatia, in 1663 (Banović 1924: 63). The symbolic function of Čaušević's pastiche is enhanced by the fact that the original phrases of Bojičić who feared God 'little / the emperor not at all / and the vizier like my own roan horse' had their own independent life, outside the epic, as a catchphrase in various situations. They were used to stress that a person was completely independent and that he would act in a way that seemed to him most appropriate, not what others might expect from him. The lines began to be used at the beginning of the nineteenth century, as an expression of the burgeoning political and social self-awareness of the Bosnian bey class, that is, the of the refusal of the newly independent Bosnian captains to comply with the decisions of the central government in Istanbul and the vizier in Travnik, its regent in Bosnia-Herzegovina (Kreševljaković 1931: 105–6)

One such independent Bosnian captain was Husein-Bey Gradaščević of Gradačac (1802–34), called the Dragon of Bosnia (*Zmaj od Bosne*). It is true he was not an epic hero in the original sense, because by the mid-nineteenth century the shaping of the epic tradition was largely completed, but he nevertheless remained in the people's memory. It is worth noting that the only two known complete epic songs about the rebellion he led come from Christian singers, although they are connected to the main trends of the Muslim epic (Buturović 1981: 152). Since the Posavina Croats also took part in the revolt, and since the guardian of the Franciscan monastery in Tolisa was Gradaščević's personal friend and adviser, there is still a positive memory of Gradaščević also among the Croats in this area of northern Bosnia.

In the first months of the Serbian aggression of 1992, Gradačac was defended by a spontaneously created unit called *The Dragon of Bosnia*. It proclaimed itself part of the otherwise non-existent Muslim-Croat Defence Council (MHVO), and the members bore on their sleeves a shield one half of which consisted of the Croatian coat of arms with its red and silver fields, while on the other was the state coat of arms of Bosnia-Herzegovina: a gold fleur-de-lys on an azure ground. But as the regular armies were created, the Croats and some Bosniaks transferred to the 108th Brčko Brigade of the HVO, and the rest of the Bosniaks and some Croats, including the commander, went over to the 107th Gradačac Brigade of the AB-H. This shows that ethnic criteria were not crucial in this reorganisation. There were no conflicts between them during the Croat-Bosniak war.

In 1942 the Bosnian Muslim writer Ahmed Muradbegović wrote a play, *Husein beg Gradaščević*, the thesis of which was the need for collaboration among Croats 'of the two faiths', along the lines of the same political idea that had been promoted a year earlier by Husein Đogo-Dubravić in his dramatisation of the shared godfathership (*šišano kumstvo*) of Mijat Tomić and Tešnjanin Alija (see p. 192). In May 1994, the play was put on by the director Gradimir Gojer, as a symbol of Bosnian resistance, but with special meaning at the time of the renewal of Croat-Bosniak collaboration after the Washington Agreement, in the Sarajevo Chamber Theatre, where I saw it on 5 June that year. The eponymous hero, who embodies Bosnian patriotism, defiantly spoke the lines about Bojičić who fears nobody, and since they do not actually appear in Muradbegović's original play, it is clear that they were put into this wartime performance precisely because they had been identified once again as a suggestive indication of indomitability: a symbolic continuity was thus established in which the spirit of Bojičić, the epic hero, is reincarnated in Gradaščević and merged with him, both of them coming to life again in the contemporary defenders of Bosnia.

It is worth mentioning one more interesting item concerning General, at the time Colonel, Stjepan Šiber. He was a Croat, who was appointed Chief of Staff of the Territorial Defence of Bosnia-Herzegovina, the only remotely organised legal military force, by the Presidency of Bosnia-Herzegovina, on 8 April 1992, two days after the beginning of all-out Serb aggression. He wrote a private diary in the first years of the war, and when he published it after the war, he dedicated the book to 'all the dragons of our state, who following the *Dragon of Bosnia*, Husein-Bey Gradaščević, set off to battle, to an unequal struggle against the aggressor, to win their way to freedom' (Šiber 2000: 11). Although there is clearly a narrower dimension to the author's inspiration, for he was born and brought up in Gradačac, the dedication indoubtedly indicates that the Ottoman period did provide stable symbols that went beyond ethnic and religious identities in the general message of patriotism and political loyalty to Bosnian identity.

But not even in Bosniak discourse, despite its apparently clearly crystallised starting point, could the attitude to the phenomenon of *'haidukery'* remain entirely unambiguous. Just as political conditions at a certain time drove Croatian discourse to *Islamise* itself, so Bosniak discourse could not always avoid a certain *Christianisation*, with changes in social and political relationships. The root of such transformations and the contradictions they entailed lies in the place where all the discourses –Yugoslav, Serbian, Croatian and Bosniak – agree: in the fact that the *haiduk*, however he is interpreted, is always the one who is fighting against the state or the political structure, the one who, appealing to universal ethical criteria, defies a certain government and rises against it with weapons in his hands. The Bosniaks never had any doubts when it was a matter of Serbian *haiduks* who did not acknowledge the legitimacy of the states of Croatia and Bosnia-Herzegovina, and nor did they when the legitimacy of the rulers in Sarajevo was contested by the Croatian *haiduks* of Mate Boban: in both cases, they were rebels, renegades, robbers and looters, exactly the kind of people they are shown to be in the Muslim epic songs.

This can be seen almost as if in a laboratory in a study that was prepared for the political leadership in Sarajevo in January 1993, when relations with the HVO had seriously deteriorated, by Colonel Fikret Muslimović, a senior officer in the military security department of the Main Staff of the AB-H. He asks first of all 'for us to recall Tuđman's term, which we like, "*haidukery*", used to express the moral turpitude and malicious intentions' of those who put up the barricades in Knin. The Bosniaks and Croats had been 'appalled' at this. And once again: 'these barricades were "*haidukery*"' but 'what should we call those who put up barricades in Herceg-Bosna and other forms of the HVO reign of terror over the Bosniaks?' (Muslimović 1995: 70–1). The question is often rhetorical – of course this is also to be called *'haidukery'* and those who put them up are simply morally despicable *haiduks*.

But with time conditions arose when terms were needed to define some of their own fellow nationals, Bosniaks who had come into conflict with the laws of their own state.

The evocation was particularly rousing if the surname of an enemy of the state should offer additional associations, as did the name of Munir Alibabić, a former officer of the Yugoslav secret service, and after the beginning of the war the controversial chief of the counter-intelligence service of Bosnia-Herzegovina, who, in circumstances that have not been entirely explained, came into conflict with Izetbegović and the top brass of the SDA and was therefore dismissed. Then a senior SDA official, the former political prisoner Omer Behmen, specifically said that Alibabić was just the tip 'of a whole layer of Ali Babas and *haiduks*' who were ready to serve anyone (*Ljiljan*, 198, 30 October 1996). On another occasion the editor of the anti-secular weekly *Ljiljan*, which functioned to transmit the thinking of SDA hardliners, described the liberal Bosniak journalists of the weekly *Slobodna Bosna* as 'cadets of the universally known Alibabić and his tabloid *haiduks*' (Hadžem Hajdarević; *Ljiljan* 206, 25 December 1996). And when the film director Emir Kusturica, who was considered a quisling by the Bosnian public for his pro-Milošević statements and his rejection of his Bosniak origins, once belittled the share that screenwriter Abdulah Sidran had in the success of his films and ascribed all their good qualities to himself, it was manifest to a Bosniak ideologue that 'this *haiduk* – in line with the age-old rules of his kind – was appropriating for himself what was not his' (Džemaludin Latić; *Ljiljan*, 209, 15 January 1997).

As can be seen, in all these examples the *haiduk* is negatively marked as a thief, a turncoat and a liar who respects neither principles nor laws, and thus fully conforms to the traditionally inherited, epic-mediated meaning. However, even with the Bosniaks, the circle would be closed when a situation was created in which it was inevitable for such a figure to be perceived not only as brigand but also as just avenger and freedom-fighter, in, one might almost say, 'the Serbian way'. The Dayton Agreement left the Bosniak village of Jusići, not far from Zvornik, in Republika Srpska, yet its exiled inhabitants wished to return to their homes despite obstacles and the overt Serb threats to prevent them. Their leader, Nekir Islamović, however, was determined that if things did not go smoothly 'we shall be, so help me Allah, the greatest of *haiduks* if we do not get back home', a statement that the editors picked out in the secondary headline, thus making it a paradigm (*Ljiljan*, 195, 9 October 1996).

A *haiduk* invoking Allah – this is at first sight quite confusing, but actually it is perfectly logical. In territory where he considered the authorities legitimate anyone would pursue *haiduks* as an *asker* (policeman). But he would naturally become a *haiduk* himself in a place where he considered the authorities illegitimate. The enduringly ambivalent nature of the historical phenomenon of '*haidukery*' had been finally copied into each of the contemporary political imaginaries and it confirmed once again that facts mediated by tradition were valued above all by the criteria of the current ideological paradigm. In the case of Franjo Tuđman the change of paradigm brought about a shift from a positive to a negative evaluation of the *haiduk*, parallel to the change in his social role, from military theorist of communist Yugoslavia to president of multi party Croatia who was then faced with a Serbian rebellion. Meanwhile, in the case of the leading figures of Bosniak discourse, the process went in the opposite direction: from an apodictic and absolutely negative stance towards a complex perception in which good and bad *haiduks* might well coexist, depending on the concrete situations and the changing relations of power at a micro-level.

With a little good-tempered irony it might be said that this was, among other things, an indirect confirmation of the historical fact that during Ottoman times there were also Muslim *haiduks*, which the Bosniak ideologues regularly passed over in silence. An additional irony is that the fearless epic hero, the *haiduk*, the just avenger that even Mate Boban would not have been ashamed of, not to mention Radovan Karadžić, should have appeared in a newspaper that most consistently idealised the Ottoman period of Bosnian history.

Armies and their imaginaries

One of the key processes in the construction of the evocation systems of public communication in the war of 1990–5 was the armies' search for symbolic support, that is, for an identity. Such symbolic underpinning in the process of developing both non-verbal identification systems and political and propaganda discourse became an organic part of the political culture, understood here as a single system of empirical beliefs, expressive symbols and values that all together defined the situation in which a given political operation was taking place.

Identity is not a state nor are identities immanent and unalterable. They are, as one of the many authors concerned with this issue put it picturesquely, 'buildings the foundations and superstructures of which are determined by the conditions in which they are erected, the power relations that are developed at the time, and the efforts made to change them'. Identities

> in interaction with the populace to which they are addressed
> process symbolic systems and manage them, produce a story with
> a mobilising objective that derives from several identity cores and
> expands [...] This process however should not be analysed only
> from the angle of manipulation: reality, the depth of these unclear
> feelings – often in registers of fear and anxiety, of rebellion against

the government, injustice or exploitation – are the necessary conditions for acceptance into the identity community to be effectuated (Martin 1993: 33).

The Serbian army – here a collective name for the JNA, VRS and SVK and all the party militias and volunteer units associated with them, which constituted a single organisation and political whole directed from Belgrade – was the first to publish its *proclamation of identity,* advertising itself as the inheritor of the *haiduk-as-avenger* tradition. Behind it lay not only what must be a partly spontaneous vernacular imaginary, but also a consistently promoted ideology that deliberately built up just such a group identity. For example, at an ambitiously conceived seminar concerning the objectives of education and upbringing in the RSK in Petrinja, a guest from Belgrade instructed local educationalists and political leaders that a necessary and vital part of the 'intellectual package' that young Serbs had to take on was 'the oral tradition and the *haiduk* summons in the free Serbian mountains.'[1] Such evocations, however, were not only explicit, but also contextual, as when Petar Štikovac (SDS), a teacher by profession – thus, as the reader has already seen, a member of a profession that since the mid-nineteenth century has been regularly met in such situations as a kind of authoritative mediator between political elites and populations in rural and suburban areas – at the Banja Luka All Serb Assembly, three months after the Serbian barricades went up, announced that the Knin Serbs 'were capable of existing in a place of dread (*na strašnu mjestu postojati*)' (*Nedjelja*, 35, 21 October 1990). Or when a secondary headline in a Belgrade fortnightly euphorically presented Mirko Jović, leader of the SNO and soon to be the founder of one of the numerous Serbian paramilitaries formed for the aggression against Croatia and Bosnia-Herzegovina, as a politician 'after the tastes of the folk songs: young, tall, strong, capable of [...] existing in the place of dread' (*Duga*, 4434, 12 October 1990). As the exalted Montenegrin reporter wrote, the JNA soldiers in the Dubrovnik war zone, showed that 'one must stand erect even in a place of dread' (*Rat za mir*, 1991: 2).

There can hardly be a single *haiduk* from whose mouth this typical epic formulation did not issue at least once, at least in one heroic song, in some variation, as proof of their courage, determination and endurance, from Starina Novak, who defined himself as one who was capable of 'arriving and avoiding (*stići i uteći*) / and existing in a place of dread', to Mijat Tomić, who took into his band only someone who 'could arrive and slip away / who

1. Milorad Zakić, 'Naša prosvetna politika [Our educational policy]', in: *Vaspitanjem i obrazovanjem u budućnost. Časopis za pitanja vaspitanja, obrazovanja, kulture i Naike,* Pedagoški fakultet, Petrinja 1993, p. 14.

was not sorry to be killed / and take a wound on himself'. The formulation can be fitted into the all-embracing Kosovo myth and thus be additionally strengthened and given almost religious force. This was done, for example, by the writer of the main ideological text in an influential Belgrade daily that devoted the whole of one number to the 600th anniversary of the Battle of Kosovo. Even in the captivity that followed the shattering of the Serbian 'earthly empire' at Kosovo, the individual and the people 'had to remain what it was, could not betray itself', had to be 'capable of arriving and slipping away' but particularly 'existing in the place of dread'. It was easy to exist in some nice place, Islamised, and to that extent devoid of any spirit, but 'to exist in a place of dread means to endure all trials and await the inevitable liberation – the avenging of Kosovo', which means to be in Lazar's heavenly empire.[1]

In Bosnian Serb newspapers, exemplary combatants were regularly compared to *haiduks*, whether in their own press statements, or whether they were so presented by journalists. 'We live like *haiduks*,' 'proudly' said a Serb leader in Trnovo, where the VRS held a strategically important road (*Javnost*, 243/244, 23 December 1995). Not just an ordinary solider, but a commander of the commandos, a major, comported himself in the war like a 'real *haiduk*'. The somewhat exalted journalist saw him in this metaphorical form – using the most typical epic lines, phrases and terms – as a member of four armies, that at the moment of the final national apotheosis and synthesis, were merged into one, into the VRS, forged in 'the fire of the Eighth Serbian Uprising that is blazing at full strength in the western Serbian *krajinas*'.

First, since he 'was driving the Turks hither and thither (*nagoni Turke na buljuke*)', this major was a reincarnation of the Kosovo warrior, for this line – which had made its way into the vernacular idiom – was used to describe the charge of Boško Jugović, the greatest Serb hero after Miloš Obilić, in the Kosovo cycle of epic songs. Secondly, since with his '*cevherdar* in his right hand (*s džeferdarom u desnici ruci*)' he 'strode the tracks and ravines of his forebears', the first phrase also being a familiar formula of the *haiduk* epic, he was also a Njegoš-inspired anti-Ottoman *haiduk*. Thirdly, since he was engaged 'in daily *meydans* with Ustashas and converted Turks (*poturice*)' he was a Chetnik version of the *haiduk* from World War II. And fourthly, since he was already in his fourth year of fighting 'in the forests and hills (*po šumama i gorama*)', as in the first line of the probably most sung Partisan song, known to everyone in Tito's Yugoslavia, he was also the Partisan version

---

1. Radomir Lukić, 'Značaj boja na Kosovu [Importance of the battle of Kosovo]', *Politika*, 28 June 1989.

High-ranking officer in the Army of Republika Srpska with a cap modelled on that of the army of the Kingdom of Serbia; on his right arm he wears the emblem of the Drina corps: the endowment bridge of Mehmed-Pasha Sokolović at Višegrad.

of the archetypal *haiduk*. This was an archetype or prototype that stretched back through history and encompassed the most diverse situations as if it had reverted to its original and absolute state. And when the exemplary major was once wounded 'like a real *haiduk*, he tended his wounds in the forest, in breaks between the daily *meydans'* (Dušan Marić; *Javnost*, 223, 01 July 1995).

It was quite natural that the commander of this archetypal army should himself be a *haiduk*: a Belgrade woman journalist saw General Ratko Mladić as a providential synthesis of 'builder and protector, *haiduk* and general' (Bulatović 1996: 7).

Finally, as a mark of the consistent definition of the army as nationally Serbian, even as the 'most Serbian', we can mention that the officers' caps in the VRS were the same as those of the army of the Kingdom of Serbia up to 1918. This was not the case even in Serbia itself, although the political and military traditions of the end of the nineteenth and the beginning of the twentieth century were otherwise vigorously revived.

This might be explained by the following difference in the positions. Serbia, that is, the Federal Republic of Yugoslavia, aspired to the annihilation only of Tito's, communist Yugoslavia, which allegedly kept down and humiliated the Serbs, but not its predecessor, centralised monarchist Yugoslavia, which it idealised and perceived as a state in which the Serbs had justifiably held the leading position. The para-state of the Serbs in Bosnia (and Croatia) symbolically annulled both Yugoslavias, for, with all their differences, each in its own way, they had both prevented the creation of a purely Serb state, in its maximum extent, and hence there was much radical harking back to pre-Yugoslav times. In addition, with some delay, the VRS had to take on an important job that Serbia itself had carried out before the end of World War I and the creation of the Yugoslav state – it had to smash the 'Ottoman Empire' and once and for all liberate itself 'from the Turks'. The caps of the Serbian officers from the Balkan Wars were clearly meant, in parallel with the *haiduk* myth, to suggest this component of their identity and historical mission.

As for the Croatian Army, its proclamation of identity on the whole included figures who evoked the medieval Croatian state and later efforts to preserve and defend this statehood: princes, kings, *bans,* noblemen and other elites, both those related to the area of the contemporary Republic of Croatia and – where the HVO was concerned, officially founded on 8 April 1992 – also those from the pre-Ottoman state of Bosnia and Hum: the kings Tvrtko Kotromanić and Stjepan Tomašević, and Duke (*herceg*) Stjepan Vukčić Kosača.

This had its own logic for 'the legitimist way of thinking was, in a sense, imposed upon the Croats'. Since all who attempted to whittle down the area of Croatia or reduce its ancient municipal autonomy, from the Habsburg court and the Venetians to Hungarian legal theorists, had resorted to historical arguments in order to do so. Therefore the 'Croat national apologetics were onesidedly historicist', rooted firmly in the belief that not only linguistic and cultural arguments but more 'the rusty weapons of historical and state right were the most effective in the struggle against Habsburg and Hungarian centralism' (Banac 1984: 74). The political discourse of Franjo Tuđman was in fact formally entirely logical although in reality an anachronistic, dysfunctional and hyperbolic continuation of the tradition, as was vividly shown by the speech at the celebration of the 400th anniversary of the Battle of Sisak.

The year 1993 saw three important Croatian anniversaries, particularly connected with the city of Sisak, some hundred kilometres to the southeast of Zagreb: the 4th centenary of the victory over the Ottoman army, which halted its inroads towards the west in that direction; then the less nicely rounded anniversary of the military squad of the local communists of 22 June 1941, which started the armed anti-fascist resistance in Croatia, and the second anniversary of the local brigade of the Croatian Army, which in autumn 1991 managed to repel a powerful attack by the JNA and Serb paramilitaries against the town.

The main speech at the major celebration of 'three anniversaries from old, modern and recent Croatian history', from which 'international factors too ought to draw certain conclusions', was given by President Tuđman. He immediately recalled, in a recognisable allusion – all the stronger since the diplomatic corps was in attendance – that in 1593 the Croatian people was 'the bulwark of Western Christendom', for then too 'it expected help from the West and obtained it in a kind of way, though not the kind it really deserved'. 'The leaders of the Muslim people in Bosnia-Herzegovina should also draw conclusions' from such events, for not even 400 years earlier

> were the parts of Croatia endangered by the Ottoman invaders, but rather by the Islamised people of Bosnia who through the janissary policy and the imposition of Islam took a considerable amount of territory and people out of the Croatian national body. Today too the leaders of Bosnia-Herzegovina should not allow the Mujahedin and fundamental extremists in their ranks to carry out the kind of policy that history has proved fatal and that today too has led to a conflict between the Croats and the Muslims.[1]

This was a typical exmple of his historicism, particularly the use of the metaphor of the *antemurale Christianitatis*, the bulwark of Christendom, common to political elites in the countries on the front line of the lengthy war with the Ottomans: Poland and Hungary, as well as the Venetian Republic and Malta. And this same metaphor, in its many variations, depending on the changing balance of power – internal and external – has remained in their political discourse and social memory to this very day (cf. Žanić 2005).

But this was also a very good example of the conflict of two perceptions and their corresponding metaphors that lay behind the otherwise politically united platforms of Tuđman's HDZ in Croatia and Mate Boban's HDZB-H in the self-styled Croatian Community of Herceg-Bosna (*Hrvatska zajednica Herceg-Bosna*). At more or less the same time, Mate Boban and his

---

1. 'Hrvati su znali obraniti slobodu', *Vjesnik*, 23 June 1993, p. 3.

men, just like the earlier Serbian agitators and propagandists, had less need of historical explanation, complex analogy or monotonous historical rhetoric for the same meanings. Everything they had to say could be condensed into the single concept – the *haiduk* – into a simple, pithy and very effective message based on typical motifs of the heroic anti-Ottoman epic. The Croat/ Bosniak alliance in the defence of Bosnia-Herzegovina was splitting at all its seams, the conflicts of the HVO and AB-H were increasingly serious, and the rhetoric of official Zagreb and particularly of its political clones in Bosnia was ever more brutally anti-Muslim. Hardly a month had passed since the open letter of Mate Boban to Cardinal Kuharić had said that it was no sin to kill non-Christians and that the *haiduk* himself determined the measure of his vengeance (see pp. 187–90). The psychological effect that Boban and his entourage achieved with such evocations of the epic world was considerable, because the period of Ottoman rule was still alive in the social memory of the Croats in Bosnia-Herzegovina (it had ceased only in 1878).

There, then, the figure of the *haiduk* was more productive in its evocations in a positive sense: the local public respected and well nigh adored Tudman as 'president of all the Croats', and people were willing to listen patiently and respectfully to lengthy and tiresome historicist speeches. But their hearts would really warm only if such things were translated into traditional categories and vernacular phraseology. The difference is visible in the different perceptions of geographical relations. Tudman speaks of the regular, imperial and royal, Christian army commanded by the legitimate Croatian *Ban*, defending a Christian city. Boban, meanwhile, talked of the *harami başis* from the *green mountain* who, if they had the power, would be happiest to attack and destroy precisely this source of all evil – the un-Christian city, where for centuries the *vizier, kadı, bey* and *haraçlis* ruled.

One detail shows in a very particular way how in Croatia itself the same political elite that was the sponsor of Boban's *haiduk* apologetics endeavoured to do away with any possibility of seeing the *haiduk* in a positive light.

Since its foundation the HV (Croatian Army) made two official proclamations of its identity: two grand parades at the Zagreb Jarun Lake – on Statehood Day, 1995, and then again in 1997. On each occasion a Historical Sub-Echelon (*Povijesni podpostroj*) stepped out from the leading Honour Echelon (*Počasni postroj*), intending to represent the national military tradition, and the elements of it that the contemporary army considered itself heir to. As the journal of the Ministry of Defence said, the Croats had 'always had to defend their land', and these groups 'in historical costumes' were supposed to represent 'part of that difficult Croatian

Members of the Boka Kotorska navy as a 'historic Croat military formation' on parade in Zagreb, May 1997.

history' (*Velebit*, 2, 02 June 1995). In the echelon there were, for example, the *Bokeljska mornarica* (Navy from Boka kotorska), the Varaždin City Guard (*Varaždinska građanska garda*), the Kumpanija Chivalric Association (*Viteško udruženje Kumpanija*) from Blato, island of Korčula, the Chivalric Alkar Association (*Viteško alkarsko društvo*) of Sinj, as well as the *Haiduks* of the Poljica Republic (*Hajduci Poljičke Republike*), which was initially their official name. They were then officially entitled the Lads (*Momci*) of the Poljica Republic, on the occasion of the same national holiday two years later.

This renaming abolished the only value-positive evocation of *'haidukery'* in the symbolic prop bag of the HV and in general in the political imaginary of independent Croatia, the last disturbance to its *imago* of state and state-building army the members of which were the heirs to 'Tomislav's warriors' and '[prince] Domagoj's sea-wolves' (Ante Matić; *Večernji list*, 30 August 1991), that is, of the 'regular' land and naval forces of the Croatian medieval kingdom, not some unpredictable arboreal outlaws. All the media implemented the same change in terminology between the two Statehood Days, clearly according to the official agenda of the celebration. In addition to the concept of *lads* being innately too general and unclear, and not at all associated with any contextually expected military tradition, the modification has no historical association whatever, indeed, it actually betrays the tradition that there is. For, however much Nedjeljko Mihanović, born in Poljica, inveighed against Serbian *haiduks* and considered them a typical expression of 'Balkan barbarianism' – throughout history inhabitants of Poljica, a small self-governing region in the hinterland of Split, in Venetian Dalmatia, had been important *haiduks*, especially during the Cretan War in the mid-seventeenth century, in no way differing from other *haiduks*. But the odium in which the term was held from the early nineties on was clearly much too strong.

The absence of the Senj Uskoks on both occasions is striking, although they can certainly not be grudged an important role in the 'long tradition of Croatian warfare' (*Vjesnik*, 31 May 1997), which was being emphasised. The reason must be the same change in the ideological paradigm that put paid to the *haiduks*. In the Yugoslav communist imaginary the Uskoks had a place right next to the *haiduks*, as protagonists of a 'markedly Partisan warfare' and sons of the people 'who – never allowing itself to be subdued – preferred death in battle on their own land than to be [...] slaves in chains on alien, Venetian galleys' (Tuđman 1970: 64, 71).

Just how intense and consistent the changes in the imaginary were may be seen in the choice of the other units: the Sinj alkars, the Knightly Defenders of Sisak (*Vitezovi branitelji Siska*, representing the 300 members of the standing city garrison in the battle with the Turks in 1593 – the other participants coming as reinforcements from outside) and the Varaždin City Guard. The proclamation of identity that has at its centre the motif or image of the *defence of the city* was additionally enhanced with the introduction of the Karlovac Citizen Guard (*Karlovačka građanska garda*) and the renaming of the Sisak men the Historical Watch of the City of Sisak (*Povijesna straža grada Siska*). Here the Croatian military and political imaginary was being consistently formed as counterpoint to the Serbian (but, and not without irony, to that of the Herzegovina Croats as well): the citizens, the burghers, or the knightly city defenders were distinguished from the peasants, that is, the *haiduks*, haters and destroyers of cities, and in one aspect also from the Turkish *askers*, in fact from all those who once sought to conquer and sack Siget and Sisak, and today Vukovar, Dubrovnik, Karlovac, Sisak again, and any other Croatian city.

The actual idea of the existence of such echelons is not uncommon: many countries, including almost all European countries, have a certain number of soldiers in the uniforms of some key period of its history. Their use, however, is restricted to a small number of situations, mainly ceremonial greetings of chiefs of states or the most important commemorations, such as, for example, in the USA, where at the central memorial cemetery in Arlington, when a head of state or guest of the same rank lays a wreath, a unit lines up in the uniforms of the War of Independence. Interestingly, in Croatia, the number of historical units suddenly multiplied: at the opening of the International Military Games in Zagreb in 1998, as many as twenty of them marched past, and this kind of review of the 'historical warriors of Croatia' showed that the Croats had 'always had a martial spirit' although the 'Greater Serbian dictatorship disputed this' and Yugoslavia disseminated propaganda about the Croats 'being an un-soldierly people'.[1] By the end of the decade, probably no one knew exactly how many of these units there were.

Another interesting feature is that in the meantime the criteria had become completely vague. Some of the echelons did indeed stem from some recognisable military tradition or some concrete battle, for example, the Otočac Border-Guard (*Otočki graničari*), which evoked the two-century-long Military Border, part of the Habsburg defensive system against the Ottoman incursions. Or, like the Sinj Alkars, it had existed for a long time as a memory of an actual battle, notably the repulsion of the Ottoman siege of Sinj in 1715 (even today the trophies of the supreme Ottoman commandant are kept as material document). Or else they were like Trenk's pandours (*Trenkovi panduri*), symbol of the regiment that the landowner and adventurer Franjo Trenk, lover of the Empress Maria Theresa, recruited in Slavonia and who – as soldiers who gave or took no quarter and were cruel looters – made their names heard from Alsace to Silesia in the War of the Austrian Succession in 1740–8 between Austria, Prussia and France.

On the other hand the 'unit' of the *Croatian Falcons* (*Hrvatski sokoli*) from Osijek was entirely remote from any military purpose, and actually refers to the men's gymnastic associations, extremely hierarchically organised, that flourished in the small Slav nations in Austria-Hungary, particularly among the Czechs, Slovenes and Croats, as a specific form of the demonstration of a national and cultural identity. Most of the city watches or guards were not originally fighting units but urban police units, in some sense forerunners of modern police forces, who, as well as having certain municipal ceremonial functions, guarded public peace and order. Almost all the other 'units' were actually derived from certain games, dances and competitions – mostly in speed and skill in tilting at the ring – of rural or urban origin, from the traditions of the artisan guilds. And yet the official state interpretation turned them overnight into an army. In short – it militarised the traditional

---

1. 'Druge svjetske vojne igre su mnogo više od igre [Second World Military Games much more than play]', *Velebit*, 221, 12 August 1999, p. 12.

past of the folk in an endeavour to create the image of a powerful feudal and bourgeois Central European tradition, as opposed to both Balkan and peasant Serbia and Yugoslav ideology, which had glorified the anti-feudal peasant rebellions, and disqualified the feudal magnates and the bourgeois as 'servants of foreigners' and 'leeches on the people'. Had it not gone to the opposite extreme and bordered on the grotesque, this action might be considered a desirable endeavour at the symbolic level to correct the previous one-sided and ideologised – often frequently grotesque – interpretation of national history and set up a more balanced perception in the eyes of the public.

This rhetorical and iconographic volte-face is seen most concretely in the official attitude to the birth houses of the two presidents, Josip Broz 'Tito' and Franjo Tuđman. By chance, the two were born some twenty kilometres distant from each other, into families of more or less equal social status. The families did not go hungry, but lived modestly, from agriculture, on smallish holdings, with a few chickens and one or two cows and pigs. Both augmented their income with a trade, the Broz family were smiths, and the Tuđmans small-time tavern-keepers. Originally, the two houses were very similar in size and appearance, and both of them, after the two presidents came to power, were renovated with state sponsorship, as open-air museums, each time with protestations that their original condition had been respected.

This was not true. Tito's birthplace was done up to make it look much poorer, while Tuđman's became considerably more prosperous, an almost bourgeois Central European house. This betrayed a real, verified symbolic authenticity: the leader who had led the oppressed peasants and their brothers, the industrial proletariat, to social liberation must have been born in a house not very different from that of his forebear, Matija Gubec. The leader who had brought national liberation to his country and created a state must have been born in a house that would fit in completely naturally with various 'city watches', even the feudal country-house lifestyle (cf. Žanić 2004).

Some of the units were completely new, but not even those that had kept up their traditions continuously in the twentieth century, even with interruptions, ever saw themselves as military in nature. For example, the custom called *kumpanija* in Korčula is actually a sword dance, one of many similar dances of the kind that is very well known in European ethnography. While the *Bokeljska mornarica* (*Navy of Boka*) has no military dimension whatsoever – its origin is in the maritime fraternities that existed in medieval times throughout Europe in cities with developed maritime commerce, such as Kotor, Tivat, Perast and other towns in the Boka, today part of Montenegro. They were, in a way, forerunners of modern trade unions.

Their aim was to help their poorer members, to take care of the families of shipwrecked mariners, and to cultivate solidarity and professional ethics, and since they were almost always in the Mediterranean under the aegis of the Church, on the feast day of their patron saint – in the case of Boka this was St Tryphon – they manifested their existence and social importance with a public appearance in ceremonial costumes that usually included the bearing of sabres and later of pistols. This detail is the beginning and end of any connection between them and the military profession.

Thus the depoliticisation of the army, the reduction of its ceremonial functions to the level usual in Europe and the efforts – in spite of resistance in the rigid sections of the Church – after the death of Tuđman and the HDZ's loss of power, to reduce in its public image the presence of Catholic elements actually meant the saving of these 'units'. On particularly ceremonial occasions the Sinj Alkars still appear here and there (and anyway, as long since generally known and recognised symbols of the military tradition they were the only ones to be present when the Croatian Army was founded, at the first public line-up of the National Guard Corps (*Zbor narodne garde*) on 29 May 1991 in Zagreb). All the others returned to the function that was most appropriate to them: they became revivers of local and regional traditions, a mark of identity of their own towns, and a tourist attraction whose appearances at traditional local and church celebrations or at the opening of some important public building, usually accompanied by majorettes and brass bands that played a popular as well as a marching repertoire, and thus did genuinely liven up public life and draw in vistors from home and abroad.

Free of any links with the army, the state and state politics, they were linked horizontally, as interest associations. They invited each other on visits, and sometimes such gatherings turned into sporting competitions. For example, the Zagreb City Watch (*Zagrebačka gradska straža*), founded in 1997 on a historical model from 1833, takes part in various quite unmilitary city solemnities, and has made international links, participating in the not even remotely militarist Review of Historical, Parade and Guard Units in France.

While the Serbian paramilitaries in Croatia and Bosnia-Herzegovina and the Army of Yugoslavia (*Vojska Jugoslavije*), as the regular military force of the post-Yugoslav Serbian and Montenegrin Federation, apart from rejecting the communist trappings of the period of 1941–5, essentially went on using the proclamation of identity of the JNA with its cult of the fearless *haiduks* as paradigmatic freedom fighters (even stepping up the anti-Muslim component), in Croatia the process of constructing the imaginary of the army entailed the expected volte-face.

This is particularly interesting if it is observed through the person of Franjo Tuđman and his personal change of ideological paradigm and dominant political objective. As a member of the Yugoslav military and political elite he celebrated, logically, the bold and freedom-loving *haiduks* as predecessors of the Partisans. Two decades later, as president of a Croatia that was obtaining its independence from Yugoslavia throught the total negation of Yugoslavia, and as supreme commander of the nascent Croatian Army, he wrote the op-ed page for the first journal of the Ministry of Defence of Croatia and the Main Staff of the HV (Croatian Army). In it, in complete accordance with the occasion, he used the opportunity to sketch out those things in national history that ought to inspire contemporary defenders of Croatia, and from which the official military tradition of the new state was to be derived. They would no longer include not only *haiduks*, who were unreservedly disqualified as 'Serbian bandits', but not even the freedom-loving incontestably *Croat* peasants Matija Gubec or Ivanić's Dalmatian commoners who in their just social anger had attacked the feudal strongholds and the palaces of the lords. Instead of these irregular, revolutionary groups, he led out onto the stage the regular armies, and in providing contents from the wars against the Ottomans, which were an important part of Croatian military history, he shifted the accent from the *haiduks* and the Uskoks to the Croatian feudal recruits, that is, an organised, state-sponsored, military force loyal to the legitimate ruler.

As he says in the editorial, the purpose of the new publication is 'the study of Croatian military history that was neglected, belittled and indeed completely negated in the Yugoslav context'. And its embryo and origin was the military power of the medieval Croatian state, including the powerful navy of King Petar Krešimir IV. Also affirmed were the armies of other states in which the Croats 'won military glory' – those of the Habsburgs and Napoleon. Even the presence of Islamised Croats in the Ottoman army, and in the service of the Moorish rulers of Spain in the ninth and tenth centuries, was positively valued because all that was proof of their military capacity and reputation.[1]

At one time, in the official Yugoslav ideological paradigm, the wars of the Croats throughout Europe under the command of the Doges of Venice, the Habsburg Emperors and of Napoleon had been negatively evaluated as serving foreign interests, with the justification that, in the power relations of the time, it had been impossible to avoid this tragic exploitation, this transformation

1. Franjo Tuđman, 'Hrvatsko vojništvo u obrambenom ratu za slobodnu i teritorijalnu cjelovitost Hrvatske [Croatian army in defensive war for free and territorial integrity of Croatia]', *Hrvatski vojnik*, 1, November 1991, p. 2.

of the Croats into the most ordinary cannon fodder. After 1990, however, this service was viewed positively, in line with the new interpretation: that the Croat was so good, naturally talented and reliable a soldier that no army that set any store by itself could do without him. An implicit condition or criterion was, of course, that the armies belonged to regular, acknowledged and properly ordered states, the subjects of international relations, that they were state-building in their purpose and role, with uniforms defined by the hierarchy. In this context it was quite natural for the Croatian soldier to stand by his monarch – be he the Holy Roman Emperor, Napoleon, the Ottoman Sultan or the Andalusian Emir.

Stemming from this, the archetypal Croatian soldier or warrior was no longer someone who attacked cities, the city being shown as a den of corruption, moral decay and the home of arrogant plutocrats who exploited the work of others. Rather he defended the city, which was redefined as the seat of legal government, a sign of the proper governance and a symbol of cultural progress and civilisation. It was threatened by savage, uncultured and rapacious rebels of all kinds, and at this level the Croatian peasants led by Matija Gubec and Slobodan Milošević's new Serbian *haiduks* were implicitly equivalent. From the revolutionary who feared no one other than God, perhaps not even God, for he did not acknowledge one, the ideal Croatian soldier had been turned into a conservative, the communists would have said a counter-revolutionary, who preserved the status quo.

And while the new image, in Croatia at least, is compact and in its way a logical product of the change in the political context, the Croat army in Bosnia-Herzegovina, the HVO (*Croatian Defence Council*), introduced a great fissure into this image, for the same reasons and in the same way that a contradiction related to the value definition of the *haiduk* had arisen in Croatian political discourse as a whole. However much they otherwise prided themselves on their authentic Croatianness, imitated the official political discourse of Zagreb, and were very largely a branch office of the Zagreb HDZ bosses, the leadership and party propagandists of HDZB-H, as well as the officers of the HVO, both during the war and after it, continued to make use of and systematise the evocations with which they had started to build their own political imaginary at the time of the breakdown of communism and the renewal of political pluralism.

On the eve of the first election after the signing of the Dayton Accords, at the central electoral meeting of HDZB-H in Tuzla, the man whose name was at the top of the proportional representation list for the county, Ivo Andrić Lužanski, received 'the biggest ovation' when he warned the 'great Pasha', the Tuzla mayor Selim Bešlagić, that his 'pashaluk was collapsing because the Croats were no longer a *rayah*' (*Slobodna Dalmacija*, 29 August 1996). A year and a half later HVO Major General Zlatan Mijo Jelić, during the ceremony of distributing decorations to HVO soldiers in Mostar, said that they were a guarantee 'that never again would the oriental tyrant oppress the Croatian people', or 'would minarets be built on the campaniles of our churches nor agas and beys collect the *harc* and the tribute in blood and gold in our Croatian areas' (*Tjednik*, 13, 23 May 1997). If the first part of the message might at first glance seem like an allusion to Milošević's Serbia, that incontrovertible originator of all the wars, the second part clearly shows that the speaker was not thinking of this enemy, rather one much further to the east, distant not only geographically but also temporally, the Ottomans, or the Bosniaks, their symbolic heirs, and it was they, and not Greater Serbian aggression, whom he considered the chief danger for the Croats in Bosnia-Herzegovina.

At the beginning of July 1999, Tomislavgrad saw the foundation and presentation in a parade through the city, together with regular units of the HVO or rather – as Dayton puts it – the Croatian component of the Army of the Federation of Bosnia and Herzegovina – of the 'historical unit of the Croatian people' named the *haiduk Band of Mijat Tomić* (*Hajdučka družina Mijata Tomića*). Afterwards, it took the oath at a formal session of the Municipal Council. It consisted of thirty-three members, precisely the number that the folk epic ascribes to such bands. What official politics in Croatia denied or hid, what a 'typical Central European and/or West European country' would naturally be ashamed of and pronounce 'typically Serbian and/or Balkan', the political elite of the Croats in Herzegovina were proud to promote as the foundation of their own military-political imaginary. No official aping of Zagreb or ambition to be as similar to Croatia as possible in all things could drive out the primordial local self-identification or hide the fact that at an unofficial or authentically living level there were two different and in many respects opposed social memories or traditions.

On the cover of an influential local monthly there was a large colour photograph of a rather grand *haiduk* band in front of the church built in 1925 in memory of the millennium of the legendary crowning of the 'first Croatian king', Tomislav, and the headline of the editorial was a recognisable quote of the epic formula *For the honoured cross and golden liberty* (*Za krst časni i slobodu zlatnu*). Under it were some thoughts about *'haidukery'* that every Croatian politician of the first half of the nineties would be indignant about (and that would soften the heart of every Serbian admirer of the

PODJELE "Globusovo" istraživanje pokazuje da lik i djelo dr. Franje Tuđmana izazivaju oprečne reakcije u javnosti

As a member of the official HDZ delegation from Bosnia-Herzegovina, one of the Mijat Tomić *Haiduk* Troop stands guard in December 2001 at the tomb of Franjo Tuđman in Zagreb, on the second anniversary of the latter's death.

untouchable Starina Novak and his band from the *green hills of Romanija*). For this editorial stated that the popular epic song taught the Croats that Mijat Tomić went into outlawry only when he was no longer able to defend 'his personal and the national dignity' from the Turkish authorities.

> For the Croats of Herceg-Bosna, to this day, he remains an emblem of the honourable battle for the honoured cross and golden freedom, an emblem of the dignity of the defender who leaves behind him no kind of unclean trace. He persistently defended his own, while the foreigner was always the foreigner, and never trusted. He did not take from other people, but did not let anyone be so bold as to take what was his [...] This nation might have forgotten everything, but not King Tomislav, and not Mijat Tomić. The reasons are clear. Both of them are the embodiment of Croatian freedom and independence in this area.[1]

---

1. 'Za krst časni i slobodu zlatnu', *Naša ognjišta*, 9, September 1991, p. 1. Colour plate 6 – On the symbolism of Tomislav and the celebration of the legendary coronation, cf. p. 182. It is worth mention that the Serbian paramilitaries in Croatia and Bosnia and Herzegovina did not create any tradition or historical ceremonial unit, not even when the last Dayton Agreement legalised them as the army of the state within the state, of Republika Srpska, although their *haiduk* cult was much older, more vigorous and comprehensive than that in Herceg-Bosna. Perhaps this was because

The *Haiduk* Band of Mijat Tomić made its official public debut in a highly symbolic moment, during the return of the restored coffin of the last medieval king of Bosnia, Stjepan Tomašević, to Jajce, on 13 September 1999. 'It was borne at exactly noon, through the centuries-old Travnik Gate, by the stout arms of members of the *Haiduk* Band of Mijat Tomić' after which 'the same powerful arms laid it down on the plateau' in front of the Culture Centre that bore the king's name.[1] They reached a kind of apogee a month later, on 16 October 1999 in Zagreb, during the reburial of the Croatian political émigré Bruno Bušić, who was murdered in 1978 in Paris by the Yugoslav secret police. They formed an honour guard together with Tuđman's Presidential Guard, thus a Balkan *harami başı* and his haiduks in untanned leather sandals stood side by side with stylised Central European hussars and grenadiers in their high, polished leather boots, homespun next to satin, *yatağans* next to sabre, Herceg-Bosna next to Croatia, Croats beside Croats, manifesting a national, historical and political unity that surmounted political borders.

But it was also very clear, for anyone who was able to see it, that this much-vaunted unity under the leadership of *the president of all the Croats* perhaps concealed many resiliently diverse and even opposed – although in principle equally valuable – experiences, aspirations and values. And that, in the end, it proved itself to be nothing but a phantom.

After 2000, the *Haiduk* Band of Mijat Tomić no longer appeared officially in Croatia, if we exclude the anniversary of Tuđman's death when, as part of the party deputation from HDZB-H it took one watch of the honour guard by his grave in Zagreb, and its participation in the local celebration of the city's patron saint, St Blaise (Vlaho), on 3 February in Dubrovnik. By contrast, in what was once Herceg-Bosna, that is in the area where the HDZB-H still holds power today, it is active on many official occasions, for example when HVO recruits take the oath, or when, in an imitation of statehood, each 7 May a wreath is placed on the grave of Mate Boban and a mass is celebrated. It also appears increasingly in tourist events and various local solemnities. It would seem that it too is being depoliticised, although more slowly than its equivalents in Croatia, at least as far as aggressive practical politics is concerned, and is becoming more and more a symbol of regional social and cultural identity.

---

the verbal proclamation of identity was quite strong enough to make a visual version unnecessary.

1. Zdenko Jurilj, 'Stjepan Tomašević bi danas bio ponosan na postrojbe HVO-a koje su oslobodile stolni grad Jajce [S.T. would be proud today of the HVO units that liberated his capital city Jajce]', *Hrvatska riječ*, 268, 18 September 1999.

Unlike the stable symbolic legitimation of the Croatian and Serbian armies, the third army, the AB-H, modified its identity several times and during the construction of this identity reconstructed and evoked several different reference worlds. At the same time, since it was chronologically the last formed – the day of its founding is officially proclaimed to be 15 April 1992, when the Presidency of Bosnia-Herzegovina published the decision that all armed formations were to be united in the Territorial Defence from which the Army of Bosnia-Herzegovina stemmed – through these successive worlds it objectively entered into polemics with the analogous Serbian and Croatian imaginaries.

At the very beginning of the war, in June 1992, the official salute was introduced: the right arm raised, bent at the elbow, fingers spread, palm turned to whoever was being saluted. Untypical in terms of the usual military standards, this gesture clearly imitated the characteristic motif from the *stećci* and in this period, when the army aspired to, and did, take in a great many Croats and Serbs committed to the idea of the defence of Bosnia-Herzegovina, it was meant to evoke pre-Ottoman Bosnia, as a joint symbolic space, free of the conflicts that followed because of the later different perceptions of the Ottoman period, and also to override the religious and national identities that derived from this time. General Stjepan Šiber, a member of the first, multi-ethnic Staff of the AB-H, later stated that it was he himself who in 1992 'took care of the procurement of the uniforms and creation of the identity of the Army of Bosnia-Herzegovina,'[1] which seems quite persuasive, since it was the Croats, thanks to the social pedagogy of the Bosnian Franciscans, who were most persistent in their cultivation of the memory of the medieval *Regnum Bosniae*, its material remains and its iconography.

The model for the salute was the famed motif from a stechak of Radimlje near Stolac that inspired Miroslav Krleža in 1954 to write that 'for a moment it seems that these hands wanted to demonstrate to future generations just how tough and defiant they were, not wanting to close before the inquisitors who had persecuted and burned Bosnia for centuries', that they are 'the emblem of a bold challenge to a duel with all the [fake] moral authorities of their time' (Krleža 1966: 245–6). It became particularly well known and visually familiar when at the beginning of the seventies it appeared as an icon on the cover of a collection of poems, *Kameni spavač (Stone Sleeper)*, by Mak Dizdar. Just before the war it was taken as a symbol by the liberal Sarajevo fortnightly *Dani*, whose multi-ethnic editorial board was consistent

1. Zvonimir Despot, 'Alija kriv za zločine nad Hrvatima, a Kordić nad Muslimanima [Alija to blame for crimes against Croats, Kordić for those against Muslims]', *Večernji list*, 05 January 2001, p. 15.

The so-called 'early-Bosnian greeting' – *stećci* at Radimlja near Stolac.

in advocating a secular state and promoting a modern, political Bosnianism, which respected all ethnic and religious identities. It was also used as the logo by the democratically oriented Croatian monthly *Stećak*, loyal to the state, which started to appear in 1993 in besieged Sarajevo.

However, a symbol so clear in one context does not necessarily remain so in another. A year later, at the time of the Croat-Bosniak war, 'the open palm with the five digits' that the Bosniak children showed the Croats in central Bosnia was interpreted by a Croat teacher from Gornji Vakuf as a menacing reminiscence of the five centuries of Turkish rule in Bosnia-Herzegovina (*Glas Koncila*, 34, 22 August 1993). On the other hand, it is impossible to rule out the possibility that in the change of political relations, and under the increasing influence of SDA ideology, which idealised the Ottoman era, some Bosniaks did indeed ascribe to the motif from the *stechak* some new meaning of that kind and used it in a new and provocatively associative complex. And thirdly, it is not improbable that it was all a quite ordinary misunderstanding, for in situations of trauma, receiver and transmitter quite spontaneously decode the message through their own primary historical memory. And in both cases, the Bosniak and the Croat, although with unequal weight, the associations with the Ottoman period outweighed the pre-Ottoman.

The evocation of the salute from the *stechak* was also compatible with the official heraldry of post-communist Bosnia-Herzegovina: its central motif was the stylised Angevin fleur-de-lys from the coat of arms of the first king of Bosnia, Tvrtko I Kotromanić (1377–91), carved over the main gate of the fort in Jajce, and an evident symbol of pre-Ottoman statehood. And the *Golden Lily* was to remain, in spite of all later vicissitudes, the most distinguished decoration for combatants of the Army of Bosnia-Herzegovina and actually its only symbolic connection with the original concept of a multi-ethnic and depoliticised army.

In such a context, this salute met with general acceptance, and even stimulated supplementary symbolic readings. Thus a year later, in April 1993, at the first anniversary of the AB-H, the chief of the Main Staff of the Armed Forces of Bosnia-Herzegovina, Sefer Halilović, a Bosniak, made a speech to the senior officers, members of the Presidency and the government. At the end of this official and ceremonial appearance, he greeted all the soldiers 'throughout the homeland' with this 'ancient salute of our Bosnia, restored in our army.' An arm raised in this way

> is a sign of the suppression of evil with good. It is a sign of our reliance on our own strength and justice. This raised hand conveys the purity of our intention and our means for achieving our objectives.

On the same occasion, Halilović attempted to extend the visual symbolism, adding to it a verbal dimension, and as he went on he suggested that to this salute, which was originally not a greeting but a prayer position,

> we add the individual Old Bosnian greeting *A SE*, which being translated means *here and now*, and which speaks most eloquently of our successes and our intentions. We are *now* in our state of Bosnia-Herzegovina and *here* we shall stay and subsist, and our Bosnia, defiant, proud, and beautiful, we shall hand down to the generations that come after us, as their inheritance, as we received it from the generations that came before us (Halilović 1997: 218).

Although it is clear that the general was directly inspired by the *stećci* and had taken care to find out about the inscriptions on them, looked at strictly linguistically his interpretation is not correct. The expression *a se*, sometimes put together as *ase*, is indeed a typical beginning of the inscription on the medieval stone monuments, particularly on *stećci* and endowment slabs. It sometimes also appears as the final part of a document, for example *A se pisa [wrote] NN*, and has a particular poignancy and poetry in the formulaic beginning of the *stechak*, *A se leži [lies] NN, on his own land, on his noble [heritage]* ... But, these two words do not mean *here and now*, rather it is a cry, in the sense of *Look! Behold*, while the *a* alone is a conjunction meaning *yet/but/and* (Dizdar 1990: 435). But, whether this was a conscious variation for the sake of a stronger effect, or just the result of not being very well informed about the cultural history and language of medieval Bosnia, the idea of the proposer here is clear and incontestable. It is precisely in keeping with the additional development of the initial symbolic conception, suffused with emotion and a romantic ardour that need not be wondered at in this dramatic moment, the source of which is probably not historical knowledge, rather the previously mentioned collection of poems by Mak Dizdar.

Halilović's position, however, at that moment was already fairly shaky, and five months later, in November, he was dismissed in circumstances indicating behind-the-scenes machinations and a different idea about the development of the AB-H, no longer as a secular and all-Bosnian rather as an ethnic, Bosniak armed force, with a new ideology that, instead of defence of the state, more frequently highlighted the Bosniak struggle for survival, together with their culture and Islam as an inseparable part of it (there was talk of 'Islamic patriotism' and 'religious patriotism'). And at the end of 1993 it slipped further into the status of the SDA party army, independent of the supervision of formal bodies of the state. Although it did not as a whole become fundamentalist, the army 'was being transformed into a Bosniak-national army committed to a national liberation struggle to which Islam was subordinated and for which it served as a badge' (Hoare 2001: 193).

During the war the archaeologist Enver Imamović became one of the main and most productive creators of the new Bosniak national ideology, particularly of its military component. In a number of lectures and newspaper articles, then in a synthesis written in parts for the weekly *Slobodna Bosna* at the beginning of 1996, and finally in a book, he endeavoured to set up a real and a symbolic continuity of what he called a 'Bosnian', which ultimately really came down to exclusively Bosniak, military tradition, starting from the armed resistance of the Illyrian tribes to Roman conquests, and ending with the AB-H. The book concludes symbolically with a photograph of one of its units marching in a ceremonial parade at a stadium, with the caption:

> The contemporary Bosnian army – the strength and guarantee of the survival of Bosnia. The descendants of the knights of [medieval ban] Kulin and [king] Tvrtko, of the janissaries of the Turkish era, Husein-Captain's *gazis* and the imperial (Franz Josef's) heroes of the First World War (Imamović 1999: 306).

This is an absolute synthesis of all periods, political systems, state structures and their military organisations, whether or not they are defined as 'our own' or 'foreign'. This is methodologically identical to the synthesis shaped by Tuđman for the Croatian army, both of them excluding the same element from the national fighting tradition – the irregular, anti-government *haiduk*, one Catholic, the other Muslim. Behind Imamović's synthesis lies an implicit and sometimes an explicit stance, that only the Bosniaks are the credible heirs of Bosnia in time and space, its 'fundamental nation', while the Serbs (Orthodox) and Croats (Catholics) are either unwanted intruders or, in a milder version, tolerated guests. Thus Imamović too joins in the revitalised romantic national ideology of the end of the nineteenth century that, in the search for a definition of the Bosnian Muslim identity in the post-Ottoman period, insisted on the continuity of Islam with the Bosnian Bogumils, a thesis with no basis whatsoever in scholarship. Along the same lines, here in a context that suggests primarily a military tradition, in the chapter concerning medieval Bosnia and its army, he prints a picture of the now well-known *stechak* with the figure raising its arm, captioned: 'The greeting of the medieval forebears (the so-called old-Bosnian salute)' (Imamović 1999: 58; see illustration p. 482).

In his book too, which presents itself as an official monograph concerning the AB-H, along with a number of obvious deceptions, there are also the usual commonplaces of such apologetic and uncritical texts, such as the notion that the Bosnian feudal knights 'obtained their knightly experience on the field of battle, unlike most European knights, who acquired it in exercises' (29), that the 'old-Bosnian army' was a 'first-rate European power' (37), that what was achieved in the Ottoman era 'in countless battles by our agas and beys – the descendants of the one-time famous old-Bosnian knights, is inscribed in golden letters in Turkish as well as in Bosnian history' (54) and when at the beginning of the nineteenth century the Empire suppressed the first Serbian insurrection, it was actually 'the heroism of the Bosnian fighters who showed their mettle in conflicts with the Serbs that frightened them so much that they trembled at the very thought of them' (111), in which it is, of course, easy to recognise quite contemporary references. In World War I, as subjects of Austria-Hungary, they defended 'the empire more ardently and devotedly than any other people' and showed that they were 'warriors for all times' (293).

In the meantime, this archetypal Bosnian warrior had undergone one more symbolic transmogrification, initially parallel and compatible with the evocation of the pre-Ottoman, independent Bosnian state that the *stechak* salute had embodied. For the core of this second identity the AB-H took the anti-fascist Yugoslav army from World War II, or Tito's Partisans, and this acquired ever greater significance when conflicts with the HVO increasingly flared up, in addition to those with the original Serbian aggressor. This level of identity was perhaps most radically expressed by the poet and influential ideologue Džemaludin Latić, who in the spring of 1995 cried: 'We [Bosniaks] today are the most forward anti-fascist squad in Europe, as was once the young Spanish Republic' (*Ljiljan*, 3 May 1995).

As early as the end of June 1992, in the introductory address at a military seminar about war-profiteering and black-marketeering in besieged Sarajevo, the Chief of Staff of the Armed Forces of Bosnia-Herzegovina, as the official name of the army then was, said that 'iron discipline and fraternal mutual relations' had to rule in it, and that 'we have to return to the original meaning of Partisan morale, not the ideological meaning, but the deep moral meaning, when a head would fall for a single stolen pear or plum' (Halilović 1997: 171). Still, a more systematic shaping of this declared identity – which, unlike the first one, led to a number of controversies and awkward moments – can be followed from the end of 1993, when the poet and celebrated screenwriter Abdulah Sidran started printing a political travelogue in instalments about visits to the soldiers in their positions at the Sarajevo daily *Oslobođenje*, ending one instalment with the conclusion: 'We shall win when we set up a system, organisation and morality analogous to the Partisan model of 1941–5' (after Matan 1998: 248).

The ideological framework for this kind of interpretation of the war in Bosnia-Herzegovina and the nature of the AB-H was created personally by the president of the SDA and the chairman of the Presidency of Bosnia-Herzegovina, Alija Izetbegović, in a speech to participants in a seminar of the Directorate of the Staff of the Supreme Command with responsibility for morale in Sarajevo's *Fleur de Lys Centre* (*Dom ljiljana*) in December 1993. Unlike Sidran's journalistic-cum-literary discourse, which above all aspired to arouse patriotism, Izetbegović as a politician and long-term political prisoner under communism was clearly very much aware of the contradictions entailed by such a selection of signs of identity. And he knew that it would become all the more apparent if there was a move away from mechanical or formal analogies to more complex, substantial or conceptual, comparisons.

> Look, you see, how history is repeating itself in a strange and ugly
> manner. You have Chetniks and Ustashas on the scene again, and
> once again you have a third army [...] and that is our people's army.
> I say to our soldiers: be like the Partisans in the last war. I had a

few complaints about this. There are some rather narrow-minded people among us. 'Don't mention them, President, after all the Partisans brought communism.' I said that I recall that war well. [The Partisans did not speak in public about communism, rather about] ... the liberation war and, the important thing, the reason why I mention this example, is that it was said of the Partisans that they were an army that did not kill the weak [...] If the Chetniks came, the people fled. If the Ustashas came, the people fled. If the Partisans came, the people did not flee. Why? Because word had spread that they did not kill women and children. The Partisans could be cruel and rough with their enemies, but they did not kill women and children. And that is why they won (Izetbegović 1995: 14–15).[1]

Yet in spite of Izetbegović's efforts (in fact, because this kind of effort was necessary at all) it was not easy to differentiate Partisans and communists unambiguously. Unlike the Chetniks and Ustashas, the Partisans did set out to fight without any plans of genocide and they were the only force that provided a political and human future and a productive model of tolerance among the Yugoslav ethnic identities. And yet they too emerged from the war with a burden of crimes against civilians against them, which they increased in particular in the triumphalistic reprisals of 1945 and later (which undoubtedly took on the dimensions they did very largely because of the uncritical acceptance of Chetniks into the ranks of the Partisans in the last two years of the war). Through the usurpation of the military victory, which was the work of a broadly based anti-fascist coalition of non-party patriots and friends of the pre-war bourgeois parties, by introducing their

---

1. The speech, under the title 'Fighter of the Army of Bosnia and Herzegovina', was used as the introduction to the first booklet of the official Military Library of the AB-H. Izetbegović developed a similar comparison even after the end of the war with the HVO, i.e. the 'Ustashas', for example in an interview for BH Television in April 1996 (*Slobodna Dalmacija,* 10 April 1996). – Speaking generally, in the Bosnian military-political and media discourse, from the beginning and quite consistently, the phrase 'Chetniks' was used for the Serbs, as in Croatia, while in connection with the Croats, for a relatively long time after the beginning of the war with the HVO, there was an attempt at a differentiating approach, with reference to the 'extreme wing of the HVO', of its 'Ustasha wing' and 'Ustasha element'. Only in the second half of 1993, when the war reached its culmination, was a generalising use of the term brought in. It is curious that Fikret Abdić used the same analogy for his National Defence of Western Bosnia: the Croat-Serb conflict in Croatia was a war between Ustashas and Chetniks, while the Abdić side considered itself the Partisans. 'They thought that their uniforms were tailored after the Partisans', or at least after the uniforms of actors in old Yugoslav films on Partisan topics.' (I. Sabalić, Ž. Godeč, T. Vučičević, 'Fikret Abdić (...) u kućnom je pritvoru', *Globus,* 245, 18 August 1995).

dictatorship and their persecution and physical liquidation of people with different political ideas, and by repressing the Church, its congregation and most of the peasantry as 'ideologically unreliable', the communists destroyed a good part of their wartime moral capital and the bases of political pluralism created in the original Partisan movement, particularly in Croatia and Slovenia.

The suggested identity of the AB-H as the *new Partisans* was less and less sustainable as the numbers of Croats and Serbs in its ranks dwindled. And also because of the increasing influence of Islamic clerics on the everyday life of the units, and ever stronger attempts to instrumentalise the army politically in order to further the aims of the SDA. It is also likely that the evocation of the Partisan movement was not so much a deliberate strategy, as a tactical reaction to the aggressive evocations of the Chetnik and Ustasha ideologies on the Serbian and Croatian sides. That is, it was an attempt to present the AB-H in this context to the Western public as an heir to the army that in the democratic world was justly perceived as an anti-fascist ally from World War II, and an army not bogged down in ethnic bias.

With respect to this foreign addressee, the identity message was undoubtedly successful and legible, and easily fitted in with schematic ideas present in some parts of the Western public and political elites. Just how superficial and uninformed this attitude was – if sometimes a politically calculated distortion of the facts or simply an unwillingness to attempt to understand what was going on in 'this complicated area of eternal hatreds and primitivism' – is shown by a document that was prepared for members of SFOR three years after the ending of the war. In it the complex events in Yugoslavia during World War II were summed up with the quite incredible sentence that 'a group of Bosniaks who were called the Partisans fought against the fascists – the Ustashas from Croatia and the Chetniks from Serbia.'[1] Such a formulation has no connection at all with events and relationships in 1941–5, but, accidentally or not, precisely repeats the scheme just shown in which the AB-H built its own declared identity in the central phase of the war in the nineties.

The remark of Croatian Prime Minister Mateša who presented this document as an example of how little international officials knew about history and 'adopted their stances about Croatia from sheer ignorance' was undoubtedly largely accurate. But the remainder of the truth tells us that this distortion of reality was greatly increased by official Croatian politics, with

---

1. D.K, 'Hrvati ustaše, Srbi četnici, Bošnjaci – partizani [Croats Ustashas, Serbs Chetniks and Bosniaks – Partisans]', *Večernji list,* 29.01.1999.

the former Partisan(!) Tuđman at its head. This cast the mass Croatian anti-fascist movement, military and political, entirely out of its political identity, and reduced the outcome of its activities to the post-war introduction of communism. The National Liberation Army of Croatia/Yugoslavia then became the immediate forerunner of the JNA that launched its attacks on Croatia in 1991, as if in the meantime nothing at all had happened. At the same time the Tuđman government openly flirted with Ustashism, and curried favour with pro-Ustasha or at least anti-communist public sentiments. Thus it happened that it was only at the great military parade of 30 May 1997, called *Rampart of Victory*, that the Croatian army placed among its precursors – at least ostensibly – the anti-fascist army from World War II. After the decorative and historically questionable 'historical units' the original wartime banners of three important and powerful Croatian wartime Partisan brigades were borne: one from Slavonia, another from northwest Croatia and a third from Istria.

The Bosniak political elite, itself militantly anti-communist, was clearly more intelligent in this respect, both towards the foreign world and the internal public, where they endeavoured to find a more balanced interpretation. In internal Bosnia-Herzegovina relations and competition for symbolic capital such a historical-political evocation for the AB-H necessarily meant a direct polemic with the Chetnik or Ustasha contents in the imaginaries of the VRS and the HVO, and functioned as their explicit and radical negation. After the outbreak of the conflicts with the HVO, the AB-H's spokesman regularly used the pairs 'Ustashas and Chetniks', 'Ustasha and Chetnik forces' or just 'Ustasha units' for the HVO in his reports and commands (cf. Halilović 1997). Apart from the heraldry, that is the frequent and tolerated, not infrequently encouraged use of Ustasha symbols, two brigades of the HVO were officially actually called after two commanders of the Ustasha Black Legion: *Jure Francetić* from Zenica and *Rafael Boban* from Grude.

These two elements undoubtedly made it possible for this kind of declared identity in the AB-H to function for some time. Although the controversies could frequently be settled only at the level of the quip, as for instance when the Serb soldier Private Simonović replied to his peasant mother, who asked what the 'Bosnian army' he had decided to join was like, and he said: 'There are Muslims, Croats. There are some Serbs too. It's a bit like the Partisans, only without the five-pointed star, thank the Lord' (*Ljiljan*, 167, 27 March 1996). It is easy to see in this ordinary soldier's simple comment echoes of the painstaking elaborations that gave the military and political elite so much trouble, above all how in Tito's army to separate the incontestable liberating role and the multi-ethnic composition from the communist ideology of its leadership and the deceptions that it carried out after the war, breaking all its promises about democracy, introducing a dictatorship and gradually Serbianisng the JNA. The contradiction was so obvious that Izetbegović himself was forced to keep intervening. Thus in a speech in November 1993 he said that 'history is repeating itself in some strange way', and that 'in Bosnia today we have a kind of image from World War II', that is, Ustashas and Chetniks. And so

> the question now arises: Where is the third side? Then the third side was the Partisans. And now there is a third side too. That is our people's Bosnian army, which has no ideological or communist marks, and which is democratic. (Isaković and Latić 1997: 8)

This essential message – Partisans, yes, but without the communist red star – was clearly heard and well remembered by Private Simonović, and he was able to give his confused mother this laconic answer. And it was followed up in many newspaper articles. The author of one of them also had no problem in settling the analogous definition of the contemporary Chetniks and Ustashas as ruthless ethnic armies that were taking over Bosnia, but the third side of the triangle stubbornly evaded any clear definition:

> Analogies go one step further: the Partisans are once again at war in Bosnia. They are waging a war of national liberation and defending a single, adapted but recognisable, formula of brotherhood and unity. In this war too the Partisans are starving and poorly armed, but superior in terms of civilisation. They react rationally, that is humanly: even when they are driven into a kind of animal existence and forced into becoming a racial or religious community, with their distinctive sensibility for 'others' they manage to avoid animosity and defend 'others' as if they were their own.

Finally, what was left was the bitter understanding that the AB-H was the heir of the Partisans only in being poorly armed and that it had somehow to keep going until allied intervention, and the ambivalent conclusion that 'today's partisans [...] are both similar to and different from those of the second war'.[1]

---

1. Edin Šarčević, 'Čekajući Amerikance [Waiting for the Americans]', *Eurobosna*, 7, 11.02.1994.

Even before Izetbegović's speech, in the middle of 1993, it could be seen that the AB-H was beginning to be dominated by a third symbolic imaginary, notably, its foundation in the Ottoman tradition. This was the more productive in that it was at the same time an unambiguous response to the well-entrenched *haiduk* imaginary of the VRS and the advanced identical process in the HVO. In other words, the Bosniak identity had to be flexible, partly from its own choice and also because all identities are by nature dynamic, and partly because it was forced to react to the messages emitted by the competing identity choices, that were already stabilised.

If the reference system was World War II, then the Army of Bosnia-Herzegovina was faced with Chetniks and Ustashas and recognised itself as analogous to the Partisan anti-fascist army. But if the reference system was the Ottoman period, then it was faced with Christian *haiduks* of both denominations, and by analogy its soldiers became *gazis*, heroes who fought for Islam just as the *haiduks* fought not only for 'golden freedom' but also for the 'honoured cross', and naturally, regular *askers* who were putting down oppressive and brutal Christian *'haidukery'*. In elaborated versions, they were 'giant-*askers* (*div-askeri*)' (Mustafa Mustafić, *Zmaj od Bosne*, 100, 5 October 1995), as when the typical collocations of the South Slav epic were used for the members of a Kalesija unit – giant-hero (*div-junak*), giant-youths (*div-mladić*), which does not mean so much physical size as strength of morality and character, or perhaps 'professional *askers*' (Mirsad Mustafić, *Bošnjak*, 38, 12 December 1995), as when the commander of a brigade from Tuzla was so named when the AB-H had already been set up as a modern army with a professional and trained officer corps. Of course, when an army symbolically defined like this liberates a city, it is primarily perceived in the function and status that it had during the time of Ottoman rule: 'The *gazis* of the Viziers' city walk through the Viziers' city of Travnik' runs the caption to one photograph in the press (Sead Suškić; *Bošnjak*, 38, 12 December 1995).

If we exclude units such as the 7th Muslim Brigade, formed along consistently religious lines, with the green flag of the Prophet as their symbol, in the phase when it did realistically become the Bosniak army, and started in its rhetoric to idealise the Ottoman period, the AB-H had a problem with the visual aspect of its identity. There was simply no tradition on which it could rely since in Bosnia the 'Muslim aristocracy had cultivated no kind of heraldic tradition as had for example the Islamised nobility on Cyprus' (Džaja 1992: 151). Thus a historically and heraldically impossible hybrid was produced: the golden Angevin (Christian) pre-Ottoman fleur-de-lys on a green ground, the colour of Islam, instead of the original blue.

In this development of its third identity the AB-H was caught up in an ever broader evocative space, which over time developed into a integral reconstruction of the Ottoman *golden age*. Of course, an evocation of the Muslim heroic epic was involved in the final version of its imaginary, on the same methodological principles as with the Serbs and Croats, as seen in the examples already mentioned of generals Dudaković, Mahmuljin and Alagić (see p. 321). At the beginning of the war fighters from the area of Kladanj and Zvornik were formed into the Sultan Fatih unit, after the nickname of Mehmed II, the Ottoman conqueror of Bosnia.[1] The Travnik municipal council, composed of members of the SDA, created a new city coat of arms with a crescent and the year 1463 on a green ground, in a combination that took the Ottoman conquest of Bosnia to be the beginning of its 'real history'.

Thus the idea of the Ottoman epoch once again came to be seen as crucial in understanding contemporary political processes. While for the Orthodox clergy and its congregation Bosnia was a 'purely Serbian country', while the Franciscans kept up the medieval political terminology and 'in all politically and religiously-cum-politically relevant documents and events of the age talked of the Bosnian kingdom and its duchy of S. Sabae', thus maintaining among the Catholics the tradition of pre-Ottoman Bosnian statehood, Muslim self-awareness was based on a powerful tradition of Bosnian autonomy within the framework of the Ottoman state; for them Bosnia was an *eyalet* or *pashalük* (Džaja 1992: 180). Although aware of their special position, the Bosnian Muslims accepted Ottoman imperial ideology, which included the celebration of the Sultan (Banac 1984: 66). An important component was the idea of its position bordering on the Christian lands, in content, function and symbol quite equivalent to the concept of the *Antemurale Christianitatis* in Croatia, Hungary and Poland. In records left by Bosnian participants in the various Ottoman military operations there was always a feeling that they were 'the chosen soldiers of the Islamic border' or that the 'Bosnian eyalet was the strong border of Islam'. The main character in a patriotic play from the end of the nineteenth century expressed the conviction that the Sultan would not allow the Austro-Hungarian occupation of Bosnia because: 'He knows well what a rampart we are / On the border, facing Europe' (Žanić 2004: 44).

Then again, the Bosniak epic song preserved the idea of Bosnia as home

---

1. Anyone who likes symbolism, even cheap symbolism, can recall that in June 1993 *Sultan Fatih* and *King Stjepan Tomašević* (the name of the Travnik brigade of the HVO – which included a fair number of Bosniaks who had fought against the Serbian aggression in 1992) found themselves drawn up oppposite each other.

in the geographical extent of the Ottoman Bosnian *eyalet*, which included Lika in the southwest and Slavonia (and almost a third of today's Hungary) to the north, before the great withdrawal of the Ottoman Empire in the wake of defeats in the wars of 1683–97 with Austria, Poland, Russia and the Venetian Republic.

A contemporary echo of this idea, and of the historical identification of the Bosnian Muslims with the Ottoman state idea, can be recognised in the image President Izetbegović used of the position of his nation in a speech at a conference of Islamic countries in Morocco in December 1994. Poetically, it is the same image of the *defence of the (besieged) city* that characterises the Croatian cultural and political imaginary at the beginning of the nineties, but the city is not in contemporary Bosnia-Herzegovina. Kaniža, as it is called in the South Slav languages, or Nagykanizsa, is today in southwest Hungary. It was taken by the Ottomans in the winter of 1599/1600 and as its governor they installed Hasan-Pasha Tiro, great hero of the Bosnian Muslim epic, a Bosnian by birth who waged war up and down the Croatian frontier, and was for some time governor of Bosnia. The way in which this 'celebrated' and 'crafty hero' soon defended the city from the Hungarian counter-attack was described as 'perhaps the greatest act of heroism ever performed by Turkish weapons' by Safvet-beg Bašagić, the creator of romantic Bosniak national ideology, who placed him at the very top of the pantheon of Ottoman Bosnia (Bašagić 1900: 53). One of the first and most extensive articles in the SDA-influenced press in the recent war about the exemplary personalities of the period was dedicated to Tiro. In the same paper Mustafa Ćeman, bibliographer and amateur historian, later explained that he was inspired to write this article about 'Sultan Mehmed III's famous general, strategist and defender of Kaniža' by 'General Atif Dudaković, defender of Bihać, which was besieged just like Kaniža, defended by Hasan-Pasha Tiro'.[1]

For this reason, and because the Bosnians always constituted the major part of the Ottoman garrison in the city, Kaniža was an important and highly symbolic locality in the traditional memory of the Bosniaks and an interesting subject long after Tiro died. There is thus nothing unusual in Izetbegović having recalled it at this meeting in Morocco, at a moment when it seemed that after three years of war the Bosniaks were facing catastrophe. Almost a century after Tiro's feat, in 1689, when the fortunes of war were reversed and Kaniža was hopelessly surrounded, its then commander wrote to the Sultan, as Izetbegović quotes, making an easily readable allusion:

1. Isnam Traljić, 'Bošnjak je utemeljio Kairo i osnovao znameniti univerzitet El Azhar [A Bosniak founded Cairo and the famed El Azhar University]', *Ljiljan*, 155, 3 January 1996.

'We are continuing to fight, waiting for good news about the movements of the powerful units of the young cavalry. We attempt to deduce it from the movements of the migratory birds that arrive from the Ottoman shores ...'

It was in vain that this humble solider hoped [...] no assistance arrived for these besieged Muslims. After three years of siege, the garrison perished to the last man, and Muslims totally disappeared in the whole of this wide region [...] Today the Muslims of Bosnia, and Sandžak, and further afield, in Kosovo, for instance, are in the same situation as the Muslims of Kaniža. We are surrounded (Izetbegović 1995: 214–5).

From a comparative perspective it can be said that this kind of conceptually founded elaboration of the military and political identity is similar to the process of building identity promoted in Croatia somewhat earlier, and not just in the parallel of metaphors of the besieged city and the *antemurale fidei*. This is not surprising, for the Serbian aggressor expressly denied both countries any historical foundation for their right to statehood, and proclaimed their religions inferior (bearing in mind that this also characterised official Croatian policy with respect to Bosnia and the Bosniaks in the same period).

For this reason it is interesting to observe the way the main political columnist of *Ljiljan* constructed a cult of the new leader, and a broader identification in the sense just referred to, based on the symbolism of the name and surname of Alija Izetbegović. With regard to the name, the premise was the comparison between the president and his namesake Alija Sirotanović, a miner from the little town of Breza in northern Bosnia. For the first two and a half decades of Tito's Yugoslavia he was the central figure in the communist album of moral examples, a cult member of the working class, several times rewarded with the symbolic title of 'shock worker' (*udarnik*) because he had 'shifted the norm', that is dug out more ore and thus accelerated the construction of socialism. A picture of him, with mining hammer over his shoulder, sooty and dirty, but with a smiling face, was even placed on banknotes.

The Bosniak journalist saw a communist trick in this, and maintained that they had chosen him as the 'ideal type of the proletarian cult worker' precisely because his surname 'was an ideal reminder for the Bosniaks of wretchedness, poverty, modesty and beggary' (Sirotanović is etymologically derived from the word *sirotan*, a poor or wretched child, or from *sirotinja*, the collective noun for the poor or poverty). But at the first multi-party election of 1990, the Bosniaks 'rose above' the semantics of the name and voted for Alija Izetbegović, because his surname showed him to be 'part of the state-building and political elite, the *eşraf* [nobility] and aristocracy'. In this way they 'confirmed the continuity of memory', from medieval Bosnia, through 'Bosnia the *sandžak*, Bosnia the *eyalet*', to today's independent Bosnia-Herzegovina.[1] Etymologically the name Izetbegović means 'descendant of Izet-Bey', and is thus an explicit contrast to the name of the poverty-stricken miner.

This shift in accent from 'poor wretch' to 'gentleman', from proletarians to bourgeoisie, from serfs to feudal aristocracy, is equivalent to the symbolic redefinitions that had already been carried out by Slovenia and Croatia. In Bosnia-Herzegovina it had two simultaneous aspects: the proclamation of the right to statehood and the negation of communism and its ideology. The miner Sirotanović, an idealised member of the working class, was the substantive and formal equivalent of the one-time equally idealised Turjak serfs and the Stubica peasant Gubec. *Bey* Izetbegović, on the other hand, was the equivalent of the Turjak counts in Slovenia, and the medieval kings Tomislav and Petar Krešimir in Croatia, like the nobility and bourgeoisie or burgher class symbolised by Tuđman's 'historical units'. For in the historical perspective, the nobility is mainly responsible for the persistence of the state or national idea.

Thus the Bosniak national-integration ideology reached back to the historical point zero, to the pre-Yugoslav period, and the kind of interpretation of Bosnian history that had been provided by Safvet-Bey Bašagić (1870-1934). This poet, historian, orientalist and publisher was the first of the Bosniaks at the turn of the century 'to create a poetic and historical symbolism for Bosnia' and fill it with motifs of the heroism of the forefathers, the *meydans*, the old pride and glory. In his vision, the key role in Bosnian history was borne by the Muslim nobility, which was the foundation he used to stress the natural continuity of 'Bosnianism' from the oldest times to the present. Working on this theoretical basis, other writers and people in public life also gave shape to 'an apotheosis of the Bosnian bey class (*begovat*) as the representative of the patriotic traditions and guardian of national interests' (Rizvić 1990: 376, 542).

Once such a basic tone is established, it naturally sucks in the hierarchically lower elements and one after another symbolically reconstructs typical situations from the exemplary period, including its zero point, the Great

---

1. Mustafa Spahić, 'Potvrđena memorija [The Memory Confirmed]', *Ljiljan*, 193, 25 September 1996.

Beginning: the gesture of the generous victor in which, at Milodraž Field near Zenica in 1463, Sultan Mehmed II El-Fatih (Conqueror) gave Fra Anđeo Zvizdović an *ahdnama* guaranteeing the Bosnian Catholics religious freedom, if they acknowledged Ottoman rule. More than five centuries later, on 19 March 1995, the Mayor of Zenica, Besim Spahić (SDA) gave Cardinal Vinko Puljić, Archbishop of Sarajevo/Vrhbosna, a replica of the *ahdnama* with a dedication that it was 'a silenced witness to the universality and tolerance of Islamic culture' (*Stećak*, 19/20, July/August 1995). In January 1996 the Executive Committee of Vareš SDA and its chairman, Avdija Kovačević, were absolutely explicit when the city's Croats protested about police harassment of the parish vicar. Kovačević answered them in writing, full of indignation and amazement that they had dared to criticise his government:

> Where are you now, Sultan Mehmed El-Fatih, to see what they are doing, they whose grandfathers knelt before your majesty and begged for mercy and protection, and you gave it them. Where are you now, Mehmed El-Fatih, to see how they return your goodness and mercy! [...] You could have taken them all away into slavery, you had the power, but you had mercy on them, you showed that you were a noble descendant of Mohammed, favourite of God [...] Good that you so acted! If only you could see how grateful the infidels' descendants are for your mercy!!![1]

This kind of SDA political imaginary, and its derivation, the ultimate identity of the AB-H as heir to the Ottoman *askers* and *gazis* from the Ottoman theocratic utopia, seen from the panoramic perspective of mutually linguistically intelligible and mutually interwoven political imaginaries in all their traditional bases, gave an objective retroactive legitimacy to the Serbian and Croatian *haiduk*, even providing a framework in which the motif of the *haiduk* epic was facilitated and its perpetuation encouraged. To speak in the same language – the Croatian, Serbian and Bosnian languages – the standardisation of which was carried out on dialect material that was typologically and generically more or less the same, does not mean only having the advantage that no translator is needed for one to be able to travel through the three states and read the best novels and watch films, as is often – and accurately – repeated in a romantic idealisation. Mutual understanding without a translator and without any special linguistic education has another

---

1. Mato Topić, 'Šablon, uzor ili prošlost? [Stereotype, model or past?]', *Svjetlo riječi*, 155, February 1996.

side as well, for then one hears the worst insults, threats and provocations uttered in these languages, a fact that is often forgotten when the linguistic similarity of the South Slav nations is uncritically celebrated. There is either full intelligibility, which includes the transmission of both good and evil, or there is none.

The inhabitant of Warsaw was not able to read the novels of Thomas Mann, unless he had specially learned German, and in 1939 nor was he able to understand the insults of the Nazi officers or the speeches of Goebbels about the inferiority of the Slav race on Radio Berlin. But the inhabitant of Vukovar or Dubrovnik, Sarajevo or Srebrenica, and indeed of Belgrade, could without the slightest difficulty understand everything. A debate about whether such a privilege was a help or hindrance to him would doubtless be endless and it is fairly certain that it would end cynically.

It is not difficult to discern why, just before he ordered the slaughter of more than 8,000 civilians, Ratko Mladić recalled and explained to journalists that it was precisely 'the Turks of Srebrenica that had committed the worst crimes against the Serbian people in the suppression of the *Revolt against the Dayis*' (Janjić 1996: 110). But it is also not difficult to guess that the job of legitimating this flagrant crime as a just balancing of the books of history was made a little easier by the statement of AB-H Brigadier Mirsad Selmanović that it was not true that 'we have no military tradition' for 'our men' had fought, as part of the Austro-Hungarian army, in the Carpathians, and the Alps, in Galicia and Lombardy, 'they had fired their weapons even earlier, throughout the Ottoman Empire', and above all, in a clear allusion to current events, it was precisely the 'Bosniaks who had, for example, put down the so-called First Serbian Insurrection in the Pashaluk of Belgrade ... And yet some would have it that we have no military tradition.'[1]

The Croatian Herzegovinian *gusle* player would, in the context of this kind of polemical or even competitive evocation of the symbolic material that they were mutually fed on, ring out a little more convincingly in the minds of his audience when on the occasion of the project for merging the AB-H and the HVO into the Army of the Federation of Bosnia-Herzegovina he sneeringly asked his fellow countryman, the Minister of Defence in the FBH:

Vlado Šoljić, big head minister
what's our army to be called –
will it be called an askeriye

---

1. Isnam Traljić, 'Bitka koja je ušla u sve historije osim u udžbenike u bivšoj Jugoslaviji [Battle that entered all histories apart from schoolbooks in the former Yugoslavia]', *Ljiljan*, 195, 9 October 1996.

or the Croat-Bosniak army?
(Šimić 1996)

On the fifth anniversary of the founding of the SDS, Radovan Karadžić proudly pointed out that the party 'had managed to turn the centuries back, to erase and cancel the ages of slavery, and grief, and suffering, and mourning' (*Javnost*, 225/226, 22 July 1995). Success or not, the fact is that it did really sweep a considerable part of the Serb population psychologically and cognitively back to the late Middle Ages, which was not actually very difficult, since it had been able to take over a well-worked-out Yugoslav political imaginary and its cognitive and perceptive schemes, and rely in organisational terms on the ramified network of *gusle* players' associations.

It was more difficult to imagine that it would not remain alone on this journey, but it was wholeheartedly joined in the same business by the HDZ and the SDA in the first half of 1993. Someone very well informed about conditions in the AB-H suggests that the process of its identification with the Bosnia of the Ottomans really gathered speed in the spring of 1993, with the mass use of the term *şehit*, martyr. The word is used of a Muslim who dies heroically in the defence of the faith. It was given not only to Bosniaks who were religiously indifferent, but also to Serbs and Croats who died in the defence of the country. The process was officially completed at the beginning of 1997, when the *nişan*, the typical Muslim gravestone, was chosen as the official emblem on the graves of all soldiers who had fallen, rather than the neutral stone slab on which every family might have a religious symbol carved as it wished, or than the stylised *stechak*, as proposed by many respected people in public life, including former members of the AB-H from its first phase, both Bosniaks and others. In the end all that is possible is the bitter conclusion that the state that 'vaunted its centuries-long statehood' was thus 'a priori rejecting the value of the non-Muslim lives woven into the defence of that statehood.'[1]

Another author considers that the key moment, at least with respect to the public flaunting of religious beliefs in the army at the highest level, was the visit of Izetbegović to the 7th Muslim Brigade in Zenica, in October 1994 (Hoare 2001: 194). This is certainly a longer process, but the fact is that from that time Islamic religious greetings started to be considered desirable in the army, despite the fact that it continued to include a relatively large number of Serbs and Croats. The commander-in-chief himself, General Rasim Delić, at the main celebration of Army Day in Sarajevo on 15 April 1995 greeted

---

1. Vildana Selimbegović, 'Pojela je politika', *Dani*, 54, travanj 1997.

the military and political elite with the religious expression *salaam* (*selam*) (Isaković and Latić 1997: 102).

And when on the occasion of the fifth anniversary celebration of the Army of Bosnia-Herzegovina an official poster was printed, showing a mosque, the editorial in the same independent weekly was similarly critical:

> Nothing would have been contentious if alongside this incontrovertible element in the identity of the army there had been room for some other mark of Bosnia and Bosnian society, which might have underlined at the symbolic level some of the sources from which the Bosnian army generates its historical role.[1]

Justly stressing its position as the regular army of an acknowledged state, the AB-H, together with the SDA, reduced this state in its imagination to the Ottoman period, giving up equally on the pre-Ottoman and post-Ottoman components of its identity. It is not in dispute that the Bosniak side was partially forced into the construction of this kind of symbolic universe by the aggressiveness of the symbolic universes of the SDS and later of the HDZ, and that the typology of rival political imaginaries in a sense compelled it to hit back with equivalent categories, justly, and, after all, in a similar way to the manner in which Croatian national ideologues had become pronouncedly historicist since the mid-eighteenth century. Nor is it in contention that the Ottoman contents created a quite natural part of the Bosniak social memory and cultural and political self-awareness and that they had to take on a more marked importance in the conditions of a struggle for sheer existence.

But it should also not be denied that there was in addition a powerful ideological current in the SDA that insisted on precisely this kind of imaginary and promoted exclusive linkage with it. This not only produced justified mistrust among the substantial number of Croats and Serbs who had remained loyal to the state of Bosnia, but also reduced the complex identity of their own community to just one component – necessarily distorted by the very act of reduction.

All this tends to confirm the accuracy of the historian Srećko M. Džaja's claim that in the Ottoman period 'the basis for a common political identity for the population of Bosnia' was 'to a large extent', if not utterly, 'destroyed'. Reduced to the administrative department of a vast empire that stretched over three continents, Bosnia ceased to exist as 'a single political being' and its 'new or rather restructured populace was non-homogeneous and each

---

1. [Unsigned], 'Armija jedne vjere', *Dani*, 55, May 1997.

group oriented itself towards some other external spiritual and political centre'. When the later Serb and Croat nationalisms attempted to rise above the Ottoman religious heritage and create political integration, they were unsuccessful because they themselves 'had the burden of their religions and because they practised a superficial and simple enlightenment' (Džaja 1992: 188).

The contemporary consequence of this was seen, among other things, most powerfully in the constant aggressive identity proclamations of the Serb paramilitaries and of the HVO, and in a slightly different way in the imaginary of the Croatian Army (HV), especially in the 1993–5 period. Bosniak nationalism too achieved a similar bottom line – anachronistic, autistic and incapable of rising above a black and white image of the world – when with political independence and international recognition Bosnia-Herzegovina was finally able freely to complete its own national-integration ideology and to form the core of its collective political imaginary. Appropriating during the war the originally all-Bosnian and secular Army of Bosnia-Herzegovina for itself alone, personally, politically and ideologically, it could not, even if it had wanted to, form its symbolic identity and traditional references in any other way than by closing once again a circle that was only just open, and slamming shut with all its force a door that was only slightly ajar.

The paradox or the irony in this is that here was the only post-Yugoslav political elite that was not a hangover from the communists and, what is more, that was very largely composed of anti-communists and former political prisoners. And yet, ultimately, it nevertheless repeated the communists' blunder of 1945.

FOURTEEN

The *Haiduk* Outside Institutions

*There were still [in 1906 in Poljica, in the central Dalmatian hinterland]
people alive who used to see haiduks going around and extorting money
from people. They roamed and hid around the mountains, spending their
days and nights there, and if they found out that someone lived well,
they told them to bring meat, bread and wine and some money. This
was certainly worth doing, it was no joking matter, because if someone
didn't respond, the haiduks would be in his house at night, robbing his
cellars and barns, slaughtering his animals, taking off whatever they
could get their hands on, and if anyone resisted, they would shoot him
or shackle his arms and legs in chains so he couldn't move until they had
finished their work around the house.*

(Ivanišević 1987: 368)

The noble brigand or Robin Hood forever

The title of this chapter might well seem tautological, a *contradictio in adjecto*.
First, by definition the *haiduk* was someone who had definitively broken with
all the established institutions of society and the state, and hence it is hardly
necessary additionally to define him as extra-institutional. Secondly, the
haiduk did in fact regularly remain integrated into his original social milieu.
He was bound to a certain section of society, which supported and protected
him, if only passively, through the agency of his harbourers (*yataks*) or some
other institutions that had grown out of the tradition and been verified by it,
such as hospitality, godfathership or variously motivated types of solidarity,
or indeed fear, for this too is a social relationship. Consequently he was, in
an idiosyncratic way, institutionalised. And in addition, these two models,
or processes, his institutionalisation and deinstitutionalisation, quite often
overlapped and interwove in various combinations.

This part of the discussion refers, however, to a particular form of the evocation of *'haidukery'* that exists even outside the official and formal political imaginaries, or the symbolic universes that were constructed in the preparations for war, or during the war, by governments, organised social groups or political parties, which have been considered above. Even these evocations could not be constructed without the spontaneous response and input of the target audience (without which it would have been quite impossible). And nor could the forms under discussion here come into being without interaction with the so-called official evocations, without connection with the overall imaginative resonances that the established political discourse stimulated when it drew terminologically or phraseologically on the vernacular culture, and quoted or imitated its patterns of discourse, motifs and ethics. In every individual case there are various indicators as to which side was dominant or took the initiative at a given moment in this interaction, but that will not be discussed here. Much of this is a matter for criminal investigation or the courts. For our purposes, it is important to try to show how some of the contents of popular (folk) culture overlapped in meaning with various wartime phenomena or were reciprocally fertilised by them.

It is also important to mention that this is relevant only in the context of the Croatian and the Bosniak political imaginaries and their stylistic and evocative terminologies because they and their corresponding discourses – with the exception of the Herzegovinian component of the Croatian one – convey an unambiguously negative evocation of the *haiduk*. Thus at least at the terminological level they create an institutional grounding in relation to which it is possible to compare the extra-institutional evocation of the same phenomenon.

In the Serbian case no such distinction exists, for there such a powerful, suggestive and all-embracing symbolic *haiduk* epic universe was constructed that all potentially competing discourses founded in other evocation matrices were eliminated from the outset. Still it is worth mentioning one contemporary treatment of the motif of the *noble outlaw* using the example of the international criminal Ljubomir Magaš aka Ljuba Zemunac, who was killed some years before the war, in 1986, as a member of the 'Yugo mafia' in Germany, in a shoot-out with Frankfurt gangs of thieves, racketeers and extortionists. The verse epitaph on his gravestone in Belgrade, put up by his friends, starts with a comparison between him and Robin Hood:

> *A warm heart he had for the weak,*
> *In a world of wrong, he had a sharp sword,*
> *Punished rapacious thugs,*
> *Travelled the ways of Robin Hood.*
> (Čolović 1993: 5–6)

Since the legal government in Bosnia-Herzegovina did not prepare for the armed defence of the country, this task was taken on first by spontaneously organised groups who partially derived from the criminal underground and were under the leadership of people who were themselves social problems, to put it mildly. Obtaining weapons privately, those of the groups that were at all organised in terms of function and hierarchy soon became the only real government in their area. They took over all the commerce – from drugs and arms to food – introduced their own taxes and charged for protection and for the deliverance of people from the besieged cities. When in the spring of 1993 the commander of the AB-H arrived in Zenica he was 'shocked' by the fact that the HVO charged Muslims and Serbs for a licence to get out of the town: it was 50 marks for an individual, or a small car, but for a truck the charge was higher. But this was not all: he soon 'understood that the local people in charge were inclined to various kinds of deals', these people in charge were the predominantly Bosniak government in the city, and 'in effect, there was active collusion between the mobs on all sides' (Halilović 1997: 104), since it was impossible to get to the safe areas without the third, Serbian, faction also agreeing to the deal. Resistance to aggression and organised crime joined as a 'kind of gangster guerrilla force' the leaders of which 'combined intimidation and crimes with expansive Robin Hood gestures' (Žunec 1997: 24).

As a sociologist researching all the effects of the war on the structure of society in Bosnia-Herzegovina, Ozren Žunec dealt with three such wartime leaders in Sarajevo – Ramiz 'Ćelo' Delalić, Mušan 'Caco' Topalović and Jusuf 'Juka' Prazina. But, apart from the apt reference to 'Robin Hood gestures', he did not go into the socio-anthropological and cultural-historical analysis of the motif of the *noble brigand* and its function in vernacular culture. And without this the wartime phenomenon cannot be fully explained. And here this is exactly what was in the foreground, with the proviso that – for a sketch of the basic parameters of this very complex and polysemic process – the three Bosniaks have to be joined by two Croats: Mladen 'Tuta' Naletilić and Vinko 'Klica' Žuljević.

In October 1992, Delalić's men carried out one of these Robin Hood gestures, when they dealt out 500 kilos of bread every day at the Sarajevo marketplace free of charge to the starving citizenry (Skrinjar Trvrz 1993: 37), thus giving public expression to characteristics that in the vernacular culture of pre-industrial Europe, from the British Isles to Greece, from Spain to Russia, had become a commonplace in the legendary biographies of people outside the law. The Scottish outlaw Rob Roy, like Robin Hood or Diego

Corrientes in Andalusia, 'gave money to a poor man who was in debt to a rich one, taking it back from the rich man soon after', while his eighteenth century contemporary the English highwayman Dick Turpin 'threw £6 into the house of a poor woman in a gesture reminiscent of the Charity of St Nicholas' (Burke 1978: 166).

In a lengthy interview in which he presents his life and worldview, Delalić sees nothing wrong in his having, for example, inflicted grievous bodily harm on the director of a bank because he was a 'thief' who 'hadn't fired a single bullet', that is, had not taken part in the armed defence of Sarajevo. Nor was it unusual to him that the government was clearly helpless when faced with his exploits, nor that on his own initiative he 'mobilised' people round the town and forced them to dig trenches in front of his units, because they were 'well fed, well trained, and so, mate, they could dig'. Having taken part in many battles, he despised professional officers because they were not 'from the people'. And he came by money in the following way:

> At that time I had the best equipped brigade. Where'd I get the money from? Course, I got it from the private businessmen who were working in the war [...] I never set the amount of money. I never brought one of them, I brought fifteen, twenty or thirty of them along, and said I needed cash, and I was collecting for weapons. And none of them said: Well, I won't give anything [...] I don't care if they did it out of fear. What's important was to give so the arms could be bought. I didn't need cash. They didn't give the money to me, but to the army.[1]

On the other hand Topalović said that he would let all those who fled from the besieged city, although he considered them 'traitors and generally worthless', come back and freely walk wherever they wanted, 'only I would take from the well-known and the rich' 'from a hundred thousand to a thousand marks, depending how much they had' to deal out among the fighters at the front line.[2]

When the authorities could no longer put up with his behaviour, at the end of October 1993 they organised a police operation to disarm this unit and then perhaps to include some parts of it in the regular military structure. In this clash Topalović was killed, as were nine members of the police specials. He was buried in an unknown spot, but three years later, when the

---

1. Senad Pećanin, Vildana Selimbegović, 'Poskidala nas vojna lica', *Dani*, 36, October 1995.
2. Senad Pećanin, 'Na svakom geleru piše ime', *Dani*, 13, 17 May 1993.

war ended, it was possible to put on a real Muslim funeral rite, the *cenaze*, at Kovači Cemetery in which the *şehits* were buried (as we have seen, *şehit* originally meant a martyr for the faith; in time, however, in official SDA rhetoric, all fallen soldiers were so called, even non-Muslims). At his funeral, attended by as many as 20,000 Sarajevo citizens, the imam pronounced him both a *gazi* (hero) and a *şehit* whose heroism had 'been admired by the whole world', one of those heroes whose 'sacrifice ensured the survival of Islam in Bosnia' and whose massive *cenaze* means the 'defeat of all *kâfirs* [infidels] and *munafiks* [those who pretend to be believers in Islam but in fact are not]'. His wartime deputy, the first speaker, said:

> It was a difficult time, harder than anyone could have guessed
> ... You, Caco, didn't have much sympathy for the models and
> mamma's boys, for those who hid in the cellars. Dear Caco, people
> have accused you of some things, but for most people you were
> a model. The cowards and the dishonest accused you, while the
> poor hailed you and defended Bosnia with you. Perhaps because
> no one knows the extent of the injustice like the poor.[1]

Prazina also shared the credit for the defence of Sarajevo in the first weeks of the war, and at the end of June 1992 he was officially appointed commander of the commandos, as Topalović was nominally commander of an AB-H brigade. Songs were sung of him, but at the same time he terrorised the town: his men seized cars and beat up members of the public, and took whatever they wanted out of the shops, sometimes leaving a receipt in order to give it an appearance of lawfulness. From time to time, with a great deal of pomp, Prazina would give some of the loot to hospitals, children and the infirm. He was the real master of a large part of the city and even made the decisions as to who would get a telephone line. While he was in town, he drove a stolen dark red Audi the license plates of which read *JUKA*, and when he went to Mt Igman in the early autumn of 1992 to the regular units of AB-H, ostensibly to help to break the siege, in the village of Šahbegovići he bought a white horse on which he intended to ride into liberated Sarajevo, completely immersed as he was in the role of the romantic hero. (The fascination with horses, and the awareness that the same fascination, deriving from the same traditional model, was shared by the target rural and semi-urban public, was shown still more vividly by Topalović when he drove up to a football match in Sarajevo in 1997 in a coach drawn by four white horses.) The ancient folk ideas about the hero sleeping underground or hidden somewhere who would return at a

---

1. Snježana Mulić, 'Ispraćaj u društvo šehida', *Dani*, 49, November 1996.

crucial moment to help his menaced community were revived in connection with Prazina. Although at the end of 1993 he was found shot on the roadside somewhere near Liège in Belgium, for two and a half years after that in Sarajevo there were 'lads who would spend hours and hours persuading you that Juka was alive and was just waiting for the right moment. He'll be here.'[1]

In Croatia, the first to evoke the figure of the *noble robber* was the union boss and secondary school teacher Vesna Kanižaj. She did this, it is true, during the war, but outside the immediate context of war, because in this context any positive evocation of *'haidukery'* – as shown above in great detail – was very difficult, if even conceivable. As organiser of a teachers' strike, and embittered at the educational policy of the HDZ government, she was, she said, particularly proud of her great-grandfather Andrija Gudelj called Velaga, 'an illiterate *haiduk* from the red-hot stones of Imotski', who, 'thinking over the future of his descendants and his nation, gave the money he had obtained through *"haidukery"*, smuggling, theft and who knows how else for a communal reading room – unlike many of today's so-called doctors of science and academicians who don't want to give anything for education'. She attempted to clarify her views further by saying that the union struggle, to which she was wholeheartedly dedicated, was nevertheless 'something other than political' and she liked strikes for the somewhat romantic reason that they 'contained important social demands' and 'a trait of rebellion against political rigidity'.[2]

Such an addition brings her statement even closer to the universal folk idea of romantic fighters for justice, against the corrupt lords, and makes her original vernacular inspiration for contemporary political action still more pronounced. It is almost possible to imagine an epic song or the popular light novel that ends with the idea that the grave of her great-grandfather the *haiduk* looks like the epitaph on the grave of Robin Hood the way it is presented by the closing stanza of an early ballad about his feats, the *Gest of Robyn Hode*:

> *Cryst have mercy on his soule,*
> *That dyed on the rode!*
> *For he was a good outlawe,*
> *And dyde pore men moch god.*

1. Vildana Selimbegović, 'Vuk ili kojot', *Dani*, 55, May 1997.
2. Vlado Vurušić, 'Ja uopće nisam Moby Dick ni Čelična Lady: ja sam samo praunuka imotskog hajduka', *Globus*, 450, 2 May 1994. For almost the same statement in another interview, in which she contrasted the 'animosity and arrogance' with which the government behaved to the unions with the 'socially active' ethics of her great-grandfather the *haiduk*, see Heni Erceg, 'Sat demokracije, uživo', *Feral Tribune*, 450, 2 May 1994.

And finally, it really was documented that at the end of the eighteenth and in the nineteenth century some *haiduks* in the South Slav lands dealt out looted food to the poor, and one from the nineteenth century in Slavonia even paid poor peasants' taxes. With a little irony it can be said that Velaga would have felt most at home in the contemporary Croatian party with which his great-granddaughter was fiercely at odds. At least if one takes into consideration the category in which the task of that party was defined by its ideologue, the writer and connoisseur of the heroic epic Ivan Aralica, deputy speaker of the Upper House of the Croatian Parliament. He resolutely rejected accusations that many members of the HDZ had got rich during the war, that it was 'a party of plutocrats because it had to carry out privatisation during the war, the worst time'. Quite the opposite, it was 'the party of the Croatian commoners that would be able to take from the rich all the riches that belonged to the people' (*Slobodna Dalmacija*, 10 February 1997). In other words, the HDZ was supposed to be a kind of collective Robin Hood, protector of the poor and avenger of the downtrodden, correcting injustice and helping the ordinary people.

Mladen 'Tuta' Naletilić from Široki Brijeg is an even more controversial figure than the three Sarajevans. He fled Yugoslavia in 1968 and spent most of his time in West Germany and Switzerland where he owned at least one casino, and came back in 1990. He claims that he then took part as a volunteer in the defence of Croatia, although he has never been able to find a single witness to confirm this, or his alleged wounding in combat near Zadar. Afterwards, in Herzegovina, he founded the Convicts' Battalion (*Kažnjenička bojna*), part of the HVO, to which serious crimes are attributed, particularly in Mostar street fighting with the AB-H, and the persecution of Bosniaks and others. The official explanation for the name of the unit was that almost all its members had been persecuted and imprisoned by the communist government in Yugoslavia because of their Croatian patriotism and democratic beliefs. But those who really had been in jail were there for far more prosaic and quite apolitical, that is, purely criminal reasons. They often did deals with the Yugoslav secret police which would amnesty them and allow them to go abroad quite legally, in return for which they would spy on and occasionally liquidate members of the real political émigré community, and as 'proven anti-communists' would infiltrate its ranks to radicalise it and by various outrages excite a police reaction from the local authorities. There are many indicators that Tuta was in fact just such an agent provocateur.

In the émigré period in Germany he joined forces with local leftist terrorists, but not 'because of their ideas, rather because of their leftist revolutionary methods', in his opinion the only proper ones for the overthrow of Yugoslavia. In a long biographical interview he condemned terrorists whose attacks targeted children and old people, but not those who 'aimed directly at the politicians'. In general, he did not think he had done anything wrong, for 'it was the state that was the terrorist, and the German radical leftists were revolutionaries. And I consider myself the same.' He admitted that some Croatian émigrés, his friends, robbed banks, but did this in order to 'finance the fight for Croatia', and he was sorry that he hadn't himself taken part instead of 'running a casino in which the poor lost their bread'. He too had a moral code similar to those of Ćelo, Caco and Juka: he did not trust the regular authorities, but he himself sought out, judged and punished persons he considered to have done something wrong. As he put it, 'I took from those who did not want to fight everything that I needed: if I needed a car, I would take it without thinking twice, whoever's it was.'[1]

In early 1997 the Croatian police arrested Naletilić on suspicion of having arranged a murder, but even then there were plenty of indications that it was a matter of far bigger crimes, war crimes, as well as the creation of a major network of organised crime. He was imprisoned in Zagreb, but in Herzegovina posters started appearing bearing his image with the inscription *Tuta – Our Victory*. The public could obtain no official details about the legal case against him, but in the 'Herzegovina taverns' news about him went round 'like the legends of the *haiduk harami başis* of the area, Mijat Tomić and Andrijica Šimić', above all that in some miraculous manner he had escaped from jail and was already residing in his luxury house on a hill above his native town.[2]

He too had no love for the *corrupt gentlemen*, or, as his fellow-townsman and former member of the Convicts' Battalion told a Zagreb journalist, 'he openly despised all the big guys, political and business'. They backed this up with the following story: when the 'president of Herceg-Bosna', Mate Boban, allowed Tuta to attend the official session of the government of Herceg-Bosna in Grude, but not the two combatants who were his escort, Tuta 'was incensed', drove Boban and the other officials out of the premises, and 'ordered a bottle of whisky, that he and the lads then drank in peace.' After they had read her an epic in decasyllabics, the journalist concluded that 'Tuta's distant forebear Mijat Tomić would have been satisfied with the entry of his descendant into national legend'.[3]

---

1. Mate Bašić, 'Čak ni svog čuvara (...) ne dam ni Interpolu ni u Haag', *Nacional*, 1, 24 November 1995.
2. Vjeran Grković, 'Terminator sa Ciganskog brda', *Feral Tribune*, 600, 17 March 1997.
3. Mare Bulić-Mrkobrad, 'Kažnjenička bojna uzvraća udarac', *Globus*, 341, 20 June

From the story it cannot be gathered whether this was her own free interpretation of the conversation or whether they were the interviewees' own words. If they had presented Naletilić in this way, then this is an additional relevant detail for understanding his status in the patriarchal setting of the living epic tradition. In truth, he was not exactly Mijat's descendant, because the Tomićes in the village of Kablići near Livno claim that honour (Mijatović 1985: 30), but the tradition still alive in our day does indeed consider the Naletilićes from the area of Široki Brijeg the descendants of his nephew and most devoted companion, Mali Marijan (Mijatović 1969: 14).

Vinko 'Klica' Žuljević from the area of Uskoplje/Gornji Vakuf was also supposed to be caught in the same police raid as Naletilić, but managed to get out, and an official warrant was put out for him. He did indeed fight as a volunteer, first in the defence of Croatia, and then in the AB-H/HVO war in central Bosnia, where he was seriously wounded. After the arrest of Naletilić, through an intermediary, he set up, with a fair amount of secrecy, a meeting with a Zagreb journalist. In the end he met her quite openly in a Mostar bar. This procedure, together with the indignation with which he reacted to the claim that he was a criminal, might remind one of the *haiduk* of the beginning of the century who asked reporters from jail to 'write nice' about him, and afterwards carefully read articles about his misdeeds and even sent corrections to the editor (Dvorniković 1991: 366). They might also recall the Ed Gein case, the quadruple American killer (and direct inspiration for that founding film of the modern psychological thriller, Hitchcock's *Psycho* of 1960) who was arrested in 1957, and when in the course of the investigation he was also indicted for shoplifting he said, annoyed and offended: 'You surely don't think I'm a thief?' And then there is the case from the chamber in The Hague, when the prosecutor mentioned that Vinko 'Štela' Martinović had fled from the scene of the crime in a Golf. The defendant leapt up from the dock and cried: 'No I didn't, it was a Mercedes!'[1]

As the journalist discovered, the story in Herzegovina is that after the raid Žuljević 'went to the *haiduks*' and that 'his countrymen' from central Bosnia, where he had fought against the AB-H, 'identified him with some Mijat Tomić who, according to *gusle* tradition, had hidden for seventeen years round the caves of Glamoč, killing Turks'. Again it is not clear which formulations are original and which are the free indirect speech of the journalist, but again it is incontestable that in the countryside Mijat Tomić and the *haiduk* tradition were in some way or other associated with the figure of Žuljević, and that

---

1997.

1. Saša Ljubičić, 'Haaška ludara', *Slobodna Dalmacija*, 6 September 2003.

this parallel really was mentioned in the interviews. From the episode in which Klica explains why he hates the Bosniaks one might conclude that he personally identified with the role, particularly that he did so during the war with the Bosniaks, or that he appropriated for himself – if we return for a moment to the categories of modern popular culture – the charisma of the high-minded terrorist who purged society of unworthy members. As he says, he was brought up 'with the *gusle* heroic songs' in which

> the Muslims are described as Turkish converts, Croats who had turned their backs on their own faith and people, outcasts of the race, who served their Turkish masters. And is there any more wretched fellow than the one who gives up his faith? And so I never accepted them as Croatian allies in the defence against the Serbs. If they had once betrayed their faith, they would sell out a second time.[1]

However different they might be, all these examples have a common trait: their protagonists are, for their original social environment, all heroes, the environment feels solidarity with them, and thinks it has to protect them, while for the government and for those segments of society that consider this government legitimate, they are criminals. When they are asked about each other, or about people with similar biographies and attitudes, they reply that they think them heroes, and they do not want to say anything about the government's different viewpoint, or else they dismiss them contemptuously. They all live with the feeling that they have been done an injustice, and that they can find genuine understanding only in each other. They speak openly about deeds that are certainly by law classified as crimes, particularly thefts, extortion, blackmail, for they do not consider them offences since they were done 'to the state' or to 'the gentry (*gospoda*)'. They all hate or despise the 'gents', they consider the state or the regular government unjust and alienated, and think its laws unrelated to real life and morality. That is why they themselves seek out and punish people they consider to have committed some offence (usually with a thrashing, sometimes with murder and in the case of Juka with a kneecapping), just as once Rade Đukić had shot his daughter's killers in the courthouse at Bijelo Polje, because he did not believe that the court would hand down what he considered an appropriate punishment, and he was warmly acclaimed by those present.

They had their own code of honour: the band or the gang was sacrosanct

---

1. Jasna Babić, 'Ako mi itko dokaže da sam prekršio zakone (...)', *Nacional*, 69, 12 March 1997.

for them. They would do anything for their own fighters, they felt that they had the right to beat them up or even kill them, a right that the soldiers themselves admitted, but they would not allow anyone from outside to do so, whatever formal and hierarchical authority they might have. Although some of them were convicted before the war, not only for theft, robbery and black-marketeering but also for rape, they vehemently deny the last, saying they would never commit any acts of violence against women, that they could not even imagine such a thing, for they had their own sisters and mothers whom they deeply loved and respected, or that such violence was simply not necessary for them, for women naturally desired them and spent time with them of their own free will. The only unforgivable offences are betrayal of the band and avoiding a fight. When the terminology is laid bare, Naletilić's depiction of the German ultra-left terrorists or bank robbers is essentially a picture of *haiduks* taking from the rich to give to the poor, or for some general benefit, just as Vesna Kanižaj describes her great-grandfather. According to them, devotion to the community, which can be only their native village or in modern times the whole nation, is the main criterion of their ethical judgments and positions. For this they are in principle ready even to be killed. As Prazina said in a long confessional interview that was printed after his death, at the beginning of 1993 the Army of Bosnia-Herzegovina ambushed and attacked his unit but 'I gave the order that no one was to return fire but they had to go back to Bjelašnica [their base]. I did not want to respond, in case they said the next day that I was a *haiduk*, that I shot at my own people.' A bit later he expressly accused the military top brass of hating him and wanting to destroy him out of envy, for 'I am the one that was a legend, and I think I am a legend now, well, who for, is not important.'[1]

Two essential things are clearly stated. First, the *noble outlaw* or, in the Balkan context, the *haiduk*, will never hit out at his own people, the people to which the ordinary soldiers of the AB-H also belong, for they, the implication goes, also respect him and have received orders to fire at him. It is only the 'office, chair-bound, officers' that are the traitors. And the meaning in which Prazina here understands the *haiduk*, that is someone who shoots at his own people, and who is therefore merely a common criminal, fits in perfectly – whether he was aware of it or not – with the Bosniak traditional and social memory and official and unofficial public discourse in which the *haiduk* is a synonym for criminal and traitor. The 'Christian' equivalent of Juka Prazina from the 1990–5 period would not have used the term in this sense and context: for someone who struck out at his 'own people' they had

---

1. Damir Hrasnica, 'Jusuf Juka Prazina', *Dani*, 28, 31 January 1995.

other terms, such as traitor or criminal.

Secondly, Prazina is fully aware of his own charisma and status among the members of his own social group in the broadest sense, that is the people, the devalued and marginalised groups who saw in him the embodiment of the cultural hero who stood for the aspiration for a different kind of society, and these myths had their own original and authentic strength that should certainly not be underrated, sneered at or denied. It is at the roots of all such mythogenesis, and if one wishes to understand how criminals or quite insignificant people can become famed and respected personalities, it is worth concentrating on the central element, which is

> the perception (conscious or unconscious) of a 'fit' in some respect or respects between a particular individual and a current stereotype of a hero or a villain [...] This 'fit' strikes people's imagination and stories about that individual begin to circulate, orally in the first instance. In the course of this oral circulation, the ordinary mechanisms of distortion studied by social psychology, such as 'levelling' and 'sharpening', come into play. These mechanisms assist the assimilations of the life of the particular individual to a particular stereotype from the repertoire of stereotypes present in the social memory of the given culture (Burke 1989: 104).

All of them, some more, of course, and some less, in the categories in which their original milieu perceives them or in which they perceive themselves, fit into the nine definitions by which Eric Hobsbawm described the typical *noble outlaw* or *soft-hearted robber*, from Robin Hood to Diego Corrientes:

1. The noble robber begins his career of outlawry not by crime, but as the victim of injustice, or through being persecuted by the authorities for some act which they, but not the custom of his people, consider as criminal.
2. He 'rights wrongs'.
3. He 'takes from the rich to give to the poor'.
4. He 'never kills but in self-defence or just revenge'.
5. If he survives, he returns to his people as an honourable citizen and member of the community. Indeed, he never actually leaves the community.
6. He is admired, helped and supported by his people.
7. He dies invariably and only through treason, since no decent member of the community would help the authorities against him.

8. He is – at least in theory – invisible and invulnerable.
9. He is not the enemy of the king or emperor, who is the fount of justice, but only of the local gentry, clergy or other oppressors (Hobsbawm 2000: 47–8).

According to the political anthropologist C. Giordano, an essential element of the public life of Mediterranean societies is the conflict between the legalism of the law and the law of culturally accepted legitimacy. A long-lasting foreign aristocracy created in such societies a peculiar historical awareness, the characteristics of which are profound distrust of the authorities and the powerful, a chasm between society and state and a conviction that every public legal judgment is in itself unjust. In such societies 'one of the basic ideas of the Western cultural heritage' – the idea of the common good in the interest of all – has still not been accepted, nor have the social actors developed a feeling of community with the mechanisms of governmental coercion. The specific models that are inherent in such a culture keep on testing out all the institutions, sanctions and other organisational proceedings that a modern state endeavours to carry out, and the laws and other regulations are systematically ignored, for

> if they are legal, they are not legitimate. For example: killing one's wife is according to the rules of the Mediterranean code of honour illegal but at the same time legitimate; the demand of the state to levy taxes is legal but not legitimate [...] The establishment of legitimacy, which is the task of the state mechanisms of coercion, is in this manner directly superimposed on the experiences internalised during many centuries (Giordano 1996: 52–3)

A newspaper report of Caco's *cenaze* covered all the essential elements in the creation of such myths about heroes and can be applied to almost all the epic and historical, imaginary and real-life *haiduk* biographies. This is an important commentary because, in addition to the dimension that Burke refers to, it also covers another no less important dimension, particularly considering that many 'war heroes' established and maintained good relations with the governmental and other established political and even religious elites, and had patrons among them for a longer or shorter period – some until the end of the war, and even beyond. Here the manipulation was a two-way affair, for the protector manipulated him in order to extend his own power domains. And this was something of which the noble outlaw was not usually aware.

Thus even Caco, at the same time as he was terrorising the citizens, enjoyed the tacit support of the major part of the establishment, which accepted him

> as an extra-institutional cure in the treatment of the institutional illness of blocked Sarajevo: war profiteering, the unjust distribution of the burden of defending the town and of rising crime. He took on the difficult task with the Robin Hood élan of a fighter who did not spare himself, even less others. Elated in his meting out of justice, in his undoubted reputation and popularity among the fighters, and the flattery of the cowards who are always to be found around such men, Caco did not even notice when he had left far behind that thin line that sometimes divides justice from injustice, heroism from crime.

When one seeks to fathom what motivation brought so many people to the *cenaze*, though, one should above all bear in mind the 'social motivations of the demobilised, the wounded and persecuted soldiers and the families of the *şehits* who had for months sought an occasion for a meaningful demonstration of their own despair'.[1] Another Zagreb woman journalist, also dedicated for years to the analysis of the mechanisms behind the wartime and post-war coalescence of the criminal mafia structures with established power-holders, in her case in Croatia and in parts of Bosnia-Herzegovina controlled by the HDZ, noticed the same important dimension in the origin and maintenance of such men, as well as in the turnabout they often undergo, the reasons for and context of which they are not always capable of understanding, as well as the lasting interweaving of spontaneous grassroots mythogenesis and interested manipulations from above. After she had talked for a long time with Klica, the following conclusion occurred to her:

> Before the signing of Dayton, while Croatian state policy was stoking the Croat-Muslim conflicts, these men delivered the punches that divided Bosnia and extended the Croatian borders. After Dayton, they became awkward and undesirable witnesses that the Croatian political leadership wanted to get rid of. But clearly it did not know how to, and it pronounced them one and all and in the same manner – criminals.[2]

---

1. Senad Pećanin, 'Cacina posljednja dženaza', *Dani*, 49, studeni 1996.
2. Jasna Babić, 'Ako mi itko dokaže da sam prekršio zakone', *Nacional*, 69, 12 March 1997.

They did in a sense truly repeat the fates of those with whom they identified or with whom they were identified by their social group. Once the *haiduk*, or the Uskok, was a pawn of higher politics and would one day be rewarded with senior commissions by the Austro-Hungarian or Venetian governments, even titles, with the appropriate equipment, giving him legal backing to make raids over the borders into Ottoman areas, motivating him with his own heroic ethos. And the very next day, when diplomacy required an alliance with Turkey, he would be arrested, he and his family would be persecuted or forcibly relocated to some distant area. Thus, willy-nilly, the modern *haiduks* really did become *haiduks*, most authentically in the respect in which they had not expected, without ever on the whole being aware of it. The sobering process, which often started with arrest and extradition to the ICTY in The Hague was undoubtedly for many of them genuinely painful or at least confusing.

Historical analogies have only a relative value, but here at least it seems cogent to recall that the model of putting criminals to work militarily and politically in Serbia, Montenegro, Bosnia-Herzegovina and Croatia in 1990–1 is in essence no different from the manner in which the Balkan *haiduks* at the end of the sixteenth century were put to work in the counter-Ottoman wars launched by Hungary and Transylvania in alliance with the Habsburgs. The *haiduk* leaders from the Bosnian and Herzegovinan mountains were on the side of the Christian rulers and obtained their special assignments within the context of the general military idea, but they had no revolutionary aims, as was later attributed to them by ideological historiography, or patriotic notions. They simply saw their own basic interest in the advantage that would accrue to them from organised brigandage in large units over a large territory instead of individually or in small bands. If such a broader context had not existed, nor the arms and logistics that they obtained from Emperor Rudolph II and his allies, the local *harami başis* would not have been able to get together and assemble as many as 1,500 or 2,000 men for raids on large and distant cities such as Plevna or Sofia.

In just the same way, 400 years later, Tuta would not have been able to organise his Convicts' Battalion of 300 members, formally in fact of 900, with the proviso that about 600 of them were only formally registered, as if they were taking part in the conflict, making ample donations in return, and they also had fictitious ranks so that they could get the maximum amount of pay out of the state. The real brigade of Mušan Caco Topalović with its 2,800 men would not have been able to exist, nor would many of the other units that had not only infantry weapons but also artillery, mortars and armour, which organised their own territories – city neighbourhoods, sometimes large rural areas – like states, including their own private jails, to which the regular police and military forces had no access. And this is not even to mention the Serbian *harami başis*, who were completely integrated into the state's military project from the very beginning.

In the intermediate space, in the society that was out of phase between legality and legitimacy, between village and city, which was in fact a *village in the city*, they themselves, and their social group, as well as the authority that pursued and punished them, were all equally confused, asking whether they were heroes or criminals. A Sarajevan citizen whom famine had forced to take the bread that Delalić's men were handing out nevertheless commented on their activities with words of outrage and condemnation: 'Nothing is going to clear them of the amount they have stolen and slaughtered' (Skrinjar Tvrz 1993: 37). Other Sarajevans, who came three years later to Topalović's *cenaze*, when asked what they thought about the killing of the nine policemen while his band was being arrested, did not believe this was something to be held against Caco. One woman blamed the government for this 'disgrace', the government that should have sent the police against the Chetniks, and not against Caco. Another citizen replied: 'I would have done the same as him. It was his way of defence. It wasn't Caco that killed those kids, the politicians killed them',[1] of course, by the mere decision to send them to arrest Caco in the first place.

We could call the first citizen a consistent legalist who, irrespective of the war, remained immune to the influence of the value system of traditional heroic culture, and the second group is the social base on which, actively or passively, people like Caco and Tuta relied. In their interaction, with the participation of the military, political, cultural and religious elites, what Rudé called *popular ideology* was created. This is most often a mixture, a fusion of two elements. He calls the first 'the "inherent", traditional element', based on 'direct experience, oral tradition or folk-memory and not learned by listening to sermons or speeches or reading books', while the second element consists of the stocks of ideas and beliefs 'that are "derived" or borrowed from others, often taking the form of a more structured system of ideas, political or religious', e.g. the Rights of Man, national sovereignty, the right to a state, nationalism, social justice and so on.

> So two things are important to note: one is that there is no such thing as tabula rasa, or an empty tablet in the place of a mind on which new ideas may be grafted where there were no ideas

---

1. Snježana Mulić, 'Ispraćaj u društvo šehida', *Dani*, 49, November 1996.

before [...]; and the second is that there is also no such thing as an automatic progression from 'simple' to more sophisticated ideas [...] The 'derived' ideology can only be effectively absorbed if the ground has already been well prepared (Rudé 1980: 28–9).

As for the mythogenesis of the *noble outlaws* in the context and categories of modern popular or mass culture, the pithiest and best commentary was given by the journalist who wrote about the controversies that came up around the third name, 'Juka' Prazina, and concluded her analysis with the words: 'Juka Prazina is the usual film story with the expected end.'[1] And not Juka alone, of course, but all the others, and all those whose heirs they are perceived as being. Finally, film is often just another name for an epic song, just as its social function often does not differ from the function of the *gusle* performance at a village gathering. Robin Hood or Starina Novak, Billy the Kid and Andrijica Šimić, Jesse James and Mladen Naletilić or Jusuf Prazina – they have all been seen before, and will be seen many times again, either in the *gusle* player's decasyllabics of folk culture, or in modern pop-culture mythology, but in each case as object of romanticisation and popularisation. And there is nothing accidental or illogical in foreign journalists, at the same time that the citizens of besieged Sarajevo were trembling before Prazina's band, seeing in him a 'Sarajevo Robin Hood', just as 120 years earlier the Oxford student Arthur Evans had seen the Sherwood forest robber with a heart of gold in the Banija and Bosnia *haiduks*.

The route they have obviously already set out on in their transformation into noble and misunderstood desperados, helpers of the weak who have, truth be told, a slightly rough but nonetheless authentic feeling for morality and justice might perhaps go along the lines of the Italian or the American or some other model. In Italy, nineteenth century bandits took on romantic connotations with the unavoidable admixture of the eternal theme of the fallen angel first of all in literature, and only then indirectly in newspaper reports. By contrast, their American contemporaries experienced their transformation into noble executers of justice above all in newspapers such as the *Police Gazette*, full of stories of the exploits of Jesse James in Robin Hood style, and hence the main source of legends that in time grew into a part of American folklore. In any case, they will certainly take some such route, for they are necessary to many, including romantic poets, not just popular ones, for the eternal topic of the 'lone fighter for justice' and to political activists of very diverse orientations and objectives, whose basic idea is the redistribution of wealth.

---

1. Vildana Selimbegović, 'Vuk ili kojot', *Dani*, 55, May 1997.

The contexts, of course, change, as do the ways in which we experience and understand them, sometimes very strangely, but the eternally romantic topic always finds a devoted public. The émigré organisation of the United Committee of South Slav Americans, which was very active in popularising Tito's anti-fascist movement in the American public and showing that the Partisan army was the only one actively to fight against the Germans, printed in 1944 a booklet with the interesting title: *Marshal Tito and His Gallant Bands*. There must have been quite a few ears that could hear in this title the enticing echo of the ancient legend, threaded through so many novels, comics, films and newspaper stories, that *in Sherwood Forest a gallant outlaw hath a band of followers and doth thwart the Prince at every turn.*

FIFTEEN

Epilogue

From me, Mijat, your servant, regards and greetings to Omer-Aga, Commander of Imotski. I heard that you took all my and my brothers' livestock and the horses too, something I didn't expect from you, nor from myself either. And yet I have done you quite a lot of good. First of all I didn't allow your cloaks to be taken away ... The second good thing I did you was when you went to Sarajevo, they were going to kill you, but I didn't allow it. The third is that when you were taking to the Pasha what you were due and when they wanted to seize it from you, I didn't permit it. And so please don't allow a friend of yours to turn into an enemy. And so please give back what you took, and if you won't, you know what you are doing.

(From a letter from the *haiduk* Mijat Tomić to the commander of Imotski Omer-Aga, about 1640; Mijatović 1985: 28)

From our master Mustaf-Aga, Captain of Udbina and Lika, to the harami başi *Petar Smiljanić, salutations and most cordial and kind greetings to our brother and friend (...) May it please your grace, greet in our name your son the* harami başi *Ilija. We have heard that he is a hero in that Krajina. God knows that this is pleasing to us, for he is ours. And thus we send him a falcon's feather, which is most fitting to him. May he wear it before the heroes (...) And may God give you all good cheer!*

(From a letter from Mustaj-Bey of Lika to the *harami başi* Petar Smiljanić in the 1640s; Nametak 1991: 245)

The heroic epic of the Serbs, the Montenegrins, the Croats and the Bosniaks is the only example 'among all known literatures' where in the same language – the same from the point of view of total mutual intelligibility on the basis of Štokavian idioms – and in the same form, there are songs and poems about the same events and the same persons on both of the belligerent sides – the other side being mainly the Muslim side of the former battlefield. Because, for example, there are no Moorish or Arab songs corresponding to the Spanish and French epics (*chansons de geste*) from the times when the members of the two faiths involved waged war in the Pyrenees, nor anything similar to the Byzantine epic of Digenis Akritas, the great hero who defeated the Saracens, from the time the two empires clashed in Asia Minor in the eighth century (Murko 1951: 222; Bowra 1978). This same perception was formulated more precisely by another researcher into the South Slav epic: 'there is almost no Christian cycle that does not have its exact equivalent on the other side, a cycle of Muslim epic songs, as its complement' (Grgec 1944: 183). To this it is only possible to add that, if they existed, the corresponding Arab-French, Arab-Spanish or Arab-Byzantine paired heroic epic songs would be unintelligible to the other parties along the former front lines because of the different languages. They would not be able to communicate with the others, lastingly, directly and dynamically on a virtually everyday basis, or produce responses and mutual inspiration at all levels – in lexis, motifs and phraseology and the whole range of value judgments.

But such interweaving, whether it is called dialogue or polemic, does have a limitation: it existed and continues to exist only in the culture of the commoners, and not in the elite culture, for by its very nature it is connected in the modern period with the concept of the nation and came into being in the context of the national integration ideologies that followed the cultural and political agendas of German pre-Romanticism and the romanticism of the Italian Risorgimento and kindred European ideational trends. Someone who belonged to a vernacular culture learned spontaneously from his or her own immediate daily life, in shared categories that cross the borders of religion and ethnicity. By contrast, a member of an elite culture would seek the same knowledge in books, in written testimonies and memoirs, sometimes in his own experience, but projected into different categories, informed by modern political attitudes, which were no longer constructed by the common people within its own pragmatic value horizons but by the educated and ambitious young middle class. In other words, a member of an elite culture was aware of the historical and ethnographic material that he needed and the way he wished to use it artistically. And this was a principle independent of whether from today's perspective this purpose should be judged noble or criminal, well-intentioned or malicious, inclusivist or exclusivist, as a tendency towards tolerance and the reconciliation of historical memories or as an attempt to exploit the historical memory as ground for new conflicts. One way or another, the age of innocence was ended, and the age of intellectual consciousness had begun.

When in the first half of the nineteenth century works started appearing in Croatian and Serbian literature with romantic and pseudo-historical and exotic themes concerning contacts between the Christian and Islamic worlds, the Muslim Bosnian milieu raised objections, despite the fact that most of the works, such as for example the novel *Zmaj od Bosne (Dragon of Bosnia)* by the Croatian writer Josip Eugen Tomić, could not be denied either generosity of intention or literary value. Indeed they showed undisguised friendliness towards the mysterious world of the Islamised Slavs in their vicinity. Nevertheless, because of 'gross errors in connection with the history, life, national and religious customs and psychology of the Muslims [Bosniaks]' these works had a 'scandalous and provocative' effect, and were sometimes seen as 'an expression of calculated malice and calumny' for their own 'original literary creations had never treated the lives of their [Christian] neighbours in this way'.

On the other hand, the attitude of overt enmity to be found in the Serbian and Croatian epic was received by the Bosniaks as 'historically natural' for they themselves, in their heroic songs, had 'the same attitude, the other way round', which has been abundantly demonstrated to the reader of this book. Particularly angry comments were provoked by literary works in which a Muslim man or woman converted to Christianity in order to be married to a Christian 'although conversion itself – but to the Islamic faith – for the sake of love is a common enough feature in the traditional Muslim folk epic' (Rizvić 1990: 97, 68).

The epic traditions referred to also had identical poetics and expressive resources, as was confirmed in the 1990–5 period. The chanting of *Alija, sokole, Krajina je uz tebe (Alija, falcon, the Krajina is with you)* at the SDA rally in Velika Kladuša at the end of September 1990, or the banner with the legend *Alija, sokole, Armija je uz tebe (Alija, falcon, the Army's with you)* that was borne by the Seventh Muslim Brigade of the AB-H on the parade ground in Zenica in April 1996, were in a poetic sense exact equivalents for the exclamations *Slobo, Srbine, Srbija je uz tebe (Slobodan, Oh Serb, Serbia's with you)* or *Slobo, sokole! (Slobo, you falcon!)* from the Serbian political rallies of 1988–90. They are so not only in rhythm and formulation, but even more so in the importance of the key heroic attribute – the falcon or hawk, *sokol*, which derives directly from the shared – transethnic and transreligious – layer of epic symbolism. That is, in the epic, the falcon symbolised the ability to make sacrifices for a common cause and virtues that set their bearer apart from his milieu. This may be seen in Njegoš's lines from *The Mountain Wreath*: 'the falcon hates the dusty plain, / will not have the marsh-bound frog, / the falcon wants the cliff-top high'; as well as the Partisan songs of World War II, created inside the single value and expressive system of vernacular culture, which called Tito a falcon, a grey falcon (*sivi sokol*), or a falcon's wing (*krilo od sokola*).

Further, the imagination of the vernacular singer often creates new songs about known heroes and interweaves characters in diverse combinations, equating various epic traditions and combining in the same song figures who were not contemporaries. Such a cavalier treatment of chronology and such combinations, when an old motif is transferred to new heroes, or an old thematic model is adapted to new heroes, are typical of the songs of the *haiduk* and Uskok cycles, and did not occur only in the Christian or only in the Muslim epic tradition but also in between them. Catholic, Orthodox and Muslim singers, that is, Croats, Serbs, Montenegrins and Bosniaks, performed the whole of the epic repertoire, Christian and Muslim to their own audiences, but quite often audiences that were mixed in terms of ethnicity and religion. The songs themselves did not deal exclusively with conflicts, they also told of examples of collaboration and mutual respect. Some singers, depicting Muslim or Christian '*haidukery*' on the border of Venetian Dalmatia or Ottoman Bosnia, preserved an awareness that every blow inflicted on Bosnian Muslim families by the Christian *haiduks* was mirrored by those received by Christian Dalmatian families from Muslim *haiduks* (Buturović 1976: 96).

Towards the end of the period of Ottoman rule, in the 1870s, the Sinj *gusle* player Božo Domnjak, who as a travelling salesmen of copper vessels walked and rode around the whole of Bosnia, Herzegovina and the Dalmatian hinterland, was singing in a watchtower in Unište on the Dalmatian-Bosnian border. The Muslim guard was happy to listen attentively to him, up until the moment when in the song the Christians started winning, and the Muslims dying. Then he jumped up from his chair saying: 'Enough, enough. By my faith, there was ill on both sides. It wasn't that our side just slept and the *giaours* slaughtered them' (Mimica 1988: 73).

Everyday life on the border was more frequently characterised by prudent coexistence than war to the death. Cross-border enmities were mitigated by many factors: lasting communication, common interest in trade, family connections and joint cultural patterns such as ideals of honour, heroism and loyalty to family and blood-brotherhood. Through these mechanisms, Christians and Muslims were able to control the damage and the bloodshed and limit conflicts that were socially and economically destructive on both sides. Stalemate or equilibrium on the border 'was based as much on the balance of power and fear as on any reciprocity of respect or tolerance' (Bracewell 1992: 187). Or, as another writer puts it in an analysis of the conditions, extremely similar in many ways, in which the *klephts* in Ottoman Greece operated, this was a matter of 'self-regulated lawlessness'. It was 'a game that required guile, calculation, acceptance of the rules by everyone concerned, and carefully measured defiance.' In addition to the outlaws, this game included a weak central government that was forced to tolerate lawlessness to a certain extent and also 'a populace at whose expense this lawlessness was practised and which essentially had no effective means of defence short of taking to the hills'. Thus the *klephts* had to operate within 'the undefined by unmistakable limits of calculated lawlessness at the expense of the weak' (Koliopoulos 1987: 34).

A proper understanding depends on a view of the epic that encompasses it, not selectively on ethnic or religious grounds, or tendentiously for some political ends, but rather panoramically in order to understand what is a world in itself with its own logic. Then it is revealed that all the heroes made and broke alliances with each other, made war and made peace, showed respect and friendship and robbed towers and villages and wreaked fearful vengeance, entered into bonds of shaved godfathership (*šišano kumstvo*) or blood-brotherhood (*pobratimstvo*), helped each other and attended each others' weddings, but also seized each others' girls and converted them to their own faith. In one song this was done by Ilija Smiljanić with the sister of Mujo Hrnjica; in another by Hrnjica with Smiljanić's sister. All in all, there is no hero who did not at some time save or spare the life of another, just as there was no one who was not at some time killed by a hero on the other side. Some of them were done to death a dozen times in diverse localities.

What is revealed, in short, is the simultaneous existence of a series of worlds that overlap, sometimes mutually excluding each other, but only an outside view could call such cases contradictory or illogical. For those on the inside such questions are never even posed, or if they are, then they have a different logic. And there is no problem about one hero being in the most diverse places, about two heroes fighting to the death in one song and in the next, which the same *gusle* player may well start to perform for the same audience, as soon as he has finished the first, forging agreements, swearing blood-brotherhood or setting off on some joint campaign or raid. Every singer has his own chronology and topography in which, of course, his own home area is the centre. This functions as the epic centre of a far broader area, indeed of the whole central South Slav geography: his fiction will bring all the heroes, wherever they were originally from, as long as they are known and valued, into the company of the local heroes. The epic poet does this intuitively, sometimes aware that his peers elsewhere are doing the same thing, pushing events, characters, subjects and places that are distant in time and space as close together as he can, thus making them more familiar, more intimate to himself and his audience. Only a professional scholar's rational and conscious analysis will reveal nuances that the authentic sharers of the vernacular culture were not aware of or did not care about, for example, that a Muslim song, with a Christian woman as a character, would actually treat her like a Muslim or that when a Christian song depicted a Muslim woman, she behaved essentially like a Christian (Rizvić 1990: 541).

In the categories of communication theory, these examples of interweaving and mixing can be understood as both a way of maintaining tension and a way of assuaging it or transferring it to a ritual and symbolic level at which conflicts are emotionally defused and politically relativised instead of happening on the field of battle, in a real shoot-out. Then they can be looked upon functionally as a kind of transposed political discourse that through symbolic activity cools polemics, as a particular kind of social dramaturgy and conversation through which communicators in the political process tone down their differences from each other by constructing a vocabulary of common meanings, expectations, assumptions – common, though never totally so (cf. Nimmo 1982).

But then, totality is not possible nor can it lead to anything good. Only dictators aspire to it, and it can be achieved only in cemeteries.

At the turn of the 1970s and 80s one could see, for instance in the Croatian village Rakitno and the Muslim village Drežnica north of Mostar, the way the two epic traditions were very much intertwined, not only at the level of poetics, but in their similar views on the conflicts between representatives of their own nation. The songs 'very often' contained messages about the need for a life together, for understanding and indeed for collaboration. And when there was a singer 'of more powerful inner potential' such as Pavle Bajčetić of Rakitno, it was even possible to speak of a 'kind of creative humanisation of the traditional forms of vernacular poetry' (Buturović 1992: 57). Some fifteen years later a Croatian singer (and there is no reason to think that such songs were not created on the other side as well) presented the relations between the two peoples in the same area as follows:

My mother wails and laments,
Dayton Agreements pain her
the Croatian mother wipes her tears
and talks of Krešimir Zubak –

may your right hand wither away
for signing this disgraceful pact
for driving your own nation
with the balijas[1] *to a federation.*
(Šimić 1996)

In sum it may be said that neither tolerance nor religious and ethnic intolerance are immanent in vernacular culture. Nor does it advocate either a merciless final reckoning or a meek silence for the sake of false peace. Quite simply it contains a range of life experiences, it reworks or selects from them in keeping with its own poetics, with the experiences of its sharers or the dominant values of the time. All the songs, living legitimately in their own worlds, live also at a higher level as a complete world. They are truth and falsehood, history and para-history.

* * *

The panoramic view mentioned above can reveal all kinds of things. There is one song in which Mali Marijan, actually the nephew of Mijat Tomić, makes his appearance as the son of Starina Novak. In principle, one does not exclude the other. Mijat in fact had two sisters, and one, Manda, had a son called Marijan, but the songs do not say who the father was, and it cannot be ruled out that it was actually Starina Novak. After all, there are songs in which Mali Marijan passes through Romanija on business, and warmly greets Novak and his band, and why indeed should one dismiss the possibility that this was the familiar greeting of father and son who because of the nature of their business had not seen each other for a long time, and not just a less sincere gesture of the interest-based solidarity of two *haiduks* who have the same non-Christian foe. On the other hand there is a song in which Marijan and Tatomir are brothers, and are attacked on Romanija by *haiduk* Mijat and 'with him thirty men of Kladuša', and Marijan is killed (Bošković-Stulli 1975: 28–30). Since in all the songs Tatomir is described as the son of Starina Novak, this would indirectly confirm the relationship of the previous song, that Marijan is Novak's son, which, of course, does not prevent Mijat from being his maternal uncle, who nevertheless killed him, in

---

1. The word *balija* (cf. wog, towelhead) is unclear in origin; perhaps it comes from the Muslim male given name Bali. It is used in Bosnia and Herzegovina by the Catholics and Orthodox populations as a derogatory name for Muslims (it is ironic that it was originally used by Bosnian beys and agas and in general by the educated Muslim class for the Muslim yokels).

company with the Kladuša Bosniaks, which cannot mean anyone but Mujo Hrnjica himself. In a third song Grujica, who is also indisputably the son of Novak, marries Hajkuna, sister of Mujo Hrnjica, and has 'a nice family' with her (Andrić 1939). This would mean that Mujo, like it or not, is involved in a pretty complex set of blood and in-law relationships.

A fourth song still sees Mijat Tomić as the maternal uncle of the famed *haiduk* Mali Radojica (Andrić 1939), who is often confused in the epic, for the names are similar, with Novak's brother Radivoje. If there was such a mix-up in this case, if, that is, the anonymous epic poet was actually thinking of Radivoje, and if we link this fact with the previous ones, then it would mean that Mijat was in an impossible situation, being at once brother-in-law and great-uncle to Novak, who was for him his brother-in-law and great-nephew.

There is also a song that says that Alija Đerzelez was the son of Deli Radivoje, who, as we know well, was Novak's brother (Milutinović 1990, no. 149), with whom hot-tempered Novak was once so terribly angry that he sold him as a servant to a Muslim woman from Sarajevo, whose name is sadly not stated. And it is not unknown in the world for a pretty but lonely lady and a virile, still young servant, although of different faiths, to find themselves in an amorous embrace, but in this case the outcome is extremely intriguing and far-reaching. For their son Alija Đerzelez grew up into such a hero that once he himself overcame and captured all three Romanija *haiduks* – Novak, Grujica and Radivoje, who after a short interlude in town had obviously taken up his old trade – but did not kill them, which was his wont as a true epic quarreller (*meydanci*), nor did he hand them over to the law, which as a legitimist and civil servant he was bound to do, rather, like a true pedagogue he advised them to turn their backs on 'devilry and *"haidukery"* because a '*haiduk* will never be a husbandman'. Most interesting of all, they heard him out and obeyed him, and went down with him to Sarajevo, where they settled down and started a new and peaceful life.

Yet another song claims that Alija Đerzelez's father was none other than Novak's son Grujica (*Bosanska vila*, IV, 17/1889), his mother was once again a Sarajevo Muslim woman, now stated somewhat more precisely to be the widow of a certain Džafer-Bey, to whom the handsome young Grujica stole one night, dressed up as a Muslim, through her bedroom window.

All in all, a fairly ramified family. Grujica and the Hrnjicas are brothers-in-law, and Marijan is another; Manda, sister of Mijat Tomić, is mother-in-law of Hajkuna Hrnjica, Starina Novak is her father-in-law, and Hajkuna's and Grujica's progeny are the great-nephews and great-nieces of Mijat Tomić.

Hajkuna is also Marijan's sister-in-law and vice versa; while for Grujica the brothers Mujo, Omer and Halil Hrnjica are his wife's family, or as the Muslims would put it, his *babaīk*. Starina Novak is Alija Đerzelez's uncle, or *amidža*, as Alija himself and all other Bosnian Muslims would call him, and Marijan and Grujica are his uncles and cousins; the Muslims would call them *amidžićes*. The Orthodox would call their relationship brothers of uncles (*braća od strica*), and Catholics would be divided by dialect: into those in Konavle, in the extreme south, close to Dubrovnik, who call them *dundićes*, and those in Imotski and Sinj, in the Dalmatian hill country, who would say that Marijan is Mijat's *netijak*.

Such connections are no less authentic than any others, and nor is this linkage in any way less natural than all the other epic combinations. There could even be an epic song in which they would all get together and have a series of stirring adventures. Perhaps such a song has existed already for a long time, only no student of folklore has yet discovered it, perhaps it is coming into being now, perhaps it is still to come – if any singer feels that an audience wants or expects it. And, given the place where it befell all these heroes to live, their adventures could really be diverse and unexpected.

For example, as far as more recent times are concerned, the same ambitious Yugoslav party secretary who might use them to praise the harmonious inter-ethnic relations in his commune, that 'bastion of brotherhood and unity and microcosm of Yugoslavia', would the very next day, were he to hear them singing some patriotic ditty of the nineteenth century, require them to be imprisoned for upsetting inter-ethnic relations and for 'counter-revolutionary separatism'. On each occasion he would receive the praise of his comrades further up the hierarchy. Then the self-styled ethnic leaders, perhaps the same people from the previous adventure, if they had managed to change their political garb fast enough, would one day puff out their chests claiming their heroism and wounds as their own, and celebrate them as model incarnations of the broad spirit of the nation that has no prejudice against other ethnic groups or religions, and then the very next day would declare them worthless trash for having made a mixed marriage and defiled the noble national bloodline and betrayed the religion of their forefathers. But nor would our heroes lack international recognition. Placed in an orderly row one next to the other, somewhat confused, with headphones on their ears for the simultaneous interpretation, they would be proudly displayed at some roundtable on the themes of multiculturalism and multiconfessionalism, as in a zoo, by every ambitious member of the appropriate international associations that make good money out of phrases about *political correctness* and *conflict resolution*.

While the very next day, at some closed diplomatic meeting, the same person will be presented as an expert on Balkan issues, and state that international intervention to end the war needs to be put on hold, because in this black hole at the edge of Europe, among those savages weighed down with their genetic hatreds, it is impossible to tell who is attacking whom and why, and that the victim who does not allow himself to be silently robbed and killed is only aggravating, with his stubborn resistance, the *intensity of the conflict*, and is thus jointly responsible for his current plight. No one, of course, would mention the word cynicism.

It is also perfectly possible to imagine a singer – Catholic, Orthodox or Muslim – performing the hypothetical song before either an ethnically homogeneous or a mixed audience, with or without appropriate modifications. It is possible to imagine the audience quarrelling and coming to blows in the middle of the performance, but also of sitting and quietly hearing it out, respecting each side's heroism – if it is chivalric, and even if it is not. And then, for hours after the performance talking over the details and analysing every aspect.

The only thing that is unimaginable is an unambiguous answer to the question of whether such a panoramic view, this kind of mixed song, is a panacea or a Pandora's box.

Acknowledgements

When the editors of the Zagreb bi-weekly *Start* invited me to join their editorial staff in the autumn of 1988, I did not hesitate for one instant. First-class reporting and, in particular, serious interviews with significant world figures had for two decades already made it into a kind of Croatian window onto the outside world, to the extent that such a thing was possible within the specific ideological framework of Yugoslav communism – and often considerably beyond that. At the time I was already contributing to the Split weekly *Nedeljna Dalmacija*, where in a regular column I used to analyse public discourse and political symbols, not just in Yugoslavia but also in an ever more turbulent European East. Those two publications, along with the Zagreb weekly *Danas*, opened hitherto taboo themes, wrote critically and with rational arguments, and promoted political dialogue and civic tolerance in Croatia, with an influence that reached also into other republics of the former Yugoslavia.

This was an unforgettable experience, a time when in long discussions on editorial committees and outside we analysed, commented upon and anticipated events, on the one hand filled with hope by the freedom that was being born, on the other filled with anxiety by something not entirely fathomable but unquestionably terrible that was heaving on the horizon.

At that time I did not travel much around Yugoslavia, but those colleagues who did so were able to convey their own experiences so vividly that I had the impression of being personally present at many of them. Among these colleagues I should like to single out in particular Ines Sabalić, who in the late eighties wrote a series of unrivalled reportages from Kosovo and later as a war reporter passed through most of the battlefields in Croatia, and Ozren Kebo and Ivan Lovrenović from Sarajevo. Special mention must be made of those honest and wise members of the Franciscan Province of Silver Bosnia: Petar Anđelić, Luka Markešić, Ivan Bubalo and others. Although based methodologically upon another type of material, this book would have been far less persuasive – insofar as it is persuasive – had it not been for our precious conversations.

Many wartime newspapers, pamphlets and other publications from Bosnia-Herzegovina, Montenegro and Serbia would have been far harder if not impossible to obtain had it not been for the kindness of Luka Gavranović from the Croatian Information Centre (HIC) in Zagreb, whither certain publications from Bosnia-Herzegovina arrived by the most incredible means, and of the Belgrade lawyer Dragoljub Todorović, who would search out even the rarest Serbian publications. In the library and archive of the Institute for Ethnology and Folklore Research in Zagreb I was able at any time to find whatever I needed thanks to the latter's marvellous librarian Anamarija Starčević-Štambuk.

Graham McMaster has been a tirelessly patient translator, who, although he certainly cannot have found it easy to deal with my constant additions and revisions, always managed to explain his every solution calmly and rationally. His ability to preserve in translation the spirit and intonation both of the classic South Slav epics and of verses from the wars of the twentieth century was admirable. The entire translation was then edited by Celia Hawkesworth, who contributed all her vast knowledge of the languages and cultural history of the South Slavs and all her experience as a translator of, inter alia, the novels and stories of the Nobel Prize-winner Ivo Andrić. To have two such people involved with my text has been a real honour.

It is hard to describe the feelings of someone writing in a 'small' language when they hear that their work will be translated into English. Doubt, bewilderment, excitement and pride because 'the whole world' will now be able to see its good sides, intermingled with unease because its flaws and deficiencies will be equally on view. Now it is too late to worry about that, but one thing is certain: it was very fortunate for me to have come to know Quintin Hoare and Branka Magaš and for us to have become friends.

The book that the reader holds is not simply a translation of the Croatian edition of 1998, with a few necessary additional explanations, but a considerably expanded and in certain aspects wholly new edition, including a new title and subtitle. There are no changes of methodology or interpretation, but it has been possible to analyse certain processes more fully from a greater temporal distance, and certain additional sources have become available to me in the meantime. I can only hope that as a result the book has become more complete and better documented. As an author, I owe sincere and lasting gratitude to my editor Quintin Hoare for readily accepting such an expansion of the original, and for investing so much understanding, time and effort in this work.

I wrote the doctoral thesis, and the book that came out of it, at a time when I was a freelancer, without any institutional framework or support, in a country moreover that was in war or its immediate aftermath. Hence, without any grant or paid academic leave, in the gaps between remunerative jobs, obliged to provide for all technical expenses and materials from my own pocket, with no small consequences for the family budget. Yet I have been aware of having a greater and more solid support than any formal institution could have furnished: my wife Mirjana, who never stopped believing that (even) this angle of research helps towards an understanding of what happened to us and around us in the 1990s. So this book belongs also to her in a unique sense, as it belongs also to our son Andrija, who unwittingly grew up with it, from a time of war to one that – I believe – will be better and nobler.

Bibliography

1. Material

1.a. Newspapers

Borba (Beograd Zagreb) • *Bosanski pogledi* (Sarajevo) • *Bošnjak* (Bihać/Travnik) • *Danas* (Zagreb) • *Dani* (Sarajevo) • *DEM [Detektivski magazin]* (Beograd) • *Državnost* (Zagreb) • *Duga* (Beograd) • *Eurobosna* (Hanau, Germany) • *Feral Tribune* (Split) • *Glas Koncila* (Zagreb) • *Glas Slavonije* (Osijek) • *Glas srpski* (Banjaluka) • *Glasnik HDZ* (Zagreb) • *Globus* (Zagreb) • *Hrvatski list* (Široki Brijeg/Mostar) • *Hrvatsko slovo* (Zagreb) • *Intervju* (Beograd) • *Iskra* (Split) • *Javnost* (Sarajevo/Pale) • *Ljiljan* (Sarajevo) • *Nacional* (Zagreb) • *Nedjelja* (Sarajevo) • *Nedjeljna Dalmacija* (Split) • *NIN* (Beograd) • *Novi list* (Rijeka) • *Novosti 8* (Beograd) • *On* (Beograd) • *Oslobođenje* (Sarajevo) • *Oslobođenje* (Sarajevo/Pale) • *Panorama* (Zagreb) • *Pobjeda* (Podgorica) • *Pogledi* (Kragujevac) • *Politika* (Beograd) • *Politika ekspres* (Beograd) • *Pravoslavlje* (Beograd) • *Republika* (Beograd) • *Slobodna Dalmacija* (Split) • *Slobodna Bosna* (Sarajevo) • *Slobodni tjednik* (Zagreb) • *Start* (Zagreb) • *Stećak* (Sarajevo) • *Svet* (Beograd) • *Svjetlo riječi* (Sarajevo) • *Tjednik* (Zagreb) • *Tomislav* (Tomislavgrad/Zagreb) • *Večernje novosti* (Beograd) • *Večernji list* (Zagreb) • *Velebit* (Zagreb) • *Vjesnik* (Zagreb) • *Vreme/Vreme International* (Beograd) • *Zapadna Bosna* (Zagreb) • *Zmaj od Bosne* (Tuzla) • *Velebit* (Zagreb) • *Vijenac* (Zagreb) • *Zapadna Bosna* (Zagreb).

NB Writings from newspapers, whether daily, weekly or monthly, are cited in this work in three ways. If details or news stories are quoted, or the statement of a person who is identified in a different way, then the source is marked with the name and date of the source in the main text. If the text is quoted at the lexical, terminological or phraseological level, the name of the author, the name and date of the printed source are supplied, also within the main text of the discussion; if major units and more complex journalistic forms are quoted, then in a note at the bottom of the page the title of the text and the name of the author and all other bibliographic details are given.

1.b. *Special newspaper editions, comic strips, pulp fiction*

Bosanski pogledi - nezavisni list muslimana Bosne i Hercegovine u iseljeništvu, Zürich 1960–7 (reprint of the whole edition), London, 1984.

Đukić, Danko (writing) and Žarko Katić (drawing) (1991) *Za slobodu Srpske Krajine.* Knindže - vitezovi Srpske Krajine, comic strip, vol. no. 2, November 1991, NIP Politika, Beograd.

Fančović, Marko (writing) and Dragoljub Savić (drawing) (1991) *Po zapovesti kapetana Dragana.* Knindže - vitezovi Srpske Krajine, comic strip, vol, no. 1, September 1991, NIP Politika, Beograd.

Krajišnik, Miloš (1991) *Demoni dolaze [Demons are coming].* Knindže - vitezovi srpske krajine [*Kninjas – knights of the Serbian Krajina*], pulp fiction, vol. no. 1, November 1991, NIP Politika, Beograd.

Rat za mir [War for Peace]. Special edition of *Pobjeda,* Podgorica, October 1991, ed. Šćepan Vuković.

Srbi u Hrvatskoj. 1. Special edition of *Duga,* Belgrade, July 1990, ed. Dragan Barjaktarević.

1.c. Gusle *players – audio cassettes*

Đukić, Božidar (1985) *Tragična pogibija Branke Đukić.* Beograd: Jugodisk BDN 0621.

Đukić, Božidar (1988) *Crnogorci - porijeklo i 'etnogeneza'. Prošlost se ne može mijenjati.* Beograd: Jugodisk BDN 3232 (written by Momčilo Lutovac).

Jeknić, Slavko (1987) *Pogibija milicionera Saveznog SUP-a na Kosovu 1981. godine.* Beograd: Jugodisk BDN 3102.

Jeknić, Slavko (1990) *Žuta greda.* Beograd-Golubac: Udruženje guslara Jugoslavija - Samostalna produkcija kaseta Jugovideo YVK 18013 (written by Svilana Karličić).

Mastilović, Ranko (1989) *Pesma o Slobodanu.* Novi Beograd: Beograd-ton K 118 (written by Novak Šojić and Tetimski).

Miljanić, Milomir (1988) *Paraćinski regruti.* Ljubljana: Helidon K-313 (written by Žarko Šobić).

Radusinović, Vojo (1989) *Sumrak bogova kod Žute grede.* Beograd: Jugodisk BDN 3513 (written by Žarko Šobić).

Rosić, Radisav (1988) *Paraćinska tragedija.* Sarajevo: Sarajevo-disk SBK 1288.

Šimić, Željko (1990a) *XIV izvanredni kongres SKJ.* Zagreb: Jugoton MC-6 3025601.

Šimić, Željko (1990b) *Ustoličenje doktora Franje Tuđmana.* Zagreb: Jugoton U 00761c.

Šimić, Željko (1996) *Herceg-Bosno, nema mi te više.* Grude: issued by the author.

Šimić, Željko (1997) *Smrt mr. Mate Bobana.* Grude: issued by the author.

1.d. Documentary films

Jukić, Ivan (1995) *Hrvatski hajduk Andrija Šimić. Po motivima knjige dr. Mije Milasa 'Hajduk Andrijica Šimić'*. A film broadcast on Channel 1 of Croatian TV, 6 November 1995 (directed and written by Ivan Jukić, screenplay associate Nera Barbarić Puharić; cameraman Mario Perušina; Andrija Šimić played by Ante Šućur).

Pawlikowski, Paul (1992) *Serbian Epics*. Film broadcast as part of the *Bookmark* literature and the arts programme on BBC1, 16 December 1992 (directed and produced by Paul Pawlikowski, with special thanks to Lazar Stojanović; research Ann Barr; cameramen Bogdan Dziworski and Jacek Petrycki; film editor Stefan Ronowicz).

1.e. Collections and anthologies of folk poems, vernacular song goods, ethnographic accounts, readers, travelogues, literature, diaries and memoirs, collections of newspaper reports and commentaries, political journalism.

*** (1926) *Narodne pjesme o 1000-godišnjici hrvatskog kraljevstva (925–1925). Herojske.* Zagreb.

*** (1926) *Narodne pjesme o 1000-godišnjici hrvatskog kraljevstva (925–1925), sv. 1. Herojske.* Zagreb.

*** (1942) *Đeneral Nedić čuva Srbiju.* Belgrade (*Narodni Guslar*).

*** (1943) *Narodna pjesma o vitezu Juri Francetiću.* Zagreb (edition signed *Narodni Guslar*).

*** (1944) *Pjesme hrvatskih vojnika.* Zagreb: Odgojni odjel Ministarstva oružanih snaga.

Abdić, Fikret (1991) *SDA hoće, može, zna.* Zagreb. Masmedia.

Abdić, Muhamed (1992) *Kraini u amanet.* Rijeka: World BiH.

Andrić, Nikola (1939) *Hrvatske narodne pjesme. VIII. Junačke pjesme.* Zagreb: Matica hrvatska.

Andrović, Ivan (1909) *Po Ravnim kotarima i kršnoj Bukovici.* Zadar: Katolička hrvatska tiskarna.

Antonić, Dragomir and Miodrag Zupanc (1988) *Srpski narodni kalendar.* Belgrade: izdanje autorâ.

Ardalić, Vladimir (1899) 'Bukovica. Narodni život i običaji' in *Zbornik za narodni život i običaje Južnih Slavena* IV: 113–126, 196–220.

Baković, Anto (1991) *Drinske mučenice. Vlastita svjedočanstva, svjedočanstva očevidaca, dokumenti.* Zagreb: published by the author.

Balić, Smail (1952) *Etičko naličje bosansko-hercegovačkih muslimana.* Beč: published by the author.

Bašagić, Safvet-beg (1900) *Kratka uputa u prošlost Bosne i Hercegovine (Od g. 1463–1850).* Sarajevo: published by the author.

Begović, Nikola (1986 [1887]) *Život Srba graničara.* Belgrade: Prosveta.

Benić, Bono (1979) *Ljetopis sutješkog samostana.* Sarajevo: IRO Veselin Masleša.

Bišćević, Hasan (1993) *Abdićev put u izdaju.* Ljubljana: NIPP Ljiljan.

Bogdanović, Bogdan (1988) *Mrtvouzice. Mentalne zamke staljinizma.* Zagreb: August Cesarec.

Bogišić, Baltazar (1874) *Zbornik sadašnjih pravnih običaja u Južnih Slovena, knj. 1.* Zagreb: JAZU.

Bonifačić, Antun (1996) *Izabrana djela.* Zagreb: Matica hrvatska.

Brković, Jevrem (1990) *Lideri, udbaši, generali..* Zagreb: Centar za informacije i publicitet.

Broz, Josip, Tito (1977) *Sabrana djela. I–XXVI.* Belgrade: Izdavački centar Komunist.

Bukša, Juraj and Antica Antoš (1966 [1961]) *Daleki vidici. čitanka za VIII razred osnovne škole.* Zagreb: Školska knjiga.

Bulatović, Ljiljana (1996) *General Mladić.* Belgrade: Nova Evropa (& Banjaluka: Glas srpski - Doboj: Grafičar).

Bušić, Bruno (1983) *Jedino Hrvatska! Sabrani spisi.* Toronto: ZIRAL.

Cindrić, Pavao (1969) *Pjesme o drugu Titu.* Zagreb.

Crnjanski, Miloš (1990) *Politički portreti.* Belgrade: Beletra.

Cvitan, Viktor, Juraj Bukša and Antica Antoš (1967) *Naše proljeće (čitanka za IV razred osnovne škole).* Zagreb: Školska knjiga.

Čajkanović, Veselin (1985) *Rečnik srpskih narodnih verovanja o biljkama.* Belgrade: SKZ - SANU.

Četnik, Milan J. (1997) *Dopisnice iz Knina. Ljetopis bune & izdaje 1989–95.* Belgrade: BiS Press.

Čolaković, Rodoljub (1977) *Zapisi iz oslobodilačkog rata. I–II.* Sarajevo: a group of publishers.

Čolaković, Rodoljub (1985/86) *Kazivanje o jednom pokoljenju. I–V.* Sarajevo.

Čubelić, Tvrtko (1956) *Epske narodne pjesme.* Zagreb: Školska knjiga.

Čubelić, Tvrtko (1966) *Ustanak i revolucija u riječi narodnog pjesnika.* Zagreb: Znanje.

Čubelić, Tvrtko (1970) *Epske narodne pjesme.* Zagreb: published by the author.

Čulinović, Ferdo (1938) *Narodno pravo. Zbornik pravnih misli iz naših narodnih umotvorina.* Belgrade: s potporom JAZU.

Ćatić, Musa Ćazim (1968) *Sabrana djela.* Tešanj: Narodni univerzitet .

Ćosić, Dobrica (1992) *Promene.* Novi Sad: Dnevnik.

Dedijer, Vladimir (1981a) *Dnevnik 1941–1945. I–III.* Rijeka - Zagreb: Liburnija - Mladost.

Dedijer, Vladimir (1981b) *Novi prilozi za biografiju Josipa Broza Tita. II.* Rijeka - Zagreb: Liburnija - Mladost.

Delorko, Olinko (1964) *Narodne epske pjesme. 1.* Zagreb: Zora.

Dizdar, Mak (1990) *Stari bosanski tekstovi.* Sarajevo: Svjetlost.

Doderović, Milorad (1990) *Kako se dogodio Šolević.* Niš: Gradina.

Drašković, Vuk (1987) *Odgovori.* Belgrade: published by the author.

Drašković, Vuk (1989) *Koekude, Srbijo.* Valjevo: Biblioteka Glas Crkve.

Drljević, Sekula (1990 [1944]) *Balkanski sukobi 1905–1941.* Zagreb: Harmica Press.

Dučić, Nićifor (1874) *Crna Gora.* Belgrade.

Dučić, Nićifor (1893) 'Putovanje kroz Crnu Goru u septembru i oktobru 1865' in *Književni radovi, knj. 3.* Belgrade.

Dujmović, Franjo (1976) *Hrvatska na putu k oslobođenju. Uspomene i prosudbe.* Rim-Chicago: ZIRAL.

Đilas, Aleksa (1995) *Raspad i nada. Eseji, članci i intervjui, 1991–1994.* Belgrade-Princip.

Djilas, Milovan (1958) *Land Without Justice. An Autobiography of his Youth.* London: Methuen.

Djilas, Milovan (1966) *Njegoš: Poet, Prince, Bishop.* New York: Harcourt, Brace and World.

Đilas, Milovan (1990) *Revolucionarni rat.* Belgrade: Književne novine.

Đilas, Milovan (1994) *Bošnjak Adil Zulfikarpašić.* Zürich-Zagreb: Bošnjački institut-Globus.

Đogo [Gjogo], Husein (1930) 'Tradicija o Mijatu harambaši', pp. 165–9 in: *Napredak-Hrvatski narodni kalendar za godinu 1931.* Sarajevo: HKD Napredak.

Đogo [Gjogo; Dubravić], Husejin (1941) 'Mijat harambaša i Tešnjanin Alija'. *Hrvatsko kolo* 22: 154–73.

Đukić, Tomo (1976) 'Tradicionalna kultura stočara na području Romanije', pp. 189–93 in: *Rad 21. kongresa Saveza udruženja folklorista Jugoslavije* Sarajevo: Udruženje folklorista BiH.

Đurić, Vojislav (1954a) *Antologija narodnih junačkih pesama.* Belgrade: Srpska književna zadruga.

Đurić, Vojislav (1954b) *Narodne junačke pesme srednjih vremena. I. O hajducima.* Belgrade: Znanje.

Evans, Arthur J. (1876) *Through Bosnia and Herzegóvina on Foot During the Insurrection, August and September 1875.* London: Longman, Green and Co.

Evans, Arthur J. (1973) *Pješke kroz Bosnu i Hercegovinu tokom ustanka avgusta i septembra 1875.* Sarajevo: Veselin Masleša.

Fleger, Josip (1935) 'Vran-planina', pp. 226–9 in: *Napredak - hrvatski narodni kalendar za 1936.* Sarajevo: HKD Napredak.

Fortis, Alberto (1778 [1774]) *Travels into Dalmatia: containing observations on the natural history of that country and the neighbouring islands* (...) Translated from the Italian under the author's inspection. J. Robson, London.

Frndić, Nasko (1969) *Muslimanske junačke pjesme.* Sarajevo: Stvarnost.

Gesemann, Gerhard (1925) *Erlangenski rukopis starih srpskohrvatskih narodnih pesama.* Sr. Karlovci: Srpska kraljevska akademija.

Giljferding, Aleksandar (1972 [1859]) *Putovanje po Hercegovini, Bosni i Staroj Srbiji.* Sarajevo: Veselin Masleša.

Grabeljšek, Brane. Anđelko Mijatović and Miroslav Vaupotić (1974) *Pjesme o hrvatsko-slovenskim. seljačkim bunama.* Zagreb - Ljubljana: Spektar - Partizanska knjiga.

Guzina, Ilija (1995) *Rat je počeo.* Čačak: Diglota.

Halilović, Sefer (1997) *Lukava strategija.* Sarajevo: Maršal.

Heneberg-Gušić, Mirjana (1930) *Etnografski prikaz Pive i Drobnjaka.* Zagreb: Etnološka biblioteka (10).

Hörmann, Kosta (1990 [1888–9]) *Narodne pjesme muslimana u Bosni i Hercegovini.I-II.* Sarajevo: Svjetlost.

Horvatić, Dubravko (1972) *Junačina Mijat Tomić. Po starim pjesmama i pripovijedanjima.* Zagreb: Mladost.

Hozić, Advan and Nusret Pašić (1983) *Romanijo, visokoga visa.* Sarajevo: Veselin Masleša.

Hudelist, Darko (1989) *Kosovo - bitka bez iluzija.* Zagreb: Centar za informacije i publicitet.

Humo, Avdo (1984) *Moja generacija.* Sarajevo: Svjetlost - Vojnoizdavački zavod - Prosveta.

Ignjatović, Jakov (1951 [1860]) 'Srbin i njegova poezija', pp. 1–79 in: *Članci (Odabrana dela, knj. VII)* Novi Sad: Matica srpska.

Imamović, Enver (1999) *Historija bosanske vojske.* Sarajevo: Studio Art 7.

Isaković, Alija (1990 [1972]) *Biserje. Antologija muslimanske književnosti.* Opatija: Otokar Keršovani.

Isaković, Zehrudin and Nedžad Latić (eds) (1997) *Armija Bosne i Hercegovine. Kraj milenija.* Sarajevo: NIPP Ljiljan.

Ivanišević, Frano (1987 [1906]) *Poljica. Narodni život i običaji.* Split: Književni krug (reprint izvornika i neobjavljena građa).

Ivanković, Željko (1995) *700 dana opsade. Sarajevski dnevnik 1992–1994.* Zagreb: Durieux.

Izetbegović, Alija (1995) *Odabrani govori, pisma, izjave, intervjui.* Zagreb: Prvo muslimansko dioničko društvo.

Jakovljević, Ilija (1999) *Konclogor na Savi.* Zagreb: Konzor.

Jančić, Miroslav (1994) *Sarajevo 92/93. Govori portparol pakla.* Ljubljana.

Janjić, Jovan (1996) *Srpski general Ratko Mladić.* Novi Sad: Matica srpska.

Jevrić, Nebojša (1995) *Srpski rulet.* Belgrade: Ikonos.

Jovanić, Đoko (1988) *Ratna sjećanja.* Belgrade: Vojnoizdavački i novinski centar (jointly published by Mladost: Zagreb).

Jovičić, Vladimir and Blagoje Jastrebić (1977) *Čovek, i drug, i vođa. Pesme i prozni odlomci o Titu.* Belgrade - Skopje: Rad - Naša knjiga.

Jović, Borisav (1995) *Poslednji dani SFRJ. Izvodi iz dnevnika.* Belgrade: Politika.

Jukić, Ivan Franjo (1973) 'Putovanje iz Sarajeva u Carigrad god. 1852, mjeseca svibnja', pp. 450–71 in: *Sabrana djela, II.* Sarajevo: Svjetlost.

Jukić, Ivan Frano and Grga Martić (1892) *Narodne pjesme bosanske i hercegovačke.* Mostar.

Kačić-Miošić, Andrija (1988 [1756]) *Razgovor ugodni naroda slovinskoga.* Zagreb: Liber.

Kadijević, Veljko (1993) *Moje viđenje raspada-vojska bez države.* Belgrade: Politika.

Kalezić, Dimitrije (1989) *Krsna slava u Srba. Porijeklo, obred, zdravice.* Belgrade: Sfairos.

Karadžić, Vuk Stefanović (1947) *Prvi i drugi srpski ustanak.* Belgrade: Prosveta.

Karadžić, Vuk Stefanović *Srpske narodne pjesme I, II, IV* (1932) *III* (1929) *V, VII* (1935) *VIII, IX* (1936) *VI* (1940). Belgrade: state published.

Karadžić, Vuk Stefanović (1898 [1852]) *Srpski rječnik.* Belgrade: III (državno) izdanje.

Kasumović, Ahmet and Ćamil Huseinbašić (2000) *Enciklopedijski rječnik odbrane Bosne i Hercegovine.* Sarajevo: Sejtarija.

Kaštelan, Jure (1949) *Pjesme o hajducima i uskocima.* Zagreb: Novo pokoljenje.

Knežević, Ivan Joko (1966) *Moja sjećanja.* Zagreb: AGM-Slobodna Dalmacija.

Koprivica, Veseljko (1996) *Sve je bilo meta. Zapisi sa dubrovačko-hercegovačkog ratišta.* Podgorica: Monitor.

Krajina, Mile (1990) *Hrvatske guslarske pjesme.* Čakovec: Zrinski.

Krajina, Mile (1994) *Vukovare, hrvatski viteže.* Čakovec: Zrinski.

Krleža, Miroslav (1966) *Eseji. V.* Zagreb: Zora.

Krleža, Miroslav (1971) *Deset krvavih godina i drugi politički eseji.* Zagreb: Zora.

Krsmanović, Jovo (1988) *Na sred gore Romanije.* Belgrade: Pan Publik.

Krsmanović, Jovo (1991) *Romanija u plamenu.* Belgrade: Pan Publik.

Krstić, Branislav (1984) *Indeks motiva narodnih pesama balkanskih Slovena.* Belgrade: SANU.

Kulenović, Džafer (1978) *Sabrana djela 1945–1956.* Buenos Aires: privatna naklada.

Kulenović, Skender (1971) 'Moji susreti sa Mažuranićevim epom', pp. 34–65 in: *Izabrana djela. IV. Eseji.* Sarajevo: Veselin Masleša.

Kulišić, Špiro, P. Ž. Petrović and N. Pantelić (1970) *Srpski mitološki rečnik.* Belgrade: Nolit.

Lopašić, Radoslav (1890) *Bihać i Bihaćka krajina. Mjestopisne i poviestne crtice.* Zagreb: Matica hrvatska.

Lovrić, Ivan (1948 [1776]) *Bilješke o Putu po Dalmaciji opata Alberta Fortisa i život Stanislava Sočivice.* Zagreb: Izdavački zavod Jugoslavenske akademije (originally in Italian as *Osservazioni di Giovanni Lovrich sopra diversi pezzi del Viaggio in Dalmazia del signor abate Alberto Fortis, coll'aggiunta della*

Vita di Soçivizca. Venezia 1776).

Lubarda, Vojislav (1982) *Anatema.* Belgrade: Zapis.

Lubarda, Vojislav (1989) *Vaznesenje.* Gornji Milanovac: Dečje novine.

Lubarda, Vojislav (1990a) *Preobraženje.* Belgrade: BIGZ.

Lubarda, Vojislav (1990b) *Svileni gajtan.* Gornji Milanovac: Dečje novine.

Lubarda, Vojislav (1993) *Srpska bespuća. Književnopolitički ogledi.* Belgrade: Književne novine-Enciklopedija.

Marek, Juraj, Nada Senić and Osman Hadžić (1966) *Čitanka za VIII razred osnovne škole.* Sarajevo: Zavod za izdavanje udžbenika.

Marić, Ante (1994) *Stante kosci.* Gorica: Ministarstvo prosvjete, znanosti, kulture i športa Hrvatske Republike Herceg-Bosne.

Martić, Grga (1991) *Izabrana djela. I–III.* Sarajevo: Svjetlost.

Martinović, Ratko (1979) *Od Ravne gore do Vrhovnog štaba.* Belgrade: Rad.

Matan, Branko (1998) *Domovina je teško pitanje. Fragmenti dnevnika 1991-1993.* Zagreb: Pres Data.

Matoš, Antun Gustav (1988) *Misli i pogledi.* Zagreb: Globus.

Matvejević, Predrag (1987) *Razgovori s Krležom.* Belgrade: BIGZ.

Mažuranić, Ivan (1979) *Sabrana djela.* Zagreb: Liber-Nakladni zavod Matice hrvatske.

Mažuranić, Matija (1992 [1842]) *Pogled u Bosnu ili Kratak put u onu krajinu učinjen 1839–40. po Jednom Domorodcu.* Zagreb: Konzor.

Mayer, Milutin (1924) *S puta na Duvanjsko polje.* Zagreb: Matica hrvatska.

Meštrović, Ivan (1993 [1962]) *Uspomene na političke ljude i događaje.* Zagreb: Nakladni zavod Matice hrvatske.

Mićanović, Slavko (1953) *Narodne pjesme o hajducima i uskocima.* Sarajevo: Seljačka knjiga.

Mihanović, Nedjeljko (1996) *Na putu do hrvatske državnosti. Govori 1990–1994.* Zagreb: Meditor-Politička uprava Ministarstva obrane.

Mihović, Dragan (1993) *Rat su započeli mrtvi.* Prosveta koprodukcija: Belgrade.

Mijatović, Anđelko (1969) *Narodne pjesme o Mijatu Tomiću.* Zagreb: Zajednica samostalnih pisaca Tin.

Mijatović, Anđelko (1974) *Uskoci i krajišnici. Narodni junaci u pjesmi i povijesti.* Zagreb: Školska knjiga.

Mijatović, Anđelko (1975) *Narodne pjesme iz Hercegovine i duvanjsko-livanjskog kraja.* Duvno-Zagreb: Naša ognjišta - HKD sv. Ćirila i Metoda.

Mijatović, Anđelko (1985) *Narodne pjesme o Mijatu Tomiću.* Sinj-Duvno: Zbornik Kačić-Sveta baština.

Milas, Mijo (1972) *Hajduk Andrijica Šimić. Tekst i pjesma.* Zagreb: published by the author.

Miletović, Olivera, Aleksandar Stefanović and Ognjen Mihajlović (1995) *Ko je ko u Republici Srpskoj.* Belgrade: Humanitarna organizacija Tamo daleko.

Milošević, Slobodan (1989) *Godine raspleta*. Belgrade: BIGZ.

Milutinović, Sima (1990 [1833. 1837]) *Pjevanija crnogorska i hercegovačka*. Nikšić: Univerzitetska riječ.

Mimica, Ivan (1988) *Za slobodu drugog puta nema. Epske deseteračke pjesme o NOB-u i revoluciji nastale u Dalmaciji*. Split: Književni krug.

Mujičić, Hasan (1995) *Peti korpus je smrt četnika u Bosni*. Zagreb: published by the author.

Muslimović, Fikret (1995) *Odbrana republike*. Sarajevo - Ljubljana: NIPP Ljiljan.

Nakićenović, Savo (1990) *Kninska krajina: naselja i poreklo stanovništva*. Belgrade - Knin: ARTEL-SKD Zora.

Nametak, Alija (1991[5]) *Junačke narodne pjesme herceg-bosanskih muslimana*. Zagreb: Nakladni zavod Matice hrvatske.

Nazečić, Salko (1954) *Epske narodne pjesme*. Sarajevo: Svjetlost.

Nazečić, Salko (1969) *Junačke narodne pjesme*. Sarajevo: Svjetlost.

Nazor, Vladimir (1977) *Sabrana djela. I–XXI*. Zagreb: NZ Matice hrvatske-Liber.

Nedeljković, Dušan (1973) *Njegoš filozof oslobodilačkog humanizma*. Belgrade: SANU.

Nikoliš, Gojko (1980) *Korijen, stablo, pavetina*. Zagreb: Liber.

Njegoš, Petar II. Petrović (1951 [1845]) *Ogledalo srpsko*. Belgrade: Prosveta-Izdavačko preduzeće. Srbije.

Njegoš, Petar II. Petrović (1969 [1850]) *Lažni car Šćepan Mali/Pisma*. Novi Sad-Belgrade: Matica. srpska-SKZ.

Njegoš, Petar II. Petrović (1987 [1847]) *Gorski vijenac*. Sarajevo: Veselin Masleša.

Opačić, Stanko (1971) *Narodne pjesme Korduna*. Zagreb: Prosvjeta.

Orahovac, Sait (1971) *Narodne pjesme bunta i otpora. Motivi iz revolucije, borbe i obnove*. Sarajevo: Svjetlost.

Owen, David (1995) *Balkan Odyssey*. London: Victor Gollancz.

Pälsi, Sakari (1996 [1930]) *Bosna ponosna. Zapisi s puta po Bosni, Hercegovini i Dalmaciji*. Sarajevo: Zid.

Pavelić, Ante (1968) *Doživljaji. I*. Madrid: privately published.

Pavlović, Vladimir (1981) 'Bičevanje helesponta', *Forum*, 6: 1050–83.

Pelagić, Vaso (1953 [1879]) *Istorija bosansko-hercegovačke bune*. Sarajevo: Svjetlost.

Pešelj, Branko (1989) *U vrtlogu hrvatske politike*. Zürich: Bošnjački institut.

Popović, Koča (1988) *Beleške uz ratovanje*. Belgrade: BIGZ.

Radica, Bogdan (1982) *Živjeti nedoživjeti. Uspomene hrvatskog intelektualca kroz moralnu i ideološku krizu Zapada*. (1984) *Živjeti nedoživjeti. Uspomene hrvatskog intelektualca kroz apokalipsu Jugoslavije*. München: Knjižnica Hrvatske revije.

Radica, Bogdan (1992 [1974]) *Hrvatska 1945*. Zagreb: Grafički zavod

Hrvatske.

Radovanović, Lazar and Branislav Lovrenski (1985) *Guslari Jugoslavije*. Belgrade: GRO D. Davidović (Smederevo).

Radović, Amfilohije (1992) *Vraćanje duše u čistotu. Besjede, razgovori, pogledi.* Nikšić-Podgorica-Priština-Belgrade: Unireks - Oktoih - Jedinstvo - Književne novine.

Raos, Ivan (1971) *Prosjaci & sinovi. I–II*. Zagreb: Matica hrvatska.

Rašković, Jovan (1990) *Luda zemlja*. Belgrade: Akvarijus.

Ravlić, Aleksandar (1987) *Velika Kladuša kroz stoljeća*. Velika Kladuša: Skupština opštine Velika Kladuša.

Renner, Heinrich (1900 [1896]) *Herceg-Bosnom uzduž i poprijeko*. Mitrovica: Hrvatska dionička tiskara (N. Dogan).

Rojnica, Ivo (1969) *Susreti i doživljaji 1938–1945*. München: Knjižnica Hrvatske revije.

Rubić, Stojan and Anđeo Nuić (1899) 'Duvno (Županjac)'. *Zbornik za narodni život i običaje Južnih Slavena* IV: 244–91.

Skrinjar Tvrz, Valerija (1993) 'Sarajevski dnevnik'. *Erasmus* 3: 28–38.

Slipičević, Fuad (1953) *Istorija naroda Federativne Narodne Republike Jugoslavije sa osnovima opšte istorije. Prvi dio (stari i srednji vijek). (1958) Drugi dio (novi vijek)*. Sarajevo: Veselin Masleša.

Stilinović, Marijan (1986) *Bune i otpori*. Zagreb: Spektar.

Šarinić, Hrvoje (1999) *Svi moji pregovori sa Slobodanom Miloševićem*. Zagreb: Globus.

Šiber, Stjepan (2000) *Prevare, zablude, istina: ratni dnevnik 1992*. Sarajevo: Rabic.

Šobić, Žarko (1983a) *Krvava svadba*. Nikšić: published by the author.

Šobić, Žarko (1983b) *Mač, oganj, ljubav*. Gornja Bijela: published by the author.

Šobić, Žarko (1987) *Jesen na Grahovu*. Gornja Bijela: published by the author.

Šunjić, Marijan (1915) *Narodne junačke pjesme iz Bosne i Hercegovine*. Sarajevo: Zbor franjevačkih bogoslova Jukić.

Tolj, Ivan, Nikola Bićanić and Kemal Mujičić (1992) *Za Hrvatsku*. Zagreb: Ministarstvo obrane Republike Hrvatske.

Topalović, Živko (1964) *Kako su komunisti dograbili vlast u Jugoslaviji*. London: Sindikalist-Naša reč.

Topalović, Živko (1967) *Borba za budućnost Jugoslavije*. Paris: Sindikalist.

Topalović, Živko (1968) *Srbija pod Dražom*. London: Budućnost.

Tošić, Desimir (1952) *Srpski nacionalni problemi*. Paris: Savez srpskih zadruga Oslobođenje.

Tovilo, Mato (1970) *Hrvatski križari*. Toronto: published by the author.

Tresić-Pavičić, Ante (1906) *Po Ravnim kotarima*. Zadar: Hrvatska knjižarnica.

Tuđman, Franjo (1970 [1957]) *Rat protiv rata. Partizanski rat u prošlosti i budućnosti*. Zagreb: Zora.

Tunjić, Andrija (1994) *Boja smrti. Bosanska ratna zbilja*. Zagreb: AGM.

Ujević, Ante (1954) *Imotska krajina. Geografsko-historijski pregled*. Split: Slobodna Dalmacija.

Ujević, Mate (1941) *Sjetva. Hrvatska čitanka za III. i IV. razred srednjih škola*. Zagreb: Nakladni odjel Hrvatske državne tiskare.

Ujević, Tin (1964) *Sabrana djela*. Zagreb: Znanje.

Valjavec, Matija (1890) *Narodne pripovjesti u Varaždinu i okolici*. Zagreb.

Veselinović, Janko (1987 [1896]) *Hajduk Stanko*. Belgrade: BIGZ.

Visković, Ante (1947) *Narodna čitanka. 2. Narodne pjesme*. Zagreb: Nakladni zavod Hrvatske.

Vrančić, Vjekoslav (1985) *Branili smo državu. Uspomene, osvrti, doživljaji. I–II*. Munich: Knjižnica Hrvatske revije.

Vrčević, Vuk (1890) *Narodne pripovijesti i presude iz života po Boki kotorskoj, Hercegovini i Crnojgori*. Dubrovnik.

Vučemil, Andrija (1990) *Duvanjska rapsodija*. Zagreb: Nakladni zavod Matice hrvatske.

Vučković, Zvonko (1980) *Sećanja iz rata*. London: Naše delo.

Vučković, Zvonko (1984) *Od otpora do građanskog rata*. London: Naše delo.

Vujasinović, Dada (1995) *Svedočenja (Iz obeščašćene zemlje). Članci o ratu u Jugoslaviji i pisma 1990–1994*. Toronto - privatna naklada Aleksandre Vujasinović-Šmic.

Vukasović, Ante (1995) *Domovinski odgoj. Priručnik za hrvatske vojnike, dočasnike i časnike*. Zagreb: Ministarstvo obrane Republike Hrvatske.

Vukić, Ante (1984) *Velebitski vukovi. Zapisi iz hrvatske križarske borbe*. Dortmund: published by the author.

Vuksanović, Mladen (1996) *Pale. Dnevnik 5.4.–15.7.1992*. Zagreb: Durieux.

West, Rebecca (1993 [1942]) *Black Lamb and Grey Falcon. A Journey through Yugoslavia*. Edinburgh: Cannongate Press.

Zečević, Vlada (1968) *I to da se zna*. Zagreb: Naprijed.

Zlatanović, Momčilo (1974) *Sija zvezda. Narodne pesme oslobodilačke borbe i socijalističke izgradnje*. Niš: Gradina.

Zupanc, Lojze (1937) *Turjačani*. Kočevje: Tiskarna Jos. Pavliček.

1.f. Collections of documents

Dedijer, Vladimir and Antun Miletić (eds) (1990) *Genocid nad Muslimanima 1941–1945. Zbornik dokumenata i svjedočenja*. Sarajevo: Svjetlost.

Požar, Petar (ed.) (1995) *Ustaša. Dokumenti o ustaškom pokretu*. Zagreb: Zagrebačka stvarnost.

Zbornik NOB – *Zbornik dokumenata i podataka o narodnooslobodilačkom ratu jugoslovenskih naroda* IV/1 (1951), IV/2 (1951), IV/3 (1952) Belgrade: Vojno-istoriski institut Jugoslovenske (narodne) armije.

2. Scholarly Literature (Studies and Treatises)

Anić, Nikola (1977) 'Pučki ustanak na Hvaru i narodnooslobodilački rat', in: *Radovi Instituta za hrvatsku povijest Sveučilišta u Zagrebu* 10: 513–32.

Aubin, Michel (1989) *Njegoš i istorija u pesnikovom delu.* Belgrade: Književne novine - Naučna knjiga-Nova knjiga (originally in French as *Visions historiques et politiques dans l'oeuvre poetique P. P. Njegoš.* Diffusion de Boccard, Paris 1974).

Azaryahu, Maoz (1992) *Die Umbennenung der Thällmannplatz. Politische Symbole im öffentlichen Leben der DDR.* Institut für Deutsche Geschichte/ Universität Tel Aviv - Bleicher Verlag: Gerlingen.

Barkey, Karen (1994) *Bandits and Bureaucrats. The Ottoman Route to State Centralization.* Ithaca: Cornell University Press.

Balcerzan, Edward (1974) 'Perspektive "poetike percepcije"', in *Umjetnost riječi* XVIII/2-4: 139–154.

Balić, Smail (1973) *Kultura Bošnjaka. Muslimanska komponenta.* Wien.

Banac, Ivo (1984) *The National Question in Yugoslavia. Origins, History, Politics.* Ithaca: Cornell University Press.

Banac, Ivo (1992) '"Emperor Karl has become a Comitadji": The Croatian Disturbances of Autumn 1918', in *Slavic and East European Review* 70:2, 284–305.

Bandić, Dušan (1974) 'Krv u religijskim predstavama i magijsko-kultnoj praksi našeg naroda'. *Glasnik Etnografskog muzeja u Beogradu* XXXVII: 141–61.

Bandić, Dušan (1990) *Carstvo zemaljsko i carstvo nebesko. Ogledi o narodnoj religiji.* Belgrade: Biblioteka XX vek.

Banović, Stjepan (1924) 'O nekim historičkim licima naših narodnih pjesama'. *Zbornik za narodni život i običaje Južnih Slavena* XXV: 57–104.

Banović, Stjepan (1933) 'Kad je živio Tomić Mijovil?' *Zbornik za narodni život i običaje Južnih Slavena* XXIX/1: 74–82.

Beardsley, Monroe C. (1967) 'The Language of Literature', pp. 289–302, in: Seymour B. Chatman and Samuel R. Levin (eds) *Essays on the Language of Literature.* Boston: Houghton Mifflin.

Berdyaev, Nicolas (1964) *The Origin of Russian Communism.* Ann Arbor: University of Michigan Press.

Berger, Peter L. and Thomas Luckmann (1971) *The Social Construction of Reality: a Treatise in the Sociology of Knowledge.* London: Penguin.

Bertoša, Miroslav (1989) *Zlikovci i prognanici. Socijalno razbojništvo u Istri u XVII. i XVIII. stoljeću.* Pula: IKK Grozd.

Bird, Elizabeth S. and Robert W. Dardenne (1988) 'Myth, Chronicle, and Story. Exploring the Narrative Quality of News', pp. 67–86, in: James W. Carey (ed.) *Media, Myths, and Narratives. Televison and Press.* Newbury Park: Sage.

Bjelajac, Mile S. (1999) *Jugoslovensko iskustvo sa multietničkom armijom 1918–*

1991. Belgrade: Udruženje za društvenu istoriju.

Bonifačić, Ruža (1995) 'Changing of Symbols: the Folk Instrument *Tamburica* as a Political and Cultural Phenomenon'. *Collegium Antropologicum* (19) 1: 65–77.

Bošković-Stulli, Maja (1973) 'Odnos kmeta i feudalca u hrvatskim usmenim predajama'. *Radovi Instituta za hrvatsku povijest* 5: 309–25 .

Bošković-Stulli, Maja (1975) *Usmena književnost kao umjetnost riječi.* Zagreb: Mladost.

Bošković-Stulli, Maja (1978) *Usmena književnost.* in: *Povijest hrvatske književnosti, knj. 1.* pp. 7–353. Zagreb: Liber-Mladost.

Bošković-Stulli, Maja (1983) *Usmena književnost nekad i danas.* Belgrade: Prosveta (Biblioteka XX vek).

Bošković-Stulli, Maja (1984) *Usmeno pjesništvo u obzorju književnosti.* Zagreb: Nakladni zavod Matice hrvatske.

Bošković-Stulli, Maja (1995) 'Uporaba narodne pjesme'. *Erasmus* 10: 42–9.

Bošković-Stulli, Maja (2002) *O usmenoj tradiciji i o životu.* Zagreb: Konzor.

Bošković-Stulli, Maja (2004) 'Vječni biseri narodni ili vječno krv i nož'. *Književna republika* 7–8: 122–9.

Bovan, Vladimir (1988) 'Preobražaj istorijskog hajduka Novaka u pesnički lik Starine Novaka', pp. 129–45. In: Radovan Samardžić (ed.) *Starina Novak i njegovo doba.* Belgrade: SANU.

Bowra, C. M. (1978 [1952]) *Heroic Poetry.* London: Macmillan.

Bracewell, Catherine Wendy (1992) *The Uskoks of Senj. Piracy, Banditry, and Holy War in the Sixteenth-Century Adriatic.* Ithaca: Cornell University Press.

Bracewell, Wendy (2000) 'Rape in Kosovo: masculinity and Serbian nationalism' *Nations and Nationalism,* 6 (4), pp. 569–90 .

Bratanić, Maja (1991) *Rječnik i kultura.* Zagreb: Filozofski fakultet.

Bratanić, Maja (1993) 'Kultura rječnika i rječnici kultura', pp. 27–32, in: Rudolf Filipović *et al.* (eds) *Rječnik i društvo. Zbornik radova sa znanstvenog skupa o leksikografiji i leksikologiji održanog 11–13.X.1989. u Zagrebu.* Zagreb: HAZU.

Bratulić, Josip (1987) *Istarske književne teme.* Pula: Istarska naklada.

Brendler, Gerhard (1977) 'O ulozi plebejaca u njemačkom seljačkom ratu'. *Radovi Instituta za hrvatsku povijest Sveučilišta u Zagrebu* 10: 227–37.

Brkić, Jovan (1961) *Moral Concepts In Traditional Serbian Epic Poetry.* 'S-Gravenhage: Mouton & Co.

Bujas, Gašpar (1939) *Katolička crkva i naša narodna poezija.* Šibenik: p.o. iz *Nove revije* XVIII/1–3.

Burke, Peter (1978) *Popular Culture in Early Modern Europe.* London: Temple Smith.

Burke, Peter (1989) 'History as Social Memory', pp. 97–113, in: Thomas Butler (ed.) *Memory: History, Culture and the Mind*. Oxford: Basil Blackwell.

Buturović, Đenana (1976a) *Studija o Hörmannovoj zbirci muslimanskih narodnih pjesama*. Sarajevo: Svjetlost.

Buturović, Đenana (1976b) 'Borbe oko torina i plijenjenje stoke u muslimanskoj epici', pp. 203–11 in: *Rad 21. kongresa Saveza udruženja folklorista Jugoslavije*. Sarajevo: Udruženje folklorista Bosne i Hercegovine.

Buturović, Đenana (1981) 'Gradaščevićev ustanak u narodnoj pjesmi', pp. 145–53 in: *Rad XXIII kongresa Saveza udruženja folklorista Jugoslavije*. Zagreb.

Buturović, Đenana (1990) *Sto godina Hörmannove zbirke*. Foreword in: Hörmann 1990: IX–LXI.

Buturović, Đenana (1991) 'Prilog povijesnom Hrnjici'. *Odjek* XLIII/15–16: 30.

Buturović, Đenana (1992) *Bosanskomuslimanska usmena epika*. Sarajevo: Institut za književnost - Svjetlost.

Calhoun, C. J. (1980) 'The Authority of Ancestors'. *Man*, XV/2: 304: 319.

Cocchiara, Giuseppe (1981) *The History of Folklore in Europe*. Philadelphia: Institute for the Study of Human Issues.

Curtius, Ernst Robert (1963) *European Literature and the Latin Middle Ages*. New York: Harper & Row Publishers.

Cvetanović, Vladimir (1988) 'Neki elementi mitskog u liku Starine Novaka kod Srba', pp. 201–9 in: Radovan Samardžić (ed.) *Starina Novak i njegovo doba*. Belgrade: SANU.

Cvetkova, Radost (1982) 'The Bulgarian *haiduk* Movement in the 15th-18th Centuries', pp. 301–38, in: Gunther E. Rosenberg, Béla K. Király and Peter F. Sugar (eds) *East Central European Society and War in the Pre-Revolutionary Eighteenth Century*. New York: Columbia University Press.

Cvijić, Jovan (1987 [1918]) *Balkansko poluostrvo i južnoslovenske zemlje*. Belgrade: SANU - Književne novine - Zavod za udžbenike i nastavna sredstva.

Čajkanović, Veselin (1941) *O srpskom vrhovnom bogu*. Belgrade: Izdanje Zadužbine M. Kujundžića.

Čale Feldman, Lada, Ines Prica and Reana Senjković (eds) (1993) *Fear, Death and Resistance: Croatia 1991-1992*. Zagreb: Institute of Ethnology and Folklore Research.

Čolović, Ivan (1985) *Divlja književnost. Etnolingvističko proučavanje paraliterature*. Belgrade: Nolit .

Čolović, Ivan (1993) *Bordel ratnika. Folklor, politika i rat*. Belgrade: Biblioteka XX vek.

Čolović, Ivan (2002) *The Politics of Symbol in Serbia*. London: C. Hurst & Co.

Čubrilović, Vaso (1938) 'Istoriska osnova Višnjićevoj pesmi "Boj na Mišaru"'. *Prilozi proučavanju narodne poezije* V/1-2: 56–67.

Čubrilović, Vaso (1939) *Prvi srpski ustanak i bosanski Srbi*. Belgrade.

Ćerić, Salim (1968) *Muslimani srpskohrvatskog jezika.* Sarajevo: Svjetlost.

Ćorović, Vladimir (1925) *Bosna i Hercegovina.* Belgrade: SKZ.

Ćorović, Vladimir (1933) *Istorija Jugoslavije.* Belgrade: Narodno delo.

Ćorović, Vladimir (1936) 'Historiska vrednost Višnjićeve pesme "Početak bune protiv dahija"', pp. 67–79 in: *Zbornik u slavu Filipa Višnjića i narodne pesme.* Belgrade: SANU.

Davidović, Svetislav (1931) *Srpska pravoslavna crkva u Bosni i Hercegovini (od 960 do 1930 god.).* Sarajevo.

Detelić, Mirjana (1992) *Mitski prostor i epika.* Belgrade: SANU.

Djordjević [Đorđević], Dimitrije (1982) 'The Role of the Military in the Balkans in the Nineteenth Century', in: *Der Berliner Congress von 1878: Die Politik der Grossmäche in Südosteuropa in der Zweiten Hälfe des 19 Jahrhunderts.* Wiesbaden, pp. 317–47.

Dragojević, Sanjin (1989) 'Ideologija i društveno komuniciranje'. *Kulturni radnik* XLII/1: 45–57.

Dvorniković, Vladimir (1990 [1939]) *Karakterologija Jugoslovena.* Belgrade - Niš: Prosveta.

Dvorniković, Vladimir (1991 [1940]) 'Hajdukovanje kao psihološka i socijalna pojava'. *Delo* XXXVII/ 9–12: 361–6.

Džaja, Srećko M. (1992) *Konfesionalnost i nacionalnost Bosne i Hercegovine. Predemancipacijski period 1463–1804.* Sarajevo: Svjetlost (originally in German as *Konfessionalität und Nationalität Bosniens und der Herzegowina – Voremanzipatorische Phase 1463–1804.* R. Oldenbourg Verlag, Munich 1984).

Džaja, Miroslav and Krunoslav Draganović (1994 [1970]) *Sa Kupreške visoravni.* Baško Polje-Zagreb: Rkt. župni ured Otinovci-Kupres.

Đorđević, Milisav (ed.) (1993) *Negovanje i vrednovanje tradicija u Vojsci Jugoslavije.* Belgrade: Vojnoizdavački i novinski centar.

Đurđev, Branislav (1964) *Uloga crkve u starijoj istoriji srpskog naroda.* Sarajevo: Svjetlost.

Ekmečić, Milorad (1973) *Ustanak u Bosni 1875-1878.* Sarajevo: Veselin Masleša.

Elbaum, Henry (1991) 'Nerazumijevanje ideološkoga diskursa SSSR dvadesetih godina XX. stoljeća'. *Filozofska istraživanja* XI/3: 715–27 [original title: 'Misunderstanding of Ideological Discourse. The USSR in 1920s].

Figes, Orlando and Kolonitskii, Boris (1999) *Interpreting the Russian Revolution. The Language and Symbols of 1917.* New Haven: Yale University Press.

Flaker, Aleksandar (1981) 'Partizanska slika svijeta'. *Forum* XX/6: 897-910.

Frye, Northrop (1971) *Anatomy of Criticism.* Princeton University Press.

Gavrilović, Slavko (1986) *Hajdučija u Sremu u XVIII. i početkom XIX. veka.* Belgrade: SANU.

Gesemann, Gerhard (1968 [1943]) *Čojstvo i junaštvo starih Crnogoraca.* Cetinje:

Obod.

Giordano, Christian (1996) 'Pravna država i kulturne norme. Antropološka interpretacija političkih fenomena u sredozemnim društvima'. *Etnološka tribina* 19: 43–59.

Grgec, Petar (1935) 'Narodna pjesma i historijski roman', pp. 123–8. In: *Napredak - hrvatski narodni kalendar za 1936*. Sarajevo: HKD Napredak.

Grgec, Petar (1940) *Na izvorima pjesništva*. Zagreb: Matica hrvatska.

Grgec, Petar (1944) *Razvoj hrvatskog narodnog pjesničtva. Književno-poviestne razprave*. Zagreb: Hrvatska školska knjižnica.

Grgić, Ivan (1958) 'Gašpar Bujas, Makarski ljetopis od god. 1773. do 1794.' *Zadarska revija* VII/1: 84–6.

Grgić, Ivan (1958) 'Uz životopis hajdučkog harambaše Stanka Radovića Sočivice'. *Zadarska revija* VII/3: 247–53.

Gross, Mirjana (1973) *Povijest pravaške ideologije*. Zagreb: Institut za hrvatsku povijest Sveučilišta u Zagrebu.

Gross, Mirjana and Agneza Szabo (1992) *Prema hrvatskome građanskom društvu. Društveni razvoj u civilnoj Hrvatskoj i Slavoniji šezdesetih i sedamdesetih godina 19. stoljeća*. Zagreb: Globus.

Hadžijahić, Muhamed (1990) *Od tradicije do identiteta. Geneza nacionalnog pitanja bosanskih Muslimana*. Zagreb: Islamska zajednica Zagreb.

Hahn, Thomas (ed.) (2000) *Robin Hood in Popular Culture. Violence, Transgression, and Justice*. Cambridge: D. S. Brewer.

Hall, Brian (1996) 'Rat Rebeke West'. *Vijenac* 67–8, 25 July 1996 [*The New Yorker* 15 April 1996]: 39–41.

Handler, Richard and Jocelyn Linnekin (1984) 'Tradition, Genuine or Spurious'. *Journal of American Folklore* (97) 385: 273–90.

Hasandedić, Hivzija (1980) *Spomenici kulture turskog doba u Mostaru*. Sarajevo: Veselin Masleša.

Hasandedić, Hivzija (1990) *Muslimanska baština u istočnoj Hercegovini*. Sarajevo: Mešihat Islamske zajednice - El-Kalem.

Hoare, Marko Attila (2001) 'Civilian-Military Relations in Bosnia-Herzegovina 1992–1995', pp. 178–99, in: Magaš, Branka and Ivo Žanić (eds) *The War in Croatia and Bosnia-Herzegovina 1991–1995*. London: Frank Cass.

Hobsbawm, Eric J. (1978) *Primitive Rebels. Studies in Archaic Forms of Social Movement in the 19th and 20th Centuries*. Manchester: Manchester University Press.

Hobsbawm, Eric J. (2000) *Bandits*. New York: The New Press.

Hrabak, Bogumil (1979) 'Haramije, odmetnici i ustanici u starim raškim oblastima od 1450-1700. godine'. *Novopazarski zbornik* 3: 3–12.

Hymes, Dell (1974) *Foundations in Sociolinguistics. An Ethnographic Approach*. Philaldelphia: University of Pennsylvania Press.

Jambrešić Kirin, Renata and Maja Povrzanović (eds) (1996) *War, Exile, Everyday*

Life: Cultural Perspectives. Zagreb: Institute of Ethnology and Folklore Research.

Jauss, Hans Robert (1982) *Towards an Aesthetic of Reception.* University of Minnesota Press.

Jelavich, Charles (1990) *South Slavs Nationalisms: Textbooks and Yugoslav Union before 1914.* Columbus: Ohio State University Press.

Jelić, Ivan (1973) 'O značenju tradicije velike seljačke bune 1573. u povijesti komunističkog pokreta i revolucije u Hrvatskoj'. *Radovi Instituta za hrvatsku povijest Sveučilišta u Zagrebu* 5: 327–41.

Jelić-Butić, Fikreta (1983) *Hrvatska seljačka stranka.* Zagreb: Globus.

Jelić-Butić, Fikreta (1986) *Četnici u Hrvatskoj 1941–1945.* Zagreb: Globus.

Kalezić, Dimitrije (1966) 'Njegoševo shvatanje junaštva. Jedno pitanje iz pesnikove epike'. *Pravoslavna misao* IX/2: 59–73.

Kalezić, Dimitrije (1969) *Etika Gorskog vijenca.* Srijemski Karlovci.

Karanović, Milan (1938) 'Čudnovata ženidba Ubojčić Alije', pp. 346–51 in: *Kalendar Gajret za 1939. godinu.* Sarajevo.

Kasumović, Ivan (1911) 'Hrvatske i srpske narodne poslovice spram grčkih i rimskih poslovicâ i krilaticâ'. *Rad JAZU* 189: 116–276.

Kilibarda, Novak *(n.d.) Poezija i istorija u narodnoj književnosti.* Belgrade: Slovo ljubve.

Kleut, Marija (1979) 'O jednom ranom prevodu Života Stanislava Sočivice'. *Zbornik Cetinske krajine* 1: 283–8.

Kolarz, Walter (1952) *Russia and her Colonies.* London: George Philip & Son.

Koliopoulos, John S. (1987) *Brigands with a Cause. Brigandage and Irrendetism in Modern Greece 1821–1912.* Oxford: Clarendon Press.

Koljević, Svetozar (1974) *Naš narodni ep.* Belgrade: Nolit.

Koljević, Svetozar (1988) 'Istorija i poezija u pesmama o hajdučkom krugu Starine Novaka', pp. 109–27. In: Radovan Samardžić (ed.) *Starina Novak i njegovo doba.* Belgrade: SANU.

Kramsch, Claire (2003) *Language and Culture.* Oxford: Oxford University Press.

Kreševljaković, Hamdija (1931) 'Husein-kapetan Gradaščević - Zmaj od Bosne', pp. 105–31 in: *Kalendar HKD Napredak za 1932. godinu.* Sarajevo.

Krippendorff, Klaus (1981) *Content Analysis. An Introduction to Its Methodology.* Beverly Hills: Sage Publications.

Krizman, Bogdan (1986a) *Ante Pavelić i ustaše.* Zagreb: Globus.

Krizman, Bogdan (1986b) *NDH izmedu Hitlera i Mussolinija.* Zagreb: Globus.

Krizman, Bogdan (1986c) *Pavelić u bjekstvu.* Zagreb: Globus.

Krnjević, Hatidža (1980) *Živi palimpsesti ili o usmenoj poeziji.* Belgrade: Nolit.

Kržišnik-Bukić, Vera (1991) *Cazinska buna 1950.* Sarajevo: Svjetlost.

Le Bon, Gustave (1982 [1895]) *The Crowd: A Study of Popular Mind.* Fraser Publishing Co.

Lešić, Zdenko (1975) *Jezik i književno djelo*. Sarajevo: Svjetlost.

Lord, Albert B. (1974) 'Uticaj turskih osvajanja na balkansku epsku tradiciju', pp. 65–83 in: Buturović, Đenana and Vlajko Palavestra (eds) *Narodna književnost Srba, Hrvata, Muslimana i Crnogoraca*. Sarajevo: Svjetlost.

Lord, Albert B. (1960) *The Singer of Tales*. Cambridge, MA: Harvard University Press.

Lovrenović, Ivan (2001) *Bosnia: A Cultural History*. London: Saqi Books in association with The Bosnian Institute.

Luburić, Andrija (1930) *Drobnjaci - pleme u Hercegovini - poreklo, prošlost i etnička uloga u našem narodu*. Belgrade.

Macan, Trpimir (1992 [1972–3]) 'Junaštvo i značaj "našega naroda" za protuturskih ratova', in: *Povijesni prijepori*. Dubrovnik: Matica hrvatska.

Maglajlić, Munib (1988) 'Mujo Hrnjica - epski i historijski', pp. 556–60 in: *Zbornik radova XXXV kongresa Saveza udruženja folklorista Jugoslavije*. Titograd: Udruženje folklorista Crne Gore.

Malcolm, Noel (1994) *Bosnia. A Short History*. Papermac/Macmillan: London.

Mamić, Mile (1992) *Temelji hrvatskog pravnog nazivlja*. Zagreb: Hrvatska sveučilišna naklada.

Maretić, Tomo (1902) 'Stajaći brojevi u narodnoj našoj epici'. *Zbornik za narodni život i običaje* VII/1: 1–56.

Maretić, Tomo (1966 [1909]) *Naša narodna epika*. Belgrade: Nolit.

Marijan, Davor (2000) 'Koliko je u Drugom svjetskom ratu bilo partizanskih divizija iz Hrvatske?' *Časopis za suvremenu povijest*, 3: 517–25.

Martin, Denis Constant (1993) 'Identiteti u politici'. *Treći program Hrvatskog radija* 41: 31–6.

Maticki, Miodrag (1982) *Epika ustanka*. Belgrade: Rad.

Matić, Vojin (1972) *Zaboravljena božanstva*. Belgrade: Prosveta.

Matić, Vojin (1976) *Psihoanaliza mitske prošlosti*. Belgrade: Nolit.

Matuz, Josef (1992) *Osmansko Carstvo*. Zagreb: Školska knjiga (originally in German as: *Das. Osmanische Reich. Grundlinien seiner Geschichte*. Darmstadt 1985).

Mayenowa, Maria Renata (1969) 'Konzistentnost teksta i primaočeva svijest'. *Umjetnost riječi* XIII/3: 163-177.

Mayenowa, Maria Renata (1974) 'Struktura književnog teksta'. *Umjetnost riječi* XVIII/2–4: 195–231.

Medenica, Radosav (1938) 'Guslar i njegovi slušaoci'. *Prilozi proučavanju narodne poezije* V/2: 171–86.

Međeši, Ljubomir (1988) 'Etička simbolika u slovenskom narodnom stvaralaštvu', pp. 501–5 in: *Zbornik radova XXXV kongresa Saveza udruženja folklorista Jugoslavije*. Titograd: Udruženje folklorista Crne Gore.

Mežnarić, Silva (1993) 'The rapists' progress: ethnicity, gender and violence'. *Revija za sociologiju* XXIV/ 3–4: 119–29.

Mićović, Dragutin (1974) 'Krajina - istorijska sadržina i epska inspiracija srpskohrvatske i albanske narodne poezije'. *Balcanica* V: 413–33.

Mihaljčić, Rade (1984) *Lazar Hrebeljanović - istorija, kult, predanje*. Belgrade: Nolit.

Mimica, Ivan (1979) 'Književne značajke Lovrićeva djela "Život Stanislava Sočivice"'. *Zbornik Cetinske krajine* 1: 239–52.

Mimica, Ivan (1988) *Život i epski svijet guslara Bože Domnjaka*. Split: Logos.

Mimica, Ivan (1990) 'Nove epske pjesme iz Dalmacije o NOB-u'. *Mogućnosti* 9–10: 1011–22.

Mirković, Nikola (1938) '"Početak bune protiv dahija" kao istorijski izvor'. *Prilozi proučavanju narodne poezije* V/2: 241–3.

Moranjak-Bamburać, Nirman (1991) 'Intertekstualnost/metatekstualnost/ alteritet'. *Književna smotra* XXIII/ 84: 27–36.

Murko, Matthias (1929) *La Poésie populaire epique en Yougoslavie au debut du XXe siecle*. Paris: Institut d'études slaves.

Murko, Matija (1951) *Tragom srpsko-hrvatske narodne epike. Putovanja u godinama 1930–1932*. Zagreb: JAZU.

Nazečić, Salko (1959) *Iz naše narodne epike. I dio/ Hajdučke borbe oko Dubrovnika i naša narodna pjesma (Prilog proučavanju postanka i razvoja naše narodne epike)*. Sarajevo: Svjetlost.

Nedeljković, Dušan (1981) 'Višestruki kontinuitet i karakter razvitka našeg narodnog pevanja ustanka', pp. 37–49. In: *Rad XXIII kongresa Saveza udruženja folklorista jugoslavije*. Zagreb.

Nimmo, Dan (1982) 'Govor u politici: simboli, jezici i javno mnenje'. *Savremenost* XII/ 7–8: 205–18 & 10–11: 135–50.

Niškanović, Miroslav (1978) 'Ilindanski dernek kod turbeta Đerzelez Alije u Gerzovu'. *Novopazarski zbornik* 2: 163–8.

Obad, Stijepo (1986) 'Kraj hajdučije u Dalmaciji'. *Radovi Filozofskog fakulteta u Zadru: Razdio povijesnih znanosti* XXV: 283–97.

Obad, Stijepo (1990) *Dalmatinsko selo u prošlosti. Od sredine osamnaestog stoljeća do prvog svjetskog rata*. Split: Logos.

Olesnicki, Aleksej (1933) 'Tko je zapravo bio Đerzelez Alija?' *Zbornik za narodni život i običaje Južnih Slavena* XXIX/1: 18–37.

Olesnicki Aleksej (1934) 'Još o ličnosti Đerzelez Alije'. *Zbornik za narodni život i običaje* XXIX/2: 20–55 .

Oraić Tolić, Dubravka (1990) *Teorija citatnosti*. Zagreb: Grafički zavod Hrvatske.

Organdžieva, Cvetanka (1985) 'O hajdučkim i razbojničkim (haramijskim) pjesmama jugoslovenskih naroda'. *Narodno stvaralaštvo-Folklor* XXIV/1–4: 1–11. Continued: (1986) *Narodno stvaralaštvo-Folklor* XXV/1–4: 23–32.

Palavestra, Vlajko (1991) *Historijska usmena predanja*. Sarajevo: Institut za književnost-Svjetlost.

Pandžić, Miljenko (1979) 'Prilozi poznavanju hajdučije u osamnaestom stoljeću na području Karlovačkog generalata i Banske krajine'. *Zbornik Cetinske krajine* 1: 107–24.

Pavličević, Dragutin (1977) 'Pučki ustanak Matija Ivanića u našoj udžbeničkoj literaturi'. *Radovi Instituta za hrvatsku povijest* 10: 533–9.

Pavličević, Dragutin (1987) 'Hajdučija u Hrvatskoj 60. godina 19. stoljeća'. *Radovi Zavoda za hrvatsku povijest Filozofskog fakulteta Zagreb* 20: 129–58.

Pejović, Danilo (1968) 'Bilo a nije prošlo. O značenju tradicije'. *Kolo* VI/1–2: 97–104.

Peričić, Šime (1991) 'Hajdučija u Dalmaciji XIX. stoljeća'. *Radovi Zavoda za povijesne znanosti HAZU u Zadru* 33: 185–204.

Perić-Polonijo, Tanja (1985) 'Usmena književnost u programu i udžbenicima književnosti'. *Narodna umjetnost* 22: 273–316.

Pešić, Vesna (1994) 'Ratničke vrline u čitankama za osnovnu školu', pp. 55–75 in: Rosandić, Ružica and Vesna Pešić (eds) *Ratništvo, patriotizam, patrijarhalnost*. Belgrade: Centar za antiratnu akciju.

Pettan, Svanibor (ed.) (1998) *Music, Politics, and War. Views from Croatia.* Zagreb: Institute of Ethnology and Folklore Research.

Plenča, Dušan (1986) *Kninska ratna vremena 1850–1946. Knin - Drniš - Bukovica - Ravni kotari.* Zagreb: Globus.

Polić, Branko (1988) *Poetika i politika Vladimira Majakovskog.* Zagreb: Globus.

Popov, Nebojša (1993) *Srpski populizam. Od marginalne do dominantne pojave.* Separat uz: *Vreme*, 135, 24 April 1993: Belgrade.

Popović, Dušan (1930) *O hajducima. Prvi deo.* (1931) *O hajducima. Drugi deo.* Belgrade: Narodna štamparija.

Popović, Miodrag (1976) *Vidovdan i časni krst. Ogled iz književne arheologije.* Belgrade: Slovo ljubve.

Popović, Miodrag (1983) *Pamtivek. Srpski rječnik Vuka St. Karadžića.* Belgrade: Zavod za udžbenike i nastavna sredstva.

Pupovac, Milorad (1987) 'Argumentacija u političkom govoru'. *SOL* II/2: 63–85.

Radenković, Ljubinko (1988) 'Mitski atributi Starine Novaka u epskoj poeziji Južnih Slovena i Rumunja', pp. 211–49 in: Radovan Samardžić (ed.) *Starina Novak i njegovo doba.* Belgrade: SANU.

Radojević, Danilo (1971) 'Problemi crnogorske historije oko prvoga svjetskog rata'. *Kritika* IV/16: 65–87.

Ređep, Jelka (1987) 'Legenda o kralju Zvonimiru'. Novi Sad: Matica srpska; p. o. iz: *Zbornik Matice srpske za književnost i jezik*, XXXIV/3 – 1986.

Rihtman-Auguštin, Dunja (1970) 'Tradicionalna kultura i suvremene vrijednosti' *Kulturni radnik*, XXIII/3: 26–45.

Rihtman-Auguštin, Dunja (1972) 'Četiri varijacije na temu kultura poduzeća'. *Kulturni radnik*, XXV/3: 121–51.

Rihtman-Auguštin, Dunja (1975) 'Folklor kao komunikacija u NOB-u', pp. 151–65 in: Jelić, Ivan, Dunja Rihtman-Auguštin and Vice Zaninović (eds) *Kultura i umjetnost u NOB-u i socijalističkoj revoluciji*. Zagreb: Institut za historiju radničkog pokreta Hrvatske - August Cesarec.

Rihtman-Auguštin, Dunja (1983) 'Etnos kao proces', pp. 806–12 in: *Zbornik 1. kongresa jugoslovanskih etnologov in folkloristov, knj. 2*. Ljubljana.

Rihtman-Auguštin, Dunja (1989) 'Vuk Karadžić: Past and Present or On the History of Folk Culture', pp. 85–94 in: Rihtman-Auguštin, Dunja and Maja Povrzanović (eds) *Folklore and Historical Process*. Zagreb: Zavod za istraživaje folklora.

Rihtman-Auguštin, Dunja (1996) 'Junaci i klijenti. Skica za istraživanje mentaliteta.' *Erasmus* 16: 54–61.

Rihtman-Auguštin, Dunja (2004) *Ethnology, Myth and Politics: Anthropologizing Croatian Ethnology*. Ashgate Publishing.

Rizvić, Muhsin (1990) *Bosansko-muslimanska književnost u doba preporoda 1887-1918*. Sarajevo: Mešihat Islamske zajednice BiH.

Rodić, Milivoj (1982) 'Narodni pjesnici Bosne i Hercegovine u NOB-u i revoluciji', pp. 105–12 in: *Rad 27. kongresa Saveza udruženja folklorista Jugoslavije*. Sarajevo: Udruženje folklorista Bosne i Hercegovine.

Roksandić, Drago (1988) *Vojna Hrvatska: La Croatie militaire. Krajiško društvo u Francuskom Carstvu 1809–1813. I–II*. Zagreb: Školska knjiga-Stvarnost.

Rosandić, Ružica (1994) 'Patriotsko vaspitanje u osnovnoškolskim udžbenicima', pp. 39–53 in: Rosandić, Ružica and Vesna Pešić (eds) *Ratništvo, patriotizam, patrijarhalnost*. Belgrade: Centar za antiratnu akciju.

Rudé, George (1980) *Ideology and Popular Protest*. London: Lawrence & Wishart.

Samardžić, Radovan (1952) *Hajdučke borbe protiv Turaka u XVI i XVII veku*. Belgrade: Prosveta.

Samardžić, Radovan (1955) *Hajdučka pisma. Prilog proučavanju naše starije pismenosti*. Belgrade: p.o. iz Zbornika Filozofskog fakulteta, knj. III.

Sa[mardžić], R[adovan] (1972) *Hajduci*, pp. 384–6 in: *Vojna enciklopedija, knj. 3 (Foča-Jajce)*. Belgrade: Redakcija Vojne enciklopedije.

Schmaus, Alois (1953) 'Studije iz krajinske epike' p.o. iz *Rad JAZU* 297: Zagreb.

Silverman, Carol (1983) 'The Politics of Folklore in Bulgaria'. *Anthropological Quarterly* (56) 2: 55–61.

Silverman, Carol (1989) 'The Historical Shape of Folklore in Bulgaria', pp. 149–58, in: Rihtman-Auguštin, Dunja and Maja Povrzanović (eds) *Folklore and Historical Process*. Zagreb: Zavod za istraživanje folklora.

Silverstone, Roger (1988) 'Television Myth and Culture', pp. 20–47, in: James

W. Carey (ed.) *Media, Myths, and Narratives. Television and Press.* Newbury Park: Sage.

Simms, Brendan (2002) *Unfinest Hour. Britain and the Destruction of Bosnia.* London: Penguin.

Skarić, Vladislav (1937) *Sarajevo i njegova okolina od najstarijih vremena do austro-ugarske okupacije.* Sarajevo.

Smailbegović, Esma (1986) *Narodna predaja o Sarajevu.* Sarajevo: Institut za jezik i književnost.

St Erlich, Vera (1965) 'Ljudske vrednote i kontakti kultura'. *Sociologija* VII/3: 27–42.

St Erlich, Vera (1978) *U društvu s čovjekom. Tragom njegovih kulturnih i socijalnih tekovina.* Zagreb: Sveučilišna naklada Liber.

Stanojević, Gligor (1970) *Jugoslovenske zemlje u mletačko-turskim ratovima XVI–XVIII vijeka.* Belgrade: Istorijski institut.

Stojanović, Dubravka (1994) 'Udžbenici istorije kao ogledalo vremena', pp. 77–103 in: Rosandić, Ružica and Vesna Pešić (eds) *Ratništvo, patriotizam, patrijarhalnost.* Belgrade: Centar za antiratnu akciju.

Stojanović, Miodrag (1984) *Hajduci i klefti u narodnom pesništvu.* Belgrade: SANU/Balkanološki institut.

Suško, Mario (1974) 'Stil kao verbalna napetost'. *Forum* XIII/ 3: 522–35.

Šagi-Bunić, Tomislav (1983) *Katolička crkva i hrvatski narod.* Zagreb: Kršćanska sadašnjost.

Šehić, Nusret (1971) *Četništvo u Bosni i Hercegovini (1918–1941).* Sarajevo: ANUBiH.

Šiber, Ivan (1992) *Politička propaganda i politički marketing.* Zagreb: Alinea.

Šimčik, Ante (1933) 'Begovi Kopčići'. *Zbornik za narodni život i običaje Južnih Slavena,* XXIX/1: 38–59.

Šišić, Ferdo (1908) 'Pogibija Smail-age Čengijića (6. oktobra 1840)'. *Hrvatsko kolo* 4: 164–81.

Šišić, Ferdo (1962) *Pregled povijesti hrvatskog naroda.* Zagreb: Matica hrvatska.

Terseglav, Marko (1988) 'Odmevi hajduštva in uskoštva v ljudski poeziji na slovenskem', pp. 540–4, in: *Zbornik radova XXXV kongresa Saveza udruženja folklorista Jugoslavije.* Titograd: Udruženje folklorista Crne Gore.

Thompson, Mark (1994) *Forging War: the Media in Serbia, Croatia and Bosnia-Herzegovina.* London: Article 19.

Tomasevich, Jozo (1975) *War and Revolution in Yugoslavia, 1941-1945. The Chetniks.* Stanford: Stanford University Press.

Turčinović, Josip (1973) *Katolička crkva u južnoslavenskim zemljama.* Zagreb: Kršćanska sadašnjost.

Veljković, Momir (1928) '"Početak bune protiv dahija". Istorisko-književna analiza'. *Književni sever* IV/7–8–9: 375–89.

Vešović, Radoslav (1935) *Pleme Vasojevići (u vezi sa istorijom Crne Gore i plemenskim životom susjednih Brda).* Sarajevo: Državna štamparija.

Vukšić, Tomo (1994) *Međusobni odnosi katolika i pravoslavaca u Bosni i Hercegovini (1878.–1903.) Povijesno-teološki prikaz.* Mostar: Teološki institut Mostar.

Zečević, Divna (1978) *Pučki književni fenomen.* In: *Povijest hrvatske književnosti, knj. 1.* pp. 356–655. Zagreb: Liber-Mladost.

Zečević, Divna (1979) 'Preporodna književna stilizacija hajdukovanja Stanislava Sočivice u "Danici ilirskoj" u odnosu na tekst Ivana Lovrića'. *Zbornik Cetinske krajine* 1: 275–81.

Zima, Luka (1988) *Figure u našem narodnom pjesništvu s njihovom teorijom.* Zagreb: Globus.

Zlatić, Slavko (1975) 'Narodno stvaralaštvo i izvorna partizanska pjesma u NOB-u', pp. 213–6 in: *Kultura i umjetnost u NOB-u i socijalističkoj revoluciji u Hrvatskoj.* Zagreb: Institut za historiju radničkog pokreta - August Cesarec.

Zuković, Ljubomir (1988) *Stazama usmenosti.* Nikšić: Univerzitetska riječ.

Zuković, Ljubomir (1989) *Vukovi pevači iz Crne Gore.* Belgrade: Rad.

Žanić, Ivo (1987) *Mitologija inflacije. Govor kriznoga doba.* Zagreb: Globus.

Žanić, Ivo (1993a) *Politički diskurs i folklorna matrica. Tradicijska kultura i politička komunikacija u Bosni i Hercegovini, Crnoj Gori, Hrvatskoj i Srbiji 1988–1992.* Zagreb (dissertation, manuscript).

Žanić, Ivo (1993b) *Smrt crvenog fiće. Članci i ogledi 1989-1993.* Zagreb: Studio grafičkih ideja.

Žanić, Ivo (1996a) 'Kletva kao element političke komunikacije'. *Medijska istraživanja* 2/1: 27–46.

Žanić, Ivo (1996b) 'Zvonimir na remontu. Politika kao pučka književnost'. *Erasmus* 15: 56–62.

Žanić, Ivo (1996c) 'Pisac na osami. Upotreba Andrićeve književnosti u ratu u BiH'. *Erasmus* 18: 48–57.

Žanić, Ivo (2002) 'South Slav Traditional Culture as a Means to Political Legitimization', pp. 45-58, in: Resic, Sanimir and Törnquist-Plewa, Barbara (eds) *The Balkans in Focus: Cultural Boundaries in Europe.* Lund: Nordic Academic Press.

Žanić, Ivo (2005) 'The Symbolic Identity of Croatia in the Triangle Crossroads-Bulwark-Bridge', pp. 35–76, in: Kolstø, Pål (ed.) *Myths and Boundaries in South-Eastern Europe.* London: Hurst & Company.

Žunec, Ozren (1995) 'Država i pobunjenici: operacija *Oluja* i njene posljedice'. *Erasmus* 13: 4–10.

Žunec, Ozren (1997) 'Socijetalne ratne štete u Bosni i Hercegovini: zašto je narod ponovo izabrao patnju'. *Erasmus* 20: 19–36.

Županov, Josip (1993) 'Dominantne vrijednosti hrvatskog društva'. *Erasmus* 2: 2–6.

Index